Anonymous

Appletons' Hand-Book of American Travel

Northern and eastern tour. Including New York, New Jersey, Pennsylvania, Connecticut, Rhode Island, Massachusetts, Maine, New Hampshire, Vermont, and the British dominions. Vol. 1

Anonymous

Appletons' Hand-Book of American Travel
Northern and eastern tour. Including New York, New Jersey, Pennsylvania, Connecticut, Rhode Island, Massachusetts, Maine, New Hampshire, Vermont, and the British dominions. Vol. 1

ISBN/EAN: 9783337212933

Printed in Europe, USA, Canada, Australia, Japan

Cover: Foto ©Andreas Hilbeck / pixelio.de

More available books at **www.hansebooks.com**

UNION ADAMS & CO.,

Hosiers, Glovers, and Shirt-Makers

No. 637 BROADWAY,

NEW YORK CITY,

Always have on hand the largest and best variety, in this country, of

FASHIONABLE

FURNISHING GOODS,

FOR

LADIES, GENTLEMEN, AND CHILDREN,

Adapted to the Seasons,

SPRING, SUMMER, FALL, AND WINTER.

Importing and manufacturing largely, we CAN and WILL offer superior inducements to every patron.

UNION ADAMS & CO.,
No. 637 Broadway, New York City.

BROWN BROTHERS & CO.,

59 WALL STREET, NEW YORK.

BILLS OF EXCHANGE ON GREAT BRITAIN & IRELAND.

COMMERCIAL

AND

TRAVELLING CREDITS ISSUED,

AVAILABLE IN

ANY PART OF THE WORLD.

TELEGRAPHIC TRANSFERS OF MONEY

MADE TO AND FROM

LONDON AND LIVERPOOL.

ADVANCES

MADE ON

COTTON, AND OTHER PRODUCE.

d

DUNCAN, SHERMAN & CO.,
BANKERS,

Corner Pine and Nassau Streets,

NEW YORK,

ISSUE

CIRCULAR NOTES, AND CIRCULAR LETTERS OF CREDIT FOR TRAVELLERS,

Available in all the principal Cities of the World.

ALSO,

Drafts on London, Paris, Ireland, Northern Europe, Berlin, Leipsic, Vienna, Leghorn, Florence, Rome, Naples, etc.,

AND ON

Havana, Lima, Valparaiso, San Francisco, and Australia.

Telegraphic transfers of Funds to

LONDON, LIVERPOOL, PARIS, HAVANA, SAN FRANCISCO, Etc.

Advance made on COTTON and other approved MERCHANDISE consigned to ourselves, or to

Messrs. BARING BROTHERS & CO.,

LIVERPOOL AND LONDON.

c

The American Banking House

OF

BOWLES BROTHERS & CO.

PARIS—12 Rue de la Paix.
NEW YORK—19 William Street.
BOSTON—27 State Street.
LONDON—449 Strand, Charing Cross.

OFFERS TO THE PUBLIC THE FOLLOWING FACILITIES:

I.—To receive Deposits at any one of said Offices, payable at any other, in FRANCS, DOLLARS, OR POUNDS STERLING, by telegraph (cable transfer), or by check, FREE OF COMMISSION.

II.—To make said Deposits payable by Drafts, Circular Credits, or Notes, at any or all other bankable points, WITH COMMISSION.

III.—To issue Circular Travelling Credits in advance of funds, upon approved personal or collateral security, payable in part or whole, at any of said points, for a commission of ONE per cent., and interest upon sum advanced thereon.

IV.—To buy or sell exchange in any currency, cash credits of other Banks, make advances upon current securities in Europe or America, and execute orders for same in either market.

V.—To effect Insurance—MARINE, FIRE, or LIFE.

VI.—To receive valuables of any kind, upon "safe deposit."

VII.—To receive, sell, purchase, deliver, FOR CASH ONLY, goods in any quantities.

VIII.—To store or forward Baggage or Express matter.

IX.—To secure passages by any line of travel, FREE OF COMMISSION.

X.—To receive, deliver, or forward, Mail matter or Telegrams.

XI.—To receive subscriptions or advertisements for prominent American journals.

XII.—To supply general information upon American affairs, through its Reading-Rooms and Registry Records, and otherwise to attend to any thing pertaining to the systematic care of American interests abroad.

Correspondents of the following Banks:

THE UNION BANK OF LONDON.
MESSRS. J. S. MORGAN & CO.
THE ORIENTAL BANK CORPORATION.

THE BANK OF CALIFORNIA.
THE NATIONAL BANK OF SCOTLAND.
MESSRS. WELLS, FARGO & CO.

THE MUNSTER BANK (LIMITED), IRELAND.

J. & W. SELIGMAN & CO.,
BANKERS,

59 Exchange Place, Corner of Broad Street,

NEW YORK,

Fiscal Agents

OF THE

UNITED STATES STATE DEPARTMENT.

Bills of Exchange, Commercial Credits, and Telegraphic Transfers on Great Britain and the Continent of Europe.

TRAVELLERS' CREDITS

PAYABLE IN

Any part of Europe, Asia, Africa, and America.

BRANCH HOUSES.

Messrs. SELIGMAN BROTHERS, London.
    "   SELIGMAN, FRÈRES & CO., Paris.
    "   SELIGMAN & STETTHEIMER, Frankfort.
    "   J. SELIGMAN & CO., San Francisco.
    "   SELIGMAN, HELLMAN & CO., N. Orleans.

Advances made on Consignments.

CIRCULAR NOTES

AND

Circular Letters of Credit,

FOR TRAVELLERS,

AVAILABLE IN ALL PARTS OF THE WORLD,

ALSO,

COMMERCIAL CREDITS,

AND

Drafts on Morton, Rose & Co., London,
The Bank of Scotland and Branches,
The Provincial Bank of Ireland and Branches,

ISSUED BY

MORTON, BLISS & CO.,

NEW YORK.

J. & J. STUART & CO.,

33 Nassau Street,

NEW YORK.

BILLS OF EXCHANGE ON MANCHESTER,

PAYABLE IN LONDON,

AT 3 AND 60 DAYS' SIGHT.

ALSO,

CHECKS ON DEMAND

ON

Smith, Payne & Smith's,

LONDON,

AND ON THE

ULSTER BANKING CO.,

BELFAST, IRELAND,

AND ON THE

NATIONAL BANK OF SCOTLAND,

EDINBURGH.

ALSO,

LETTERS OF CREDIT.

DABNEY, MORGAN & CO.,
BANKERS,
53 Exchange Place,

NEW YORK,

Draw Bills of Exchange on England and San Francisco,

AT CUSTOMARY USANCES.

TELEGRAPHIC TRANSFERS OF MONEY

MADE TO OR FROM

EUROPE, SAN FRANCISCO, OR HAVANA.

As Agents and Attorneys for

Messrs. J. S. MORGAN & CO.,

LONDON,

Commercial and Travelling Credits issued,

AVAILABLE IN ANY PART OF THE WORLD.

AS AGENTS FOR THE

London and San Francisco Bank (limited) of London and San Francisco,

Banking Transactions undertaken with the Pacific Coast,

INCLUDING

SHIPMENTS OF BULLION

FROM

SAN FRANCISCO TO CHINA AND JAPAN.

j

IMPORTANT FOR EUROPEAN TRAVELLERS.

Just Ready,

SKELETON TOURS

Through England, Scotland, Ireland, Wales, Denmark, Norway, Sweden, Russia, Poland, and Spain,

With various ways of getting from place to place, the time occupied, and the cost of each journey to a party of four; with some of the principal things to see, especially country-houses.

By HENRY WINTHROP SARGENT.

One vol., 12mo, limp covers. Price, $1.00.

Sent free, by mail, to any address in the U. S., on receipt of the price.

D. APPLETON & CO., Publishers.

Important to Railway Travellers.

In order to save trouble and anxiety in reference to which route to select previous to commencing your journey, be careful and purchase a copy of

Appletons' Railway Guide.

Thousands and tens of thousands of Railway Travellers would as soon think of starting on their journey without a copy of the GUIDE as without their brggage. It contains—

I. IMPORTANT INSTRUCTIONS TO RAILWAY TRAVELLERS, in reference to purchasing tickets, checking baggage, etc.

II. ONE HUNDRED RAILWAY MAPS, representing the principal railways of the country West, South, North, and East, in connection with the timetable of the line.

III. INDEX TO UPWARD OF EIGHT THOUSAND TOWNS, VILLAGES, and Cities, in connection with the various railways, the important railways being represented by map.

IV. TOURIST GUIDE TO THE WATERING-PLACES and Places of Fashionable Resort throughout the United States and the Canadas.

V. MONTHLY ACCOUNT OF RAILWAYS AND THEIR PROGRESS.

VI. ANECDOTES AND INCIDENTS OF TRAVEL.

VII. NEW TIME-TABLES TO DATE, etc., etc.

D. APPLETON & CO., Publishers,

549 & 551 BROADWAY, NEW YORK.

APPLETONS' JOURNAL
OF LITERATURE, SCIENCE, AND ART.

APPLETONS' JOURNAL is published weekly, and consists of thirty-two quarto pages, each number attractively illustrated. Its contents consist of serial Novels and short Stories, Essays upon Literary and Social Topics, Sketches of Travel and Adventure, and papers upon all the various subjects that pertain to the pursuits and recreations of the people, whether of town or country.

PRICE 10 CENTS PER NUMBER, OR $4.00 PER ANNUM, IN ADVANCE.

SUBSCRIPTIONS RECEIVED FOR TWELVE OR SIX MONTHS.

TERMS FOR CLUBS.—Any person procuring FIVE Yearly Subscriptions, and remitting $20, will be entitled to a copy for one year GRATIS; FIFTEEN Yearly Subscribers, and remitting $50.00, will entitle sender to a copy one year GRATIS.

THE NEW AMERICAN CYCLOPÆDIA, edited by GEORGE RIPLEY and CHAS. A. DANA, 16 vols., 8vo, cloth, price $80, will be given to any person sending 50 Subscribers, and remitting $200.

The postage within the United States, for the JOURNAL, is 20 cents a year, payable yearly, semi-yearly, or quarterly, in advance, at the office where received. Subscriptions from Canada must be accompanied with 20 cents additional, to prepay the United States postage. New York City subscribers will be charged 20 cents per annum additional, which will prepay for postage and delivery of their numbers.

In remitting by mail, a post-office order, or draft, payable to the order of D. Appleton & Co., is preferable to bank-notes, as, if lost, the order or draft can be recovered without loss to the sender. In ordering the JOURNAL, the name should be clearly given, with the post-office, county, and State, in full.

Reading Cases for APPLETONS' JOURNAL, arranged to hold thirteen numbers. In half leather, price $1.00. Binding Cases for vols. 1 and 2, cloth, gilt, price 75 cents each. Mailed post-free on receipt of price.

Appletons' Journal and either Harper's Weekly, Harper's Bazar, Harper's Magazine, Putnam's Magazine, Lippincott's Magazine, the Atlantic Monthly, or the Galaxy, for one year, on receipt of $7. Appletons' Journal and Littell's Living Age, for $10. Appletons' Jounal and Oliver Optic's Magazine, for $5; or the Riverside Magazine, for $5.50.

The publication of the JOURNAL began April 3, 1869. Back numbers can always be supplied. Third Volume began with No. 40, January 1, 1870.

APPLETONS' JOURNAL is also issued in MONTHLY PARTS, price 50 cents each, or $4.50 per annum, in advance.

D. APPLETON & CO., Publishers,
549 & 551 BROADWAY, NEW YORK.

New York Belting and Packing Company,

The oldest and largest Manufacturers in the United States of

VULCANIZED RUBBER FABRICS,

ADAPTED TO

MECHANICAL PURPOSES,

invite the attention of all who are interested in the sale or use of such articles to the high standard quality and low prices of their various manufactures, comprising

Machine Belting, Steam Packing, Leading Hose, Suction Hose, Car Springs, Wagon Springs, Billiard Cushions, Grain-Drill Tubes, etc.

"TEST" HOSE

made expressly for the use of Steam Fire Engines, and will stand a pressure of 400 pounds per square inch. Officers of Fire Departments, requiring New Hose, will find this much superior in strength and quality to any other.

PATENT SOLID EMERY VULCANITE WHEELS.

A composition of rubber and emery, making a very hard uniform substance of the nature of stone throughout. These Wheels, for grinding and polishing metals, "gumming" saws, etc., are the most economical and effective tools that can be used.

These Wheels were patented in 1859, and are the ORIGINAL SOLID EMERY WHEELS, of which all other kinds are mere imitations, and greatly inferior.

WAREHOUSE, 37 & 38 PARK ROW, NEW YORK.
JOHN H. CHEEVER, Treasurer.

Price-lists and further information may be obtained by mail, or otherwise, on application.

Established 1855.

KISSINGEN AND VICHY WATERS, Etc.

THESE POPULAR REMEDIES,

AS MANUFACTURED BY

DR. HANBURY SMITH,

ARE DAILY GROWING IN FAVOR IN CONSEQUENCE OF THEIR

Purity, Freshness, and Reliability.

They keep better than the natural; produce precisely the same effects as those do when in their best condition, and are not, like them, variable in composition.

NEW YORK, *March 2, 1870.*

Having carefully examined the improved process adopted in the laboratory of Dr. HANBURY SMITH, and **ANALYZED** samples of the MINERAL SPRING WATERS which he offers for sale, I am prepared to testify that the waters are manufactured with the most intelligent and conscientious care, and are every way reliable substitutes for the natural waters. The public estimation in which Dr. SMITH'S preparations are held is thus amply justified by my investigations and analyses.
CHARLES A. SEELEY.
Late Prof. of Chemistry and Toxicology in the New York Medical College, and of Chemistry and Metallurgy in the New York College of Dentistry.

Beware of the spurious and inferior articles with which the market is flooded.

EXAMINE THE BRAND ON THE CORK,

HANBURY SMITH AND HAZARD,
35 Union Square, New York.

WESTMINSTER HOTEL,

ON THE EUROPEAN PLAN,

Cor. of Irving Place and 16th Street, one Block from Union Square,

NEW YORK.

This house is in a very quiet locality, and yet in close proximity to Broadway and all the principal places of public amusement. Its *cuisine* enjoys an unrivalled reputation, and its appointments are, in every respect, of the most perfect description.

To travellers of taste, culture, and refinement—to those who appreciate the comforts of a home, united with those of a sumptuously appointed hotel, the WESTMINSTER commends itself very strongly indeed.

The following extract of a letter written by Mr. Charles Dickens, on his return to Europe, gives assurance of the esteem in which the WESTMINSTER HOTEL was held by that distinguished writer.

CHARLES B. FERRIN, Proprietor.

"ON BOARD THE RUSSIA, OFF QUEENSTOWN, Thursday night, *April* 30, 1868.

"* * * * When we parted I thanked you for all your great care of me in your excellent Hotel, and for having made it quite a home for me; but I did not say half enough to satisfy myself. I shall always remember my old rooms in the Westminster gratefully and pleasantly, and shall always feel a personal interest in the House and its prosperity.

"Be sure that it shall have my thoroughly well-earned recommendation on this side of the Atlantic.

"Believe me, always, very faithfully yours,
"CHARLES DICKENS."

STEREOSCOPIC VIEWS
OF
AMERICAN SCENERY.

The most Extensive Assortment in the World.

FOR SALE BY

E. & H. T. ANTHONY & CO.,

591 Broadway, New York,

OPPOSITE METROPOLITAN HOTEL.

Manufacturers, Importers, and Jobbers of

Stereoscopes and Views, Chromos and Frames, Photographic Materials, and Albums.

BREVOORT HOUSE,
NEW YORK.

THIS WELL-KNOWN HOTEL IS LOCATED ON

Fifth Avenue, corner of Eighth Street, near Washington Park,

one of the most delightful locations, combining the quiet retirement of a private mansion with easy access to all parts of the city. The

BREVOORT

has always been a favorite with Europeans visiting the United States, the plan upon which it is kept being such as to specially commend it to those accustomed to European habits.

CLARK & WAITE, *Proprietors.*

o

RHODE
NT,

SKILLS,
ICE,

SHING

N Y,

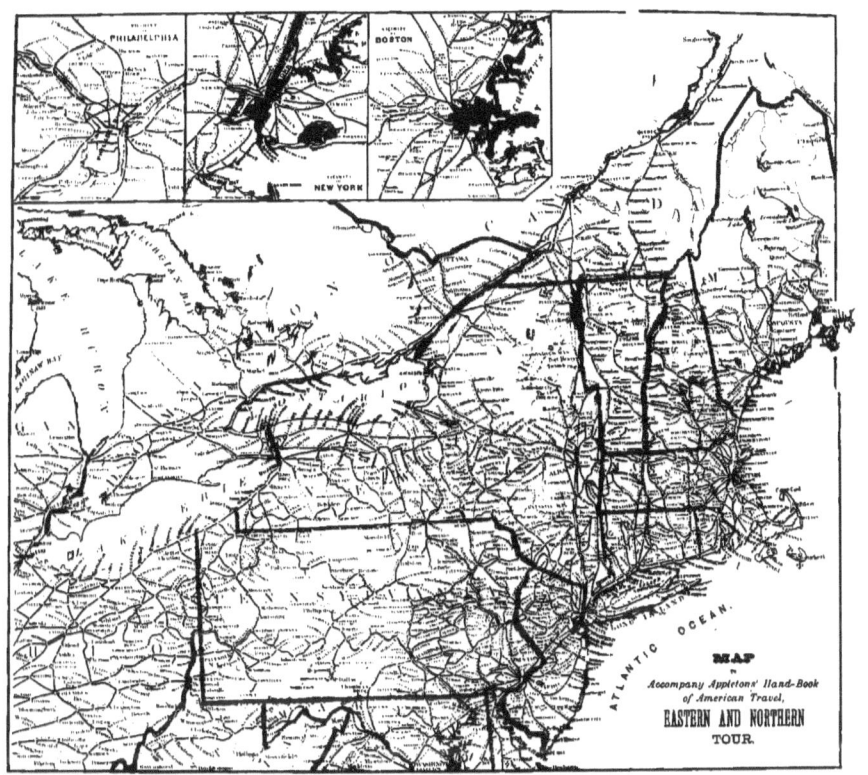

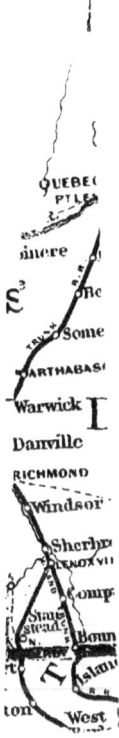

one of the n
private man:

has always l
plan upon w
accustomed

OF

AMERICAN TRAVEL.

Northern and Eastern Tour.

INCLUDING

NEW YORK, NEW JERSEY, PENNSYLVANIA, CONNECTICUT, RHODE ISLAND, MASSACHUSETTS, MAINE, NEW HAMPSHIRE, VERMONT, AND THE BRITISH DOMINIONS.

BEING A GUIDE TO

NIAGARA, THE WHITE MOUNTAINS, THE ALLEGHANIES, THE CATSKILLS, THE ADIRONDACKS, THE BERKSHIRE HILLS, THE ST. LAWRENCE, LAKE CHAMPLAIN, LAKE GEORGE, LAKE MEMPHREMAGOG, SARATOGA, NEWPORT, CAPE MAY, THE HUDSON, AND OTHER FAMOUS LOCALITIES;

WITH FULL DESCRIPTIVE SKETCHES OF THE

CITIES, TOWNS, RIVERS, LAKES, WATERFALLS, MOUNTAINS, HUNTING AND FISHING GROUNDS, WATERING-PLACES, SEA-SIDE RESORTS, AND ALL SCENES AND OBJECTS OF IMPORTANCE AND INTEREST WITHIN THE DISTRICT NAMED.

WITH MAPS, AND VARIOUS

SKELETON TOURS,

ARRANGED AS SUGGESTIONS AND GUIDES TO THE TRAVELLER.

NEW YORK:
D. APPLETON AND COMPANY,
549 & 551 BROADWAY.
LONDON: SAMPSON LOW, SON, AND MARSTON.
1872.

F106
.A66

By Transfer.
NOV 22 1910

ENTERED, according to Act of Congress, in the year 1870, by
D. APPLETON & CO.,
In the Clerk's Office of the District Court of the United States for the
Southern District of New York.

TO TRAVELLERS.

The Hand-Book of Travel is in three parts—the "Northern and Eastern Tour," the "Western Tour," and the "Southern Tour," each forming a volume separately.

In addition to the Hand-Book of Travel, a copy of Appletons' Railway Guide, with time-tables always corrected to date, is necessary to the traveller. Price twenty-five cents, published semi-monthly.

By the aid of the Table of Contents and the Index this book will be readily understood by the traveller. The Table of Contents, and the aid of Skeleton Tours (page 272), will enable him to consult special routes, and the Index is a complete guide to all places. In the Index, bays, falls, islands, mountains, rivers, and valleys, are indexed in groups.

The rate of charge on railways in the Northern and Eastern States varies from two to three cents per mile. It rarely exceeds this, and in New York it is commonly two cents per mile. Excursion tickets (see Skeleton Tours) to almost all points of interest are issued during the summer travelling season, at a considerable reduction of price. Some of these excursions include a grand round trip through New York and the New-England States. Average speed on express trains is about thirty miles per hour.

In calculating cost, from two to three dollars a day should be added for meals. Sleeping-berths on night trains are extra, usually two dollars.

The charge at first-class hotels is from $4 to $4.50 per day. Board for a length of stay can usually be arranged for at a lower price. In some of the rural places, the charge is not over three dollars per day. Travel on the steamboats is somewhat less than by rail. The steamers on Long Island Sound, the Hudson River, Lake Champlain, Lake Ontario, and the St. Lawrence, are all excellent boats. Those on Long Island Sound and the Hudson are famous the world over for their noble proportions and sumptuous arrangements. The night-boats on the Hudson are the largest and handsomest, but the day-boats are swift and well fitted up. The rates of fare do not ordinarily include meals. Sleeping-berths are provided without extra charge, in most cases, but in all instances state-rooms are an additional charge. During the height of summer travel the state-rooms are usually all engaged several days in advance, and hence the traveller desiring a room should secure one at least three days before his contemplated journey.

TO TRAVELLERS

It is the custom in America to deliver baggage to a person known as the baggage-master, who will give in return a "check" for every piece, on presentation of which the baggage is delivered. Baggage may be checked over long routes in this way, and the traveller, no matter how many times he changes cars or vehicles, has no concern about his trunks. The companies are responsible if the baggage should be injured or lost, the check being evidence of delivery into their hands. The traveller, arriving at the station, should first procure his ticket at the ticket-office, and then, proceeding to the baggage-car, or proper station of the baggage-master, have his trunks checked. The baggage-master usually requires the traveller to exhibit his ticket before he will check the trunks. Arriving at his destination, the check may be handed to the hotel-porter, always in waiting, who will procure the various articles, and have them sent to the hotel. The traveller in the United States, by the system now in vogue, is almost entirely relieved from any care or concern about his luggage.

It is not necessary to fee porters and waiters in the States, as it is in Europe, but the practice has some slight and irregular observance. The traveller is free to do as he pleases in the matter. Nothing of the kind is ever demanded. In all large cities there are coaches or omnibuses at the station on the arrival of every train, which connect directly with the principal hotels. A small charge is made for this conveyance, which, in some cases, is paid to the omnibus porter, and in others is regularly charged to the traveller in the hotel bill.

Travellers from abroad will understand that the present currency in the United States, with the exception of California, is exclusively bank-notes. These are issues of the national Treasury, commonly known as *greenbacks*, and the notes of the national banks. They are taken everywhere without hesitation, and serve every practical purpose of coin. All prices are understood to be in this currency, which is at a discount for gold ; or, as the phrase is here, gold is at a premium— now of about ten per cent. In the British Provinces, the circulating medium is coin, or the notes of the local banks, which are at par. In California, gold and silver are exclusively used.

As regards outfit, it is important for the traveller that he should be dressed with sufficient warmth. Our climate is very changeable, and the traveller had better suffer at noonday under too much clothing, than expose himself at night in storms, or to sudden changes of the atmosphere, with too little. One should wear woollen under-clothing, and always have a shawl or extra wrapper of some kind. The traveller's own judgment will suggest to him that strong suits of gray or brown are more convenient and suitable than darker colors.

In a country where changes are so frequent as in America, it is difficult to keep a book of this character always up to date in every particular. This edition of the HAND-BOOK was entirely rewritten for the summer of 1870, and revised for the summer of 1871.

CONTENTS.

NORTHERN AND EASTERN TOUR.

	PAGE
THE UNITED STATES	1
Census Returns of Population, 1870	2
NEW YORK	5
New-York City	6
Long Island	31
Brooklyn	31
Trips through Long Island	35
ROUTE I.—Trip up the Hudson, by Steamer	38
By Hudson River Railway	50
" II.—New York to Albany, *via* New York & Harlem Railway	51
" III.—Albany to Saratoga, Lakes George and Champlain	52
" IV.—To the Adirondacks	58
" V.—Albany to Buffalo and Niagara Falls, *via* N. Y. Central Railroad	62
Branch Routes on the New-York Central Railroad	66
" VI.—Albany & Susquehanna Railway	75
" VII.—Erie Railway and Branches	76
" VIII.—Hudson to Rutland, Vt	84
" IX.—Troy to Castleton, Vt	85
Ogdensburg & Lake Champlain Railway	85
Rome, Watertown & Ogdensburg Railway	85
Syracuse, Binghamton & New York Railway	86
New York & Oswego Midland Railway	86
NEW JERSEY	87
ROUTE I.—New York to Philadelphia, *via* New Jersey Railway	87
" II.—New York to Philadelphia, *via* Camden & Amboy Railway	90
" III.—New York to Long Branch, Atlantic City, and Philadelphia	91
" IV.—Jersey City to Easton, Pa., Delaware Water-Gap, etc., *via* Central Railway of New Jersey	93
" V.—Jersey City to Easton, Pa., *via* Morris & Essex Railroad	95
" VI.—Jersey City to Piermont	97
" VII.—Jersey City to Paterson	97
" VIII.—Philadelphia to Cape May, *via* West Jersey Railway	98
" IX.—Philadelphia to Manunkachunk and Delaware Water-Gap, *via* Belvidere Delaware Railway	99

CONTENTS.

	PAGE
PENNSYLVANIA	100
Philadelphia	101
ROUTE I.—Philadelphia to Harrisburg, *via* Pennsylvania Central Railway	118
" II.—Philadelphia to Reading, Pottsville, and Williamsport, *via* Philadelphia & Reading, and Catawissa Railways	125
" III.—Philadelphia to Erie and the Oil Regions, *via* Philadelphia & Erie Railway, Atlantic & Great Western Railway, Lake Shore Railway, etc.	128
" IV.—Philadelphia to Bethlehem, Easton, Allentown, Wilkesbarre, Lehigh and Wyoming Valleys, Scranton, etc., *via* North Pennsylvania, Lehigh Valley, Lehigh & Susquehanna, and connecting Railways	133
" V.—Philadelphia to the Erie Railway at Binghamton	136
" VI.—Easton to Harrisburg and the Cumberland Valley	139
" VII.—To Gettysburg, Pa., and Elmira, N. Y.	140
CONNECTICUT	144
ROUTE I.—New York to New Haven, New London, Stonington, etc.	144
" II.—Bridgeport to Pittsfield, Mass.	152
" III.—New Haven to Lake Memphremagog and the White Mountains, including Hartford, Springfield, etc.	153
" IV.—New Haven to Brattleboro, Vt., White Mountains, Quebec, Montreal, etc., etc.	157
" V.—To White Mountains, *via* New London	158
" VI.—Waterbury to Providence, R. I.	159
RHODE ISLAND	161
ROUTE I.—Stonington, Conn., to Providence	162
" II.—Waterbury to Providence	164
" III.—Providence to Bristol	164
" IV.—Providence to Newport	164
" V.—Providence to Worcester, Mass.	165
MASSACHUSETTS	167
Boston	168
ROUTE I.—New York to Boston, *via* New York & Boston Express Line	178
" II.—New York to Boston, *via* Shore Line, Stonington & Providence	180
" III.—New York to Boston, *via* various Steamboat Lines	180
" IV.—New York to the Housatonic Region, etc.	180
" V.—New York to the White Mountains, Franconia Mountains, etc., *via* Connecticut River Railway	185
" VI.—New London to White Mountains, Lake Memphremagog, Quebec, Montreal, etc., etc.	188
" VII.—New London to Worcester and Fitchburg	189
" VIII.—Boston to Plymouth, New Bedford, Cape Cod, etc.	190

CONTENTS.

MASSACHUSETTS—(Continued). PAGE
  ROUTE IX.—Boston to Bellows Falls and Lake Champlain................. 193
    " X.—Boston to the White Mountains, Green Mountains, Adirondacks, Lake Memphremagog, and Canada...................... 194
    " XI.—Boston to Portsmouth, N. H., Portland, Me., and Eastern Massachusetts.. 195
    " XII.—Boston to Lawrence, White Mountains, Portland, Me., and to the North.. 199
    " XIII.—Boston to Albany... 201
    " XIV.—Boston to the Hoosac Tunnel.............................. 201
  Vermont and Massachusetts Railway................................... 202
NEW HAMPSHIRE... 203
  ROUTE I.—To the White Mountains, Lake Memphremagog, and Canada.... 203
    The White Mountains.. 207
    " II.—Boston to the White Mountains, via Boston & Maine and Dover & Winnipiscogee Railways, Steamer on Lake, etc.... 214
    " III.—Boston to Montpelier, Vt., Green Mountains, Adirondacks, etc.. 216
    " IV.—Boston to Bellows Falls and Lake Champlain................. 218
    " V.—Boston to Portsmouth, N. H., etc., to Quebec, and all parts of Maine, via Eastern Railway and connections............... 219
    " VI.—Portsmouth to Manchester, to the White Mountains, Green Mountains, Lake Champlain, etc., via Concord and Dover, and connecting Routes.. 221
    " VII.—To the White Mountains at Gorham, and to the St. Lawrence River, via Grand Trunk Railway........................ 221
VERMONT... 222
  ROUTE I.—New York to Green Mountains, Lake Memphremagog, etc..... 222
    " II.—Boston to Montpelier, Green Mountains, Montreal, etc........ 226
    " III.—Boston to Bellows Falls, Saratoga Springs, Lake George, Canada, etc.. 230
    " IV.—New York to Rutland, Green Mountains, Lake Champlain, and Canada.. 232
MAINE... 235
  ROUTE I.—Boston to Portland, and all parts of Maine................... 236
    " II.—To the White Mountains, Canada, and the West.............. 238
    " III.—To Augusta and the Valley of the Kennebec.................. 239
    " IV.—To Bangor and the Valley of the Penobscot.................. 241
    " V.—Brunswick to Farmington................................. 243
  Places of Interest, Lakes and Mountains, not on any Railway Route..... 244
THE BRITISH PROVINCES.... 247
  ROUTE I.—Quebec to Montreal, Toronto, and the West................ 249
  Quebec.. 249
  Montreal.. 252
  ROUTE II.—Through Canada from Buffalo to the West................. 257

CONTENTS.

THE BRITISH PROVINCES—(*Continued*).   PAGE

  ROUTE III.—Trip down the St. Lawrence............................ 258
  Trip up the Saguenay... 264
  New Brunswick... 266
  Nova Scotia.. 268
  Trip to the Upper Lakes.. 271
  Cape Breton.. 271

  Skeleton Tours 272
  Index.. 275

APPLETONS'
HAND-BOOK OF AMERICAN TRAVEL.

THE UNITED STATES.

THE territory of the United States, without including the recently-acquired possession of Alaska or Russian America, covers an area of 2,963,666 square miles—not much less than the entire Continent of Europe, including all its outlying islands. This extreme extent of territory gives every variety of climate, products, and geographical features; and, with the means of rapid communication at the command of the traveller, a few days' time suffices to pass from the cold regions of the North to the warm latitude of the Gulf, or from the Atlantic to the Pacific Ocean.

The extreme length of the United States proper is 2,700 miles from north to south, and its breadth 1,600 miles from east to west, and the entire frontier line exceeds 10,000 miles; to which must be added the great unexplored Territory of Alaska, which extends to sixty-six degrees north latitude, or nearly to the Arctic circle.

DIVISIONS.—The United States is divided into thirty-seven States and twelve Territories, the District of Columbia, which was ceded by the State of Maryland as the seat of the U. S. Government, having been made a Territory by Act of Congress in the winter of 1871.

The States, for convenience of reference, have always been divided into arbitrary sections, according to their geographical position.

POPULATION.—The total population, according to the census of 1870, is 38,750,033. As this census has not yet been published in detail, the populations of cities and towns, as stated in this volume, are, with the exceptions of the large cities, only estimates, but will be found substantially correct. The following figures are accurate:

THE UNITED STATES.

THE EASTERN, OR NEW ENGLAND STATES

Maine (Me.)	626,463	Massachusetts (Mass.)	1,457,351
New Hampshire (N. H.)	318,300	Rhode Island (R. I.)	217,338
Vermont (Vt.)	330,552	Connecticut (Conn.)	537,418

Total.. 3,487,422

THE MIDDLE STATES.

New York (N. Y.)... 4,374,703
New Jersey (N. J.).. 905,794
Pennsylvania (Pa.).. 3,519,601

Total.. 8,800,098

THE SOUTHERN STATES.

Virginia, (Va.)	1,224,830	Maryland (Md.)	780,894
West Virginia (W. Va.)	462,032	Alabama (Ala.)	996,988
North Carolina (N. C.)	1,071,135	Louisiana (La.)	726,927
South Carolina (S. C.)	705,169	Texas (Tex.)	810,218
Georgia (Ga.)	1,195,338	Mississippi (Miss.)	834,984
Florida (Fla.)	189,995	Arkansas (Ark.)	483,179
Kentucky (Ky.)	1,321,001	Tennessee (Tenn.)	1,257,495
Delaware (Del.)	125,015		

Total..12,285,200

THE WESTERN STATES.

Ohio (O.)	2,662,330	Missouri (Mo.)	1,719,978
Indiana (Ind.)	1,673,941	Oregon (Or.)	90,922
Minnesota (Minn.)	436,058	California (Cal.)	556,615
Illinois (Ill.)	2,539,638	Kansas (Kas.)	379,497
Michigan (Mich.)	1,184,296	Nebraska (Neb.)	123,160
Wisconsin (Wis.)	1,055,167	Nevada (Nev.)	42,491
Iowa (Io.)	1,191,720		

Total..13,655,813

The District of Columbia (D. C.)................................... 131,706

TERRITORIES.

New Mexico	91,852	Dakota	14,181
Washington	23,901	Idaho	14,998
Utah	86,786	Arizona	9,658
Colorado	39,706	Indian Territory, estimated	17,000
Montana	20,594	Alaska, estimated	62,000
Wyoming	9,118		

Total.. 389,794

RECAPITULATION.

Eastern States.. 3,487,422
Middle States... 8,800,098
Southern States...12,285,200
Western States..13,655,813
District of Columbia... 131,706
Territories... 389,794

Total..38,750,033

THE UNITED STATES.

The population of the country is largely and steadily augmented by immigration. From 1847 to 1860, 2,598,214 immigrants arrived, and since the close of the late war the number of arrivals has averaged two hundred and fifty thousand a year. They come mainly from Germany and the British Isles.

GOVERNMENT.—The Government of the United States is a confederation of the several States, delegating a portion of their power to a central government, whose laws are always paramount to State authority. The governing power is divided into legislative, judicial, and executive. The executive power is vested in a President and Vice-President, elected by the people, who hold their office for four years. The legislative power is exercised by a Congress composed of two branches, a Senate and House of Representatives; the former representing the several States in their sovereign capacity, and the House of Representatives the people of each State. The members of the national legislature are respectively known as Senators, members of Congress, and delegates, or Territorial members. The Congress is held annually at Washington. The judiciary consists of a supreme court, nine circuit and numerous district courts. The Supreme Court is presided over by a chief and eight associate justices. For each circuit there is a circuit judge, who must reside therein, and for each district a district judge. Each judge of the Supreme Court is assigned to one of these circuits, and must attend at least one term of the court in the circuit to which he is assigned, once in two years. All the judges of the U. S. Courts are appointed by the President, with the concurrence of the Senate, and hold their offices during life or good behavior.

HISTORY, ETC.—The earliest settlements within the present territory of the United States were made by the Spaniards in Florida, about 1565; but, as this State was not acquired till 1819, it is usual to date the commencement of the settlement of the colonies which formed the foundation of the present Union, from the settlement of Jamestown, Virginia, in 1607. New York was settled by the Dutch, in 1614; Massachusetts, at Plymouth, in 1620; and New Hampshire and Maine, in 1623. Washington, D. C., is the capital of the United States, and New York its chief commercial city. Next to the latter, the most important cities are Philadelphia, Baltimore, Boston, Brooklyn, New Orleans, Cincinnati, St. Louis, Chicago, San Francisco, Buffalo, Pittsburg, Detroit, Cleveland, Charleston, Mobile, Savannah, Louisville, Albany, and Providence.

The military history of the nation is properly divided into four periods or epochs, known respectively as the War of the Revolution, the War of 1812, the War with Mexico, and the Rebellion. The first of these closed with the surrender of Cornwallis at Yorktown, October 19, 1781. The

War of 1812 is conspicuous for the battles of Lundy's Lane and New Orleans, the former of which was fought July 25, 1814, and the latter, January 8, 1815. The war with Mexico commenced May 8, 1846, and virtually closed with the occupation of the city of Mexico (September 20, 1847) by the United States forces under General Scott. The late Rebellion commenced with the attack on Fort Sumter, in the harbor of Charleston, South Carolina, April 11, 1861, and closed with the occupation of Richmond and the surrender of Generals Lee and Johnston, April, 1865.

The leading military movements which have at different times been carried on within the territory of the United States will be found briefly recorded in the chapters descriptive of the localities in which they occurred, as will also the leading subjects of interest throughout the country.

THE NORTHERN AND EASTERN TOUR.

NEW YORK.

The first State in the Union in population, in wealth, and in commercial importance, exceeded by none in the fertility of its soil and the healthfulness of its climate, unsurpassed in the variety and beauty of its natural scenery, and in its historical associations, New York is appropriately called the Empire State.

Its length from east to west is 335 miles, and its breadth about 300 miles, embracing an area of 47,000 square miles, or about 30,000,000 acres.

The earliest settlements within the State were made by the Dutch, at Fort Orange (Albany), and at New Amsterdam, now New York City. This was in 1614, five years after the voyage of Hendrick Hudson up the waters of that river which now bears his name.

In 1664 the colony fell into the possession of the English, was recaptured by the Dutch in 1673, and finally came again under British rule in 1674, and so continued until the period of the Revolution. Many stirring events occurred within this territory during the wars between France and England, in 1690, 1702, and 1744, and through all the years of the War of Independence. These events the traveller will find duly chronicled as he reaches the various locations where they occurred, in the course of our intended travels.

Every variety of surface and every character of physical aspect are found within the great area of New York; vast fertile plains and grand mountain-ranges, meadows of richest verdure, and wild forest-tracts, lakes innumerable and of infinite variety in size and beauty, waterfalls unequalled on the continent for extent and grandeur, and rivers matchless in picturesque charms. We need not now recount these wonders, as our rambles will afford us, by-and-by, abundant opportunity to see them all in turn and time—the peaks and gorges of the Adirondacks and the Catskills, the floods of Niagara, and the ravines of Trenton, the pure placid waters of Lake George, the mountain-shores of Champlain, the deer-filled wildernesses and the highland passes of the Hudson, and all the intricate reticulation of cities, towns, villages, villas, and watering-places.

The principal cities of the State are the metropolis New York, Brooklyn, Buffalo, Albany, Troy, Rochester, Syracuse, Utica, Elmira, etc.

Though originally settled by the Dutch, and in the social features of many portions of its extended territory still partaking largely of the characteristic traits of that people, the constant and increasing infusion of New England and of foreign population has contributed to give to New York a more thoroughly cosmopolitan character than is enjoyed by any other State or people of the Union.

The internal improvements of the State are vast and important. Among the most prominent public works are the Erie Canal, 304 miles long, completed in 1825, at a cost of $7,000,000. This work, with its numerous branches and feeders, embracing a system of artificial communication of nearly 1,000 miles, constitutes by far the most important line of public works on the continent. But New York has natural advantages greater far than canal or railway alone can bestow. She has 365 miles of lake coast, 206 miles of interior lake, and 245 miles of river navigation.

NEW YORK CITY.

The city of New York, the largest and most important city of the Western Continent, is situated at the mouth of the Hudson River, on New York Bay, in latitude about 41°, longitude 74°. The city and county are identical in limits, and occupy the entire surface of Manhattan Island; Randall's, Ward's and Blackwell's Islands, in the East River; and Bedloe's, Ellis's, and Governor's Islands, in the bay—the last three being occupied by the United States Government.

Manhattan Island, on which the city proper stands, is thirteen and a half miles in length, with an average breadth of one and three-fifths miles, forming an area of nearly twenty-two square miles, or fourteen thousand acres. The islands in the East River and the bay make four thousand additional acres.

New York Island is bounded on the north by Harlem River, on the east are East River and Long Island Sound, with its clusters of beautiful islets, and on the west the Hudson River.

A rocky ridge originally ran from the southern point of the island northward, sending out several jagged spurs, which, after branching irregularly for several miles, culminated in Washington Heights (two hundred and thirty-eight feet above tide-water), and in a sharp, precipitous promontory, one hundred and thirty feet high, at its northern extremity. Most of the lower portion is composed of alluvial sand-beds.

The city proper extends from the southern extremity (Battery Point), and is compactly built for a distance of about six miles, and irregularly, on the east side, to Harlem, four miles farther. On the west side, it is almost solidly built to about Fifty-second Street, and thence irregularly to above Bloomingdale (Seventy-eighth Street), whence occur the refreshing greenness, and long lines of country-seats and elegant suburban residences of Manhattanville and Washington Heights. The harbor of New York is one of the finest and most beautiful in the world. The outer bar is at Sandy Hook, eighteen miles from the Battery, and is crossed by two ship-channels, which are from twenty-one to thirty-two feet deep at low, and from twenty-seven to thirty-nine feet at high tide, admitting vessels of the heaviest draught. The Narrows and the rivers surrounding the city are very deep, with strong tidal currents, keeping them in winter almost constantly clear of ice.

The history of the city of New York is somewhat remarkable. Scathed by war, fire, riot, and pestilence, its growth from a village of 1,000 inhabitants, in 1656, to 1,000,000 at the present day—its vast public works, its magnificent buildings, its leagues of roaring thoroughfares, and its colossal commerce—afford an imposing monument of the speed with which a youthful people may stride to opulence and power.

As the steamer from abroad enters New York Bay from the sea, and sails between the villa-crowned shores of Staten and Long Islands, through that contracted passage known as the Narrows, on the left are seen the massive battlements of Fort Richmond, and the water-battery of Fort Tompkins, on Staten Island. These fortifications are quite new, are constructed of gray-stone, mounted with guns of huge caliber, and are among the most imposing objects that first greet the vision of the passenger from the water-waste. The water-battery is the most fort-like in appearance, but, in the event of a fleet of iron-clads undertaking to force an entrance, would probably prove more vulnerable than the batteries on the heights, from which a continuous volley of plunging shot could be directed with as much effect as from Gibraltar or any stronghold in the world.

Opposite, on the Long Island shore, is the formidable Fort Hamilton, which numbers in its armament several of the celebrated Rodman guns, whose iron spherical shot of one thousand pounds would prove disagreeable to almost any iron ship-of-war that floats; and also the old, round, red Fort Lafayette, isolated in the waves, more famous as a rebel prison than as a fortress.

Passing amid these noble guardians of the harbor, with a fleeting glimpse of the foam-fringed neck of Coney Island, the panorama of the great island-city of the Western Hemisphere is at once unfolded. To the left is Bedloe's Island, a mere

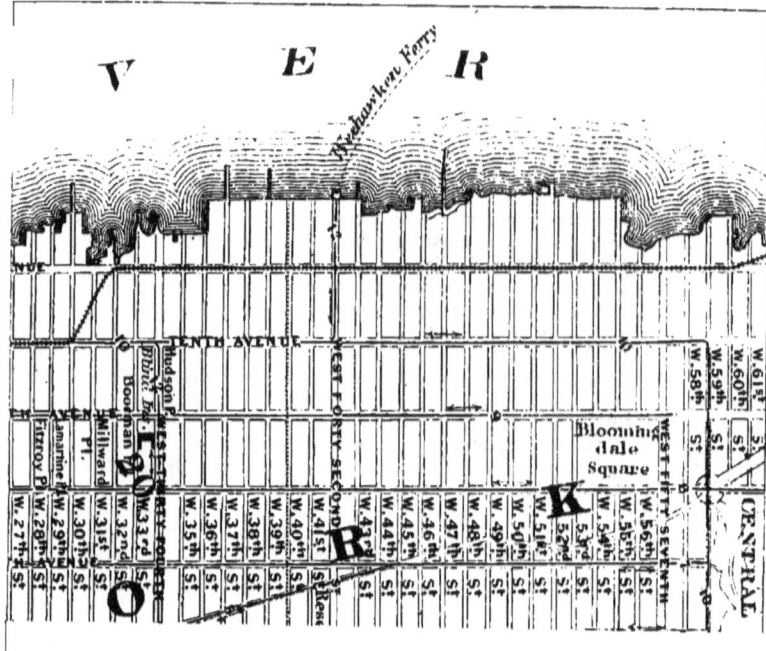

Fold-out
Placehol

This fold-out is being digitized, and
future date.

bank in the water, almost made for the convenience of the United States Government in the construction of a fort. Another island-fort (Ellis's Island), smaller and more insignificant, stands still farther toward the Jersey shore; and then, well round the point of Governor's Island, stands old Fort Columbus. Passing beyond the westerly point of Governor's Island, in the upward sweep to a North River pier, the entire length of the empire city is spread out to view. There are to be seen the crowd of sail upon the rivers, the puffing and busy tugs, the numerous ferry-boats, "the forests of masts," the big ships, the mammoth steamboats, Trinity spire, looming up so nobly, the dome of the City Hall, the well-known Castle Garden, and the crowded Brooklyn and Jersey shores.

The early history of the city of New York is involved in no inconsiderable degree of uncertainty. The Norse or Northmen, as is affirmed by Scandinavian records, visited these shores, which were then known as part of the ancient Vineland, as early as 1014. The generally acknowledged commencement of European civilization in this part of the newly-discovered continent, however, commenced with the arrival, in the bay of New York, of Hendrick Hudson, an Englishman in the service of the Dutch East India Company, who arrived at the site of the present city, September 3, 1609. He afterward sailed up the river which now bears his name in a vessel called the Half Moon. In 1614 an expedition under Captains Black and Christianse arrived, and commenced the settlement of the future city. At the close of that year the future metropolis of New York consisted of a small fort, on the site of the present Bowling Green, and four houses, and was known as "Nieuw Amsterdam." As late as 1648 it contained but 1,000 inhabitants. In 1664 it was surrendered to the British, and, passing into the hands of the Duke of York, was thenceforward known as New York. In 1677 it contained 384 houses. In 1700 the population had increased to about 6,000. Eleven years subsequently, a market for slaves was opened in Wall Street; and in 1725 a weekly paper, the *New York Gazette*, the fifth newspaper published in the colonies, made its first appearance. On June 28, 1776, the British army and fleet entered the bay of New York, and effected a landing on Staten Island. Crossing the Narrows, they encountered the American forces near Brooklyn (August 22d), and fought the battle of Long Island. For eight years succeeding this battle, New York remained the headquarters of the British troops. The British forces evacuated the city November 25, 1783, which has since been known as Evacuation Day, and is annually celebrated. Within ten years after the War of Independence, New York had doubled its population. In 1807 the first steamboat to navigate the Hudson was built. The completion of the great Erie Canal followed in 1825, and the Croton Aqueduct in 1842, since which time the progress of the city, in spite of fire and pestilence which have often visited it, has been rapid and permanent.

Among the few historical localities and objects of interest which the rapid growth of New York, and the constant change incident to war, increase in population and trade, have left for the contemplation of the citizen and stranger, the following will be found best worthy attention.

Broadway, as the representative street and leading thoroughfare of the past, as well as of the present city, furnishes the best field for observation, and the Battery the best point from which to start on our antiquarian tour.

Bowling Green in the times of the Dutch was the court end of the town; that part of Broadway then called the "Heere Straas," in contradistinction to the Heere Wegh, which was the name of the highway beyond the walls, was already a popular part of New Amsterdam, and no doubt presented the most pleasing features of the town. On the opposite or east side of the street for a short distance, measured by its present length, seems to have been inhabited by the humbler and poorest classes, being mainly composed of hovels and small shanties. In front (south) of the Green, was the Parade, which also served as the market-place. The Bowling Green was first enclosed in 1732. The row of six buildings facing the Green on the south, and ex-

esting relics now left standing. It occupies the site of the "Kocks Tavern," built by Peter Kocks, an officer in the Dutch service, and an active leader in the Indian war of 1643. In colonial times it was the heart of the highest fashion in the colony, having been successively the residence and headquarters of Lords Cornwallis and Howe, General (Sir Henry) Clinton, and General Washington. Arnold occupied No. 5 Broadway, and in Clinton's headquarters his treasonable projects were concerted. Fulton died in a room in the present Washington Hotel, then No. 1 Marketfield Street. It was then (1815) used as a boarding-house, and was kept by a Mrs. Avery. Since 1849 it has been occupied as a hotel.

The freight-shed just north of the Kennedy House stands on the spot occupied during colonial times by the "Burns Coffee-House," and upon or near the site of the Dutch Tavern of Burgomaster Martin Crigier. Subsequently (1763) it was known as the "King's Arms." In 1765 General Gage held his headquarters here. During the British possession of the city, the traitor Arnold lodged here. It served in turn as boarding-house, tavern, and beer-garden, being last known as the Atlantic Garden, when it was numbered 11 Broadway. Previous to the present century, Chancellor Livingston resided at No. 5 in this block.

On the southerly corner of Morris Street stood the residence or parsonage of the Dominie Megapolensis. This afterward became the property of Balthasar Bayard, kinsman of Governor Stuyvesant, who erected a brewery on the premises, near the river-shore, the access to which ... a lane on the present line of Mor- North of and adjoining Morris

Street, erected by Walton, in 1754, is one of the few old structures remaining in the city.

HOTELS, RESTAURANTS, AND CLUBS.

HOTELS.—On arriving in a city where one cannot at once proceed to a home, the first thought that suggests itself to any one is, "Where shall I go?" and in New York the only difficulty in answering the question lies in the embarrassment consequent upon too many desirable places, for the unsurpassed excellence of its hotel accommodations is known the world round. There is no place where the traveller can find more solid comfort, combined with the most sumptuous elegance, or, if necessity or inclination call for economy, where comfort and attention can be secured at a smaller outlay. To those who object to a hotel life, and who intend passing any length of time in the city, a very large number of boarding and lodging houses afford an opportunity of almost unlimited choice, from the elegantly-appointed suites of apartments in the fashionable and exclusive localities to the modest room in a cheaper locality. To those who are so occupied by business as to be necessarily absent from their regular meals, the most pleasant and convenient course is to stay at some hotel kept upon the European plan—taking furnished rooms, and eating at some one of the numerous restaurants with which the city abounds, several of the most prominent of which will be mentioned hereafter.

One hundred and fifty-three hotels are given a place in the City Directory, and among such a number it would seem as if all tastes could be suited. From among them we have selected the most popular of each class, and our readers may confidently rely upon polite attention at any of those we mention, though the expense is often greatly modified by the class of room occupied. In our list we first mention the more fashionable and higher-priced hotels, afterward naming a few of those that are principally frequented by business-men and country merchants.

The *Albemarle* is a quiet house on the European plan, situated at the corner of Broadway and Twenty-fourth Street.

The *Astor House*, at the lower end of the Park, has a front on Broadway, extending from Vesey to Barclay Street, and is now conducted exclusively upon the European plan; a change much regretted by its old customers.

The "*Brevoort*," 11 Fifth Avenue, corner of Eighth Street (Clinton Place), (Clarke & Waite), is on the European plan. It is large, well kept, and in a desirable location.

The *Clarendon* (60 Union Place), corner of Seventeenth Street and Fourth Avenue, is a very fashionable house, of special repute among English travellers. It is kept by Charles H. Kerne.

The *Coleman House* (Robert B. Coleman & Co.) is on Broadway, corner of Twenty-seventh Street. It contains about 200 rooms, and is kept upon the European plan.

The *Everett House* (William B. Burroughs) is on the corner of Seventeenth Street and Fourth Avenue, fronting on Union Square. It is on the European plan.

The *FifthAvenue Hotel* (Darling, Griswold & Co.) fronts on Madison Square, and occupies the entire block from Twenty-third to Twenty-fourth Street. It is admirably kept, and has accommodations for 1,100 guests.

The *Gramercy Park House* (Curtis Judson) is in East Twentieth Street, fronting on Gramercy Park. It is essentially a family hotel, and has a very pleasant location.

The *Grand Hotel*, corner of Broadway and Thirty-first Street, is new and large. The proprietors claim that it is the most handsomely-furnished and best-appointed hotel in the world. It is on the European plan.

The "*Great Central*" is a hotel of very large capacity, just completed, being enlarged from what was recently known as the *Southern Hotel*, and originally as the *La Farge House*. It is situated on Broadway, between Bleecker and Amity Streets.

The *Madison Park Hotel*, Twenty-second Street, Broadway and Fifth Avenue, is a first-class quiet family house.

The *Hoffman House* (Mitchell & Reed), 1114 Broadway, between Twenty-fourth and Twenty-fifth Streets, is another fashionable hotel on the European plan.

The *Metropolitan* (S. Leland & Co.), corner of Prince Street and Broadway, is one of the largest and best hotels in the

The *New York Hotel* (D. M. Hildreth & Co.) occupies the whole square bounded by Broadway, East Washington Place, and Waverley Place. It is very popular among Southerners.

The *St. Cloud* (Rand Brothers, European plan) is on the corner of Broadway and Forty-second Street. It is farther up-town than any other first-class hotel in the city, and possesses superior accommodations for families.

The *St. Denis* (Mosber & Reed), corner of Broadway and Eleventh Street; the *St. Elmo*, Twenty-ninth Street and Broadway; the *St. George*, Twentieth Street and Broadway; and the *St. James* (Elias Hitchcock), corner of Broadway and Twenty-sixth Street, are all first-class houses kept upon the European plan.

The *St. Nicholas* (S. Hawk), Broadway, between Broome and Spring Streets, is large, well kept, and very popular.

The *Westminster* (Palmer & Ferrin), 119 East Sixteenth Street, is a noted hotel, on the European plan, and is habitually frequented by many distinguished persons.

In addition to the above, are a number of *family hotels*, which bear a deservedly high reputation, such as the *Irving House* (George P. Harlow), 49 East Twelfth Street; *Lenox House* (James Slater), 72 Fifth Avenue; *Spingler House* (F. H. Orvis, 5 Union Place; *Union Place* (H. C. Fling), 58 East Fourteenth Street; *Union Square* (A. J. Dam & Co.), 18 Union Place; *Wadsworth House* (D. P. Peters), 63 Fifth Avenue; and the *Westmoreland* (George Roberts), Union Place, corner of East Seventeenth Street.

BUSINESS HOTELS.—In the lower part of the city, surrounded by the wholesale houses, are a number of hotels, the charges in all of which are moderate, and which are principally supported by country merchants. Among the most popular are *Bang's*, 251 Canal Street; *Brandreth* (William J. Kerr), corner of Broadway and Canal; *Continental*, 442 Broadway; *Cosmopolitan*, corner of Chambers Street and West Broadway; *Earl's*, 241 Canal Street; *French's*, 1 Chatham Street, opposite the City Hall; *Merchants'* (Clarke & Schenck), 41 Cortlandt, and *National* (Arthur T. Halliday), 5 Cortlandt Street; *Park*, G. W. J. Wright, ʌkman Street; *Prescott House* (David

Hexter), 531 Broadway; *Stevens House* (Allen & Bodwell), 25 Broadway; and *United States* (George N. Terry), 198 Water Street.

It is impossible to give a correct scale of prices; but it is safe for any one to be prepared to pay well if good accommodations are desired in fashionable localities. In the down-town hotels good rooms can be had, without board, from $1 to $2 per diem.

RESTAURANTS.—The city is filled with restaurants, and the ordinary traveller requires no guide to find them; for, wherever he may turn, a short walk will bring him to one. But, as many ladies do not know where they can go with comfort, it may be well to mention a few of the leading places where accommodations are especially provided for them. In the first place, with every hotel on the European plan is connected a restaurant, and any lady can, with propriety, visit any of these alone, if the house itself is first-class.

In the *Astor House* is a fine restaurant.

Bigot, 42 Fourteenth Street, between Fifth Avenue and Broadway, keeps a ladies' restaurant, which is quiet and respectable.

A. Iauch keeps a well-known and popular place at 864 Broadway, a short distance above Union Square.

Delmonico's, in Fifth Avenue, corner of Fourteenth Street, is the largest and most elegantly-appointed restaurant in New York.

The *New York Restaurant* (L. A. Geyer), 734 and 736 Broadway, opposite the New York Hotel, is pleasantly located and admirably kept.

Parker's, Broadway and Sixth Avenue, between Thirty-third and Thirty-fourth Streets, has for some time been favorably known as a gentleman's eating-house. An excellent ladies' department has recently been added.

E. Solari's, in University Place, corner of Eleventh Street, is noted for its dinners and suppers.

William Taylor, 555 Broadway, keeps an excellent restaurant, which may be visited by ladies without any hesitation.

Of the leading restaurants frequented by business men, Delmonico keeps three: one at the corner of Broadway and Chambers Street; one in Broad Street, near the Stock Exchange; and the third, No. 2 South William Street.

Crook, Fox & Nash keep a popular place at No. 39 Park Row.

Rudolph has two restaurants in Broadway; one below Lispenard Street, and the other below John Street.

There are very many other capital places of the same kind; but enough have been mentioned to afford an ample opportunity to make a selection.

CLUBS.—The clubs of New York are very numerous; and some of them, being of great wealth, own elegant buildings, the exterior being about all with which the ordinary traveller can delight his sense of the beautiful; though, if he happens to have any friends among the members, he can obtain the *entrée* subject to certain conditions. Among the most prominent of these clubs are the *Century*, 109 East Fifteenth Street; *City*, 31 East Seventeenth Street; *Manhattan*, 96 Fifth Avenue; *Travellers'*, 222 Fifth Avenue; *Union*, corner of Fifth Avenue and West Twenty-first Street; and *Union League*, Madison Avenue, corner of East Twenty-sixth Street.

CONVEYANCES.

ONCE comfortably settled in the city, the visitor naturally inquires "where to go and how to get there?" but we will give an inverted answer, and, after detailing the different means of communication, will name the places of amusement, the churches, and the parks, and will then visit the principal buildings, streets, and avenues.

In a city like New York, where distances are so great, and where the city proper is surrounded by broad and deep rivers, the means of communication must be numerous and varied in their character. Within the city proper are *omnibuses*, *hackney* and *livery coaches*, *horse-cars*, and, to the more remote portions, *steam-cars*.

OMNIBUSES, formerly very numerous, have, by the introduction of street railways, been greatly reduced in number, and at present there are but seven lines in the city, as follows: 1. From South Ferry to Thirty-second Street *via* Broadway and Fourth Avenue. 2. From South Ferry to Thirtieth Street depot, N. Y. C. & H. R. R. R. *via* Broadway, Twenty-third Street, and Ninth Avenue. 3. From. South Ferry to Tenth Street Ferry and Dry Dock *via* Broadway and Eighth Street. 4. Wall Street Ferry to Fortieth Street *via* Broadway and Madison Avenue. 5. From Fulton Ferry to Forty-third Street *via* Broadway and Fifth Avenue. 6. From the Jersey City Ferry to the Williamsburgh Ferry *via* Broadway, Bleecker, and Second Streets. 7. The free line of the Erie Railway from the corner of Twenty-third Street and Broadway to the ferry foot of Twenty-third Street, Hudson River. With the exception of the Second Street line, which is eight cents, and the last-named line, fares are ten cents for each person.

HORSE, STREET RAILWAYS.—This mode of conveyance has now become thoroughly popularized throughout the United States, and has come to be considered indispensable in our principal cities. The routes of the different street railroads are given below, *fares* in all cases being *five cents* for each adult, except where otherwise stated.

Central Park, North and East River (Belt Line), *Western Division.*—From Fifth Avenue entrance, Central Park, *via* Fifty-ninth Street to First Avenue; thence to Fourteenth Street, then through Fourteenth Street, Avenues C and D, and several minor streets, to Grand Street and East River; thence down South, Water, and Front Streets to South Ferry, at the Battery.

Second Avenue.—From Harlem, through Second Avenue to Twenty-third Street, First Avenue, Allen, and Grand Streets, Bowery, Chatham, and Pearl Streets, to Peck Slip, East River, returning through South and Oliver Streets, Bowery, Grand, and Chrystie Streets, to Second Avenue, thence to Harlem.

Third Avenue.—This is a direct route from the Astor House through Park Row, Chatham Street, Bowery, and Third Avenue, to Harlem—a route eight miles in length.

Fourth Avenue.—This road belongs to the New York and Harlem Railway, and runs from foot of East Thirty-fourth Street past the depot of the Harlem Road, on Fourth Avenue, to the Astor

11

House. A branch extends through Madison Avenue to Central Park. Fare *six cents*.

Broadway. — From Central Park to Astor House, through Seventh Avenue, Broadway, University Place, Houston, and Canal Streets, to West Broadway, and thence through Barclay Street to terminus; returning by same route, except that Church and Greene Streets are substituted for West Broadway and Wooster Streets. Branch to corner of Broome Street and Broadway.

Sixth Avenue.—From Central Park to Astor House, through Sixth Avenue, Carmine, Varick, and Canal Streets, West Broadway, and Vesey Street. Branch to corner of Canal Street and Broadway.

Seventh Avenue.—Central Park to Astor House through Seventh and Greenwich Avenues, Macdougal, Thompson, and Canal Streets, West Broadway, Barclay, and connecting streets; returning through Church and Sullivan, instead of Barclay and Macdougal Streets.

Eighth Avenue.—From Manhattanville (One Hundred and Twenty-fifth Street) to Astor House, through Eighth Avenue, Hudson and Canal Streets, West Broadway, and Vesey Street. Branch to corner Canal Street and Broadway. *Fare above Fifty-ninth Street five cents additional.*

Ninth Avenue.—From corner of Fifty-first Street, through Ninth Avenue, Washington and Fulton Streets, to corner of Fulton Street and Broadway.

Central Park, North and East River (Belt Line), *Eastern or Tenth Avenue Division.*—From Central Park, through Fifty-ninth Street, Tenth Avenue, West Street, Battery Place, State and Whitehall Streets, to South Ferry.

These may be called the grand trunk lines, either running the entire length of the city or connecting with through-lines.

The shorter lines, whose general direction is the same, as nearly as the shape of the island permits, but which are not so long, are—

Avenue B.—From Thirty-fourth Street Ferry, through Avenue A, Fourteenth Street, Avenue B, Second Street, Avenue A, Essex Street, East Broadway, Chatham Street, and Park Row, to the lower end of City Hall Park; returning, passes through the same or parallel streets.

Dry Dock and East Broadway.—From Fourteenth Street and Avenue B, along Fourteenth Street, Avenue D, Eighth Street, Lewis and Grand Streets, East Broadway, Chatham Street, and Park Row, to the Astor House.

Dry Dock and East Broadway Company (Avenue D Line).—The route of this road is so nearly identical with the preceding one as only to be of interest to those living along its line.

We have now disposed of all the street horse-railway companies, except those known as the cross-town lines, which are four in number. As it would consume too much space to designate the details of their respective routes, we will content ourselves with giving their termini, and the principal streets through which they pass.

Bleecker Street and Fulton Ferry.—This road connects the Fulton Ferry (for Brooklyn) with the Twenty-third Street Ferry of the Erie Railway on the Hudson River. Running from Twenty-third Street and the Hudson River, it passes through Fourteenth, Hudson, Bleecker, and Crosby, to corner of Canal, where it divides; about two-thirds of the cars proceed by way of the City Hall and Beekman Street to Fulton Ferry. The other third turn off at Canal Street, and run to the ferry by way of Bowery and Franklin Square.

Grand and Cortlandt Street Ferries.—This road connects the Grand Street Ferries (for Williamsburgh) with the Jersey City Ferry, Cortlandt Street, by as direct a route as the topography of the city will permit.

Grand Street.—This is an almost air line, from the Williamsburgh Ferry, at Grand Street, to the Jersey City Ferry, at Desbrosses Street (near Canal Street), and traverses the entire length of Grand Street.

Forty-second Street and Grand Street Ferry.—This road is quite a long one, and pursues a somewhat devious route from the Weehawken Ferry, at the foot of Forty-second Street, Hudson River, to the Grand Street Ferries for Williamsburgh.

Houston and Prince.—Runs from foot of East Seventeenth Street (East River) through Avenue C, Third Street, First

Avenue, Houston and Washington Streets, to foot of Duane Street, Hudson River; returns through Duane, Greenwich, Charlton and Prince Streets, Bowery, Stanton and Pitt Streets, and Avenue C. Connects with Greenpoint Ferry (East River), and Houston Street Ferry to Williamsburgh, and with Fort Lee, Desbrosses Street (for Jersey City) and Pavonia Ferries.

There is yet one street railway to be mentioned, and that is the Elevated Railway through Ninth Avenue and connecting streets, from Thirtieth Street to the Battery. The track is perched upon iron pillars, and the motion originally was communicated to the cars by means of an endless chain, connecting with engines, placed under the sidewalk, at intervals of half a mile. This plan not proving satisfactory, small dummy engines have been placed on the track. A second track will be necessary before the road can be extensively used.

Though not an enjoyable means of locomotion, the cars of the Third, Fourth, Sixth, Seventh, and Eighth Avenues, and of the Broadway lines, will give a traveller who wishes to obtain an idea of the city, as it is, and at the same time to economize time and money, more satisfaction than any other that he could select, for they pass in their routes among the business houses and residences of almost every class of people.

The hackney-coaches and livery-carriages are very much the same as those of other large cities, and the amount a person pays rests in a great measure with himself. If he sends to a livery-stable, he is charged according to the time he uses the conveyance and its character. If he takes a hackney-coach, he is not compelled to pay more than is authorized by the municipal law, which not only fixes the rates of fare, but provides that a card having these rates shall be prominently posted in every carriage. If, as is often the case, a driver attempts to be extortionate, an appeal to the first policeman will soon bring him to terms.

Suburban Communication, by means of trunk lines of horse-cars, has already been noted, but this is altogether too slow, and of inadequate capacity to accommodate the large population in the upper part of this island, and the adjoining county of Westchester; and consequently frequent "accommodation trains" are run on the railroads entering the city from the north, arriving and departing at intervals of not more than fifteen to thirty minutes each, and stopping every two or three miles at the little stations with which the lines are dotted.

One of these roads, the "New York Central and Hudson River," has its terminal station in the square bounded by Twenty-ninth and Thirtieth Streets and Ninth and Tenth Avenues; and the other two, the Harlem and the New Haven roads, entering the city by the same track, have their terminal stations at the corner of Thirty-second Street and Fourth Avenue. These roads need no further mention here, as they have been treated under the general head of "railroads."

FERRIES.

The ferries connecting New York with its adjacent cities and towns are twenty-six in number, as follows:

To Astoria.—Foot of East Ninety-second Street, to which the most available means of access are the Second and Third Avenue Railroads.

To Brooklyn.—Catherine Slip to Main Street. From 5 A. M. to 9 P. M. every five minutes; from 9 to 12 P. M. every twenty minutes. Reached by Second Avenue cars, and cars of Eastern Division of Central Park, North and East River Railroad, known as "Belt Line."

Fulton Street to Fulton Street.—From 3 A. M. to 12 P. M. every three minutes; from 12 to 3 A. M. every fifteen minutes. Reached by Fifth Avenue stages, Bleecker Street cars, and the cars of the Eastern Division of the Belt Line.

Jackson Street to Hudson Avenue.— From 5.30 A. M. to 10 P. M. Reached by cars of Eastern Division of the Belt Line.

Wall Street to Montague Street.—From 5 A. M. to 8 P. M. every five minutes; from 8 P. M. to midnight every twenty minutes. Reached by Madison Avenue stages and cars of Eastern Division of the Belt Line.

South Ferry.—Whitehall Street to Atlantic Street. From 5 A. M. to 11 P. M. every *twelve* minutes; from 11 P. M. to 5

A. M. every half hour. Reached by Twenty-third Street, Fourth Avenue, and Eighth Street lines of stages, and by the cars of both divisions of the Belt Line.

Hamilton Ferry.—Whitehall Street to Atlantic Dock. From 7 A. M. to 6.30 P. M. every five minutes; 6.30 P. M. to 9 P. M. every fifteen minutes; from 9 P. M. to 7 A. M. every half hour. Reached by same conveyances as South Ferry.

New Chambers Street to Bridge Street. —From 5 A. M. to 10 P. M. every fifteen minutes. Reached by Second Avenue cars, and cars of the Eastern Division Belt Line.

To Brooklyn, E. D. (Williamsburgh).— Peck Slip Ferry.—Roosevelt Street to Broadway. From 5 A. M. to 8 P. M. every *ten* minutes; from 8 P. M. to 5 A. M. every twenty minutes. Reached by cars of Eastern Division Belt Line.

East Houston Street to Grand Street. Reached by Houston Street cars, and cars of Eastern Division Belt Line.

Grand Street to Grand Street, and Grand Street to Broadway. Reached by cars of Belt Line, and of both Grand Street lines.

To Greenpoint.—East Tenth Street and East Twenty-third Street to L Street. Reached by cars of the Eastern Division Belt Line, East Broadway cars, and by Eighth Street stages.

To Hunter's Point.—East Thirty-fourth Street.—From 4.30 A. M. to 12 P. M. every *fifteen* minutes; after 8 P. M. every thirty minutes. Reached by the Fourth Avenue cars, and the cars of the Eastern Division Belt Line. From James Street every half hour. Reached by the cars of the Eastern Division Belt Line.

To Staten Island (Tompkinsville, Stapleton, and Vanderbilt Landings.—From Whitehall Street (at Battery).—From 5 A. M. to 9 P. M. every hour; then at 11.45 P. M. The 5, 7, and 9 A. M., and the 1, 4, 5, and 6 P. M. boats connect with the trains of the Staten Island Railway. Reached by same conveyances as South Ferry.

Elm Park, Factoryville, Port Richmond, and Snug Harbor.—From Pier 19, Hudson River, between Cortlandt and Dey Streets, 7.30, 9.30, and 11 A. M., and 12.30, 2, 4, 5, and 6.30 P. M. Reached by cars of Ninth Avenue and Western Division Belt Line Railroads.

To Jersey City.—Cortlandt Street to Montgomery Street.—From 7 A. M. to 10 P. M. every ten minutes; from 10 P. M. to 12 P. M. every fifteen minutes; from 12 P. M. to 4 A. M. every thirty minutes; from 4 A. M. to 7 A. M. every fifteen minutes. Reached by the cars of the Western Division Belt Line, of the Grand and Cortlandt Street line, and by the Broadway and Second Street line of stages.

Desbrosses Street to Exchange Place. —This ferry lands in Jersey City, at the Camden and Amboy Railroad Depot. Reached by Grand Street, Houston Street, and Belt Line Railways.

To Pavonia.—From Chambers Street, Hudson River, to Long Dock, from 1 A. M. to 7 P. M. every fifteen minutes; from 7 P. M. to 1 A. M. every half hour. Reached by cars of Western Division of Belt Line.

Twenty-third Street to Long Dock.— Connects with all trains on the Erie Railway. Reached by Bleecker Street cars, and Erie line of Twenty-third Street stages.

To Hoboken.—Barclay Street to Henry Street. Reached by Ninth Avenue cars, and cars of Western Division Belt Line.

Christopher Street to Henry Street.— From 7.45 A. M. to 7.30 P. M. every fifteen minutes. Reached by cars of Houston Street and Western Division Belt Line Railroads.

To Weehawken.—Foot of West Forty-second Street. From 6 A. M. to 9 P. M. every twenty minutes. Reached by Grand and Forty-second Street cars, and by Western Division Belt Line.

To Fort Lee and Pleasant Valley.—From Pier 51, Hudson River, between Christopher and West Tenth Street. Runs only in summer. Reached by Houston Street cars, and Western Division Belt Line

To Fort Lee, Shady Side, Bull's Ferry, and Pleasant Valley.—From Spring Street (North River). Four times a day in summer; in winter 10.30 A. M., and 4.45 P. M. Sundays 10 A. M. and 4.30 P.M. Reached by Houston Street cars, and Western Division Belt Line.

To Communipaw.—From Liberty Street (North River). Reached by cars of Western Division Belt Line.

PLACES OF AMUSEMENT.

There probably is no city in the world more abundantly furnished with places of amusement than New York, and probably there is nowhere a greater variety of entertainments, to suit all tastes, from the lecture-rooms of the scientific and educational institutions to the cellar concert-halls of Chatham Street. Those mentioned in this book can be classed as opera-houses, legitimate theatres, variety theatres, museums, concert-halls, lecture-rooms, Ethiopian minstrels; and the circus.

There are three opera-houses, named, respectively, Academy of Music, French Theatre, and Grand Opera-House.

The *Academy of Music* is at the corner of Fourteenth Street and Irving Place, a short distance east of Broadway. It is the home of Italian opera in New York, and is also used for grand balls and large public gatherings.

The *French Theatre* is on Fourteenth Street, about one hundred feet west of Sixth Avenue. It is, as its name indicates, especially designed for French artistes, but is also used for English opera and dramatic representations, and, during the winter, for balls, being admirably adapted for the purpose.

The *Grand Opera-House*, one of the handsomest buildings in the city, is at the corner of Eighth Avenue and Twenty-third Street. Besides being one of the largest and most elegant places of amusement in the United States, it is noted for the care which the management bestows upon the scenery and stage appointments. It is only occasionally occupied by an opera troupe, being chiefly used for dramatic representations.

The legitimate theatres are seven in number. *Booth's Theatre*, at the corner of Sixth Avenue and Twenty-third Street, was built expressly for the production of Shakespearian and other plays of the highest class, and during the regular season is devoted exclusively to that purpose. Mr. Booth bestows the greatest care upon all the appointments of the plays presented; scenery, costumes, and stage furniture, being of the most accurate description. The building is of the finest Concord granite, is in the Renaissance style of architecture, and is considered one of the finest structures in New York.

The *Bowery Theatre*, in the Bowery, below Canal Street, seats over 3,000 people. To suit the tastes of its peculiar audiences, the performances are always of a strikingly sensational character.

The *Fifth Avenue Theatre*, on Twenty-fourth Street, in the rear of the Fifth Avenue Hotel, is a charming little box. It is principally used for light operas, and for legitimate comedies, and is one of the most fashionable resorts in the city.

Niblo's is entered from Broadway, above Prince Street, through the Metropolitan Hotel. With the exception of the Bowery, it is the oldest theatre in the city, but is still as popular as when first opened. It is well ventilated and pleasant, and at one time was greatly frequented by people who, while they saw no wrong in a comedy, pantomime, or ballet at "Niblo's Garden," would not visit a *theatre*.

The *Olympic*, on Broadway, above Houston Street, has passed through the hands of a number of managers, and is not noted for adhering especially to any particular class of performances. It was in this theatre that Mr. Sothern made his reputation as Lord Dundreary, and it was also here that Mr. Jefferson became prominent as a comedian.

The *Stadt Theatre*, in the Bowery, between Bayard and Canal Streets, is a large building used for German theatrical and operatic performances.

Wallack's, corner of Broadway and Thirteenth Street, is devoted to legitimate comedy. The company is always good, the plays mounted with the greatest care, and the audience refined and cultivated. Until within a very short time it has had no rival in these respects.

Union League Theatre.—This is a beautiful private theatre, in the Union League Club Building, corner of Twenty-sixth Street and Madison Avenue. Until recently it was only used for amateur performances, but is now occasionally thrown open to the public.

There are but three variety theatres, the Théâtre Comique, Tony Pastor's, and the Globe.

The *Globe*, on the east side of Broadway nearly opposite the New York Hotel, was for many years used as a church, was afterward changed to a theatre, and now, after a number of failures as a legitimate theatre, has finally succeeded as at present managed; the entertainment consisting of singing, dancing, negro minstrelsy, farces, and gymnastic performances.

Tony Pastor's "*Opera House*," as it is called, is on the east side of the Bowery, below Houston Street, and for several years has been the most steadily popular place of amusement on the Bowery. It is almost invariably crowded at every performance. The entertainment is of the same character as that at the Globe.

The *Théâtre Comique*, Broadway, opposite the St. Nicholas Hotel, is of the same character as Tony Pastor's.

To the curious, the museums of New York furnish few attractions, though the probability is that, in course of time, the museum at the Central Park, which at present is almost in an embryo state, will become an institution worthy of the name. At present the small collection of specimens is in what is known as the Armory, a short distance from the Fifth Avenue entrance.

Wood's Museum, Broadway, corner of Thirtieth Street, has a fair collection of curiosities and quite a number of wild animals. Connected with it is a theatre, in which dramatic performances are given every afternoon and evening. This museum is the only legitimate successor of the famous "Barnum's."

The *Museum of Anatomy*, on Broadway, above Houston Street, is of more interest to the medical student and practical anatomist than to the casual visitor. To a sensitive person, unaccustomed to the wards of a hospital, it is a perfect chamber of horrors.

The reputable concert-halls are of two classes, those known as "gardens," and those used only for occasional musical entertainments. Of the first named, the Central Park Garden and the Atlantic Garden are the best known and the largest.

The *Central Park Garden* is a large frame building at Central Park terminus of the Seventh Avenue and Broadway Railroads. In the rear is an open-air promenade, which is called a "garden." Every evening during the summer season choice music is rendered by a fine orchestra to large audiences, who, seated around small tables, can enjoy the music, and at the same time partake of any of the delicacies provided at a first-class restaurant. It is frequented by people of all classes.

The *Atlantic Garden* is in the Bowery, next door to the Bowery Theatre. It is conducted on the same principle as the Central Park Garden, but is seldom frequented by any but Germans.

There are many others of a similar class scattered through the city.

Steinway Hall, on Fourteenth Street, east of Broadway, is the leading hall for concerts, and is the favorite with the leading musicians, as it is not only an elegant room, but possesses fine acoustic properties.

The hall of the Cooper Institute, Apollo Hall, Irving Hall, Trenor's Lyric Hall, and many others, are used from time to time for concerts, lectures, etc.

Two first-class places of Ethiopian entertainment are open all the year round: "*Dan Bryant's*," Twenty-third Street, near Sixth Avenue, and "*Birch, Wambold, and Backus, San Francisco Minstrels*," on Broadway, opposite the Metropolitan Hotel. The performances consist of delineations of negro peculiarities, singing, and dancing. Persons wishing to enjoy a hearty laugh cannot do better than to visit either of these places.

The *New York Circus* is on Fourteenth Street, nearly opposite the Academy of Music.

There is still another class of places of amusement which it is difficult to place under any distinct head, as they combine the attractions of music, dancing (not ballet), gymnastics, eating, drinking, and out-of-door exercise. They are known by the name of "Gardens," which in some respects they merit, but they possess so many other attractions, that the garden, or *al fresco* department, is one of the least thought of. These gardens are very numerous, and are, as a rule, located in the upper part of the city, in Hoboken, and in Jersey City; among them are the Lion Park Garden, on Eighth Avenue; Jones's Wood, on the

East River, reached by Second or Third Avenue cars; Lanman's Park, on Third Avenue; Elm Park on the Bloomingdale Road, and Funke's Park, foot of Sixty-seventh Street, East River. These gardens are principally frequented by Germans, though the natives of the United States and other countries are gradually falling into the German custom of devoting their holidays to this kind of pleasure.

CHURCHES.

There are 333 places of public worship in New York City, as follows: Baptist, 30; Congregational, 5; Friends, 3; Jewish, 27; Lutheran, 13; Methodist Episcopal, 45; Presbyterian, 55; Protestant Episcopal, 73; Reformed (Dutch), 18; Roman Catholic, 39; Unitarian, 3; Universalist, 4; and of miscellaneous creeds, 18.

A few of the leading churches of each denomination are mentioned below, and strangers may always be sure of receiving polite attention, and of being shown to the best available seats.

Baptist.—Calvary, 50 West Twenty-third Street; R. J. W. Buckland, Minister. Fifth Avenue, West Forty-sixth Street, near Fifth Avenue; Thomas Armitage, Minister. Freewill Baptist, 104 West Seventeenth Street; C. E. Blake, Minister. Madison Avenue, corner East Thirty-first Street; Henry G. Weston, Minister. Murray Hill, Lexington Avenue, corner East Thirty-seventh Street; Sidney A. Corey, Minister. Tabernacle, 162 Second Avenue; J. R. Kendrick, Minister.

Congregational.—Church of the Pilgrims, 365 West Forty-eighth Street; Seymour A. Baker, Minister. New England, West Forty-first Street, near Sixth Avenue; Lyman Abbott, Minister. Tabernacle, Sixth Avenue, cor. West Thirty-fourth Street; J. P. Thompson, Minister.

Friends.—East Fifteenth Street, corner of Rutherford Place. Twentieth Street, East Twentieth Street, near Third Avenue. Twenty-seventh Street, 43 West Twenty-seventh Street.

Jewish Synagogues.—Temple, Fifth Avenue, cor. East Forty-third Street. Adas Jeshurun, West Thirty-ninth Street, near Seventh Avenue. Adereth El, 135 East Twenty-ninth Street. Beth Cholim, 138 West Thirty-eighth Street. Beth El, 248 West Thirty-third Street.

Lutheran.—Gustavus Adolphus, 91 East Twenty-second Street. Holy Trinity, West Twenty-first Street, near Sixth Avenue; G. F. Krotel, Minister. Lutheran, Avenue B, corner East Ninth Street; F. W. Foehlinger, Minister. St. James, 216 East Fifteenth Street; A. C. Wedekind, Minister. St. Luke's, 318 West Forty-third Street; G. W. Drees, Minister.

Methodist Episcopal.—Eighteenth Street, 307 West Eighteenth Street. Fifty-third Street, 231 West Fifty-third Street. Forty-third Street, 253 West Forty-third Street. John Street, 44 John Street. Ladies' Five Points Home Mission, 61 Park Street. Rose Hill, 221 East Twenty-seventh Street. St. Paul's, Fourth Avenue, cor. East Twenty-second Street. Trinity, 248 West Thirty-fourth Street. Twenty-fourth Street, 359 West Twenty-fourth Street.

Presbyterian.—Brick, Fifth Avenue, cor. West Thirty-seventh Street; Gardiner Spring, Minister. Church of the Covenant, Fourth Avenue, cor. East Thirty-fifth Street; George L. Prentiss, Minister. Fifth Avenue, cor. East Nineteenth Street; John Hall, Minister. First, Fifth Avenue, corner West Eleventh Street; W. M. Paxton, Minister. Fortieth Street, East Fortieth Street, near Lexington Avenue; John E. Annan, Minister. Forty-second Street, 233 West Forty-second Street; W. A. Scott, Minister. Fourth Avenue, 286 Fourth Avenue; Howard Crosby, Minister. Lexington Avenue, cor. East Forty-sixth Street; Joseph Sanderson, Minister. Madison Square, Madison Avenue, corner East Twenty-fourth Street; William Adams, Minister. Rutgers, Madison Avenue, cor. East Twenty-ninth Street; N. W. Conkling, Minister. Twenty-third Street, 210 West Twenty-third Street; H. D. Northrup, Minister. University Place, corner Tenth Street; A. H. Kellogg, Minister.

Protestant Episcopal.—Calvary, Fourth Avenue, cor. East Twenty-first Street; E. A. Washburn, Rector. Christ, Fifth Avenue, cor. East Thirty-fifth Street; F. C. Ewer, Rector. Du St. Esprit, 30 West Twenty-second Street; A. Verren, Rector. Grace, 800 Broadway; Henry Potter, Rector. St. Alban's, Lexington Avenue, corner East Forty-seventh Street;

C. W. Morrill, Rector. St. Ann's, 7 West Eighteenth Street; Thomas Gallaudet, Rector. St. George's, Rutherford Place, corner East Sixteenth Street; Stephen H. Tyng, Rector. St. John's, 46 Varick Street; S. H. Weston, Rector. St. Mark's, Stuyvesant Street, near Second Avenue; A. H. Vinton, Rector. St. Paul's, Broadway, corner Vesey Street; B. I. Haight, Minister. St. Thomas's, Fifth Avenue, cor. West Fifty-third Street; W. F. Morgan, Rector. Trinity, Broadway, corner Rector Street; and the Chapels of St. Paul's, St. John's, and Trinity Chapel; Morgan Dix, Rector; F. Vinton and F. Ogilby, Assistant Ministers. Trinity Chapel, 15 West Twenty-fifth Street; C. E. Swope and C. T. Olmsted, Assistant Ministers. Transfiguration, East Twenty-ninth Street, near Fifth Avenue; G. H. Houghton, Rector.

The services at Trinity and Trinity Chapel are conducted in the English cathedral manner, with full choir of boys. Christ Church is Ritualistic, and St. Alban's represents the most advanced views of the Ritualists. St. George's Church is the largest and most influential of those belonging to the "Low Church" portion of this denomination.

Reformed (Dutch).—Collegiate, Lafayette Place, corner East Fourth Street; North Dutch, cor. William and Fulton Streets; Fifth Avenue, cor. West Twenty-ninth Street; Lecture-room, West Forty-eighth Street, near Fifth Avenue; Thomas Dewitt, T. E. Vermilye, T. W. Chambers, Ministers. North Dutch, J. L. McNair, Missionary; 103 Fulton Street. South, Fifth Avenue, cor. West Twenty-first Street; E. P. Rogers, Minister. Washington Square, Washington Square, east corner Washington Place; Mancius S. Hutton, Minister.

Roman Catholic.—St. Ann's, 149 Eighth Street, T. S. Preston, Priest. St. Francis Xavier, 36 West Sixteenth Street; J. Loyzance, Priest. St. Patrick's Cathedral, cor. Mott and Prince Streets; Most Rev. John McCloskey, Archbishop; Very Rev. William Starrs, Vicar-General; T. S. Preston, Chancellor; F. McNeirny, Secretary; P. F. McSweeney, J. H. McGean, and J. Kearney, Priests. St. Peter's, corner Barclay and Church Streets; William Quinn, Priest. St. Stephen's, 149 East Twenty-eighth Street; E. McGlynn, Priest. St. Vincent de Paul, 127 West Twenty-third Street; Annet La Font, Priest. Most Holy Redeemer (German), 165 Third Street; M. Leimgruber, Priest. St. Francis Xavier is the Church of the Jesuits.

Unitarian.—All Souls, Fourth Avenue, cor. East Twentieth Street; H. W. Bellows, Minister. Messiah, East Thirty-fourth Street, cor. Park Avenue; George H. Hepburn, Minister. Third, West Fortieth Street, near Sixth Avenue; O. B. Frothingham, Minister.

Universalist.—Third, 206 Bleecker St.; D. K. Lee, Minister. Fourth, Fifth Avenue, cor. West Forty-fifth Street; E. H. Chapin, Minister. Our Saviour, 65 West Thirty-fifth Street; James M. Pullman, Minister.

The following churches will be found especially attractive to the stranger, either on account of their architectural beauty, the character of the services, or the associations connected with them:

Trinity (Episcopal), Broadway, at the head of Wall Street. It is built of solid brown-stone, from foundation to spire, with the exception of the roof, which is wood. The walls of the church are fifty feet in height, and the whole edifice is generally recognized as one of the most elegant and cathedral-like on this continent. The height of the steeple is 284 feet. The graveyard of old Trinity occupies nearly two acres of ground (or it did so at one time), and within it are many venerated tombs. Among them, those of Alexander Hamilton, who was shot by Aaron Burr; of Captain Lawrence, the hero of the "Chesapeake;" of the unfortunate Charlotte Temple, and of many other distinguished people.

The chief monument in the graveyard is that erected to the memory of the American patriots who died in British prisons while the city was under British rule. It is a very simple shaft of brown-stone, resembling the monumental crosses often found in European cities, and, in purity of Gothic architecture, surpasses the church itself. Trinity is the oldest organized church in the city. The first edifice was destroyed by fire in 1776, and was rebuilt in 1790. It was afterward (in 1839) pulled down. The present noble structure was finished and consecrated in 1846. The view from the lookout in Trinity tower is the finest that can be afforded in the city of New York. It extends from the Highlands of New Jersey (and, in clear weather, from Sandy Hook), far up into the Palisades, and up among the picturesque islands that throng the throat of Long Island Sound. The perquisite received by the sexton is merely nominal, and no stranger should quit the metropolis without making this famous ascent.

St. Paul's (Episcopal), corner Broadway and Vesey Street. The oldest Episcopal Church in the city is St. Paul's, which, like Trinity, is surrounded by the graves of a generation passed away. It is a chapel of Trinity. In the churchyard are monuments of great interest, among them the splendid obelisk in memory of Robert Emmet, and the monument to George F. Cooke the actor, erected by Edmund Kean. Most interesting of all, is the monument to General Montgomery, which is built into the wall of the church fronting Broadway.

Grace Church (Episcopal), Broadway, corner of Eleventh Street. The most prominent object on Broadway is Grace Church, which, standing just at the point where that street deflects to the left, appears to block the way. It gracefully lifts its decorated, white, and slender spire above the gayety and worldliness below. The architecture, with that of the adjoining rectory, is light and pleasing.

St. George's (Episcopal), corner Rutherford Place and East Sixteenth Street. This is an elegant specimen of the purest Romanesque, or Byzantine, order of architecture, and, with its two lofty towers looking to the east, and immense depth and height of wall, is certainly entitled to the first rank among the religious edifices of America. It is built of solid brownstone, was erected in 1849, and its original cost, including the adjoining chapel and rectory, was $280,000. The interior was completely destroyed by fire on the 14th of November, 1865, but was immediately refitted, and it now—unsupported by any visible columns either to gallery or roof—presents an appearance of refined yet sumptuous magnificence. Its length from the rear of the chancel-recess to the outer walls of the towers is 150 feet, and its width, from inner wall to wall, 75 feet. The height from the ground to the peak of the roof is 100 feet—to the top of the towers about 245 feet. The ceiling, though of the simple, open order, is one of the most striking and effective features of the interior. The staining of the upper or loftier sections is a marvel of beauty and art, as are also the rose windows over the chancel.

Christ (Episcopal), corner Fifth Avenue and Thirty-fifth Street. This church is built of brown-stone, but has no windows. It is lighted by glass domes, and the interior is elaborately and splendidly painted.

The *Church of the Transfiguration* (Episcopal) is situated on the north side of Twenty-ninth Street, just east of Fifth Avenue, and, with its adjoining chapel and rectory, more interesting from its quaint irregularity and air of seclusion than for any architectural pretensions. Indeed, it may be said to have no architecture at all. The original edifice was erected about fourteen years ago. From time to time, as the congregation grew in numbers and wealth, additions were made, by appending a little chapel at this end, a porch at that end, and a wing at the side, until finally the original building itself disappeared, and gave place to another equally quaint and plain. It is known as the "little church round the corner."

The principal feature of the interior is the picture, directly behind the pulpit, of the Ascension, a copy from Raphael; and the entire interior is in keeping with the picturesqueness of the church as seen from the street.

Trinity Chapel (Episcopal), Twenty-fifth Street, near Broadway. This is an elegant church, extending from Twenty-fifth to Twenty-sixth Street. The service is *choral*.

St. Thomas's (Episcopal) is a very elegant church in all its appointments, corner of Fifth Avenue and Fifty-third Street.

Tabernacle (Congregational) Sixth Avenue, corner West Thirty-fourth Street. The style of this church is Gothic, and its interior arrangements are in perfect accord with its elegant exterior. The pulpit and organ screen are beautifully carved.

St. Paul's (Methodist Episcopal), Fourth Avenue, corner Twenty-second Street, is one of the finest churches in the city. It is in the Romanesque style, and is built entirely of white marble.

Brick Church (Presbyterian), Fifth Avenue, corner West Thirty-seventh Street. This is a large church, and is particularly interesting as the successor of the "Old Brick Church," which once stood on Park Row, at the corner of Beckman Street. Rev. Dr. Spring, the pastor, is the oldest clergyman in New York.

University Place (Presbyterian). University Place, corner Tenth Street, is handsomely built of stone. Over the main entrance is a fine Gothic window.

First Presbyterian, Fifth Avenue, corner West Eleventh Street, is also a fine stone building.

Washington Square (Dutch Reformed), East Washington Place, fronting Washington Square. This church is built of rough granite in the Gothic style, having two towers. The interior is striking, and the carved work of the pulpit, etc., is very fine.

St. Patrick's Cathedral (Roman Catholic), corner of Mott and Prince Streets, will accommodate two thousand people. The exterior is unattractive, but the interior is quite striking. The ceiling is very lofty, and is supported by massive pillars.

Church of the Most Holy Redeemer (Roman Catholic), 165 Third Street, near Avenue A, is a German church, which cost over $100,000. It is in the Byzantine style of architecture, and has a superbly-ornamented interior. The columns supporting the roof are of white marble, and the spire is two hundred and sixty-five feet in height.

St. Stephen's (Roman Catholic), 149 East Twenty-eighth Street, extends from Twenty-eighth to Twenty-ninth Street. It is a very large church, and possesses the most expensive and elegant altar in the country, while the paintings with which it is adorned are exquisite works of art.

St. Peter's (Roman Catholic), Barclay, corner of Church Street, is one of the oldest churches in the city.

The Unitarian *Church of the Messiah*, occupying a commanding site at the northwest corner of Thirty-fourth Street and Park Avenue, was only completed in April, 1868. The architecture may be best expressed as the Rhenish-Gothic style. It is built of brick, with gray sandstone trimmings, and covers a space, including the chapel, of eighty by one hundred and forty-five feet. The entrance, on Thirty-fourth Street, is of light-colored stone, elaborately carved, and a little gem as a piece of architecture.

Immediately adjoining the Church of the Messiah, and occupying the avenue block between Thirty-fifth and Thirty-sixth Streets, is the larger and more elaborate *Presbyterian Church of the Covenant*. Its dedication dates three years prior to that of its neighbor. It is of the Lombardo-Gothic style of architecture, and, in many of its characteristics, is worthy the attention of the student in that branch of art. It faces the avenue, and is built of rich gray-stone.

The new *Jewish Synagogue*, on Fifth Avenue, corner of East Forty-third Street, is worthy of study, as the purest example of the Moresque style of architecture in this country.

The churches here specified are but a very small proportion of those worthy of a visit, and the tourist will find in his walks through the city elegant churches in every quarter.

St. Patrick's Cathedral, Fifth Avenue, corner Fifty-first Street, is now slowly building. It was projected by the late Archbishop Hughes, who laid the corner-stone in 1858. The ground occupied (extreme length, 332 feet; general breadth, 132 feet, with an extreme breadth at the transepts of 174 feet) is the most elevated on Fifth Avenue, there being a gradual descent both toward the south, and toward Central Park, on the north. A stratum of solid rock—which in some places is 20 feet below the surface, necessitating a cutting into steps to receive the mason-work—supports the foundations, which are of immense blocks of stone, laid by derricks in cement mortar. The first base-course is of Maine granite. The material above the base-course is of white marble—a highly crystalline stone, productive of very beautiful effects, especially in the columns and elaborations of the work. The style of the building is decorated Gothic. The height of the two towers will be 328 feet each.

PARKS AND PUBLIC SQUARES.

The great boast and pride of New York is its *Central Park*, a rectangular area of 843 acres, extending from Fifty-ninth to One Hundred and Tenth Street, and from Fifth to Eighth Avenue.

The first surveys for the park were commenced in June, 1856, and, in the fourteen years which have elapsed since that time, the swamps, bowlders, and rugged spurs of bare rock, which then existed, have been transformed into a scene of rare beauty: swamps have been changed into beautiful lakes; the bare rocks have been covered with earth; large trees now stand where then all was desolation; bowlders and spurs have been changed to mounds and hills; the level portions have become lawns of emerald, and the very defects which once seemed fatal have, by means of engineering skill, become the most attractive features. With admirable forethought, the designer of the park provided for the inevitable business transportation across its width, by means of four sunken roads, or subways, so that they do not interfere in any way with the beauty of the scenery or the pleasure of visitors.

The Old and New Reservoirs constitute prominent features of the park. The former is 1,826 feet in length, and 835 feet wide, and has a capacity of 150,000,-000 gallons. The latter, constructed at the time of the park, is a gigantic work, and, considered in connection with the Croton Aqueduct and the admirable water system of New York, is worthy the attention of every stranger. The area of this vast basin is 106 acres, and its capacity over 1,000,000,000 gallons. The nearest approach is by the gates at Ninetieth and Ninety-sixth Streets, on the Fifth Avenue. The summit of the reservoir walls serves as a pleasant promenade, and commands a fine view. The gate-houses are massive structures of granite.

The Lakes are among the most attractive features of the park; they are five in number, and embrace an area of $43\frac{1}{2}$ acres. The largest is a beautiful sheet of water, lying between Seventy-second and Seventy-ninth Streets. Upon its surface are numerous pleasure-boats, which, in summer, are generally filled with gayly-dressed visitors, and, with the beautiful swans, produce a charming effect.

The Mall is a delightful promenade, perfectly level, and terminating in the Terrace. It is provided with seats, and it is here that the free, open-air concerts are given. It always presents an animated appearance.

Descending from the Terrace which forms the upper part of the Mall, and the plateau which it traverses, the visitor is conducted by a flight of stairs to the Lake. The Ramble, covering an area of 36 acres of sloping hills, extends from the Old Reservoir to Central Lake. It abounds in pleasant, shady walks, and is much frequented by park visitors. The Stone Arch, on the western slope of the Ramble, is much admired. The Cave and the Tunnel are also objects of interest.

The Belvedere is located upon the rocky point at the southwestern corner of the small reservoir, on the highest ground in the Ramble. As the name indicates, its object is to afford to visitors a suitable place from which to obtain comprehensive views of the park.

The style of architecture is different from any thing in this country, and, as some portions are left open, the whole presents an entirely different appearance from every point of view, the general effect being that of a cluster of quaint houses around a tower, such as is often seen upon the Rhine. A due regard to the laws of architectural harmony has been observed, and there is no such extent of front, or altitude of tower, as would tend to dwarf the other structures in the park. The tower, on the southeasterly extremity of the building, is so located as to be in the central line of the Mall, and is therefore the first and most prominent object upon which the eye rests, as one walks up the Mall toward the lake. It commands attractive views of the whole of

21

the lower park and of the expanse of the two reservoirs, together with glimpses of many of the most beautiful spots in the upper park. Every convenience will be afforded to visitors to avail themselves of the advantages of the Belvedere.

The Museum is contained in a castellated structure formerly occupied as a State arsenal, near Fifth Avenue and Sixty-fourth Street. The art collection is small, but of much promise. Here, during the winter months, are housed the few animals which it is intended shall form the nucleus of a future Zoological Garden. The Green, Play-ground, Dovecot, and the Knoll, are all frequented spots.

In the upper park are the ruins of the redoubts used in the Revolutionary War, guarding McGowan's Pass, where there was some sharp fighting. In the northeastern portion is still to be seen a part of the "Old Boston Road," the first road ever made out of New York on the east side of the island.

There are about ten miles of carriageways, six of bridle-paths, and thirty of foot-paths in the park, and additions are constantly being made to them. The refreshment-saloons, bridges, shelters, arches, and, in fact, all the architectural features of the park, are in perfect harmony with the scenery.

The means of conveyance to the park are the Third Avenue, Broadway, Sixth, Seventh, and Eighth Avenue cars, and by the Belt Line. Once at the park, carriages are found at the entrances for hire, and also the Central Park omnibuses, which are so constructed as to afford every passenger a good view, only carry as many as can comfortably sit in them, and charge twenty-five cents for each passenger. In each trip they pass through all those portions of the park accessible by carriages, stopping at the most desirable points for views.

Mount Morris Square is an abrupt hill, rising from a plain where there are no other hills. It has an area of about twenty acres, "heads off" Fifth Avenue at One Hundred and Twentieth Street, and extends as far north as One Hundred and Twenty-fourth Street.

Hamilton Square, fifteen acres in extent, is bounded by Sixty-sixth and Sixty-ninth Streets, and Third and Fourth Avenues.

Reservoir Square extends from Fifth to Sixth Avenue, between Fortieth and Forty-second Streets, and has an extent of several acres. The granite "Distributing Reservoir" of the Croton Aqueduct stands on the portion bounded by Fifth Avenue.

Madison Square is six acres in extent, and lies between Twenty-third and Twenty-sixth Streets, and Madison and Fifth Avenues. The Fifth Avenue Hotel, Hoffman House, and many other fine hotels, the Union League Club-house, and numerous elegant private residences, surround this, which is one of the most fashionable squares in the city. On the west side, at the junction of Broadway and Twenty-fifth Street, stands a monument to General Worth.

Tompkins Square, between Avenues A and B, and Seventh and Tenth Streets, contains between ten and eleven acres, and is paved in concrete, being used as a military parade-ground.

Stuyvesant Square is divided in the centre by the passage of the Second Avenue. It extends from Fifteenth to Seventeenth Street. Saint George's Church (Rev. Dr. Tyng) is upon the west side of this park. The enclosure consists of three acres, and was presented by the late P. G. Stuyvesant to the church.

Gramercy Park, on Twentieth Street, a little to the northeast of Union Square, is a charming ground, belonging to the owners of the elegant private homes around it. Lexington Avenue and Irving Place are in the immediate vicinity.

Union Park was at one time one of the most aristocratic portions of New York. It is of an oval shape, forms the centre of Union Square, and is bounded by Fourteenth and Seventeenth Streets, Broadway, and Fourth Avenue. It is filled with trees, has a fountain in the centre, as have almost all the parks, and is generally thronged with people passing to and fro, or resting under the trees. At its lower eastern extremity is the bronze equestrian statue of Washington by Henry K. Browne, and a companion statue of Lincoln will soon be erected at the lower western extremity. It is surrounded by elegant hotels and residences, which are rapidly yielding to the pressure of business, and becoming replaced by stores.

Washington Square (Parade-ground) is a pleasant down-town park, a little west of Broadway, with Waverley Place and Fourth Street on the north and south sides, and upon the east the grand marble edifice of the New York University and Dr. Hutton's beautiful Gothic church. A fountain occupies the centre of these grounds, which embrace about nine acres. This square was originally the "Potter's Field" of New York, and it is estimated has received the remains of over 100,000 beings. During the winter and spring of 1871, Fifth Avenue was extended to Laurens Street, crossing and bisecting this park, and opening another artery through the city.

The *City Hall Park* has almost ceased to exist as such, and is now more a reservation for public buildings. It is a triangular piece of ground, containing about nine acres. It contains at its upper end the City Hall, New Court-house, and several other public buildings. The lower end has been sold to the United States for the site of the new Post-Office, which is now in process of erection.

Bowling Green, so called from the fact that, previous to the Revolution, it was used as such, is near the Battery, at the commencement of Broadway. It is of an oval form, surrounded by an iron railing, and is the oldest public ground in the city, having served as the Dutch parade-ground and market-place. It was enclosed in 1732, and was once the central point of the most aristocratic neighborhood in the city.

The *Battery* was once a most beautiful spot, and the favorite promenade of all classes. About ten acres in extent, and at the most southern point of the island, at the confluence of the Hudson and East Rivers, it was surrounded by the most elegant private residences, while under its shady trees both rich and poor could enjoy the magnificent view of the bay and the bracing sea-air. Connected with it was a fortification, which still exists under the name of Castle Garden, having been first a fort, then an opera-house, and now a receiving depot for immigrants. The limits of the Battery are now in process of extension; though not yet finished, much has been done within the past year to restore this spot to its original beauty.

PUBLIC AND PROMINENT BUILDINGS, AND PLACES NOT OTHERWISE CLASSIFIED.

MUNICIPAL.

City Hall, in the Park, is a white marble building, one of the finest in the country. The library, Governor's room, etc., etc., are all worth visiting.

The *New Court-house*, in the rear of the City Hall, is a fine building of white marble. The Chambers Street portico is to have a row of Corinthian columns, and when completed will be the most beautiful in America. The dome is to be like that of the Capitol in Washington.

There are several other city buildings in the Park of no particular interest.

The *Tombs* is a granite prison occupying the entire square bounded by Centre, Leonard, Elm, and Franklin Streets. It is pure Egyptian in its architecture.

City Arsenal, Seventh Avenue, corner of Thirty-fifth Street, is a large brick building, pierced for musketry, and so arranged that it could easily be defended against a mob.

Washington Market, foot of Fulton Street, on the Hudson River, is the representative market of the city. Here, especially on a Saturday morning in summer, we will find, radiating from the market building as a centre, miles upon miles of market-wagons, extending upon both sides of the convergent streets. The crowd of eager buyers and sellers, and the clamor of drivers and vehicles, form the most exciting scene that New York ever presents.

The *Distributing Reservoir* of the Croton Aqueduct, Fifth Avenue, from Fortieth to Forty-second Street, is of granite, in the Egyptian style of architecture.

NATIONAL.

Custom-House.— Wall Street, cor. of William. This building, at one time, was known as the Merchants' Exchange, famous for the great granite plinths of the columns that support the pediment of the front elevation. Its dimensions are a depth of 200 feet, a frontage of 144 feet, and a rear breadth of 171 feet. Its height to the top of the central dome is 124 feet. Beneath this dome, in the interior of the building, is the Rotunda, around the sides of which are eight lofty columns of Italian marble, the superb Corinthian capitals of which were carved in Italy. They support the base of the dome, and are probably the largest and noblest marble columns in the country.

The *Sub-Treasury and Assay-Office* is a white marble building at the corner of Nassau and Wall Streets. It was constructed for, and long used as, the Customhouse of the port of New York, now removed to the neighboring premises formerly known as the Merchants' Exchange. The building is a handsome and imposing one, and is a fine specimen of the Doric order of architecture. It is 200 feet long, 80 feet wide, and 80 feet high. The main entrance on Wall Street is made by a flight of eighteen marble steps, while on Pine Street, in the rear, the acclivity of the ground brings the entrance almost on a level with the street. The old Federal Hall used to stand on this same site, and the spot is rendered classic from its being that whereon Washington delivered his inaugural address.

Standing at the corner of the Treasury, a person beholds an extraordinary scene. At the head of Wall Street, on Broadway, the lofty spire of Trinity towers far above us; looking down, we can, through the vista of banks and brokers' offices, catch a glimpse of Brooklyn and the East River; a turn of the head, and narrow, busy-thronged Nassau Street stretches out like a gorge of brick and stone, while a glance down Broad Street gives a view of a series of elegant buildings on either side of the way, for a block and a half. Chief among these is the handsome edifice mainly occupied by the Board of Brokers, on the right-hand side looking down.

The *Post-Office*, at the corner of Nassau and Liberty Streets, is an irregular, unsightly, and uncouth edifice, moulded from an old Dutch Church, which, in the time of the Revolution, was used by the English as a cavalry-stable.

The *New Post-Office*, which is now building at the lower end of the Park, will, when finished, be one of the most magnificent buildings in the city.

EDUCATIONAL AND CHARITABLE.

The *New York University* occupies a grand Gothic edifice of white marble, upon the east side of Washington Square, Wooster Street, corner Waverley Place. This structure is a fine example of pointed architecture, not unlike that of King's College, Cambridge, England. The chapel—in the central building—is, with its noble window, 50 feet high and 24 feet wide, one of the most beautiful rooms in the country. The whole edifice is 200 feet in length, and 100 feet deep. It was founded in 1831. A valuable library and philosophical apparatus are attached to the University.

Columbia College, on Fiftieth Street, near Fifth Avenue, is an ancient establishment, having been chartered by George II. in 1754, under the title of King's College. Until within a few years back, it occupied a site in Park Place. The green lawns adjoining its old site have long since been built over. The college has a president and twelve professors, a library of 20,000 volumes, and a museum.

The *College of the City of New York*, in Twenty-third Street, corner of Lexington Avenue, is a Gothic structure well suited to the purpose for which it is designed. It is a part of the common-school system, and is free.

Rutgers Female College is immediately opposite the Distributing Reservoir, on Fifth Avenue. It was removed to its present locality only a short time ago, and has proved very successful. The building, or series of buildings, were originally erected for dwellings—as, indeed, the two end buildings are at present occupied, the College using the central portion.

The *General Theological Seminary of the Episcopal Church* occupies the entire square bounded by Ninth and Tenth Avenues, and Twentieth and Twenty-first Streets.

The *College of St. Francis Xavier* (Roman Catholic) was founded in 1850. It is on Fifteenth Street, between Fifth and Sixth Avenues.

The *Union Theological Seminary*,

founded in 1836, is at 9 University Place, just above the New York University.

Ladies of the Sacred Heart, Manhattanville. (See " Places of Interest above Central Park.")

Five Points House of Industry, 155 Worth Street, and *Five Points Mission,* 61 Park Street, face each other on what was once the most dangerous and vilest portion of the city.

Roman Catholic Orphan Asylums (Girls), corner Prince and Mott Streets; (Boys), Fifth Avenue, corner Fifty-first Street. These are both large and prosperous institutions, as are many others of a similar character. Those located above the entrance to Central Park are described in "Places of Interest above Central Park" (page 26).

New York Institution for the Blind. This is a large and handsome building on Ninth Avenue, between Thirty-third and Thirty-fourth Streets. The pupils are of two classes—those whose circumstances enable them to pay for their board and tuition, and those who are poor. The expenses of the latter are borne by the State. Visitors received on Wednesdays from 9 A. M. to 5 P. M.

St. Luke's Hospital, on Fifth Avenue, corner of Fifty-fourth Street, is one of the most noticeable objects on the avenue.

Bellevue Hospital (City) is at the foot of East Twenty-sixth Street, and is the largest hospital in the city.

OTHER PLACES AND BUILDINGS OF INTEREST.

The *Kennedy House,* No. 1 Broadway, facing the Bowling Green, was, during the Revolution, successively the residence of Lord Cornwallis, General Clinton, Lord Howe, and General Washington.

The *Corn Exchange,* located at the upper end of Whitehall Street, was erected a few years ago. It is built of brick, is a noble structure, and will amply repay a visit of inspection.

The *Stock Exchange and Gold Room* are in Broad Street, below Wall Street.

The *Equitable Life Assurance Company's Building,* at the corner of Cedar Street and Broadway, is built of granite, and is probably the most solid and substantial structure in the city. Doric is the pattern of the lower stories, composite of those immediately above, and the upper part is finished in the *renaissance* or *Mansard* roof style. The entire building has a frontage of 87 feet on Broadway, is 187 feet deep on Cedar Street, and is 137 feet high.

The *Park Bank,* one of the most striking fronts on Broadway, and *New York Herald Building,* which holds the same place in regard to the newspaper offices of the city, are both built of white marble. They occupy the site of the old " Barnum's Museum," on Broadway, at the foot of the Park, opposite "old St. Paul's."

New York Life Insurance Company Building, at the corner of Broadway and Leonard Street, is one of the handsomest structures in the city. The exterior of the building is very imposing. It is of pure white marble, in the Ionic order of architecture, the design having been suggested by the Temple of the Erechtheus, at Athens. The chief entrance is highly ornamented, and the entire cost was about one million dollars.

The *Freight Depot of the New York Central and Hudson River Railroads* is in Hudson Street, below Canal Street, occupying the site of St. John's Park. This depot, besides being notable for its immense size, is surmounted by the great "Vanderbilt Bronze," the largest in the world, and illustrating the entire life of Cornelius Vanderbilt.

Stewart's Retail Store is the largest in the world. It occupies the entire square bounded by Ninth and Tenth Streets, Broadway and Fourth Avenue. It is built of iron, and is considered fire-proof.

The *Mercantile Library,* Clinton Hall, is in Eighth Streect near Broadway, and in the immediate vicinity of the Cooper Institute, the Astor Library, and Bible House. It was founded in 1820, and was first opened at 49 Fulton Street. This building was, originally known as the Astor Place Opera-House, and was the scene of the great Macready riots in 1848.

The *Astor Library,* on Lafayette Place near Astor Place, was founded by John Jacob Astor, who endowed it with the sum of $400,000. The building, erected in 1853, 65 feet by 120, was enlarged in 1857 by the addition of another building corresponding in size to the original. It is of brick, ornamented with brown-stone in the Romanesque style, and cost $140,000. The Library Hall is 50 feet high, and approached by a flight of 38 marble steps. The collection of books constitutes one of the largest and most valuable public libraries on the continent. Open daily (except Sundays and holidays), from 9 to 5 o'clock.

The *Cooper Institute* (*Union*) occupies a magnificent brown-stone edifice opposite the Bible House on Astor Place, at the point where the union of the Third and Fourth Avenues forms the Bowery. Its main front, 143 feet long, is on Eighth Street. It was founded by the generous munificence of Peter Cooper, an eminent merchant of New York. It is devoted to the free education of the *people* in the practical arts and sciences, and was publicly opened in November, 1859, with over 2,000 students, and contains a free reading-room and library. One of its departments is a School of Design for women. The basement is devoted to the purposes of a lecture-room. The building cost $600,000.

The *Bible House* is a conspicuous edifice, occupying the space bounded by Third and Fourth Avenues and Eighth and Ninth Streets. It has a street frontage of 700 feet, and is six stories high. The principal entrance, on Fourth Avenue, has four columns, surmounted by a cornice. It is built of brick, and cost $300,000. It is the property of the American Bible Society, and here all the operations of that important organization are carried on. Upward of 500 operatives are employed.

The *New York Historical Society* building is on the corner of Second Avenue and Tenth Street, is fire-proof, is built of stone, and contains a library of rare books, pertaining to the history of the country; also medals, coins, etc., the Nineveh Marbles, Dr. Abbott's Egyptian Collection, and many other objects of interest.

New York Society Library, No. 67 University Place, contains the oldest and one of the most valuable collections of books in the city. The "Public Library," commenced 1700, during the provincial governorship of the Earl of Bellamont, formed the nucleus of the present library.

The *National Academy of Design*—the chief art institution of America—was founded in 1826, since which time it has steadily advanced in influence and usefulness. It occupies a prominent *locale* at the corner of Fourth Avenue and Twenty-third Street, fronting on the latter. The front is constructed of Westchester County marble, banded with *greywacke ;* is in the Gothic style of architecture of the thirteenth century, and presents a unique and pleasing appearance.

Young Men's Christian Association Building, directly opposite the Academy of Design, on the southwest corner of Fourth Avenue and Twenty-third Street, is the building of the Young Men's Christian Association. Its dimensions are 175 feet on Twenty-third Street, 83 feet on Fourth Avenue, and 97 feet at the rear. The material is New Jersey brown-stone, and the yellowish marble from Ohio, in almost equal parts. The building contains twenty-five apartments in all, including gymnasium, library, lecture-rooms, offices, etc., and has cost about $300,000.

Park Avenue, as that portion of Fourth Avenue is called which is arched to permit the passage of the Harlem cars, is very beautiful, the centre of the avenue, beneath which the road passes, being laid out as a succession of grass-plats and flower beds.

Broadway, from the Battery to Union Square, is lined with splendid stores.

Fifth Avenue, above Twenty-third Street, presents a succession of elegant residences and churches.

Stewart's Palace.—Of all the splendid buildings on Fifth Avenue, none will probably ever be so famous as the marble palace of Mr. A. T. Stewart, at the corner of Thirty-fourth Street. It is the most costly and luxurious private residence on the continent. It is built of white marble, and cost over $2,000,000.

For prominent Club-Houses, see p. 11.
For Churches, see page 17.
For Places of Amusement, see page 15.
For Parks, etc., see page 21.

PLACES OF INTEREST ABOVE CENTRAL PARK.

The following places are reached by what is known as the Bloomingdale Road, which is merely a continuation of Broadway.

The *Bloomingdale Asylum for the Insane* (*Lunatic Asylum*), and the *New York Orphan Asylum*, are in the upper part of the island, on the line of one of the pleasantest drives about New York. It occupies a most attractive and commanding site on West One Hundred and Seventeenth Street, near Tenth Avenue. The principal building is 211 feet in length, and four stories high. The Orphan Asylum, on Bloomingdale Road, near Seventy-fourth Street, is 120 feet long by 60, and has nine acres of ground attached, commanding a fine view of the river on either side.

The following places are reached by the Bloomingdale Road, also by the drive through Central Park and Harlem Lane, to the Bloomingdale Road at One Hundred and Twenty-fifth Street, and by Hudson River Railway, or Eighth Avenue cars, to One Hundred and Twenty-fifth Street (Manhattanville). Stages beyond.

Manhattan College, a large and flourishing Roman Catholic institution in Manhattanville.

Convent of the Ladies of the Sacred Heart.—This convent and school for young ladies is beautifully situated on a hill at about One Hundred and Thirtieth Street. It is surrounded by park-like grounds, and has one of the most charming little chapels in the country.

Sheltering Arms.—An infant asylum of the Episcopal Church, is situated on One Hundred and Twenty-eighth Street.

The *Colored Orphan Asylum* is a large and handsome building, near One Hundred and Forty-third Street.

The *Deaf and Dumb Asylum* occupies a conspicuous *locale* at Fanwood, West One Hundred and Sixty-second Street, near Bloomingdale Road (Washington Heights). It is reached by the cars of the Hudson River Railroad. The principal building, 110 by 60 feet, and five stories high, has accommodation for between 200 and 300 pupils. Admission daily from 12 to 4 o'clock, P. M.

The *New York Juvenile Asylum*, One Hundred and Seventy-fifth Street, near Tenth Avenue and High Bridge, is a *noble charity*.

Audubon Park is on the Hudson River, foot of One Hundred and Fifty-fourth Street. It is one of the most charming collection of private residences in the country. It was formerly the residence of Audubon the naturalist, and his house still remains.

For *Fort Washington*, One Hundred and Eighty-first Street and Hudson River, *Fort Tryon*, One Hundred and Ninety-fifth Street and Hudson River, and *King's Bridge*, see "Trip up the Hudson," page 30.

High Bridge, by which the Croton Aqueduct is carried across the Harlem River, can be reached in a variety of ways, for which see page 29.

The material employed in erecting this magnificent structure—the most important connected with the Croton Aqueduct —is granite throughout. It spans the whole width of the valley and river, from cliff to cliff, at a point where the latter is six hundred and twenty feet wide, and the former a quarter of a mile. It is composed of eight arches, each with a span of eighty feet, and the elevation of the arches gives one hundred feet clear of the river from their lower side. There are, besides these, a number of arches rising from the ground, with an average span of forty-five feet each. The water is led over the bridge, a distance of one thousand four hundred and fifty feet, in immense iron pipes, as great in diameter as the stature of a tall man, and over all is a pathway for pedestrians. On the lofty bank at its southern end, the officers of the Croton Aqueduct are constructing an immense reservoir for the supply of the upper portion of the city, which is too high ground to receive a supply from the level of the aqueduct. The water will be raised into this reservoir by powerful engines. From this point is to be had a most comprehensive and beautiful view of the city, the islands in the East River, Long Island, the Harlem River, and Spuyten Duyvel Creek, and the elegant farms and villas of Westchester County.

CEMETERIES.

Calvary.—Newtown L. I. Two miles from East Tenth Street Ferry.*

---

* Reached from ferries by horse or steam railways, or both; an inquiry at any of the ferries will afford the stranger information as to his best route.

Cypress Hills.—Myrtle Avenue and Jamaica Plank Road, five miles from the Williamsburgh ferries.*

Evergreen.—Between Cypress Hills and Williamsburgh.*

Greenwood.—Gowanus Heights, Brooklyn.*

Lutheran.—Jamaica turnpike near Middle Village, L. I. Four miles from Williamsburgh ferries.*

Mount Olivet.—On the old Flushing Turnpike, near Maspeth, 3½ miles from Williamsburgh ferries.†

Trinity Church.—From Hudson River to Tenth Avenue, between One Hundred and Fifty-third and One Hundred and Fifty-sixth Streets.

ART GALLERIES, ETC.

ACADEMY OF DESIGN.—Fourth Avenue, corner of Twenty-third Street. This is the chief art institution of America, is considered a very beautiful building, and contains a central hall, picture-galleries, and sculpture-room, lecture, reading, library, and council-rooms.

Goupil's (Knoedler's), corner of Fifth Avenue and Twenty-second Street, *Schaus's*, 749 Broadway, and *Snedecor's*, 768 Broadway, are well-known art emporiums.

There are a number of fine private collections in the city, to which access can only be had through an introduction from a friend.

SHORT PLEASURE EXCURSIONS.

Astoria, L. I.—Academy, gardens, etc. (See "Trip up the East River.") Reached by ferries. (See FERRIES.)

Babylon.—Fishing, etc. (See "Trips through Long Island," No. 2.)

Bay Side.—Clams and beautiful scenery. (See "Trips through Long Island," No. 3.)

Bedloe's Island.—Fort. (See "Trip down the Bay.")

Blackwell's Island.—Reformatory Institutions. (See "Trip up the East River.")

Brighton.—Fashionable resort. (See "Staten Island," "Trip down the Bay.")

Brushville.—Popular resort. (See "Trips through Long Island," No. 1.)

Cedarmere.—Home of William C. Bryant—beautiful scenery. (See "Trips through Long Island," No. 1.)

College Point.—Summer resort. (See "Trips through Long Island," No. 3.)

Coney Island.—Bathing. (See "Trip down the Bay.")

Croton Dam.—The head of the Croton Aqueduct. Reached by steamer on the Hudson, by N. Y. Central and Hudson River Railroad to Croton Station, and by Harlem Railroad to Croton Falls, thence by private conveyance. (See "Trip up the Hudson.")

East Hampton.—Retired bathing. (See "Trips through Long Island," No. 1.)

Ellis Island.—Fort. (See "Trip down the Bay.")

Fire Island.—Fishing, bathing, and boating. (See "Trips through Long Island," No. 2.)

Fishing Banks.—During the season, special popular excursions by steamers are of almost daily occurrence. They convey passengers to the best localities for sea-fishing, furnishing all the necessary conveniences. (See advertisements in the papers.)

Flatbush.—Battle-ground. (See "Trips through Long Island," No. 4.)

Flushing.—Botanical Garden, etc. (See "Trips through Long Island," No. 3.)

Fordham.—Westchester County. A pleasant place, the seat of one of the leading Roman Catholic colleges in the country. Reached by Harlem Railroad, or by private conveyance.

Fort Lee.—Popular resort. (See "Trip up the Hudson.") Reached by ferry, which see.

Fort Hamilton.—Large fortification on Long Island, five miles from the city. (See "Trip down the Bay.")

Glen Cove.—Fishing, boating, etc. (See "Trips through Long Island," No. 1.)

Governor's Island.—Fortifications. (See "Trip down the Bay.")

Gravesend.—Fishing and shooting. (See "Trips through Long Island," No. 4.)

Great Neck.—Clams. (See "Trips through Long Island," No. 3.)

Greenpoint.—Bathing and Fishing.

---

* Reached from ferries by horse or steam railways, or both; an inquiry at any of the ferries will afford the stranger information as to his best route.
† Reached by ferries, street-cars, and stages.

(*See* "Trips through Long Island," No. 1.)
Greenwood Cemetery.—(*See* BROOKLYN.) Reached by street cars connecting with ferries.
Hell Gate.—Dangerous tideway. (*See* "Trip up East River.")
Hempstead.—Stewart's new village for working-men. (*See* "Trips through Long Island," No. 1.)
High Bridge of the Croton Aqueduct across Harlem River.—One of the finest bridges in the world. Reached by Third Avenue Railroad, Eighth Avenue Railroad, Harlem Railroad, and connecting stages, by private conveyance, or by Harlem River excursion steamers, which touch at several East River slips, commencing at Peck Slip. The Eastern Division Belt Line Railroad passes all these slips. By taking this route, the visitor obtains a fine view of the city, and of the islands in the East River.
Hoboken and Weehawken, N. J.—Two charming summer resorts on the Hudson River, opposite the city. The Elysian Fields are in Hoboken, and it was at Weehawken that Burr killed Hamilton. Reached by Hoboken ferries, which see.
At *Secaucus*, on the plank-road from Hoboken to Paterson, and about five miles from the former point, are the race-course of the Hudson County Association, and the training-stables of Colonel McDaniels.
Hyde Park.—(*See* "Trips through Long Island," No. 1.)
Islip.—Bathing, boating, and fishing. (*See* "Trips through Long Island," No. 2.)
Jamaica.—Union race-course, beautiful bay. (*See* "Trips through Long Island," No. 1.)
Jerome Park.—A fashionable and beautiful race-course in Westchester County, near the Harlem River. Reached by private conveyance or Harlem Railroad. Persons visiting this park can secure a most charming drive, by going by the way of King's Bridge, and returning by Macomb's Dam Bridge, at Harlem. They will thus ride nearly the whole length of Spuyten Duyvel Creek and the Harlem River, and pass through the most beautiful suburbs of the city.
Long Branch, N. J.—Fashionable watering-place. (*See* NEW JERSEY, Route iii.)

Reached by steamer from pier 32, North River, to Monmouth, thence by rail.
Patchogue.—Bathing, boating, etc. (*See* "Trips through Long Island," No. 2.)
Paterson, N. J.—Beautiful falls. (*See* NEW JERSEY, Route vii.)
Quogue.—Fishing and bathing. (*See* "Trips through Long Island," No. 1.)
Randall's Island.—Juvenile Reformatory Institutions. (*See* "Trip up East River.")
Rockaway Beach.—Bathing, fishing, etc. (*See* "Trips through Long Island," No. 2.)
Ronkonkoma Pond.—Boating and fishing, etc. (*See* "Trips through Long Island," No. 1.)
Staten Island.—Fine drives, beautiful views, etc. Reached by ferries from New York and Brooklyn. (*See* FERRIES; also see "Trip down the Bay.")
Throgg's Point, L. I.—(*See* "Trip up the East River.")
Ward's Island.—Emigrant hospitals, etc. (*See* "Trip up the East River.")
Whitestone.—Summer resort. (*See* "Trips through Long Island," No. 3.)
Willett's Point.—Summer resort. (*See* "Trips through Long Island," No. 3.)
For all places between New York and Albany, see "Trip up the Hudson."

NOTE.—To obtain the latest information in reference to the time and place of departure of railway trains, see APPLETONS' RAILWAY GUIDE. For steamers, see "*Mackey's Office Directory*," which can be found in every hotel and large business house in the city.

TRIP DOWN THE BAY.

The more easily and logically to notice the islands in the harbor, and in the East River, we have concluded to make two trips in our own steamer, touching at these points, and informing our readers how they can reach the same points in a less direct manner.

We will start from the Battery, and first stop at—

Governor's Island, opposite the Battery. It is scarcely more than a mile in circumference, yet it contains Fort Columbus, Castle Williams, a powerful water battery, and a United States Arsenal. It is now used as a receiving depot for recruits, but the fortifications are heavily mounted with sea-coast guns. Access is secured by means of small boats, which can be hired at Whitehall, by the post and ordnance-barges which leave the barge-house on the Battery, and by the Government steamer, which makes two trips a day from Whitehall pier, next to the South Ferry. The barges are only used by the officers and their friends.

Ellis Island, an insignificant point rising but little above the water, and hardly large enough to hold the fort upon it. The same Government steamer that runs to Governor's Island touches here also. The nearest approach by small boats is from the pier of the New Jersey Railroad, Jersey City.

We now turn toward Staten Island, stopping at—

Bedloe's Island, another island fort larger than the one last mentioned, and, though insignificant in appearance, likely to prove a serious impediment in the way of any hostile war-vessel. The Government steamer above mentioned stops here also. The hours of the steamer can always be obtained at the Governor's Island barge-house on the Battery.

Having thus paid our respects to the islands under the control of the United States Government, we will run over to—

Staten Island, the largest in the harbor, where we will find splendid scenery, handsome villas, and charming rides. We will find Brighton, Tompkinsville, and other beautiful villages, and we will visit "The Sailor's Snug Harbor," a home for worn-out sailors, and the "Marine Hospital." The Staten Island Railroad, thirteen miles in length, runs from Vanderbilt Landing to Tottenville, with stations at Garretson's, New Dorp, Court-House, Gifford's, Eltingville, Annadale, Huguenot, Prince's Bay, Pleasant Plains, and Richmond Valley.

On the heights is Fort Richmond, and below it, on the lower shore, the water battery of Fort Tompkins commanding the "Narrows," as the channel between Staten and Long Islands is called. Directly opposite, on Long Island, are Fort Hamilton, and Fort Lafayette, the celebrated "prison fort," during the rebellion.

Brighton is a very fashionable resort, and visitors will find "St. Mark's," "Pavilion," and "Belmont Hall," first-class hotels.

Elm Park, a popular resort, is on the Jersey side of the island.

Staten Island is reached from New York by two lines of ferries—for which, see FERRIES. The lower or Jersey-facing side of the island is best reached by taking the boat which leaves Pier 19, North River, and plies through the Kills, as the long sea-inlets separating the island from Jersey are termed. By this route we pass the neat and pleasant buildings of Sailor's Snug Harbor. The shores of the island facing the Kills are garnished with even more fine country-seats than the other side, and the waters are favorite offings for our yachtmen and boating-parties.

We will conclude our trip down the bay by a visit to—

Coney Island, which was once the only fashionable sea-bathing resort for New Yorkers. Its nearness to the city, and the increased facilities for reaching it, soon popularized it to such an extent that the "exclusives" found it necessary to seek more remote and expensive places. It is the great resort of people of moderate means, who can spare a few hours from their business for recreation, and is reached by boats from Pier 1, North River, and by cars which connect at Brooklyn with all the ferries. As the boats are the favorites with the noisy element of the frequenters of the island, and are often overcrowded, it is better for family parties to take the cars, which do not go to the same portion of the island as the boats. The boats, however, are not as crowded in the morning trips as in the afternoon ones.

Fort Hamilton, on the Long Island shore of the Narrows, is a splendid fortification and a pleasant resort. It is reached by street cars from Brooklyn, and by the Coney Island boats.

TRIP UP THE EAST RIVER.

To secure a view of the islands and shores of the East River, take a steamer from Pier 24, at Peck Slip, foot of Beekman Street, for Glen Cove, L. I.

Blackwell's Island is the first one passed. It extends from opposite the foot of East Forty-sixth Street to East Forty-eighth Street, and upon it are located the lunatic asylum, almshouse, penitentiary, charity-hospital, small-pox hospital and workhouse, all built of granite, quarried on the island by the convicts. The "Crazy-man's Fort," at the upper end of the island, is worth a visit. The steamer Bellevue leaves the foot of Twenty-sixth Street, East River, daily at 10.30 A. M., and 1.30 P. M., for Blackwell's, Ward's, and Randall's Islands—fare 15 cents. No one is allowed to visit either of these Islands without permits, which may be procured at the office of the Commissioners of Public Charities and Corrections, corner of Eleventh Street and Third Avenue.

Hell Gate, long the terror of all steamers and vessels coming to or leaving the city by way of Long Island Sound, is the next object of interest, though by the labors of years it has been shorn of most of its dangers, and all the resources of engineering skill are being used to render it perfectly safe. It is a collection of rocks in the channel, opposite the mouth of the Harlem River, which offer so much opposition to the flow of the tide as to cause a succession of whirlpools and rapids.

Ward's Island divides the Harlem from the East River. Upon it are located the emigrant hospital and other buildings, and inebriate asylum, and lunatic asylum. (For means of access, see BLACKWELL'S ISLAND.)

Randall's Island, the last of the group, is separated from Ward's Island by a narrow channel. It is the site of the House of Refuge, hospitals, schools, and other charities provided by the city, for destitute and abandoned children, and is well worth a visit. Means of access the same as those for Blackwell's Island.

The picturesque villages of Astoria and Flushing are soon in sight upon the Long Island shore. The academy and botanic gardens of the former are worthy a visit, and an interesting feature of its location is the singular whirlpool of Hell Gate, which is strongest and most turbulent at this point. It is reached by ferry—(*see* FERRIES).

Throgg's Point is only reached by private conveyance. It is the termination, at Long Island Sound, of Throgg's or Throgmorton's Neck, and, from the summit of the bold headland, which divides East River from the sound, a noble prospect is obtained. The little archipelagoes of green and rocky islets gleam brightly in the sunshine, or appear and disappear strangely in the foggy morning, and, with the broken and wooded Westchester shore, eight or ten miles away, form a sunrise or a sunset scene in the spring or fall of the year, which has often attracted the pencils of our most prominent sketchers. The fishing among these islands is also most excellent, especially for sea-bass and blackfish.

Fort Schuyler, on the point, and Pelham Bridge—both interesting and romantic localities—may likewise be embraced in this excursion.

LONG ISLAND.

Long Island, part of the State of New York, is 115 miles in length, and, at some points, twenty miles in breadth; bounded by the Atlantic on the south, and by Long Island Sound on the north. The upper part of the island is agreeably diversified with hills, though the surface is, for the most part, strikingly level. The coast is charmingly indented with bays; and delicious fresh-water ponds, fed by springs, are everywhere found on terraces of varying elevation. These little lakes, and the varied coast views, give Long Island picturesque features, which, if not grand, are certainly of most attractive and winning character, heightened by the rural beauty of the numerous quiet little towns and charming summer villas. Along the lower shore of the island, which is a network of shallow, land-locked waters, extending seventy miles, fine shooting and fishing are to be had. Hotel and boarding-house accommodation is abundant.

BROOKLYN.

The city of Brooklyn is the second in size in the State of New York, and the third in the Union, but is considered as being, in fact, a part of the city of New York, since a great portion of its inhabitants transact all their business in New York; while the majority of the manufactories, etc., located within its limits, are but the workshops of New York firms. It embraces Brooklyn proper, designated Western District (W. D.), and Williamsburgh, Green Point, and Bushwick, known as the Eastern District (E. D.). South Brooklyn and East New York are outlying portions of the city, which are rapidly growing. It is divided from New York by the East River, and is connected with it by numerous ferries, all of which are mentioned under the head of "Ferries," in the description of New York, where they can be referred to.

Brooklyn was settled in 1625, near Wallabout Bay, by a band of Walloons; and, during the Revolutionary War, was the scene of events that give great interest to some of its localities. On the Heights, back of the city, the battle of Long Island (August 26, 1776) was fought, and the Americans defeated, with a loss of 2,000 out of 5,000 men.

Brooklyn is known as the "City of Churches," and it merits the appellation, from the fact that within its limits are 226 places of worship; while several others are building; but it is also a city of residences, and, while filled with handsome houses, it has not many notable places of business.

Hotels.—There are but few hotels, the principal ones being the Pierrepont House, corner of Montague and Hicks Streets, and the Mansion House, 117 Hicks Street.

Street Railroads.—The street railroads of Brooklyn afford means of communication to all parts of the city. All of them have their *termini* at the ferries; and all either start from, or connect with, the Fulton Ferry.

PUBLIC INSTITUTIONS AND PROMINENT BUILDINGS.

The *United States Navy Yard* is situated on the point of land between the East River and the Wallabout, in the northeast portion of Brooklyn proper. It occupies nearly forty acres of ground, and contains property worth many millions of dollars. There are ship-houses for vessels of the largest class, with workshops, and every requisite for an extensive naval depot. At almost all times representative vessels of every kind used in the Navy may be found at this yard; while the trophies and relics preserved at this point are of great interest to visitors. A large dry-dock has been constructed here, at an expense of about $1,000,000. The United States Naval Lyceum, an interesting place, also in the Navy Yard, is a literary institution, founded in 1833 by the officers of the Navy connected with the port. One of the most interesting objects at the Navy Yard is the receiving-ship North Carolina, the representative of that class of huge men-of-war, now superseded by monitors and small steamers. Reached by cars from all the ferries.

Marine Hospital.—On the opposite side of the Wallabout, half a mile east of the Navy Yard, is the Marine Hospital, a handsome granite building, located in the midst of extensive grounds. It has a capacity for 500 patients. Reached by the same lines of cars as the Navy Yard.

The Atlantic Dock is located at the other end of the city, about a mile below the Brooklyn terminus of the South Ferry, within what is called Red-Hook Point, the outside pier extending some 3,000 feet on the "Buttermilk Channel." This channel, now of sufficient depth to float ships of the deepest draught, is said to have been so shallow in the days of the Revolution, that at low tide the cows would sometimes wade over to "Governor's Island." The dock is a very extensive work, and worthy the attention of strangers. The company was incorporated in May, 1840, with a capital of $1,000,000. The basin within the piers contains 42¼ acres, with sufficient depth of water for the largest ships. The piers are of solid granite. Many of the warehouses and buildings in this neighborhood are of enormous size and capacity. The best approach from New York is by the Hamilton Ferry. (*See* "Ferries," New York.)

The *Water-Works.*—Within the past few years Brooklyn has been, for the first time, supplied with water from any source, except wells and cisterns; and the completion of the water-works was the occasion of a general celebration. The sources whence the water is obtained are Rockville reservoir and others, in the vicinity of Hempstead. From thence it is conveyed by an open canal to Jamaica reservoir, and thence through a conduit to Ridgewood reservoir, and the reservoir on Flatbush Avenue, opposite Prospect Park. From these reservoirs it is distributed throughout the city.

Home for Aged Indigent Females, 224 Washington Avenue, corner of De Kalb Avenue.—It is one of the oldest and best endowed institutions of the kind in the United States, and is handsomely located in the middle of a plat of ground occupying half a block.

Long Island College Hospital.—This is a large and elegant building, with grounds enclosed, on Henry Street, near Pacific Street. It is a fine institution, and is liberally endowed.

The *City Hall*, at the junction of Court and Fulton Streets, is one mile distant from the ferry. It is a handsome building in the Doric style, and is built of white marble from the Westchester quarries. Its length is 162 feet, and its height to the top of the cupola is 253 feet. Cost, $200,000.

The *County Court-house*, fronting on Fulton Street, in the immediate vicinity of the City Hall, is an imposing edifice, though seen to poor advantage. It is 140 feet wide, and extends 315 feet back to Livingston Street. It is in the Corinthian style of architecture, and cost $543,000.

Kings County Jail is in Raymond Street. It is a heavy-looking, castellated Gothic edifice of red sandstone. The *State Arsenal* and *City Hospital* are also in the vicinity.

The *Post-Office* is in Washington Street, north of Myrtle Avenue.

The *New Mercantile Library* is on Montague Street, near Court. It is a handsome specimen of Gothic architecture.

The *Long Island Historical Society Rooms* are in the Mercantile Library Building, and are full of interesting relics.

The *Academy of Music* is opposite the Mercantile Library. It possesses no special architectural merit, but has handsome interior decorations.

The *Packer Collegiate Institute* is a large and handsome institution for the education of young ladies. It is on Joralemon Street, near Court, and its chapel is often used for lectures, readings, etc.

The *Polytechnic Institute* is a beautiful modern edifice, devoted to the education of young lads. It is on Livingston between Court and Bocrum streets.

CHURCHES.

A few of the most prominent churches are—

Baptist: First, Rev. H. M. Gallagher, Nassau, near Fulton Street.
First, of *Williamsburgh*, cor. of South Fifth and Fifth Streets, Rev. Mr. Brackett.
Congregational: Clinton Avenue, Rev. W. Ives Buddington, Clinton Avenue, corner Lafayette Avenue.
Church of the Pilgrims, Rev. R. S. Storrs, Jr., Henry, corner Remsen Street.
Plymouth, Rev. Henry Ward Beecher, Orange, north of Hicks Street. This is the great attraction of Brooklyn, and, though it has sittings for 2,500 persons, is always densely crowded.
Dutch Reformed: Church on the Heights, Rev. Zachary Eddy, Pierrepont, near Monroe Place. This is a remarkable building. Its interior is exceedingly beautiful, and is said to have been modelled after the earliest Christian Church, built by the mother of Constantine.
Methodist Episcopal, De Kalb Avenue: Rev. W. H. Wardell, De Kalb Avenue, near Franklin Avenue.
St. John's, Bedford Avenue, corner Wilson Street, Rev. J. A. M. Chapman.
A new Methodist Episcopal church on Willoughby, near Carleton Street, was completed in 1870, and is one of the handsomest in the city.
Presbyterian: Lafayette Avenue, Rev. Theodore L. Cuyler, Lafayette Avenue, corner of Oxford Street.
Classon Avenue, Rev. Joseph T. Duryea, Classon Avenue, corner of Monroe Street.
Second, Rev. Mr. Kennedy, Clinton, near Fulton Street.
Protestant Episcopal: The Church of the Holy Trinity, Rev. Charles H. Hall, Rector, corner of Clinton and Montague Streets.
Grace, Rev. Benjamin H. Paddock,

Rector, Brooklyn Heights, Grace Court, corner Hicks Street.

St. Ann's (New), Rev. Noah Hunt Schenck, Rector, Clinton, corner Livingston Street.

St. John's (Old), Douglass Street, corner Seventh Avenue. (New), Fronting Prospect Park, Rev. Alexander Burgess, Rector.

Christ, Rev. E. H. Canfield, Rector, Clinton, corner Harrison Street.

Roman Catholic: St. James's Cathedral, Right Rev. John Loughlin, Bishop; V. Rev. John F. Turner, Rev. Thomas J. Gardner, and Rev. Eugene McSherry, Priests, Jay, corner Chapel Street.

St. Mary's, Star of the Sea, Rev. Eugene Cassidy, and Rev. Michael J. Goodwin, Priests, Court, corner Luqueer Street.

St. Patrick's, Rev. Edward G. Fitzpatrick, and Rev. Michael Moran, Priests, Kent Avenue, corner Willoughby Avenue.

St. Paul's, Rev. R. J. McGuire, Rev. Edward O'Reilly, and Rev. William Lane, Priests, Court, corner Congress Street.

St. Peter's and St. Paul's, Rev. S. Malone, Rev. John N. Campbell, and Rev. John Fagan, Priests, Second, near South Second Street.

A new cathedral is building for the Archbishop, which is to occupy the entire block bounded by Greene, Lafayette, and Vanderbilt Avenues, and Claremont Street. When completed, it will, with the exception of the new cathedral in New York, be the largest and handsomest ecclesiastical building on the continent.

Unitarian: The leading Church is the *Church of our Saviour*, Rev. A. P. Putnam, Pierrepont, corner Monroe Place.

Universalist: Church of the Redeemer, Rev. E. C. Bolles, Greene Avenue, near Carlton Avenue.

Many of the other churches are equally attractive with those which have been named, but enough have been given to afford a visitor an ample choice.

PARKS, CEMETERIES, AND OTHER POINTS OF INTEREST.

Prospect Park is to Brooklyn what Central Park is to New York. It is over 600 acres in extent, and is yet in its infancy. It is noted for beautiful distant views, and fine groves of forest-trees. Excavators are now at work upon a spot which will soon be transformed into a lake of fifty acres' extent. The largest and most beautiful fountain in America will throw its waters heavenward, and all that artistic and engineering skill can accomplish will be done to make it a credit to the country, and a spot of rare beauty. The well recently completed is said to be the largest in the world, and is one of the most important features of the park. The outer wall is fifty feet in diameter, two feet thick, and fifty-four feet high. The inner curb or wall is thirty-five feet in diameter and two feet thick, having a depth of ten feet. The masonry, as seen from the top of the structure, is a marvel of neatness and solidity. The water surface in the well is thirteen feet above high-tide level, and the depth of water in the well is fourteen feet. The pump is the Worthington patent, and, with a pressure of forty pounds, is capable of raising one million gallons of water, every twenty-four hours, a height of 176 feet. In case of any accident to the Brooklyn Waterworks, this well has more than the necessary capacity to supply the park abundantly with water. The special work of the well will be to supply the pools at an elevation of 133 feet, and from the pools the water is conducted to the lake. The main entrance is at the junction of Park, Flatbush, and Vanderbilt Avenues, and is especially fine. It is a large circle, called the "Plaza," in the centre of which stands a statue of Abraham Lincoln. Reached by cars from any of the ferries.

Washington Park (Fort Greene) is on an elevated plateau, to the northeast of the City Hall, between Myrtle and De Kalb Avenues. During the Revolutionary War, it was the site of extensive fortifications, of which the ruins of Fort Greene are now all that remain. It is pleasantly shaded, and commands an extensive view.

There are several other smaller parks.

Greenwood Cemetery is in the south part of Brooklyn, at Gowanus, about three miles from Fulton Ferry landing. Access is had by the cars, which pass the cemetery gates every fifteen minutes throughout the day. Free entrance is allowed to persons on foot during week days, but on the Sabbath none but the proprietors of lots and their families, and persons with them, are admitted; others than proprietors can obtain a permit for carriages on week-days. Office, 30 Broadway, New York. This cemetery was incorporated in 1838, and contains 242 acres of ground, about one-half of which is covered with wood of a natural growth. These grounds have a varied surface of hills, valleys, and plains. The elevations afford extensive views; that from *Ocean Hill*, near the western line, presents a wide range of the ocean, with a portion of Long Island. *Battle Hill*, in the northwest, commands an extensive view of the cities of Brooklyn and New York, the Hudson River, the noble bay, and of New Jersey, and Staten Island. From the other elevated grounds in the cemetery there are also fine prospects.

Greenwood is traversed by winding avenues and paths, twenty miles in extent, which afford visitors, with sufficient time at their disposal, an opportunity of seeing every part of this extensive cemetery. Several of the monuments, original in their design, are very beautiful, and cannot fail to attract the notice of strangers. Those to the memory of Miss Canda, of the Indian Princess Dohumme, and the "mad poet," McDonald Clark, near the Sylvan Water, are admirable; as also are the memorials to the pilots and to the firemen. The proceeds arising from the sale of lots are devoted to the preservation, improvement, and embellishment of the cemetery. Visitors, by keeping the main avenue, called *The Tour*, as indicated by *guide-boards*, will obtain the best general view of the cemetery, and will be able to regain the entrance without difficulty. Unless this caution be observed, they may find themselves at a loss to discover their way out. To the east of Greenwood, distant about four miles, are the cemeteries of the *Evergreens* and *Cypress Hills*.

Wallabout Bay is between the Navy Yard and Williamsburgh (Brooklyn, E. D.), and is a most unattractive place. It is interesting as being the place where were stationed the Jersey and other prison ships of the English during the Revolutionary War, in which, it is said, 11,500 American prisoners perished from bad air and ill-treatment. In 1808 the bones of the sufferers, which had been washed out from the bank where they had been slightly buried, were collected and deposited in thirteen coffins, inscribed with the names of the thirteen original States, and placed in a vault beneath a wooden building erected for the purpose, in Hudson Avenue, opposite to Front Street, near the Navy Yard.

Clinton Avenue is the most beautiful street in Brooklyn, it is lined with fine residences, and is a delightful place for a drive.

Fort Hamilton, one of the most powerful fortifications in the harbor, is reached by cars from Brooklyn, and by the boat down the bay. It is so situated as to command the narrows from the Long Island Shore.

Fashion Race-course.—This celebrated course is a short ride from Brooklyn. It is reached, by private conveyance from New York, via Thirty-fourth Street Ferry and the road to Flushing.

TRIPS THROUGH LONG ISLAND.

NO. I.

The *Long Island Railroad* runs from Hunter's Point to Greenpoint, on the Sound, at the eastern end of Long Island, with branches from *Mineola* to Locust Valley, and from *Hicksville* to Northport, and *Manor* to Sag Harbor. It is reached by the Hunter's Point Ferries from James Slip and Thirty-fourth Street, New York, and by street cars from Brooklyn.

Jamaica is the first station, ten miles from Hunter's Point. It is an interesting old town on Jamaica Bay, settled in 1656. The *Union Race-course* is in this county.

Brushville ("Queen's" Station) is three miles from Jamaica, and is an attractive resort during the summer.

Hyde Park, the next station, formerly the seat of Hon. George Duncan Ludlow, is where, in 1818, William Cobbett composed his English Grammar.

Hempstead Village, in the township of North Hempstead, 21 miles east of Brooklyn, was originally bought by the Dutch, in 1640, who gave the place its name Heemsteede (homestead), since corrupted to Hempstead. It was afterward (1684) settled by New-Englanders, who came hither by way of Stamford. It contains two hotels, and a population of nearly 2,000. The park is prettily laid out. The Rev. Richard Denton, and his son, Daniel Denton, the historian, were among the first settlers of Hempstead. *Hempstead Plains* was an open space of 12,000 acres, embracing the New Market Race-course. Seven thousand acres of this plain were recently purchased by Alexander T. Stewart, and upon it he is building a town for the purpose of affording, to people of small means, homes at reasonable prices.

Success Pond, famous for its perch-fisheries, and *Lakeville*, a little village which has sprung up on its margin, are both in the town of North Hempstead.

Cedarmere, the residence of William Cullen Bryant, is near the pretty village of Roslyn, which is about half-way between Hempstead and Glen Cove, on the Glen Cove Branch. It is a spot of great though quiet picturesque beauty, overlooking Hempstead Bay, and the Connecticut shore across the Sound. Many of the charming terraced spring-water lakes, of which we have spoken already as among the pleasant and unique features of the Long Island landscape, are found within the domain of Cedarmere, and in the neighborhood of Roslyn. Within a pleasant stroll of Mr. Bryant's residence is Hempstead Hill, said to be the highest land on Long Island. This fine eminence overlooks the Sound and inlets on the one hand, and the ocean-beach on the other; at its base the village of Roslyn is nestled among green trees and placid lakelets. Roslyn is the residence of Joseph W. Moulton, author of a "History of New York." It is also reached by steamer from Peck Slip, Pier 24, East River.

Glen Cove, six miles from Hempstead, is a pleasant place for a quiet day's enjoyment, and has a good hotel. It is also reached by steamer from Peck Slip, Pier 24, East River.

Oyster Bay, or "*Syosset*," *Huntington*, *Centreport*, and *Northport*, villages on Long Island Sound, are all reached by the Northport Branch.

Riverhead and *Mattituck*, near the terminus of the main line, are also summer resorts.

Greenport, the terminus of the road, 94 miles from Hunter's Point, about six hours' ride from New York, is a retired but delightful little watering-place. It possesses the advantages of fine scenery, bathing, boating, and fishing, as well as several good hotels.

Rockaway Beach can be reached by this route, by leaving the road at Jamaica, and riding eight miles in a stage over a good road. The South Side Road is nearer. (*See* "Trip No. 2.")

Quogue, on Shinnicock Bay, a place of resort for fishing and bathing, is reached by Sag Harbor Branch, now completed to that point.

East Hampton, one of the quietest of all quiet places, is on the south shore of Long Island, about 15 miles from Montauk Point, the eastern extremity of the island. It has no hotels, but many families will entertain visitors (for a consideration). There is very fine surf-bathing. For a person tired of noise and travel, this is a desirable place. Reached by stage from Riverhead, and from Bridge Hampton on Sag Harbor Branch; also by steamer from Peck Slip to Sag Harbor, thence by six or seven miles' staging.

Ronkonkoma Pond is situated about the centre of the island, and is a most peculiar sheet of water. Just three miles in circumference, it has neither inlet nor outlet: for four years its waters steadily fall, and then for four years they rise again, and this peculiarity has always existed. The pond is full of the most delicious fish, and upon its banks are several inns, where boats, fishing-tackle, etc., can be procured. The nearest station is *Lakeland*, distant about two miles.

NO. II.

The *South Side Railway* is the next in importance. Its terminal station is at the foot of South Eighth Street, Brooklyn (E. D.), reached by Grand and Roosevelt Street Ferries from New York, and by street cars from Brooklyn. It extends to Patchogue, 54 miles from New York.

Jamaica has already been mentioned in "Trip No. 1."

Woodsburgh (17 miles) has sprung up since January 1, 1870. It contains a number of pretty cottages, and the *Pavilion*, the best hotel on Long Island, kept by James P. M. Stetson. There is fine stillwater and surf-bathing within half a mile—carriages free. Time from New York, 1 hour 16 minutes, over a very pleasant road.

Far Rockaway and *Rockaway Beach* are respectively 20¼ and 21¼ miles from New York, and are regarded as one place. The beach is very fine, looking out upon the Atlantic. The principal village is at Far Rockaway, where there are a number of small hotels, the best being the *National* and *United States*. At the Beach are the *Bay View* and *Sea View* hotels, and the commodious refreshment-rooms provided by the Railway Company. There are six trains daily from New York.

Babylon is a small village, resorted to for its fishing.

Fire Island is a long, narrow slip of sand, in the great South Bay, about 35 miles from New York, and is reached by steamer across the bay from Bayside, the first station beyond Babylon. It contains two hotels, but possesses no advantages except a very fine beach, fresh ocean-breezes, sailing, and superb fishing, the bluefish being very plentiful in this vicinity. Persons desiring the pleasures of riding and driving can find good boarding on the Long Island shore, across the bay. Good hotel on the island.

Islip, 43 miles from New York, is pleasantly situated on Great South Bay, and is a favorite resort during the summer months. The *Pavilion* is the leading hotel.

Patchogue, the terminus of the road, is a regular "*New England Village*" of about 3,000 inhabitants, on the south shore of Long Island, about three miles from that long, narrow bay, some four miles wide, which runs the whole length of the island, and is only separated from the Atlantic by a breakwater of sand about 200 yards wide. Sweetser, in his "Book of Summer Resort," says: "There are two or three pretty good hotels in the place; but, if you can get in, go to Mrs. Willett's," and then eulogizes her farm-house. This place is also reached by four miles' staging over a pleasant road, from Medford, on the Long Island Railroad (Bellport Station), about 56 miles from New York.

NO. III.

The third route is the short line of the New York and Flushing Railroad, extending from Hunter's Point to Great Neck, a journey of one hour and thirty minutes. It is reached by the James Slip and Thirty-fourth Street Ferries from New York, and by street cars from Brooklyn.

Flushing, forty minutes' ride from Hunter's Point, is a favorite suburban retreat for New-Yorkers. It is situated at the head of Flushing Bay, at the entrance of Long Island Sound, and is noted for the celebrated *Linnæan Botanic Garden*. Though the railroad is more expeditious, the traveller will find the boat which leaves Peck Slip, Pier 24, East River, a pleasanter means of conveyance, as will be seen by referring to the "Trip up the East River."

College Point, *Whitestone*, and *Willett's Point*, all pleasant resorts, can be reached by private conveyance from Flushing, or by steamer from Pier 26, East River.

Bay Side, four miles beyond Flushing, is a delightful place for a day's excursion; the scenery is beautiful, and the bay is famous for its clams—a roast or a chowder, served up in primitive style, being one of the features of the place. A pleasant way of going to Bay Side is to take a private conveyance from Flushing, where carriages can be procured at moderate rates.

Great Neck, the terminus of the road, is celebrated for its clams.

NO. IV.

The *Coney Island Railroad*, from Fulton Ferry to Coney Island, is the last and shortest trip; it passes through the scene of one of the most memorable events of the Revolutionary War, the battle of Long Island.

Flatbush is about five miles from Brooklyn, has a flourishing educational institution and several churches, but its principal interest consists in that it was in this immediate vicinity the *Battle of Long Island* was fought (August, 1776). The thoughts of the tourist on the quiet plains of Long Island will revert with interest to that eventful night when the British troops, under Sir Henry Clinton, Lord Cornwallis, and General Howe, made their silent, unsuspected march, from Flatlands through the swamps and passes, to Bedford Hills, stealing upon the rear and almost surrounding the patriot lines—"that able and fatal scheme, which cost the Americans the deadly battle of Long Island, with the loss of nearly 2,000 out of the 5,000 men engaged." The surprise of the attack, the obstinacy of the conflict, the bold retreat, and the loss of the city of New York, to which it led, make this battle one of the most romantic episodes in the history of the Revolution.

Gravesend, the Long Island terminus of the Coney Island Railroad, is a small but handsome place. Its shores abound with clams, oysters, and fowl, and are much resorted to.

Coney Island. (See "Trip down the Bay.")

ROUTE I.

TRIP UP THE HUDSON.—(By Steamer.)

The Hudson received its name in honor of Hendrick Hudson, a Dutch navigator, who discovered it, and ascended its waters for the first time in his vessel, the Half Moon, in 1609. It is also known as the North River, which name was given to it by the original Dutch colonists, to distinguish it from the South (Zuyd), as they called the neighboring floods of the Delaware. Its source is in the mountain-region of the Adirondacks, in Essex County, east of Long Lake, in the upper portion of New York, whence it flows in two small streams—the one from Hamilton and the other from Essex County. These waters, after a journey of forty miles, unite in Warren County. Its head-waters are nearly 4,000 feet above the sea-level. The course of the Hudson varies from south by east for some distance, but at length drops into a straight line, and continues thus nearly southward, until it falls into the Bay of New York. Its entire extent is about 325 miles; its navigable length, from the sea to Albany, is nearly half that distance. Its breadth, near the head of steamboat navigation, varies from 300 to 900 yards; and at the Tappan Bay, twenty miles above the city of New York, it widens to the extent of over four miles. Ships of the first class can navigate the river as far as Hudson, 117 miles, and small sailing-craft may reach the head of tide-water (150 miles) at Troy. To the Hudson belongs the honor, not only of possessing the finest river steamboats in the world, but of *having borne upon its waters the first steamboat that ever succeeded*, when Robert Fulton ascended the river in the Clermont, in 1807, exactly two centuries after the first voyage of Hendrick Hudson in the Half Moon.

The visitor or tourist up the Hudson has every possible facility for seeing its various points to advantage; he can proceed either by steamer or by railway, morning, noon, or night. The former is much the more desirable during the summer months. The boats of the day-line start from piers foot of Vestry and Thirty-fourth Streets, at 8.45 and 9 A. M.; and those of the night (People's line), from foot of Canal Street, N. R., at 6 P. M. No Sunday boat on either line.

If the traveller accompany us up the Hudson, he will take passage in one of the splendid steamers already mentioned, which leave New York every morning and night.

Passing in full view of the city of Hoboken, and village of Weehawken, on the New Jersey shore (*see* page 29), we shortly reach the "*Palisades.*" These grand precipices, rising in many places to the height of 300 feet, follow, in unbroken line, as far as the great bay of the river, called the Tappan Zee, a distance of twenty miles. They do not wholly terminate, however, until we reach Haverstraw, a distance of thirty-six miles from New York. The rock is trap, columnar in formation, somewhat after the fashion of the famous Giant's Causeway, in Ireland, and of Fingal's Cave in Scotland.

Bull's Ferry, opposite Ninetieth Street, New York, now lies upon our left. It is a favorite summer resort for excursionists from New York. In the hot months, the ferry-boats, continually plying thither at a fare of only 12½ cents, are thronged with passengers.

Bloomingdale, now absorbed by the city, but once a suburban village, six miles from the City Hall, lies on the right. The Orphan Asylum here, with its fine lawns sloping down to the river edge, forms a conspicuous feature of the landscape.

Fort Lee, ten miles up the river, and opposite One Hundred and Sixtieth Street, New York, now calls us back again to the western shore. It crowns the lofty brow of the Palisades, 300 feet above the river. A fortification, called Mount Constitution, stood here during the Revolution; and here it was attempted, by command of the Continental Congress, to obstruct the navigation of the river by every art and at whatever expense, "as well to prevent the egress of the enemy's frigates, lately gone up, as to hinder them from receiving succors." A large force of Americans, in retreating from Fort Lee, were overpowered, and either slain or taken prisoners by a greatly superior body of Hessian troops.

Fort Washington, another spot of deep historical interest, stands on a steep projecting cliff, between One Hundred and Eighty-first and One Hundred and Eighty-fifth Streets, New York, nearly opposite Fort Lee. It fell into the hands of the enemy, November 16, 1776, and the garrison of 3,000 men became prisoners of war. Two days after, Lord Cornwallis, with 6,000 men, crossed the river above, at Dobb's Ferry, and attacked Fort Lee. The garrison there, then commanded by General Greene, made a hasty retreat to the encampment of the main army, under Washington, five miles back, at Hackensack. All the baggage and stores fell into the hands of the enemy. The fort was a strong earthwork, of irregular form, covering several acres. Some twenty pieces of ordnance, besides small arms, bristled upon its walls, though its strength lay chiefly in its position. The very spot where the old fort once stood, as well as all the region round, is now covered by the peaceful and fragrant lawns and gardens of elegant villa residences. Just below the high grounds once occupied by Fort Washington (*Washington Heights*), and close by the river, is the promontory of Jeffrey's Hook. A redoubt was constructed here as a covering to the *chevaux-de-frise* in the channel. The banks of this work are still plainly to be seen. Above Fort Washington, on the same side of the river, was Fort Tryon. The site now lies between One Hundred and Ninety-fifth and One Hundred and Ninety-eighth Streets, New York. Not far beyond it is the northern boundary of Manhattan Island—the little waters, famous in history and story as Spuyten Duyvel Creek. *King's Bridge,* built in 1693, by Frederick Phillips, marks the meeting of the waters which flow from the East into the North River, and form the Island of Manhattan. Hard by (Two Hundred and Seventeenth Street) was a redoubt of two guns, called Cock Hill Fort; and upon Tetard's Hill, across the creek, was Fort Independence, a square redoubt with bastions.

Upon the heights on each side of King's Bridge a bloody fight took place between the British and American forces, January, 1777. The heights command an extended and picturesque view.

There was still another military work here, strengthened by the British in 1781, and named Fort Prince.

Mount Saint Vincent.—Fifteen miles from New York is the seat of the Convent of St. Vincent, under the charge of the "Ladies of the Sacred Heart." Among the buildings is the castellated structure known as "*Fonthill,*" the celebrated residence of Edwin Forrest, the tragedian. After his divorce he sold it to the "Ladies of the Sacred Heart," who have erected suitable additional buildings, which are now used as a convent and academy for young ladies. The group of buildings presents a striking but not very pleasing appearance from the river.

Yonkers—(HOTEL, *Getty House*), seventeen miles up the river, is an ancient settlement at the mouth of the Neperan, or Saw-mill River. Since the opening of the Hudson River Railway, it has become a fashionable suburban town of New York, as the short distance thence permits pleasant, speedy, and cheap transport by land or water. Yonkers was the home of the once famous family of the Phillipses, of which was Mary Phillips, the first love of General Washington. The *Manor House,* a spacious edifice of stone, built in 1682, is still to be seen. The existing front was added in 1745. It is now occupied by its present owner, Mr. Woodworth, who has preserved its interior construction with scrupulous care. East of the Phillips manor-house is *Locust Hill,* where the American troops were encamped in 1781. In 1777 a naval action occurred in front of Yonkers, between the American gunboats and the British frigates Ross and Phœnix.

Hastings, three miles north of Yonkers, is a thriving little village; the vicinity contains many beautiful residences. It has large marble-yards.

Dobb's Ferry, two miles yet beyond, and still upon the eastern bank of the river, is an ancient settlement, with a new leaven of metropolitan life, like all the places within an hour or two's journey from New York. The village has a pleasant air, lying along the river-slope, at the mouth of the Wisquaqua Creek. Its name is that of an old family which once possessed the region and established a ferry. Remains of military works still exist at Dobb's Ferry. *Zion Church* is an old and interesting edifice.

Piermont, on the western shore, marks the sinking of the Palisades. It was once the main and now is a branch terminus of the Erie Railroad. It takes its name from its pier, one mile long from the shore to the channel of the river, which is here three miles wide. It (the pier) marks the boundary line between New York and New Jersey. Communication is had with the eastern shore by ferry to Irvington. Between Dobb's Ferry and Irvington is *Nevis,* once the homestead of Colonel James Hamilton. It contains many reminiscences of Hamilton, among which is Washington's last portrait, by Stuart. In the immediate neighborhood of Nevis is the residence of Mr. Cottinet, built of Caen stone, and said to be the most elegant house on the Hudson.

Three miles S. W. of Piermont is the old town of *Tappan,* interesting as having been one of the chief of Washington's headquarters during the Revolution, and as the spot also where Major André was imprisoned and executed. The home of the commander-in-chief, and the jail of the ill-fated officer, are still in good preservation, though the latter house has been somewhat modified in its interior arrangements of late years, to suit its present occupancy as a tavern, under the style and title of the "'Seventy-six Stone House." The old Dutch church, in which André was tried, stood near by, but it was torn down in 1836, and a new one reared upon its site. The spot where the execution took place (October 2, 1780) is within a short walk of the *Old Stone House,* in which the prisoner was confined.

Irvington & "Sunnyside." —Irvington, four miles above Dobb's Ferry, on the right bank, was once called Dearman, and was rechristened Irvington, in honor of the late Washington Irving, whose unique little cottage of *Sunnyside* is close by, upon the margin of the river, hidden from the eye of the traveller only by the dense growth of the surrounding trees and shrubbery. It is a pretty stone cottage, the eastern side embowered in ivy, the earlier slips of which were presented to Irving by Sir Walter Scott, at Abbotsford, and were planted by Irving himself. The original house was built by Wolfert Acker, in the days of the Dutch governors, and bore over the door the inscription "Lust in Rust," the meaning of which is "pleasure in quiet." Irving has made this house the subject of one of the sketches in his work entitled "Wolfert's Roost."

Nyack, a healthful and charming summer residence, is on the west side of the river, above Piermont, reached by ferry from Tarrytown. A railroad from Piermont was opened May 21, 1870.

Tarrytown, twenty-six miles from New York, is a prosperous little town on the eastern bank of the Hudson. It has many attractions, historical, pictorial, and social; elegant villas, chiefly occupied by New York gentlemen, having gathered thickly around it, as about all this part of the river's margin within the past few years. A short distance up Mill River is the quiet little valley of *Sleepy Hollow,* the scene of some of Irving's happiest fancies. *Carl's Mill* and the bridge over the brook are still standing. The principal objects of interest in the village are those connected with Irving's life and memory, the *Old Dutch Church,* and *Christ Church,* where Irving always attended service, of which he was a warden at the time of his death, and in which a handsome tablet has been erected to his memory. The *Old Dutch Church* was built in 1615, and is near where Ichabod Crane, the village schoolmaster, encountered the "headless horseman," and but a few yards from the spot where André was captured.

During the Revolution, Tarrytown witnessed many stormy fights between those lawless and marauding bands of both British and Americans, known as "Skinners" and "Cowboys." It was upon a spot, now in the heart of Tarrytown, that Major André was arrested, while returning to the British lines, after a visit to General Arnold. At *Greensburg*, three miles east of Tarrytown, is a monument to Isaac Van Wart, one of the captors, who died in 1828.

Upon a high promontory below Tarrytown stands the "Paulding Manor," the residence of Philip R. Paulding. It is one of the finest specimens of the Pointed Tudor style of domestic architecture in the United States, and is the most conspicuous dwelling to the eye of the traveller on the lower Hudson.

Sing Sing (33 miles) is on the right bank, and in its acclivitous topography, upon a slope of 200 feet, it makes a fine appearance from the water. The greatest breadth of the Hudson, nearly four miles, is at this point. Many fine country-seats crown the heights of this pleasant village. It is distinguished for its educational establishments; for its vicinage to the mouth of the Croton River, whence the city of New York derives its abundant supply of water; and for being the seat of the State Prison. The name is derived from an Indian word, meaning "Stony Place." The *great Croton Aqueduct* at this point is especially interesting, being carried over the Sing Sing Kill by an arch of stone masonry 88 feet between the abutments, and 100 feet above the water.

The *State Prison* is located on the banks of the Hudson, nearly three-quarters of a mile south of the village. The buildings are large structures, erected by the convicts themselves, with material from the marble and limestone quarries which abound here, and which many of them are continually employed in working. The prisons form three sides of a square. The main edifice is 484 feet long, 44 feet wide, and five stories high, with cells for 1,000 occupants, 869 of which were filled in 1852. In 1861 over 1,300 were confined here. The female prisoners are lodged in a fine edifice, some 30 or 40 rods east of the male department. The prisoners are guarded by sentinels, instead of being enclosed by walls. The whole area covered by the establishment is about 130 acres. The railway passes through and beneath the prisons, but from the river they are seen to advantage.

Rockland Lake, the source of the principal ice supply of the city of New York, and the headwaters of the Hackensack River, is an oval lake, 150 feet above the level of the Hudson, and is directly opposite Sing Sing. It is upon what is known as *Verdrieteges' Hook*, a commanding height, with such a deceptive appearance, viewed from the river above and below, of a grand headland, that it has been christened *Point-no-Point*. Intervening hills hide the lake, and the village upon its banks, from the traveller, but its site is marked by a collection of dwellings and ice-houses clustered round the pier, whence the ice is shipped by barges to New York.

Croton (*Teller's*) **Point**, a prominent headland dividing Haverstraw Bay from the Tappan Zee, four miles above Sing Sing, is noteworthy for its famous lake which supplies the metropolis with water. The dam is 250 feet long, 40 feet high, and 70 feet thick at the base. The capacity of the lake is 500,000,000 gallons, and it discharges 40,000,000 to 60,000,000 daily. Another and much larger reservoir is now nearly completed, and it is anticipated that, when it is finished, all danger of a short supply of water, caused by continued dry weather, will be obviated by the immense reserve collected at this point. The dam can be reached by carriages from Sing Sing, from Croton, and from Croton Falls on the Harlem Railroad.

The great bay above Croton Point is called Haverstraw Bay, on the western shore of which are the following points of interest:

Haverstraw, a pretty little village, where, upon what is known as "Treason Hill," stands the house of Joshua Hett Smith, where André and Benedict Arnold met to arrange the terms of the surrender of West Point. It is of stone, with a piazza in front, and stands on the hill-side beyond the flats. Above Haverstraw is a line of limestone cliff about half a mile in length and very valuable, producing a million bushels of lime

41

every year, besides stone for rough masonry, and for macadamizing roads.

Grassy Point is a little village two miles above Haverstraw; and one mile above this is Stony Point, the site of a fort during the Revolution. The fort was captured by the English, June 1, 1779; was stormed and recaptured by General Anthony Wayne, July 16, 1779, and was then abandoned to the enemy for want of sufficient force to hold it. The present light-house and bell-tower mark the site of the magazine of the old fort, and are always pointed out.

Verplanck's Point, on the east side, is the spot at which Hendrick Hudson's ship, the Half Moon, first came to anchor after leaving Yonkers. Topographically, Verplanck's Point may be described as a peninsula, gradually rising from a gentle surface, until it terminates at the river, in a bold bluff of from forty to fifty feet elevation. A small fortification, called *Fort Fayette*, once existed on the western extremity of Verplanck's Point, many remains of which are yet distinctly visible. It was captured by the English June 1, 1779.

Peekskill, forty-three miles, is one of the most interesting places on the Hudson. It is near the mouth of the Peekskill or Annsville Creek, which enters the Hudson a short distance above. The town was settled by John Peck, in 1764, an early Dutch navigator of the Hudson, who, as popular tradition runs, mistaking this creek for a continuation of the main stream, ran his boat ashore, and commenced the future town. In 1797 Peekskill was the headquarters of General Putnam, where, on the 7th of August, he hung the British spy, Palmer. The oak-tree on which Palmer was hung is, we believe, still standing.

The *Van Cortlandt House*, in the vicinity, is an object of interest, as the ancient seat of an ancient family, and as the temporary residence of Washington. Near by is a venerable church, erected in 1767, within whose graveyard there is a monument to the memory of John Paulding, one of the captors of Major André. A pleasant ride from Peekskill is to *Lake Mahopac*, a fashionable summer resort for the pleasure-seekers of New York. (*See* page 51.) *Lake Mohen-*

sick, about six miles east of Peekskill, and 900 feet above the Hudson, is a tributary of the Croton. It has a circumference of about four or five miles, and is famed for its magnificent views.

Caldwell's Landing, opposite Peekskill, at the foot of Dunderberg Mountain, three miles above Stony Point, was long a calling-place for the river steamers. The passengers for Peekskill, opposite, were then always landed at Caldwell. This spot is memorable for the search so seriously and actively made for the treasure which the famous pirate Captain Kidd was supposed to have secreted at the bottom of the river here. Remains of the apparatus used for this purpose are still seen, in bold, black relief, at the Dunderberg Point, as the boat rounds it, toward the Horserace. At Peekskill the river makes a sudden turn to the west, which is called the race.

We have now reached

THE HIGHLANDS,

and the scenery from this point to Newburg is said to equal and in some places to surpass that of the Rhine itself. On our left is Dunderberg Mountain, and at its base a broad deep stream, called Fort Montgomery Creek, which, a short distance from its mouth, makes its descent to the river in a beautiful cascade. On its south side stood Fort Montgomery, and on its north side Fort Clinton. In October, 1777, they were both captured by the English, and the chain which had been stretched across the river at this point removed. Near this point is Sinnipink Lake, or *bloody pond*, as it is sometimes called, from its waters having become discolored by the blood of the slain who were thrown into it, during an engagement in the Revolutionary War. It is now one of the sources from which the ice for New York is brought.

Anthony's Nose is a rocky promontory on our right, which rises to the height of 1,128 feet, the base of which has been tunnelled by the railway a length of 200 feet. Two miles above is *Sugar-Loaf Mountain*, with an elevation of 865 feet. Near by, and reaching far out into the river, is a sandy bluff, on which *Fort Independence* once stood. Farther on is *Iona Island*, and in the extreme distance *Bear Mountain*.

On the west side of the river, below West Point, the *Buttermilk Falls* are seen descending over inclined ledges, a distance of 100 feet.

In the heart of the Highland pass, and just below West Point, on the west bank, is *Cozzens's*, a spacious and elegant summer hotel, which comes most charmingly into the pictures of the vicinity. It is accessible, as is West Point, at the same time, from the railway on the opposite side of the river, by a steam-ferry from *Garrison's Station* (51 miles from New York), between Peekskill below and Cold Spring above. The concourse of sail sometimes wind-locked in the angles of this mountain-pass presents a novel sight.

Constitution Island, with the Rocky plateau of West Point, now bars our view of the upper portion of the Highland passage. Rounding it, we come into that wonderful reach of the river, flanked on the west by *Cro'nest* and *Butter Hill*, or *Storm King*, and on the east by the jagged acclivities of *Breakneck* and *Bull Hill*, with the pretty village of Cold Spring beneath. Constitution Island, called, prior to the Revolution, Martelear's Rock, was fortified, together with West Point, in 1775–'76. The remains of the magazines and other portions of the fort are still standing.

West Point.—HOTELS, *The West Point* (T. Cozzens), on the Post, and *Cozzens* (Sylvanus T. Cozzens), 1½ miles below.

West Point (51 miles), on account of its famous military school and historical associations, and for its varied scenic attractions, is one of the most charming places on the Hudson. The hotels, though well kept, are not large enough always to accommodate those desiring board; and those intending to make a stay there, *en route* to or from New York, would do well to order rooms in advance. Cozzens's was first opened in 1849, since which time the late Lieutenant-General Scott was accustomed to make it his summer headquarters.

The *United States Military Academy*, established in 1802, will first attract the visitor's attention. The buildings embrace the barracks, with accommodation for 250 cadets; a large stone building for cavalry exercises, a laboratory, observatory, chapel, hospital, mess-building, and quarters for officers. The academy is of stone, 275 feet long by 75 feet wide, and three stories high. The United States lands (2,105 acres) were purchased, and control over 250 acres in extent, was ceded by New York to the General Government in 1826. Among the objects of interest to be seen in and around the academy buildings are Revolutionary relics, cannon captured in the Mexican War, and a brass mortar taken from the British at Stony Point. *The Chapel* is an interesting edifice, rendered more so by the associations connecting it with the obsequies of Lieutenant-General Scott, who died at West Point, May 29, 1866. The afternoon military exercises on the Plain afford a characteristic and striking phase of West Point life.

Kosciusko's Garden and Monument are on the river-bank near the camp-ground. The monument is of white marble. It was erected by the corps of cadets in 1828, and cost $5,000. Near Kosciusko's Garden is a fine spring, said to have been discovered by Kosciusko himself. An attractive path leads from here to the North Wharf, called *Chain Battery Walk*. The ruins of Forts Clinton, Putnam, Webb, and Wyllys, are sometimes visited. From the walls of *Putnam*, on Mount Independence, 600 feet above the river, a view is obtained which will well repay the labor of reaching it. The visitor will delight his eye at all points, whether he gaze upon the superb panorama of the river as he sits upon the piazza of the hotel, or as he looks upon the scene from the yet loftier eminence above, crowned by the ruins of ancient fortresses.

The Robinson House, occupied by Arnold at the time of his treason, and whence he made his escape to a British vessel, the Vulture, lying near by, is on the opposite (east) bank of the Hudson, at the foot of Sugar-Loaf Mountain.

An excursion to West Point from New York and return will occupy one day. By steamer, landing at eleven o'clock A.M., and return steamer at two; or by Hudson River Railroad, station at Garrison's, opposite, connected by ferry. To go by steamer and return by rail gives more time at the Point and varies the excursion.

43

Cold Spring is two miles north of Garrison's Station, on the Hudson River Railway. It has large founderies and machine-shops.

Cro'nest, above West Point, on the same side of the river, casts its broad shadow upon us as we continue our northward voyage. This is one of the highest mountains found in the Highland group. Its height is 1,428 feet. It is the scene of Rodman Drake's poem of "The Culprit Fay."

Butter Hill ("Boterberg") is the next mountain-crest, and the last of the Highland range upon the west. It is 1,529 feet high.

Between Cro'nest and Butter Hill, and in the laps of both, is a lovely valley, replete with forest and brook beauties, called *Tempe*.

Cold Spring and "Undercliff."—Cold Spring is one of the most picturesque of the villages of the Hudson, whether seen from the water, or from the hills behind, or in detail amid its little streets and villa homes. It is built upon a steep ascent, and behind it is the massive granite crown of *Bull Hill*. This noble mountain overshadows the beautiful terrace upon which the poet Morris lived in the rural seclusion of "*Undercliff*" for many years. It is scarcely possible to find a spot of sweeter natural attractions than the site of Undercliff, looking over the pretty village to the castellated hills of West Point, across the blue Hudson to old Cro'nest, or northward beyond the Newburg Bay, to the far-away ranges of the Kaatskill. Near Cold Spring is the celebrated foundery of R. P. Parrott, the inventor of the Parrott gun.

Beyond Cold Spring, and still on the east bank of the river, the Highland range is continued in the jagged precipices of the *Breakneck* and *Beacon Hills*, in height, respectively, 1,187 and 1,685 feet. These mountains are among the most commanding features of the river scenery.

Cornwall Landing is a rugged and picturesque little place, on the west bank. Back from the landing is the pleasant village of *Canterbury*.

"*Idlewild*," Mr. Willis's romantic home, occupies a lofty plateau above, and north of the village. It is easily reached by either the Newburg or Cornwall road.

New Windsor, between "Idlewild" and Newburg, and once the rival of the latter, is a straggling hamlet of Revolutionary memory. Washington established his headquarters at New Windsor, June 23, 1779, and again in 1780. His residence, a plain Dutch house, has long since passed away, as has also the famous "Temple of Virtue." *Plum Point*, on the west side, has some residences.

Newburg, with a population of nearly 15,000, and its social and topographical attractions, is one of the largest and most delightful towns on the Hudson. Rising, as it does, rather precipitously from the water to an elevation of 300 feet, it presents a very imposing front to the voyager. The higher grounds are occupied by beautiful residences and villas. The place was originally settled by emigrant Palatines, in 1798. It has immediate railway communication westward up the Quassic Creek, via Chester (20 miles), by the Newburg branch of the Erie Railway. It is a place of considerable trade, and has some extensive manufactories. The home of the lamented landscape gardener and horticultural writer, Downing, was here. Newburg was the theatre of many interesting events in the War of the Revolution. *Washington's Headquarters*, an old gray stone mansion, built by Mr. Hasbrouck, in 1750, stand a short distance south of the village. It was here the Revolutionary army was finally disbanded at the close of the war, June 23, 1783. Apart from the historical interest connected with the site, it commands a fine view of the great pass of the Highlands. It is owned by the State. The principal hotels are the *Powelton* and *Orange*. The *Wharton House* was used during the Revolution as a barracks. Many of the scenes in Cooper's novel of "The Spy" are laid in Newburg. It is reached by ferry from *Fishkill Landing*.

Fishkill Landing, 60 miles from New York, and opposite Newburg, like that village and all the region round, abounds in natural beauties and elegant residences. It is a small place, with a population of 1,800. It lies in the lap of a lovely, fertile plain, which reaches back from the landing to the base of a bold mountain-range. A portion of the Continental army was encamped here. The village of *Fishkill* is situated on a creek of the same name, five miles east of the river.

Two miles northeast of Fishkill Landing is the *Verplanck House*, interesting as having once been the headquarters of Baron Steuben, and the place in which the famous *Society of the Cincinnati* was organized in 1783. *Matteawan*, a manufacturing point, is about a mile from the landing.

Low Point, three miles above Fishkill Landing, is a small river hamlet.

New Hamburg comes next, near the mouth of Wappinger's Creek, and a little north is the village of *Marlborough*, with *Barnegat*, famous for its limekilns, two miles yet beyond.

Poughkeepsie (75 miles) is one of the largest towns between New York and Albany. Its population is 17,000. It contains about twenty churches, four banks, and three or four newspapers. It has a variety of manufactories; and the rich agricultural region behind it makes it the depot of a busy trade. *College Hill*, the site of the boys' boarding-school, half a mile northeast, is a commanding elevation, overlooking the river and the region around. The *Gregory House* and the *Exchange* are the leading hotels. The *Vassar Female College*, which is one of the finest in the country, occupies a commanding position a short distance back of the town. Poughkeepsie was founded by the Dutch in 1705. It is symmetrically built upon an elevated plain half a mile east of the river. It has no historical associations of especial interest. Prof. Morse, the inventor of the electric telegraph, and Benson J. Lossing, author of the "Field Book of the Revolution," reside here.

New Paltz Landing, on the opposite side of the river, is reached by ferry.

Hyde Park, 80 miles above New York, is a quiet little village on the east side of the river, in the midst of a country of great fertility, and thronged with wealthy homesteads and sumptuous villas. It is named after Sir Edmund Hyde, Lord Cornbury, one of the early provincial governors. *Placentia*, once the home of Paulding, is near by, and commands a magnificent view of the river windings far above, even to the peaks of the distant Kaatskills. *Staatsbury* is upon the railway five miles above.

Rondout, near the mouth of Rondout Creek, is the terminus of the Delaware and Hudson Canal, and connects with Rhinebeck by ferry. It has extensive manufactories of cement, and a population of 7,500, chiefly Germans and Irish.

Kingston, two miles above Rondout, is a thriving and pleasant place. It was settled by the Dutch (1663), about the time of the settlement of Albany and New York. It was burnt by the British (1777). The first Constitution of New York was framed and adopted in a house still standing here. It was the birthplace of Vanderlyn the painter. He died here in 1853.

Rhinebeck Landing, 90 miles from New York, is on the railway opposite Kingston, and is connected with that village by a ferry. The river presents some attractive views at this point. The village of *Rhinebeck* is two miles back from the landing. It was founded by William Beekman in 1647. The *Beekman House* is one of the best specimens of an old Dutch homestead to be found in the valley of the Hudson.

Saugerties and **Tivoli**, the one on the west and the other on the east bank of the river, next attract our attention. Saugerties is a picturesque and prosperous manufacturing village, at the *débouché* of the beautiful waters of Esopus Creek. *Rokeby*, the estate of William B. Astor, is a short distance south of Barrytown. Between Barrytown and Tivoli are *Annandale* and *Montgomery Place*, the seats of John Bard and Edward Livingston.

Passing *Malden*, on the left, and *Germantown*, on the right bank, we reach Oakhill Station, the point of departure on the Hudson River Railway for Kaatskill. Opposite Malden stands *Clermont*, the seat of the late Chancellor Livingston. At *Annandale* is a beautiful little church on the border of a fine park, built by Mr. John Bard, as a free chapel for the inhabitants of the neighborhood; and near it is "St. Stephen's College," built by

45

the same gentleman, as a training-school for young men about to enter the General Theological Seminary of the Episcopal Church in New York.

Of *Montgomery Place*, Mr. Lossing, in his "Hudson," says: "Of all the fine estates along this portion of the Hudson, this is said to be most perfect in its beauty and arrangements." It was built by the widow of General Montgomery, who here passed fifty years of widowhood.

Kaatskill, or *Catskill*, lies at the mouth of the Kaatskill Creek, on the west bank of the Hudson. The site of the town is somewhat elevated, and commands extensive views of the river and distant hills. The banks of the creek abound in varied and attractive scenery, and are annually the resort of city artists, bent on obtaining fresh studies. Here the lamented Cole painted his "Course of Empire" and "Voyage of Life." The *Prospect Park Hotel* (a new hotel, recently erected), by Beach & Co., affords excellent accommodation for those visiting Kaatskill village. The *Catskill House*, opposite the stage-office, is also a well-kept house. This is the spot where we leave the river to visit the celebrated

KAATSKILL MOUNTAINS,

there being immediate connection between the landing and the Mountain House by stage-line.—Fare, $2.

The *Kaatskills* are a part of the great Appalachian chain, which extends through the eastern portion of the Union from Canada to the Gulf of Mexico. Their chief ranges follow the course of the Hudson River for 20 to 30 miles, lying west of it, and separated by a valley stretch of 10 to 12 miles. These peaks lend to the landscape, of that part of the Hudson from which they are visible, its greatest charm. The *Mountain House* is reached by a pleasant stage-coach ride, which usually occupies three hours. *Bloom's* Half-way House affords refreshment for stage-passengers. Two miles from the summit the coach stops at *Sleepy Hollow*, a spot usually conceded to be the site of Rip Van Winkle's famous nap. Here a house of refreshment has recently been built; it is known as the "Rip Van Winkle House." The *Mountain House* is an excellent one, combining all the comforts and many of the luxuries of more pretentious establishments. The last three miles of the journey to the hotel is up the side of the mountain, made easy by a good winding way. *Moses Rock*.—The path leading to this retired spot is passed on the left of the road, a short distance south of the hotel. A most superb view of the Hudson River and valley, and of the mountain-ranges of New England in the distance, is had from the piazza of the hotel. In favorable weather the cities of Albany and Troy can be seen with the aid of a good glass.

North Mountain furnishes a pleasant ramble for the visitor at the Mountain House; the best view is obtained from Table Rock, three-quarters of a mile north of the hotel. *South Mountain* is another favorite ramble, commanding a view of the Kaaterskill Pass. The *Two Lakes*, north and south, are reached in a short stroll from the hotel, being on the direct road to the falls. They afford good fishing.

The *Kaaterskill* or *High Falls* are two miles west of the Mountain House, easily reached by stage, or boat on the lake. The *Laurel House* commands an excellent view of the falls, and of *Round Top* and *High Peak*, in the immediate neighborhood. The descent of the first cascade is 180 feet, and of the second 80 feet; below these is another fall of 40 feet, making the total descent 300 feet. The Kaaterskill has a devious and rapid course of eight miles to the Kaatskill, near the village. To see the falls to the best advantage, the visitor should descend the winding stairs leading from the platform of the hotel, and spend an hour or two in exploring the gorge and glen below. Refreshments, if desired, can be supplied from the dizzy height by means of basket and rope. Mr. Scutt, the proprietor of the falls, resides at the Laurel House, and personally provides for the wants of visitors. Guides to the falls and to the neighboring *Cloves* are furnished at the Laurel House; a charge of 25 cents is made to each passenger for showing the falls.

This branch of the Kaaterskill comes from the waters of the two lakes on the plateau above; and, as the supply has to be economized in order that the cascades may look their best when they have company, the stream is dammed, and the flood is let on at proper times only. We have now peeped at all the usual "sights" of the region; but there are other chapters of beauty, perhaps yet more inviting. Let the tourist, if he be adventurous and is a true lover of Nature, follow the brook down from the base of the cataracts we have just described, into the principal clove; then let him ascend the main stream for a mile over huge bowlders, through rank woods, and many by-cascades, which, if smaller, are still more picturesque than those "nominated in the bond;" or, let him descend the creek two miles, sometimes by the edge of the bed of waters, and, when that is impracticable, by the turnpike-road, which traverses the great clove or pass. At every turn and step there will be a new picture—sometimes a unique rapid or fall, sometimes a soaring mountain-cliff, sometimes a rude bridge across the foaming torrent, sometimes a little hut or cottage, and at last, as he comes out toward the valley on the east, the humble village of *Palenville*. This portion of the Kaatskills is that most preferred by artists for study, and the inns at Palenville are often occupied by them, though they offer but little inducement to the ease and comfort-loving tourist to tarry.

Another nice excursion from the Mountain House is a ride along the ridge five or six miles, to the entrance of the *Stony Clove* (Bear's Gap), and thence through the wilderness of this fine pass. The *Mountain Home*, at Tannersville, is a desirable stopping-place for visitors to this region.

High Peak, the most elevated of the Kaatskill summits, towering 4,000 feet high, should certainly be climbed, in order to see the region fairly. It is six miles west of the Mountain House, is a long and toilsome journey for many, but it well repays for the labor of reaching it. The Mountain House, seen from High Peak, looks like a pigmy in the vale.

Plauterkill Clove is another grand pass on the hills, five miles below the Kaaterskill passage. A mountain-torrent, full of beauties in glen, and rock, and cascade, winds through it.

To visit the Kaatskills comfortably, three days will suffice for the journey thence by rail from New York, for the stay, and the return to the city. Not less than four, however, ought to be thus invested, if one would make sure of a satisfactory dividend; and if a week is at command, so much the happier he who commands it.

Hudson.—HOTELS: *The Hudson House, Worth House.*—Passing *Mount Merino*, about four miles above Kaatskill, the city of Hudson, 115 miles from New York, is next reached. It was settled in 1784 by Quakers from New England. The main street (Warren), which runs through the heart of the city from east to west, terminates at the river extremity in a pleasant little park called *Promenade Hill*, on a bold promontory, rising abruptly 60 feet above the water; while the other terminus climbs to the foot of *Prospect Hill*, an elevation of 200 feet. From these heights the views of the Kaatskills, on the opposite side of the Hudson River, and of the river and city of Hudson, are incomparably fine. It is at the head of sloop navigation on the river. It contains a fine court-house of marble, several elegant church edifices, and a Female Seminary, which occupies the former Lunatic Asylum. It is the terminus of the Hudson and Boston Railway. Population, 13,000.

New Lebanon Springs have fine medicinal properties, and are much resorted to during the summer months. The route thither from Hudson is by the **Hudson and Boston Railroad** to Chatham, and there change cars. The manufacture of thermometers and barometers is extensively carried on here. There are ample accommodations for the traveller at this favorite watering-place, in a well-appointed hotel, a water-cure establishment, etc., pleasantly perched on a hill-slope, overlooking a beautiful valley. There are pleasant drives all around, over good roads, to happy villages, smiling lakelets, and inviting spots of many characters. Trout, too, may be taken in the neighborhood. The water of the Spring flows from a cavity 10 feet in diameter, and in sufficient volume to work a mill. Its temperature is 72°. It is soft, and, pleasantly suited for bathing uses, is quite tasteless and inodorous. For cutaneous affections, rheumatism, nervous debility, liver-complaint, etc., it is an admirable remedial agent. *Columbia Hall* is the best hotel. These Springs may also be reached from the Harlem Railroad. (*See* Routes II, and VIII.)

The *Shaker Village*, with its unique features of social life, is worth visiting. The settlement is two miles from the Springs, and is situated in a charming valley, richly skirted by woods. The *Herbery* for the vegetable-curing process, in which the Shakers are so proficient, and many of the farms, are well worth the attention of strangers.

Columbia Springs, five miles from Hudson, is a summer resort of great value to invalids, and of interest to all. In the immediate neighborhood, moreover, there is a pleasant lake, offering all the country charms of boating and fishing. The hotel here is large and well appointed. The *Claverack Falls*, some eight miles off, should not be overlooked by the visitor. The falls have a clear leap of nearly 90 feet.

Athens is a little village, with a population of 2,000, directly opposite Hudson, and connected with it by a steamferry. It is also the terminus of a branch of the New York Central Railroad from Schenectady.

Stockport and **Coxsackie** are bustling and thriving little places immediately beyond Athens.

Kinderhook Landing.—The village of Kinderhook, about five miles east of the landing, on the east side of the river, is the birthplace of Martin Van Buren, the eighth President of the United States. His estate of "Lindenwald," where he spent the last years of his life, is situated two miles south of the village. *New Baltimore* and *Coeymans* are now passed on the left, and *Schodack* and *Castleton* on the right. Two miles below Albany, at a place called *Renwood*, is an immense stone dike, built by the Government in 1832, at the cost of $250,000.

Albany.—HOTELS: *The Delavan House*, *Stanwix Hall.*

Albany was founded by the Dutch, first as a trading-post, on Castle Island, directly below the site of the present city, in 1614. Fort Orange was built where the town now stands, in 1623; and, next to Jamestown in Virginia, was the earliest European settlement in the original thirteen States. The town was known as *Beaver Wyck*, and as *Williamstadt*, before it received its present name in honor of James, Duke of York and Albany, afterward James II., at the period when it fell into British possession, 1664. It was chartered in 1686, and made the State capital in 1798. It is divided into 10 wards, and had a population in 1870 of over 69,000. It has a large commerce, from its position at the head of sloop navigation and tidewater upon the Hudson, as the *entrepôt* of the great Erie Canal from the west, and the Champlain Canal from the north, and as the centre to which many routes and lines of travel converge. The boats of the canal are received in a grand basin constructed in the river, with the help of a pier 80 feet wide and 4,300 feet long.

Albany, seen from some points on the river, makes a very fine appearance, the ground rising westward from the low flats on the shore to an elevation of some 220 feet. State Street ascends in a steep grade from the water to the height crowned by the State capitol. The water-works, built 1852-'53, at a cost of $1,000,000, are worth seeing.

Among the public buildings are the *Capitol*, the *State-house*, the *City Hall*, the *Hospital*, the *Penitentiary* (a model prison), the *Almshouse*, and more than 50 church edifices. Of the latter, the cathedral (*Immaculate Conception*), on Eagle Street, and the *Church of St. Joseph*, on Ten Broeck Street, corner of Second, are the most prominent structures. The cathedral has sittings for 4,000, and a powerful organ. The stained windows, by Gibson, of New York, are among the finest specimens of art in the country. The *Capitol* occupies the west side of the public square, the State-house and City Hall the east. The latter, completed December, 1832, is built of marble, surmounted by a dome, from which a fine view is obtained. The *State Library*, adjoining the Capitol, has upward of 60,000 volumes. The *Dudley Observatory*, founded by the munificence of Mrs. Blandina Dudley, was erected at a cost of $25,000, and has been further endowed to the amount of $100,000. It stands on Observatory Hill, near the northern limits.

The *State Arsenal*, on Eagle Street, is a large, gloomy structure, in the castellated style. The *University* of Albany was incorporated in 1852. The Law Department is now one of the best in the Union. The *Medical College*, which was founded in 1839, is a prosperous establishment, with an extensive Museum. The *State Normal School* was organized successfully in 1844, for "the education and practice of teachers of common schools in the science of education and the art of teaching." The *Albany Institute*, organized 1791, for scientific advancement, has a library of 9,000 volumes. Admission through a member. The *Young Men's Association*, 38 State Street, has a collection of 12,000 volumes; the *Apprentices' Library*, 5,000. The edifice on State Street, where are deposited the public collections in Natural History, and in Geology and in Agriculture, is most interesting. The *Orphan Asylum* and other benevolent establishments of this city are well worth the consideration of the tourist. The distinguished sculptor, E. C. Palmer, resides here. His studio, No. 5 Fayette Place, is frequently visited by strangers.

In the northern part of the city, extending from Broadway to the river, surrounded by large and beautiful grounds, is the *Van Rensselaer Manor House*, one of the most attractive town residences in the State. It is over two hundred years since the mansion of the first *Patroon* was built upon this spot, and some portions of the present house were built in 1765.

Above the city on the flats is the *Schuyler House*, an exceedingly plain and antiquated dwelling. It was here that Colonel Peter Schuyler, the first Mayor of Albany, the Indian commissioner, who took four sachems of the Mohawks to England, and presented them to Queen Anne, resided. After his death, his own son Phillip lived in the house, which in the summer of 1759, eighteen months after his death, was destroyed by fire. It was immediately rebuilt, portions of the original walls still remaining.

Trains leave Albany, for New York, by the Hudson River and Harlem Railways, almost hourly; for the west, by the Central, and for Boston by the Western (Mass.) Railway, several times each day. For Saratoga and the north, one express through-train leaves early in the morning. The great *Railroad Bridge* across the Hudson is a massive structure, and entirely obviates those delays formerly incidental to ferrying passengers and freight. Day boats down the Hudson at 7½ A. M., and night boats at 8 P. M. To Kaatskill, steamers daily.

Greenbush, the former terminus of the Hudson River Railway, is immediately opposite. It is now connected with Albany by bridge. It is incorporated, and includes *Bath* and *East Albany*. Population, 4,000.

Troy.—HOTELS: *American Hotel, Mansion House, Troy House*. Troy is a large and beautiful city of 46,471 inhabitants, and including suburban settlements 60,000. It stands upon both banks of the Hudson, at the mouth of the Poestenkill Creek, 148 miles from New York, and six from Albany. It is built upon an alluvial plain, overlooked on the east side by the classic heights of *Mount Ida*, and on the north by the barren cliffs of *Mount Olympus*, 200 feet high. These elevated points command superb views of the city and its charming vicinage, and of the great waters of the Hudson. Troy lies along the river for the length of three miles, and extends back a mile from east to west. It boasts many fine churches and public buildings, and several handsome private mansions and cottages; among the former the Episcopal churches of *St. Paul* and *St. John* are best worthy notice. The *Female Seminary*, established in 1821, and the *Rensselaer Polytechnic Institute*, are flourishing institutions. It has extensive manufactures, and enjoys a large and growing trade by river and rail. Four main lines of railway meet at this point, viz.: the Hudson River, the Troy and Boston, the Schenectady and Troy, and the roads which are united in one depot by means of the Union (city) Railroad. Cars leave Troy for Greenbush (six miles) every hour. Horse-cars to Albany, Cohoes, Lansingburg and various neighboring points.

West Troy, a suburb of Troy, on the other side of the river, is a rapidly-growing place. The inhabitants are employed principally in manufactures. A fine macadamized road leads from West Troy to Albany, a distance of six miles. Horse-cars to Albany every fifteen minutes. The *Watervliet* (*U. S.*) *Arsenal*, in West Troy, has a large and constant supply of small-arms, and various munitions of war. This is one of the most important of the national depots, and is worthy the attention of the traveller. It was built in 1814, and occupies 100 acres of ground. *Green Island Village*, near West Troy, has an extensive car and coach factory. *Oakwood* and *Mount Ida Cemeteries* are worth visiting. The former is in Lansingburg, and occupies a beautiful site overlooking the city. *

By the Hudson River Railway.

The journey by the Hudson River Railway, 144 miles, to Albany, though less popular with pleasure-travellers during the heats of summer than the steamboat route, is nevertheless a most interesting one. The road lies on the eastern bank of the river, touching its waters continually, and ever and anon crossing wide bays and the mouths of tributary streams. Great difficulties were surmounted in its mountain, rock, and water passage, and all so successfully and so thoroughly, that it is one of the securest routes on the continent. Opened 43 miles to Peekskill, September 29, 1849, and opened through, October 8, 1851. It has eight tunnels, with an aggregate length of 3,595 feet. The total amount expended in building and equipping the line was $12,700,000. With its heavy business, its history is happily free from any considerable record of collision or accident. This is owing as much to the vigilant management and the admirable police as to the substantial character of the road itself. The flag-men are so stationed along the entire line, at intervals of a mile, and at curves and acclivities, as to secure unbroken signal communication from one end to the other. Six through express trains daily from Thirtieth Street depot. Time, $4\frac{1}{2}$ to $5\frac{1}{4}$ hours.

STATIONS.—Manhattan, 8 miles; 152d Street, 9; Fort Washington, 10; Spuyten Duyvel, 13; Riverdale, 14; Mt. St. Vincent, 15; *Yonkers*, 17; Glenwood, 18; Hastings, 21; Dobb's Ferry, 22; Irvington, 24 (ferry to Piermont, terminus of Piermont Branch of Erie Railway); Tarrytown, 27 (ferry to Nyack); Scarborough, 31; Sing Sing, 32; Croton, 36; Cruger's, 37; Montrose, 41; *Peekskill*, 43; Fort Montgomery, 47; Garrison's, 51 (ferry to West Point); Cold Spring, 54; Cornwall Station, 56; Fishkill, 60 (ferry to Newburg, terminus of Newburg Branch of Erie Railway); Low Point, 64; New Hamburgh, 66; Milton Ferry, 71; *Poughkeepsie*, 75; Hyde Park, 80; Stattsburg, 85; Rhinebeck, 90; Barrytown, 96; Tivoli, 100; Germantown, 105; Catskill Station, 111; *Hudson*, 115 (connects with Hudson & Boston Railway); Stockport, 119; Coxsackie Station, 123; Stuyvesant, 125; Schodack, 132; Castleton, 135; East Albany, 144; *Albany* (connects with New York Central and Albany & Susquehanna Railways); *Troy*, 150 (connects with Troy & Boston and with Rensselaer & Saratoga Railways).

* There are several celebrated iron-founderies in Troy, and manufactories of stoves and machinery. It is famous for its laundries, and has the largest linen, collar and cuff manufactories in the United States, employing thousands of young women. There is a fine Roman Catholic College at Troy.

Rensselaer Park, reached by horse-cars, has a fine half-mile race-track.

Lansingburg is a thriving suburb of Troy. It has among other manufactories a large brush-factory.

Cohoes is an important manufacturing city on the banks of the Mohawk, which affords fine water-power. The falls are very beautiful.

ROUTE II.

NEW YORK TO ALBANY.

Via N. Y. & Harlem Railway.

This route extends from the heart of the city of New York to the State capital, skirting in its course the eastern portions of all those counties lying upon the Hudson and traversed by the river railway. The distance between the termini is 151 miles, seven miles longer than that of the Hudson River. The stations and towns upon the Harlem road are, for the most part, inconsiderable places, many of them having grown up with the road. The country passed through is varied and picturesque in surface, and much of it is rich agricultural land. It does not compare with the river route in scenic attractions.

STATIONS.—Twenty-sixth Street Station; Forty-second Street, 1½ miles; Harlem, 5; Mott Haven, 6; Melrose, 7; Morrisania, 8; Tremont, 9; Fordham, 10; Williams Bridge, 12 (Junction of the New York and New Haven Road); Bronxville, 16; Tuckahoe, 17; Scarsdale, 20; Hart's Corners, 21; White Plains, 24; Kensico, 26; Unionville, 29; Pleasantville, 32; Chappaqua, 34; Mount Kisco, 38; Bedford, 40; Katonah, 43; Golden Bridge, 45; Purdy's, 47; Croton Falls, 49; Brewster's, 53; Dykman's, 56; Towner's, 59; Paterson's, 61; Pawlings, 65; South Dover, 71; Dover Plains, 78; Wassaic, 82; Amenia, 86; Sharon Station, 89; Millerton, 94; Mount Riga, 97; Boston Corners, 100; Copake, 106; Hillsdale, 110; Bains, 113; Martindale, 116; Philmont, 120; Ghent, 126; Chatham Four Corners, 128 (junction with railway route from Albany and from Hudson for Boston); East Albany, 151 miles, connects with Troy and Greenbush Railway.

On leaving the city streets, the road passes under a considerable extent of tunnelling and continued bridging across thoroughfares, and reaches the extremity of the island and city of New York at Harlem, where it crosses the Harlem River into Westchester County.

Melrose (7 miles) is where the Port Morris Branch to Long Island Sound, 2 miles long, diverges. The Spuyten Duyvel and Port Morris Railway, to be completed within the year, will intersect at this point.

Fordham (10 miles) is noted for its fine Roman Catholic College. It can also be reached by private conveyance from New York. It is from this station that *Jerome Park* is reached.

Williams Bridge (12 miles) is at the junction with the New York and New Haven Road. One mile beyond is *Woodlawn*, one of the most beautiful cemeteries in the vicinity of New York.

White Plains (24 miles) is interesting as the scene of important events in the Revolution. An eventful battle was fought here, October 28, 1776. A residence of Washington (in which there are some attractive relics) is yet standing in the vicinage.

Chappaqua, Mount Kisco, and **Bedford,** are summer resorts for New-Yorkers.

Katonah (43 miles) is named after an Indian chief who once owned the land in the vicinity. It has grown up since 1847, when the first house was built, and is now quite a pretty place.

Croton Falls (49 miles), upon the river which supplies the great Croton Aqueduct to the city of New York, are worth seeing. Passengers for *Lake Mahopac,* 5 miles distant, take stage here.

Lake Mahopac.—HOTELS: *Gregory's, Baldwin's,* and *Thompson's.* This pleasant summer resort lies in the western part of the town of Carmel, Putnam County. The lake is nine miles in circumference, is about 1,800 feet above the sea, and is 14 miles from the Hudson at Peekskill. It is one of the principal sources of supply to the Croton, and is the centre of a group of 22 lakes, lying within a circle of 12 miles' radius, all of which, with two exceptions, are feeders of the Croton. Though the landscape has no very bold features, and but little to detain the artist, yet its quiet waters, its pretty, wooded islands, the romantic resorts in its vicinage, the throngs of pleasure-seeking strangers, the boating and fishing, and other rural sports, make it a most agreeable spot for either a brief visit or a long residence. There are many attractive localities of hill and water scenery around Mahopac. The pleasant hotels are well filled during the season by boarders or by passing guests. It is a nice retreat to those whose business in the great city below forbids their wandering far away.

Brewster's (53 miles) is noted for its iron-mines, the product of which is largely shipped to Pennsylvania, to be used in the manufacture of steel by the Bessemer process. The *Boston, Hartford and Erie Railway* will intersect at this point (*see* Route VI. of CONNECTICUT).

Pawlings (65 miles). All trains stop for refreshments.

Dover Plains (78 miles) is 20 miles east of Poughkeepsie, and is surrounded by much pleasing landscape. It is a flourishing village, containing several churches and a number of stores.

Amenia (86 miles) is a pleasant village, containing the Amenia Seminary, a fine preparatory school for Yale and other colleges; several churches, a bank, and a number of stores. This is the point of departure from this road for *Sharon*, and the splendid scenery of the *Housatonic Region*, described in Route II. of CONNECTICUT.

Millerton (94 miles) is the junction of the *Western Connecticut Railway*, and is to be the junction of the *New York, Housatonic, and Northern Railway*. This is the point of departure for *Salisbury*.

Boston Corners (100 miles). One-half mile north of this station, on the east, is a gorge through which the east and northeast winds sometimes sweep with great fury.

Copake (106 miles) is within half a mile of the *Bash-Bish* fall, and is in the vicinity of other charming scenery (*see* page 153).

Hillsdale (110 miles) is also delightfully situated, being surrounded by superb scenery.

Chatham (128 miles) is the junction of the *Boston and Albany Railway* (*see* MASSACHUSETTS), and the road to *Lebanon Springs* (*see* Route VIII.).

Albany (151 miles) (*see* page 48).
Troy (157 miles) (*see* page 49).

ROUTE III.

ALBANY TO SARATOGA, LAKES GEORGE AND CHAMPLAIN.

Via *Rensselaer and Saratoga* (*Consolidated*) *Railway.*

STATIONS.—Troy Union Depot; Green Island, 1 mile; Waterford, 4; Albany Junction, 6; Mechanicsville, 12; Ballston, 25; Saratoga, 32; Gansevoort, 48; Moreau, 49; Fort Edward, 52; Dunham's Basin, 57; Smith's Basin, 61; Fort Anne, 65; Comstock's Landing, 71; Junction, 73; Lake Champlain Junction, 77; Fairhaven, 79; Hydeville, 81; Castleton, 84; West Rutland, 91; Rutland, 95.

Ballston Spa is upon the Kayaderosseras Creek, a small stream which flows through the village, 25 miles from Troy, and 7 miles from Saratoga Springs. Its mineral waters, which were discovered in 1769, are celebrated for their medicinal qualities, although not so popular as they were formerly, those of Saratoga being now generally preferred. A flourishing seminary has been established near the centre of the village on the site of the former *Sans-Souci Hotel*. The village has railway connection with Schenectady, distant 15 miles. *Long Lake*, a famous fishing-resort, is five miles distant.

Saratoga Springs.—HOTELS: the most desirable hotels are the *Union Hall*, the *Clarendon*, and *Congress Hall*. Besides these houses, there are many of less fashion and price, and numerous private boarding-houses, where one may live quietly at a moderate cost. The prices of the principal hotels are $4.50 per day. Attached to the *Union* is an opera-house, capable of seating 1,500 persons, billiard-rooms, baths, etc. Fine bands of music perform on the broad, shady piazzas, and in the ballrooms at the dinner and evening hours.

ROUTE.—From Boston by the Western Railway, 200 miles to Albany; or, from New York, by the Hudson River line or steamboats, 144 miles to Albany, or 150 miles to Troy. From either place, by the Rensselaer and Saratoga Railway, through Ballston Springs.

The short ride from Troy to the Springs is a most agreeable one. The route crosses and follows the Hudson and the Mohawk Rivers, to Waterford, at the meeting of these waters, four miles above Troy, and near the *Cohoes Falls*—a much-admired and frequented resort upon the Mohawk—thence continuing upon the west bank of the Hudson, eight miles farther to Mechanicsville. It afterward crosses the canal, passes Round Lake, and enters Ballston Springs.

During the summer, a car, on the Hudson River Railway express trains from New York, passes through to the Springs without change. Passengers *via* Albany for the Springs change cars at Albany.

Saratoga has been for many years one of the most famous places of summer resort in the United States, frequented by Americans from all sections, and by foreign tourists from all parts of Europe. During the height of the season the arrivals frequently outnumber a thousand in a single day. There is nothing remarkable about the topography or scenery of Saratoga; on the contrary, the spot would be uninteresting enough but for the virtues of its waters and the dissipations of its brilliant society. The village streets, however, are gratefully shaded by fine trees, and a little respite from the gay whirl may be got on the walks and lawns of the pretty rural cemetery close by. The springs, from which the fame of Saratoga is derived, however much fashion may have since nursed it, are all in or very near the village. There are many different waters in present use, but the most sought after of all are those of the Congress Spring. This spring was discovered in 1792, though it was long before known to and esteemed by the Indians.

After the Congress waters, which are bottled and sent all over the world, the springs most in favor and use at Saratoga are the Empire, the Hathorn, the Columbian, the High Rock, the Red, the Pavilion, and Putnam's. The Excelsior, Minnehaha, Star, and Saratoga Springs, are also popular. The *Empire Spring*, the most northerly one in the village, has grown greatly in repute of late years. The *Hathorn Spring*, recently discovered, is now one of the most popular. The *High Rock Spring*, not far from the Empire, is much esteemed both for its medicinal virtues and for the curious character of the rock from which it issues, and after which it is named. It was first known by the discovery of Sir William Johnson, in 1767. This singular rock has been formed by the accumulated deposits of the mineral substances (magnesia, lime, and iron) held in solution by the carbonic acid gas of the springs. The circumference of the rock, at the surface of the ground, is 24 feet 4 inches, its height 3 feet, with an aperture of nearly one foot diameter. The centennial anniversary of its discovery was celebrated August 23, 1866. The *Seltzer Spring* is newly opened. In the immediate vicinity of the springs is pointed out the spot upon which the battles of Saratoga and Stillwater were fought in 1777.

The Alpha and the Omega of the daily Saratoga programme are to drink and to dance—the one in the earliest possible morning, and the other at the latest conceivable night. Among the out-door diversions is a jaunt to *Saratoga Lake*, an attractive resort six miles distant. The lake is nine miles in length and very nearly three in width. The marshes around it prevent access, except here and there. *Moon's* and *Abell's* Lake Houses are well-kept houses, with conveniences for boating, fishing, etc. *Snake Hill* is the name given to an eminence upon the eastern side of the lake. During the summer a line of stages runs between the village and the lake. The *Indian Camp, Circular Railway,* and *Archery Ground,* are immediately south of Congress Spring, and the Victoria Walk. The peculiarity of the Camp is that the Indians are almost all white, and of marked Milesian features. The village has two newspaper offices, several churches, and a resident population of 8,000, which is increased to nearly 30,000 during the months of July and August.

The trip from Saratoga to *Lake Luzerne* is one of the pleasantest in the State. (*See* page 60.)

Leaving Saratoga by railroad, we will pursue our northward journey as far as **Glen's Falls,** on the upper Hudson, whence Lake George is reached by a stage-ride of nine miles. The wild and rugged landscape is in striking contrast with the general air of the country below—there, quiet, pastoral lands; here, rugged rock and rushing cataract. This is a spot trebly interesting, from its natural, its poetical, and its historical character. The passage of the river is through a rude ravine, in a mad descent of 75 feet over a rocky precipice of 900 feet in length. Within the roar of these rapids were laid some of the scenes in Cooper's story of the "Last of the Mohicans." They are generally associated with our romantic memories of Uncas and Hawkeye, David Duncan, Haywood and his sweet wards, Alice and Cora Munro.

The village built up round these falls was almost wholly destroyed by fire in May, 1863. It was, at that time, one of the most attractive little places in the State, and has been rebuilt in such a manner as to even exceed its former beauty. The inhabitants number nearly 5,000, and are principally engaged in manufacturing pursuits. Marble of fine quality is quarried here.

When within four miles of the lake, we pass a dark glen, in which lie hidden the storied waters of *Bloody Pond,* and close by is the historic old bowlder, remembered as *Williams's Rock.* Near this last-mentioned spot, Colonel Williams was killed in an engagement with the French and Indians, September 8, 1775. The slain in this unfortunate battle were cast into the waters near by, since called Bloody Pond. It is now quiet enough, under its surface of slime and dank lilies.

Our road from the falls descends to the lake shore, the gleaming floods and the blue cliffs of Horicon closing in the distance. The first broad view of the beautiful lake, seen suddenly as our way brings us to the brink of the highlands, above which we have thus far travelled, is of surpassing beauty, only exceeded by the thousand-and-one marvels of delight which we afterward enjoy in all the long traverse of its famous waters.

Lake George. *Caldwell,* at the southern end of Lake George (the Indian name of which was *Horicon*), is the termination of our ride. Here we find two excellent hotels, the *Lake House,* and the *Fort William Henry Hotel,* besides several smaller inns. At these hotels every convenience is afforded for boating, fishing, etc. Fort William Henry Hotel stands upon the site of the old fort of that name, while the ruins of *Fort George,* about a mile to the southeast, are visible from the piazza of the Lake House, which commands also a fine view of French Mountain and Rattlesnake Hill, and of the islands and hills down the lake.

The passage of Lake George, 36 miles, to the landing near the village of Ticonderoga, and four miles from the venerable ruins of Fort Ticonderoga, on Lake Champlain, is made by the steamer *Minnehaha,* the trip down to the fort and back occupying the day very delightfully. Leaving Caldwell after breakfast, we proceed on our voyage down the lake. After passing the fine residence of Mr. Cramer, the first spot of especial interest which we pass is *Diamond Island,* in front of Dunham Bay. Here, in 1777, was a military depot of Burgoyne's army, and the scene of a skirmish between the garrison and a detachment of American troops.

North of Diamond Isle lies *Long Island,* in front of long Point, which extends into the lake from the east. *Harris's Bay* lies between the north side of this point and the mountains. In this bay Montcalm moored his boats and landed in 1757. *Doom,* or *Fourteen Mile Island,* is passed in the centre of the lake, some 12 miles north of Caldwell. Putnam's men took shelter here while he went to apprise General Webb of the movements of the enemy, at the mouth of the *Northwest Bay.* Upon the island is Derrom's

Hotel. A small pleasure-steamer named the *Ganouskie* makes regular morning trips to the island from Caldwell. In the afternoon it can be chartered for excursions. It was built on the lake. Northwest Bay lies in one of the most beautiful parts of Lake George, just beyond *Bolton Landing*, where there is an inviting place to sojourn, called the "Mohican House."

Four miles from Bolton, on the east, is an hotel called *Trout Pavilion*. There is no village, but visitors at the hotel enjoy the very best fishing, on the lake. The finest fishing-grounds of Lake George are in that part of the waters which we have already passed, in the vicinity of Bolton Landing, Shelving Rock, and thence to Caldwell, though fine trout and bass are freely caught from one end of the lake to the other. The bay extends up on the west of the *Tongue Mountain* some five miles. On the east side of the bay, the Tongue Mountain comes in literally like a tongue of the lake, into the centre of which it seems to protrude, with the bay on one side and the main passage of the waters on the other. On the right or east shore, in the neighborhood, and just as we reach the Tongue and enter the "Narrows," is the bold semicircular palisades called *Shelving Rock*. Passing this picturesque feature of the landscape, and, afterward, the point of the Tongue Mountain, we enter the *Narrows* at the base of the boldest and loftiest shores of Horicon. The chief peak of the hills here is that of *Black Mountain*, with an altitude of 2,200 feet. The islands of this lovely lake number more than 300.

The water is wonderfully clear, and is 400 feet deep. This is the most beautiful part of the lake, and by enthusiastic writers is said to be unsurpassed for beauty by any of the famed lakes of Switzerland or Scotland.

Sabbath-Day Point.—Emerging from the Narrows, on the north, we approach a long projecting strip of fertile land, called Sabbath-Day Point—so named by General Abercrombie, from his having embarked his army on the spot on Sunday morning, after a halt for the preceding night. The spot is remembered also as the scene of a fight, in 1756, between the colonists and a party of French and Indians. The former, sorely pressed, and unable to escape across the lake, made a bold defence and defeated the enemy, killing very many of their men. In 1776 Sabbath-Day Point was again the scene of a battle between some American militia and a party of Indians and Tories, when the latter were repulsed, and some 40 of their number were killed and wounded. This part of Horicon is even more charming in its pictures, both up and down the lake, than it is in its numerous historical reminiscences. On a calm sunny day the romantic passage of the Narrows, as seen to the southward, is wonderfully fine; while, in the other direction, is the broad bay, entered as the boat passes Sabbath-Day Point, and the summer landing and hotel at "Garfield's," soon to be abruptly closed on the north, by the huge precipices of Anthony's Nose on the right, and Roger's Slide on the left. This pass is not unlike that of the Highlands of the Hudson as approached from the south.

Rogers's Slide is a rugged promontory, about 400 feet high, with a steep face of bare rock, down which the Indians, to their great bewilderment, supposed the bold ranger, Major Rogers, to have passed, when they pursued him to the brink of the precipice.

Two miles beyond is *Prisoner's Island*, where, during the French War, those taken captive by the English were confined; and directly west is *Lord Howe's Point*, where the English army, under Lord Howe, consisting of 16,000 men, landed previous to the attack on Ticonderoga. We now approach the termination of our excursion on this beautiful lake, and in a mile reach the steamboat landing near the village of *Ticonderoga*, whence stages run a distance of three miles, over a rough and romantic road, to *Fort Ticonderoga*—following the wild course of the passage by which Horicon reaches the waters of Lake Champlain—a passage full of bold rapids and striking cascades.

Time is given visitors to see and explore the picturesque ruins of the fort, to dine at the hotel, and to return to Caldwell by the steamer, in time for tea. Fare for the round trip, $2.

Postponing our visit to Fort Ticonderoga, until we reach it in our trip up Lake Champlain, we will return to Fort Edward, on the Saratoga and Whitehall Railway, to which point we have already followed it in our visit to Lake George.

To Whitehall the country is exceedingly attractive, much of the way, in its quiet, sunny valley beauty, watered by pleasant streams, and environed in the distance by picturesque hills. The Champlain Canal is a continual object of interest by the way; and there are also, as in all the long journey before us, everywhere spots of deep historic charm, if we could tarry to read their stories—of the memorable incidents which they witnessed, both in French and Indian and afterward in the Revolutionary War. In the valley regions of the Hudson, which lie between Albany and Lake Champlain, are many scenes famous for the struggles between the colonists and Great Britain —the battle-grounds of Bemis Heights and Stillwater (villages of the upper Hudson), and of Saratoga, which ended in the defeat of Burgoyne and his army.

Three miles north of Moreau Station we pass *Fort Edward*, the scene of the murder of Jane McCrea by the Indians; and, twelve miles farther on, *Fort Anne*, a pleasant village of Washington County, on the canal. Remains of the fortification from which the place is named, and which was erected during the French War of 1756, are still to be seen.

Whitehall, 77 miles north of Albany, was a point of much consideration during the French and Indian War, and through the Revolution. In former times it was called *Skenesborough*. It is at the south end or head of Lake Champlain, within a rude, rocky ravine, at the foot of Skene's Mountain. The Champlain Canal to Troy terminates here. Pawlet River and Wood Creek, which enter the lake here, furnish abundant water-power; population, 4,500. There is nothing in the vicinage to delay the traveller. From Whitehall we can either continue our journey down Lake Champlain, 156 miles, to St. John, or proceed by railway through Vermont, via Castleton, Rutland, Burlington, etc., to Rouse's Point, and thence to Montreal. The boat or lake route is preferable, as affording greater variety and more attractive scenery.

LAKE CHAMPLAIN.

Lake Champlain, one of the most important and attractive features of the northern tour, lies between New York and Vermont, in latitude between 43° 30' and 45° 6' north. It varies in breadth from half a mile to 10 miles, and in depth from 50 to 280 feet. Its principal tributaries are the Saranac, Au Sable, and Winooski, and its principal outlet the Sorel or Richelieu River, through which it discharges into the St. Lawrence, 50 miles below Montreal. The name is derived from that of Samuel de Champlain, who discovered it in 1609. Navigation open from May to November. One of the U. S. mail steamers leaves Whitehall on the arrival of trains from Albany, etc. The narrowness of the lower part of Lake Champlain gives it much more the air of a river than a lake. For 20 miles the average breadth does not exceed half a mile; and at one point it is not more than 40 rods across. It afterward becomes quite wide; but whether broad or narrow, the voyage, in large and admirable boats, over its mountain-environed waters, is always a pleasure to be greatly enjoyed and happily remembered. On the east rise the bare peaks of the Green Hills of Vermont, the bold Camel's Hump leading all along the line; and on the west are the still more varied summits and ridges of the Adirondack Mountains in New York.

Ticonderoga, the point where the lake widens and becomes a lake in fact as well as in name, is the site of *Fort Ticonderoga*, of which the ruins only are visible, was erected by the French in 1756, and called by them "Carrillon." It was originally a place of much strength; its natural advantages were very great, being surrounded on three sides by water, and having half the fourth covered by a swamp, and the only point by which it could be approached, by a breastwork.

Fort Ticonderoga was one of the first strongholds taken from the English in 1775, at the commencement of the Revolutionary War. Colonel Ethan Allen, of Vermont, at the head of the Green Mountain Boys, surprised the unsuspecting garrison, penetrated to the very bedside of the commandant, and, waking him, demanded the surrender of the fort. "In whose name, and to whom?" exclaimed the surprised officer. "In the name of the great Jehovah and the Continental Congress!" thundered the intrepid Allen, and the fort was immediately surrendered.

It was afterward, however, easily reduced, by an expedient adopted by General Burgoyne—that of placing a piece of artillery on the pinnacle of *Mount Defiance*, on the south side of the Lake George outlet, and 750 feet above the lake, and entirely commanding the fort, from which shot was thrown into the midst of the American works.

Mount Independence lies in Vermont, opposite Ticonderoga, about a mile distant. The remains of military works are still visible here. *Mount Hope*, an elevation about a mile north of Ticonderoga, was occupied by General Burgoyne previous to the recapture of Ticonderoga, which took place in 1777, nearly two years after its surrender to the gallant Allen.

Crown Point, thirty-five miles from Whitehall, was the site of Fort Frederick, erected by the French in 1731. Its history is strikingly similar to that of Ticonderoga. In 1759 the English took possession of this whole region, and in 1775 the fort was taken by Ethan Allen at the time he captured Ticonderoga. Opposite Crown Point is *Chimney Point*, at the mouth of *Bullwaggy Bay*.

Port Henry, forty-four miles from Whitehall, is surrounded by some of the prettiest scenery on the lake. It is an attractive place.

Westport, fifty-five miles, and *Essex*, sixty-five miles from Whitehall, are gates to the Adirondack region, as are *Crown Point* and *Port Kent*.

Port Kent, ninety miles from Whitehall, is where tourists leave the boat and take the stage for Keeseville, in visiting the Au Sable Chasm, which is described in the "Trip to the Adirondacks." The most interesting feature of the town is the old stone mansion of Colonel Elkanah Watson, on the hill near the lake. From this vicinity, whether on land or on water, the landscape in every direction is striking and beautiful.

Burlington, Vt., is on the east side of Burlington Bay. The first permanent settlement was made in 1783. In 1865 the township was divided into the city of Burlington and the town of South Burlington. The view of the city, as approached from the lake, is very fine, as it is built upon ground which rises from the lake-shore to a height of 367 feet in the distance of a mile, the summit being crowned by the university buildings. The city is handsomely laid out, and many of the residences and churches are noticeable for their beauty.

The *University of Vermont*, located here, was incorporated in 1791, and organized in 1800. The corner-stone of the dormitory was laid by General Lafayette in 1825, and in 1865 the Agricultural College was united with it. The view from the dome of the principal building is superb, including Lake Champlain and the mountains of Vermont, and the Adirondacks, over sixty peaks being in sight. There are numerous places of interest in the vicinity, and many beautiful drives. *Green-Mount Cemetery*, where Ethan Allen was buried in 1789, affords a fine view of the Winooski Falls and village. The shaft of granite which marks Allen's grave is to be surmounted by a statue. The lumber-trade of Burlington is very great. The only large hotel is the *American*. The depôt of the Vermont Central, Vermont and Canada, near the wharf, is an elegant building, and should by all means be visited.

Plattsburg.—HOTEL: "*Fouquet's.*" Terms $3.00 per day. Twenty-four miles above Burlington, and on the opposite shore, is the pleasant village of

Plattsburg, where the Saranac River comes in from its lake-dotted home, at the edge of the great wilderness of northern New York, 30 miles westward. Plattsburg is connected with Montreal by the P. & M. Railway. *Cumberland Bay*, into which the Saranac enters, was the scene of the victory of McDonough and Macomb over the British naval and land forces, under Commodore Downie and Sir George Provost, familiarly known as the *Battle of Lake Champlain*. Here the American commodore awaited the arrival of the British fleet, which passed Cumberland Head about eight o'clock in the morning of September 11, 1814. The first gun from the fleet was the signal for commencing the attack on land. Sir George Provost, with about 14,000 men, furiously assaulted the defences of the town, while the battle raged between the fleets, in full view of the armies. General Macomb, with about 3,000 men, mostly undisciplined, foiled the repeated assaults of the enemy, until the capture of the British fleet, after an action of about two hours, obliged the English to retire, with the loss of 2,500 men, and a large portion of their baggage and ammunition.

Twenty-five miles farther we reach *Rouse's Point*, on the west side of the lake. This is our last landing before we enter Canada. It is the terminus of the Lake Champlain Railway to Ogdensburg, 118 miles. Railways from the Eastern States through Vermont come in here, and are prolonged by the Montreal and Champlain road to Montreal. If the traveller toward Canada prefers to continue his journey otherwise than *via* Plattsburg, or Rouse's Point, he may go on by steamboat to the head of navigation in these waters to St. John's, and thence by Lachine to Montreal.

(*See* CANADA, for the tour of the St. Lawrence and Lake Ontario from Quebec *via* Montreal to Niagara.)

ROUTE IV.

TRIPS TO THE ADIRONDACK REGION.

In the northern portion of the State of New York is a wilderness as large as the entire State of Connecticut, and known under the general name of the "Adirondack Region," though in different portions it is called by various names indicating special localities, such as "Brown's Tract," which is the most southerly portion; the "Saranac region," in the northeast, and the "Long Lake," or "Adirondacks," in the central and northwestern portions. The "Chateaugay Woods" and "Lake Pleasant" regions are the names applied to other portions. There are over a dozen different routes by which this wilderness may be entered, all of which are given further on, though we shall pursue the most popular, that by the way of Lake Champlain.

Port Kent (for which *see* page 57) is the gateway by which we propose entering this maze of woods, lakes, rivers, and mountains. We will leave the boat and at once take the stage over the plank road to Keeseville, where we will stop with the Boynton Brothers at the *Adirondack House*, and visit one of the greatest natural wonders on the continent—**The Walled Banks of the Au Sable,** which are described as follows in Sweetzer's "Book of Summer Resorts:" "About a mile and a half from Keeseville, the Au Sable River makes a leap of some 30 feet, into a semicircular basin of great beauty; a mile farther down, another precipice, greatly resembling Niagara in general contour, dismisses the river to a course 150 feet below, amid the wildest scenery. Following the stream, now rapidly narrowing, deepening, and foaming, yet farther down, we come to the chasm—a section fully rivalling in grandeur anything east of the Rocky Mountains. At the narrowest point in the river, where a wedged bowlder cramps the channel to a width of little over five feet, a great curiosity is noticed, in that the walls of the river, varying hereabouts from 90 to 125 feet in height, appear on one side inclined and worn, as though some great torrent had swept over them; while the opposite wall stands erect and jagged. Still lower down, toward the lake (Champlain), the walls stand apart about 50 feet, more than 100 feet high, descending quite to the water's edge in a sheer perpendicular line, and extending this mammoth canal, with occasional windings, for more than half a mile."

Source of the Hudson.—

One of the greatest attractions of this section of the wilderness is the source of the Hudson River, which is in Essex County, in the Indian Pass, a savage gorge in the wildest part of the Adirondack Mountains. The springs which form the source are found at an elevation of 1,800 feet above the sea, in rocky recesses, in whose cold depths the ice of winter never melts entirely away. Here, in the centre of the Pass, rise also the springs of the Au Sable, whose waters reach the Atlantic, through the mouth of the St. Lawrence, hundreds of miles from the mouth of the Hudson; and yet so close are the springs of the two rivers, that the wildcat, lapping the water from the one, may bathe his hind-feet in the other. The main stream of the Au Sable flows from the northeast portal of the Pass, the Hudson from the southwest. It is locally known as the Adirondack River, not taking the name Hudson until after passing through Lakes Henderson and Sandford.

Having laid aside your ordinary travelling and donned your backwoods costume, leaving behind all baggage not absolutely necessary, you will take the stage at Keeseville for a 56-mile ride over the plank-road to Baker's, or Martin's, on the Lower Saranac, where you are joined by your guide with his shell of a boat, in which you are to make your explorations; for travelling in the Adirondacks is always by boat, its recesses being penetrated in every part by connecting lakes and streams, an occasional short portage being all the land travel necessary.

The Saranac Lakes.—

We have now reached the Saranac Lakes, about a dozen of the wonderful links in the chain of mountain waters in upper New York. They lie principally in Franklin County, and are most easily reached by the route we have followed. There is a little village and an inn or two at this point, and here guides and boats, with all proper camp-equipage for forest-life, may be procured. For this route the tourist must engage a boatman, who, for a compensation of two or three dollars per day—the price will be no more if he should have extra passengers—will provide a boat, with tent and kitchen apparatus, dogs, rifles, etc. The tourist will supply, before starting, such stores as coffee, tea, biscuit, etc., and the sport by the way, conducted by himself or by his guide, will keep him furnished with trout and venison. If camp-life should not please him, he may, with some little inconvenience, so measure and direct his movements as to sleep in some one or other of the shanties of the hunters, or of the lumbermen found here and there on the way. The tent or bark shanty in the forest, however, is preferable.

Returning from *St. Regis*, and back *via* the Upper to the Middle Saranac, we continue our journey, by portage, to the *Stony Creek* ponds—thence three miles by Stony Creek to the Racquette River—a rapid stream, with wonderful forest vegetation upon its banks. This water followed for some 20 miles brings us to *Tupper's Lake*—the finest part of the Saranac region. Tupper's Lake is the largest of this chain, being seven miles long, and from one to two miles broad. The shores and headlands and islands are especially picturesque and bold, and at this point the deer is much more easily found than elsewhere in the neighborhood. Below Tupper's Lake—the waters commingling—is *Lough Neah*, another charming pond. The chain continues on yet for miles, but the Saranac trip, proper, ends here. This mountain-voyage and the return to Lake Champlain might be made in a week, but two or three, or even more, should be given to it. It is seldom that ladies make the excursion, but they might do so with great delight. The boatmen and hunters of the region are fine, hearty, intelligent, and obliging fellows.

Hammond, in his excellent work, "Hills, Lakes, and Forest Streams," gives an excellent route from Dannemora, in Clinton County, *via* Chazy Lake, Bradley's Pond, the Upper Chateaugay, Ragged Lake, Indian and Meacham Lakes, Big Clear Pond, St. Regis Lake, to the Upper Saranac.

Leaving the Lower Saranac, we will pass pleasantly along some half-dozen miles—then make a short portage, the guide carrying the boat by a yoke on the back, to the Middle Saranac—there we may go on to the upper lake of the same

59

name, and thence by a long portage of three miles to Lake St. Regis. These are all large and beautiful waters, full of picturesque islands, and hemmed in upon all sides by fine mountain-ranges. Trout may be taken readily at the inlets of all the brooks, and deer may be found in the forests almost at will.

The Adirondack Mountains.—The Adirondack region embraces the eastern portion of the plateau which forms the Wilderness of Northern New York. It may be reached by private conveyance over a rude mountain-road from *Pottersville*, above Lake George, or more conveniently from Crown Point village, just beyond the ruins of Fort Ticonderoga, on Lake Champlain. The distance thence is some 30 miles, and requires a day to travel, either to Root's, on Schroon River, or to John Cheeney's, in a different direction, some 6 miles from the lower works, and 20 from Long Lake. The tourist in this region will move about by land more than by water, as among the Saranacs; for, although the lakes are numerous enough, it is among and upon the hills that the chief attractions are to be found. The accommodations, though still rude enough, are much better than in former years. Stopping at either of these points, as headquarters, he may make a pleasant journey down *Lake Sandford* near by, on one side, and upon *Lake Henderson* on the other hand. In one water he ought to troll for pickerel, and in the other cast his fly for trout; and upon both enjoy the noble glimpses of the famous mountain-peaks of the Adirondack group, the cliffs of the *Great Indian Pass*, of *Mount Colden*, *McIntyre*, *Echo Mountain*, and other bold scenes. It will be a day's jaunt for him afterward to explore the wild gorge of the *Indian Pass*, five miles distant; another day's work to visit the dark and weird waters of *Avalanche Lake*; and yet another to reach the *Preston Ponds*, five miles in a different direction. He will find, indeed, occupation enough for many days, in exploring these and many other points, which we cannot now catalogue. In any event he must have two days to do the tramp, *par excellence*, of the Adirondacks, to visit the summit of *Tahawus*, or Mount Marcy, the monarch of the region. Tahawus is 12 miles away, and the ascent is extremely toilsome. The Adirondacks (named after the Indian nation which once inhabited these fastnesses) lie chiefly in the county of Essex, though they extend outside the limits of that county. *Mount Marcy*, or Tahawus, "the Cloud Splitter," is 5,467 feet high. *Mount McIntyre* has an elevation almost as great. The *Dial Mountain*, *McMartin*, and *Colden*, are also very lofty peaks, impressively seen from the distance, and inexhaustible in the attractions which their ravines and waterfalls present. *Blue Mountain*, *Dix's Peak*, *Nippletop*, *Cove Hill*, *Moor Mountain*, *White Face*, and other grand peaks, belong to the neighboring range called the Keene Mountains. White Face is the most northern, and, except Mount Marcy, the loftiest of the wilderness crests.

Long Lake is one of the most important features of this region. It is 10 miles long. The *Racquette River* enters its head, and affords an approach to the most beautiful of all the Adirondack waters, the Racquette and Saranac Lakes.

Lake Pleasant.—To reach Lake Pleasant and the adjoining waters of Round, Piseco, and Louis Lake—a favorite and enchanting summer resort and sporting-ground—take the Central Railway from Albany, 33 miles to Amsterdam, thence by stage or carriage to *Holmes's Hotel*, on Lake Pleasant. The ride from Amsterdam is about 30 miles. The stage stops overnight at a village, *en route*. Mr. Holmes's house is an excellent place, with no absurd luxuries, but with every comfort for which the true sportsman can wish. It is a delightful summer home for the student, and may be visited very satisfactorily by ladies. The wild lands and waters here are a part of the lake region of Northern New York, of which we have already seen something on the Saranacs, among the Adirondacks. The Saranac region is connected with Lake Pleasant by intermediate waters and portages. The deer and other game are abundant here in the forests, and fine trout may be taken in all the brooks and lakes. *Lake Pleasant* and its picturesque surroundings lie in Hamilton County.

Lake Luzerne is 25 miles from

Saratoga, on the Adirondack Company's Railroad, which, when completed, will extend to Lake Ontario, near Cape Vincent, opening to the world the immense iron and lumber regions of the State. It runs from Saratoga straight up the mountain, ascending 700 feet in the first 6 miles. It is a most picturesque route, and in one place it passes over a trestle-work 1,310 feet long. It crosses the *Sacandaga* by a bridge between 400 and 500 feet long, and 90 feet high. It passes near *Corinth Falls*, where the Hudson, with a width only of 50 feet, makes a leap of 60 over the precipice. The lake itself is beautiful, and the visitors at Rockwell's Hotel generally number about 150. In addition to the standard amusements of fishing, hunting and boating, picnics are greatly in vogue among the guests.

The Northern Wilderness of New York is similar in its attractions to the wilderness in the upper part of the State of Maine. The following synopsis of routes to the different parts of the Wilderness, gleaned mainly from Alfred B. Street's excellent work, "Woods and Waters," will be found useful to the traveller in that region:

Some of the Principal Routes into the Northern Wilderness from Eastern, Southern, and Western New York.

I.—INTO THE CHATEAUGAY WOODS.

1. From Plattsburg to Dannemora State Prison, and Chazy Lake, 25 or 30 miles.

2. From Rouse's Point to Chateaugay Four Corners and Chateaugay Lakes.

II.—INTO THE SARANAC REGION.

3. By steamboat to Port Kent (or steamboat or railroad to Burlington, opposite), on Lake Champlain. Thence by post-coach to Keeseville (Essex County), 4 miles. From Keeseville, 16 miles, to *Baker's* Saranac Lake House, 2 miles short of the Lower Saranac Lake; or to *Martin's*, on the banks of the Lower Saranac; or to *Bartlett's*, between Round Lake and Upper Saranac Lake, 13 miles from Martin's. The Keeseville road is a good travelling road, planked from Keeseville to Franklin Falls, 30 miles from Keeseville.

At the village of Au Sable Forks, 12 miles from Keeseville, the visitor can turn off into a road through the village of Jay, intersecting the Elizabethtown road, about 12 miles from Baker's. This road leads through the famous *White Face* or Wilmington notch.

4. By steamboat to Westport, on Lake Champlain. Thence to Elizabethtown, and thence to Baker's or Bartlett's, or to Martin's. This route is about the same distance as the Keeseville route, but the road is by no means so good.

III.—INTO THE ADIRONDACK, RACQUETTE, AND HUDSON RIVER REGIONS.

5. From Crown Point, on Lake Champlain, to *Root's*, about 20 miles. From Root's to the Adirondack Lower Works, 20 miles; thence to Long Lake, 20 miles. From the Lower Works to Adirondack village or Upper Works, by water (through Lake Sandford), 10 or 12 miles; by road, same. From the Upper Works to Mount Tahawus (Mount Marcy), 4 miles, and 3 miles to top. From the Upper Works to the famous *Indian Pass* (the most majestic natural wonder, next to Niagara, in the State), 4 miles. From the Indian Pass to *Scott's*, on the Elizabethtown road (through the woods, with scarcely a path), 7 miles; thence to Baker's (over a road), 14 miles.

6. From Glenn's Falls to *Root's*, over a good road, 30 miles, viz.: From Glenn's Falls to Lake George, 9 miles; thence to Warrensburg, 6 miles; thence to Chester, 8 or 10 miles; thence to Pottersville, 6 or 8 miles; thence to Root's, and thence to Long Lake, or the Lower or the Upper Works; or from Pottersville to the Boras River, 15 miles.

7. From Carthage, in Jefferson County (by way of the Beach Road), to Long Lake, 40 or 50 miles; thence to Pendleton, 10 miles; thence to Hudson River Bridge, about 5 miles; thence to the Lower Works, about 5 miles. Can drive the whole distance from Carthage to the Lower Works.

8. From Fort Edward to Glenn's Falls and Lake George; thence to Johnsburg; thence to North Creek; thence to

Eagle Lake or Tallow Lake (the middle of the three Blue Mountain Lakes). From North Creek to Eagle Lake, 20 miles.

9. By road from Saratoga Springs to Lake Pleasant and Pisco.

IV.—INTO THE JOHN BROWN TRACT REGION.

10. From Utica by railroad to Booneville; thence to Lyonsdale and Port Leyden, 7 miles by stage-road; thence to Deacon Abby's place, 5½ miles, over a good road; thence to Arnold's (over rather a poor road, although passable by wagon), 14 miles.

11. From Utica by railroad to Booneville; thence to Booth's mills, 11 miles, over a good wagon-road; thence to Arnold's by pack-horses (sent by Arnold to Booth's mills), 14½ miles, over a rather rough road.

12. From Utica by railroad to Alder Creek; thence by road to the Reservoir Lakes.

13. From the village of Prospect (Oneida County, reached by railroad), through Herkimer County, to Morehouse, in Hamilton County.

14. From Ogdensburg to Potsdam, on the Racket River, by *Ogdensburg and Lake Champlain Railroad;* thence to Colton by stage, 10 miles; thence to the foot of the Little Bog at McEwen's, on the Racquette River, 12 miles, by private conveyance, over a good road; thence by boat 1½ miles, to Bog Falls; thence a short portage on east side of river; thence to Harris's place, 4⅜ miles, opposite the mouth of the Jordan River; thence 3½ miles by wagon-road to John Ferry's; thence 3 miles farther on, same road, to foot of Moose-Head Still Water; thence through the latter, 6 miles; thence 9 miles to Racquette Pond; and thence 5 miles to Big Tupper's Lake.

ROUTE V.

FROM ALBANY TO BUFFALO AND NIAGARA FALLS AND POINTS OF INTEREST NEAR THE ROAD.

Via N. Y. Central and Hudson River Railway Branches and Connections.

STATIONS.—*Main Line to Buffalo.*—Albany, Schenectady, 17 miles (junction with Rensselaer & Saratoga R. R.). Amsterdam, 33. Fonda, 44. Palatine Bridge, 55 (stages for Sharon Springs). Fort Plain, 58 (stages for CherryValley and Cooperstown on Otsego Lake). St. Johnsville, 64. Little Falls, 74. Herkimer, 81 (stage for Richfield Springs). Frankfort, 86. Utica, 95 (connects with Utica, Chenango, and Susquehanna Valley Railroad, and with Utica and Black River Railroad, *via* Trenton Falls). Rome, 110 (connects with Rome, Watertown, and Ogdensburg Railroad). Verona, 118. Oneida, 122 (connects with New York and Midland Railroad). Canastota, 128. Chittenango, 134. Syracuse, 148 (connects with "Old Line," *via* Canandaigua, and with Oswego and Syracuse Railroad). Jordan, 165. Port Byron, 173. Clyde, 186. Lyons, 193. Newark, 199. Palmyra, 206. Fairport, 218. Rochester, 229 (junction with "Old Line" *via* Canandaigua; with Niagara Falls and Suspension Bridge Division; with Rochester Branch, Buffalo Division of Erie Railway; and with Rochester and Charlotte Railroad). Chili, 239. Bergen, 246. Byron, 253. Batavia, 261 (junction with Canandaigua, Batavia, and Tonawanda Branch with the Batavia and Attica Railroad, and with Buffalo Division, Erie Railway). Corfu, 273. Buffalo, 298.

This great route traverses from east to west the entire length of the Empire State. It has two termini at the eastern end, one at Albany, and the other at Troy, the branches meeting, after 17 miles, at Schenectady. It then continues in one line to Syracuse, 148 miles from Albany, when it is again a double route for the remainder of the way: the lower line, *via* Auburn and Canandaigua, being looped up to the other at Rochester, about midway between Syracuse and Buffalo. The upper route is the more direct, and the one which we shall now follow. The great Erie Canal traverses the State of New York from Albany to Buffalo, nearly on the same line with the Central Railroad.

Schenectady.—HOTELS: *Carley* (late *Eagle*), *Given's Hotel*. At Schenectady the railways from Albany and Troy meet, and the Rensselaer and Saratoga Railroad diverges. By the road access is had to Saratoga (*see* page 52), to Lakes George and Champlain (*see* pages 54 and 56), and to the Adirondacks (*see* page 58). Schenectady is upon the right bank of the Mohawk River. It is one of the oldest towns in the State, and is distinguished as the seat of *Union College*, founded in 1795. The council-grounds of the Mohawks once formed the site of the present town. A trading-post was established by the Dutch as early as 1620. In the winter of 1690 a party of 200 Frenchmen and Canadians and 50 Indians fell at midnight upon Schenectady, killed and made captive its people, and burned the village to ashes — 69 persons were then massacred, and 27 were made prisoners. The church and 63 houses were destroyed. It was afterward taken in the French War of 1748, when about 70 people were put to death. Population upward of 10,000.

Leaving Schenectady, the road crosses the Mohawk River and the Erie canal, upon a bridge nearly 1,000 feet in length.

Palatine Bridge (55 miles) is where visitors to Sharon Springs take the stage. (*See* SHARON SPRINGS, page 66.)

Fort Plain (58 miles) is two miles from old Fort Plain of Revolutionary memory. It is a flourishing village, and is in the vicinity of some fine stone quarries. A regular line of stages runs from this point to Cherry Valley and Cooperstown. (*See* page 66.)

St. Johnsville (64 miles) is a large and prosperous manufacturing town on the banks of the Mohawk. There is fine scenery in the vicinity.

Little Falls (74 miles) is remarkable for a bold passage of the Mohawk River and Erie Canal through a wild and most picturesque defile. The scenery embracing the river, rapids, and cascades, the locks and windings of the canal, the bridges, and the glimpses far away of the valley of the Mohawk, are especially beautiful.

Herkimer (81 miles), the county-seat of Herkimer County, is a flourishing manufacturing village. It is noted for its fine paper-mills, which are worth a visit.

Utica (95 miles) is a large and handsome city on the south bank of the Mohawk. It stands upon the site of old *Fort Schuyler*, and was incorporated as a village in 1817. The *State Lunatic Asylum* is situated here, and consists of several stone edifices. The *City Hall* is a handsome building, and many of the churches, dwellings, stores, etc., are noteworthy. The *Erie Canal* passes through the city; the *Chenango Canal* terminates here; it is the terminus of the *Utica, Chenango and Susquehanna Railroad* (Utica to Binghamton), and of the *Utica and Black River Railway*, by which Trenton Falls are reached. (*See* page 66.) Utica has many extensive manufactures.

Rome (110 miles) is at the junction of the Rome, Watertown, and Ogdensburg Railroad, and of the "Black River" and "Erie" Canals. It is the summit level between the Hudson and Lake Ontario, the Mohawk flowing through its east part and entering the former, while Wood Creek, only three-fourths of a mile west of the Mohawk, flows into the latter. It is a flourishing place, and contains several fine buildings, the handsomest of which is the seminary. It is one of the best lumber-markets in the State, and possesses an excellent water-power. Rome occupies the site of Fort Stanwix and Fort Bull, famed in the early history of the State as two of the strongest fortifications on the then northern frontier.

Verona (118 miles) is a small village on Oneida Lake.

Oneida (122 miles) is on the shore of *Oneida Lake*, a beautiful sheet of water, abounding in fish, and surrounded by some of the most fertile and highly-cultivated land in the State. The New York and Oswego Midland Railway crosses the line of the Central at this point.

Chittenango (134 miles) lies at the entrance of the deep, narrow valley through which the waters of Cazenovia Lake find an outlet by way of Chittenango Creek. The village is noted for its iron and sulphur springs, which were once very popular, but are now frequented principally by invalids, who are deriving great benefits from the fine medicinal qualities of its waters. There is an excellent physician in charge of the springs, and there are hotel accommodations for 100 guests.

Syracuse. — HOTELS: The *Globe*, the *Syracuse*, the *Onondaga*. At Syracuse, 148 miles from Albany, the Central road connects by rail with Binghamton, on the Erie route, and with Oswego, 35 miles northward. The "Old Line" *via* Canandaigua also diverges at this point. It is pleasantly situated on the south end

63

of Onondaga Lake. The most extensive salt-manufactories in the United States are found here. It is famous, too, as the meeting-place of State, political, and other conventions. Incorporated as a village in 1825, and as a city in 1848. It has a population of over 43,000. Between Syracuse and Rochester are seven flourishing towns, the names and distances of which may be seen by referring to the list of stations at the head of this chapter.

Rochester. HOTELS: The *Osborn* (new), the *Brackett*, and the *Congress Hotel*, are among the many excellent houses here.

Rochester is the largest and most important city upon our present route between Albany and Buffalo, its population being 62,424. It was settled in 1812, and named after Colonel Nathaniel Rochester. It is the seat of the *Rochester University*, founded by the Baptists in 1850. There is also here a Baptist *Theological Seminary*, founded in 1850. The *Rochester Athenæum* has a library of 14,000 volumes. Among its picturesque attractions, are the *Falls of the Genesee*, upon both sides of which river the city is built. The *Mount Hope Cemetery*, in the vicinity, is also a spot of much natural beauty. *St. Mary's Hospital* is an imposing edifice of cut stone, with accommodation for 1,000 patients. The *Western House of Refuge*, for Juvenile Delinquents, a State institution, a very extensive establishment, of brick, is about one mile from the centre of the city. The cut-stone aqueduct by which the Erie Canal is carried across the Genesee River is worthy of notice. Rochester is connected by railway with the New York and Erie route at Corning, and with Niagara Falls direct, by the Rochester, Lockport, and Niagara Falls division of the New York Central road (*see* page 69), and by the Rochester and Charlotte Railroad and connecting steamboats, with all ports on Lake Ontario. This is also the point of reunion of the old with the main line of the Central Railroad.

The *Genesee Falls* are seen to the best advantage from the east side of the stream. The railroad cars pass about 100 rods south of the most southerly fall on the Genesee River, so that passengers in crossing lose the view. To see the scene properly, the visitor will cross the bridge over the Genesee above the mill, and place himself immediately in front of the fall. This railway bridge is 800 feet long and 25 feet high. Some distance beyond, a stairway conducts to the bottom of the ravine, whence you may pass in a boat, or pick your way along beneath the spray of the tumbling floods. The walls of this gorge are of slate-stone; they rise to a height of more than 300 feet, and, in the many and sudden turnings of the way, offer a grateful succession of noble pictures. These falls have three perpendicular pitches and two rapids; the first great cataract is 80 rods below the aqueduct, the stream plunging perpendicularly 96 feet. The ledge here recedes up the river from the centre to the sides, breaking the water into three distinct sheets. From *Table Rock*, in the centre of these falls, Sam Patch made his last and fatal leap. The river below the first cataract is broad and deep, with occasional rapids to the second fall, where it again descends perpendicularly 20 feet. Thence the river pursues its course, which is noisy, swift, and rapid, to the third and last fall, over which it pours its flood down a perpendicular descent of 105 feet. Below this fall are numerous rapids, which continue to Carthage, the head of navigation on the Genesee River from Lake Ontario.

Of the five stations between Rochester and Buffalo, there is but one which we need notice.

Batavia (261 miles) is noted for its wide streets, pleasantly shaded by rows of beautiful trees, and for its cultivated society. It is something of a railroad centre, as will be seen by referring to its railroad connections in the list of stations. Within the year 1869, a superb public edifice—the State Institution for the Blind—has been erected at this place. In architectural beauty, and perfection of internal arrangement, it is said to be the best building of its class in the State.

OAK ORCHARD ACID SPRINGS.—There are nine of these springs issuing from the earth within the limits of a circle 50 rods in diameter, three of them coming from the same mound within ten feet of each other. Curious to say, the water of no two is alike. They are 12 miles northwest of Batavia, and are reached by a road from that place.

Buffalo, the third city in size in the State of New York, had, at the time of the census of 1870, a population of 118,050, which shows an increase of 36,921 since 1860. It is situated at the mouth of Buffalo Creek and head of Niagara River, at the eastern end of Lake Erie, and possesses the largest and finest harbor on the lake. It is also the terminus of the Erie Canal, the New York Central Railroad, and numerous other lines of road connecting it with all parts of the country.

The city has a water-front of about 5 miles, half of which is upon the lake and half upon the Niagara River. A portion of the river-front is a bold bluff about 60 feet above the level of the river, and the more elevated portions afford fine views of the city, Niagara River, Canada shore, the lake, the bay, and the hilly country to the southeast. Buffalo, in the main, is handsomely built. Its streets are broad and straight, and for the most part laid out at right angles. Main, Niagara, and Delaware Streets are especially worthy of mention. The streets in the more elevated portions of the city are bordered with a profusion of shade-trees, and the more important avenues have many fine residences. Shade-trees adorn the public squares, five in all, named respectively, Niagara, Lafayette Place, Franklin, Washington, Delaware Place, and Terrace Parks. Among the principal public buildings are the *City Hall, Penitentiary, U. S. Custom-House* and *Post-Office, Court-House, Jail, State Arsenal,* and Market-Houses. The Young Men's Association Building and 70 churches, of which *St. Paul's* and *St. John's* (Episcopal), *St. Joseph's Cathedral* (Roman Catholic), the *North, Central,* and *Delaware* Street Churches (Presbyterian), and the *New* Universalist Church, are especially worthy of notice. Among the prominent literary, educational, and charitable institutions of Buffalo, are the *Buffalo University,* and *Medical School,* chartered in 1846; the *Young Men's Association,* with a library of 20,000 volumes; the *Grosvenor Library,* liberally endowed ($30,000), by Seth Grosvenor, formerly an opulent merchant of New York; the Episcopal *Church*

Charity Foundation, a fine building overlooking the outlet of Lake Erie into Niagara River; the *State Normal School,* a large and imposing edifice. The new State *Insane Asylum,* to cost $500,000, has been located in Buffalo, and is to be built immediately; the *Buffalo Female Academy,* on Delaware Street; the Buffalo and St. Vincent's *Orphan Asylums;* the *City* and *Marine Hospitals,* the latter founded in 1833; the *Hospital of the Sisters of Charity,* etc. The city has extensive manufactures of iron, being second only to Pittsburg in that important branch of industry.

The position of Buffalo, at the foot of the great chain of lakes, makes it the great *entrepôt* through which nearly three-fourths of the commerce between the East and the great Northwest must pass, and an idea of the magnitude of the lake commerce may be formed from the fact that, in 1870, the total number of vessels employed was 5,343, of which 641 were steamers with a tonnage of 142,474. The aggregate tonnage was 680,462.

The leading hotels are the *Mansion House* and *Tifft's Hotel,* on Main Street; the *Western Hotel,* on the Terrace; the *Genesee House,* on Genesee Street; the *Courter House,* on Erie Street; the *Revere House,* near Niagara Depot; *Bonny's Hotel,* corner of Washington and Carrol Streets, and *Bloomer's Hotel,* on Eagle Street. Among the places particularly worthy of a visit are the spacious passenger depots of the Central and Erie Railroads, and the immense freight depots of the same roads, also the piers, the canal basin, and some of the iron-works. No tourist should leave Buffalo without crossing the Niagara River and visiting the ruins of Fort Erie, where an old soldier is to be found who is still able to point out all objects of interest, and to amuse the visitor with personal reminiscences of the War of 1812. As this is the scene of the last Fenian invasion of Canada, he will probably find something to say about that.

Buffalo has immediate connection with Niagara Falls (22 miles), five times daily, via Black Rock and Tonawanda.

The foregoing description is taken mainly from *Lippincott's Gazetteer.* Having now finished a trip over the main line of

65

the road, we will take up the diverging routes in the order in which we passed them, merely omitting the Saratoga route, which has been already described.

BRANCH ROUTES ON THE NEW YORK CENTRAL RAILROAD TO POINTS OF INTEREST.

Sharon Springs.—At *Palatine Bridge*, 55 miles from Albany, tourists take the stage over the hills to Sharon Springs, a 10-mile ride over a good plank-road. A curious feature of these springs is the existence of five different kinds of water issuing from apertures near each other. They are white sulphur (very similar to the Virginia White Sulphur Springs), magnesia, blue sulphur, chalybeate, and pure water. The waters are pure and clear, and, although they flow for one-fourth of a mile from their source with other currents, they yet preserve their own distinct character. The fall here is of sufficient force and volume to turn a mill. It tumbles over a ledge of perpendicular rocks, with a descent of some 65 feet. The principal hotels are the *Pavilion* (the largest), and the *Eldridge*, both good houses. Sharon may also be reached by Albany and Susquehanna Railroad. (*See* page 75.) Cherry Valley is near Sharon, and may be found mentioned below.

TRIP TO OTSEGO LAKE.

Leaving the railroad at *Fort Plain* (58 miles from Albany), and taking a stage for Otsego Lake, over a beautiful road, the traveller passes through the classic grounds of

Cherry Valley, now a pretty little village, and a place of great interest as the scene of one of the most atrocious massacres that ever disgraced any war. Here, in August, 1778, the Tories and Indians fell upon the unprotected settlers, and, without making any distinctions of age or sex, either killed or took captive the entire population.

Cooperstown, the former residence of James Fenimore Cooper, is beautifully situated at the south end or outlet of Otsego Lake. High up in the mountains, with a clear bracing atmos-

phere, in the midst of the most beautiful scenery, and provided with good hotels, it is a charming summer resort.

Otsego Lake, upon which Cooperstown is situated, is the source of the main branch of the Susquehanna River. It is 9 miles in length, from 1 to 2 in width, and is surrounded by hills of at least 400 feet in height. The waters are clear, the fishing, swimming, and boating excellent, and, to add to the interest of the spot, it has been immortalized in Cooper's "Leather Stocking," many scenes in which will be recognized by the tourist. *Canaderaga*, a smaller lake, is in the same county (Otsego). These places may be reached by Albany and Susquehanna Valley Railroad. (*See* page 75.)

TRIP TO RICHFIELD SPRINGS.

Richfield is a quiet yet pleasant resort, where a few weeks can be passed with great benefit and enjoyment. It is 22 miles west of Sharon, near the head of Canaderaga, or Schuyler's Lake, and is within a few miles' ride of Cooperstown and Cherry Valley. It is noted for its springs, and possesses the advantages of beautiful drives and walks, fine boating, bathing, and fishing, and a good hotel, the *Spring House*, within the limits of which the springs are situated—is reached by the Utica, Chenango and Susquehanna Railway (from Utica to Binghamton).

TRIP TO TRENTON FALLS.

At Utica there are two divergent lines. The southern, called the "Utica, Chenango and Susquehanna Railway," runs through a beautiful country and passes a number of prosperous villages, the principal of which are Waterville (22 miles), Sherburne (43 miles), and Norwich (54 miles). The northern, or "Utica and Black River Railway," then, is the one we will take for our purposed trip.

Trenton Falls (17 miles) is the place, above all others, where it is a luxury to stay—which one oftenest revisits, which one most commends to strangers. "In the long corridor of travel between New York and Niagara, Trenton," says Mr. Willis, "is a sort of alcove aside —a side-scene out of earshot of the crowd—a recess in a window, whither you draw a friend by the button for the sake of chit-chat at ease." Trenton Falls is rather a misnomer, for the wonder of Nature which bears the name is a tremendous torrent, whose bed, for several miles, is sunk fathoms deep into the earth —a roaring and dashing stream, so far below the surface of the forest, in which it is lost, that you would think, as you come suddenly upon the edge of this long precipice, that it was a river in some inner world (coiled within ours, as we in the outer circle of the firmament), and laid open by some Titanic throe that had cracked clear asunder the crust of this "shallow earth." The idea is rather assisted if you happen to see below you, on its abysmal shore, a party of adventurous travellers; for at that vast depth, and in contrast with the gigantic trees and rocks, the same number of well-shaped ants, dressed in the last fashion, and running at your feet, would be about of their apparent size and distinctness.

Trenton Falls are upon the West Canada Creek, a branch of the Mohawk, 17 miles from Utica. The descent of the stream, 312 feet in a distance of 2 miles, is, by a series of half a dozen cataracts, of wonderful variety and beauty. Every facility of path and stairway and guide, for the tour of the Trenton ravine, has been provided by Mr. Moore, who has for many years resided on the spot, and has been always its Prospero, and its favorite host. A walk of a few rods through the woods brings the visitor to the brink of the precipice, descended by secure stairways for some hundred feet. The landing is a broad pavement, level with the water's edge, often, in times of freshet, the bed of foaming floods. Here is commanded a fine view of the outlet of the chasm, 45 rods below, and also of the first cascade, 37 rods up the stream. The parapet of the First Fall, visible from the foot of the stairs, is, in dry times, a naked perpendicular rock, 33 feet high, apparently extending quite across the chasm, the water retiring to the left, and being hid from the eye by intervening prominences. But in freshets, or after rain, it foams over, from one side of the gorge to the other, in a broad amber sheet. A pathway to this fall has been blasted at a considerable cost, under an overhanging rock and around an extensive projection, directly beneath which rages and roars a most violent rapid. The passage, though at first of dangerous aspect, is made secure by chains well riveted to the rock wall.

Passing to the left, yet a few rods above, we come to *Sherman's Fall*, 35 feet high, so named in memory of the Rev. Mr. Sherman, whose account of the spot we are now closely following. He was one of the earliest pioneers of the Trenton beauties, and it was by him that the first house, called the "Rural Resort," for the accommodation of visitors, was built. The fall has formed an immense excavation, having thrown out thousands of tons from the parapet rock, visible at the stairs, and is annually forcing off slabs at the west corner, against which it incessantly forces a section of its powerful sheet. A naked mass of rock, extending up 150 feet, juts frowningly forward, which is ascended by natural steps to a point from which the visitor looks securely down upon the rushing waters.

Leaving this rocky shelf, and passing a wild rapid, we come suddenly in sight of the *High Falls*, 40 rods beyond. This cascade has a perpendicular descent of 109 feet, while the cliffs on either side rise some 80 feet yet higher. The whole body of water makes its way at this point—divided by intervening ledges into separate cataracts, which fall first about 40 feet; then, reuniting on a flat below, and veering suddenly around an inclination of rocky steps, they plunge into the dark caldron beneath. The *Rural Retreat*, 20 feet above the summit of the High Falls, is readily reached by a flight of stairs.

The opening of the chasm now becomes considerably enlarged, and a new variety of scene occurs. *Mill-Dam Fall*, 14 feet high, lies some distance beyond, reaching across the whole breadth of the chasm.

Ascending this fall, the visitor comes to a still larger platform of level rock, 15 rods wide at low water, and 90 in length, lined on each side by cedars. At the extremity of this locality, which is known as the *Alhambra*, a bare rock 50 feet in height reaches gradually forward from the mid-distance; and, from its shelving top, there descends a perpetual rill, which forms a natural shower-bath. A wild cataract fills the picture on the left. Here the wide opening suddenly contracts, and a narrow aperture only remains, with vistas of winding mountain, cliff, and crag. Near by is a dark basin, where the waters rest from the turmoil of the wild cascade above. In this vicinage is an amphitheatre of seemingly impossible access, replete with ever-new surprises and delights. Yet beyond is the *Rocky Heart*, the point at which the traverse of the ravine usually ends, though, despite the difficulties and dangers of the way, even ladies frequently penetrate beyond, as far as the falls at *Boon's Bridge*, the terminus of the gorge.

The scene at Trenton varies much, according as the drought or freshet dries or fills the stream, and passages are easy enough at one time, which are utterly impracticable at others. It is difficult to say when the glen is the most beautiful, whether with much or with little water.

The *John Brown Tract* of the Adirondacks is reached by taking this (Black River) road to Alder Creek, 10, or Boonsville, 18 miles beyond Trenton Falls. (*See* page 66.)

THE OLD LINE OR "AUBURN" ROAD.

STATIONS.—Syracuse, 148 miles from Albany; Marcellus, 158; Skeneateles, 165; Auburn, 174; Cayuga, 185; Seneca Falls, 190; Waterloo, 193; Geneva, 200; Phelps, 208; Clifton Springs, 212; Shortsville, 217; Canandaigua, 223 (junction of Canandaigua Br. N. Y. C. R. R.); Victor, 233; Pittford, 234; Rochester, 242.

Skeneateles, 165 miles, is a manufacturing point of some importance. It lies at the foot of *Skeneateles Lake*, a charming water 16 miles long, with picturesque shores, and good supplies of trout and other fish. A steamboat plies on the lake during the summer.

Auburn, 174 miles, the capital of Cayuga County, is delightfully situated near *Owasco Lake*, a beautiful sheet of water 12 miles in length, which finds its outlet through the town. It is well laid out, and the streets are pleasantly shaded. The *State Prison* is a massive stone structure. The *Theological Seminary* and *Academy* are prominent institutions. The former, founded in 1821, has a fine library. Genesee Street is the principal business thoroughfare. Auburn has long been the residence of Hon. Wm. H. Seward. The principal hotels are the *American*, *National Hotel*, and *Exchange*.

Owasco Lake is a favorite resort of the residents of Syracuse and of Auburn, which is its nearest railroad station, being distant 7 miles. It is a beautiful sheet of water, upon which plies a little steamer between Moravia and Owasco Village. At the former is the *Moravia House*, and at the latter the *Skidmore*. Terms, $2.50 per day. Board can also be had at farm-houses.

Cayuga (185 miles) is the point where the railroad crosses Cayuga Lake by a bridge, over a mile in length. The tourist should leave the cars at this point, if he would not miss seeing one of the wonders of America, Taghkanic Falls. Taking the boat up the lake (south), the first landing is *Springport*, where the present Emperor of the French lived for some time while in this country. The next stopping-place, *Aurora*, claims the honor of being the prettiest town in the country. The last landing is called "*Frog Point*," or *Trumansburg*, the nearest approach to our destination.

(The following description is condensed from Sweetser's "Summer Resorts.")

Taghkanic Falls.—The tourist may land here, visit the falls hurriedly, and get back to the wharf in time to take the same boat, after it has completed its trip to Ithaca and returned hither. A wiser course, however, will at least be to spend a day at the falls. Leaving the boat, you find a stage ready to convey you up the steep hill (1 mile, 25 cents) to the Taghkanic House, just in front of Taghkanic Falls, the highest in New York State. Mr. J. S. Halsey is landlord here, and has the reputation of keeping an excellent country hotel. Terms $2.50 per day, $14 per week. P. O. address, Trumansburg, Tompkins Co., N. Y. Halsey or Taghkanic Creek flows through a rich and flourishing country, until, about a mile and a half from the lake, it reaches a rocky ledge rising some 50 or 60 feet in height, directly in its bed. But the stream has succeeded in excavating for itself a channel from 100 to 400 feet in depth, and 400 feet across at its lower extremity. Through this chasm the waters hurry on to the precipice, where they fall perpendicularly 215 feet into a rocky basin, forming a cataract more than 50 feet higher than Niagara. The jagged rock-rift, through which the river rolls before it makes the plunge, is some 200 feet in depth, the rocky channel becoming a triangle at the brink. At the bottom of the fall the ravine is upward of 400 feet perpendicular height. "The fall is in truth," says Dr. George B. Cheever, who visited the place in 1859, "the Staubbach of Switzerland most absolutely reproduced, and of concentrated beauty and grandeur."

Ithaca, at the head of Cayuga Lake, and the principal town on its borders, is 38 miles from Cayuga. In its immediate vicinity are 15 waterfalls, varying from 80 to 160 feet in height, 5 of them being 100 feet or more. The celebrated Cornell University is situated at this place. It can also be reached by the Cayuga division of the Erie Railway.

Seneca Falls (190 miles) is pleasantly situated at the outlet of Seneca Lake, and is the first stopping-place after resuming the cars at Cayuga.

Geneva (200 miles) is a flourishing city of between 7,000 and 8,000 inhabitants. It is the seat of *Hobart College* (an Episcopal institution founded in 1823); also of the *Medical Institute* of Geneva College, and the *Geneva Union School.* The site of Geneva is admirably chosen on the banks of *Seneca,* which is one of the largest and most beautiful of the lakes of Western New York. It is 40 miles long, and from two to four wide. It is very deep, and never freezes over. Steamboats run between *Jefferson,* at the south end of the lake, and *Geneva,* at the north end. *Watkins Glen,* one of the natural wonders of the State, is situated at the southern extremity of the lake. As the most convenient approach is *via* Elmira, it is described in the Erie Railway Route. (*See* page 76.)

Clifton Springs (212 miles) is a very popular watering place, the springs being noted for their beneficial effects in cutaneous and bilious disorders.

Canandaigua (223 miles), at the junction of the "Canandaigua Branch R. R. from Rochester to Elmira," of the "Canandaigua, Black Rock and Tonawanda R. R.," and of the "Old line of the N. Y. Central," is a beautiful town, at the north end of Canandaigua Lake, 29 miles east of Rochester. Incorporated in 1815, it now contains 6,000 people. The lake is about 15 miles in length and is well stocked with fish.

At Rochester the "Old" and "Main" lines are reunited.

NIAGARA FALLS AND SUSPENSION BRIDGE BRANCH.

STATIONS: **Rochester,** 229 miles from Albany; Brockport, 246; Albion, 260; Medina, 269; Lockport, 285; Suspension Bridge, 304; Niagara Falls, 309.

Though this is called a branch, it is in fact the continuation of the main trunk line, and the main line from Rochester to Buffalo the branch, as by far the greater portion of the freight and passengers never go to Buffalo.

Brockport, Monroe County, on the Erie Canal, 17 miles west of Rochester, is famous for its pump-manufactures.

Albion (260 miles), the seat of justice of Orleans County, is a place of considerable trade, with a population of 2,000.

Medina (269 miles) is a thriving manufacturing village.

Lockport, 21 miles east of Niagara Falls, is a thriving town in the midst of a rich agricultural region. It is famous for its limestone quarries and its manufacture of flour. Its population in 1860 was nearly 15,000, since which time it has constantly been increasing. It is situated at that point of the Erie Canal where it descends by ten double locks from the level of Lake Erie to the Genesee Level. These locks may be seen from the windows of the cars. By means of these locks an immense water-power is obtained, the water drawn from the Erie Level being used over and over again before it is returned to the canal at the Genesee Level. The roar of the great cataract can be heard here in favorable conditions of the atmosphere.

Suspension Bridge is a small village at the American end of the *Suspension Bridge,* which spans the river two miles below the Falls. The total length of the bridge, from centre to centre of the

69

towers, is 800 feet; its height above the water, 258 feet. The first bridge, which was built by Mr. Charles Ellett, was a very light and fairy-like affair, in comparison with the present substantial structure. The bridge, as it now stands, was constructed under the direction of the late John A. Roebling, at a cost of $500,000. The towers are 66 feet high, 15 feet square at the base, and 8 feet at the top. The bridge is supported by four cables, each being nine and a half inches in diameter, and composed of 8,000 wires. It was first crossed by a locomotive March 8, 1855. Twenty-eight feet below the floor of the railway tracks a carriage and foot way is suspended. This bridge is used at present by the New York Central, the Erie, and the Great Western (Canada) roads. Having examined the bridge, we will now cross it to the opposite shore. Taking a carriage at our hotel, on the American side, we may "do" the Canadian shore very comfortably between breakfast and dinner, if we have no more time to spare. The regular price of carriage-hire at the livery stables is one dollar per hour. Make your contract when you engage, as overcharges are fashionable. On the plank road, going and returning, the toll is five cents; at the bridge, for each foot-passenger, going and returning the same day, 25 cents, or 12½ each way. If the passenger does not return, the bridge toll is still 25 cents. For each carriage (two horses), going and returning, 50 cents for each passenger, and 50 cents besides for the carriage. A plank-road leads from the opposite terminus of the bridge to the Clifton House. At the bridge is shown a basket in which Mr. Ellett, his wife, and other ladies and gentlemen, crossed over the river on a single wire, about one inch in diameter. A perilous journey across such a gorge, and at an elevation in the air of 280 feet! Two or three persons thus crossed at a time, the basket being let down on an inclined plane to the centre of the towers (this was during the building of the first suspension bridge), and then drawn up by the help of a windlass to the opposite side. The usual time in crossing was from three to four minutes. By the means of this basket the lives of four men were once saved, when the planks of the foot-bridge were blown off in a violent storm, and they were suspended over the river by only two strands of wire, which oscillated, with immense rapidity, 60 or 70 feet. The basket was sent to their relief, at a moment when the hurricane grew less fearful, and they descended into it by means of a ladder, one at a trip only, until all were released from their terrible position. The exploits of Blondin and Leslie, with which our readers are all doubtless familiar, have since thrown these ventures far in the shade. The *Monteagle*, at Suspension Bridge, is a fine hotel. *De Veaux College for Orphans*, an institution founded and endowed by the late Stephen De Veaux, of Niagara Falls, is located a short distance from the bridge. It is under the control of the Episcopal Church of that diocese. The building is a large one, of stone. The land and property bequeathed by Mr. De Veaux have so rapidly increased in value, that the present income is ample for all expenditures.

Niagara Falls.—HOTELS: upon the American side of the river, the *Cataract House* and the *International Hotel* are most excellent homes for the tourist; on the Canada side, is the *Clifton*.

The falls are situated on the river of the same name, a strait connecting the floods of Lakes Erie and Ontario, and dividing a portion of the State of New York on the west from the Province of Ontario. The cataracts thus lie within the territory both of Great Britain and the United States. They are some 20 miles below the entrance of the river, at the northeast extremity of Lake Erie, and about 14 miles above its junction with Lake Ontario.

The *River Niagara* (signifying in the Iroquois language "Thunder of Waters") takes its rise in the western extremity of Lake Erie, and after flowing 33½ miles enters Lake Ontario, which is 334 feet below Lake Erie. The waters for which the Niagara is the outlet cover an area of 150,000 square miles—floods so grand and inexhaustible as to be utterly unconscious of the loss of the *hundred millions of tons* which they pour every hour, through succeeding centuries, over these stupendous precipices.

The Approach.—The best approach to

the Falls is that most usually taken, viz., by the American shore. "The descent of about 200 feet, by the staircase, brings the traveller directly under the shoulder and edge of the American Fall, the most imposing scene, for a single object, that he probably has ever witnessed. The long column of sparkling water seems, as he stands near it, to descend to an immeasurable depth, and the bright sea-green curve above has the appearance of being set into the sky. The tremendous power of the Fall, as well as the height, realizes his utmost expectations. He descends to the water's edge and embarks in a ferry-boat, which tosses like an egg-shell on the heaving and convulsed water, and in a minute or two he finds himself in the face of the vast line of the Falls, and sees with surprise that he has expended his fullest admiration and astonishment upon a mere thread of Niagara—the thousandth part of its wondrous volume and grandeur. From the point where he crosses to Table Rock, the line of the Falls measures three-quarters of a mile in length; and it is this immense extent which, more than any other feature, takes the traveller by surprise. The current at the ferry sets very strongly down, and the athletic men who are employed here keep the boat up against it with difficulty. Arrived near the opposite landing, however, there is a slight counter-current, and the large rocks near the shore serve as a breakwater, behind which the boat runs smoothly to her moorings."

It is from the American side of the river that access is had to the hundred points of interest and surprise in the famous Goat Island vicinage, with its connecting bridges, its views of the Rapids, of the Cave of the Winds, of the scene of Sam Patch's great leap, and of its bold overtopping tower; and in other neighborhoods of the Whirlpool, of the Chasm Tower, and the Devil's Hole.

A totally different and not less wonderful gallery of natural master-pieces is opened upon the Canada shore — the mighty Horseshoe Fall; the noble panorama from the piazzas of the Clifton House, the Burning Spring, the historical village of Chippewa, and the battle-field of Lundy's Lane, Bender's Cave, etc.

Goat Island. (American side.)—Leaving the Cataract House, take the first left-hand street, two minutes' walk to the bridge, which leads to the toll-gate on Bath Island. This bridge is itself an object of wonder, in its apparently rash and dangerous position. It is, however, perfectly safe, and is crossed hourly by heavily-laden carriages.

The *Rapids*, as seen on the way to Goat Island, are impressive. The river descends 51 feet in a distance of three-quarters of a mile by this inextricable turmoil of waters. It is one of the most striking features of the Niagara scenery. Standing on the bridge, and gazing thence up the angry torrent, the leaping crests seem like "a battle-charge of tempestuous waves animated and infuriated against the sky. Nearer the plunge of the Fall, the Rapids become still more agitated, and it is impossible for the spectator to rid himself of the idea that they are conscious of the abyss to which they are hurrying, and struggle back in the very extremity of horror. This propensity to invest Niagara with a soul and human feelings is a common effect upon the minds of visitors, in every part of its wonderful phenomena. The torture of the Rapids, the clinging curves with which they embrace the small rocky islands that live amid the surge; the sudden calmness at the brow of the cataract, and the infernal writhe and whiteness with which they reappear, powerless, from the depths of the abyss—all seem, to the excited imagination of the gazer, like the natural effects of impending ruin—desperate resolution and fearful agony on the minds and frames of mortals."

Chapin's Island is upon the right of the bridge, within a short distance of the American Fall. It is named in memory of a workman whose life was imperilled by falling into the stream, and he was laboring upon the bridge. Mr. Robinson went gallantly and successfully to his relief in a skiff.

The *Toll Gate* is upon Bath Island, where baths, warm and otherwise, are accessible at all times to visitors. A fee of 25 cents paid here gives you the freedom of Goat Island, during all your stay, be it for the year or less. Near this point are Ship and Big Islands. There is here a very extensive paper-mill. Crossing

71

another small bridge, we stand upon *Iris Island*. (See PROSPECT TOWER.) The only place of habitation here is a house at which the traveller can supply himself with refreshments of all inviting kinds, and store his trunks with every variety of samples of Indian ingenuity and labor.

The place is called the *Indian Emporium*. Three routes over the island diverge at this point. The principal path followed by most visitors is that to the right, which keeps the best of the sights, as Wisdom always does, until the last, affording less striking views of the Falls than do the other routes at first, but far surpassing them both in its grand *finale*. This way conducts to the foot of the island, while the left-hand path seeks the head, and the middle winds across. Taking the right-hand path, then, from the Toll Gate, we come, first, to the centre Fall, called *The Cave of the Winds* (see TERMINATION ROCK), mid-distant nearly between the American and the Horseshoe Falls. This wonderful scene is best and most securely enjoyed from the spacious flat rock beneath. The cave is 100 feet high, and of the same extent in width. You can pass safely into the recess behind the water, to a platform beyond. Magical rainbow pictures are formed at this spot; sometimes bows of entire circles, and two or three at once, are seen. At the foot of Goat Island the *Three Profiles* form an object of curious interest. These profiles, seemingly some two feet long, are to be seen, one directly above the other, as you look across, the first sheet of water, directly under the lowest point of rock. They are sometimes called the *Three Sisters*.

Luna Island is reached by a foot-bridge, from the right of Goat Island. It has an area of some three-quarters of an acre. The effective rainbow forms, seen at this point, have given it the name it bears. A child of eight years once fell into the torrent at this point, and was lost, together with a gallant lad who jumped in to rescue her. *Biddle's Stairs*, on the west side of the island, was named after Nicholas Biddle, of United States Bank fame, by whose order they were built. "Make us something," he is reported to have said to the workmen, "by which we may descend and see what is below."

At the base of these spiral stairs, which are secured to the rocks by strong iron fastenings, there are two diverging paths. The *up* river way, toward the Horseshoe Fall, is difficult, and much obstructed by fallen rocks; but down the current a noble view is gained of the centre Fall or Cave of the Winds.

Sam Patch's Leap.—It was upon the west side of Goat Island, near Biddle's Stairs, that the renowned jumper, Sam Patch, made two successful leaps into the waters below, saying, as he went off, to the throng of spectators, "that one thing might be done as well as another!" The fellow made one jump too much, within the same year (1829), over the Genesee Falls, at Rochester.

Reascending the Biddle Stairs, we come, after a few rods' travel, to a resting-place at a little house, and thence we go down the bank, and, crossing a bridge, reach *Prospect* (*Terrapin*) *Tower*. This precariously placed edifice, which seems to have "rushed in, as fools do, where angels fear to tread," is on Iris Island, very near the edge of the precipice, above which it rises some 45 feet in the air. From the top, which is surrounded by an iron railing, a magnificent scene is presented—a panorama of the Niagara wonders—the like of which can be seen from no other point. Here a register for visitors is kept.

The Horseshoe Fall—always marvellous from whatever position it is viewed—forms the connecting link between the scenes of the American and Canadian sides of the river. This mighty cataract is 144 rods across, and it is said by Prof. Lyell that fifteen hundred millions of cubic feet of water pass over its ledges every hour. One of the condemned lake ships (the Detroit) was sent over this fall in 1829, and, though she drew 18 feet of water, she did not touch the rocks in passing over the brink of the precipice, showing a solid body of water, at least some 20 feet deep, to be *above* the ledge. We shall return to the Horseshoe Fall from the Canada side.

Gull Island, just above, is an unapproachable spot, upon which it is not likely or possible that man has ever yet stood. There are three other small isles seen from here, called the *Three Sisters*. Near the Three Sisters, on Goat Island, is the spot remembered as the resort of an eccentric character, and called, after him, the *Bathing-Place of Francis Abbott, the Hermit*. At the head of Goat Island is *Navy Island*, near the Canada shore. It was the scene of incidents in the Canadian rebellion of 1837–38, known as the McKenzie War. *Chippewa*, which held at that period some 5,000 British troops, is upon the Canadian shore, nearly opposite. It was near *Fort Schlosser*, hard by, that, about this period, the American steamboat Caroline was set on fire, and sent over the falls, by the order of Sir Alan McNab, a Canadian officer. Some fragments of the wreck lodged on Gull Island, where they remained until the following spring.

Grand Island, which contains 11,000 acres, was the spot on which Major M. M. Noah hoped to assemble all the Hebrew populations of the world. Near the ferry there was once an observatory or pagoda, 100 feet high, from which a grand view of the region was gained. This spot is called *Point View*.

The Whirlpool.—Three miles below the Falls (American side) is the Whirlpool, resembling in its appearance the celebrated Maelstrom on the coast of Norway. It is occasioned by the river making nearly a right angle, while it is here narrower than at any other place, not being more than 30 rods wide, and the current running with such velocity as to rise up in the middle 10 feet above the sides. This has been ascertained by measurement. There is a path leading down the bank to the Whirlpool on both sides, and, though somewhat difficult to descend and ascend, it is accomplished almost every day.

The *Devil's Hole* is a mile below the Whirlpool. It embraces about two acres, cut out laterally and perpendicularly in the rock by the side of the river, and is 150 feet deep. An angle of this hole or gulf comes within a few feet of the stage-road, affording travellers an opportunity, without alighting, of looking into the yawning abyss. But they should alight, and pass to the farther side of the flat projecting rock, where they will feel themselves richly repaid for their trouble. Into the Devil's Hole falls a stream known by the unpoetical name of the *Bloody Run*.

Chasm Tower, three and a half miles below the Falls, is 75 feet high, and commands fine views (seen, if you please, in all hues, through a specular medium) of all the country round. A fee is required.

Bender's Cave is midway between the Suspension Bridge and the Clifton House. It is a recess six feet high and twenty in length, made by a decomposition of the limestone.

Table Rock exists now only in name, and the sort of posthumous interest which attaches to the spot where it stood. The grand overhanging platform called Table Rock, and the fearful abysmal scene at the very base of the mighty Horse-shoe Fall, once constituted one of the cardinal wonders of Niagara. This famous rock fell in 1862, but the vicinity is still a place much resorted to by visitors at the Falls. If one would listen to the terrible noise of the great cataract, let him come here, where the sound of its hoarse utterance drowns all lesser sounds, and his own speech is inaudible to himself.

Termination Rock occupies a recess behind the centre of the Horse-Shoe Fall, reached by the descent of a spiral stairway from Table Rock, the traverse for a short distance of the rude marge of the river, and then of a narrow path over a frightful ledge and through the blinding spray, behind the mighty Fall. Before descending visitors should make a complete change of toilet for a rough costume more suitable for the stormy and rather damp journey before them. When fully equipped, their ludicrous appearance excites for a while a mirthful feeling, in singular contrast with the solemn sentiment of all the scene around them. This strange expedition, often made even by ladies, has been thus described: "The guide went before, and we followed close under the cliff. A cold, clammy wind blew strong in our faces from the moment we left the shelter of the staircase, and a few steps brought us into a pelting fine rain, that penetrated every opening of our dresses and made our foothold very slippery and difficult. We were not yet near the sheet of water we were to walk through; but one or two of the party gave out and returned, declaring it was impossible to breathe; and the rest, imitating the guide, bent nearly double to keep the beating spray from their nostrils, and pushed on, with enough to do to keep sight of his heels. We arrived near the difficult point of our progress; and in the midst of a confusion of blinding gusts, half deafened, and more than half drowned, the guide stopped to give us a hold of his skirts and a little counsel. All that could be heard amid the thunder of the cataract beside us was an injunction to push on when it got to the worst, as it was shorter to get beyond the sheet than to go back; and with this pleasant statement of our dilemma, we faced about with the longest breath we could draw, and encountered the enemy. It may be supposed that every person who has been dragged through the column of water which obstructs the entrance to the cavern behind this cataract, has a very tolerable idea of the pains of drowning. What is wanting in the density of the element is more than made up by the force of the contending winds, which rush into the mouth, eyes, and nostrils, as if flying from a water-fiend. The 'courage of worse behind' alone persuades the gasping sufferer to take one desperate step more."

The *Museum*, near Table Rock, contains more than 10,000 specimens of minerals, birds, fishes, and animals, many of which were collected in the neighborhood of the Falls. Admittance—which includes the use of the dress and admission to the Cave of the Winds, 50 cents. The *Burning Spring* is near the water, two miles above the Falls. The carbonated sulphuretted hydrogen gas here gives out a brilliant flame when lighted. The height of the American Fall is 164 feet, that of the Canadian or Horseshoe, 150 feet. The former is 900 feet across, the latter 1,900. The roar of the waters has been heard at Toronto, 44 miles away, and yet in some states of wind and atmosphere it is scarcely perceptible in the immediate neighborhood. Niagara presents a new and most unique aspect in winter, when huge icicles hang from the precipices, and immense frozen piles of a thousand fantastic shapes glitter in the bright sunlight. Father Hennepin, a Jesuit missionary, was the first European who ever saw Niagara. His visit was in 1678. In 1869 a suspension bridge, 1,268 feet long, for carriages and pedestrians, was completed just below the falls, connecting the village of Niagara Falls with Clifton. It is 150 feet above the water.

In the vicinity of Niagara is *Lewiston*, seven miles distant, at the head of navigation on Lake Ontario—and directly opposite Lewiston is Queenstown. *Queenstown* is well worthy a visit from the sojourner at the Falls, and affords a most delightful drive. It is historically as well as pictorially interesting. Here General Brock and his aide-de-camp McDonnell fell, October 11, 1812. *Brock's Monument*, which crowns the heights above the village, is 185 feet high, surmounted by a dome of nine feet, which is reached by a spiral flight of 250 steps from the base inside. The remains of Brock and his comrade lie in stone sarcophagi beneath, having been removed thither from Fort George. This is the second monument erected on the spot, the first having been destroyed by Lett, in 1840.

ROUTES: From New York, *via* Hudson River or Hudson River Railroad to Albany, 144 miles; from Albany to Buffalo, *via* N. Y. Central R. R., 298 miles; from Buffalo, by Buffalo, Niagara Falls, and Lewiston R. R., 22 miles. Total, 464 miles. Same to Rochester, 373 miles; and thence by Rochester, Lockport, and Niagara R. R., 77 miles. Total, 450 miles. From New York, *via* New York and Erie R. R., to Buffalo, 422 miles; Buffalo (as above), by Buffalo, Niagara Falls, and Lewiston R. R. (to Niagara), 22 miles. Total, 444 miles. From *New York*, by New York and Erie R. R. to Elmira, 274 miles; from Elmira to Niagara, by Elmira, Canandaigua, and Niagara Falls R. R., 166 miles. Total, 440 miles. From *New York* to *Albany*, by Hudson River, 144 miles; thence to Troy, six miles. Railway from Troy to Whitehall, 65 miles; from Whitehall by steamer on Lake Champlain, to St. Johns, 150 miles; St. Johns to La Prairie Railroad, 15 miles; La Prairie, by steamboat on the St. Lawrence to Montreal, nine miles; from Montreal (Grand Trunk Railroad and other lines to Niagara), railroad and steamboat, 436 miles. Total, 727 miles.

ROUTE VI.

ALBANY AND SUSQUEHANNA RAILWAY.

This road, which runs from Albany to Binghamton, on the Erie Railway, is of considerable importance; and the great contest between the Erie and Central roads, known as the "Erie War," was caused by a desire on the part of each of these roads to obtain possession of the line.

STATIONS.—Adamsville, 6 miles from Albany; Slingerlands, 7; New Scotland, 11; Guilderland, 14; Knowersville, 17; Duanesburg, 24; Quaker Street, 27; Esperance, 31; Schoharie, 36; Howe's Cave, 39; Cobleskill, 45; Richmondville, 50; East Worcester, 57; Worcester, 62; Schenevus, 67; Maryland, 70; Junction Central and Schoharie Valley, 75; Colliers, 76; Emmons, 79; Oneonta, 82; Otego, 90; Wells's Bridge, 95; Unadilla, 99; Sidney, 103; Bainbridge, 108; Afton, 114; Harpersville, 120; Tunnel, 127; Osborn Hollow, 132; Port Crane, 135; Binghamton, 142.

Schoharie (36 miles) connects with Schoharie Valley and Middleburg and Schoharie Railroad, and stages for Gilboa, Moresville, Roxbury, Livingstonville, Preston-Hollow, Cooksburg, Durham, and Oak-Hill. This station, like *Howe's Cave*, is in the midst of caves and lakes. Howe's Cave is but 3 miles distant, while within 2 miles is *Ball's Cave*, which is large and interesting. A stream which may be explored in a boat runs through it for a considerable distance. In the course of this stream are several falls. There are many other caves worth visiting in the vicinity; also a pretty little body of water called *Utsayantha Lake*. The principal hotels are the Mansion and the Franklin, $2 50 per day. Carriages, guides, etc., may be procured at either of them.

Howe's Cave (39 miles). The limestone region of this part of the State is filled with caves, from the largest of which this station takes its name. This cave, which was discovered by Lester Howe in 1842, is entered from a point about 50 feet below the Cobleskill, and contains several chambers—its length being probably about 4 miles, though some persons have claimed for it a length of 20 miles. Like all large caves, it has one large chamber called "the Chapel." It also possesses a narrow passage, through which the visitor must crawl upon all-fours, and a subterranean lake or rather pool of pure water, 30 feet long, 20 feet wide, and 10 feet deep. The distant murmur of an invisible river and waterfall may be heard by the attentive listener. The cavern is full of wonderful beauties.

Not far from this cave there once existed a heap of small flat stones, 4 rods long, 1 or 2 wide, and from 10 to 15 feet high. It was thrown up by the Indians, who, influenced by some superstition or tradition, never passed it without adding a stone. Some years since the owner of the land destroyed this monument, using the stones for a fence. There is a hotel at the station, where guides, costumes, etc., can be procured.

Cobleskill (45 miles). The Sharon Springs and Cherry Valley Branch diverges here. (*See* page 66.)

Colliers (76 miles), a small village on the Susquehanna River, connects with *Cooperstown* by Cooperstown Railroad. Two trains daily from Albany and from Binghamton. (*See* COOPERSTOWN, page 66.)

Bainbridge (108 miles), a flourishing village. In 1852 a steamboat was built here to run on the Susquehanna to Lanesboro, 30 miles. Stages run from this place to Norwich, Greene, Oxford, Coventry, and Guilford.

Afton (114 miles). Visitors to *Vallonia Springs* take stages here.

Vallonia Springs is a little village some 600 or 700 feet above the level of the Susquehanna River, and about 1 mile distant from it, a little to the east of the centre of Broome County. It possesses fine mineral waters, and is in the midst of splendid scenery, while in the vicinity are fine hunting and fishing. The hotel is the Spring House. It is reached by Albany and Susquehanna Railway to Afton, thence by stage.

Binghamton (142 miles). *See* page 80.

ROUTE VII.
ERIE RAILWAY AND BRANCHES.
New York to Dunkirk.

This great route claims especial admiration for the grandeur of the enterprise which conceived and executed it, for the vast contributions it has made to the facilities of travel, and for the multiplied and varied landscape beauties which it has made so readily and pleasantly accessible. Its entire length, from New York to Dunkirk on Lake Erie, is 460 miles (including the Piermont and the Newburg branches, it is 497 miles), in which it traverses the southern portion of the Empire State in its entire extent from east to west, passing through countless towns and villages, over many rivers, now through rugged mountain-passes, and anon amid broad and fertile valleys and plains. In addition, it has many branches, connecting its stations with other routes in all directions, and opening up new stores of pictorial pleasure.

The road was first commenced in 1836. The first portion (46 miles, from Piermont to Goshen) was put in operation September 23, 1841, and on May 15, 1851, the entire line to Lake Erie was opened amid great rejoicings and festivities, in which the President of the United States and other distinguished guests of the company assisted. Four daily trains leave for the West on this route, from the foot of Chambers Street, and foot of Twenty-third Street, North River.

STATIONS.—Rutherford Park, 10 miles; Passaic, 12; Paterson, 17 (junction of Newark Branch); Ridgewood, 22; Hohokus, 24; Allendale, 26; Ramsey's, 28; Suffern's, 32 (branch to Piermont); Ramapo, 34; Sloatsburg, 36; Southfields, 42; Greenwood, 44; Newburg Junction, 46 (junction of Newburg Branch); Turner's, 48; Monroe, 50; Oxford, 52; Chester (Greycourt), 54 (junction of Warwick and Newburg Branches); Goshen, 60 (junction of Montgomery Branch); Hampton, 64; Middletown, 67 (junction of Unionville Branch); Howell's, 71; Otisville, 76; Port Jervis, 88; Lackawaxen, 111 (junction of Honesdale Branch); Mast Hope, 117; Narrowsburg, 123; Cochecton, 131; Hancock, 164; Deposit, 177; Susquehanna, 193; Great Bend, 201 (junction of Delaware, Lackawanna and Western Railway); Kirkwood, 206; Binghamton, 215 (junction of Syracuse and Binghamton, and Albany and Susquehanna Railways); Owego, 237 (junction of Cayuga Division of Delaware, Lackawanna, and Western Railway); Barton, 249; Waverley, 256 (junction of Lehigh Valley Railway); Chemung, 261; Wellsburg, 267; Elmira, 274 (junction of Elmira and Williamsport Railroad, and Canandaigua Division Northern Central Railway); Big Flats, 284; Corning, 291 (junction of Rochester Division and Corning, Blossburg, and Tioga Railway); Painted Post, 293; Addison, 302; Rathboneville, 307; Adrian, 323; Hornellsville, 332 (junction of Northwestern Division); Alfred, 341; Andover, 350; Genesee, 358; Philipsville, 366; Belvidere, 370; Hinsdale, 390; Olean, 395; Carrollton, 408 (junction of Bradford Branch); Great Valley, 411; Salamanca, 414 (junction of Atlantic and Great Western Division); Cattaraugus, 429; Dayton, 438; Perrysburg, 441; Forestville, 452; Dunkirk, 460 (connects with Lake Shore Line).

The first 31 miles of the Erie route lie through the State of New Jersey, from Jersey City, opposite New York, to "Suffern's," and consists of parts of three different railways, though used of late years for all the general business of the Erie road, and with its own broad gauge and cars. The original line of the road is from Suffern's eastward, 18 miles, to Piermont, and thence 24 miles down the Hudson River. This route is now employed only for freight and for local travel. It leads through a rude but not uninteresting country, with here and there a fine landscape or an agreeable village. Passing then through the New Jersey towns (see chapter on NEW JERSEY, page 98), we begin our mention of places and scenes of interest on the Erie route at the New York State line.

Suffern's Station (32 miles) is where the original Piermont and the present Jersey City lines meet. The *Ramapo Valley* commences at this point, and in its wild mountain-passes we find the first scenes of especial remark in our journey. Fine hill-farms surround us here, and on all our way through the region of the Ramapo for 18 miles.

Ramapo (34 miles) is near the *Torn Mountain*, the chief attraction of the *Ramapo Gap*, which is seen on the right, near the entrance to the valley. This is historic ground, sacred with memories of the movements of the Revolutionary army, when it was driven back into New Jersey from the Hudson. Washington often ascended to the summit of the Torn Mountain, to overlook the movements of the British. On one such occasion, anecdote says that he lost his watch in a crevice of a rock, of which credulity afterward heard the ticking in the percolations of unseen waters. Very near the railway at Suffern's the *débris* of old intrenchments are still visible, and marks of the camp-fires of our French allies, of the period, may be traced in the woods opposite. Near by is an old farm-house, once occupied by the commander-in-chief. The Ramapo is a great iron ore and iron manufacturing region, and it was here that the chain which was stretched across the Hudson, to check the advance of the English ships, was forged, at the spot once called the Augusta Iron-Works, now a poetical ruin by a charming cascade with overhanging bluff, seen close by the road, on the right, after passing Sloatsburg. The *Ramapo Brook* winds attractively through the valley, and beautiful lakelets are found upon the hill-tops. There are two such elevated ponds near Sloatsburg.

Sloatsburg (36 miles) is one of the points from which to take a stage for *Greenwood Lake*, which can also be reached from Chester and from Monroe.

Greenwood Lake.—HOTEL: The *Windermere House.*

To Greenwood Lake, sometimes called Long Pond, is a very agreeable jaunt from the metropolis, whether for the pure air of the hills, the pleasant aspects of Nature, or for the sports of the rod and the gun. Greenwood lies in Orange County, 8 miles southwest of Chester, in the midst of a very picturesque mountain-region. It is a beautiful water of seven miles in extent, and all about it, in every direction, are lesser but scarcely less charming lakes and lakelets, some of which, in a ride or ramble over the country, delight the eye where least dreamed of. Such an unexpected vision is *Lake Macopin*, and the larger waters of the *Wawayandah*. The last-mentioned lake is situated in the Wawayandah Mountains, about 3½ miles from the New York and New Jersey boundary-line. The word Wawayandah signifies winding stream, and is very characteristic of the serpentine course of the outlet of this lake toward the Wallkill. Wawayandah is almost divided by an island into two ponds, and thus gets its *home* name of "Double Pond." It is very deep, and abounds in fine trout. This varied hill and lake neighborhood presents in its general air an admirable blending of the wild ruggedness of the great mountain-ranges and the pastoral sweetness of the fertile valley lands, for it possesses the features of both, though of neither in the highest degree.

Newburg Junction (46 miles) is the junction with the branch road to Newburg. (*See* NEWBURG, page 44.)

Turner's (48 miles) possesses some interest to the hungry traveller, from the fact that it is one of the principal eating-places on the road. All trains stop here for meals. It has the reputation of being the most picturesque station on this section of the line. The view from the hill north of the station is superb, the Hudson River with Fishkill and Newburg being in sight. The following lakes are near the station, the most remote, "*Truxedo,*" being within 6 miles: "*Ramsey's,*" "*Round,*" "*Little Long,*" "*Mount Basha,*" and "*Slaughter's.*"

Monroe (50 miles) is connected with Greenwood Lake by a stage-line. From *Monroe* onward through *Oxford, Chester, Goshen, Hampton, Middletown, Howell's,* and *Otisville,* to *Port Jervis* (or Delaware), we are in the great dairy region of Orange County, New York, which sends a train of cars laden with milk daily to the New York market. A very charming view is seen south from the station at Oxford, led by the cone of the Sugar Loaf, the chief hill feature of the vicinage.

Greycourt, formerly called Chesterville (54 miles), is the point where the branch road from Newburg, on the Hudson River, to Warwick, 29 miles, intersects the main line. From this point, as well as from Sloatsburg and Monroe, passengers for Greenwood Lake (8 miles) take stage.

Middletown (67 miles) is a flourishing town in Orange County, having a population of over 6,000 inhabitants, various grades of schools and academies, churches of every denomination, and manufactories of all descriptions. It is generally conceded to be the handsomest village on the line of the Erie Railway.

Howell's (71 miles) is where the picturesque scenery seen all the way onward to Port Jervis commences.

Otisville (76 miles). On approaching Otisville, the eye is attracted by the bold flanks of the *Shawangunk Mountain,* the passage of which great barrier (once deemed almost insurmountable) is a miracle of engineering skill. A mile beyond Otisville, after traversing an ascending grade of 40 feet to the mile, the road runs through a rock-cutting 50 feet deep and 2,500 feet long. This passed, the summit of the ascent is reached, and thence we go down the mountain-side many sloping miles to the valley beneath. The scenery along the mountain-slope is grand and picturesque, and the effect is not lessened by the bold features of the landscape all around—the rugged front of the Shawangunk, stepping, like a colossal ghost, into the scene for one instant, and the eye anon resting upon a vast reach of untamed wilderness. In the descent of the mountain the embankment is securely supported by a wall 30 feet in height and 1,000 feet long. Onward the way increases in interest, until it opens upon a glimpse, away over the valley of the mountain spur, called the *Cuddeback;* and, at its base, the glittering water is seen now for the first time, of the Delaware and Hudson Canal, whose *débouché* we have looked upon at Kingston, in our voyage up the Hudson River. Eight miles beyond Otisville we are imprisoned in a deep cutting for nearly a mile, which prepares us for the brilliant surprise which awaits us. The dark passage made, and yet another bold dash through rocky cliffs, and there lie suddenly spread before us, upon our right, the rich and lovely valley and waters of the Neversink. Beyond, sweeps a chain of blue hills, and at their feet, terraced high, gleam the roofs and spires of the village of *Port Jervis;* while onward, to the south, our eye first beholds the floods of the Delaware.

Guymard (81 miles), surrounded by beautiful scenery, has a good hotel, and first became a summer resort in 1870.

Port Jervis, formerly Delaware, as the station was called, is the terminus of the eastern division, one of four great sub-sections into which the road is divided. It is a point which should not pass unnoticed by the tourist who can spend several days in viewing the route. The vicinage is replete with pictorial delights, and with ways and means for rural sports and pleasures. Charms of climate and of scenery, with the additional considerations of a pretty village and a most excellent hotel (the Delaware House), have made Port Jervis a place of great and continuous summer resort and tarry. The *Falls of the Sawkill,* 6 miles distant, are reached by stage.

This stream, after flowing sluggishly for some miles through level table-land, is here precipitated over two perpendicular ledges of slate-rock—the first of about 20 feet, and the second about 60 feet—into a wild gorge. The brook still continues, dashing and foaming on for a quarter of a mile, over smaller precipices, and through chasms scarcely wide enough for the visitor to pass. The beetling cliffs that form the sides of the gorge are surmounted and shaded by cedars and hemlocks, that lend a peculiarly sombre air to the scenery. The sojourner here should not omit a tramp to the top of *Point Peter*, which overlooks the village.

At Port Jervis commences the second division of the road which carries us onward, 104 miles farther, to *Susquehanna*. The canal keeps us company, nearer or more remote, for some miles, and by-and-by we cross the Delaware on a fine bridge of 800 feet, built at a cost of $75,000. The river, from this point, is seen, both above and below, to great advantage. Here we leave Orange County and New York for a little incursion into the Keystone State, for which privilege the railway company pays Pennsylvania $10,000 per year. The canal, and its pictures and incidents, are still the most agreeable features of our way, though at Point Eddy we open into one of the wide basins so striking in the scenery of the Delaware.

Shohola (107 miles). We are now among some of the greatest engineering successes of the Erie route, and some of its chief pictorial charms. Here the road lies on the mountain-side, several feet above the river, along a mighty gallery, supported by grand natural abutments of jagged rock. It is a pleasant scene to watch the flight of the train upon the crest of this rocky and secure precipice; and the impressiveness of the sight is deepened by its contrast with the peaceful repose of the smiling meadow-slopes on the opposite side of the river below. Upon three miles along this Shohola section of the road no less than $300,000 were expended.

At **Lackawaxen** there is a charming picture of the village, and of the Delaware, bridged by the railway and by the grand aqueduct for the passage of the canal, supported by an iron-wire suspension bridge. This is the point of junction of the Honesdale Branch.

Narrowsburg (123 miles from New York) has a good hotel. Beyond Narrowsburg, for some miles, the traveller may turn to his newspaper or book for occupation awhile, as the scenery here presented is not so particularly interesting as that which we have lately witnessed. Some compensation may be found in recalling the stirring incidents of Cooper's novel of "The Last of the Mohicans," of which this ground was the theatre.

At **Callicoon,** a brook full of wild and beautiful passages and of bright trout enters the Delaware.

Hancock (164 miles) is one of the most important places of this division of our route, and in every way a pleasant spot for sojourn.

At **Deposit** (13 miles beyond Hancock) we bid good-by to the Delaware, which we have followed so long; refresh ourselves at the restaurant, and prepare for the ascent of a heavy grade over the high mountain-ridge which separates it from the lovely waters of the Susquehanna. As the train descends into the valley there seems no promise of the wonders which are awaiting us, but they come suddenly, and before we are aware we are traversing the famous *Cascade Bridge*, a solitary arch, 250 feet wide, sprung over a dark ravine of 184 feet in depth. No adequate idea of the bold spirit and beauty of the scene can be had from the cars; indeed, in the rapid transit, it is often passed before the traveller is aware of its approach. Since the above appeared in a previous edition of this work the bridge has been transformed into a high embankment by filling the ravine beneath the arch.

The Cascade Bridge crossed, the view opens almost immediately at the right— deep down upon the winding Susquehanna, reaching afar off amid a valley and hill picture of delicious quality, a fitting prelude to the sweet river-scenes we are henceforth to delight in. This first grateful glimpse of the brave Susquehanna is justly esteemed as one of the finest points in the varied scenery of the Erie Railway route. It may be looked at more leisurely and more lovingly by him who tarries to explore the Cascade Bridge hard by, and the valley of the Starrucca, with its grand viaduct, which we are now rapidly approaching. The *Starrucca Viaduct* is one of the greatest engineering achievements of the entire route. It is 1,200 feet in length, and 110 feet high, and has 18 grand arches, each 50 feet span. The cost was $320,000. From the vicinity of *Susquehanna*, the next station, the viaduct itself makes a most effective feature in the valley views. A little beyond the viaduct, and just before we reach the Susquehanna station, we cross a fine trestle bridge, 450 feet long, over the *Cannewacta Creek*, at Lanesborough. We are now fairly upon the Susquehanna, not in the distance, but near its very marge, and, anon, we reach the end of the second grand division of our route, and enter the depot of Susquehanna.

Susquehanna (193 miles from New York) is an important railroad station and manufacturing point. Just beyond the Susquehanna depot we cross to the right bank of the river, and, after two more miles' ride, yet amidst mountain-ridges, we reach

Great Bend (201 miles). The village of this name lies close by, at the base of a bold, cone-shaped hill. Leaving Great Bend, we enter upon the more cultivated landscape of which we lately spoke, and approach villages and towns of great extent and elegance.

Near **Kirkwood**, the next station, 6 miles from Great Bend, there stands an old wooden tenement, which may attract the traveller's notice as the birthplace of the Mormon prophet, Joe Smith.

Binghamton.— HOTELS: *American, Lewis, Exchange, Spaulding's.*

Binghamton (215 miles from New York) is, with its population of about sixteen thousand people, one of the most important places on the Erie route, and indeed in Southern New York. It is a beautiful town, situated upon a wide plain, in an angle made by the meeting of the Susquehanna and the Chenango Rivers. Binghamton was settled in 1787 by Mr. Bingham, an English gentleman, whose daughters married the brothers Henry and Alexander Baring, the famous London bankers. The State Inebriate Asylum is located here. The Chenango Canal, extending along the Chenango River, connects Binghamton with Utica, 95 miles distant; and it is also the junction of the Delaware, Lackawanna, and Western Railway, the southern terminus of the Syracuse and Binghamton Railroad, 80 miles long, and of the Albany and Susquehanna Railway, for which, and the pleasant places along its line, *see* page 75.

Owego.—HOTELS: *Ahwaga, Park, Central,* and *United States.*

Owego (237 miles) is another large and handsome town, almost rivalling Binghamton in beauty and importance. It was settled in 1791, and incorporated in 1827. Owego is surrounded by a landscape not of bold but of very beautiful features. Many noble panoramas are to be seen from the hill-tops around, overlooking the village and the great valley. The Owego Creek, which enters the Susquehanna here, is a charming stream. Just before its meeting with the greater waters, it passes through the meadow and at the base of the hill-slopes of "*Glenmary*," once the home of N. P. Willis, and now one of the Meccas of the vicinage, to which all visitors are won by the charms and spells the fancy of the poet has cast about it. It was here that Mr. Willis wrote his famous "Letters from under a Bridge." Population, 6,000. There are 7 churches, and, besides the hotels already mentioned, several smaller ones. The business of the place is chiefly commercial, though there is some manufacturing. At this point the Susquehanna is spanned by a fine iron bridge, about 1,150 feet long. The Cemetery, situated opposite the village, on the north side of the Susquehanna River, is upon an eminence about 200 feet high, and commands a number of fine views. The Cayuga division of the *Delaware, Lackawanna, and Western Railroad* diverges here, some 30 miles, to Ithaca, on Cayuga Lake. (*See* ITHACA, page 69.) The *Southern Central Railway,* now under construction, is in full operation to Auburn. When completed, it will extend from Little Sodus Bay, near Oswego on Lake Ontario, to Waverly, on the Erie Railway, where it will connect with the railways to the Pensylvania coal-regions.

Elmira.—HOTELS: *Rathbun House* and *Hathaway House*.

Passing the half dozen intermediate stations, we reach Elmira, 274 miles from New York, and 37 from Owego. This beautiful town is the largest inland city on the line of the road, with the same charming valley-nest and the same environing hill-ridges as Binghamton and Owego. It was settled in 1788, and, in 1860, had a town population of 14,000. Its present population is estimated at 20,000. The Elmira Female College is a large and prosperous institution of a high literary standard. There is at this point a popular water-cure. The Newton Creek and the Chemung River, near the junction of whose waters Elmira is built, lend a picturesque beauty to the vicinage. The *Canandaigua Division of Northern Central Railway* diverges here, and connects the town with Rochester, Niagara Falls, and the Canada lines. This road affords one of the pleasantest summer routes from New York to the Falls of Niagara, and enables the tourist to visit Watkins Glen, one of the natural wonders of the country. (*See* page 83.) The Pennsylvania Northern Central Railroad connects with lines leading to Philadelphia, Baltimore, and Washington. The Chemung Canal also connects Elmira with *Seneca Lake*, 20 miles distant. The Junction Canal leads from Elmira to the coal-fields of Pennsylvania. Two other railroads are building, having a terminus at Elmira—the Lehigh Valley road, having connections with New York and Philadelphia, and the Utica and Elmira Railroad. Two daily and three weekly newspapers are published in Elmira, the *Daily and Weekly Advertiser*, the *Daily and Weekly Gazette*, and the *Saturday Review*. The *Advertiser* has a large circulation at home and through the surrounding counties, and possesses an establishment that is a model in every way. Five miles beyond Elmira our route lies over the Chemung River. The new State Prison, authorized to be built by the Legislature of 1869, has been located in Elmira.

Corning (291 miles) is an important point on the Chemung River. The feeder of the Chemung Canal extends hither from Elmira. It is the depot of the *Corning and Blossburg Railroad*, which connects it with the coal-beds of Pennsylvania. Incorporated, 1848. Present population, about 8,000. At Corning terminates also the branch road to Rochester (90 miles), and Buffalo, *via* Avon Springs, 142 miles.

Hornellsville (332 miles). Here we enter upon the fourth division of the Erie route; it is yet 128 miles to Dunkirk. The country through the rest of our way is comparatively new, and no important towns have yet grown up within it. Pictorially, this division is the least attractive of the whole route, though beautiful scenes occur at intervals all along. Beyond Hornellsville we enter the valley of the Canisteo River. *Almond* and *Alfred* lie upon the banks of this charming stream.

Reaching *Tip Top Summit* (the highest grade of the Erie road, being 1,700 feet above tide-water), we commence the descent into the *valley of the Genesee*. The country has but few marks of human habitation to cheer its lonely and wild aspect, and for many miles onward our way continues through a desolate forest tract, alternated only by the stations and little villages of the road. Beyond *Cuba Summit* there are many brooks and glens of rugged beauty. Passing *Olean*, on the Alleghany River, we come into the lands of the Indian Reservation, where we follow the wild banks of the Alleghany, between lofty hills as wild and desolate as itself.

Salamanca (414 miles from New York) is important as the junction of the *Erie* and *Atlantic and Great Western Railways*, which unitedly form the great thoroughfare of travel between New York and Cincinnati and the Great West. At *Cattaraugus*, 428 miles from New York, and 31 from Dunkirk, we traverse a deep valley, where the eye is relieved for a little while with scenes of gentler aspect than the unbroken forest we have long traversed, and are to traverse still. Three miles beyond *Perrysburg* we catch glimpses of the great Erie waters, toward which we are now rapidly speeding. Yet a few miles and we are out of the dreary woods, crossing again through the more habitable lands which lie upon the lakes.

Dunkirk.—HOTEL: *The Eastern*.

Dunkirk, on Lake Erie, is the western terminus of the Erie road, connecting with the Lake-Shore line from Buffalo to the West. It is a port of entry, and possesses a safe and commodious harbor. Dunkirk has a large trade, which is steadily increasing, and, as the branch road from Carrollton has opened up a route to the coal-regions of Pennsylvania, it bids fair to become an important coal-depot. We have reached our destination within the State (New York), and refer our travelling friends to Route III of Pennsylvania for further information.

BRANCHES TO BUFFALO.

There are two branch roads to Buffalo, and, from their importance, we will take them up before mentioning the other branches, which, from their geographical position, should precede them.

VIA CORNING.

STATIONS.— Corning, 291 miles from New York; Painted Post, 2 miles from Corning; Cooper's, 5; Campbell's, 9; Savona, 14; Bath, 20; Avoca, 28; Wallace's, 31; Liberty, 35; Blood's, 40; Wayland, 46; Springwater, 50; Conesus, 57; South Livonia, 61; Livonia, 65; Hamilton's, 67; Avon, 76; Caledonia, 83; Le Roy, 90; Stafford, 95; Batavia, 100; Alexander, 108; Attica, 111; Darien, 117; Alden, 123; Town Line, 128; Lancaster, 132; Buffalo, 142.

Bath (20 miles from Corning, and 311 from New York) is a thriving manufacturing town, surrounded by a rich and populous agricultural country. It is the county seat of Steuben County.

Avon (76 miles from Corning) is beautifully situated on the right bank of the Genesee River, about 18 miles from Rochester. It is upon a terrace, 100 feet above the river, and commands a beautiful view in all directions. Some 2 miles from the village are two mineral springs, which are considered as very beneficial to invalids suffering from rheumatism, indigestion, or cutaneous affections. The hotel accommodations are capital, the *Knickerbocker* being the principal house. A railway, 16 miles in length, connects it with the flourishing villages of Geneseo, Cuylerville, and Mount Morris. Avon is connected with Rochester, 18 miles distant, by a branch road. (For Rochester, see page 64.)

Batavia (100 miles from Corning) is also on a branch of the New York Central Railroad. (*See* page 64.)

Attica (111 miles from Corning) is a prosperous village, and is the junction of Corning Branch with the Hornellsville Branch (or Buffalo division Erie Railroad), and a branch of the New York Central Railroad.

Buffalo, the terminus of the line, is, by this route, 433 miles from New York. (For *Buffalo, see* page 65.)

VIA HORNELLSVILLE (BUFFALO DIVISION).

STATIONS.—Hornellsville, 332 miles from New York; Burns, 340; Canaseraga, 344; Garwood's, 346; Swain's, 349; Nunda, 356; Hunt's, 358; Portage, 362; Castile, 365; Gainesville, 368; Warsaw, 375; Dale, 381; Linden, 385; Attica, 392; Griswold, 395; Darien, 398; Alden, 403; Town Line, 409; Lancaster, 412; Checktowaga, 415; Buffalo, 423.

Hornellsville (332 miles). (*See* page 81.)

Nunda (356 miles) is a beautiful and prosperous manufacturing village.

Portage (362 miles) is a village of great interest, and no traveller who can spare the time should fail to stop here for a few hours at least. It is situated on the Genesee River, and is remarkable for its waterfalls and glorious scenery, as well as for the aqueduct of the Genesee Valley Canal, and the great railroad trestle-bridge. The *Portage Falls*, three in number, are each of sufficient beauty and grandeur to repay one for a visit. About three-quarters of a mile below the village are the Upper, or Horseshoe, Falls, having a vertical descent of 70 feet. Next come the Middle Falls, a quarter of a mile below. They are the most imposing of the three, the river falling in one unbroken sheet 110 feet into a chasm formed by perpendicular ledges of rock. The action of the water has worn a cave or hollow in the west bank, which is called the Devil's Oven. In time of high water, this cavern is filled with water; but, when the river is low, it is large enough to hold 100 people. The river, for 2 miles below the Middle Falls, pursues a devious course between vertical walls, the channel being very narrow. It then runs down a series of steps in the rock, passes under a rock, and descends to a narrow passage some 15 feet in width. It falls vertically 20 feet, and, recoiling from the base of the rocks, turns nearly a right angle in its course, and falls into a deep hole overhung with rocks. The *Sugar-Loaf* is a point of rock 100 feet in height, and 15 feet in diameter, which, at a bend in the river, rises abruptly from its centre, dividing its swift current in two portions. The greatest height of the vertical bank on the west side is 380 feet.

The Aqueduct, by which the Genesee Valley Canal crosses the river, is visible from the railroad bridge, it being located farther up the river, running parallel to it on the east side, and passing under the railroad bridge at a considerable elevation above the bed of the river.

The Trestle Bridge, by which the railroad crosses the river, is the largest wooden bridge in the world, and is sustained by 13 stone piers. The trestle-work rises 234 feet above the piers (which themselves are far above high-water mark), and is 800 feet long. There is enough lumber in the bridge to build a large village, and the cost was over $175,000. The construction is such that any timber in the bridge can be removed at pleasure and replaced by another, without injury to the structure. The two upper falls can be seen from the bridge, but no adequate idea can be formed of their grandeur until they are seen from below. There is a good hotel at the bridge, and also one at Portageville, 1¼ miles distant.

Gainesville (368 miles) possesses a large female seminary on the Mount Holyoke system. It is principally interesting from its proximity to Silver Lake, where the alleged sea-serpent was said to have been seen in 1855.

Warsaw (375 miles) is situated in a deep valley, about a mile from the station. It is the county seat of Wyoming County.

Attica (392 miles). (*See* page 82.)

Buffalo (423 miles). (*See* page 65.)

OTHER BRANCH AND CONNECTING ROADS.

Having disposed of the routes to Buffalo, we will return to the eastern line of the State, and take up the connecting and branch roads in their order.

BRANCH TO PIERMONT AND NYACK.— This branch runs from *Suffern's* to *Piermont* and *Nyack*, and was originally the main line. (*See* page 40.)

BRANCH TO NEWBURG AND WARWICK.— This branch runs from Greycourt (Chester). For Newburgh, *see* page 44. *Warwick* is a small village in Orange County.

MONTGOMERY BRANCH.—From Goshen for Montgomery and Guilford, two flourishing villages noted for their dairies.

UNIONVILLE BRANCH.—From *Middletown* to Unionville, 14 miles.

HONESDALE BRANCH.—From Lackawaxen to Honesdale.

DELAWARE, LACKAWANNA, AND WESTERN RAILWAY.—Connects at Binghamton. This road passes through the "Delaware Water-Gap." (*See* page 137.)

ALBANY AND SUSQUEHANNA RAILWAY. —Connects at Binghamton. (*See* page 75.)

SYRACUSE AND BINGHAMTON RAILWAY. —This is a road 80 miles in length, connecting the Central and Erie Roads.

CAYUGA DIVISION DELAWARE, LACKAWANNA, AND WESTERN RAILWAY.—Two daily trains run from Owego to Ithaca, on Cayuga Lake, whence *Taghkanic Falls*, and other points of interest on Cayuga Lake, can be reached by steamer, besides the 15 waterfalls which are in the vicinity of Ithaca. (*See* pages 68 and 69.)

LEHIGH VALLEY RAILWAY, at Wellsburg, connects with Lehigh Valley Railway, which runs through some wild scenery and through the mining regions of Pennsylvania. (*See* PENNSYLVANIA.)

ELMIRA AND WILLIAMSPORT RAILWAY connects at Elmira. (*See* PENNSYLVANIA.)

CANANDAIGUA DIVISION NORTHERN CENTRAL RAILWAY, connects at Elmira.

STATIONS.—Horseheads, 6 miles; Pine Valley, 10; Millport, 13; Havana, 19; Watkins, 22; Starkey, 33; Penn Yan, 45; Hall's, 55; Gorham, 58; Hopewell, 63; Canandaigua, 69.

Watkins (22 miles) is the first station of interest. It is at the head of Seneca Lake, and is connected with *Geneva* (*see* page 69) by a daily line of steamers. Its great attraction is its celebrated chasm and water-falls, known as

Watkins Glen, a natural curiosity, which was considered by Secretary

Seward of such interest that he brought the whole Diplomatic Corps to visit it on the occasion of that tour in which he showed them some of the wonders of this country. This glen is nothing more nor less than a vertical rift or gorge in a rocky bluff some 500 or 600 feet in height. It opens abruptly upon Franklin, the principal street in the village, about half a mile from the hotel. First entering a huge amphitheatre, to which there is no apparent exit, the visitor looks up at the rocks towering above his head, and then follows the path to the western end, where he finds that, instead of meeting, the walls of rock overlap each other, leaving a narrow passage through and up which he passes by a steep stairway to the *First Glen*. This is a narrow gorge, about half a mile in length, through which runs a stream, along the bank of which a narrow path has been cut. In the warmest weather a cool shade prevails here, the overhanging rocks, with their fringe of trees, nearly meeting far above his head. At the upper end is a waterfall some 70 or 80 feet in height.

Ascending a staircase, which may almost be termed a ladder, to the top of this fall, the Mountain House, as the refreshment-saloon is called, is reached. A short rest is taken here, and then the *Second Glen*, which is oval in form, with perpendicular walls, and through which the stream runs quietly, spread over a smooth and shallow bed. There are three more glens filled with wild and picturesque beauties, though in ascending them in their numerical order, the banks and cascades continually diminish in height. The great attraction of the *Fourth Glen* is the *Rainbow Fall*, behind which the path passes.

On returning to the village, the visitor will do well to make a digression at the Mountain House, and climb to the summit of the mountain, whence a splendid view of Seneca Lake and the surrounding country can be obtained. The population of Watkins is about 3,000, and, of its four or five hotels, the Jefferson House and the Fall Brook House are the best.

Havana, three miles from Watkins, is a thriving village, and has a glen very similar to that at Watkins, though not so well known.

Penn Yan (45 miles) has a population of about 2,500, and is a prosperous place. It is at the north end of *Crooked (Keuka) Lake*, and is connected with Hammondsport by a steamboat line. It has ample hotel accommodations.

Crooked Lake (hereafter to be called Keuka) is a very beautiful sheet of water, about 18 miles in length, and very narrow, its greatest breadth being 1¼ miles. At the foot, or north end, it divides into two forks, the one 8 and the other 5 miles long. Between these forks is a point of land of rare beauty. This lake is a favorite resort of those who have once visited it.

Hammondsport is at the head of Crooked Lake. It is the centre of a fine grape-growing and wine-making district, and has good hotels. It is reached by steamer from Penn Yan.

Canandaigua (69 miles) is the terminus of the road. (*See* page 69.)

CORNING, BLOSSBURG, AND TIOGA R. R. runs south from Corning 47 miles, to Blossburg, in the Tioga Valley, in the coal-regions of Pennsylvania.

ATLANTIC AND GREAT WESTERN RAILWAY.—This road leaves the track of the Erie at Salamanca, and runs west through the oil-regions of Pennsylvania, and across the State of Ohio to Cincinnati.

ROUTE VIII.

FROM HUDSON TO RUTLAND, VT.

Via Hudson & Boston and Bennington & Rutland Railways.

STATIONS.—Hudson, Claverack, Mellenville, Pulver's, Ghent, Chatham Four Corners (connects with Harlem Railway), Chatham, 7 miles from Chatham Four Corners; New Lebanon, 19; Lebanon Springs, 20; Stephentown, 25; Berlin, 36; Petersburg Junction, 47; Rutland, 114.

Hudson, 115 miles from New York via Hudson River Railway. (*See* page 47.)

Chatham Four Corners, 131 miles from New York, is where the Hudson & Boston Railway connects with the Harlem, the Boston & Albany, and the Bennington & Rutland Railways.

New Lebanon (19 miles) is a celebrated Shaker settlement. (*See* page 48.)

New Lebanon Springs (20 miles.) (*See* page 47.)

Petersburg Junction (47 miles); connections are made here with the *Troy & Boston Railway*, by which the celebrated Hoosic Tunnel can be reached. This is the last station in New York. (For the remainder of this route *see* Route IV of VERMONT.)

ROUTE IX.

TROY TO CASTLETON, VT.

Via Troy & Boston and Rensselaer & Saratoga Railways.

STATIONS.—Troy; Lansingburg, 4 miles; Grant's, 9; Schaghticoke, 13; Valley Falls, 14; Johnsonville, 17; Buskirk's, 21; Eagle Bridge, 23 (connects with Rutland & Washington Railway). Cambridge, 29; Shushan, 34; Salem, 41; Rupert, 49; Pawlet, 56; Granville, 59; Middle Granville, 61; Poultney, 67; Castleton, 84.

Lansingburg (4 miles) is a thriving manufacturing town upon the Hudson River. It has considerable river trade.

Schaghticoke (13 miles) is a manufacturing town on the Hoosic River, which furnishes a fine water-power.

Eagle Bridge (23 miles) is the junction of the *Troy & Boston* and *Rensselaer & Saratoga Railways*.

Salem (41 miles) is the semi-capital of Washington County, and is situated upon *White Creek*. From this station the road makes a detour into Vermont, and runs near the boundary for some miles until at Granville it again comes into New York for a short distance, finally leaving the State near Poultney.

Castleton, Vt. (84 miles), is a manufacturing town at the junction of this road with the *Saratoga and Castleton Railway*. It is the seat of a Seminary and a Medical College.

OTHER ROUTES.

OGDENSBURG & LAKE CHAMPLAIN RAILWAY.

This road, 118 miles in length, runs from Rouse's Point, on Lake Champlain, to Ogdensburg, on the River St. Lawrence.

Ogdensburg is a flourishing commercial town of about 8,000 inhabitants. Being on the frontier, it is one of the points around which public interest centres on the occasion of every threatened Fenian invasion of Canada.

ROME, WATERTOWN, AND OGDENSBURG RAILWAY.

This road extends from Rome, on the New York Central Railroad, to Ogdensburg, on the St. Lawrence, a distance of 142 miles. It is connected by branches with Oswego, Sackett's Harbor, Cape Vincent, and the Ogdensburg and Lake Champlain Railway, and in its course skirts the western and northwestern edge of the Adirondack region.

Rome is 110 miles from Albany, on the New York Central Railway. (*See* page 63.)

Richland (42 miles from Rome) is where the Oswego Branch, 29 miles in length, diverges.

Pierrepont Manor (54 miles) is the terminus of the stage line to Sackett's Harbor, 18 miles.

Sackett's Harbor is situated about 8 miles from Lake Ontario, on the south side of Black River Bay, the best harbor on the lake. Sackett's Harbor, in the War of 1812, was a naval station of great importance, and has since been a military post. The trade of the place is on the decline, and the short line of railway by which it was reached has been torn up and abandoned.

Watertown (72 miles) is on the south side of the Black River, which is at this point 180 feet wide, and affords a valuable water-power, there being a vertical fall of about 25 feet, besides three or four miles of rapids below the town. The branch to Cape Vincent, 25 miles in length, diverges here.

Cape Vincent is the point where the St. Lawrence River leaves Lake Ontario. There is a ferry here to Kingston, on the Grand Trunk Railway of Canada.

De Kalb Junction (123 miles) is where the branch for Potsdam and the Ogdensburg and Lake Champlain Railway diverges.

Ogdensburg (142 miles.)

OSWEGO AND SYRACUSE R. R.

This road is the most northern division of the Delaware, Lackawanna, and Western Railway, which runs from Jersey City to Oswego, although known by four different names, having originally been built by as many different companies. This division is 35 miles long.

Oswego, the northern terminus, is the largest city on Lake Ontario, having a population of over 21,000. It has naturally a fine harbor, formed by the mouth of the Oswego River, and this harbor has been greatly improved by two piers, one 1,259 and the other 200 feet in length. Its shipping and grain interest is very large, and, with the exception of Rochester, there is more flour manufactured here than in any city in the country. The river has a fall of 32 feet within the city limits, thus affording an unsurpassed water-power. The city is handsomely built, and is laid out with broad streets crossing at right angles. Oswego was settled by the French, who built a fort here soon after the settlement of Quebec, since which time it has always been a military post, Fort Ontario, on the east side of the river, now standing upon the site of a fort erected by the English in 1775.

Oswego is not only the terminus of the road we are describing, but also of the Oswego branch of the Rome, Watertown, Ogdensburg, and Oswego Railway, of the New York and Oswego Midland Railway, and of the Oswego Canal.

Syracuse (35 miles) is the junction of this road with the New York Central and with the Syracuse, Binghamton, and New York R. R. (For description, *see* page 63.)

SYRACUSE, BINGHAMTON, & NEW YORK RAILWAY.

This road is now a division of the Delaware, Lackawanna, and Western Railway, forming the connecting link, 80 miles in length, between the Oswego Division and Pennsylvania portion of the line.

STATIONS.—Syracuse connects with N. Y. Central and Oswego & Syracuse Railways; Jamesville, 7; Lafayette, 14; Apulia, 19; Tully, 21; Preble, 26; Homer, 33; Cortland, 36; Blodget's Mills, 40; State Bridge, 45; Marathon, 50; Lisle, 57; Whitney's Point, 59; Chenango Forks, 69, connects at Chenango Forks with trains both ways, for Greene, Oxford, Norwich, and other places in the Chenango Valley; Binghamton, 80, connects with Erie Railway, Albany and Susquehanna Railway, and Delaware, Lackawanna, and Western Railway, for which, *see* Pennsylvania Routes. The last link in the chain is the Morris and Essex Division, for which, *see* New Jersey, Route V.

NEW YORK & OSWEGO MIDLAND RAILWAY.

This road, when completed, which will be within the summer of 1871, will be a continuous road 400 miles in length from Jersey City to Oswego, and crossing Orange, Ulster, Sullivan, Delaware, Madison, and Cayuga, and the great midland counties of New York. Work is progressing rapidly along the whole line, and now (April, 1871) trains are running regularly from Oswego to Sidney Plains, a distance of 124 miles.

STATIONS.—Oswego, Seneca Hill, 6; Battle Island, 9; Fulton, 11; Ingall's Crossing, 16; Pennellville, 19; Caughdenoy, 23; Central Square, 26; West Monroe, 30; Constantia, 33; Bernhard's Bay, 38; Cleveland, 40; West Vienna, 43; North Bay, 47; Fish Creek Station, 50; State Bridge, 53; Durhamville, 55; Oneida, 57 (connects with New York Central Railway); Oneida Community, 61; Bennett's Corners, 62; Cook's Corners, 64; Munnsville, 66; Pratt's Hollow, 71; Morrisville Station, 73; Eaton, 76; Smith Valley, 80; Earlville, 84; Smyrna, 88; Sherburne Four Corners, 91; Junction U., C. & S. V. R., 92; North Norwich, 94; Norwich, 99 (connects with Utica, Chenango & Susquehanna Valley Railway); Lyon Brook Bridge, 105; Oxford, 109; Guilford, 114; Guilford Centre, 116; East Guilford Junction, 121; Sidney Plains, 124. It will connect with every road running between New York and the West.

NEW JERSEY

SETTLEMENTS were made in this State at Bergen, by the Dutch, soon after their arrival in New York. In 1627 a Swedish colony was founded near the shores of the Delaware, in the southwestern part of the State. A droll account of the quarrels of these Swedish folk with the Dutchmen of New Amsterdam may be found in "Diedrich Knickerbocker's" solemn "History" of the New Amsterdam colonists. New Jersey is one of the original thirteen States. She did her part nobly in the long War of Independence, and her historical record is of the most eventful and interesting character—the famous battles of Trenton, of Princeton, and of Monmouth, at all of which Washington was present and victorious, occurred within her limits. Morristown was the winter camp of the American army in 1776 and 1777.

New Jersey is bounded on the north by New York, on the east by the Atlantic Ocean and Hudson River, south by Delaware Bay, and west by Delaware River. It is 163 miles long, and from 40 to 70 miles wide, and includes an area of 8,235 square miles. Though small in extent, New Jersey yet presents many natural attractions to the traveller. Her sea-coast abounds in favorite bathing and sporting resorts, much visited by the citizens of New York, Philadelphia, and Baltimore. Among these summer haunts are Cape May, Long Branch, Sandy Hook, Atlantic City, Deal, Squam Beach, and Tuckerton. In the southern and central portions of this State the country is flat and sandy; in the north are some ranges of picturesque hills, interspersed with charming lakes and ponds. Some of the Alleghany ridges traverse New Jersey, forming the spurs known as Schooley's Mountain, Trowbridge, the Ramapo, and Second Mountains. In the northwestern part of the State are the Blue Mountains. The Neversink Hills, on the Atlantic side, rising nearly 400 feet, are usually the first and last land seen by ocean voyagers as they approach and leave New York. The celebrated Palisade Rocks of the Hudson River are in this State.

New Jersey lies between New York and Philadelphia, and hence is the great highway of travel between those two cities. There are two routes commonly travelled, known respectively as the *New Jersey*, and the *Camden and Amboy*. There is a third route over the *New Jersey Southern Railway*, formerly known as the *Raritan and Delaware Bay Railway*, but this is not much travelled. During the summer months steamers connect the two cities by the "outside" or ocean route.

ROUTE I.
NEW YORK TO PHILADELPHIA.
Via the New Jersey Railway.

THIS route passes over the New Jersey, Philadelphia, and Trenton Railroads. Trains leave New York (by ferry across the Hudson, from the foot of Cortlandt Street to Jersey City) several times each day. Distance, 90 miles. Time, three and one-half hours.

STATIONS.—Jersey City, 1 mile; Newark, 9; Waverley, 12; Elizabeth, 15; Linden, 17; Rahway, 19; Uniontown, 23; Metuchin, 27; New Brunswick, 32; Dean's Pond, 39; Kingston, 45; Princeton, 48; Trenton, 58; Bristol, 69; Cornwells, 74; Tacony, 80; Kensington, 86; West Philadelphia, 90. The region through which this line passes is populous and opulent, and covered with towns, villages, and villas; for 20 or 25 miles from each terminus, over which the two cities spread their suburbs, the crowded local trains are passing and repassing continually.

Jersey City.—Hotels: *American*, 9 and 11 Montgomery Street, *Fisk's*, near the ferry, and *Gallagher's*, on Greene Street, near Montgomery. Jersey City is on the Hudson, opposite the city of New York, with which it is connected by numerous ferries. Practically it is a portion of New York, a large portion of its inhabitants having their places of business in that city. Being also one of the principal gateways of the metropolis, it is the greatest thoroughfare in the country. The present population is about 83,000. Jersey City is the New York terminus of all railways from the south, and of all from the west except the *New York Central and Hudson River Railway*. It is also the terminus of the *Morris Canal*, and is the berth of the *Cunard* and *White Star* lines of transatlantic steamers. The steamers of the *Bremen* and *Hamburg* lines sail from Hoboken. (For Hoboken, see page 29.)

The Hudson River forms the eastern boundary of the city, while on the south is a water front on New York Bay, an indentation at the eastern point being called Communipaw Cove, which is to be filled up for business purposes. Below this cove and beyond the depot of the Central Railway of New Jersey, which is on the south side, lies that portion of the township of Bergen, known as Communipaw, described by Irving in his "Knickerbocker's History of New York," but now noted for its extensive and admirably conducted slaughter-houses, known as "abattoirs," where the animals are killed by puncturing the base of the brain with a sharp lance, causing instantaneous and painless death. These abattoirs are remarkably free from the usual disagreeable concomitants of places devoted to this purpose, and are well worth visiting. Three miles from the ferry is the suburb, known as *Claremont*, which is merely a collection of private residences; and one mile farther is *Greenville*, the site of the *New York Bay Cemetery*, from which fine views of the bay are obtained. It is also the site of many beautiful villas. Continuing in this direction, we come to *Saltersville*, *Bayonne*, and *Centreville*, once distinct villages on the line of the Central Railway of New Jersey, but now rapidly becoming integral parts of the city. They have not lost their rural air, and are full of beautiful villas and residences.

The streets of Jersey City are broad and handsome, intersecting each other at right angles. The churches are numerous and beautiful, and the school facilities are good. Water is supplied by an aqueduct, the reservoir being on Bergen Hill. The water-works are at Belleville.

Newark.—Hotel, *Newark*.—Newark, nine miles from New York and 78 from Philadelphia, was settled in 1666. It is built on an elevated plain, upon the right bank of the Passaic River, four miles from its entrance into Newark Bay, and is regularly laid out in wide streets, crossing at right angles. Many portions of the city are very elegant, and in its most fashionable quarter are two charming parks, filled with noble elms. Broad Street, its main thoroughfare, is a splendid avenue. Among its principal public edifices are the *Court-House*, the *Post-Office*, the *Custom-House*, and *City Hall*, and many handsome churches.

Of the literary institutions, the most noteworthy are the *Library Association*, the *State Historical Society*, and the *Newark Academy*. From the grounds attached to the Academy an extended view of the Passaic valley is had.

Newark is distinguished for its manufactures of jewelry, carriages, and leather. It has upward of 550 manufactories. Enormous quantities of lager-beer are made in this city. The *Newark and Bloomfield Railway*, a branch of the Morris and Essex, connects with the pleasant suburban towns of Roseville, Bloomfield, and Mont Clair. The vicinity has many pleasant drives and walks. Population, 105,542.

Waverley (12 miles). The grounds of the New Jersey State Agricultural Society are located here.

Elizabeth (15 miles) is the handsomest city in the State, and is growing with wonderful rapidity. It is noted for its broad streets, beautiful churches and dwellings, and the wealth of its residents. It is the greatest coal-shipping port in the Union, and is noted for its oil-cloth and other manufactories. It has two daily and three weekly papers, of which the principal is the *Herald.* Population, 20,974. The *Elizabeth River* empties here, and the *New Jersey* and the *Central Railways* intersect at this point. The *Sheridan House* is new and handsomely furnished.

Linden (17 miles) is laid out for suburban residences, and is the summer residence of many New-Yorkers. Hon. Ferd. Blancke's model farm is here.

Rahway. — HOTEL, *De Graw's.* Rahway (19 miles) lies on both sides of the Rahway River. It is noted for its manufacture of carriages, stoves, hats, earthenware, etc. A large portion of the vehicles made here are for the Southern market. It was settled in 1720. Population, 10,000. One mile south, the *Perth Amboy and Woodbridge Branch* diverges.

Perth Amboy.—HOTEL : *Brighton House.*

Perth Amboy (27 miles) is one of the oldest cities in the State, having received its charter one day before the city of New York. It has always been a port of entry. It is much frequented during the summer for its sea-breezes, and a mineral spring near the city. The fire-brick manufactured here are considered the best in the United States, and a large trade is done in exporting kaolin and other fine clays. It is connected with Staten Island and South Amboy by ferry. Population, 5,000.

New Brunswick. — HOTELS : *Railroad, City,* and *Bull's Head.* New Brunswick (32 miles), founded 1770, is pleasantly situated at the head of steamboat navigation on the Raritan River. This is the seat of *Rutgers College* and *School,* and also of a Theological Seminary of the Dutch Reformed Church, known as *Hertzog Theological Hall.* The most prominent buildings are the *Court-House* and other *County Buildings,* occupying a square in the centre of the city. The *Roman Catholic Cathedral,* in which a fine chime of bells is about to be placed, *St. James's Methodist Episcopal,* and other churches. A new *Masonic Hall* has been commenced, which is to cost $100,000, and will contain a large public hall. There are numbers of manufactories here, one of which is noted for the superior quality of the hosiery it produces. The city is, from its location, very healthy, the hills of red-shale upon which it is built affording natural drainage. The drives in the vicinity are pleasant and picturesque. The streets on the river are narrow and crooked, and the ground low; but those on the upper bank are wide, and many of the dwellings are very neat and even elegant, being surrounded by fine gardens. From the site of Rutgers College on the hill there is a wide prospect, terminated by mountains on the north and by Raritan Bay on the east. The Delaware and Raritan Canal extends from New Brunswick to Bordentown, on the Delaware River, 42 miles. This canal is 75 feet wide and 15 feet deep, and is navigable by sloops and steamboats of 150 tons. This fine work cost $2,500,000. The railway here crosses the Raritan River. Population, 17,000.

Monmouth Junction. At this point the *Freehold and Jamesburg Railway* diverges to the southeast, and the *Kingston and Rocky Hill Railway* to the northwest.

Princeton, built on an elevated ridge two and a half miles north of Princeton Junction, 48 miles from New York, is a pleasant little town of literary and historical interest. It is the seat of *Princeton College,* one of the oldest and most famous educational establishments in the country. It was founded by the Presbyterians at Elizabethtown, 1756, and removed to Princeton in 1757. The college buildings, including the chapel, dormitories, and the halls of the literary societies, form a group of venerable looking structures, the principal of which, known as *Nassau Hall,* is a spacious edifice, 176 feet by 50 feet, and three stories high. The Hall stands in the centre of handsome grounds fronting on Main Street. Peale's picture of Washington, in the College Library, is an object of considerable interest. Here also is the *Theological Seminary* of the Presbyterian Church, founded in 1812. About one and a quarter miles south of Princeton is the battle-ground where was fought the memorable conflict of January 3, 1777, between the American forces under General Washington, and those of the British under Lieutenant-Colonel Mawhood, in which the latter were vanquished. The house in which General Mercer died, near the Trenton turnpike, is still pointed out.

Trenton.—HOTELS: *Trenton House, American House.*

Trenton, the capital of New Jersey, is on the left bank of the Delaware, 30 miles from Philadelphia and 58 from New York. The city is regularly laid out, and has many fine stores and handsome dwellings. The *State-House*, which is 100 feet long and 60 feet wide, is built of stone, and stuccoed so as to resemble granite. Its situation on the Delaware is very beautiful, commanding a fine view of the river and vicinity. Here is the *State Lunatic Asylum*, founded in 1848, and also the *State Penitentiary, State Arsenal,* and *Normal Schools. White Hall,* used for barracks by the Hessians in 1776, is still to be seen on the south side of Front Street. Trenton has three daily and three weekly newspapers, twenty-four churches, and a city and State Library, in both of which are many rare and valuable books and manuscripts. The Delaware and Raritan Canal, forming an inland navigation from New Brunswick, passes through Trenton to the Delaware at Bordentown. It is supplied by a navigable feeder, taken from the Delaware, 23 miles north of Trenton. It was completed in 1834, at a cost of $2,500,000. This canal passes through the city, and connects it with New York and Philadelphia. The *Belvidere and Delaware Railroad* runs hence, 63 miles, to Belvidere, on the Delaware River. (*See* ROUTE IX.) Trenton was first settled by Phineas Pemberton and others about 1680, and was named in 1720 after Colonel William Trent, Speaker of the House of Assembly. The *Battle of Trenton* was fought December 26, 1776. On Christmas night, in 1776, and during the most gloomy period of the Revolutionary War, General Washington crossed the Delaware with 2,500 men, and early on the morning of the 26th commenced an attack upon Trenton, then in possession of the British.

So sudden and unexpected was the assault, that, of the 1,500 Hessian troops encamped there, 906 were made prisoners. This successful enterprise revived the spirit of the nation, as it was the first victory gained over the Hessian soldiers. General Washington immediately recrossed the river with his prisoners. About the 1st of January he again crossed below the city, and fired upon it from the south side of Assunpink Creek. Leaving his camp-fires burning, by a rapid movement he marched to *Princeton*, and fought the battle of January 3, 1777.

Trenton was selected as the State capital in 1790, and incorporated in 1792. Its present population is about 20,000. Here the traveller can take the Branch Road, six miles to Bordentown, and thence by Camden and Amboy line, or continue, as we now do, by Philadelphia and Trenton route.

Bristol, Pennsylvania (69 miles), founded in 1697, is a beautiful village on the west bank of the Delaware, nearly opposite Burlington. The Delaware division of the Pennsylvania Canal, which communicates with the Lehigh at Easton, terminates here in a spacious basin on the Delaware. It has a valuable mineral spring. Daily communication with Philadelphia by boat. Population, 3,500.

Frankford, Tacony, and *Kensington,* are within the corporate limits of Philadelphia, and are there described.

ROUTE II.

NEW YORK TO PHILADELPHIA.
Via Camden and Amboy Route.

FROM Pier No. 1, N. R., New York, daily (Sundays excepted) for South Amboy, by steamer 30 miles, and thence by rail.

STATIONS.—New York, South Amboy, 30 miles; South River, 38; Spotswood, 40; Jamesburg, 44; Prospect Plains, 46; Cranberry Station, 48; Hightstown, 51; Windsor, 54; Newtown, 57; Bordentown, 64; Burlington, 74; Beverly, 77; Delanco, 79; Palmyra, 84; Camden, 91; Philadelphia, 92.

In the summer season no more delightful journey can be made than the first 30 miles of our present route across the lovely bay and harbor of New York, to South Amboy, past the villaged and vil-laced shores of Staten Island and the Raritan River. (*See* "Trip down the Bay," page 29.)

South Amboy (30 miles) is the steamboat landing-place, and the northern terminus of the *Camden and Amboy Railroad*. It is at the mouth of the Raritan River, at the entrance of Raritan Bay. Upon arriving here, passengers are transported in a short space of time from the steamboat to the railroad cars; and, after a slight detention, proceed on the journey up a steep ascent from the river, and soon enter a deep cutting through the sand-hills. The road is then continued through a barren and uninteresting region of country toward the Delaware at Bordentown.

Jamesburg (44 miles). Junction of *Freehold and Jamesburg Railroad.*

Bordentown (64 miles) is situated on a steep sand-bank, on the east side of the Delaware. The principal objects of interest here are the extensive grounds and mansion formerly occupied by the late Joseph Bonaparte, ex-King of Spain. Although in a commanding situation, the view is greatly obstructed from the river. This is a favorite resort of the Philadelphians during the summer season. The Delaware and Raritan Canal here connects with the Delaware River. A branch road, 6 miles long, on the bank of the canal and river, unites this town with Trenton. Bordentown was incorporated in 1825, and has a population of 6,000. The extensive car-shops, locomotive-works, and general depot of supplies of the Camden and Amboy road, are at Bordentown.

Burlington.—HOTELS: *City, Belden's.*

Burlington (74 miles) is a port of entry on the Delaware, 19 miles from Philadelphia. *Burlington College*, founded by the Episcopalians in 1846, is located here, and there are besides, upon the banks of the river, two large boarding-schools, one for each sex. Burlington is connected with Philadelphia by steamboat, and is a place of great summer resort thence. It was settled in 1667, was originally called New Beverly, and has a population of 6,000. A branch road to Mount Holly, 6 miles.

Beverly, built on the banks of the Delaware since 1848, has now a population of 1,500. It is a suburb of Philadelphia, distant 15 miles.

Camden is at the terminus of our route, upon the east bank of the Delaware River, immediately opposite the city of Philadelphia, with which there is constant communication by ferry. It is the terminus also of the *West Jersey* and *Camden and Atlantic Railroads.* It was chartered in 1831, and already contains nearly 20,000 inhabitants. The vicinity abounds in fruit and vegetable gardens. (*See* "Philadelphia and Vicinity.")

ROUTE III.

NEW YORK TO LONG BRANCH, ATLANTIC CITY, AND PHILADELPHIA.

Via *New Jersey Southern Railway* (formerly "*Raritan and Delaware Bay Railway*"), *Long Branch and Sea-Shore Railway,* and *Camden and Atlantic Railway.*

THIS is a pleasant and expeditious summer route to Red Bank, Long Branch, Deal, Squan Beach, Tom's River, and Atlantic City. From Pier No. 28, N. R., by steamboats to Sandy Hook and Port Monmouth, and thence by rail.

The New Jersey Southern Railroad (from Port Monmouth), and the Long Branch and Sea-Shore Railroad (from Sandy Hook), being now under one management, a junction has been made at Long Branch, and a Union Depot built. For summer travel, the route *via* Sandy Hook is preferable.

STATIONS (*on New Jersey Southern Railroad*).—Navesink, 22 miles (stages for Navesink, Riceville, and New Monmouth); Middletown, 23; Red Bank, 26 (stages for Rumsom, Fair Haven, Port Washington, Little Silver and Newman Springs); Shrewsbury, 28; Eatontown Branch, 30; Oceanport, 31; Branchport, 33 (stages for Deal and Mechanicsville); Long Branch, 34 (stages for Deal and Pleasure Bay); Shark River, 36 (stages for Squan Beach); Farmingdale, 39 (Junction of Freehold and Jamesburg Railroad—stages for Point Pleasant); Squankum, 41; Bricksburg, 47 (stages for Burrsville and Point Pleasant); Manchester, 55; Tom's River (branch), 62 (stages for Cedar Creek,

Forked River, Waretown, Barnegat, Tuckerton, and Manahawkin); Whitings, 61 (junction of branch to Camden, known as the "Atco Spur" or "Atco Branch)'"; Woodmansie, 68; Shamong, 73; Atsion, 94 (junction of Camden and Atlantic). *On Long Branch and Sea-Shore Railroad.*—Sandy Hook, 20 miles; Highlands, 24; Sea Bright (Rumsom), 26; Atlanticville, 29; Long Branch, 30 (stages for Deal and Pleasure Bay).

Port Monmouth Pier, the terminus of the *New Jersey Southern Railroad*, and **Sandy Hook Pier,** the terminus of the *Sea-Shore Railroad*, are each 20 miles from New York by steamer. The trip from New York affords to the traveller a charming series of views of the upper and lower bays, with their numerous islands. There is good fishing at either pier.

Highlands of Navesink (24 miles from New York, *via* Sandy Hook).— These are well-known bluffs, extending from Sandy Hook to Raritan Bay, and are also known as the "Neversink Hills." The highest point, "Mount Mitchell," is 282 feet above the level of the sea. These highlands are usually the first land seen on approaching New York from the ocean, and the last to sink beneath the horizon on leaving. There are two lights, about 100 feet apart: the Southern, a revolving "Fresnel," 248 feet above the water, being the best on the Atlantic coast. This is a very attractive resort, there being good fishing and bathing, romantic walks and fine scenery, with two good hotels, "*Thompson's Atlantic Pavilion*," and "*Schenck's Hotel*," besides numerous cottages. The Neptune Club-House is in this vicinity. Hotels open from about the first of June until autumn. The Red Bank boat touches at the wharf daily during the summer.

Red Bank (26 miles *via* Port Monmouth, and 38 miles *via* Sandy Hook) is a remarkably pretty town, on the Shrewsbury River, famed among artists for its lovely views. It possesses, among its other attractions, sailing, boating, fishing, and bathing. Shell-fish of all kinds abound, and it is in the vicinity of some of the finest oyster-beds in the world. Being within easy drive of Long Branch (8 miles), over excellent roads, many summer visitors who wish to be within reach of that fashionable resort, and yet away from its noise and excitement, pass their time here. The *Globe*, *Atkins*, and *French's Hotels* are open all the year round. Terms, $2.50 to $3.50 per day. Reached also by daily boats from foot of Warren Street, New York.

Oceanport (31 miles) is so near Long Branch as almost to be a portion of it. It is here that the *Dunbarton House*, a fashionable hotel, is located, and here, too, are to be found numerous private boarding-houses, at prices from $8 to $15 per week. It is 4 miles from the beach. *Chamberlain's* "*National*" *Trotting Park*, in the preparation of which $250,000 was expended, is on the outskirts of the village. This park was finished in the summer of 1870, and, it is claimed, far surpasses any thing of the kind in the United States.

Long Branch (30 miles *via* Sandy Hook, and 35 *via* Port Monmouth), the most attractive of all the sea-side resorts in the vicinity of New York, is famed for its bathing, its sea-breezes, its shell-fish, and its hotels, as well as for the pleasant resorts in its immediate vicinity. Its proximity, both to New York and Philadelphia, and its consequent ease of access, contribute greatly to its popularity. The drives are over good roads, which are well cared for, and lead in most cases to desirable localities, one of the favorite places being *Mineral Spring*, about 2 miles distant, near Oceanville. On the drive to Eatontown, is "*Turtle Mill*," which was running during the Revolution, and is still in operation. The *Park*, upon the bluff, *Newman Springs*, and the wrecking-station, with life-car and apparatus, should all be visited. Among the handsome summer residences at the Branch are those of Messrs. John Hoey, General Grant, Lester Wallack, and J. W. Wallack. The largest hotels are as follows:

Continental, south of the depots, 700 feet front, with a portion running back 250 feet. It has a capacity for 800 to 1,000 guests. Terms, $3 to $5 per day. *Stetson House*, about 1 mile south of the depots. Capacity, 600 to 800 guests. Terms, $5 per day. *Metropolitan*, about 300 yards from the Sea-Shore Railway depot. Capacity, 600 guests. Terms $3 to $5 per day. *Mansion House*, near the Continental. Capacity, 300 to 400 guests. Terms, $4 per day. *Howland's Hotel*, north of the Stetson. Capacity, 300 guests. Terms, $3 to $5 per day. These hotels are all provided with fine bands during the season. Among the other hotels are the *Pavilion, United States, Clarendon, Atlantic, Cooper Cottage*, and *Charles Jackson's Cottage*.

Fare, $1—or $1.50 for the round trip.

Among the places of interest in the vicinity of Long Branch are:

Pleasure Bay, distant about 1 mile. It is on the Shrewsbury River, and is a favorite place with persons fond of boating, fishing, etc. It is noted for its oysters, crabs, etc. The principal hotel is the *New York Hotel*.

Deal is 5 miles south of the Branch. It has two hotels, *Hathaway's* and *Abner Allen's*, with an aggregate capacity for 650 guests.

Shark River (36 miles from New York on the railroad) is a short distance south of Deal. It is a favorite place for picnic parties from Long Branch, and is noted for its oysters, which possess a peculiarly fine flavor. The village is reached by stage from the railroad station of the same name, which is 4 miles distant. Passengers for Squan Beach leave the train at Shark River, and take stage.

Farmingdale (39 miles) is a thriving village, the junction of the *Freehold and Jamesburg Railroad*. Around it lie extensive beds of marl. The well-known beds of the Squankum Marl Company lie 2 miles to the south, where the marl is dug by a powerful steam-dredge.

Tom's River, on the *Tom's River Branch Railroad* (62 miles from New York) is one of the prettiest villages on the coast. It is situated at the head of Barnegat Inlet, about 6 miles from the beach. The opportunities for sailing, boating, bathing, and fishing are excellent. A new Hotel, to accommodate 300 guests, is being built; and it is expected the natural advantages of the place will attract many visitors.

In the fall the place is much sought by sportsmen, it being a favorite resort of wild duck and geese.

Whitings (61 miles from New York) is the junction of the *Pemberton and New York Railroad*, which, in connection with the Camden and Burlington County Railroad, will furnish a new, short, and very attractive route between Philadelphia and New York, *via* Long Branch.

Atco (formerly Jackson Junction), (93 miles). This is the junction with the Camden and Atlantic Railway, from Philadelphia to Atlantic City.

CAMDEN AND ATLANTIC RAILWAY.

This road, which is 60 miles long, is the connecting link between New York, Philadelphia, and Atlantic City. The only stations of importance are its *termini*. In the following list of stations, the distances given are those from *Cooper's Point*, at Camden, which is 1 mile from Vine Street Ferry, Philadelphia. The distances from New York can be found by adding 93 miles to the distance of any station from *Jackson Junction*.

STATIONS.—*Cooper's Point*, Haddonfield, 7 miles; Ashland, 10; White Horse, 12; Berlin, 17; Atco, 19; Jackson Junction, 20; Waterford, 23; Spring Garden, 25; Winslow, 27; Hammonton, 30; Da Costa, 32; Ellwood, 37 (stage daily to Tuckerton, Manahawkin, Barnegat, Wiretown, Forked River, Cedar Creek, etc.); Egg Harbor, 41 (stage daily to May's Landing and Tuckahoe — tri-weekly to Cape May, and Court-house); Pomona, 47; Absecon, 52 (stage daily to Leed's Point, Somers's Point, etc.); Atlantic City, 59.

Camden.—(*See* page 91.)

Atlantic City.—HOTELS: The *United States, Surf House*.

Atlantic City (60 miles from Philadelphia, and 133 from New York) may be reached from the former city twice daily by the *Camden and Atlantic Railroad*. It has fine accommodation for bathing, and is a place much resorted to by visitors from Philadelphia. The season at Atlantic City and Cape May opens about July 10th, and closes September 15th.

ROUTE IV.

FROM JERSEY CITY TO EASTON, PA., DELAWARE WATER GAP, WILKES-BARRE, ETC.

Via Central Railway of New Jersey.

FROM foot of Liberty Street, New York (Pier 15, N. R.), to Jersey City, and thence by rail, *via* Bergen Point.

This road forms the first link in the great chain of roads known as the "Allentown Line." It also with its connections forms a direct route to all parts of Central and Northern Pennsylvania, as well as Southern New York.

STATIONS.—Pier 15, N. R.; Jersey City, 1; Bergen Point, 8; Elizabeth, 13; Roselle, 15; Cranford, 17; Westfield, 20; Fanwood, 22; Plainfield, 24; Dunnellen, 27; Bound Brook, 31; Somerville, 36; Raritan, 37; North Branch, 41; Whitehouse, 46; Lebanon, 50; Clinton, 52; High Bridge, 54; Spruce Run, 58; Junction, 59; Asbury, 62; Valley, 64; Bloomsbury, 67; Springtown, 69; Phillipsburg, 74; Easton, 75.

Jersey City and suburbs have already been described under the head of Route I.

Bergen Point (8 miles) is the southern extremity of the peninsula between Newark Bay and the Kills, and is an extremely desirable place of residence for business-men, being connected with Jersey City Ferry by horse-cars and dummy. The steamers to the south side of Staten Island, to Elizabethport, and to Newark, also stop here, thus (including the trains on the Central Railway of New Jersey) affording communication with the city of New York between fifty and sixty times every day. Bergen Point boasts of numerous beautiful residences and churches, and, though the elevation of the land is not particularly great, affords a series of comprehensive and beautiful views. New York, Brooklyn, Jersey City, Elizabeth, and Newark, Newark Bay, and beyond it Eagle Rock, New York Bay, its islands, and the broad salt marshes of New Jersey, can all be seen from the summit of the hill. HOTEL, *Latourette House.*

Newark Bay is crossed from Bergen Point by a pile bridge more than a mile in length, which is provided with an iron draw of two spans of 75 feet opening each.

Elizabeth (13 miles) has been described in Route I., though the fact was there omitted that the shipments of coal from *Elizabethport*, which is within its corporate limits, were among the largest in the country.

Roselle (15 miles) is a town of suburban residences. HOTEL: *Mansion House*

Cranford (17 miles) is a pleasant village on Rahway River.

Westfield (20 miles) is a prosperous town of over 2,000 inhabitants.

Scotch Plains, Fanwood (22 miles), is a favorite summer resort. Just north of the village is a beautiful stream called Green Brook.

Plainfield (24 miles) is a prosperous place, surrounded by a level and fertile country, near a ridge which is the continuation of Orange Mountain. It is a pleasant place, and has many summer visitors. To the north (on the right hand of the traveller) is *Washington's Rock*, a point near the top of the range of hills, from which Washington often watched the movements of the enemy, the view being very extended, since between these hills and the eastern coast the country is level. On a clear day the spires and masts of New York, and all the intervening New Jersey towns, can be seen. The rock is opposite a point on the railway two miles from Plainfield, and may be distinguished by the extensive clearings and the hotel in the vicinity.

Dunnellen (27 miles). Here the road makes a curve and runs directly west.

Bound Brook (31 miles) is on the Raritan River, at the mouth of the brook from which it takes its name. Here the Raritan Valley is reached.

Somerville (36 miles) is a flourishing village on the Raritan River. There are many fine views and drives in the vicinity, and copper-ore has been found in the neighboring mountains. The South Branch Railroad diverges at this point to *Flemington*, where it connects with a branch of the Belvidere Delaware R. R. running to Lambertville, on the Delaware.

Raritan (37 miles) is a village noted for its manufactures. The *North Branch* diverges here.

Whitehouse (46 miles) is a thriving village. The hill on the left, near the village, is named *Pickle Mountain.*

Lebanon (50 miles) has a population of about 800. The railroad here enters a fertile limestone country.

Clinton (52 miles) is a large village, having two or three hotels and a number of mills. It is noted for its limestone quarries

High Bridge (54 miles) is where the road crosses the South Branch of the Raritan by an embankment 1,300 feet long and 105 feet high, which was built at an expense of $180,000. The view from this embankment is remarkably fine. The *Taylor Iron Works*, at this place, are noted for the manufacture of car-wheels and axles.

Spruce Run (58 miles) is at the opening of a gap in the ridge, called "Spruce Run Valley," through which the road enters the valley of the Musconetcong River.

Junction (59 miles), a little southwest of the village of New Hampton, is in Hunterdon County, 16 miles northwest of Flemington. This is the southern terminus of the *Delaware, Lackawanna, and Western Railway* of Pennsylvania, which leads through the Delaware Water Gap to Scranton, Great Bend, Binghamton, and the North.

Asbury (62 miles) and **Valley** (64 miles) are small stations in the Musconetcong Valley, and are in the midst of most beautiful scenery.

Bloomsbury (67 miles) is pleasantly situated on the Musconetcong River, on the boundary-line of Warren and Hunterdon Counties. From this point the road passes along the side of the Pohatcong Mountain into the Pohatcong Valley.

Phillipsburg (74 miles). HOTELS: *Bennet's, Reese's*. This is an important iron-manufacturing town on the left bank of the Delaware, opposite *Easton*, Pa., with which it is connected by three bridges. Here connections are made with the *Lehigh Valley Railroad*, the *Lehigh Coal and Navigation Company Railroad*, the *Belvidere Delaware* and *Lehigh & Susquehanna Railways*.

Easton (75 miles). (*See* Route IV., PENNSYLVANIA.)

ROUTE V.

FROM JERSEY CITY TO EASTON, PA., AND DELAWARE WATER-GAP.

Via Morris and Essex Division of Delaware, Lackawanna, and Western Railway.

THIS road, like the Central of New Jersey, is one of the first links of the chain of roads running to the West, the eastern terminus of which is practically Jersey City, though the actual terminus is in Hoboken. Like the Central, it runs to Phillipsburg and Easton, but it takes a more northerly course, and with its branches affords a means of access to the lake and mountain regions of Northern New Jersey, as well as with the net-work of railways through the mineral regions of Pennsylvania.

STATIONS.—Foot of Barclay Street and foot of Christopher Street, New York, to Hoboken, by ferry. Hoboken, 1 mile; Newark, 9 (connects with Newark and Bloomfield Railway for Bloomfield, Montclair, etc.); Orange, 13; South Orange, 15; Milburn, 19; Summit, 22; Chatham, 25; Madison, 27; Morristown, 31; Denville, 38 (connects with Boonton Branch for Boonton, 44 miles from N. Y.); Rockaway, 40; Dover, 43 (connects with Chester Railway for Succasunna, 49, and Chester, 56 miles from N. Y.); Drakesville, 48; Stanhope, 53; Waterloo, 56 (connects with Sussex Railway for Andover, 62, and Newton, 67 miles from N. Y.); Hackettstown, 62; Washington, 71 (connects with Delaware, Lackawanna, and Western Railway for the North); Broadway, 76; Stewartsville, 80; Phillipsburg, 85 (connects with Belvidere Delaware Railway); Easton, 86 (connects with Lehigh Valley Railway for Bethlehem, Allentown, Mauch Chunk; and also with Lehigh and Susquehanna Railway for Mauch Chunk, Wilkesbarre, and Scranton, and all points in the Pennsylvania coal regions).

Hoboken (1 mile) has been described in the chapter on New York, page 29.

Newark (9 miles). (*See* Route I.)

Orange (13 miles) has a population of about 5,000. It is a flourishing suburban town, is connected with Newark by horse-railway, and is very largely peopled by persons doing business in New York.

Milburn (19 miles) is where the road passes round the extremity of Orange Mountain, the grade at this point being 80 feet to the mile.

Summit (22 miles) is the crest of the mountain, and is noted for the extent and beauty of its views.

95

Chatham (25 miles) is a handsome village on the Passaic River, having a population of about 3,000. As far as this place the road has passed through a succession of beautiful gardens.

Madison (27 miles) is a prosperous and rapidly-growing village, and is the point where the road first enters the borders of the mountain-region, which continually grows more picturesque as the traveller proceeds westward. The Drew Theological Seminary is located at this point.

Convent Station (29 miles) is the site of an extensive Roman Catholic convent and school.

Morristown (32 miles), the capital of Morris County, is splendidly situated on the *Whippany River*, standing upon a plain surrounded by hills. It is noteworthy as having been, during the Revolution, the headquarters of the American army on two occasions. The house occupied by General Washington and the ruins of a fort in the rear of the Court-house are still pointed out. The town contains a fine public square, court-house and several churches. Population, 4,000. *Speedwell Lake* is not far from the hotels.

Denville (38 miles) is where a branch six miles in length leads to *Boonton.* It is a small village, and has one hotel.

Boonton (44 miles), the terminus of the Boonton Branch, is an important manufacturing town on the Rockaway River, the Morris Canal also passing through it. It is particularly noted for its iron-manufactory, which consists of a blast-furnace, a rolling-mill, and a nail-factory, forming in the aggregate an unusually large and complete establishment. The town is in a very mountainous region, and from its high location is visible for many miles.

Rockaway (40 miles) has a population of between 5,000 and 8,000, and is an extensive iron-manufacturing town on the Rockaway River and Morris Canal. It is located in the richest portion of the iron-regions of New Jersey.

Dover (43 miles), like Boonton and Rockaway, is situated on the Rockaway River and Morris Canal, and like them is supported by its iron-manufactories, possessing forges, rolling-mills, founderies, steel-furnaces, and spike-factories. It is in the centre of the "Lake Region," and has two good hotels, *Mansion House* and *Stickle House.* Though there are other stations nearer to some of the places of interest, Dover, on account of its superior hotel and livery accommodations, is the general headquarters. Distances are: Schooley's Mountain, 20 miles ; Lake Hopatcong (Brookland Pond), 6 miles ; Long Pond, 10 miles; Green Pond, 30 miles ; and Seneeawana (Budd's) Lake, 7 miles.

The road to Chester (13 miles) branches here.

Succasunna (49 miles) is on the Chester Branch.

Chester (56 miles) is the terminus of the Chester Branch. It has a population of about 300, and is in the midst of retired and pleasant surroundings. Summer board may be had at the *Young Ladies' Institute* at reasonable rates.

Drakesville (48 miles) is on the Morris Canal, 12 miles northwest of Morristown. It is but four miles from this station to *Lake Hopatcong.*

Stanhope (53 miles) is on the Morris Canal and Muscouetcong River, and contains a mill and several iron-forges. Three miles to the south of it is **Budd's Lake**, a beautiful circular lake of pure mountain-water, deep, clear, and well filled with fish. Hotel, the *Forest-Grove House,* from which the whole lake is visible. The atmosphere is bracing, and the class of visitors at the hotel very select.

Lake Hopatcong (Brookland Pond), a very beautiful sheet of water, much larger than *Budd's Lake,* lies a few miles to the north of Stanhope, and is the source of the Muscouetcong, one of the affluents of the Delaware, and a feeder of the Morris Canal. The Indian name means "Stone Water," a name given on account of a causeway of stone from one of the islands to the shore, built by the Indians, but now covered by water. Opposite the island once stood an Indian village. The scenery around the lake is varied and beautiful, and the surface of the water is dotted with islands. A few yards from the hotel is Southard's Peak, from which the Delaware Water-Gap and the Bloomfield Mountains are both visible. A small steamboat plies upon the lake. The hotel, the *Lake Hopatcong House*, has not very extensive accommodations, but has a fashionable class of *habitués*. The lake is 720 feet above tide-water. It can be reached from *Stanhope* or *Dover*, or from *Andover* or *Newton* on the Sussex Railway.

Waterloo (56 miles) is where the Sussex road to Newton connects. The "Andover" and "Tar" Iron-mines are both in Newton township.

Hackettstown (62 miles) is on Musconetcong Creek, near the Morris Canal, about 50 miles north of Trenton. It is noted for its flouring-mills. There are two hotels, the *American* and the *Warren House*. There is a large seminary at Hackettstown, under the charge of the Methodists. Population, 2,000.

Schooley's Mountain (2¼ miles from Hackettstown) is a noted and popular resort. The drives in the vicinity are delightful, and the hotels, the *Belmont House*, and *Heath House*, are good. The mountain itself is an extensive ridge, upon one portion of which is Budd's Lake. Its height is about 1,100 feet above the sea. Springs, containing muriate of soda, of lime, carbonate of magnesia, silex, and carbonated oxide of iron, are near its summit.

From New York it is reached by the route we have indicated, and also by private conveyance from Dover or any other of the stations in its neighborhood. Visitors from the South proceed *via* Philadelphia and New Brunswick, connecting with the *New Jersey Central Railway* at Bound Brook, and from this line as above.

Washington (71 miles) is the junction with the Delaware, Lackawanna, and Western Railway for the Delaware Water-Gap and the splendid mountain scenery of Northeastern Pennsylvania.

Broadway (76 miles), and **Stewartsville** (80 miles), are two thriving villages.

Phillipsburg (85 miles) has already been described. (*See* page 95.)

Easton (86 miles). (*See* Route IV., PENNSYLVANIA.)

ROUTE VI.

JERSEY CITY TO PIERMONT.

Via Northern Railway of New Jersey.

This road runs parallel to the Hudson River, behind the Palisades, and at a distance of from two to three miles from the river. It serves as a means of access to the succession of pretty suburban towns between Jersey City and Piermont, on the Hudson, and along the Hackensack valley. The distances given in the following list of stations are from the depot in Jersey City, and is reached by the ferries from the foot of Chambers Street and Twenty-third Street : New Durham, 6 miles; Granton, 8; Ridgefield, 9; Leonia, 10; Englewood, 12; Highland, 15; Tenafly, 16; Cresskill, 17; Closter, 18; Norwood, 20; Tappan, 22; Upper Piermont, 23; Piermont, 24.

The road passes through the celebrated Bergen Tunnel, which is over a mile in length.

Leonia (10 miles) is where passengers for Fort Lee leave the road.

The other stations on the road are of the general character indicated in the introductory remarks.

Piermont (24 miles), the former terminus of the Erie Railway, and now the terminus of one of its branches, has been described in the "Trip up the Hudson."

ROUTE VII.

JERSEY CITY TO PATERSON AND THE NEW YORK STATE LINE.

Via Erie Railway, New Jersey Division.

This road is reached from New York by ferry from foot of Chambers Street and foot of Twenty-third Street. As it runs almost entirely within the limits of the State of New York, it has, with the exception of the following places, been described as Route No. VII. of New York.

STATIONS.—Jersey City, 1; Rutherford Park, 10; Passaic, 12; Paterson (junction of Newark Branch), 17; Ridgewood, 22; Hokokus, 24; Allendale, 26; Ramsey's, 28.

Paterson and the Passaic Falls.—*Paterson* (17 miles), the capital of Passaic County, is finely situated on the right bank of the Passaic River, immediately below the falls. It was founded in 1791 by Alexander Hamilton, in the cotton interest, and many of its cotton-factories are now quite extensive. In point of population, it is the third city of the State, in manufactures the second. One of the most extensive silk-mills in the United States is located here, employing nearly 800 hands. It is connected by bridges with the village of Manchester and with Newark by a branch railway. There are two large locomotive-manufactories here which do a heavy business. In 1860 the population was 19,586. It is now over 31,000 and is rapidly growing, the rate of increase having been greater between 1860 and 1870 than in the preceding ten years.

The Passaic Falls were originally but 70 feet in height, but have been raised to 90 by a dam at the top, by which they are converted into a powerful agent to drive the machinery of the numerous manufactories in the vicinity. The falls are still very beautiful and attractive.

The remaining stations are not particularly noticeable, until reaching the State of New York. (For the portion of the Erie road in that State, see NEW YORK, Route VII.)

HACKENSACK BRANCH.

This branch of the Erie Railway diverges, after passing through the Bergen Tunnel. Its total length is but 14 miles.

STATIONS.—Carlstadt, Woodbridge, Lodi Junction, and Hackensack.

Hackensack, the chief town of Bergen County, is pleasantly situated on the west bank of the Hackensack River, from which it derives its name, 13 miles north by west of New York. It contains about 250 dwellings, and several church edifices.

ROUTE VIII.

PHILADELPHIA TO CAPE MAY.

Via West Jersey Railway.

THIS road connects Philadelphia with Cape May, but lies wholly within the State of New Jersey. It runs through an un-

interesting section of country, and no tourist is at all likely to stop at any of the stations between its terminal points.

STATIONS.—Camden, Gloucester, 3 miles; Westville, 5; Woodbury, 8; Mantua, 11; Barnsboro', 13; Marlboro', 15; Glassboro', 18 (junction of branch to Salem and Bridgeton); Fisherville, 21; Franklinville, 24; Crane's, 26; Malaga, 28; Lake, 29; Forest Grove, 33; Vineland, 35; Millville, 40; Manumuskin, 46; Belleplain, 53; Woodbine, 56; Mount Pleasant, 59; Seaville, 62; Swain, 66; Miller-ton, 73; Rio Grande, 75; Bennett's, 78: Cape May, 81.

Cape May is the extreme southern point of New Jersey, forming, with Cape Henlopen, in Delaware, the gate through which Delaware Bay enters the Atlantic Ocean. The beach is over 5 miles long, and, being firm and hard, makes a splendid drive. The bathing is fine, and all the usual amusements of a watering-place are provided for the guests. The hotels, cottages, etc., are on a small piece of land, about 250 acres in extent, which is known as Cape Island. Cape May has always been a favorite resort for Southerners, and is also popular with Western people, besides being *the place*, of all places, for Philadelphians. The principal place of resort in the vicinity is *Cold Spring*, 2 miles north of the beach, on the line of the railroad, which affords a pleasant drive and picnic-place. No hotel accommodation yet at this spring. The hotels are huge affairs, and very well kept, besides being numerous. The leading houses are the *Stockton House*, *Congress Hall*, *Columbia*, *United States*, and *West Jersey*. There are also the following: *Delaware House, Atlantic Hotel, Centre House, Washington Hotel, Tremont Hotel, National Hotel, City Hotel, Sherman House, American Hotel,* and *Merchants' Hotel.*

ROUTE.—From *Philadelphia*, as above stated. From *New York*, every evening by steamboat.

ROUTE IX.

PHILADELPHIA TO MANUNKA CHUNK AND DELAWARE WATER-GAP.

Via Belvidere Delaware Railway.

THIS road follows the northern bank of the Delaware River from *Trenton* to *Manunka Chunk*. Trains on this road connect with trains from Philadelphia, which is regarded as being, in point of fact, its southern terminus. Taking Philadelphia, then, as a point of departure, the distances are as follows:

STATIONS.—Trenton, 30 miles; Asylum, 34; Greensburg, 36; Washington's Crossing, 39; Titusville, 41; Moore's, 43; Lambertville, 46 (junction of the Flemington Railway); Stockton, 50; Bull's Island, 53; Point Peasant, 55; Tumble, 57; Frenchtown, 62; Milford, 65; Holland, 68; Riegelsville, 72; Carpenterville, 75; Phillipsburg, 81 (connecting with Lehigh Valley, Lehigh & Susquehanna, Morris & Essex, and New Jersey Central Railways); Martin's Creek, 87; Belvidere, 95; Manunka Chunk, 98 (connects with Delaware, Lackawanna and Western Railroad).

Trenton (30 miles). (*See* page 90.)

Washington's Crossing (39 miles) is the point where General Washington made the celebrated passage of the Delaware, when he surprised and defeated the Hessians at *Trenton*.

Lambertville (46 miles) is the largest town in Hunterdon County, having a population of over 3,000. It possesses a fine water-power, which supplies a number of mills, factories, machine-shops, locomotive-works, car-shops, etc. It is connected with the Central Railroad, of New Jersey, by the Flemington Railway for the lakes and mountains of New Jersey.

Phillipsburg (81 miles). Connections are made here with the Central Railway of New Jersey, and with all the roads to the north and west radiating from Easton, Pa. (For description of Phillipsburg, *see* page 95.)

Belvidere (95 miles) is situated on both sides of Pequest Creek, where it empties into the Delaware. It has a fine water-power, is a considerable manufacturing place, and has a population of over 2,000.

Manunka Chunk (98 miles) is the junction with Delaware, Lackawanna, and Western Railway, to the Delaware Water-Gap, Erie Railway, and northern connections. (*See* PENNSYLVANIA, Route V.)

PENNSYLVANIA.

Pennsylvania is, in point of population, the second State in the Union, and in all respects one of the most important and interesting. A very singular fact in her history—singular because it has no parallel in the annals of any other member of the American Union—is, that her territory was settled without war or bloodshed. The doctrines of peace and good-will, taught by William Penn and his associates, when they pitched their tents upon the sunny banks of the Delaware, long served, happily, as a charm over the savage natures of their Indian neighbors. We have no record of battle and siege in the story of this State, from the time of the first settlement at Philadelphia, in 1682, until the date of the French and Indian War in 1755. During this year the famous defeat of Braddock, in which Washington, then in his early youth, distinguished himself, occurred at Pittsburg. In 1763 the massacre of the Conestoga Indians took place in Lancaster County. In 1767 the southern boundary of the State, which has since become famous as Mason and Dixon's line, was made. Pennsylvania is memorable in the annals of the American Revolution, in which she played a conspicuous part. Upon her soil occurred the important battles of Brandywine and Germantown (1777). The traveller will seek here also for the scenes of those celebrated events, the massacres of Wyoming and Paoli. Valley Forge was the chief headquarters of General Washington, and is made yet more interesting by the memory of the sufferings there of the patriot army during its winter encampment in 1777–'78. Philadelphia was the national capital until 1789—a period of nearly ten years—and here the earliest American Congresses assembled. The memorable revolt, called the Whiskey Insurrection, happened in Pennsylvania, in 1794. Among the great men whom this State has given to the Republic, we may cite the honored names of Franklin (though born in Boston), Robert Morris, Fulton, Rush, and Rittenhouse, James Buchanan, Thaddeus Stevens, etc. Pennsylvania furnished upward of 360,000 troops for the national defence in the war of 1861–'65.

The landscape of Pennsylvania is extremely diversified and beautiful. One-fourth of her great area of 46,000 square miles is occupied by mountain-ranges, sometimes reaching an elevation of 2,000 feet. These hills, links of the great Alleghany chain, run generally from northeast to southwest, through the eastern, central, and southern portions of the State. The spur of this hill-range is called South Mountain, where it rises on the Delaware, below Easton. Next, as we go westward, come the Kittatinny, or Blue Mountains, and the Broad Mountains, south of the North Branch of the Susquehanna. Across the river is the Tuscarora. South of the Juniata are the Sideling Hills, and, lastly, come the Alleghanies, dividing the Atlantic slope from the great Mississippi valley region. West of the Alleghanies, the only hill-ranges in the State are the minor ones called the Laurel and the Chestnut ridges. This belt of mountains extends over a breadth of 200 miles, enclosing numberless fertile valleys, many charming waters, and the greatest coal-fields and iron deposits in the Union. Pennsylvania cannot boast the marvellous lake scenery of the Empire State; indeed, she has no lakes, if we except the great Erie waters which wash the shore of the north-

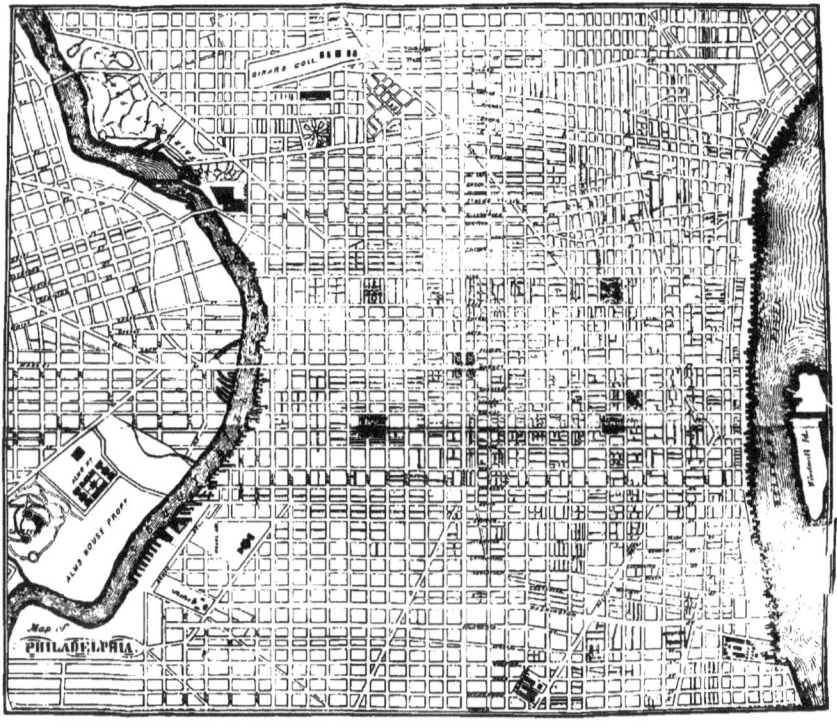

west corner of the State. For this want, however, the charms of her many picturesque rivers fully compensate. Her valleys are even more inviting and beautiful than her mountains. The Delaware, the Lehigh, the Wyoming, the Schuylkill, and the Lackawanna, abound in scenic attractions.

RIVERS.

The *Susquehanna*, the largest river of Pennsylvania, and one of the most beautiful in America, crosses the entire breadth of the State, flowing 400 miles in many a winding bout, through mountain-gorges, rocky cliffs, and broad, cultivated meadows. (*See* SUSQUEHANNA RIVER, page 142.)

The *Juniata* is the chief affluent of the Susquehanna. It enters that river from the acclivities of the Alleghanies in the west, through a mountain and valley country of great natural attractions. (*See* JUNIATA RIVER, page 121.)

The *Delaware* flows 300 miles from its sources in the Catskill Mountains to the Delaware Bay, forming the boundary between Pennsylvania and New Jersey, and afterward between New Jersey and Delaware. It is one of the chief features of the varied scenery of the *New York and Erie Railway*, which follows its banks for 90 miles. (*See* ERIE R. R., page 76.) Lower down, its passage through the mountains forms that great natural wonder of the State, the *Delaware Water-Gap*. (*See* DELAWARE WATER-GAP (page 137). The navigation of the Delaware is interrupted at Trenton, New Jersey, by falls and rapids. Philadelphia is on this river, about 40 miles above its entrance into Delaware Bay. The river was named in honor of Lord De La Ware, who visited the bay in 1610. The shores of the Delaware and its smaller tributaries are fine gunning-grounds in the autumn months. *Reed-birds* and *rail* are found in great abundance.

The *Lehigh* is a rapid and most picturesque stream. Its course is from the mountain coal-districts, through the famous passage of the Lehigh Water-Gap, below Mauch Chunk, to the Delaware at Easton. Its length is about 90 miles.

The *Schuylkill* flows 120 miles from the coal-regions north, and enters the Delaware five miles below Philadelphia. We shall review it as we call at the towns and places of interest upon its banks.

The *Alleghany* and the *Monongahela Rivers*—one 300 and the other 200 miles in length—unite at Pittsburg and form the Ohio. The *Youghiogheny* is a tributary of the Monongahela.

The *Lackawanna* is another mountain-stream, which takes its rise in the northeast part of the State, and it falls into the north branch of the Susquehanna River, 10 miles above Wilkesbarre. The valley of the Lackawanna is noted for its rich coal-mines.

PHILADELPHIA.*

Philadelphia, the largest city as to area in the United States, and, in point of population, second only to New York, lies between the Delaware and Schuylkill Rivers, five miles above their junction, and nearly 100 miles, by the Delaware Bay and River, from the Atlantic. Its precise latitude is 39° 57' north, and longitude 75° 10' west, being 136 miles northeast of Washington City, and 87 miles southwest of New York. The site of the city is so low and level, that it does not make a very impressive appearance from any approach. But the elegance, symmetry, and neatness of its streets, the high cultivation and the picturesque character of the higher suburban land to the northward, fully compensate for this want. In the most densely-built section, streets extend from river to river, and are crossed by other streets at right angles. This portion of the city covers an area of nearly nine square miles, and embraces Chestnut and Market Streets, Second and Seventh, Third (the Wall Street of Philadelphia), and other leading thoroughfares and business marts of the city proper. Within this area are located the Exchange, State-House, Post-Office, Custom-House, the large banking-houses, insurance and newspaper offices, warehouses, wholesale stores, etc. The entire length of the city north and south is 20 miles, and from east to west 8 miles, and, with its rapid growth west of

* For routes to New York, *see* NEW JERSEY.

the Schuylkill, it will soon exceed even these magnificent dimensions.

The city, as originally incorporated (1701), was bounded by the rivers Delaware and Schuylkill, and Vine and South Streets; but in 1854 the adjoining districts of Spring Garden, Penn, Northern Liberties, Kensington, and Richmond, on the north, West Philadelphia, etc., on the west, and Southwark, Moyamensing, and Passyunk, on the south, were consolidated with the city, into one municipal government. Within this area are over 300 miles of paved streets, and more buildings than in any other city in the country.

The history of Philadelphia, though of more recent date than that of many other American cities, is both interesting and eventful. To William Penn is almost universally credited the first settlement and foundation of the city (1682), though the local record is by no means clear on that point. In the year 1681 the first settlers arrived from London, in the ship "Sarah and John," Captain Smith. William Penn, accompanied by a colony of English Friends, or Quakers, in 1682, planned and settled Philadelphia after a regular purchase from the Indians, ratified by treaty in due form. However this may be, certain it is that the *sobriquet* of the "City of Brotherly Love," which it now bears, was given to it by Penn himself. At the time of Penn's arrival, the site of the city was owned and occupied principally by Swedes, whose claims were subsequently disposed of to Penn, in exchange for lands on the Schuylkill, near what was then called "Swedes' Ford." The original plan of the city was made by Thomas Holmes, and surveyed in 1683. The first house recorded to have been erected was that built by George Guest, and subsequently known as the "Blue Anchor" Tavern. This stood near the mouth of Dock Creek (northwest corner of Dock and Front Streets), then known as "Sandy Beach." The first *daily* newspaper published in the country was published here. It was called the *American Daily Advertiser*. It was established by Mr. Dunlop in 1771, and first issued as a daily in 1784, by D. C. Claypole, who sold out to Zacharia Poulson. In 1840 it was merged in the *North American*. The *Weekly Mercury* was first issued December 22, 1719. No striking events mark the history of Philadelphia down to the days of the Revolution. The first Congress assembled here, as did also subsequent Congresses, during the continuation of the war. The Declaration of Independence was signed and issued here, July 4, 1776. The Convention which formed the Constitution of the Republic assembled here, May, 1787. Here resided the first President of the United States, and here, too, Congress continued to meet until about 1797. The city was in possession of the British troops from September, 1777, to June 11, 1778, a result of the unfortunate battles of Brandywine and Germantown.

In 1844 riots broke out between the Protestant and Catholic population in the northern and southern suburbs. The military were called out and quiet restored, but not until several Catholic churches had been destroyed, and many lives lost.

The streets running north and south are named numerically from the Delaware—thus, 1st (or Front), 2d, 3d, 4th, etc.

The streets running east and west are numbered from First (or Front) Street, east and west. (In the old part of the city, Front Street being the bank of the Delaware, no mention is made of east and west in the numbering.) Those running north and south are numbered from Market Street each way. A marked peculiarity is observed with regard to the numbering of the buildings, which, though somewhat novel to strangers, is easily understood, and generally approved. It consists in allowing a hundred numbers for each square: thus, if one is advancing west, the first figure or figures of the first house, after crossing a street, is the name of that street: thus, if you have passed Sixteenth Street, the first house upon the right, or north side, is 1,601; upon the left, or south side, 1,602; and so numbered regularly, until Seventeenth Street is passed, when it is 1,701 north, and 1,702 south side. In like manner the streets running north and south are allowed 100 numbers for every square they are distant from Market Street, either north or south.

Thus, you are told that a friend resides at 1,511 North Twentieth Street, the number itself informs you that his house is twenty squares west of the Delaware, and fifteen squares north of Market Street, and the fifth house from the corner. This plan is also very convenient in going about the city, as, whenever one can see a number—and they are usually very conspicuous—he can calculate his exact distance from Market Street or the Delaware.

Fourteenth Street is usually called Broad Street. It is very wide, and when fully completed will extend in a straight line, and of equal breadth, about 23 miles, and is the longest street in the city. The *Opera-House, Union League Club, La Pierre House*, and very many of the finest residences, are upon this street, which is also the most fashionable drive and promenade within the city.

The census returns made for the several decades will best illustrate the growth of the city in population and trade. In 1684, it contained 2,500 inhabitants; in 1777, 21,167; in 1790, 42,520; in 1800, 70,287; in 1810, 96,287; in 1820, 119,325; in 1830, 167,325; in 1840, 258,037; in 1850, 408,762; in 1860, 565,529. The population, as was ascertained by the census of 1870, was 673,726. Its present annual increase is estimated at 25,000.

A week well employed will suffice, in moderately favorable weather, to show the visitor the principal objects of interest in and around Philadelphia, though a fortnight might be profitably spent there. To those desirous of "doing it," as the phrase goes, in the shortest possible time, the street-cars offer the cheapest, and, all things considered, the most expeditious means. For a complete list of the several main and branch roads and routes, of which there are twenty-two, under the control of nineteen companies, the stranger had better consult the City Directory, published annually, and to be found at all the hotels. As these routes are frequently miles in length, and are laid, in many cases, through the principal thoroughfares and streets, the stranger is enabled to see many of the objects described in these pages, without so much as moving from his seat.

HOTELS, RESTAURANTS, AND CLUBS.

HOTELS.—The hotels of Philadelphia, though neither so numerous nor extensive as those of New York, are nevertheless conspicuous for the comfort of their internal arrangements and the excellence of their *cuisine*. Among the most desirable are the following:

The *Continental*, on Chestnut and Ninth Streets, opened in 1860, has a reputation second to no hotel in the United States. Under the proprietorship of Messrs. J. E. Kingsley & Co., its well-deserved reputation has been fully sustained. The Chestnut Street front, 200 feet long, is of Pictou sandstone, six stories high, and is much admired.

The *La Pierre*, at the intersection of Chestnut and Broad Streets, has been recently refurnished throughout, and is now one of the most elegant houses in the country. It is in the immediate neighborhood of the Union League Club-rooms, and the Opera-House, and has accommodations for upward of 300 guests.

The *Girard House*, on Chestnut Street, opposite the Continental, is a commodious, handsomely-furnished, and well-kept house, with an excellent table, and a corps of attentive and obliging waiters. The *Merchants' Hotel*, on Fourth Street, and the *American*, on Chestnut, near Fifth Avenue, are popular houses, at medium prices. Charges at the Continental and La Pierre, $4.50, at the Girard $3.50, per day.

Furnished apartments in private houses are readily obtained by those desiring them. The best locations are to be found in Chestnut Street above Twelfth Street, in Arch Street, and in and around Franklin, Penn, and Logan Squares. Furnished apartments, with good board, can be had at about one-half the hotel rates.

RESTAURANTS.—Of late, the restaurant has become a feature of Philadelphia life, though in so essentially a domestic and home community it will be long before it becomes fashionable.

CLUBS.—The *Union League of Philadelphia*, on Broad Street, corner of Sansom, offers the greatest attractions to gentlemen visiting or making a stay in the city. Files of the leading European and American magazines and journals are to be found here. Attached to it is the best refectory in Philadelphia. No more elegant place to beguile an hour can be found in the city. Upward of one hundred and seventy-six thousand dollars were expended on the construction of this building, an amount which has been largely increased by outlays subsequently made to repair the damages caused by the fire of September 6, 1866. The list of members numbers (1870) about 1,760. A member's introduction and ticket will secure the visitor the privileges of the club for one month.

CONVEYANCES.

STREET RAILWAYS.—Philadelphia has the most complete system of city passenger railways on the continent. The lines are 22 in number. By the use of transfer or "exchange" tickets almost any point within the city limits can be reached by rail at a uniform fare of *nine* cents, single fares *seven* cents. The Merchants' Exchange is the principal car station.

HACKS, ETC.—(Fares regulated by law.) One passenger, with trunk, valise, carpet-bag, or box, distance not exceeding one mile, 50 cents. Distance over a mile, and not exceeding two miles, 75 cents. Each additional passenger, 25 cents.

If the distance be over two miles, each additional mile, or part of a mile, 25 cents, in addition to the sum of 75 cents for the first two miles, and for every additional passenger 25 cents. If engaged by the hour, with the privilege of going from place to place, and stopping as often as may be required, $1 per hour. In case of dispute, call a policeman, or apply at the mayor's office.

FERRIES.

There are six ferry lines running to and from Philadelphia, as follows, viz. :

West Jersey.—Market Street, Philadelphia, to Market Street, Camden ; fare, five cents.

Camden and Philadelphia.—Market Street, Philadelphia, to Federal Street, Camden ; fare, five cents.

Camden.—South Street, Philadelphia, to Kaigu's Point, Camden ; fare, five cents.

Gloucester.—South Street, Philadelphia, to Gloucester, N. J. ; fare, five cents.

Red Bank.—South Street, Philadelphia, to Red Bank, N. J. ; fare, ten cents.

Cooper's Point.—Vine Street, Philadelphia, to Cooper's Point ; fare, five cents.

Shakamaxon.—Fare, five cents.

Besides these ferries, numerous steamers ply on the Delaware, affording easy and pleasant communication during the summer between Philadelphia and Arlington, Chester, Delanco, Trenton, Burlington, Bristol, Newcastle, Tacony, Bridgeport, etc.

BRIDGES.

There are nine bridges in and near Philadelphia. The following are best worthy a visit, viz.: Iron Bridge, across the Schuylkill, at Chestnut Street. It was commenced September 19, 1861, and completed July, 1866, and is the first cast-iron bridge built in the United States. It is 390 feet long, 42 feet wide, and 40 feet above high water. It is 1,200 tons' weight, and cost half a million dollars. The *Fairmount Suspension Bridge* is an elegant structure, built (1841) by Mr. Ellet, and closely resembling the Niagara suspension bridge, was the first of the kind in this country. The *Market Street Bridge* is of wood, resting on stone piers. It was erected in 1798, and cost $300,000. It is in contemplation to bridge the Schuylkill at every alternate street.

PLACES OF AMUSEMENT.

Theatrical exhibitions were introduced into Philadelphia in 1754. The first performances were held in a store-house in Water Street, near Pine. Subsequently a suitable building was erected in South Street, but it was not until 1791 that the theatre (since removed) on Chestnut Street, west of Sixth Street, was built. In 1809 the Olympic (now Walnut Street Theatre) was built, since which time the drama may be said to have flourished.

The *Academy of Music* (Opera-House), on Broad and Locust Streets, is one of the most complete establishment of its kind in the United States. The first story is of brown-stone and the rest of pressed brick, with brown-stone dressing. The front, on Broad Street, is 140 feet, and presents a substantial appearance. Its extent on

Locust Street is 268 feet. The *auditorium* is 102 feet deep, 90 feet wide, 70 feet high, and has sittings for upward of 3,000 persons. The first-class seats number 1,692, and are divided into the parquet, parquet circle, balcony, first tier, boxes, and six proscenium-boxes. The *foyer*, or retiring-room, in the second story front, is a handsome apartment, supported by sixteen Ionic columns. The chandelier in the centre has 240 lights, and is much admired. The Academy was first opened January 26, 1857.

The *Walnut Street Theatre* is at the corner of Walnut and Ninth Streets. It was built in 1809 as the "Olympic," and enlarged and remodelled in 1865.

Arch Street Theatre is in Arch Street, above Sixth. The *New Chestnut Street Theatre* is a commodious and well-arranged establishment. It fronts on Chestnut Street, west of Twelfth Street. The *Musical Fund Hall*, 806 Locust Street, between Eighth and Ninth Streets, is a favorite concert and lecture room. It was erected in 1824, and cost $27,500. It has seats for 2,500 persons. The other places of amusement are: *Carncross & Dixey's Opera-House* (Ethiopian), Eleventh Street, above Chestnut; *Duprez & Benedict's Opera-House* (Ethiopian), Seventh Street, below Arch, late Theatre Comique; *Concert Hall*, 1221 Chestnut Street; *National Hall*, 1226 Market Street; the *Assembly Buildings*, southwest corner of Chestnut and Tenth Streets, and the *American Theatre*, Walnut near Eighth Street.

The *American Museum*, corner Ninth and Arch Streets, has a good dramatic company. A fine German theatre was built in the course of the year 1870. There are several other halls, concert and lecture rooms, in the more remote parts of the city.

The *Gymnasium*, under the management of Professor Lewis, is open daily at the northeast corner of Arch and Ninth Streets. Choice seats at all the above places can be secured at the leading hotels up to 6½ P. M. each day.

CHURCHES.

The wish of the city's founder, Penn, that every one might worship God according to the dictates of his own conscience, seems to have been most scrupulously carried out by its citizens. Religious societies have multiplied exceedingly, and church edifices have kept pace in increase. These now number 293 against 139 in 1818, of which 81 belong to the Presbyterian denomination, 63 to the Episcopal, and 35 to the Roman Catholic. But 13 belong to the Friends or Quakers. We enumerate those only best worthy the stranger's attention:

The *Cathedral Church of St. Peter and St. Paul*, on Logan Square, Eighteenth Street, is built of red-stone, and is the largest and most imposing church edifice in the city. The plan of the edifice is that of the modern Roman cruciform churches, having a nave in the centre. It was commenced in September, 1846, from designs by Le Brun, and opened for worship in 1862. The front portico was designed by Notman, and is much admired. The dome rises to a height of 210 feet. It has a fine organ and fresco paintings. The altar-piece, by Brumidi, is conspicuous for its fine coloring.

The *Church of St. Mark* (Episcopal), on Locust Street, near Sixteenth Street, is a beautiful Gothic edifice of light-red sandstone, with a tower and steeple of admirable grace. It was erected in 1849, from designs by Notman.

St. Paul's (Episcopal), on Third Street, is also a noted church.

Christ Church, on Second Street, above Market, with its lofty spire, is a very interesting object in its ancient and quaint aspect. In the steeple, which is 196 feet high, is a fine chime of bells. It was commenced in 1727, and completed in 1753. This church was organized in 1695, and, until the erection of the present building, worship was conducted in a log chapel. The communion service, presented by Queen Anne in 1708, is unique. Washington attended this church.

The *Church of the Incarnation*, southeast corner of Broad and Jefferson Streets, the corner-stone of which was laid July 28, 1866, is a handsome edifice. It is of Liperville granite, relieved by corners of Pictou stone.

The new *Baptist Church*, at the corner of Broad and Spruce Streets, is a very beautiful building.

The *Church of Calvary* (Presbyterian),

in Locust Street, and the *Baptist Church* in Broad and Arch Streets, are of sandstone, with imposing towers and spires. We may also mention among the churches of the greatest architectural interest, *St. Stephen's* (Episcopal), on Fourth Street, below Market, built 1823, in the Gothic style, and the *Catholic Church of the Assumption*, *St. Jude's*, the *Presbyterian churches* upon Arch and Eighteenth Streets, and upon Arch and Tenth Streets; the *Church of the Nativity*, and the *Baptist churches* on Chestnut and Fifth Streets.

St. Peter's Church, at the intersection of Pine and Third Streets, is a venerable edifice, founded 1758, and finished 1761. In the yard is a monument to Commodore Decatur. In the towers of St. Peter's, St. Stephen's, and of Christ Church, there are chimes of bells.

The *Swedes' Church*, Southwark, in the vicinity of the Navy-Yard, should not be forgotten by the visitor. It is the oldest church edifice in the city, having been erected in 1700. Previous to that year, the site upon which it stands was occupied by a log building, which served both as a place of worship, and a block-house to protect against Indian attacks. This building, which constituted the original *Swedes' Church*, was erected in 1677, four years before the arrival of Penn. In the yard of the present edifice is the grave of Wilson the ornithologist.

The meeting-houses of the Friends are interesting only from association. The first, erected in 1685, has long since been torn down. Previous to that the meeting of the Friends took place near the Treaty-Ground, at Shackamaxon (1681). That on the corner of Arch and Fourth is best worth a visit. Next to the Swedes' Church it has the oldest burying-ground in the city. William Penn spoke over the grave of the first person buried here. The building on Arch Street, corner of Fifth, is interesting as having been built and used by the "Fighting Quakers" of the Revolution. It is now occupied as the *Apprentices' Library*.

St. Andrew's Church, on Eighth Street, near Spence, has an imposing façade. It is copied from the *Temple of Bacchus* at Taos, and is considered the most perfect specimen of the Grecian Ionic order in the city.

PARKS AND PUBLIC SQUARES.

Fairmount Park.—Twenty-five years ago, the city became the owner of "Lemon Hill," a finely-wooded tract of about seventy acres, lying immediately contiguous to the small plot occupied by the Fairmount Water-works and gardens; but it was only after thirteen years that the Lemon-Hill Park was opened, from which time (1856) may be dated the practical beginning of the present Fairmount Park. This Park now contains an area of sixteen hundred and eighteen acres, including the water area of the Schuylkill River (two hundred and seventy acres) within its boundaries.

The grounds lie on both sides of this beautiful stream, extending, on the eastern or cityward side, from old Fairmount, in a northeasterly direction as far as the Wissahickon, and stretching, on the western side, from a point nearly opposite Fairmount to the Falls of the river at Manayunk.

The eastern portion of the park comprises only three hundred and fourteen acres, and, with the exception of the ground immediately around Fairmount proper, consists of a narrow belt of land running directly along the river-bank. Upon the western side of the river, however, the park extends upward and backward from the stream, and embraces a wide and varied landscape of hill and dale, woodland, meadow, and lawn, in an area of one thousand and thirty-four acres.

This portion of the park is especially fortunate in having been laid out originally by enlightened taste and skill as private country estates, and under culture many years before it finally passed by purchase or gift into the ownership of the city.

The last, and perhaps, so far as scenic attractions are concerned, the most valuable addition to this part of the park, is the eighty-acre plot known as "George's Hill," which was recently presented to the city by its proprietors, Mr. and Miss George.

From the top of this hill a magnificent panoramic view is obtained, not only of the river to its mouth, and the entire park, but of the city, and the surrounding landscape for many miles in all directions.

Fairmount Park is all natural landscape and water view. In it no structural effects are needed other than the bridges which will cross the river here and there, and a few rustic pavilions, or similar fanciful additions to the rural *ensemble*.

The finest roadway in the park is "Vista Drive," which is remarkable for the varied and romantic beauty of its views. It winds for some seven miles through the entire length of the park, along the sides of the western hills overlooking the river, and presents a series of natural vistas of land and water scenery.

The *Fairmount Water-works* are worthy special notice. They supply a large portion of the city with water, are on the east bank of the Schuylkill, about two miles northwest from the heart of the city, occupying an area of 30 acres, a large part of which consists of the "mount," an eminence towering far above the falls and river below, and about 60 feet above the most elevated ground in the city. The top is divided into four reservoirs, capable of containing 26,896,636 gallons, one of which is divided into three sections for the purpose of filtration. The whole is surrounded by a beautiful gravelled walk, from which may be had a fine view of the city. The reservoirs contain an area of over six acres; they are 12 feet deep, lined with stone, and paved with brick, laid in a bed of clay, in strong lime cement, and made water-tight. The power necessary for forcing the water into the reservoirs is obtained by throwing a dam across the Schuylkill; and by means of wheels moved by the water, which work forcing-pumps, the water of the river is raised to the reservoirs on the top of the "mount." This dam is 1,600 feet long, and the race upward of 400 feet long and 90 wide, cut in solid rock. The mill-house is of stone, 238 feet long and 56 wide, and capable of containing eight wheels, and each pump will raise about 1,250,000 gallons in 24 hours. The water raised by these pumps is sufficient, not only for the reservoirs above-named, but also for the reservoir corner of Corinthian Avenue and Poplar Street, which is 124 feet above high water, and has a capacity of 37,500,000 gallons. The wards of the city, numbered from 1 to 10, are supplied with water by these works; the first four drawing their quota from the Corinthian Avenue Reservoir; the other six from the Fairmount Reservoirs.

The *Schuylkill Water-works* are above Fairmount, at the foot of Thompson Street, and supply the 11th, 12th, 13th, 14th, and 15th wards, distributing the supply from the Schuylkill Reservoir, which has a capacity of 9,800,000 gallons. It is at the corner of 26th and Master Streets, 124 feet above high water.

The *Delaware Water-works*, foot of Wood Street, on the Delaware River, supply the wards numbered from 16 to 20 inclusive. The reservoir for these works is 117 feet above high water, and has a capacity of 9,400,000 gallons.

The *24th Ward Water-works* are on the Schuylkill, opposite Fairmount. They have no reservoir, the stand-pipe acting as a pressure and supply regulator. This stand-pipe is a beautiful tower, which is an ornament to the city, and from which a superb view may be secured.

A large basin is now building at George's Hill, for the purpose of supplying the higher portions of the city with water.

Washington Square, a little southwest of the State-House, is finely ornamented with trees and gravelled walks, is surrounded by a handsome iron railing with four principal entrances, and is kept in exellent order. During the War of Independence upward of 2,000 American soldiers were buried in this spot, which went by the name of the "Potter's Field." No traces of their graves can now be seen. It was made a public square and promenade in 1815. It is very celebrated for containing every, or nearly every tree that will grow in this climate, whether indigenous or otherwise. There is a map of the square showing the position of each tree. In summer it is wonderfully variegated and very beautiful. There is no other spot of land on this continent containing so great a variety of forest-trees within an equal space.

Independence Square, in the rear of the State-House, was purchased by the Provincial Assembly in 1782 for the erection of State buildings, etc. It is enclosed by a solid brick wall, rising three or four feet above the adjacent streets, surmounted by an iron railing. The entire area is laid off in walks and grass-plots, shaded with majestic trees. It was within this enclosure that the Declaration of Independence was first publicly read, July 4, 1776, and at the present day it is frequently used as a place of meeting for political and other purposes. The buildings facing this square on Walnut Street occupy the site of the "Old Prison," the "British Provost" of the Revolution. The new Court-House has been erected near the northwest corner of the square.

Franklin Square, between Race and Vine, and Sixth and Franklin Streets, is an attractive promenade, with a fountain in its centre, surrounded by a marble basin; it is embellished with a great variety of trees.

Penn Square, at the intersection of Broad and Market Streets, is now divided into four parts by Market and Broad Streets being cut through it. It was formerly the site of the old water-works.

Logan Square, the largest in the city, is on Eighteenth Street, between Race and Vine Streets. The Sanitary Fair was held here, June, 1864. The great Roman Catholic Cathedral fronts the square.

Rittenhouse Square is between Eighteenth and Nineteenth Streets and Walnut and Locust Streets. The palatial residence of Mr. Joseph Harrison fronts this square, which is the aristocratic quarter of the city.

Jefferson Square is embraced within Third and Fourth, Washington Avenue and Federal Streets.

Hunting Park, on the York Road, contains 48 acres, and a fine avenue of tulip poplars.

Philadelphia has few monuments worthy special observation. That erected to perpetuate *Penn's Treaty with the Indians* is the most noteworthy. It stands on Beach Street, above Columbia Avenue.

PUBLIC AND PROMINENT BUILDINGS AND PLACES NOT OTHERWISE CLASSIFIED.

MUNICIPAL.

The most interesting object in Philadelphia, and the one most frequently visited, is the *State-House* or *Independence Hall*. It fronts on Chestnut Street, and, including the wings, which are of modern construction (1813), occupies the whole block, extending from Fifth to Sixth Street. The centre edifice was built by Edward Woolley, from designs by Governor Andrew Hamilton. It was commenced in 1729, and completed in 1734, at a cost of £5,600. In the following year it was occupied by the General Assembly, who continued its occupation until the removal of the seat of government to Lancaster, in 1799. In 1740 two wings were erected, which were connected with the main building by an arcade, with stairs leading to the upper rooms. At a later period there were added at the Fifth and Sixth Street corners oblong wooden buildings or sheds, which were used for storage and other purposes. The old wings and arcade were torn down in 1813, and the present two-story edifice was erected on their site. The *City Hall*, corner of Fifth Street, was erected in 1790, and the *County Court-House* commenced in 1789, and finished in 1791, an addition to it being made in 1797. In the east room of the State-House, known as *Independence Hall*, on July 4, 1776, the Declaration of Independence was adopted by Congress, and publicly proclaimed from the steps on the same day. The room presents now the same appearance as it did at that time in furniture and interior decorations. It contains a *statue of Washington*, portraits of William Penn, by Henry Inman; of John Hancock, of Marquis de la Fayette, by Sully; of Baron Steuben, Commodore Porter, Roger Sherman, and numerous other pictures, and many curious Revolutionary relics. Descriptive catalogues of the pictures can be obtained of the superintendent, at the Hall. Admission daily, from nine o'clock until two. Here also is preserved the old "Liberty Bell," imported from England, but which, as the visitor is informed, "got cracked by the stroke of a hammer in trying the sound." It was recast by Isaac Morris, and was the first bell in the United States rung after the passage of the immortal Declaration. It bears the following inscription:

"PROCLAIM LIBERTY THROUGHOUT THE LAND TO ALL THE PEOPLE THEREOF."

A small bell, made from the filings of the original, is to be seen in the rooms of the Historical Society, Athenæum Building. The *Statue of Washington* is wrought in wood, and was executed by Rush, of Philadelphia. Near it is a piece of stone, said to be a part of the step of the balcony upon which John Nixon stood while reading the Declaration of Independence. Up-stairs, over Independence Hall, is the "Lobby," famed in colonial days as the scene of many a sumptuous feast. In it were confined the American officers captured at the battle of Germantown. The original steeple, having become much decayed, was taken down in 1774, twenty-six years before the removal of the Government to Washington, and the present one erected in 1828. In front of the main entrance of Independence Hall is a statue of the Father of his Country, which has recently been erected, the expense being defrayed by contributions from the children of the Public Schools. The statue is by Bailley, and is pronounced a superior work of art.

The *State Arsenal* is at the corner of Sixteenth and Filbert Streets. The *Soldiers' and Sailors' Home* has suitable quarters in the building. To the Home is attached a library of 3,000 volumes for the use of the inmates. The *City Arsenal* is on Race Street, below Broad.

NATIONAL.

The *Custom-House*, formerly the United States Bank, on Chestnut Street, between Fourth and Fifth Streets, is a chaste specimen of the Doric order of architecture, modelled after the Parthenon at Athens, with the omission of the colonnades at the sides. The Chestnut Street and Library Street fronts have each eight massive columns. It was commenced in 1819, and completed in about five years, at a cost of half a million dollars.

The *United States Mint* is on Chestnut Street, corner of Juniper Street, and fronts on the former 122 feet. It is built of white marble, in the style of a Grecian Ionic temple, and comprises several distinct apartments. The corner-stone of the present building was laid in 1829; the edifice cost $200,000. Coining is among the most interesting and attractive of processes to those who have never witnessed such operations. The collection of coins preserved here is among the largest and most valuable in the Union. Visitors are admitted during the morning of each day, Sundays excepted, from 9 to 12 o'clock, on application to the proper officers.

The *United States Navy-Yard* is located on Front Street, below Prime, 1½ miles southeast of the State-House, and contains within its limits about 12 acres. It is enclosed on three sides by a high and substantial brick wall; the east side fronts on and is open to the Delaware River. Entrance from foot of Federal Street. The yard contains every preparation necessary for building vessels of war, and has marine barracks, with quarters for the officers. The sectional floating dock in this yard, built in 1850, cost nearly one million dollars. Admission daily from 10 A. M. to 5 P. M. *League Island*, a tract of land on the Delaware, was accepted in 1867, by act of Congress, as the permanent site of a new Navy-Yard, but as yet has not been occupied for that purpose.

Nearly opposite the Navy-Yard, extending to the Schuylkill River (Gray's Ferry Road), is the *United States Naval Asylum*, founded in 1835, and constructed of white marble, with a front of 380 feet. The grounds are extensive, and tastefully laid out. Application for admission should be made at the gate.

For *Post-Office* and *Sub-treasury*, see Merchants' Exchange.

The United States Government has two arsenals in the neighborhood of Philadelphia; one on *Gray's Ferry Road*, south of the Naval Asylum, the other near *Frankford*. The latter has one of the largest powder-magazines in the United States. Applications for admission are received by the commandant of the post.

EDUCATIONAL AND CHARITABLE.

Girard College is situated on Ridge Avenue, in a northwest direction from the city proper, about two miles from the State-House. It was founded by Stephen Girard, a native of France, who died in 1831. He bequeathed $2,000,000 for the purpose of erecting suitable buildings "for the gratuitous instruction and support of destitute orphans." The site of the edifice and grounds embrace an area of 42 acres, and crown the summit of a slope at once commanding and attractive. The corner-stone was laid July 4, 1833. The buildings were completed in 1847, and the institution went into operation January 1, 1848. The central, or college building, is 218 feet long, 160 broad, and 97 feet high, and is a noble marble structure, of the Corinthian order. Six other buildings, each 125 feet by 52, and three stories high, flank the main edifice on either side. The library is in the central building, to the right of the main entrance. A statue of the founder, said to be a truthful likeness, stands at the foot of the grand stairway of the college. Underneath the statue his remains are interred. The easternmost building embraces four separate and complete dwellings for the several officers of the college. The number of orphans at present in the college is 470. An *Infirmary* was added in 1859-'60. The whole is enclosed by a stone wall 10 feet high, which is in singular contrast to the splendid edifice within. The whole cost of the ground and structure was $1,933,821.78. Permits to visit the college and grounds may be obtained at the principal hotels, of the Secretary, or of the Directors. Principal entrances on the north and south fronts. Clergymen are not admitted.

The *University of Pennsylvania*, Ninth Street, between Chestnut and Market Streets, is a prominent edifice, occupying the greater portion of the entire square. The University was founded as a charity school and academy in 1745, erected into a college in 1755, and subsequently into a university in 1797. In 1798, the trustees of the University purchased from the State what was then the President's (United States) House. This building was enlarged in 1807, and finally removed in 1828, to make way for the present structures. The University embraces four departments, viz.: the Academical the Collegiate, the Medical, and the Law. The medical department, which is one of the most prominent schools of medicine in the country, has a European as well as local reputation, and graduates from this institution are regarded with great favor in the French, English, and German universities. The College of Philadelphia was instituted in 1749, and was the first medical college in the United States. In 1779 its charter was abrogated; and the University of Pennsylvania, which had been first established (1744) as an academy, was organized. In 1789 the charter and privileges of the college were restored by the Legislature, and in 1791 the two institutions were united as the University of Pennsylvania. It has a large and valuable library, and an extensive and valuable anatomical collection. This institution is largely indebted for its establishment and success to Drs. William Shippen and John Morgan, whose portraits adorn its walls.

Jefferson Medical College, situated in Tenth Street, below Chestnut, was established in 1825, and was originally connected with the college at Canonsburg, but is now an independent institution. The number of pupils averages about 300 annually. It has an *anatomical museum* and *lecture-room*, open to visitors.

The *College of Physicians*, instituted in 1787 and chartered 1789, is one of the principal sources from which proceeds the Pharmacopœia of the United States. The *College Hall* is located at the northeast corner of Locust and Thirteenth Streets, and contains a large and valuable medical library.

The *Philadelphia College of Pharmacy*, in Filbert Street, above Seventh, established in 1821, was the first regularly organized institution of its kind in the country. The hall was built in 1832.

Besides these, Philadelphia has an *Eclectic and Homœopathic Medical College*, a *Female Medical College*, *College of Dental Surgery*, and several other prominent medical institutions.

The *Polytechnic College of Pennsylvania*, on West Penn Square, Market Street, is organized on the plans of the Industrial Colleges of France and Germany, and comprises a Scientific School, and six Technical Schools. It was incorporated in 1853.

The *Wagner Free Institute*, the gift of Professor Wagner, is near the corner of Columbia Avenue and Thirteenth Street. The fine residences of Edwin Forrest and Thomas J. Mackenzie are in the neighborhood.

The hospitals, asylums, and other charities of the city, number more than 100. The following are the most noteworthy:

The *Pennsylvania Hospital*, in Pine Street, between Eighth and Ninth Streets, is an admirable institution, founded in 1751. It contains an anatomical museum and a library of more than 10,000 volumes. In the rear of the lot, fronting on Spence Street, is a small building, which formerly contained West's celebrated picture of *Christ Healing the Sick*, presented to this institution by its author, and now in the Insane Asylum. Admission, Monday and Thursday afternoons. The cornerstone of the east wing was laid May 28, 1755; the west wing was erected in 1796, and the centre in 1805. A statue of Penn stands in the lawn facing Pine Street.

The *County Almshouse*, situated on the west side of the Schuylkill, facing the river opposite South Street, is an immense structure, consisting of four main buildings, each 500 feet front, covering and enclosing about 10 acres of ground. The site is much elevated above the bank of the river, and commands a fine view of the city and surrounding country. Connected with the Almshouse is a hospital with accommodations for 600 patients.

Pennsylvania Insane (Asylum) Hospital, West Philadelphia, between Westchester and Haverford roads. It contains male and female departments, and was first opened in 1841. The grounds attached to it embrace 114 acres. The main front is 430 feet long. *Christ Healing the Sick*, by West, is on exhibition here. Visitors admitted every day, except Saturday and Sunday. The Market Street (W. P.) cars run direct to the Hospital.

The *Hospital of the Protestant Episcopal Church in Philadelphia* is at the corner of Huntingdon and Front Streets. The hospital buildings are, excepting only Girard College, the most imposing range of buildings in the city. They are fine specimens of the Norman Gothic style of architecture, but are not entirely completed, though there is already accommodation for over 200 patients. All who can be accommodated are admitted, irrespective of creed, color, or nationality.

The *United States Marine Hospital*, founded 1835, has a handsome situation on the east bank of the Schuylkill, below South Street. It is for the use of invalid seamen and officers disabled in the service (see U. S. NAVAL ASYLUM, page 109).

The *Pennsylvania Institute for the Deaf and Dumb* is situated on the corner of Broad and Pine Streets. The present building was erected in 1825, from designs by Haviland, at a cost of $80,000.

Pennsylvania Institution for the Instruction of the Blind. This is not an asylum, but a school, in which the unfortunate persons for whose benefit it was founded are instructed in useful trades, in music, and in the usual branches taught in schools. The exhibition of the acquirements of the pupils is given every Wednesday afternoon at 3.30 P. M. From 2.30 to 3.30 the workshops are open to inspection. Visitors are charged a trifling admission fee, which is devoted to a fund, from which outfits are purchased for graduating pupils. The institution is located at the corner of Twentieth and Race Streets, and is reached by the Race and Vine, Arch Street, and Seventeenth and Eighteenth Street Railways.

The *Preston Retreat*, another famous charity, the bequest of Dr. Jonas Preston, occupies the square bounded by Twentieth, Twenty-first, Hamilton, and Spring Garden Streets. Admission daily.

The *House of Refuge* is on Twenty-second Street and Girard Avenue, in the rear of the Penitentiary; the *House of Correction* is at Bush Hill; and *Wilt's Hospital* is on Race Street, opposite Logan Square.

LITERARY AND SCIENTIFIC.

There are upward of 20 public libraries in Philadelphia, containing 300,000 volumes.

The *Philadelphia Library*, sometimes called the *Franklin Library*, founded in 1731, through the influence of Benjamin Franklin and the members of the "Junto," stands on South Fifth (No. 125), near Chestnut Street. The first importation of books was received October, 1732. In 1744 the *Union Library Company* was incorporated with it. The corner-stone of the present library building was laid August 31, 1789. Over the front entrance is a marble statue of Franklin, executed in Italy, by order of William Bingham. The library is rich in early printed works, and works on American history. Valuable donations of books have been made by William Logan, Samuel Preston, Robert Barclay, and William Mackenzie. The number of volumes, including the Loganian Library, is 90,000, and is increasing at the rate of 2,000 annually. Admission free from 10 o'clock till sunset.

The *Mercantile Library*, near the Philadelphia Library, was founded in 1821, and the present building erected in 1845 at a cost of $23,190. Library numbers over 50,000 volumes. Open from nine A. M. to ten P. M. daily.

The *Athenæum*, on Sixth Street, corner of Adelphi, is generally visited by strangers. This institution was established February 9, 1814, and opened in the following month, over "Cary's book-store," southeast corner of Chestnut and Fourth Streets. The corner-stone of the present edifice was laid November 1, 1845, and the hall opened in 1847. Cost $50,000. The second story contains a *library, news and reading rooms*, and a *chess-room*. The library numbers 25,000 volumes. In a hall in the third story of the *Athenæum* is the *Library of the Historical Society of Pennsylvania*.

The *Apprentices' Library*, corner of Fifth and Arch Streets, has 25,000 volumes. It was founded in 1821, and is open to the youth of both sexes.

Friends' Library, 304 Arch Street, has 10,000 volumes.

Law Association Library, Court-House, southeast corner of Chestnut and Sixth Streets, organized 1862; 8,000 volumes.

The *American Philosophical Society*, founded in 1743, has its hall at the southwest corner of South Fifth and Chestnut Streets. It owes its origin mainly to the efforts and influence of Franklin, Governor John Penn, and the active members of "the Junto," a once celebrated scientific association, organized in 1727. The site of the present building was donated by the State (1785), and the building erected and occupied in 1790. It has a library of 30,000 volumes, and a choice collection of minerals, fossils, and ancient relics. The Committee-Room should be visited. For admission to the hall, apply to the librarian.

The *Franklin Institute*, situated at No. 155 Seventh Street, below Market, was incorporated in 1824. Its members are very numerous, composed of manufacturers, artists, mechanics, and persons friendly to the mechanic arts. The annual (October) exhibitions of this Institute never fail to attract a large number of visitors. It has a library of about 10,000 volumes, and an extensive reading-room, where most of the periodicals of the day may be found. Lectures are given on Tuesday and Thursday of each week, from October to April. Strangers admitted on application to the secretary.

The *Academy of Natural Sciences*, founded 1812, incorporated 1817, is well worthy a visit. The present building, which is at the intersection of Broad and Sansom Streets, in the immediate vicinity of the Union League and La Pierre House, was commenced May 25, 1839, and enlarged in 1847-1853. The main hall is 45 feet by 28, with spacious galleries. The library is one of the most complete of its kind in the United States, containing over 30,000 volumes. The *Collection of Ornithological Works and Specimens* is especially rich, as is also the Cabinet of Botany. The Cabinets of Geology and Mineralogy are also very complete. The entire collection of the Museum embraces over 200,000 specimens. It is shortly to be removed to more commodious quarters on Tenth Street, above Chestnut, where an elegant building is to be erected. Admission by members' tickets on Tuesday and Friday afternoons. Tickets also of E. Parish, 800 Arch Street.

The *Historical Society of Pennsylvania*, founded for the purpose of diffusing a knowledge of local history, especially in relation to the State of Pennsylvania, has its rooms in the upper floor of the Athenæum Building, corner of Sixth and Adelphi Streets. It has caused to be published a large amount of information on subjects connected with the early history of the State, and is now actively engaged with similar pursuits. Here are preserved an original portrait of Penn, believed to be the only one in existence, the *belt of wampum* presented to Penn, by the Leni-Lenapé sachems, at the famous treaty in 1682, and other interesting relics. Its library, though small, contains many valuable works. The collection of official documents relating to the early French Revolution preserved here numbers 1,000. The medical history of the American Revolution, known as the "Potts Papers," and the original manuscript report of Mason and Dixon's surveys, are also kept here, together with many other objects of great interest to the antiquarian. An antique clock by Fromantell, of Amsterdam (1659), is worthy of notice. The whole number of volumes, bound and unbound, is 18,470. Open every Monday (July and August excepted).

ART GALLERIES.

The *Pennsylvania Academy of Fine Arts*, founded in 1805, and incorporated 1806, has a fine building, with a noble suite of galleries on Chestnut Street; entrance, 1025 Chestnut Street, between Tenth and Eleventh Streets. It possesses a very valuable and permanent collection of pictures, and holds an annual exhibition of new works (April to June). Among the more prominent pictures on exhibition are, *Death on the Pale Horse*, and *Christ Rejected*, by West; and the *Dead Man Restored*, by Washington Allston. The *Relief of Leyden*, by Wittkamp, is also a fine picture. The walls are adorned by highly-meritorious works from the pencils of Stuart, Sully, Neagle, Hamilton, Rothermel, Bonfield, Williams, Russell, Smith, Moran, Lewis, Leslie, and others. Admission 25 cents; catalogue extra.

The *School of Design for Women*, established in 1850, is on Penn Square and Filbert Street.

PRISONS.

The prison or penitentiary system of Philadelphia, first adopted in 1794, and perfected in 1829, reflects lasting credit on its projectors.

The *Eastern Penitentiary*, in the north-west part of the city, is situated on the property once known as Cherry Hill, on Coates Street, corner of Twenty-fifth Street, and south of Girard College. It covers about 10 acres of ground, is surrounded by a wall 30 feet high, and in architecture resembles a baronial castle of the middle ages. It is constructed and conducted on the principle of strictly solitary confinement in separate cells, and is admirably calculated for the security, the health, and, so far as is consistent with its objects, the comfort of its occupants. It was finished in 1829, at a cost, including the purchase of the site, of $600,000. The average number confined here yearly is 350. Previous to the erection of this penitentiary, the old Walnut Street Prison was used for the custody of convicts.

The *County* (*Moyamensing*) *Prison*, situated on Passyunk road, Moyamensing District, below Tenth Street, is a spacious Indo-Gothic building. It is constructed of Quincy granite, is three stories high, and presents an imposing appearance. It is appropriated to the confinement of persons awaiting trial, or those who are sentenced for short periods. It is managed by a board of 15 inspectors. Admission by ticket.

The *Debtors' Prison*, adjoining the above on the north, is constructed of red sandstone, in a style of massive Egyptian architecture. It is no longer used as a debtors' prison.

The *House of Refuge* is situated on Parish Street, between Twenty-second and Twenty-fourth Streets, near Girard College. City office, northeast corner of Arch and Seventh Streets. Visitors admitted Monday, Wednesday, and Friday afternoons. Every needful facility for visiting the above prisons will be furnished on application at the Mayor's office, or to Mr. Richard Vaux, No. 520 Walnut Street.

OTHER BUILDINGS AND PLACES OF INTEREST.

The *Girard National Bank*, on Third Street, below Chestnut, is a stately edifice, originally built for the first United States Bank (1795–'98). It was the first public building with portico and columns ever built in Philadelphia. The design is copied from that of the Dublin Exchange. After the closing of the "Bank of the United States," this building was occupied by the banking-house of Stephen Girard until the time of his death. The north end of the first floor is now occupied by the City Treasurer, and the south end by the bank.

The *Philadelphia Bank*, an imposing granite structure, is on Chestnut Street, between Fourth and Fifth. It was chartered in 1804. This edifice, as well as that of the *Farmers' and Mechanics' Bank* adjoining, are among the finest bankinghouses in the city. The *First National Bank* is a solid granite structure, on Chestnut Street, near Third.

The *Merchants' Exchange*, situated between Dock, Walnut, and Third Streets, is of white marble. It is a beautiful structure, and, of its kind, one of the finest in the country. The Board of Brokers and Commercial Association have rooms here. The *Merchants' Reading-Room*, in the rotunda of the second story, is ornamented with designs in fresco.

One of the most striking buildings in the city is the office of the *Public Ledger*, corner of Sixth and Chestnut Streets, which holds the same relation to the newspaper offices of Philadelphia which the *Herald* does to those of New York.

The *Bank of North America*, on Chestnut Street, built of brown-stone, in the modern Florentine style, is worthy of notice as having been the first bank established in this country, December, 1781.

The rooms of the *Numismatic Society of Philadelphia* are at 524 Walnut Street, facing Independence Square (former number 927 Market).

The new hall of the *Horticultural Society*, south of the Academy of Music, is a handsome edifice, completed in 1870.

The numerous *Markets* of Philadelphia are many of them worthy of special notice, for their great extent and admirable appointment, and will amply repay the visitor. The largest are on Market Street, or near it, in the intersecting streets. They are nearly all of an ornamental, yet solid, character. The Mercantile Library was originally a market-house.

OLD PHILADELPHIA.

After visiting the more important public works and buildings of the city, and the objects and points of interest in its vicinity, a stroll in the Old District, or what was once "the city" of Philadelphia, will well repay the stranger. Among the relics of the past still left undisturbed by the march of improvement, is the *Penn Cottage*. It is located in Letitia Street, which is not a street, but a narrow, dingy court or lane, opening out from Market Street, between First and Second. It is thought to have been the first brick building erected in Philadelphia, and was the residence of William Penn during his first visit to the city (1682–'83). Since then it has been successively occupied as a tavern, bakery, and cigar-store, and is now used as a lager-bier saloon and Gasthaus by Adam Best, whose sign-board, embellished with a foaming tankard, surmounts its humble doorway. It is still in a good state of preservation, but is almost lost to view in the maze of buildings which surround it.

The *Slate-Roof House*, another interesting old landmark, until recently stood on the corner of Second and Gothic Street (Norris Alley), and immediately opposite the Old Bank of Pennsylvania. The year of its erection is uncertain. William Penn and his family occupied it in 1700. It was sold to William Trent, the founder of New Jersey, in 1703. In it John Penn, "the American," was born. There Generals Forbes and Charles Lee died. It was also occupied at different times by Adams, Hancock, De Kalb, and other distinguished men. Arnold also occupied it while military governor of this city in 1778. It was removed, to make way for the new Corn Exchange. Soon not a relic of the early days of Pennstown will be left. On Third Street, between Willing's Alley and Spence Street, the *Washington Hall* occupies the site of the old Bingham mansion. Penn's country residence (palace) was at Pennsbury Manor, above Bristol. Here was the famous *Hall of Audience*.

Carpenter's Hall, south of Chestnut Street, below Fourth, should be visited. Here assembled the first Congress of the United Colonies. It is a plain brick building of two stories, surmounted by a cupola.

Loxley's House (home of Lydia Darrack, and headquarters of the British army) is now a clothing-store.

The *Indian Queen Hotel*, where Jefferson resided, still stands at the corner of Front and Market Streets.

Hultsheimer's New House, where Jefferson penned the Declaration of Independence, is still standing, at the southwest corner of Market and Seventh Streets. The chamber is frequently visited, and should continue to be, as long as it stands.

Solitude, once the country residence of John Penn, is on the west bank of the Schuylkill, and may be seen not far from the falls, by the visitor at Fairmount. It is built of rough-cut stone.

The *Grave of Franklin* is at the southeast corner of Arch and Fifth Streets. For the purpose of affording to passers-by the privilege of looking upon the resting-place of this great man, iron palings have been substituted for the brick wall of the cemetery, opposite the grave.

The *Elm-Tree*, under which the famous treaty between Penn and the Indians was made, was blown down in 1809. A chair made from the wood is preserved in the collection of the Historical Library Association.

CEMETERIES.

Philadelphia can boast a larger number of beautiful cemeteries, perhaps, than any other city of the Union. First and most attractive among them is *Laurel Hill*. This beautiful rural burying-ground, the second in respect to age, and by many esteemed the first in point of beauty in the Union, is situated on Ridge Avenue, near the "falls" of the Schuylkill, on the east bank of that picturesque stream. It is easily reached by the street-cars from any portion of the city, or by boat up the Schuylkill from Fairmount. The bank, upon which a great portion of the original Laurel Hill is laid out, and many of the finer monuments are erected, is 110 feet high, and commands a most charming view of the river. No more fitting or beautiful spot for a cemetery is to be found in the country. *Old* (North) *Laurel Hill* was founded in 1835, and laid out by John Jay Smith, Esq., President of the present Laurel Hill Company; it embraced originally but 20 acres. The surface is undulating, prettily diversified by hill and dale, and adorned with a number of rare and beautiful trees. The irregularity of the ground, together with the foliage, shrubs, and fragrant flowers, which here abound, with an extensive and diversified view, make the whole scene highly impressive.

The additions to the cemetery-grounds embrace more than 130 acres, and are respectively known as "Central" and "South Laurel Hill." Approaches to the different portions of the entire cemetery lead from Ridge Avenue, which bounds it on the east. The western or river front extends more than a mile in length. North Laurel Hill, being the oldest and most finished, should be visited first. The group near the main entrance, known as "Old Mortality," by Thom, is finely executed and will command attention. The *Chapel* on the brow of the hill, a little to the right of Old Mortality, is a Gothic structure with a large stained-glass window. Improvements are being made hereabouts which will add much to the beauty of the ground. The *Superintendent's bell* is close by the chapel. Opposite the chapel is the monument to General Hugh Mercer, who fell at Princeton, and not far off is the tomb of Commodore Hull. The remains of Commodores Murray, Lavalette, and Hassler are also near by. The vault of Dr. Kane, the Arctic explorer, is underneath the brow of the hill, overlooking the Schuylkill, and is cut from the solid rock. Among the more prominent monuments recently erected at Laurel Hill are those to General F. Patterson, Henry P. Voorhees, Mrs. Kempton, and Miss Bailey. The last, which is of Aberdeen granite, is much admired. The granite obelisk to Charles Thomson, perpetual Secretary of the Continental Congress, and the Hassler monument, are both fine specimens of art. Godfrey, the inventor of the quadrant, Judge Conrad, the author of "Jack Cade," Dr. R. M. Bird, and Brown, the novelists, Joseph C. Neal, the author of the "Charcoal Sketches," and Joseph S. Lewis, the projector and builder of Fairmount Water-works, are all buried here. But the great attraction of Laurel Hill, and that which preëminently distinguishes it among other public burying-grounds, is its unique garden landscape, and the profusion of valuable trees, shrubs, and flowers, which adorn and beautify it. Among the former, of more than ordinary interest are some cedars of Lebanon, the first which bore fruit in the United States, and noble specimens of the weeping ash which thrive finely. Admission every day, except Sunday, from nine o'clock until sunset. No tickets are necessary except to drive in, and these are occasionally furnished on application to the secretary or treasurer at 524 Walnut Street, Philadelphia.

Glenwood, at the intersection of Ridge Road and Islington Lane, is prettily situated on the ridge which divides the waters flowing into the Delaware from those falling into the Schuylkill. It contains 21 acres. Office, 16 North Seventh Street.

Mount Vernon, on Ridge Avenue, opposite Laurel Hill, will repay a visit. It has a handsome entrance.

Monument Cemetery, situated on Broad Street, in the vicinity of Turner's Lane, about three miles from the State-House, was opened in 1838, and now contains many handsome tombs. Office, 141 North Sixth Street.

Ronaldson's Cemetery is in Shippen Street, between Ninth and Tenth. *Odd-Fellows' Cemetery*, Twenty-fourth Street, and Islington Lane, contains 32 acres, and is intersected by spacious avenues.

Woodlands, on the Darby road, beyond the Schuylkill, though comparatively a new cemetery, has many attractions, and commands some fine views. It is 80 acres in extent.

Mount Moriah, on the Darby road, in the southwest part of the city, is an attractive place.

The burying-grounds attached to the Swedes' and Christ Churches, and the *Friends' Burial-Ground*, at the junction of Arch and Fourth, contain some interesting monuments. (*See* CHURCHES.)

VICINITY.

The vicinity of Philadelphia abounds in pretty romantic spots, and picturesque drives and walks. Laurel Hill and neighboring cemeteries, Girard College, and the famous water-works at Fairmount, have already been described. After visiting Fairmount, the visitor should extend his ride up the *Wissahickon Creek*, a stream remarkable for its romantic and beautiful scenery, which falls into the Schuylkill about five miles above the city. It has a regular succession of mill-dams, which in the aggregate amount to about 700 feet. Its banks, for the most part, are elevated and precipitous, covered with a dense forest and diversified by moss-covered rocks of every variety. The banks of the beautiful Wissahickon afford one of the most delightful drives in the vicinity of Philadelphia. The route is *via* Ridge Avenue past Laurel Hill, to Manayunk, and thence *via* Wissahickon road. A charming trip may be made from Fairmount by steamer up the Schuylkill to Mount Pleasant, Laurel Hill, etc.

The scenery along the shores of the Schuylkill River is famous for its varied beauty.

Excursion-boats every hour daily during the summer months.

On leaving Fairmount an extensive view of the west front of the city is presented, embracing the Gas-works, the Suspension Bridge, Penitentiary, and Girard College, and several handsome private mansions, among which are Solitude, more fully noticed in our brief sketch of old Philadelphia, Egglesfield, and Sweet Brier.

Fountain Green, on the eastern bank, was until late years a rural spot of much beauty. Nearly opposite to this are seen the ruins of the *Lansdowne Manor-house*. This old relic, built by John Penn, and interesting as the headquarters of General Washington during the War of Independence, was almost entirely destroyed by fire a few years ago. It is now in the hands of a land company. A fine view is had from the site. The boats on the river call at Mount Pleasant landing, and afford opportunities for passengers to visit the neighborhood.

The *Schuylkill Viaduct*, three miles northwest from the city, is 980 feet in length, and is crossed by the *Reading Railroad*.

Moore's Cottage, an old white cottage building, which stands on the west bank of the Schuylkill, above the *Reading Railroad* bridge, and opposite Peter's Island, is pointed out as having been once the residence of Tom Moore the poet, and the spot where he wrote his poem—

"Alone by the Schuylkill a wanderer roved,
And dear were the flowery banks to his eye."

This is traditionary, however, and is doubted by many early settlers and local historians. It is known that Moore visited Philadelphia; but that he had any fixed *abode*, or even temporary *residence* in this locality, is extremely doubtful.

From the landing at Laurel Hill (four miles) that beautiful ground and the adjoining cemeteries on Ridge Avenue are easily accessible. The *Falls of the Schuylkill* (four miles) are seen to advantage from the boat.

Manayunk, seven miles from the centre of the city, is a large manufacturing place. It is indebted for its existence to the water-power created by the improvement of the Schuylkill, which serves the double purpose of rendering the stream navigable, and of supplying hydraulic power to the numerous factories of the village. It is reached by street-cars on Ridge road, as well as by the boat on the river, and may best be visited in connection with the cemeteries, the falls on the Schuylkill, and the Wissahickon, which lie between Manayunk and the city on the same route.

Bartram, the elegant country-seat of Andrew M. Eastwick, Esq., will well repay a visit. It is on the west bank of the Schuylkill, in the immediate vicinity of the Eastwick Skating Park, and is easily reached from Gray's-Ferry road by the Darby car-line.

The *Old Bartram Mansion*, which occupies the centre of the present grounds (garden) was built by John Bartram in 1731. It is in good preservation, and affords a fine specimen of the prevailing style of country-house architecture at that day. It is of stone, and occupies an eminence commanding an extended view of the Schuylkill winding to its juncture with the Delaware at League Island. During the occupancy of Philadelphia by the British, the building was used as headquarters by some of the British officers, and thus escaped damage. It was a favorite resort of Washington, and was frequently visited by Jefferson, Franklin, and other distinguished persons. Here resided William Bartram, son of the original proprietor, and distinguished as one of the leading botanists and writers on botany and ornithology in the country. Here, and in the adjoining garden, Alexander Wilson and Thomas Nuttall pursued many of their life-long scientific labors. *Nuttall's chamber*, in the mansion, is still pointed out. The *Botanic Garden*, adjoining, is the pride of Bartram. It was pronounced by the lamented Downing "the most interesting garden in America to every lover of trees." In 1815 it came into the possession of the late Colonel Robert Carr, who served in the War of 1812, and in 1850 it was purchased by its present owner.

Whitehall is that portion of the city on the line of the Central Railway, ten miles from the depot. On the left of the road, surrounded by an extensive lawn, is *Haverford College*, belonging to an association of Friends. Near by is the birthplace of Benjamin West. *Villa Nova*, a short distance farther on, is the seat of a Roman Catholic college.

Penn's Rock, a mile-stone, raised by William Penn, and bearing his coat-of-arms, is still standing on the road to Haddington. On this rock, tradition says, "Penn and his wife ate their dinners," while the founder of the city was engaged in laying out the Haverford road.

Germantown, now included in the twenty-second ward of the city, was laid out in 1684, and consists mainly of one long street. It is six miles north from Chestnut Street, and may be reached every fifteen minutes by city railroad and steam-cars. The street-car route lies up Eighth Street and Germantown road, and terminating at Mount Airy. The *battle of Germantown* was fought October 4, 1777. *Washington's headquarters*, on Market Square, and *Button-ball Tree Tavern*, are still to be seen. Here are fine cricketing and base-ball grounds. *Chew's House* is a noteworthy object. Many handsome private residences are seen from the Germantown road. *Nicetown*, through which the street railway passes, is a pleasant rural village, inhabited mainly by Germans and Swiss.

Greenwich Point, about three miles below the city, and *Gloucester Point*, directly opposite, are favorite places of resort through the summer season. Ferry from South Street, Philadelphia.

Camden, New Jersey, opposite Philadelphia, is the terminus of the *Camden and Amboy*, the *Camden and Atlantic*, and *West Jersey* (Cape May) *Railways*. It was incorporated in 1831, and is a place of considerable trade and manufacture, and has a population of nearly 20,000. Four steam-ferry lines connect it with Philadelphia. (*See* FERRIES.)

Red Bank, on the Jersey shore of the Delaware, five miles below Philadelphia, has some interesting historical associations. Here (at *Fort Mercer*) a battle was fought, October 22, 1777. The embankment and trenches of the fort are still seen. The house of *Whitehall*, the Tory Quaker, and *Count Donop's* grave, are both pointed out. Opposite Red Bank, on Great Mud Island, is *Fort Mifflin*. A marble monument, 15 feet high, erected October 22, 1829, to commemorate the battle, stands within the northern line of the fort. Lying between Forts Mercer and Mifflin is *League Island*, the accepted site of the new Navy-Yard, not yet established.

Chestnut Hill affords a pleasant drive or ride. It is within the corporate limits, 12 miles north of the State-House, and can be reached by the *Philadelphia, Germantown, and Norristown R. R.*

Whitemarsh is interesting as the scene of a skirmish following the battle of Germantown, and as the headquarters of Washington. It is situated in a beautiful little valley north of Chestnut Hill, 14 miles from Philadelphia, and 6 from Germantown.

Norristown, the county seat of Montgomery County, is on the left bank of the Schuylkill, 16 miles from Philadelphia. It is the seat of justice of Montgomery County, and contains a fine *Court-House* of marble, and *prison buildings*. The Schuylkill is here spanned by two bridges, which connect Norristown with Bridgeport.

Westchester is a beautiful suburb of Philadelphia, finely situated on elevated ground, 22 miles west of the city. The *Court-House* and *Military Academy* are worthy of notice. Reached by cars almost hourly, either on *Westchester and Philadelphia Railway*, via Media, or on the *Central Railway*, via Paoli.

ROUTE I.

PHILADELPHIA TO HARRISBURG, ALTOONA, AND PITTSBURG.

Via Pennsylvania Central Railway.

STATIONS.—Philadelphia; Paoli, 20 miles; Westchester Int., 22 (Junction of Westchester and Philadelphia Railway); Downington, 33 (connects with Chester Valley Railway); Coatesville, 39; Parkesburg, 45; Christiana, 49; Gap, 52; Leaman Place, 58 (connects with Strasburg Branch); Lancaster, 70; Dillerville, 71 (eastern terminus of Columbia Branch); Landisville, 77 (connects with Reading and Columbia Railway); Mount Joy, 82; Elizabethtown, 88; Col. Branch Int., 96 (western terminus of Columbia Branch); Middletown, 97; Harrisburg, 107 (connects with Northern Central, Cumberland Valley, Lebanon Valley, Philadelphia, and Erie, and Schuylkill, and Susquehanna Railways); Marysville, 113 (point of departure for Erie Railway); Duncannon, 122; Newport, 135; Mifflin, 156; Lewistown, 168; Mount Union, 193; Huntingdon, 204 (connects with Huntingdon and Broad Top Railway); Tyrone, 224 (connects with Tyrone and Clearfield and Bald Eagle Valley Branches); Altoona, 239 (connects with Branch to Holidaysburg); Gallitzin, 250; Cresson, 253 (connects with Ebensburg Branch); Summerhill, 266; Conemaugh, 274; Johnstown, 277; New Florence, 290; Blairsville Int., 301 (connects with Indiana Branch); Latrobe, 314; Greensburg, 324; Irwin's, 333; Wall's, 341; Brinton's, 343; Pittsburg, 355.

This fine line constitutes one of the great highways from the Atlantic to the Mississippi States. It extends 355 miles from the city of Philadelphia through the entire length of Pennsylvania, to the Ohio River at Pittsburg, connecting there with routes for all parts of the Southwest, West, and Northwest. Through-trains (13½ hours to Pittsburg) run, morning, noon, and night. Philadelphia station, corner of Thirty-first and Market Streets.

Paoli (20 miles), the scene of an action (September 20, 1777) between the American forces, under General Wayne, and a detachment of British troops, under

Gray, better known as the Paoli massacre, from the fact that a large number of the Americans were killed after they had laid down their arms. A monument, erected September, 1817, marks the spot. The scenery beyond Paoli, through the limestone valley of Chester County, is picturesque. Chester is famous for its highly-cultivated farms and extensive dairies. Two miles beyond Paoli the *Westchester Railway* intersects the main line.

Downington (33 miles) is a pretty rural village, on the north branch of the Brandywine Creek. Waynesburg Branch diverges. It is the western terminus of the Chester Valley Railroad, a short line, traversing one of the most beautiful valleys on the continent. A fine view of this valley is had from the windows of the cars on the Central Road. *Chad's Ford*, 15 miles distant, was the scene of the engagement known as the *Battle of Brandywine*. The *Birmingham Friends' Meeting-house*, where the conflict raged hottest, is farther up the stream.

Coatesville (39 miles) is delightfully situated, and is a thriving place. Near here the road crosses the west branch of the Brandywine, on a bridge 850 feet long and 75 feet high.

Parkesburg (45 miles), in Chester County, contains several large machine-shops, an hotel, and a population of 600. It is a large depot for lumber and coal. On the north side of this bridge is located a large iron-foundery. The town grows fast, and now (1871) has probably 1,500 inhabitants. It has good hotel accommodations.

Christiana (49 miles) has an active trade, an iron foundery, and a machine-shop. It was the scene of a riot in 1851.

Gap (52 miles) has an active trade in coal and lumber. It is named from its location, being in the gap through which the road runs in passing from the Chester to the Pequea Valley. The scenery in the vicinity is attractive.

Leaman Place (58 miles) is the junction of the branch road to the flourishing village of Strasburg.

Lancaster (70 miles) is prettily situated near the Conestoga Creek, which is crossed in entering the city. It was incorporated in 1818, was at one time the principal inland town of Pennsylvania, and was the seat of the State government from 1799 to 1812. In population (20,000) it now ranks as the fifth city in the State. It is pleasantly situated in the centre of a rich agricultural region, is well built, and has many fine edifices, public and private. The *Court-House* is an imposing edifice in the Grecian style of architecture. Lancaster is the seat of *Franklin and Marshall College*, organized in 1853, by the union of Marshall with the old establishment of *Franklin College*, which was founded in 1787. *Fulton Hall*, an edifice for the use of public assemblies, is a noteworthy structure, as are some of the church edifices. The oldest turn-pike-road in the United States terminates here, 62 miles from Philadelphia. Besides the large locomotive-works, one of the sources of prosperity of Lancaster is in the navigation of the Conestoga, in a series of nine locks and slack-water pools, 18 miles in length from the town of Safe Harbor on the Susquehanna, at the mouth of the Conestoga Creek. With the help of Tidewater Canal to Port Deposit, a navigable communication is opened to Baltimore. The *Ephrata Springs* and the Moravian *Village of Litiz* are reached from Lancaster. The principal hotels are *Michael's* and the *City*.

Dillerville (71 miles) is the eastern terminus of the Columbia Branch.

Columbia, 12 miles from Lancaster, and about the same distance from Middletown, on the Columbia Branch Railway, is situated on the left bank of the Susquehanna, and is the western terminus of the Philadelphia and Columbia Railway. A part of the town occupies the slope of a hill, which rises gently from the river, and the business part of the town lies along the level bank of the river, for the convenience of shipping lumber, which is the great trade of the place. The scenery from the hills in the vicinity is highly pleasing. The broad river, studded with numerous islands and rocks, crossed by a long and splendid bridge, and bounded on every side by lofty hills, makes a brilliant display. A fine bridge, more than a mile in length, crosses the Susquehanna to Wrightsville. In 1865, during the invasion of Pennsylvania by the Confederates, this bridge was burned by the

Union troops, but has since been rebuilt. Population, 6,000.

Landisville (77 miles) is at the crossing of the Reading and Columbia Railway.

Mount Joy (82 miles) is situated in a rich and populous district; it has two churches and a seminary. Population about 4,000.

Middletown (97 miles), at the mouth of Swatara Creek, on the Susquehanna River, nine miles east of Harrisburg, has a population of 2,500. It is one mile west of the intersection of the Columbia Branch, of which it is the western terminus. The *Union Canal* terminates here.

Harrisburg (107 miles).—HOTELS —The *Lochiel* (formerly Herr's), on Market Street, is the leading house; *Bolton's* (formerly the Beuhler House) is a commodious, well-kept house, on Market Square; the *Jones House* is also a centrally-located and well-ordered establishment. This city is beautifully situated on the east bank of the Susquehanna. It was laid out by John Harris in 1785, previous to which date it was known as *Lewiston*, and still earlier as *Harris's Ferry*. In 1791 it was made a town. In 1812 it was made the capital of Pennsylvania; and on the 19th of March, 1860, it was incorporated into a city, with six wards. It now has a population of about 20,000.

The *State-House* occupies a picturesque and commanding position upon a natural eminence, a little north of the centre of the city; and from its dome a fine view is obtained of the wide and winding river, its beautiful islands, its bridges, and the adjacent ranges of the Kittatinny Mountains. It contains the State Library, and on the grounds is erected a beautiful monument to the deceased soldiers of the Mexican War.

Adjoining the State-House, or capitol building, are two brick edifices, the one on the right being occupied as the Land, the other as the State Department. The Arsenal building stands south of the former edifice. Among the other prominent buildings are the *Court-House*, and the Old and New School Presbyterian churches. The former is a handsome edifice of stone, fronting on the Capitol Square. The Court-House is a stately brick edifice, surmounted by a dome, and stands on Market Street, opposite the Lochiel House. *Front Street* is a handsome, wide avenue, overlooking the Susquehanna, and affords the most attractive promenade in the city. Here are many of the finest residences in the city. *Harris Park*, at the intersection of Front Street and Washington Avenue, is usually visited by strangers. At the crossing of State and Second Streets is a fine brown shaft erected to the memory of the soldiers of Dauphin County who fell in the late war. Harris's grave and tree occupy the centre of the enclosure. Facing it is the *Harris Mansion*, now owned and occupied by Hon. Simon Cameron, ex-Secretary of War. The extensive rolling-mill and works of the *Lochiel Iron Company* are near the town. There are also steel-works of large capacity. During the war Harrisburg was threatened by the Confederates; and would probably have been captured, had it not been for the destruction of bridges across the Susquehanna, and the consequent hinderance to the invaders. The earthworks thrown up for the defence of the city are still visible from the railroad.

From Harrisburg diverge the following railways: *Cumberland Valley Railway* to Carlisle (18 miles); Chambersburg (52 miles); Hagerstown, Md. (74 miles). This road is replete with interest growing out of the rebel raids during the late war. (From Newville, on this line, stages run to the Sulphur Springs.) The *Lebanon Valley Railway* (branch of *Philadelphia and Reading Railroad*) to Lebanon (26 miles), and Reading (54 miles), and the *Northern Central Railway* south to Baltimore, Md., and north to Elmira and Canandaigua, N. Y., excepting 40 miles of the Philadelphia and Erie Railway from Sunbury to Williamsport. This road connects at Lebanon with *Pine Grove and Lebanon Railway* to Pine Grove (24 miles), also with *Lebanon and Cornwall Railway* to celebrated Iron Ore Mountains (6 miles). Passengers for Gettysburg can either take the *Cumberland Valley* line (52 miles) to Chambersburg, and thence by stage, or the *Northern Central* to *Hanover Junction* (39 miles), and thence by rail (30 miles) to the battle-field. The latter is the most expeditious and generally-travelled route. There is a detention of one hour at Hanover Junction on the morning train from Harrisburg. Two days will suffice to make this trip comfortably. (*See* GETTYSBURG, page 141.)

About five miles above Harrisburg the railroad crosses the Susquehanna on a splendid bridge 3,670 feet long, the view obtained from the centre of the bridge being one of the finest on the line. The *Cove Mountain* and *Peter's Mountain* are seen near Cove Station, 10 miles west of Harrisburg. From this point to within a short distance of Pittsburg the scenery is superb, and in places grand beyond description.

Duncannon (122 miles) is the point of departure for the Juniata Valley, which is followed for about 100 miles to the base of the Alleghanies. Here are situated very extensive iron-works.

The Juniata.—This beautiful river, whose course is closely followed so many miles by the *Pennsylvania Central Railroad* and Canal, rises in the south central part of the Keystone State, and, flowing eastward, falls into the Susquehanna about 14 miles above Harrisburg. The landscape of the Juniata is in the highest degree picturesque, and many romantic summer haunts will be found among its valleys; though at present very little tarry is made in the region, from its attractions being little known, and the comforts of the traveller being as yet but inadequately provided for. The mountain background, as we look continually across the river from the cars, is often strikingly bold and beautiful. The little Juniata, which with the Frankstown branch forms the main river, is a stream of wild, romantic beauty. The entire length of the Juniata, including its branches, is estimated at nearly 150 miles, and its entire course is through a region of mountains in which iron-ore is abundant, and of fertile limestone valleys. The Raystown Branch, which rises in the southwest part of Bedford County, enters the Juniata near Huntingdon.

Newport (135 miles) is located at the confluence of the Little Buffalo Creek with the Juniata. Five miles farther on is Millerstown, near the confines of Perry County. The passage of the Juniata through the Great Tuscarora Mountain,

one mile west of this station, is worthy of notice.

From the point of *Law's Ridge*, along the face of which the line runs west of *Perrysville*, a fine view of Mifflin is obtained.

Mifflin (156 miles), the county seat of Juniata County, is beautifully situated on the right bank of the Juniata. It is a flourishing place, and is four miles east of the wild spot known as the "Long Narrows."

Lewistown (168 miles) is the best point from which to visit the Juniata. It is at the outlet of the valley of Kishicoquillas, once the camping-ground of Logan, the Indian chief. The *National Hotel* has good accommodation. Mifflin and Centre County Branch connects here.

Mount Union Station (193 miles) is at the entrance of the gap of Jack's Mountain. Three miles beyond is the famous *Sidling Hill*, and still west the Broad Top Mountain.

Huntingdon (204 miles)—*Exchange Hotel*—is a place of some antiquity, having been laid out previous to the Revolution. It was named after the Countess of Huntingdon. This is another good point from which to see the beauties of the Juniata. The *Huntingdon and Broad Top Railway* to Broad Top Mountain (24 miles), and Mount Dallas (44 miles), joins the main line here. From Mount Dallas to Bedford Springs by stage, six miles.

Bedford Springs, located one mile from the village of Bedford, on the Raystown branch of the Juniata, and reached by the route above indicated, is an attractive place for invalid summer resort. The water contains carbonic acid, sulphate of magnesia, sulphate of lime, and muriate of soda. Excellent hotel accommodation for visitors.

At **Petersburg**, seven miles west of Huntingdon, the railroad parts company with the canal, and follows the Little Juniata, which it again leaves at Tyrone City.

Tyrone City (224 miles)—*Ward House*—at the mouth of Little Bald Eagle Creek, is famous for its manufactures of iron. The line here enters *Tuckahoe Valley*, noted for its iron-ore. A branch (Bald Eagle) road extends 81 miles,

through Bellefonte and Lock Haven. At *Lock Haven* (55 miles) it connects with the Philadelphia and Erie Railway to Williamsport. The Tyrone and Clearfield branch also extends 24 miles to Phillipsburg, and to Clearfield, 43 miles.
Altoona (239 miles), at the head of Tuckahoe valley, and at the foot of the Alleghanies, is important to every traveller, as the best point at which to make a short stay, as well for refreshment as for observation. No tourist should be willing to pass through this region except by daylight, so as not to miss the views in crossing the mountains, described below.

The *Logan House* has complete accommodation for 500 guests. The workshops of the railway company are the most extensive in the State. In 1856 the town contained but one log house. It has now a population of nearly 1,500. A branch road extends eight miles to *Hollidaysburg*, whence stages run to *Bedford Springs*, 27 miles.

The Alleghanies.—At Altoona the western-bound traveller commences the ascent of the Alleghanies. In the course of the next 11 miles some of the finest views and the greatest feats of engineering skill on the entire line are to be seen. Within this distance the road mounts to the tunnel at the summit by so steep a grade that, while in the ascent double power is required to move the train, the entire 11 miles of descent are run without steam, the speed of the train being regulated by the "breaks." At one point there is a curve as short as the letter U, and that too where the grade is so steep that in looking across from side to side of the curve it seems that, were the tracks to be laid contiguous to each other, they would form a letter X. The road hugs the side of the mountains; and from the windows next to the valley the traveller can look down on houses and trees dwarfed to toys, while men and animals seem like ants from the great elevation. Going west, the left-hand, and, going east, the right-hand side of the cars is the best to enjoy the scenery. The summit of the mountain is pierced by a tunnel 3,670 feet long, through which the train passes before commencing to descend the western slope.

Gallitzin (250 miles), the first station after passing through the tunnel, is named after a Russian prince who settled at Rosetta, Cambria County, in 1789.
Cresson Springs (253 miles), on the summit of the Alleghanies, is a pleasant summer resort. The village is 3,000 feet above sea-level, and is much esteemed by invalids for the purity of its air. The hotels and cottages have accommodation for upward of 2,000 persons. The *Mountain House* is well kept. In descending the mountain from this point the remains of another railroad are constantly seen, sometimes above and sometimes below the track. This old road was merely a system of inclined planes by which loaded canal-boats were carried over the mountain, the boats being built in sections which were separated at the foot of the mountains and joined together again after making the portage. The stream, which is almost constantly in sight during the descent, is the *Conemaugh*, which is crossed by a stone viaduct at Horseshoe Bend, near *Conemaugh Station* (274 miles), the terminus of the mountain division of the road. From Cresson Springs there is a branch to Ebdensburg (12 miles), the county town of Cambria, and a place of note.

Johnstown (277 miles), at the junction of Stony Creek with Conemaugh River, commands some attractive scenery. The *Cambria Iron-Works*, seen to the right of the road, are among the most extensive in the country. This is one of the most thriving towns in the State, numbering now (1871) 15,000 inhabitants. It has several fine churches. The *Scott* and *Foster Hotels* are the best. Just beyond, the road takes leave of the Conemaugh, after following its course fifty miles from the slope of the Alleghanies.

Blairsville Intersection (301 miles) is where the branches to Blairsville (3 miles) and to Indiana (19 miles), and from Blairsville to Alleghany City (64 miles), diverge. One mile east of the station is the celebrated cutting in the *Saddle Rock* mountain. From this point the Central forks and runs by the two independent routes to Alleghany and Pittsburg. The north branch follows the course of the Conemaugh and Kiskiminetas to their junction with the Alleghany

River, which it crosses, and, keeping closely on its western side, unites again with the southern branch at Alleghany City. The southern branch goes to Greensburg, through Latrobe, and from it, via Brinton's and Wilkinsburg, enters Pittsburg. On the south branch the road passes

Greensburg, 324 miles from Philadelphia and 31 from Pittsburg, is the county seat of Westmoreland County, and a thriving trading-point. Lines of stages connect it with neighboring towns in Pennsylvania and Maryland. In the yard of the Presbyterian Church, seen as you enter the town, is a monument to Major-General Arthur St. Clair, a British officer in charge of Fort Legonier at the close of the French War. *Penn Station* and *Manor*, a short distance west of Greensburg, are interesting as having formed part of the Penn estate.

Brinton's (343 miles). Here the Connellsville branch joins the main line. *Braddock's Field*, the battle-ground on which General Braddock was defeated by the French and Indians (July 9, 1755), is in the neighborhood, nine miles from Pittsburg. The point where Braddock's army crossed the river in their march on Fort Du Quesne is seen to the left of the line west of Brinton's.

Wilkinsburg (7 miles east of Pittsburg), a thriving town of 1,000 inhabitants, having a number of stores and good hotel accommodations.

The north branch passes Saltzburg, Kiskiminetas, Leechburg, and crosses the Alleghany at Freeport, running thence along the river to Alleghany City. The Meadville Railroad keeps on the east side, so the traveller has the option of landing either at Pittsburg or Alleghany. Over either route he passes over a country most beautiful and picturesque.

Saltsburg, on this route, is a place of consequence, growing rapidly, and an important station on the road.

Kiskiminetas is a thriving town of 2,500, situated on the river of the same name.

Leechburg and **Freeport** are small places, but important depots on the route.

The only other places necessary to mention are the small villages of *Vernon*, on the east, and *Sharpsburg*, on the west side of the river.

Pittsburg (355 miles). HOTELS, the *Monongahela House*, *Union Depot*, *St. Charles*, and *Merchants' Hotel*.

Pittsburg is at the head of the Ohio River, at the confluence of the Alleghany and the Monongahela. It is situated in a district extremely rich in mineral wealth, and the enterprise of the people has been directed to the development of its resources, with an energy and success seldom paralleled. The city of Pittsburg also enjoys, from its situation, admirable commercial facilities, and has become the centre of an extensive commerce with the Western States; while its vicinity to inexhaustible iron and coal mines has raised it to great and merited distinction as a manufacturing place. The internal revenue returns show that the amount of capital invested at this point amounts to over $200,000,000.

The city was laid out in 1765, on the site of Fort Du Quesne, subsequently changed to Fort Pitt, in honor of England's prime minister, William Pitt. The city charter was granted in 1816. Pittsburg is connected with the left bank of the Monongahela by two bridges, 1,500 feet long, which was erected at a cost of $102,000. Five excellent bridges cross the Alleghany River, connecting Pittsburg with Alleghany City. It is usual to speak of extensive manufactories as being in Pittsburg, though they are not all within the limits of the city proper, but are distributed over a circle of five miles' radius from the Court-House on Grant's Hill. This space includes the cities of Pittsburg and Alleghany, the boroughs of Birmingham and Lawrenceville, and a number of towns and villages, the manufacturing establishments in which have their warehouses in Pittsburg, and may consequently be deemed, from the close connection of the general interests and business operations, a part of the city. The stranger in Pittsburg will derive both pleasure and instruction by a visit to some of its great manufacturing establishments, particularly those of glass and iron.

The immense extent of these manufactures, and of the coal and oil trade of the city, can be realized when it becomes known that actual measurement shows that, in the limits of what is known throughout the country as Pittsburg, there are thirty-five miles of manufactories of iron, of glass, of steel, of copper, of oil, of woods, of cotton, and of brass, alone, not to include manufactories in other materials, nor including any of less grade than manufactories of chains in iron, or ploughs in wood. A measurement of the ground also shows that these thirty-five miles of factories are so closely contiguous that, were they placed in a single row, each factory would have but about 400 feet of front space for its workings. These factories are 475 in number.

At the present time the coal-trade of the city amounts to about $10,000,000 annually, and there are in the vicinity of Pittsburg 103 colleries, the value of whose lands, houses, improvements, cars, etc., amount to about $11,000,000.

Oil is another great staple, and there are in Pittsburg fifty-eight refineries, in which is invested a capital of nearly $8,000,000 in buildings and machinery, and, in the tanks and barges necessary to the carrying on of the business, nearly $6,000,000 more. The oil-trade of the city for the five years from January, 1863, to January, 1868, amounted to about $56,000,000, or an average of about $11,000,000 annually. During those five years the entire exportation of petroleum from the United States was 217,948,692 gallons, and the shipments east from Pittsburg was 132,396,179 gallons, showing that Pittsburg supplied over sixty per cent. of the whole foreign exportation of petroleum in the period cited.

As nearly as can be ascertained, one-half of the glass factories of the United States are located at Pittsburg, where there are forty firms engaged in the manufacture of glass, who run sixty factories producing the various descriptions of green, window, flint, and lime glass, employing over four thousand workmen, and producing between four and five millions' worth of glass.

In iron and steel Pittsburg claims and maintains to be the great market of the country. The exact money market of this great trade has always been difficult to arrive at. Much of the iron is shipped by rail to various points, and much by river. By figures we have at command of the shipments of plate, bar, sheet, and rod iron and steel from Pittsburg in the year 1865, it would seem that there were exported, by rail alone, to twenty-four different States, over 143,000 tons, and 180,000 kegs of nails to twenty different States—these railroad exportations, it must not be forgotten, are not probably half the manufacture—that of castings there were shipped by rail alone 5,143,008 pounds in 1864 to twenty-two different States, and that by one railroad alone there were received, in 1864, into the city, 107,000 tons of pig-iron and blooms, exclusive of the yield of six or eight furnaces running in the city of Pittsburg, and the imports by river and other railroads. It is estimated that, of shipments made from Pittsburg, at least as much is sent by river as by rail. There are over thirty iron-rolling mills in Pittsburg, six steel-mills, and between fifty and sixty iron-foundries. These figures but feebly indicate the full extent of the great iron and steel trade of the city, of which the sales alone of articles made of iron subject to tax, made and returned in the city, was from March, 1865, to March, 1866, over $27,000,000.

The *American Iron-Works* of Jones and Laughlins' cover seventeen acres of ground, giving employment to 2,500 hands, and contain twenty-five engines, aggregating 2,750 horse-power. The works contain a machine-shop; a nail-factory 166 feet by 65, two stories in height; a blacksmith-shop, 40 by 75 feet, containing eight fires; a 600-pound steam-hammer, and other mechanical necessaries; a foundery 125 feet by 85 feet, with an air-furnace and two cupolas, having a melting capacity of fifty tons, in which foundery all the machinery for the works are cast; a pattern and carpenter-shop 40 feet by 140, and two rolling-mills, one 280 feet by 130, and the other 325 feet by 185. There is also a spike, bolt, and nut factory 50 feet by 125; also an annealing-house, 60 by 20 feet, for sheet-iron; also a store-house, 375 feet by 30. There also several blast-furnaces attached to the works, located on the opposite side of the river.

The city proper has a population of 86,000, and including its suburban towns, which are now (1871) incorporated with it, the number will fall little short of 180,000. The city is divided into 22 wards, and contains 173 church edifices, among which are several of large size, surmounted by lofty spires. The Roman Catholic *Cathedral of St. Paul*, at the corner of Fifth and Grant Streets, is an imposing edifice of brick, with a fine tower. The *First* and *Third Presbyterian* and the *First Baptist Church*, are also handsome structures. The *Court-House*, facing the cathedral, is a solid stone edifice, surmounted by a dome. The *Custom-House* and *Post-Office* is a commodious stone building, and there are several large and substantial public school-houses. The *Mercantile Library Hall*, costing over $250,000, and the new *City Hall*, costing $750,000, are nearly completed. But the iron-rolling mills, oil-refineries, and other extensive manufactories in the vicinity, constitute the absorbing interest and most characteristic feature of the town. In the vicinity of the city proper there are four cemeteries. They are named and located as follows, viz.: *Alleghany Cemetery*, adjoining Lawrenceville; *St. Mary's Cemetery*, on Greensburg Pike; *Hilldale Cemetery*, adjoining Alleghany City; and *Mount Union Cemetery*, adjoining Manchester, in McClure township. The street-cars connect the city proper with all objects worth visiting in the suburbs. Pittsburg has direct railway communication with the principal cities East and West by means of the *Pennsylvania Central; Pittsburg, Columbus, and Cincinnati; Pittsburg, Fort Wayne, and Chicago Railways*, and with Lake Erie by the *Pittsburg and Cleveland* and *Pittsburg and Erie Railways*. The *Alleghany Valley Railway* to Kittanning (44 miles); and Mahoning (55 miles); Franklin (123 miles); and Oil City (131 miles); and the *Pittsburg and Connellsville Railway* to Connellsville (57 miles), and to Uniontown (72 miles), also diverge here. Boats daily up and down the Ohio River during the season of navigation. There are several places in the vicinity of Pittsburg which, as they may be considered parts of one great manufacturing and commercial city, are entitled to notice here. *Alleghany City*, opposite to Pittsburg, on the west side of the Alleghany River, is the most important of them. The elegant residences of many persons doing business in Pittsburg may be seen here, occupying commanding situations. It contains 115 streets and 41 courts and alleys. Here is located the *Western Theological Seminary of the Presbyterian Church*, an institution founded by the General Assembly in 1825, and established in this town in 1827. Situated on a lofty, insulated ridge, 100 feet above the Alleghany, it affords a magnificent prospect. The *Theological Seminary of the United Presbyterian Church*, established in 1826, and the *Alleghany Theological Institute*, organized 1840 by the Synod of the Reformed Presbyterian Church, are also located here. The *Western Penitentiary* is an immense building, in the ancient Norman style, situated on the "common" of Alleghany City. It was completed in 1827, at a cost of $183,000. The *United States Arsenal* is located on the left bank of the Alleghany River, within the city limits.

Birmingham is another considerable suburb of Pittsburg, lying about a mile from the centre of the city, on the south side of the Monongahela, and connected with Pittsburg by a bridge, 1,500 feet long, and by a ferry. It has important manufactories of glass and iron.

Manchester, now a part of Alleghany, is two miles below Pittsburg, on the Ohio. Here is located the *House of Refuge*, incorporated in 1850. The *Passionist Monastery* is near here. The *United States Marine Hospital* is yet below.

East Liberty, five miles from Pittsburg, on the line of the Central Railroad, is a thriving suburb, containing some fine residences, and affording a delightful drive to and from the city. The capacious edifice of the *Western Pennsylvania Hospital*, erected in 1860, at Dixmount, is seen in approaching the city on the *Pittsburg, Fort Wayne, and Chicago Railroad*.

ROUTE II.

PHILADELPHIA TO READING, POTTSVILLE, AND WILLIAMSPORT.

Via Philadelphia & Reading, and Catawissa Railways.

STATIONS.—Philadelphia and Reading R. R., Philadelphia: Manayunk, 7 miles;

Conshohocken, 14; Norristown, 17 (Connects with Philadelphia, Germantown & Norristown, and Chester Valley Railways) Port Kennedy, 21; Perkiomen Junc., 25 (connects with Perkiomen Railway to Swenkville); Phœnixville, 27; Royer's Bridge, 32; Limerick, 34; Pottstown, 40 (connects with Colebrookdale Railway to Mt. Pleasant, 13 miles); Douglasville, 44; Birdsboro', 48 (connects with Wilmington and Birdsboro' Railway); Reading, 58 (connects with Lebanon Valley Branch, Columbia and Reading Railway, Lancaster and Reading Branch, and E. Penn. Railways). Leesport, 66; Mohrsville, 68; Hamburg, 75; Port Clinton, 78 (connects with Little Schuylkill, and Catawissa Railways). Auburn, 83 (connects with Schuylkill & Susquehanna Railway). Landingville, 86; Schuylkill Haven, 89 (connects with Mine Hill & Schuylkill Haven Railway). Pottsville, 93 (connects with Port Carbon and Schuylkill Valley Railways).

Catawissa Railway: Port Clinton, 78; Tamaqua, 98; E. Mahanoy Junction, 102 (connects with Schuylkill Railway). Quakake, 106 (connects with Lehigh Valley Railway). Summit, 109; Girard, 113; Mahanoy, 117; Ringtown, 122; Beaver, 129; McAuley, 135; Mainville, 138; Catawissa, 145; Rupert, 147 (connects with Lackawanna & Bloomsburg Railway). Danville, 154; Mooresburg, 160; Milton, 170 (connects with Philadelphia & Erie Railway). Watsontown, 175; Dewart, 177; Montgomery, 181; Muncy, 185; Williamsport, 187 (connects with Northern Central Railway).

The passenger station in Philadelphia is at the corner of Callowhill and Broad Streets. The Philadelphia and Reading road runs through the valley of the Schuylkill, a distance of 58 miles to Reading, and thence 35 miles to Pottsville, and connects the great anthracite coal-fields with tide-water. It was opened in 1842, and has cost upward of $16,000,000. It has several tunnels and numerous fine bridges.

In leaving the city by this line, the fine stone bridge over the Schuylkill is crossed in full view of Laurel Hill, Fairmount Park, and other objects of interest already noticed in our sketches of the vicinity of Philadelphia.

Norristown (17 miles) is the capital of Montgomery County, and has a population of about 15,000. The town is neatly and substantially built, and is especially noted for its Court-house, which is built of a light-gray marble. The town contains 11 churches, three boarding-schools, 14 factories, mills, etc., the county prison, and supports four newspapers. It is the eastern terminus of the Chester Valley Railway.

Valley Forge (23 miles) is memorable as the headquarters of General Washington during the winter of 1777. The building he occupied is still standing near the railroad, whence it can be seen.

Phœnixville (27 miles) is noted for its rolling-mill and furnaces, supposed to be the largest in the Union. It has a population of over 7,000. Within the township limits are mines of copper and iron. Near here the railroad passes through a tunnel nearly 2,000 feet in length. It was here that the iron for the dome of the Capitol at Washington was made.

Pottstown (40 miles) is prettily situated on the left bank of the Schuylkill. It was incorporated in 1815, and has a population of 6,000. The houses, which are built principally upon one broad street, are surrounded by fine gardens and elegant shade-trees. The scenery of the surrounding hills is very fine, especially in the fall of the year, when the foliage is tinged with a variety of rich autumnal tints. The *Reading Railroad* passes through one of its streets, and crosses the Manatawny on a lattice bridge, 1,071 feet in length.

Reading (58 miles) is the third city in the State in manufactures, and the fourth in population. It was founded in 1748 by William and Richard Penn. The plain on which Reading is built rises gradually from the Schuylkill River, and is enclosed on the East by Penn's Mount, which is several hundred feet high, and forms a part of the South Mountains. Among the most striking buildings in the city is the Court-house, a splendid building, 200 by 220 feet, with a portico, supported by six columns of red sandstone. The *Episcopal Church*, on North Fifth Street, is built of sandstone, and has a steeple 180 feet high. This church is considered one of the handsomest in the State. The *German Lutheran* is also a beautiful church, with a spire of 210 feet. The immense furnaces, mills, railroad-shops, etc., at this point give employment to more than 1,200 men. The capital employed is over $3,000,000, and the annual value of the manufactures exceeds $18,-000,000.

The principal places of interest in the vicinity of Reading are: The *Mineral Spring*, one mile and a half to the east; *Andalusia Hall*, one mile north, where there are fine accommodations for boarders, and the *White-House Hotel*, a mile and a half to the southeast, and about 300 feet above the river. *White Spot* on Penn's Mount, 1,000 feet above the river, is famed for its view. There are numerous hotels in Reading, the leading one being the *Mansion House*, one of the best kept in the State. The population is but a trifle over 34,000. The Lebanon Valley, Reading and Columbia, and East Pennsylvania Railroads connect here.

Hamburg (75 miles) is at the foot of the Blue Mountain.

Port Clinton (78 miles) is a pleasant place, at the mouth of the Little Schuylkill. This is the point of junction with the *Little-Schuylkill* and *Catawissa* roads.

Auburn (83 miles) is the connection of the Schuylkill and Susquehanna Railway.

Schuylkill Haven (89 miles), on the banks of the Schuylkill, is in the midst of a very interesting landscape region. The *Mine Hill* branch road (distance 24 miles) comes in here from the great coal-district.

Pottsville (93 miles) is the terminus of the Philadelphia and Reading route. It is upon the edge of the great coal-basin, in the gap by which the Schuylkill breaks through Sharp's Mountain. The annual yield of the Schuylkill coal-field is between 3,000,000 and 4,000,000 tons. This enormous product annually reaches market through the Reading Railway and Schuylkill Navigation Companies' lines. The city, commenced in 1825, has already a population of 15,000. The *Cathedral*, *Town-Hall*, and *Jail*, are worthy of notice. The mountains which surround Pottsville are too rugged and sterile for cultivation, and the town relies for its prosperity upon the mineral wealth in the vicinity. The Port Carbon and Schuylkill Valley railways connect at this point.

To pursue his journey over the wild and attractive *Catawissa Route*, the traveller will retrace his way to *Port Clinton*, 12 miles, or take the Schuylkill Valley road to *Tamaqua*, 17½ miles.

Tamaqua (98 miles) is beautifully situated on the Little Schuylkill, in the midst of a rich coal-region. The population is over 5,000.

E. Mahanoy Junction (102 miles) is the point of intersection with the Schuylkill Railway.

Quakake (106 miles) is the junction of the Lehigh Valley Railway.

Catawissa (145 miles) is in the midst of a varied and beautiful scenery, and the views from the surrounding hilltops are superb. The *Susquehanna* is a good hotel. The *Lackawanna* and *Bloomsburg Railway* intersects the Catawissa road at *Rupert*, two miles west of this place.

Danville (154 miles) has a population of between 8,000 and 10,000, and, being surrounded by mines of iron and coal, possesses unrivalled advantages for the manufacture of iron. The Montour Iron-Works are noted for their railroad iron. The Lackawanna and Bloomsburg Railway connects this place with Wilkesbarre and Scranton.

Milton (170 miles) is the largest town in Northumberland County. It is the junction of the road with the Philadelphia and Erie Railway, the track of which it follows to Williamsport.

Williamsport (197 miles) is the principal town on the west bank of the Susquehanna River. It is the capital of Lycoming County, is handsomely laid out, and contains a number of fine buildings. The population is variously estimated at from 18,000 to 22,000, and the city itself is ranked as one of the great business centres of the State. It is especially noted for its lumber manufactories, which are about fifty in number. Thirty of these are saw-mills, with an aggregate annual capacity of 225,000,000 feet of lumber. The great boom in the Susquehanna at this point will hold 300,000,000 feet of lumber at one time. Within two miles of the city are fine quarries of black marble, said to be almost inexhaustible, and the only quarries in the Middle, Western, or Southwestern States. The Dickinson Seminary is a noted educational institution. Among the hotels the *Herdic House*, the *City Hotel*, and the *American Hotel*, rank as first class. The Northern Central Railway (*see* page 140), and the Philadelphia and Erie, pass through this place.

ROUTE III.

FROM PHILADELPHIA TO ERIE AND THE OIL REGIONS, AND ACROSS NORTHWEST CORNER OF PENN-SYLVANIA.

Via Philadelphia and Erie Railway, Atlantic and Great Western Railway, Lake Shore Railway, and their connections.

This road properly commences at Sunbury, and was originally known as the *Sunbury and Erie Railway*. Passengers by this route pass over the Pennsylvania Railway to Harrisburg, and thence to Sunbury over the Northern Central Railway. In the following list of stations the distances given are from Philadelphia:

Sunbury, 163 miles (connects with Northern Central and Shamokin Railways); Northumberland, 165 (connects with Lackawanna and Bloomsburg Railway); Lewisburg, 172; Catawissa Junction, 175; Milton, 176 (connects with Catawissa Railway); Watsontown, 180; Dewart, 183; Montgomery, 187; Muncy, 191; Williamsport, 203; Newberry, 205; Linden, 208; Jersey Shore, 215; Wayne, 223; Lock Haven, 228 (connects with Bald Eagle Valley Railway); Whetham, 243; Renovo, 255; Keating, 267; Sinnemahoning, 280; Driftwood, 283; Sterling, 292; Cameron, 296; Emporium, 301; St. Mary's, 323; Ridgeway, 332; Wilcox, 347; Kane, 356; Wetmore, 361; Sheffield, 371; Pattonia, 378; Warren, 385; Irvineton, 390 (connects with Oil Creek and Alleghany Railway); Youngsville, 393; Pittsfield, 396; Garland, 400; Spring Creek, 406; Columbus, 411; Corry, 413 (connects with Atlantic and Great Western, Cross Cut, and Oil Creek Railways); Lovell's, 417; Concord, 419; Union, 424; Waterford, 432; Jackson's,

438; Erie, 451 (connects with all roads passing through or terminating at Erie).

In the following description only the principal stations will be mentioned:

Sunbury (163 miles) is pleasantly located on the east bank of the Susquehanna, and is the point of intersection of the *Philadelphia and Erie*, the *Northern Central*, and the *Shamokin Railways*.

Northumberland.—The west branch of the Susquehanna unites two miles above Sunbury with the main or north arm; and the village, the pleasantest of all the region round, is built upon the point formed by the confluence of the two waters. The quiet, cultivated air of Northumberland, and its excellent hotel (*Central*) will attract the not over-hurried traveller. From this point to Williamsport the river scenery is very fine.

A pleasant detour may be made from this point over the *Lackawanna and Bloomsburg Railway* to the Wyoming valley.

Milton (176 miles). Junction with Catawissa Railway. (*See* page 127.)

Williamsport (203 miles) has already been described. (*See* page 127.)

Lockhaven (228 miles) is one of the great centres of the lumber-trade, the annual amount of logs received in the boom on the West Susquehanna at this point being about 400,000,000 feet, which, when standing, covered about 100 square miles. The scenery in the vicinity is described as charming. In the town are many handsome residences, and three good hotels: the *Fulton House*, the *Irvin House*, and the *Montour House*. The population is between 6,000 and 8,000. Besides the Philadelphia and Erie and the Bald Eagle Valley Railroads, the town is connected with the "Bald Eagle Cross Cut," a feeder of the Pennsylvania Canal.

Renovo (255 miles) is a creation of the railroad. It is situated in a beautiful valley, surrounded by mountains. The air of the place is exceedingly healthy, and it is said that a fog is an unheard-of thing. This valley combines in itself beauty, healthy location, fertility, and fine trout-fishing. The construction-shops and founderies of the railroad company are located here, while in the vicinity are five fine veins of bituminous coal. The population, now about 1,500, is rapidly increasing.

Cameron (296 miles) is a small village, with a large hotel, and is owned by the Cameron Coal Company. This company own, and are now working, several veins of rich bituminous coal, which is particularly suitable for the generation of gas.

For the next forty miles the road passes through what, until its construction, was an unknown land, even to its nearest neighbors—a favorite refuge of outlawed criminals. It is the section of country known as the "*Great Horseshoe of the Alleghany*," which in its circuitous and rocky course encompassed and isolated it. The railroad has now changed all this, and its mineral and agricultural wealth is becoming known and developed.

Emporium (301 miles) is an entirely new town, having sprung from the merest village into existence as a town since 1863. It is the county-seat of Cameron County, and is rapidly growing. It is situated in the narrow valley of the Driftwater, a tributary of the Susquehanna, the sides of which rise abruptly from 700 to 1,000 feet. This place has been built up and supported chiefly by its large lumber interest. The vicinity is abundant in salt water, and in one well which has been bored the water was found equal to the best Salina water. It is therefore probable that the salt manufactures will become leading features of the region.

St. Mary's (323 miles) is surrounded by numerous veins of the richest bituminous coal, which are being worked by energetic companies. There are also veins of iron-ore and fire-clay, and an abundance of fine timber. There are two religious houses here: St. Mary's Convent of Benedictine Nuns, and St. Mary's Priory, a Benedictine monastery. The convent is the oldest of the order in the United States, and is called the "Mother House." The hotels at St. Mary's are the *Alpine House*, the *St. Mary's*, the *Luhr House*, and the *Franklin House*.

Ridgeway (332 miles) was laid out in 1843, and is a small but prosperous town. It is built on both sides of Clarion River, in a picturesque location. The large hemlock-forests in the vicinity will probably cause it to become the site of numerous tanneries. As throughout all this region, there are fine veins of bituminous coal. Population, 1,000. HOTEL: The *Hyde House*.

Wilcox (347 miles) is noted as the site of the largest tannery in the world. HOTEL: The *Wilcox House*.

Kane (356 miles) is where the road leaves the "unknown land," or "*Wildcat Country*." It is situated on what is called the Big Level, an undulating tableland four to eight miles in width, and 50 to 60 in length, from northeast to southwest, forming the boundary from north to south of the great coal and oil region of Northwestern Pennsylvania. *Kane* is at the narrowest point in this level, and is the summit whence trains descend by heavy grades to Lake Erie and to the Atlantic. It is designed to make this one of the principal places on the road. A fine hotel, repair, and locomotive shops, are now in operation. In view of the future prosperity of the place, and its becoming a popular summer resort, extensive hotel parks have been laid out, and also a public park of 600 acres. By the terms of the deeds conveying these parks, the original forest-trees are never to be cut down, nor can the land ever be devoted to any other purpose. The hotel has accommodations for from 300 to 400 guests.

Sheffield (371 miles) is noted for its immense tannery.

Warren (385 miles), on the Alleghany River at its junction with the Conewango, is one of the handsomest towns in the State, having wide rectangular streets. It contains the Warren County buildings, an academy, and, as both rivers are navigable, it has an extensive boat trade. It is the site of extensive tanneries, has an abundance of light sandstone for building-purposes, and lies between the coal and iron, and the oil regions of Pennsylvania, having communication with both. The Dunkirk, Warren, and Pittsburg Railway will pass through this place.

Irvineton (390 miles) is the junction of the Oil Creek and Alleghany River Railway, formerly Warren and Franklin Railroad, which leads directly into the oil regions; described under the head "Oil Regions," at the end of this route.

Corry (413 miles) is the junction of the Philadelphia and Erie, Atlantic and Great Western, and Buffalo, Corry, and Pittsburg Railways. It came into existence as the result of the discovery of oil, the first building ever erected there being a small eating-house, in August, 1861. It promises to become an important manufacturing town and railroad centre.

Erie (451 miles) opposite Presque Island, formerly a peninsula, is the Lake Erie terminus of the road. It is a flourishing place, with a large trade, and possesses a fine land-locked harbor 3¼ miles in length, and one in width, with a depth of water varying from 9 to 25 feet. This is one of the United States naval stations. The population is about 15,000. It contains a fine court house, an academy, several hotels, and twelve churches. The Erie Extension Canal connects the city with the Ohio River and Beaver Canal, and affords a fine water-power, which is used for a number of manufactories. Within a few years it has become one of the principal places for working Lake Superior iron, and has extensive rolling-mills. It is supplied with water which is forced by powerful engines to the top of a tower over 200 feet high, whence it is distributed by mains. The pressure is so great that, by affixing a pipe to one of the street fire-hydrants, water can be thrown over any building in the city. It was from Erie that Perry's fleet sailed on the occasion of his memorable victory. The *Erie and Pittsburg Railway* and the *Lake Shore Railway* connect with the Philadelphia and Erie at this point. The *Reid House* is the principal hotel. It is handsome, large, and well kept.

NEW YORK TO OHIO.

Via Lake Shore Railway.

This road passes along the southern shore of Lake Erie from Buffalo, N. Y., to Toledo, Ohio, crossing Pennsylvania. The stations in New York were not mentioned in the chapter on that State, as the only two of importance, Buffalo and Dunkirk, were described, the former in *Route V. of New York*, and the latter in *Route VII. of New York*. The only station of note in Pennsylvania is *Erie*, which is described above. (For the remainder of this road, see HAND-BOOK, WESTERN TOUR, Route II.)

NEW YORK TO OHIO.

Via Atlantic & Great Western Division of Erie Railway.

This great line extends from the city of New York to Cincinnati, Ohio, crossing the northwestern corner of the State of Pennsylvania. The portion in New York has been described in *Route VII. of New York*. The stations given below are those from the junction with the Erie Railway, to the Ohio State line. The distances given are from the New York City.

STATIONS.—Salamanca, 415 miles; Red House, 420; Steamburg, 425; Randolph, 431; Kennedy, 438; Jamestown, 448; Ashville, 454; Panama, 458; Freehold, 465; Columbus, 471; Corry, 474 (connects with Philadelphia and Erie, and Oil Creek and Alleghany River Railways); Union, 486; Mill Village, 493; Miller's, 498; Cambridge, 502; Venango, 505; Sægertown, 510; Meadville, 516 (Junction of Franklin and Oil City Branch); Sutton's, 524; Evansburg, 529; Adamsville, 534; Greeneville, 542; Clarksville, 548 (connects with Erie and Pittsburg Railway).

Salamanca (415 miles) is the junction with the Erie Railway (for description, see NEW YORK, Route VII.).

Jamestown, N. Y. (448 miles), is at the outlet of Chautauque Lake, upon which there is a small steamer which runs to *Maysville*, 21 miles distant. The lake furnishes water-power for several mills, manufactories, etc. The population is between 3,000 and 4,000. This is a popular summer resort.

Freehold (465 miles) is the first station in Pennsylvania, and is on the north boundary of the State, 15 miles from Warren. Population, 2,000.

Corry (474 miles) connects with *Philadelphia & Erie* and *Alleghany River* Railways.

Venango (505 miles) is on French Creek, along the banks of which are several of the principal wells in the oil region.

Meadville (516 miles) is a flourishing city, and the centre of a large trade with the oil region. It is one of the oldest towns west of the Alleghanies. It lies on the west bank of French Creek, at one time called Venango River. It is the seat of *Alleghany College*, founded in 1816, and of the *Western Theological Seminary*, founded in 1844. Among the more prominent edifices are several churches, a State arsenal, and an academy. The *Franklin and Oil City Branch* road to Reno and Oil City, 36 miles, comes in here. The *McHenry House* is the leading hotel, and is well kept. Population, 6,000.

Clarksville (548 miles) is the junction with the *Erie and Pittsburg Railway*, and is the last station in Pennsylvania.

(For continuation of this line, see OHIO, in WESTERN TOUR.)

OIL REGIONS.

The *Warren and Franklin Railway*, now consolidated with the Farmer's and Oil Creek Railway to form the Oil Creek and Alleghany River Railway, was not opened until 1866, previous to which time access to this region was only had from the North by way of *Corry*. The routes at present are: From New York via *Atlantic and Great Western* to *Corry* and *Meadville*: From Philadelphia via *Philadelphia and Erie* to *Irvineton*, or to *Corry*: From Pittsburg via *Alleghany Valley Railway* to *Franklin, Reno,* and *Venango City*, connecting at Franklin with the *Oil Creek and Alleghany River Railway.*

The most celebrated oil-wells, as yet discovered and operated on the American Continent, are located in the western part of Pennsylvania, principally in Venango, Crawford, and Warren Counties.

Oil Creek, which has become celebrated as the site of the richest oil-producing region of the continent at the present day, is a tortous mountain-stream, taking its rise in the northern part of the State of Pennsylvania, near the south line of Erie County, and, with its tributaries, waters Crawford and Warren Counties, and, after a course of about thirty miles through these counties, empties into the Alleghany River, seven miles above the town of Franklin. The valley through which Oil Creek takes its course is narrow, and flanked on each side by high and rugged hills, on the top of which are broad fields of excellent farming-land. The scenery on Oil Creek at one time, no doubt, was quite picturesque; but now the bottom-lands are dotted with tall derricks, wooden engine-houses, and iron smoke-stacks.

Petroleum, under the name of "Seneca oil"—so called from the tribe of Indians of that name who once inhabited the country—became early of great importance to the settlers, both as a medicine and for burning and lubricating purposes. The greater portion of the oil was obtained from two natural springs. One of these was in the immediate neighborhood of Titusville, on the lands now owned by the "Watson Petroleum Company" of New York, and on the spot where now stands the old "Drake Well." The other spring was on the farm of Hamilton McClintock, within four miles of the mouth of Oil Creek. During the year 1853, Dr. F. B. Brewer, of the firm of Brewer, Watson, & Co., conceived the idea of collecting surface-oil by means of absorbing it in blankets, and wringing the oil out. Great quantities were collected in this novel manner, and used for burning-purposes in the lumber-mills of the Oil Creek region. The oil produced from the oil springs became so necessary and useful as to suggest the formation of an oil company, in 1854, called "The Pennsylvania Rock-Oil Company." This was the first oil company ever formed, and preceded the sinking of any well, or before such a thing was suggested. Although Professor Silliman, of New Haven, had in 1854 analyzed the rock-oil, and pronounced upon its properties, no further developments of any importance took place until the winter of 1857, when Colonel E. L. Drake, of Connecticut, arrived at Titusville. He was the first man who attempted to bore for oil. He was obliged to go 50 miles to a machine-shop every time his tools needed repairing; but, after many delays and accidents, on the 29th day of August, 1859, at the depth of 69 feet 6 inches, he struck a vein of oil, from which he afterward pumped at the rate of 35 to 40 barrels per day. This is now known as the "Drake Well." It was the first well ever sunk for oil, and yielded the first

131

petroleum ever obtained by boring. One experiment followed another in rapid succession, until the different farms on Oil Creek became centres for oil operations. The Barnsdell, Mead, Rouse, and Crosley wells were opened in 1860. In 1861 numerous wells were sunk in the since famous localities known as the "McIllheny," "McClintock," "Tarr," and "Buchanan" farms. The Empire and the Sherman Wells were opened in 1862, and the Delameter Well in the following year. In fact, a complete furor of folly and speculation, arising mainly from geological ignorance, seems at that time to have seized hold of the public mind, and it is not hazarding much to say that more money changed from the hands of fools to the pockets of sharpers in that "oil fever" period, than the Government revenues for any one year.

The great excitement which prevailed, during the first few years subsequent to the discovery of oil in great quantities, has entirely subsided, and the business is now carried on in a systematic manner.

OIL CREEK AND ALLEGHANY RIVER RAILWAY.

This road runs in a curve through the heart of the oil region from *Irvineton* on the Philadelphia and Erie Railway, to *Corry* on the same road at its junction with the Atlantic and Great Western Railway.

STATIONS.—Irvineton, 390 miles from Philadelphia; Cobham, 9 miles from Irvineton; Tidioute, 15; East Hickory, 23; Jamison, 28; Tionesta, 30; Stewart, 35; Eagle Rock, 38; Oleopolis, 41 (connects with Oil City and Pithole Branch Railway, 7 miles long); Rockwood, 47; Oil City, 50 (connects with Franklin Branch of Atlantic and Great Western Railway); Rouseville, 54; Rynd Farm, 55; Tarr Farm, 56; Columbia, 56; Petroleum Centre, 57; Pioneer, 59; Shaffer, 61; Miller Farm, 62; Titusville, 68; Hydetown, 71; Tryonville, 76; Spartansburg, 86; Corry, 95 miles from Irvineton and 474 from N. Y.

FRANKLIN BRANCH OF ATLANTIC AND GREAT WESTERN RAILWAY.

This Branch, 36 miles in length, has but three stations of importance, Meadville, 516 miles from New York, Franklin, 28 miles from Meadville, and Oil City, 36 miles, where it connects with the Oil Creek and Alleghany River Railway, and the Alleghany Valley Railway to Pittsburg, and the Jamestown and Franklin Railway, which connects the routes centring at Franklin, with the Pittsburg and Erie Railway.

It is not necessary to refer to more than one or two of the principal places in this region, as they are all of the same general character, and are entirely devoid of interest, except such as is the result of the oil business.

Meadville was described under the head "Atlantic and Great Western Division of Erie Railway." (*See* page 130.)

Franklin is the great railroad centre of the region from whence all the main lines diverge, and is also connected with Pittsburg by a line of small steamers running on the Alleghany River. It is the county-seat of Venango County, and occupies the site of *Fort Franklin*, at the confluence of French Creek with the Alleghany River. The town was laid out in 1795, and is substantially built on high land. Population nearly 6,000. The *Exchange* is the principal hotel. (For railway connections, *see* lists of stations above.)

Oil City, the centre and chief city of the oil region, is on the Alleghany River, at the mouth of Oil Creek, which here enters the Alleghany, and is spanned by a bridge. It will afford the visitor, in a few short rambles, the best opportunity of witnessing the varied operations of obtaining, refining, barrelling, shipping, and generally manipulating the precious petroleum. It is not perhaps the most attractive place to pursue his researches—for the odor and aspect of every thing are smoky, oily, and dirty.

Oil Creek derives its name from a spring from which large quantities of bituminous oil are obtained—the Indians valuing it highly. It is claimed that when, by treaty, the Seneca nation sold the western part of the State, they made a reservation around this spring of one mile square. For about a mile above Oil City, on the right-hand side of the stream, the bank rises in an abrupt bluff, at the foot of which a very substantial road has been constructed. The city is built on the flats that run along the base of the high bluffs, and has but one street. Directly across the creek, on Cottage Hill, fine dwellings have been erected. (For means of access, consult tables of railroads, page 132.)

Titusville, 28 miles east of Meadville, and 27 miles south of Corry, by the Oil Creek and Alleghany River Railway, is in Crawford County. It is one of the most important towns in the oil region, and contains three banks and several churches and hotels. Of the last-named institutions, the *Crittenden* and *Bush* are the best. This is another good point from which to visit the oil wells and refineries which abound on the creek, both above and below the town.

Reno (4 miles from Franklin), on the Alleghany River, has obtained great prominence in connection with the oil business of this region. Here large quantities of oil are received, and shipped by river and rail. The view of the river at this point presents a characteristic phase of life in the oil region. The trains usually stop long enough to afford a good view of the town and river from the train. It is a station of the Alleghany Valley Railway, 129 miles from Pittsburg.

Venango City, 132 miles from Pittsburg, is the terminus of the Alleghany Valley Railway.

ROUTE IV.

PHILADELPHIA TO BETHLEHEM, EASTON, ALLENTOWN, WILKES-BARRE, LEHIGH AND WYOMING VALLEYS, SCRANTON, THE DELAWARE WATER-GAP, THE ERIE RAILWAY AT WAVERLY, GREAT BEND AND LACKAWANNA, AND THE PENN HAVEN & MOUNT CARMEL BRANCH OF THE LEHIGH VALLEY RAILWAY.

Via North Pennsylvania, Lehigh Valley, Lehigh and Susquehanna, and connecting Railways.

NORTH PENNSYLVANIA RAILWAY.

STATIONS.—Philadelphia: Fisher's Lane, 4; Green Lane, 5; Old York Road, 7; Abington, 10; Fort Washington, 14; Ambler, 15; Penllyn, 17; Gwynedd, 18; North Wales, 20; Lansdale, 22 (connects with Doylestown Branch); Hatfield, 25; Souders, 28; Sellersville, 32; Quakertown, 38; Coopersburg, 44; Centre Valley, 46; Hellertown, 50; Bethlehem, 54 (connects with Lehigh Valley and Lehigh and Susquehanna Railways).

The depot of this road, in Philadelphia, is corner of Berks and America Streets. The first fifteen miles of its length is now within the corporate limits of Philadelphia, and any places of interest have already been mentioned under the head of PHILADELPHIA.

Gwynedd (18 miles) is a Welsh settlement, with a population of about 2,000. Near it is a fine tunnel, which is one of the most extensive and costly works on the whole line. A single mile cost over $300,000.

Lansdale (22 miles) has a good hotel. The Branch to Doylestown diverges here.

Sellersville (32 miles) is where the road crosses *Landis Ridge*, which divides the waters of the Schuylkill and Delaware Rivers. From the summit one mile west of the station a fine view of Limestone Valley and Quakertown is obtained.

Hellertown (50 miles) has extensive iron and zinc mines, occupying the sites of the old Moravian farms. An extended view of the hills skirting the Lehigh valley is obtained in this vicinity. Settled in 1856. Population, 6,000.

Bethlehem, upon the Lehigh River, 54 miles from Philadelphia, and 87 miles from New York, is a delightful place to make a short stay *en route.* It is the principal seat of the United Brethren, or Moravians, in the United States, and was originally settled under Count Zinzendorf in 1741. The village contains a stone church, 142 feet long and 68 feet wide, and capable of seating 2,000 persons. It is the site of *Lehigh University,* which was inaugurated September 1, 1866. This university was founded by Hon. Asa Packer, who gave the land upon which it is located (56 acres) and in addition the sum of $500,000. The site is admirably chosen upon a declivity of the Lehigh Mountain range. It is surrounded by forest-trees, and has an unobstructed view of twenty miles. The *Moravian Boys' School* stands near the church, and there is also a *Moravian Female Seminary,* of high repute, founded in 1788.

133

The old Moravian buildings for the most part still remain, and the principal ones, which are built of stone and stand in Church Row at the foot of Broad Street, are in a good state of preservation. Washington in his retreat across the Delaware removed his hospital and supplies to this point, and the Moravians gave up these buildings for the use of the government. The banner which the "Single Sisters" of Bethlehem gave to Count Pulaski is now in the rooms of the Historical Society at Baltimore. Bethlehem is noted for its iron and zinc manufactories. It has several good hotels, among which the *Sun*, established in 1808, is the best.

The *Lehigh Valley* and *Lehigh and Susquehanna Railways* connect with the North Pennsylvania at this point. These two roads run parallel to each other from Easton to Pittston, generally on opposite banks of the Lehigh River. We give below the stations on each of these, but in our description shall confine ourselves to the Lehigh Valley Railway, which we shall follow to Waverly on the Erie Railway, making a digression at Penn-Haven junction. We shall then return to Pittston and follow the Lehigh and Susquehanna Railway to *Scranton* and *Green Ridge*. The Delaware Water-Gap and the road to Great Bend will be described in Route V., with which connection is made at *Scranton*. The distances given are from Easton, unless otherwise stated. To obtain distance from New York, add 86 miles. For distance from Philadelphia, add 54 miles.

LEHIGH VALLEY RAILWAY.

STATIONS.—Easton; Lime Ridge, 7 miles; Freemansburg, 9; Bethlehem, 12 (connects with North Pennsylvania Railway); East Pennsylvania Junction, 17 (connects with East Pennsylvania Railway); Allentown, 17; Furnace, 18; Catasauqua, 20 (connects with Catasauqua and Foglesville Railway); Hokendauqua, 21; Coplay, 22; White Hall, 24; Laury's, 26; Rockdale, 29; Slatington, 33; Lehigh Water Gap, 35; Parryville, 40; Lehighton, 42; Mauch Chunk, 46; Penn-Haven Junction, 53 (connects with branches to Hazelton and Audenried and Mount Carmel); Rockport, 61; Mud Run, 64; Hickory Run, 66; Tannery, 69; White Haven, 71; Fairview, 85; Newport, 92; Sugar Notch, 97; S. Wilkesbarre, 100; Wilkesbarre, 101; Plainsville, 106; Pittston, 110; L. & B. R. R. Junction, 111; Falls, 122; McKune's, 126; Tunkhannock, 134; Meshoppen, 148; Wyalusing, 166; Towanda, 186; Waverly Junction, 206 (connects with Erie Railway).

Easton (86 miles from New York and 66 miles from Philadelphia) is one of the great railroad centres of the country. It is the western terminus of the Central Railroad of New Jersey (*see* Route IV., NEW JERSEY), the Morris and Essex Railroad (*see* Route V., NEW JERSEY), and the Morris Canal. The Lehigh Valley Railroad and the Lehigh Coal Navigation Company's Railroad and Canal extend from here to the coal regions. By the Belvidere Delaware Railroad, it is connected with Philadelphia below, and with Belvidere, the Water-Gap, and the Lackawanna coal regions above (*see* Route IX., NEW JERSEY). The Allentown route, from Allentown through Harrisburg to Pittsburg, connects it with all points west.

The town is located at the junction of the Delaware, Lehigh, and Bushkill Rivers, and is regularly laid out. On the east is Lafayette College on Mount Lafayette, a richly-endowed institution, with a full staff of professors, an extensive library, and a fine mineral cabinet. *Durham Cave* is near here, and *Mount Jefferson* is an abrupt peak in the centre of the town. At Easton are extensive iron manufactories, as well as mills, distilleries, etc. There are several fine bridges, one of which, of iron, 500 feet long, is particularly noticeable. Easton has two banks and eight newspapers, is one of the most flourishing towns in Pennsylvania, and has a population of 15,000.

Lime Ridge (7 miles) is on the Lehigh River, and is noted for its beautiful scenery. A short distance below the station is Smith's Island, a favorite picnic ground.

Bethlehem (12 miles), junction with North Pennsylvania Railway. (*See* page 133.)

Allentown (17 miles) has two stations, one known as *Allentown*, the other, as *East Pennsylvania Junction*. It is a beautiful city, and is built upon an eminence between Jordan Creek and the Lehigh River. The streets are well laid out, and many of the houses are very pretty. It has large iron and other manufactories, and is at the junction of the East Pennsylvania Railroad, to Reading, with the road now under consideration. "*Big Rock*," 1,000 feet in height, is near the city, as are also several mineral springs. There are several hotels, the best of which is the *American*.

Catasauqua (20 miles) has a population of about 4,000. It has a large manufacturing interest, being especially noted for its large blast-furnaces, one of which turns out 250 tons of iron per week, a yield scarcely equalled elsewhere. The *Catasauqua and Fogleville Railway*, which comes in here, was built to bring coal and iron from the mines in the vicinity.

Slatington (33 miles) is in the most extensive slate region ever discovered. The slate on the capitol at Washington, half an inch in thickness, came from this place. The village is charmingly located about one-half mile from the station, and is a pleasant summer resort.

Lehigh Water-Gap (35 miles) or "The Gap" as it is familiarly known, is where the road crosses Lizard Creek, a small stream, that opens a path for the Lehigh River through Blue Mountain. Through this gap a distant view of the Lehigh Mountains can be obtained from the cars. The scenery is wild and inexpressibly grand.

Lehighton (42 miles) is on the Lehigh River, at the mouth of Mahoning Creek. The old Moravian Cemetery stands on a hill, from which may be had a fine view of the Mahoning Valley, and at the foot of which twelve settlers were murdered by the Indians in 1775. At *Weissport*, on the opposite side of the river, formerly stood Fort Allen, built by William Penn. There are here extensive iron works. Its site is occupied by the *Fort Allen Hotel*.

Mauch Chunk (46 miles), on the Lehigh, is noted as being in the midst of some of the wildest and most picturesque scenery in America, the town being surrounded by mountains rising abruptly from 700 to 1,000 feet. It is situated in the midst of extensive coal-beds, and its principal traffic is in " black diamonds." One of its most notable features is the inclined railroad up Mount Pisgah, and the Gravity road connected therewith. The coal-mines are situated nine miles back from the Lehigh River, and the coal is brought this distance with no other motive power than that of gravity. The empty cars ascend Mount Pisgah by means of an inclined plane with a stationary engine at the top (ascent 700 feet in 2,340); the cars then, over a downward grade, proceed by their own weight to Summit Hill, and thence to the mines in the valley. The loaded cars, by other inclined planes, are lifted to the Summit, and then run by gravity the entire distance to the river, where they are discharged into waiting boats. Small pleasure-cars for the use of travellers make this trip once a day, the jaunt being both novel and of great interest. Time required about three hours. The view from Mount Pisgah is remarkably fine, and the approach to the town on the Gravity road, which lies far below, huddled in among the hills, is very picturesque. The street scenes in Mauch Chunk are very quaint. The town is but one street wide, and the valley is so narrow that the houses are crowded up against the hill-sides, with outhouses and gardens perched above the roofs. Besides ascending Mount Pisgah and viewing the coal-mines, the tourist will do well to visit *Moer's Falls* on Moer's Creek, near the "*Turn Hole*" in the Lehigh River. They are three in number, being respectfully 40, 70, and 35 feet high, and *Prospect Rock*, near the Mansion House. The *Mansion House* is the principal hotel.

Penn Haven Junction (53 miles) is surrounded by the wildest scenery. It is at the mouth of Quakake Creek, and is at the junction of the branches to *Mahanoy and Mount Carmel* and to *Hazleton and Audenried*. The first of these, 46 miles in length, intersects the *Catawissa Railway* at *Quakake*, and the *Shamokin Valley and Mine Hill Railway* at *Mount Carmel*. The road to *Hazleton and Audenried* crosses the mountain opposite the station, to the coal-mines. The inclined planes by which it descends the mountain can be seen from the cars. Near here the road crosses the Lehigh by an iron bridge, from which can be seen the tunnel of the Lehigh and Susquehanna Railway.

Whitehaven (71 miles) has a population of about 1,500. The road here crosses the river, affording a good opportunity to see the large dams at this point, which are usually filled with immense numbers of logs. This town is called after Whitehaven in England, remarkable for having the deepest coal-mine in the world.

Fairview (85 miles) is the summit of the mountain, and the descent to the Wyoming Valley commences.

New Port (92 miles) is near the top of the mountain, and affords a perfectly magnificent view of the Wyoming Valley. The Susquehanna is visible for more than 20 miles, from its entry through Lackawannock Gap near Pittston, to its departure through Nanticoke Gap near Shickshinny. Solomon's Gap, where the Lehigh and Susqehanna Railway formerly crossed the mountain by a series of inclined planes, is also visible. These planes are only used now for heavy coal-trains.

Wilkesbarre (101 miles) is situated on the Susquehanna River, in the *Wyoming Valley*. It is reached by the following railroads: *Lehigh Valley, Lehigh and Susquehanna*, and *Lackawanna and Bloomsburg*. (For description, see page 138).

Pittston (110 miles) is the point where this road intersects the Lackawanna and Bloomsburg railway. (For description, see page 138).

Tunkhannock (134 miles), the county seat of Wyoming County, is at the mouth of Tunkhannock Creek, on the Susquehanna River, and is a thriving place of 1,000 inhabitants.

Towanda (186 miles) is the last station in Pennsylvania. It is at the mouth of Towanda Creek, on the Susquehanna, and has a population of about 2,000.

Waverly Junction (206 miles) is the point where this road connects with the Erie Railway. (*See* Route VII. of NEW YORK.)

LEHIGH AND SUSQUEHANNA RAILWAY.

STATIONS.—All the stations of note on this line have been described in the account of the Lehigh Valley Railway as far as Pittston, where the two roads diverge. The remaining stations on this line are Spring Brook, 113 miles from Easton, Minooka, 116, Scranton, 119 (connects with Delaware, Lackawanna and Western Railway); Green Ridge, 120 (connects with Delaware and Hudson Railway).

Scranton, formerly called Lackawanna (119 miles), is an important manufacturing town, being especially noted for its immense iron-works and its great coal-trade. It was incorporated as a city in 1866, and is handsomely laid out with broad streets. It boasts of 24 churches and 4 academies, besides numerous handsome residences, fine stores, etc. It is the junction of the *Delaware, Lackawana and Western*, the *Lehigh and Susquehannna*, and the *Lackawanna and Bloomsburg, Railways*. Passengers for *Binghamton*, via the Erie Railway, take the trains northward; and for the Delaware Water-Gap, the trains southward on the D., L. and W. Railway, which is described as Route V. Passengers for *Lackawanna* take the L. and B. Railway, which is also described in Route V.

ROUTE V.

FROM PHILADELPHIA OR NEW YORK, TO THE DELAWARE WATER-GAP, TO THE ERIE RAILWAY AT BINGHAMTON, AND TO SUNBURY ON THE PHILADELPHIA AND ERIE.

Via Delaware, Lackawanna, and Western, Lackawanna and Bloomsburg, and Pennsylvania Coal Company's Railways.

DELAWARE, LACKAWANNA, AND WESTERN RAILWAY.

THIS line of road, and under four different names, extends from Jersey City to Oswego, on the shore of Lake Ontario, crossing the States of New Jersey, Pennsylvania, and New York. The portion in New Jersey known as the *Morris and Essex Railway* has been described in *Route V. of New Jersey*. The portion in New York is known as the *Oswego and Syracuse* Division (page 86), and the *Syracuse, Binghamton and New York* Division (page 83). This road is reached from New York by the *Morris and Essex Railway*, which connects at Washington, 71 miles from Jersey City, and by the *Central Railway of New Jersey* which connects at Washington by a branch from *New Hampton*, or "Junction Station." (See Route IV. of NEW JERSEY.)

The connection from Philadelphia is by the *Belvidere Delaware Railway* described as Route IX. of New Jersey. The distances given are from New York. To obtain the distance from Philadelphia, add 16 miles to the distance from New York.

STATIONS.—Manunka Chunk, 82 miles; Delaware, 84; Mount Bethel, 87; Water-Gap, 92; Stroudsburg, 96; Spragueville, 101; Henryville, 104; Oakland, 109; Forks, 115; Tobyhanna, 122; Gouldsboro, 128; Moscow, 136; Dunning, 139; Scranton, 149 (connects with Lackawanna and Bloomsburg Railway, and Delaware and Hudson Canal Company's Railway); Clark's Summit, 156; Abington, 159; Factoryville, 164; Nicholson, 170; Hopbottom, 176; Montrose, 183; New Milford, 190; Great Bend, 196; connects at Great Bend with the Erie Railway, and with the line to Lake Ontario.

Manunka Chunk, N. J. (82 miles), is the junction of the Belvidere Delaware Railway. Within sight of the station the Delaware, Lackawanna, and Western Railway passes through the Manunka Chunk Mountain by the Voss Gap Tunnel, about 1,000 feet long, and through which also runs a small stream of water.

Delaware, N. J. (84 miles), is the last station in New Jersey, the road crossing the Delaware into Pennsylvania over a long bridge. All trains stop here for meals.

Mount Bethel (87 miles) is at the verge of the celebrated "Delaware Water-Gap," and may fairly be said to be under the shadow of the "*Blue Mountains.*" From this point the scenery is grand beyond description.

Delaware Water-Gap (92 miles) is where the Delaware River forces its way through the Blue Mountains, after a journey of about 200 miles through a wild, rugged, and romantic country. It rises from two sources in the Catskill Mountains, the two branches uniting at Hancock, on the Erie Railway; thence it forms the boundary between New York and Pennsylvania as far as Port Jervis, on the Erie road, where it turns to the southwest and runs along the base of the *Kittatinny* or *Blue Mountain*, until it finds a passage through this Gap. The Gap is about two miles long, and is a narrow gorge between walls of rocks some 1,600 feet in height, and so near to each other at the southeastern entrance as hardly to leave room for the railroad.

Among the numerous places of interest is *Moss Cataract*, where a small stream of water, tumbling down the moss-covered side of the Kittatinny Mountain, scatters its spray in all directions. *Lover's Leap* (for this, like most other well-known resorts in the United States, possesses the original) affords a fine view. *Prospect Rock* is at the end of a wearisome climb of two miles, but once reached repays the visitor with the finest and most extensive view in the vicinity. The mountain on the right of the track is "Jersey Mountain," that on the left "Kittatinny." Above the station, on the mountain from which it takes its name, stands the *Kittatinny House*, a good hotel. As the road emerges from the Gap, it crosses Broadhead's Creek, and passes through a cut in "Rock Difficult," so called from the difficulty in making a passage through its flinty mass.

Stroudsburg (96 miles) is the first station beyond the Gap. Two miles from the station and three from the Gap is a pleasant summer resort, the *Highland Dell House.*

Spragueville (101 miles). Here the ascent of Pocono Mountain, the eastern slope of the Alleghany range, commences, the grade for 25 miles being at the rate of 65 feet to the mile.

Oakland (109 miles). Just beyond this station the road passes through the Pocono Tunnel near the top of the mountain, a point from which the view, extending more than 30 miles, is most sublime.

Tobyhanna (122 miles) is the point where the descent of the western slope of the mountain commences.

Moscow (136 miles) is in the midst of a lumber-district. Game and trout abound in the vicinity. Its hotels are *Moscow and Delaware, Lackawanna and Western.*

Dunning (139 miles) is a small

village. The railroad which is here seen on the opposite side of *Roaring Brook* is the *Pennsylvania Coal Company's Railroad* which extends from Pittston on the Susquehanna to Hawley on the Delaware and Hudson Canal, where it connects with the *Hawley Branch* of the Erie Railway from Lackawaxen.

Scranton (149 miles) connects with *Lackawanna and Bloomsburg* and *Delaware and Hudson Canal Company's*, and *Pennsylvania Coal Company's Railways*. (*See* page 136.)

Factoryville (164 miles) is a thriving village, having several mills.

Great Bend (196 miles). Here the road connects with the Erie Railway, the track of which it follows to Binghamton to connect with its northern divisions. (*See* Route VII. of NEW YORK, and pages 83 and 86.)

LACKAWANNA AND BLOOMSBURG RAILWAY.

This road is operated as a branch of the one just described. The distances given below are from *Scranton*. For distances from New York, add 147 miles. For distances from Philadelphia, *via Belvidere Delaware Railway*, add 166 miles.

STATIONS.—Scranton ; Lackawanna, 6 miles ; Pittston, 9 (connects with Lehigh and Susquehanna and Lehigh Valley Railways) ; Wyoming, 13 ; Kingston, 17 ; Plymouth, 20 ; Nanticoke, 25 ; Hunlock's Creek, 27 ; Shickshinny, 32 ; Hick's Ferry, 37 ; Beach Haven, 41 ; Berwick, 43 ; Lime Ridge, 50 ; Bloomsburg, 56 ; Rupert, 58 (connects with Catawissa Railway) ; Catawissa Bridge, 60 ; Dunville, 68 ; Chulasky, 71 ; Northumberland, 80 (connects with Philadelphia and Erie, and Northern Central Railways).

This road traverses the celebrated Wyoming valley throughout its length, and therefore, before commencing the description of the principal towns, we will give a brief notice of the valley.

The Wyoming Valley is about 25 miles long and 3 miles wide, being formed by two parallel ranges of mountains ; averaging, on the west, about 800 and on the east 1,000 feet in height. It is reputed one of the most beautiful on the continent. The *Wyoming Massacre* took place in this valley on the 3d of July, 1778, and, as in the Cherry Valley massacre, the victors spared no one, killing all their prisoners.

Pittston (9 miles) is where this road intersects the *Lehigh Valley* and *Lehigh and Susquehanna Railways*. It is on the Susquehanna, just below the mouth of Lackawanna Creek, from which point it follows the river to Northumberland. West of the town are the Lackawannock Mountains, filled with rich coal-mines, which here find an outlet. A prominent object of interest in the vicinity is *Campbell's Ledge*, a point from which a charming view of the valley is obtained.

Kingston (17 miles) is opposite Wilkesbarre, with which it is connected by a bridge. Within its limits is the site of "*Fort Forty*," where the Wyoming Valley massacre took place, the spot being marked by the *Wyoming Monument*, an obelisk of granite 62½ feet high, with appropriate inscriptions. In this township there still exists, on the north side of *Toby's Creek*, about 150 feet from the bank, and half a mile from the Susquehanna, a defensive mound which was erected by some race who inhabited the country even before the Indians, who had no traditions concerning their builders or their design.

Wilkesbarre (18 miles), on the opposite bank of the Susquehanna, the largest town in the valley, was settled in 1773. Its broad, well-shaded streets add much to its attractions, while from the facts that 9 or 10 large coal-mines here find a place of shipment, and that there are a number of manufactories in active operation, its importance as a business centre is by no means inconsiderable. A bridge across the river connects it with Kingston. The population is 5,000. Its attractions to the tourist consist in its charming vicinage, and the historical interest connected with it. In the rear of the town is *Prospect Rock*, from which a good view of the valley can be obtained. The *Lehigh Valley*, *Lehigh and Susquehanna*, and *Lackawanna and Bloomsburg* Railways, afford ample means of communication with the sea-board. The leading hotels are the *Wyoming* and *Phœnix Houses*. One of the principal resorts in the vicinity of Wilkesbarre is *Harvey's Lake*, which abounds in fish, and around which is capital hunting. There is a hotel here, called the *Lake House*.

Plymouth (20 miles) is not far from the Wyoming Falls of the Susquehanna, about the middle of the valley.

Nanticoke (25 miles) is a little coal village, near the southern extremity of the valley. Looking northward from the hills on the east side of the river near here, a beautiful view of the Wyoming is presented, and the scenes below, from the banks of the river and the canal, are most varied and delightful. Two or three miles below, is *Jessup's*, a very cosy, lone inn, upon the west shore, whence are seen striking pictures of the river and its bold mountain-banks both above and below. The hills in all this vicinity are impressively bold and lofty, making the comparatively narrow channel of the river seem yet narrower, and enhancing the quiet beauty of the many verdant islands which stud its waters.

Shickshinny (32 miles), at the outlet of the valley, is a little place in the midst of a rugged hill and valley country. The Bank of Wapwollopen, on the east shore, is the barren peak of its namesake mountain. All the streams from Nanticoke down are adorned with cascades of great beauty, and abound in trout, and the river with salmon. From this point there is a little of especial interest to the tourist, except the fine river and mountain scenery along the entire length of the road, the towns all possessing the same characteristic iron manufactories and coal-mines.

Rupert (58 miles) is the point of connection with the *Catawissa Railway*. (*See* Route II.)

Danville (68 miles) is also on the Catawissa Railway. (For description, see page 127.)

Northumberland (80 miles), the terminus of the road at its junction with the *Philadelphia and Erie Railway*, has been described on page 128.

ROUTE VI.

EASTON TO READING, HARRISBURG, AND THE CUMBERLAND VALLEY.

Via "Allentown Line," consisting of the Lehigh Valley Railway, and the East Pennsylvania and Lebanon Valley Branches of the Philadelphia and Erie Railway connecting with the Cumberland Valley Railway.

THE distances given are from Easton, which is 85 miles from New York, until the Cumberland Valley Railway is reached, when distances are given from Harrisburg, which is 182 miles from New York, 107 from Philadelphia, and 248 from Pittsburg.

STATIONS.—"*Allentown Line*," Lehigh Valley Railway, Easton; Lime Ridge, 7 miles; Freemansburg, 9; Bethlehem, 12 (connects with North Pennsylvania Railway); Allentown, 17; *East Pennsylvania Railway*, Emaus, 23; Alburtis, 29; Shamrock, 32; Topton, 34; Bowers, 37; Lyons, 38; Fleetwood, 42; Blandon, 45; Temple, 48; Reading, 53; *Lebanon Valley Railway*, Robesonia, 66; Womelsdorf, 68; Myerstown, 75; Lebanon, 81; Palmyra, 91; Hummelstown, 98; Harrisburg, 107 (connects with all Railways passing through Harrisburg).

STATIONS.—*Cumberland Valley Railway*, Harrisburg, Shiremanstown, 5 miles; Mechanicsburg, 9; Kingston, 13; Middlesex, 15; Carlisle, 18; Good Hope, 23; Alterton, 26; Newville, 30; Oakville, 35; Shippensburg, 41; Scotland, 47; Chambersburg, 52; Marion, 58; Greencastle, 63 (connects with daily stages to Mercersburg and Waynesboro', Pa.); State Line, 68; Morgantown, 70; Hagerstown, 74 (connects with Baltimore and Ohio Railway and with stages to Martinsburg, Hancock, and Frederick City, Md.).

Easton (*see* page 134).

Lime Ridge (7 miles). (*See* page 134.)

Bethlehem (12 miles). (*See* page 133.)

Allentown (17 miles). (*See* page 134.)

Alburtis (29 miles). A branch road to the mines intersects at this point.

Lyons (38 miles) is a small village. It is the only place at which express trains stop between Reading and Allentown. Numbers of visitors resort to this place during the summer. The hotels are the *American*, and *Lyons House*. From here to Reading the road passes through a handsome and exceedingly fertile section of country. About 1½ miles from Lyons is *Kutztown*, an old and well-known town, beautifully situated in a rich farming district, and the seat of the Keystone State Normal School. Population, 1,700.

Reading (53 miles). (*See* p. 126.)

Wernersville is nine miles from Reading, on the line of the road, to the south of which on the mountains is *Ephrata Springs*, a very popular resort for invalids. Near the springs is an extensive water-cure called the *Hygiene House*.

Womelsdorf (68 miles), one of the largest towns in Berks County, is within one mile of the road. Near it is a large and beautiful spring, where a fine hotel has been built, which is a favorite resort for picnic parties from Harrisburg and Reading. The *South Mountain House* is much frequented.

Lebanon (81 miles), on the Swatara River, is the capital of Lebanon County, and is a large and prosperous place. Seven miles south of the town are the Cornwall Ore Banks, which are three hills formed of masses of iron-ore, and called Grassy, Middle, and Big Hill. It has been estimated that Big Hill contains 40,000,000 tons of ore above the surface of the ground, yielding 70 per cent. of pure iron to the ton. Veins of copper are found among the iron, and six miles from Lebanon a quarry of fine gray marble has been opened. Population, about 10,000.

Hummelstown (98 miles) is a pretty village on the Swatara River. A large *cave* to the south of the village is an interesting place to visit. The first chamber is 400 feet in length, at the end of which there is a descent of twenty feet to the principal cavern, which is some four miles long, and possesses all the usual features of limestone caves.

Harrisburg (107 miles) is where the traveller changes cars. If he is going west, he takes the *Pennsylvania Central*; if north or south, the *Northern Central*; if bound for Chambersburg and the Cumberland Valley, he takes the Cumberland Valley Railway. (For description, *see* Route I., page 120.)

CUMBERLAND VALLEY RAILROAD.

Carlisle is a beautiful and interesting town, with a population of 7,000. It lies in the limestone valley country, between the Kittatinny and the South Mountains. *Dickinson College* (Methodist), which is located in Carlisle, is one of the most venerable and esteemed institutions in Pennsylvania. General Washington's headquarters were here in 1794, at the time of the Whiskey Rebellion. Some years before, Major André was a prisoner of war in Carlisle. It was shelled by the rebels during their invasion of the State (July, 1863). *Carlisle Springs*, four miles north of the town, is a place of pleasant summer resort.

Chambersburg (52 miles) is pleasantly situated, surrounded by a highly-cultivated country, forming part of the limestone valley which extends along the south base of the Blue Mountain. Conechocheague Creek flows through the town. It reaches from Philadelphia, via Harrisburg, or from Baltimore by the *Baltimore and Ohio Railway*, to Frederick; thence by stage to Hagerstown. Hotel, *Brown's*.

Hagerstown (74 miles), capital of Washington County, Maryland, with a population of about 5,000, is a prosperous place, 26 miles northwest of Frederick, from which it may be easily reached by stage. It is pleasantly situated on the west bank of Antietam Creek, nine miles from the Potomac River. It is well located in the midst of a fine agricultural district, is well built, and contains several substantial edifices. The *Washington* is the principal hotel. The Baltimore and Ohio Railway connects at this point.

ROUTE VII.

BALTIMORE, MARYLAND, TO GETTYSBURG, PENNSYLVANIA, AND TO ELMIRA, NEW YORK.

Via Northern Central Railway.

THIS road, having neither of its termini in Pennsylvania, crosses the State from north to south, and is essentially a Pennsylvania route. In the following description no especial mention will be made of any except Pennsylvania towns. The distances are given from Baltimore.

STATIONS.—Baltimore (connects with railways diverging from Baltimore); Relay, 7 miles (connects with Western Maryland Railway); Timonium, 12; Cockeysville,15; Monkton, 23; Parkton, 29; Freelands, 35; Glenrock, 42; Hanover Junction, 46 (connects with Hanover Branch, and Gettysburg Railway); Glatfelters, 49; York, 57 (connects with Wrightsville, York, and Columbia Railway); Goldsborough, 72; Bridgeport, 84 (connects with Cumberland Valley Railway); Harrisburg, 85 (connects with Pennsylvania Central, Lebanon Valley, and Schuylkill and Susquehanna Railways); Marysville 91; Dauphin, 93; Clark's Ferry, 99; Halifax, 106; Millersburg, 111; Georgetown, 122; Trevorton Junction, 126; Selin's Grove, 133; Sunbury, 138 (connects with Philadelphia and Erie Railway); Williamsport, 178, (connects with Catawissa Railway); Trout Run, 192; Ralston, 202; Canton, 218; West Granville, 225; Troy, 231; Columbia X Roads, 236; Elmira, 256 (connects with Erie Railway and with branches for Rochester and Niagara Falls).

Hanover Junction (46 miles) is the first station in Pennsylvania which we shall mention. Its principal importance lies in the fact that it is the junction of the Gettysburg Branch road, 30 miles in length.

Gettysburg, the county town of Adams County, and the western terminus of the *Gettysburg Railway*, is pleasantly situated on a gently rolling and fertile plain, surrounded by hills, from which extensive views of the village and adjacent country are obtained. It is 69 miles from Harrisburg, and 76 from Baltimore, *via* Hanover Junction. It is reached from New York in one day, by the *Jersey Central Railway* to Reading, and thence, *via* Columbia and York. The principal hotel is the *Eagle*, which has accommodation for about 80 guests. The Lutheran *Theological Seminary*, founded in 1826, and the *Pennsylvania College*, are among the most prominent institutions of the place. The former has a fine library. A *mineral spring*, possessing valuable medicinal qualities, forms one of the novel and attractive features of the place. The water is said to resemble that of the celebrated Vichy Springs in Germany.

A great battle was fought on the 1st, 2d, and 3d of July, 1863, between the Union forces, under General Meade, and the Confederate army, under General Lee, in which the latter was defeated, with a loss in killed, wounded, and prisoners, of 23,000 men.

A day, well employed, will suffice to show the stranger, at Gettysburg, the battle-field and cemetery, while a second and third may be spent in visiting the springs and the several objects of interest in and round the village. The best approach to the battle-field is that by the Baltimore turnpike, which leads southwardly from the village directly to Cemetery Hill, distant half a mile from the Eagle Hotel. *Cemetery Hill* forms the central and most striking feature at Gettysburg. Here General Howard established his headquarters; upon this point the heaviest fire of the enemy was concentrated; and here is most appropriately located the National Cemetery, where are interred a large number of the Union soldiers who fell during the engagement. It was known as Cemetery Hill long before the battle, the eastern slope of it having been enclosed and used as the village burying-ground. The view from the crest of the hill is open and extended, affording every facility for following the movements of the respective armies. The *Village Cemetery*, sometimes called the Citizens' Cemetery, in contradistinction to the National or Soldiers' Cemetery, which adjoins it, is entered through a lofty arched gateway from the Baltimore road. Following the main avenue southward, a short walk brings the visitor to a circular lot, almost covered with stones, which are to be used in the construction of a vault. They present an aspect at once striking and suggestive. They cover the spot selected by General Howard on the morning of the engagement as his headquarters, and the heaviest fire of the rebel batteries, numbering nearly two hundred guns, was concentrated. The marble monument erected to General Gettys, the founder and early proprietor of Gettysburg, occupies a prominent position on the right of the avenue between the entrance and this lot. Standing on Cemetery Hill, the visitor has the key to the position of the Union forces during those eventful "three days of July." Cemetery Hill proper is

141

the termination of the ridge which runs southward, between the roads leading respectively to Taneytown and Emmettsburg. Westward the horizon is bounded by the long range of the "South Mountain," beyond which lie Chambersburg and Hagerstown. In the same direction, a little to the right, and rather more than a mile distant, is the *Seminary*, near which began the battle of the 1st, which terminated so disastrously to Reynolds's corps. From Seminary Ridge, General Lee opened a furious bombardment of the Union position on Cemetery Hill. On the gateway to the Cemetery are inscibed the names (eighteen in number) of the States represented by those buried within. The *monument*, the foundation of which was laid November 19, 1863, was dedicated July 4, 1868. It is 60 feet high, and crowned with a statue of Liberty. At the base of the pedestal are four buttresses, surmounted with allegorical statues, representing War, History, Peace, and Plenty. The monument occupies the crown of the hill, and around it, in semicircular slopes, are ranged the dead, each State being represented by a separate section. The divisions between the States are marked by alleys and pathways, radiating from the monument to the outer circle, the coffin-rows being divided by continuous granite blocks about six inches high, upon which are inscribed the name and regiment of each soldier, as far as ascertained. Between Emmettsburg pike and Cemetery Hill lies the scene of Pickett's bloody and disastrous charge, in which, 18,000 men are estimated to have been engaged. Following Cemetery Ridge, and keeping before him Round Top Mountain, a short walk will bring the visitor to one of the most interesting spots on this famous battle-field. This is a bunch of wood to which a few of the boldest and bravest of Pickett's charging column, on the 2d July, attained. *Seminary Ridge, College Hill, Culp's Hill, Round Top,* and *Little Round Top,* are generally visited; and *Willoughby Run,* where General Buford's cavalry held in check the rebel column under Hill for nearly two hours, is pointed out.

York (57 miles) is ten miles southwest of the Susquehanna, upon the Codorus Creek, 28 miles south-southeast of Harrisburg, and 92 from Philadelphia.

With all these cities, and with yet other points, it is connected by railway. The *Northern Central Railway* unites at York with the *Wrightsville, York, and Columbia Railway*. The Continential Congress met here in 1777, during the occupation of Philadelphia by the British troops. The *Court-House* is an imposing granite edifice, built in 1842, at a cost of $150,000. The *National Hotel* has good accommodation for visitors. Population, 12,000.

Harrisburg (85 miles) has been described in Route I. (*See* page 120.)

Susquehanna River. The line of the *Northern Central Railway* follows the Susquehanna, from a few miles below Harrisburg, to Sunbury, and then runs along the bank of the Western Branch, as far as Williamsport. This is the largest and most beautiful of the rivers of Pennsylvania, traversing as it does its entire breadth from north to south, and in its most interesting and most important regions. It lies about midway between the centre and the eastern boundary of the State, and flows in a zigzag course, now southeast, and now southwest, and so on over and over, following very much the windings of the Delaware, which separates the State from New Jersey. The Pennsylvania Canal accompanies it throughout its course, from Wyoming on the north to the Chesapeake Bay on the south. All the great railroads intersect or approach its waters at some point or other, and the richest coal-lands of the State lie contiguous to its banks. The main branch rises in Otsego Lake, in the east central part of New York, and pursues a very tortuous but generally southwest course. This main, or North, or East branch, as it is severally called, when it reaches the central part of Pennsylvania, after a course of 250 miles, is joined at Northumberland by the West Branch, 200 miles long, which flows from the declivities of the Alleghanies. The course of this arm of the river is nearly eastward, and, like the North Branch, through a country abounding with coal and other valuable products. It is also followed by a canal for more than a hundred miles up. The route of the *New York and Erie Railway* is upon or near the banks of North Branch of the Susquehanna in Southern New York, and occasionally across the Pennsylvania line for 50 miles, first touching the river near the Cascade Bridge, nearly 200 miles from New York, passing the cities of Binghamton and Owego, and finally losing sight of it just beyond Barton, 250 miles from the metropolis. The scenery along the line from Harrisburg to Williamsport is very fine, but none of the stations possess any special attractions for the tourist.

Sunbury. (138 miles) has been described in Route III., page 128.

Williamsport (178 miles). (*See* Route II., page 127.)

Columbia Cross Roads (236 miles) is the last station in Pennsylvania.

Elmira (256 miles), the terminus of the road and junction with the *Erie Railway*, and branches for the north, has been described in Route VII. of New York.

RAILROADS NOT DESCRIBED.

Of the other railways in Pennsylvania, the tourist will find descriptions as follows:

To the West, from Pittsburg, in the HAND-BOOK, WESTERN TOUR. *To the South*, from Philadelphia, in HAND-BOOK, SOUTHERN TOUR. The principal places on the lines of road lying entirely within the State have already been mentioned in the descriptions of the main lines, with which these shorter roads connect.

CONNECTICUT.

The scenery of Connecticut is delightfully varied by the passage of the Connecticut, the Housatonic, and other picturesque rivers; and of several low hill-ranges. Spurs of the Green Mountains rise here and there, in isolated groups or points through the western portions of the State. The Talcot, or Greenwood's, Range extends from the northern boundary almost to New Haven. Between this chain and that in the extreme west, lies another ridge, with yet two others on the eastward—the Middletown Mountains, and the line across the Connecticut, which is a continuation, most probably, of the White Hills of New Hampshire. Lying between these mountain-ranges are valleys of great luxuriance and beauty. The valley of the Connecticut, now traversed by rail through a greater part of its length, affords some of the most picturesque scenery in New England. The lakes among the mountains of the northwestern corner of the State are extremely attractive. The Long Island Sound, which waters the entire coast of Connecticut, is 140 miles long and 24 wide, and affords some fine scenery. If we except a small trading-house built by the Dutch at Hartford, in 1631, the first colony planted in Connecticut was the settlement of some of the Massachusetts emigrants at Windsor. Soon afterward Hartford fell into the possession of the English colonists. Wethersfield was next occupied, in 1636, and New Haven in 1638. The State had its share of Indian troubles in its earlier history, and of endurance, later, in the days of the Revolution. Hartford and New Haven are the capitals, and chief cities of the State. Norwalk, Bridgeport, and New London, are all important and prosperous places.

ROUTES.—The situation of Connecticut, and its system of railways, running through rather than terminating within its borders, renders it impossible to select any point within the State as a centre from which to cause a system of routes to radiate. The plan which will be followed will be to make the line of railroad from New York, along the shore of Long Island Sound the entire length of the State, the initial route; then to take the roads running north from this line, as they connect in succession from west to east, and finally to take the line of road crossing the centre of the State from east to west.

ROUTE I.

NEW YORK TO NEW HAVEN, NEW LONDON, STONINGTON, AND POINTS IN RHODE ISLAND AND EASTERN MASSACHUSETTS.

Via New York and New Haven, and Shore Line Railways.

STATIONS.—New York, City Hall (passengers take city cars, opposite the Astor House, at least 30 minutes earlier than time given for leaving Twenty-seventh Street); Twenty-seventh Street and Fourth Avenue, 2; Forty-second Street, 3; Harlem, 8; Williams Bridge, 14 (New York and New Haven Railway diverges from New York and Harlem Railway); Mount Vernon, 17; New Rochelle, 20; Mamaroneck, 24; Rye, 27; Port Chester, 29; Greenwich, 31; Cos Cob, 32; Stamford, 37; Noroton, 39; Darien, 41; Norwalk, 45 (connects with Danbury and Norwalk Railway); Westport, 48; Southport, 52; Fairfield, 54; Bridgeport, 59 (connects with Housatonic Railway); Stratford, 62; Naugatuck Railroad Junction, 64 (connects with Naugatuck Railway); Milford, 67; New Haven, 76 (connects with New Haven, New London and Stonington, and Northampton Railways, and river steamers; Fair Haven, 78; East Haven, 81; Branford, 84; Stony Creek, 87; Guilford, 92; East River, 94; Madison, 96; Clinton, 99; Westbrook, 104; Saybrook, 108; Connecticut River, 109; Lyme, 109; Black Hall, 112; South Lyme, 115; East Lyme, 119; Waterford, 123; New London, 126 (connects with New London Northern, and Stonington and Providence Railways); Groton, 127; Poquonnock Station, 129; West Mystic, 133; Mystic, 134; Stonington, 138.

(For New York, Harlem, and Williams Bridge, *see* NEW YORK CITY, and Route II. of NEW YORK.)

Mount Vernon (17 miles) is a flourishing village of about 6,000 inhabitants, in Westchester County, New York. It contains the residences of many New York business men.

New Rochelle (20 miles), in Westchester County, New York, is pleasantly situated on Long Island Sound. It was settled by Huguenots from Rochelle, in France. It was the residence of Thomas Paine, who died here, June 8, 1809. A monument to his memory still stands near where he was first buried. This is one of the favorite places of residence for wealthy New-Yorkers, and is surrounded by beautiful villas.

Mamaroneck (24 miles), **Rye** (27 miles), and

Port Chester (29 miles), all partake of the same general characteristics as *New Rochelle*. Their proximity to *Rye Beach*, on Long Island Sound, adds to their popularity as quiet but remarkably pleasant summer resorts.

Greenwich (31 miles), the first station in Fairfield County, Connecticut, commands a fine view of the Sound and Long Island. It has three large churches, and several handsome residences. Greenwich is famous as the scene of "Putnam's breakneck ride" down the rocks. The spot known as "Put's Hill" can be seen from the train after leaving the depot, a little to the east of the churches.

Stamford (37 miles), at the mouth of Mill (or Ripowam) River, has of late years been much resorted to by visitors during the summer months, and affords quiet and healthful homes to large numbers of persons going daily to their business in New York. It has eight churches, excellent schools, and numerous beautiful residences. Among the many pleasant drives in the neighborhood, one around *Shippan Point*, two miles south of the village, is particularly attractive.

Stamford has a good harbor for light-draught vessels; and a canal, recently enlarged, enables the steamers running daily to New York to connect with the New York and New Haven and New Canaan Railroads, at the wharf of the latter near the depot.

The population of the town in 1860 was 7,000, and is now estimated at about 10,000.

Its manufactures of iron, woollens, and dyestuffs, are considerable.

Indian Harbor is the headquarters of the celebrated *Americus Club*.

Norwalk.—HOTEL, *Alliss House.*

Norwalk (45 miles) is a pleasant village, upon Norwalk River. It was burnt by the British, July 11, 1779. The quiet rural beauties of Norwalk, and its proximity to New York, make it one of the most desirable as well as available summer resorts of Connecticut. The oyster business is extensively carried on here, as is also the manufacture of hats. This is the junction with the *Danbury and Norwalk Railway*, 24 miles in length. About a mile from the railroad; to the north, is to be seen the splendid residence of Le Grand Lockwood.

Southport (52 miles) is a beautiful little place, the population in 1870 having been about 1,500. It has a good harbor for vessels of not over 100 tons' burden, and boasts of a very fine school-house.

Fairfield (54 miles) was settled in 1659, and on the 7th of July, 1779, was burnt by Governor Tryon. It is noted for its fine air and beautiful scenery, and, being a place of great resort in summer, supports an immense hotel called the *Marine Pavilion*. The village itself is about half a mile from the beach, and is beautifully built, but the township comprises within its limits the village of *Black Rock*, which has the finest harbor on the

Connecticut coast, except that of New London. In its northern portion is *Greenfield Hill*, the scene of Dwight's poem of that name, and in the west is *Southport*, already described.

Bridgeport (59 miles) is upon an arm of Long Island Sound, at the mouth of the Pequonnock River. A terrace height of 50 feet, occupied by beautiful private mansions and cottages, commands a charming view of the town and the Sound. *Washington Avenue* and *Seaside Parks* are fine public grounds. The town is celebrated for its manufactures of sewing-machines and fire-arms. Among the most extensive establishments are those of the Wheeler & Wilson and Howe Sewing-Machine Companies, the Union Metallic Cartridge Company, the New Haven Arms Company, and one of the largest carriage-manufactories in the United States. In Bridgeport was born the famous dwarf, Charles S. Stratton, *alias* "Tom Thumb." The harbor is broad, but will not admit vessels of very great size, as the depth of water on the bar is but 13 feet at high tide. It is the southern terminus of the *Housatonic Railway* and of the *Naugatuck Railway*. There is also a line of steamers to New York. The population of Bridgeport is about 20,000.

Stratford (62 miles), 3¼ miles from Bridgeport, has long been celebrated for its rural beauty and refined society. It has very little local business, either connected with manufacturing or trade, being, in fact, in all business matters, a suburb of Bridgeport.

Milford (67 miles) presents a picturesque appearance. The streets are lined with stately elms. In the cemetery near the railway, east of the depot, is a monument 30 feet high, erected over the remains of the American soldiers brought here from New York, January, 1777.

West Haven (73 miles), a suburban village, 2 miles from New Haven, is seen spread out below the railway, which passes through it on a slight elevation. It is located near the sea-shore, and connected with New Haven by a horse-railroad, which runs to the *Savin Rock House*, 4 miles from New Haven, and a favorite resort for sea-side visitors in the summer season.

After leaving West Haven Station, the railroad passes over extensive flats, or "salt meadows," on the opposite side of which New Haven and its harbor come into view. West and East Rocks, two abrupt promontories, 400 and 300 feet in height, are also seen in the distance, West Rock, on the northern side of the railroad, being the most conspicuous.

New Haven, or the "City of Elms" (inhabitants, by census of 1860, 39,267, by census of 1870, nearly 51,-000), one of the two capitals of Connecticut, settled in 1638 by a colony from London, lies chiefly upon a broad plain, surrounded by hills of moderate height, at the head of a small bay which juts in from Long Island Sound. *East and West Rocks*, two bluffs of trap-rock, rising about 400 feet above the plain on the north, are conspicuous in all the approaches of the city, and are attractive resorts to those who love fine views. On the top of the West Rock there is a group of bowlders called the "*Judges' Cave*," because, in 1661, Goffe and Whalley, two of the judges of King Charles I. of England, were here secreted for a little while. The poet Hillhouse suggested the name of "*Regicide*" for West Rock, and of "*Sassacus*" for East Rock, but these designations are not in common use. Besides these rocks, there are many other interesting places to visit within a distance of five miles from the centre of New Haven; e. g., *Savin Rock*, a bathing-place with summer hotels, on Long Island Sound, southwest of the city; *Maltby Park*, a wild, picturesque drive; *Edgewood*, the residence of D. G. Mitchell (Ik Marvel); *Wintergreen water-fall*, and the tributary lake on West Rock; *Sachems' Wood* (the Hillhouse residence), and the *Prospect Street Drive* beyond; *Whitneyville*, and the Mill-river reservoir; *Fair Haven*, including a drive to the hill near Mr. Charles Ives's house; *Saltonstall Lake*, a retired sheet of water three miles long; *Fort Hale*, wholly rebuilt during the recent war; the *Light House*, and *South End*.

Yale College.—New Haven is famous as the seat of Yale College, founded in 1700, and numbering, in 1869-'70, 59 instructors and 736 students. Its chief departments are: 1. The Academic Department or the old Classical College, the nucleus of the institution, now attended by 518 students; 2. The Scientific School, having 141 students; 3. The Theological School; 4. The Medical School; 5. The Law School; 6. The School of the Fine Arts. The most noteworthy buildings are the *Library* (containing 78,000 vols.); the *Art-building*, containing the Trumbull collection of historical paintings, the well-known "Jarves collection" of early Italian pictures, some interesting casts from Grecian antiques, and a few modern works of art; the *Graduates' Hall*, in which are hung portraits of distinguished officers and graduates of the College; the *Cabinet of Minerals*, etc., to be removed to the Peabody Museum of Natural History. These are all on the College Square. Just north of it is a new building erected in 1870 for the *Theological School;* and still farther north the hall of the *Sheffield Scientific School*, with its laboratories, library, scientific collections, etc. The clock on this building regulates the time for the city, by sending a telegraphic signal to the City Hall and elsewhere.

PUBLIC BUILDINGS, etc.—The public square or "*Green*" in the centre of the town has in it the *State-House* (where the Legislature assembles in 1870, and every alternate year), the *Centre Church*, the *North Church*, and *Trinity Church*. On the east side of it is the *City Hall*, a new and interesting building, in which the courts are held, and the city, county, town, and school district, have their local offices. The other public buildings (not specifying churches) are the *U. S. Post-Office, Custom House*, and *Court Room* in Church Street, the *State Hospital*, the *Medical College*, the *County Prison*, and several good public-school houses.

Temple Street, Elm Street, Hillhouse and Whitney Avenues, Dwight Place, and West Chapel Street, are well-shaded streets, lined with pleasant residences.

CEMETERIES.—The *Old Burying-Ground* in Grove Street contains many interesting monuments, among which are those which mark the graves of Theophilus Eaton (first Governor of the New Haven Colony), Roger Sherman (signer of the Declaration), David Humphreys, Roger S. Baldwin (Governor and U. S. Senator); of Ezra Stiles, Timothy Dwight, Benjamin Silliman, James L. Kingsley, Jonathan Knight, N. W. Taylor, and other college officers; of James Hillhouse and James A. Hillhouse; Noah Webster, Jedediah Morse, Eli Whitney, Theodore Winthrop, William Croswell, father and son, etc. The *New Cemetery* on the bank of West River is worth visiting. The Centre Church marks the site of the earliest burying-ground, and in its rear may be seen the grave of the regicide John Dixwell, marked by a marble monument.

PARKS.—The Green, Wooster Square, Hamilton Park (with race-course, fair-ground, etc.), Maltby Park.

MANUFACTORIES.—In New Haven these are numerous and important, including machinery, hardware, locks, clocks, fire-arms, carriages and carriage fixtures, shirts, etc.

Trade with the West Indies is a noteworthy feature in the New Haven business.

Five railroads connect New Haven with (1) New York, (2) Hartford, (3) New London, (4) Northampton, and (5) Middletown. The last named was first opened in 1870; a sixth road is building to Derby. Steamboats ply daily to and from New York.

Westville, *Whitneyville*, and *Fair Haven*, are villages lying partly within the limits of the town.

HOTELS.—The largest and best is the *New Haven Hotel;* the *Tontine* and *Tremont* houses are also good; and there are several smaller houses, chiefly near the railroad station.

Fair Haven (78 miles), a suburb of *New Haven*, is situated on both sides of the Quinnepiac River, over which is a railroad bridge of wood, 40 feet above the water, and a bridge for ordinary travel, of iron, about 900 feet long. The views from the left bank, which rises to the height of 100 to 150 feet, greatly enchance its value as a site for villas. Fair Haven is especially noted for the extent of its oyster-trade.

East Haven (81 miles) has large copper-smelting works. Near it is *Saltonstall Lake*, the source of the principal ice-supply for New Haven.

Branford (84 miles) has within its

limits Branford Point, a favorite watering-place.

Guilford (92 miles) is a pretty town built around a public square, shaded with fine trees. Fronting the square are five churches, the leading stores, and the hotel. A fine stone school-house was built in 1854, at a cost of $40,000. The point south of the village is a popular summer resort. This was the birthplace of Fitz-Greene Halleck, the poet, who died there on the 17th of November, 1867.

New London (126 miles) is the oldest town in Eastern Connecticut, having been settled by John Winthrop, Jr., in 1645.

It is pleasantly situated on the west bank of the river Thames, covering a narrow strip of land from its mouth three miles north. It possesses one of the finest harbors in the United States, well land-locked, and never obstructed by ice. It is defended by Fort Trumbull, a strong granite fortification, on the western shore, and Fort Griswold, earth-works, on the eastern bank of the river. The town was burned during the Revolutionary War by Benedict Arnold, September 6, 1781, and a tall granite monument on the opposite bank of the Thames commemorates that event, and the fearful massacre at Fort Griswold the same day.

New London has a good system of free education, embracing common and high schools, and was the first town in the State to establish free high and evening schools at public expense. The ancient burial-ground in this town is a place of special interest to the antiquarian, and contains many well-preserved stones with legible inscriptions, dating prior to 1700. In 1850 a new cemetery of 40 acres was opened, and in entering it a stranger cannot fail to be impressed with its rural beauty and its monuments. It is called the *Cedar Grove Cemetery*.

A polished freestone *City Hall of Records*, granite *Custom-House*, and some especially fine stores and private residences, are found in the city. It contains ten houses for Christian worship, of which two, Congregational, are of granite, and one, Episcopal, of freestone. One of the former, Second Congregational, is a new edifice of unusual taste and beauty in its interior finish.

The "*Pequot House*," a favorite place of summer resort, is delightfully situated at the mouth of the river, and is always filled with visitors during the pleasure season. A number of private summer residences and cottages, owned by the proprietor of the Pequot, surround the house. On the eastern side of the river are many smaller houses, which accommodate visitors by the day or week during the summer months.

New London was formerly largely engaged in the whale-fishery, and has still a number of ships and smaller vessels engaged in the trade, and ranks as the third town in whaling tonnage in the United States. A large fleet of schooners and sloops pursue the cod and other fresh fisheries from this port. It has one woollen and several iron and other manufactories, several marine railways, and one large dry-dock.

New London has excellent steamboat and railroad accommodations. Two steamers leave daily for New York, and during the summer one boat runs between Hartford and Sag Harbor, *via* New London. It is the terminus of the New London Northern Railway, 100 miles, the Shore Line, running 50 miles south or west, to New Haven, and the New London, Stonington, and Providence, 63 miles to Providence. Eight trains leave daily for Boston, and five for New York.

The city of New London and the State of Connecticut have given to the United States about 80 acres of land on the eastern bank of the Thames, as a site for a Navy-Yard.

Groton (127 miles) just across the river from New London, was originally a part of that town. The events connected with the Revolutionary War, in the western part of Groton, have made it a place of historic interest. A brave band of about 150 men, many of them farmers and artisans, hastily gathered within the walls of Fort Griswold, September 6,1781, defended that fortification against very great odds, and finally, when completely overpowered, surrendered. As the conquerors entered the gates, the leading British officer cried out, "Who commands this fort ;" Colonel Ledyard replied, " I did, sir—you do now," raising and lowering his sword, in token of submission, and advancing to present it to him. The ferocious officer received the sword, and *plunged it up to the hilt in the owner's bosom*. Eighty-five men were killed in the fort, and thirty-five dangerously wounded. A granite monument, erected by the State of Connecticut, to the memory of Colonel Ledyard, stands in the Ledyard burial-ground, a neatly-enclosed lot on the brow of the hill, south of the Groton monument.

Mystic (134 miles) is a prosperous village in the towns of Groton and Stonington, and situated on both sides of the Mystic River. It is the site of the celebrated Pequot massacre, May 26, 1637, when the colonists, under John Mason, annihilated the tribe, burning their forts and shooting down their men, women, and children. It has of late years been famous for its ship-building; many fine steamers and sailing-vessels have been constructed in its yards, and no other place between Boston and New York has contributed an equal amount of new tonnage to the commercial marine of the country during the last twenty years.

Stonington (138 miles) was originally a part of New London, and settled with that town in 1649. It was organized as a separate township in 1665, and a part of it incorporated as a borough in 1801. A brave and successful resistance was made by the inhabitants of this town in the War of 1812 to the attack of Sir Thomas Hardy, commanding a British squadron. The Stonington Railway to Providence, R. I., completed in 1835, was the first line built in Connecticut. The harbor is protected by a substantial breakwater, built many years ago by the U. S. Government, at a cost of $100,000. In summer this is a favorite watering-place. The *Waddamonoch* is a fine hotel, situated on a slight eminence, commanding an excellent view of *Fisher's Island Sound* and the ocean in the distance. There are several fine private residences in Stonington, and a good line of steamers connects it with New York. It is the last station, on the Shore Line, in Connecticut.

SHORT DIVERGENT ROADS.

Danbury and Norwalk Railway.

This road is but 24 miles in length, and the distances given below are from its southern terminus. To obtain the distance from New York, add 45 miles.

STATIONS.—South Norwalk; Norwalk, 2; Winnipauk, 3; Kent, 5; Wilton, 8; Cannon's, 9; Georgetown, 12; Ridgefield, 13; Sanford's, 15; Reading, 17; Bethel, 21; Danbury, 24.

South Norwalk was formerly known as *Old Well*, and is two miles from the village of Norwalk. It is at this point that on the 6th of May, 1853, a locomotive and two passenger cars plunged through an open drawbridge, involving the loss of 47 lives. There is a steamboat line between this line and New York.

Norwalk (2 miles). (*See* p. 145.)

Ridgefield (13 miles) contains a few manufactories. The village is about 3 miles from the station, and is a very pleasant town, it is on high ground with a wide street, and an abundance of fine shade-trees. A branch from the Danbury and Norwalk Railroad is now being built to it.

Danbury (24 miles) is the northern terminus of the road, and has a population (1870) of about 10,000. It is a pleasant place, on the *Still River*, which furnishes numerous hat-factories, almost all its inhabitants being engaged in that branch of business. It is the semi-capital of the county, and contains the county-buildings, several churches, two banks, etc. The town was burnt by the British troops under General Tryon in 1777, and the military stores destroyed. General Wooster was wounded in an engagement with the enemy in their retreat, and died in Danbury. A monument was erected to his memory in the new cemetery in 1854 by the Masonic fraternity, to which he belonged, aided by the State and citizens of Danbury. The principal public school is one of the finest and best arranged in the State, and will accommodate 600 scholars.

HOTELS: The *Wooster House* (near the depot), *Pahquioque Hotel*, and *Turner House*, are the principal hotels.

N. B.—Pahquioque is the Indian name for Danbury.

When the *Boston, Hartford, and Erie Railway* is completed, it will pass through this place. (*See* Route V.)

[DERBY.] CONNECTICUT. [WATERBURY

NAUGATUCK RAILWAY.

This road, commencing at Bridgeport, follows the line of the New York and New Haven Railway 5 miles through Stratford and across the Housatonic River; it then turns northward, and follows the left bank of the Housatonic River 9 miles to Derby, then the valley of the Naugatuck, nearly to Winsted.

STATIONS.—Bridgeport, 59 miles from New York; Stratford, 3 miles from Bridgeport; Junction, 5; Derby, 14; Ansonia, 16; Seymour, 20; Beacon Falls, 23; Naugatuck, 27; Union City, 28; Waterbury, 32 (connects with Hartford, Providence, and Fishkill Railway); Waterville, 35; Plymouth, 41; Camp's Mills, 47; Litchfield, 49; Wolcottville, 52; Burville, 57; Winsted, 62.

Bridgeport (see page 146).

Derby (14 miles) is at the junction of the Housatonic and Naugatuck Rivers, and at the head of navigation. It is an old town, having formerly a West Indian trade and considerable ship-building. The village of *Birmingham*, picturesquely placed on a high point of land between the two rivers, is now, owing to its manufactures, the important part of the town. A dam across the Housatonic at this point, now nearly finished, will afford the largest water-power in the State. The manufactures are steel, pins, tacks, hoop-skirts, etc. Commodore Isaac Hull and General David Humphreys were natives of Derby. A railway from here to New Haven (10 miles) is building. It has steamboat communication with New York during the summer. It has a bank, a weekly newspaper, a public reading-room, and several fine churches and other public buildings.

Ansonia (16 miles), an important manufacturing village in the town of Derby, has a fall on the Naugatuck River of 32 feet. It was established by Phelps, Dodge & Co., about 1838, and named from Anson G. Phelps, Esq. It has 11 rolling-mills, 2 founderies, white-lead works, woollen-mills, extensive clock-factories, hoop-skirt factories, etc. This village has a good public water-works, a bank, several churches, and quite a number of fine private residences.

Seymour (20 miles), formerly a part of Derby, and called Humphreysville, but now a separate town, was founded mainly by General Humphreys, in connection with his endeavors to foster the growth and use of fine Spanish wools in this country. It has good water-power on the Naugatuck River, and contains quite a number of manufacturing establishments of various kinds, but has not increased much for some years past. The rocks at the falls near the centre of the village on the west side of the river contain some of the largest and finest specimens of "pot-holes" to be found in the country; some of these are 2 feet in diameter and 6 or 8 feet deep.

Beacon Falls (23 miles). Here are the large shawl-mills of the Home Woollen Company.

Naugatuck (27 miles), formerly a part of Waterbury, and called Salem Bridge, has large india-rubber goods factories, woollen-mill, agricultural tools, and a considerable number of manufactories of less note.

Union City (28 miles) is a part of Naugatuck. Here are Tuttle & Whittemore's malleable-iron foundery and several smaller works.

Waterbury (32 miles), the principal place of the valley, is the fifth city of the State in population, of which at least one-half is foreign (population, 1860, 10,000, 1870, estimated, 16,000). Its situation is picturesque. The hills, which closely hem in the Naugatuck above and below, here recede on the north and east, leaving an elevated triangular plateau, measuring about one mile on each side, and on the adjacent slopes and surrounding hill-sides, the city is built. A noisy mill-stream, called the *Mad River*, comes down on the east side, and *Great Brook*, another mill-stream, flows nearly through the centre of the town. The manufactories being mostly on the outskirts of the town, the central part has a neat and tasteful appearance, unusual in manufacturing towns.

Manufactures, to which Waterbury owes its growth, employ a capital of upward of $7,000,000. The main business is the manufacture of rolled brass and German silver, and wire, and, as incident to this, all manufactures that consume these materials in large quantities are pursued and encouraged. Fine steel rolls are manufactured here so superior, that they have been ordered for the British and Belgian Mints.

PROMINENT BUILDINGS.— These are mostly about *Centre Square*, a small park of three or four acres, neatly planted and lying in the centre of the town. The *City Hall*, built in 1869, at a cost of about $140,000, is a fine building, with brownstone front and clock-tower, and contains, besides the public offices, a fine court-room and an elegant public hall, for concerts, lectures, etc., seating about 1,500. The *First Congregational Church* (of wood) is on the north side of the square, the *Second Congregational Church* (of stuccoed brick) at the east end, and *St. John's Episcopal Church* at the west end. This building was destroyed by fire, December 24, 1868, but is now being rebuilt in granite, trimmed with Ohio stone—pointed Gothic style, at a cost of about $150,000. The *Methodist* and *Roman Catholic* Churches, on East Main Street, and the *Baptist* Church on Bank Street, all near, but not on Centre Square, are brick structures of some elegance. The *Scoville House*, a very comfortable hotel, is on the south side of the square, and about one-fourth of a mile from the railroad station. *The Silas Bronson Library*, a public library, free to all inhabitants of the city, founded by the late Silas Bronson, of New York, with a permanent fund of about $200,000, has just been opened, with a circulating library, of about 10,000 volumes.

Riverside Cemetery, on the south side of the Naugatuck, though small (about 40 acres), is one of the most beautiful rural cemeteries in the country.

The *Hartford, Providence and Fishkill Railway* extends from this place to Providence. A branch road to *Watertown* (5¼ miles) is now in operation. It was finished in 1870.

Watertown is a very fine agricultural town, and is a pleasant summer residence, the *Warren House* being an excellent hotel. It has several manufactories, the largest being one of sewing-silk.

Waterville (35 miles) is noted for its manufacture of pocket cutlery.

Plymouth (41 miles) contains three villages, Thomaston, on the railroad, Plymouth Hill, 1 mile east, and Torryville, 3 miles east. Thomaston, the most important, contains a brass rolling-mill, extensive clock-works, etc. About 2 miles below Thomaston, the road passes fine quarries of white granite, belonging to the Plymouth Granite Company.

Litchfield Station (49 miles). The village of Litchfield, 4 miles west of here, reached by stage from this point, is in the county of the same name, and is the county seat. The village is 1,100 feet above tide-water, near *Bantam*, the largest lake in the State, the outlet of which furnishes a large water-power. The two principal streets are broad, shaded with grand old elms, with pleasant parks at their intersection. The drives and scenery in the vicinity are very attractive. This was the seat of the famous Law School of Judges Reeve and Gould, and of Miss Pierce's Young Ladies' School, the earliest institution of its kind in this country. Here was brought, in the early days of the American Revolution, to the residence of Governor Oliver Wolcott (a signer of the Declaration of Independence), the leaden equestrian statue of George III., from the Bowling Green in New York, and by the Governor's daughters and their companions melted into bullets for our armies. His son, Oliver, Washington's Secretary of the Treasury, subsequently Governor of Connecticut, also lived here; the dwelling still stands. Here also the famous Lyman Beecher, D. D., the father of "all the Beechers," spent the prime of his life. The town contains several deposits of nickel-ore, and at the outlet of the lake, three or four mills, etc. The village is chiefly built upon two streets crossing each other at right angles, and contains a handsome park, and several churches. Dr. H. W. Buel has here a private infirmary for insane patients. HOTELS: *Mansion House* and *United States*.

Wolcottville (52 miles) is a prosperous manufacturing village, in the township of Torrington, containing several churches. The woollen mill of the Union Manufacturing Company is a commodious building. There is also a large brass rolling-mill, manufactory of plated goods, gilt cornices, window trimmings, etc. Between Wolcottville and Winsted, the road crosses the line separating the watershed of the Naugatuck from that of the Farmington River, on whose head-waters Winsted lies.

Winsted (62 miles), the terminus of the road, the principal village in the town of Winchester, and the largest village in Litchfield County, is situated at the outlet of *Long Lake*, which furnishes a valuable water-power, the village being built along the stream. It contains numerous manufactories, mostly of various forms of iron and steel, such as scythes, hoes, and forks, several handsome buildings and a good hotel, the *Beardsley House*, which is supplied with water from the lake in pipes.

ROUTE II.

BRIDGEPORT TO PITTSFIELD, MASS.

Via Housatonic Railway.

In the following list of stations none in Massachusetts are named except Pittsfield, as they will all be found in Route IV. of Massachusetts.

The distances are from Bridgeport, which is 59 miles from New York.

STATIONS.—Bridgeport; Stepney, 10 miles; Botsford, 15; Newtown, 19; Hawleyville, 23; Brookfield Junction, 27 (connects with New York, Housatonic, and Northern Railway); Brookfield, 29; New Milford, 35; Merwinsville, 42; Kent, 48; Cornwall Bridge, 57; West Cornwall, 61; Falls Village, 67; Canaan, 73 (connects with Western Connecticut Railway); Pittsfield, 110 (connects with Boston and Albany, and Pittsfield and North Adams Railways).

Bridgeport. (*See* page 146.)

Brookfield (29 miles) is the junction of the *New York, Housatonic, and Northern Railway*, a short road to Danbury, on the *Danbury and Norwalk Railway*. (*See* page 149.)

New Milford (35 miles), on the Housatonic River, is a large and very beautiful village, with broad, well-shaded streets. It is the site of several manufactories. From this point to the terminus of the road the scenery is ever changing and of rare beauty.

Kent (48 miles), on the Housatonic River, has three blast-furnaces. It is a quiet little village, with the river running through it. *Hatch* and *Swift* lakes or ponds are visible from the railway. There is also a hill which rises to a height of 1,000 feet, crowned by *Spectacle Pond*, a pair of twin lakelets of oval shape, connected by a strait. The view from this hill is grand. Looking westward, the *Catskills* are in sight, 60 miles distant, and between them and the spectator four other mountain-ranges.

Cornwall Bridge (57 miles), surrounded by beautiful scenery, is a manufacturing village, and contains a blast-furnace.

Falls Village (67 miles) is at the falls of the Housatonic, which are the largest and finest in the State. They are bold and picturesque, descending 60 feet over a ledge of limestone. Not far from the village is *Prospect Hill*, from which the finest views in the vicinity can be obtained. Near to it is a wild cleft in the rocks, known as the *Wolf's Den*.

Canaan (73 miles) is the last station in Connecticut, and, like *Falls Village*, is in the midst of splendid scenery.

Salisbury is a few miles to the southwest of *Canaan*, and is in the township of the same name, so noted for its varied and beautiful scenery, its charming lakes, and its fruitful valleys. Upon *Mount Riga*, at an elevation of 1,000 feet, is a lake which furnishes a fine water-power. The celebrated *Salisbury iron-beds* are upon this mountain, furnishing ore to a number of iron-works in the vicinity. It is here that the Ames wrought-iron cannon are made.

Mr. Beecher, in his "Star Papers," describes this section of the country as follows, the only liberty we have taken being to add a few notes for the guidance of the traveller, and to italicize names:

"If one has not leisure for detailed explorations, and can spend but a week, let him begin, say at *Sharon*, or *Salisbury*, and both accessible from the *Harlem Railroad*.* On either side, to the east and to the west, ever-varying mountain-forms frame the horizon. There is a constant succession of hills swelling into

---

* *Amenia Station*, on the Harlem Road, or *Canaan* on the Housatonic Road, for *Sharon* and *Millertown*, or *Falls Village* on the Housatonic, for *Salisbury*.

mountains, and of mountains flowing down into hills. The hues of green in trees, in grasses, and in various harvests, are endlessly contrasted. There are no forests so beautiful as those made up of both evergreen and deciduous trees. At *Salisbury* you come under the shadow of the *Taconic range*. Here you may well spend a week, for the sake of the rides and the objects of curiosity.* Four miles to the east are the *Falls of the Housatonic*, called *Canaan Falls*, very beautiful and worthy of much longer study than they usually get. *Prospect Hill*, not far from *Falls Village*, affords altogether the most beautiful view of any of the many peaks with which this neighborhood abounds. Many mountain-tops of far greater celebrity afford less various and beautiful views. Near to it is the *Wolf's Den*, a savage cleft in the rocks, through which you grope as if you had forsaken light and hope forever. On the west of *Salisbury* you ascend *Mount Riga* to *Bald Peak*, thence to *Brace Mountain*, thence to the *Dome*, thence to that grand ravine and its wild water, *Bash-Bish*, a ride in all of about 18 miles, and wholly along the mountain-bowl. On the eastern side of this range, and about four miles from *Norton's House*, in Salisbury, where you will, of course, put up, is *Sage's Ravine*, which is the antithesis of *Bash-Bish*. *Sage's Ravine*, not without grandeur, has its principal attractions in its beauty; *Bash-Bish*, far from destitute of beauty, is yet most remarkable for grandeur. I would willingly make the journey once a month from New York to see either of them. Just beyond *Sage's Ravine*, very beautiful falls may be seen just after heavy rains, which have been named *Norton's Falls*. Besides these and other mountain scenery, there are the *Twin Lakes* on the north of Salisbury, and the two lakes on the south, around which the rides are extremely beautiful."

The rest of this route will be described in Route IV. of Massachusetts.

---

* There is a good hotel.

ROUTE III.

THE CONNECTICUT RIVER VALLEY FROM NEW HAVEN TO LAKE MEMPHREMAGOG AND THE WHITE MOUNTAINS, INCLUDING HARTFORD, SPRINGFIELD, etc.

Via New Haven, Hartford and Springfield, and Connecticut River Railways, or via New Haven and Northampton Railway, etc.

[NOTE.—Although the above announcement of this route is so comprehensive, only those portions of these lines which lie within the limits of Connecticut will be described here. In the chapter on Massachusetts it will be resumed as Route V, and in Vermont as Route I.

NEW HAVEN, HARTFORD, AND SPRINGFIELD RAILWAY.

This road, as far as Springfield, is one of the main highways to Boston, and it continues on to the Canadian frontier as the best route from New York to the White Mountains and to Quebec. The valley of the Connecticut is one of the most beautiful in the country, but the tourist sees but little of the lower river from the cars, the track not running along the river-bank until after passing above Hartford.

STATIONS.—New Haven, 76 miles from New York; North Haven, 7 miles from New Haven; Wallingford, 12; Yalesville, 16; Meriden, 18; Berlin, 26 (connects with Middletown Branch); Newington, 31; Hartford, 36 (connects with Hartford, Providence and Fishkill Railway); Windsor, 42; Windsor Locks, 48; Warehouse Point, 49; Thompsonville, 53; Longmeadow, 58; Springfield, 62 (connects with Boston and Albany Railway, and with Connecticut River Railway).

New Haven (76 miles from New York). (*See* page 146.)

Wallingford (12 miles) is a beautiful summer resort, with broad and handsome streets, and several manufactories. It has an excellent hotel—*Beach House.*

Meriden (18 miles) is beautifully situated upon a hill. It has several large manufactories, and is noted for its clocks. "In Meriden," says S. G. Goodrich, "is a natural ice-house, in a narrow defile, between ridges of greenstone. The defile is choked up with the ruins of the rocks which have fallen from the ridges, and form a series of cavities overgrown with trees, and strewn with thick beds of leaves. The ice is formed in the cavities of these rocks, and remains the whole year. A portion of it melts during summer, causing a stream of cold water to flow perpetually from the spot."

Berlin (26 miles) is a thriving manufacturing village at the junction of the branch road to Middletown.

Middletown is a city, situated on the western bank of the Connecticut River, at the head of ship navigation, having 10 feet of water at its wharves. It possesses numerous handsome residences, many of them surrounded with extensive ornamental grounds. The Berkeley Divinity School (Episcopalian) is situated on Main Street. Its chapel, dedicated to St. Luke, is an exquisite specimen of Gothic architecture. Upon an eminence overlooking the city stands the Wesleyan University, controlled by the Methodists. The university possesses a library of about twenty thousand volumes, a somewhat extensive cabinet of natural history, and one of the finest telescopes in the country. Among the university buildings, the most noticeable are the Memorial Chapel, Rich Hall, and Judd Hall. Rich Hall is occupied by the library, and Judd Hull is devoted to the department of Natural Science. These are all elegant and substantial buildings, of Portland sandstone. The quarries whence this excellent stone is obtained are situated on the east bank of the river, directly opposite Middletown. The region is one of considerable interest to mineralogists, and the characteristic minerals of the locality are well represented in the collections in Judd Hall. The feldspar, which occurs very abundantly in a coarse granite, is quarried in several localities near the city, and largely used in the manufacture of porcelain. A lead and silver mine, formerly worked a short distance below Middletown, is now abandoned. The Connecticut Hospital for the Insane, and an Industrial School for Girls, are located near the city. The manufactories of Middletown are quite varied and extensive, including webbing, pumps, hardware, indian-rubber goods, silver-plated ware, sewing-machines, shirts, etc. A branch of the Hartford and New Haven Railroad extends from Berlin to Middletown, a distance of 10 miles. Two other railroads are in process of construction through this city. One of these, the New Haven, Middletown, and Willimantic, will form a part of the "Air line" from New York to Boston, and was opened from New Haven to Middletown in the summer of 1870. The other will run from Hartford to the mouth of the Connecticut. The steamers running between New York and Hartford stop here. The *McDonough* is the leading hotel.

Hartford (36 miles), the seat of government of the State, and one of the most beautiful cities in all New England, is situated at the head of sloop navigation on the Connecticut River. It was first settled by the Dutch, 1633, and the site of the first houses at the junction of the Connecticut and Park Rivers is still known as "Dutch Point." In 1635 the first English colony settled here, and named the place in honor of Hartford, England, the birthplace of one of their ministers. The business of Hartford is very extensive, not only on account of its numerous manufactories, but also because it is one of the great centres of the fire and life insurance companies of the United States, the aggregate capital of those located here being immense. The distinguishing features of this city are its benevolent, educational, and charitable institutions, its handsome buildings, and its beautiful residences, all of which may be reached or at least approached by the street railway through Main Street, upon or near which most of the principal buildings stand.

The *Asylum for the Deaf and Dumb* is beautifully situated on the hill, near the depot, in the midst of extensive grounds. It was founded in 1817 by Rev. T. H. Gallaudet, LL. D., and was the first institution of the kind in America.

The *Retreat for the Insane*, founded in 1824, stands upon elevated ground in the southwest part of the city, and is a prominent object. It has extensive and highly-ornamental grounds, from which fine views of the city and of the Connecticut Valley can be obtained.

The *Hartford Hospital*, located on Hudson Street, in the southern portion of the city, near the Retreat, is a handsome building, of Portland stone. It was established in 1854, and the present building dedicated in 1859.

Trinity College, the leading educational institution, is under the management of the Episcopal Church, by which it was founded in 1823. The buildings are of stone, and are named Seabury, Jarvis, and Brownell Halls. They stand upon an eminence, surrounded by extensive and beautiful grounds, laid out as a park, through which runs the Park River. They are to the east of the railway, and can be seen from the depot. Its libraries contain about 15,000 volumes. A bronze statue, 11 feet high (exclusive of the pedestal), of the late Bishop Brownell, by Rogers, cast at the Royal Foundery, at Munich, has been erected on the grounds west of the college.

The new *High School*, which can be seen on the left of the railroad, just before entering the city, and which is a conspicuous object from the park, and the new *Brown School*, on Market Street, are among the finest school-houses in the land.

The *Theological Institute of Connecticut*, under the control of the Congregationalists, incorporated in 1834, and formerly located at East Windsor, is situated at the corner of Prospect Street and Wadsworth's Alley. Its library contains about 7,000 volumes.

The *Wadsworth Athenæum* is a fine granite edifice, in the castellated style. The central portion is used as a fine-art gallery; the southern portion by the museum, library, and other rooms of the State Historical Society, through which is the entrance to the Wilkinson Library, a free public library containing about 20,000 volumes. The northern portion is occupied by the Young Men's Institute, which has a large library. No person stopping in Hartford should neglect visiting this institution.

The *State-House* was built in 1794, and contains the public offices and the State Library. In the secretary's office is the famous charter. In the Senate-chamber is a full-length portrait of Washington, by Stuart, pictures of former colonial and State Governors, and an elegant chair made from the Charter Oak. From the cupola on the top of the building there is a fine view.

The *City Hall* is a handsome building in the Grecian style of architecture. It fronts on Market Square.

There is a fine *Opera-House*, a large concert and lecture hall—*Allyn Hall*—and a very large *Skating-Rink*.

The *Charter Oak*, once the pride of the city, was blown down during a storm in 1856, and the spot where it stood is now marked by a marble slab.

Churches.—Among the many beautiful churches, the most noticeable are the *Church of the Good Shepherd* (Episcopal), built by Mrs. Colt; *Christ Church* (1827), corner of Main and Church Streets, a remarkable specimen of Gothic architecture for the time when it was built; *Asylum Hill* and *Park Churches* (Congregational), and the *Pearl Street Church*, which has a graceful stone spire.

Colt's Fire-Arms Manufactory and the *Willow-Works* form a village of themselves, in the southeast portion of the city. The dwellings for the employés are near the workshops. The grounds extend from the river to Main Street, upon which stands the elegant "Colt Mansion," surrounded by immense green-houses, graperies, etc.

The residence of the late Mrs. L. H. Sigourney, the poetess, stands on Asylum Street, near the railway depot.

CEMETERIES. — The *Ancient Burying-Ground*, containing the ashes of the first settlers, is in the rear of the *Centre Church*, on Main Street. The largest cemetery is in the north part of the city; but the *Cedar Hill Cemetery* should be visited, to see the Colt Monument, the Beach Monument, and the fine prospect over the surrounding country.

The vicinity of Hartford abounds in picturesque drives and walks. The drives to *Tumble-Down Brook*, 8 miles west, on the Albany Road, to *Talcott Mountain*, to *Prospect Hill*, and to *Wethersfield*, are the most frequented.

The best hotels are the *Allyn House* and the *United States*.

Wethersfield (6 miles) is the most ancient of the river towns, dating from 1636. It contains a number of venerable residences, an old church which Vandal hands have recently modernized, and the old cemetery where generation after generation lay mouldering to dust. The *State Prison* is located here. The Main Street Railway extends to Wethersfield.

Windsor (42 miles) is on the right bank of the Connecticut, and is the first English settlement in the State. It was the birthplace of Roger Wolcott, once Governor of Connecticut, and Oliver Ellsworth, once Chief Justice of the Supreme Court of the United States.

Warehouse Point (49 miles) is a flourishing manufacturing village. The Connecticut River is here crossed by an iron-truss bridge 1,525 feet long. The frame of the bridge was put together in England. Its erection was commenced June, 1865, and it was completed February, 1866. Of its 17 spans, the largest is 177½ feet.

Thompsonville (53 miles) is the last station in Connecticut.

(For continuation, *see* Route V of MASSACHUSETTS.)

NEW HAVEN AND NORTHAMPTON RAILWAY.

The New Haven and Northampton Railroad, from New Haven to Williamsburg, Massachusetts, 84 miles, and branch from Farmington to New Hartford, Connecticut, of 14 miles, was leased for 20 years, to the New York and New Haven Railroad, but reverted to its owners July 1, 1869. It has since been entirely renovated and put in first-class order, furnished with an entirely new outfit of locomotives, cars, shops, wharf facilities, etc., and now ranks with any of the roads centring in New Haven, as a first-class route. Following the line of the old Farmington Canal, it runs through the centre of the State, to the Farmington Valley, up the valley to the Massachusetts line, crossing that great thoroughfare to the West, the Boston and Albany Railroad, at Westfield, thence on to Northampton and Williamsburg, where it rests for the present, looking for a good outlet to the great northern valleys beyond.

STATIONS.—New Haven, Ives's, 8 miles; Mount Carmel, 9; Cheshire, 15; Hitchcock's, 20; Plantsville, 21; Southington, 22; Plainville, 27 (connects with Hartford, Providence, and Fishkill Railway, for Waterbury, Hartford, Willimantic, Plainfield, and Providence); Farmington, 31 (trains leave Farmington for New Hartford at 8.30 A. M., and 12.56 and 7.20 P. M.); Avon, 37; Weatogue, 40; Simsbury, 42; Granby, 47; Southwick, 55; Westfield, 61 (connects with Boston and Albany Railway for Boston, Springfield, Worcester, Albany, Troy, Saratoga, and the West); Southampton, 68; Easthampton, 71; Northampton 76 (connects with Connecticut River Railway); Florence, 79; Leeds, 81; Haydenville, 83; Williamsburg, 84.

Cheshire (16 miles from New Haven), a large farming town, midway between Meriden and Waterbury, is the seat of a flourishing Military School, and of the most extensive barytes-mines in the country, has some manufactures, and is delightfully located.

Southington (22 miles) is a flourishing manufacturing town, noted for its great variety of articles made from iron and steel.

Plainville (27 miles), the crossing of the *Hartford, Providence and Fishkill Railway*, is an enterprising manufacturing village of some 2,000 inhabitants.

Farmington (31 miles) is a beautiful and prosperous village, on the Farmington River; the scenery in the vicinity is very picturesque, and *Round Hill*, which is near the village, is a great natural curiosity. Misses Porters' Young Ladies Seminary, at this place, is widely known. The Branch to Collinsville and New Hartford diverges here.

Unionville (34 miles from New Haven), on the branch road, is a flourishing manufacturing village, mostly engaged in paper production.

Collinsville (39 miles), the former terminus of the branch, is especially noted for the largest axe-manufactory in the United States. Ploughs and cutlery are also extensively manufactured here; and here old John Brown, whose soul is still "marching on," procured his famous pikes, which opened the war, and began the end of slavery.

New Hartford (45 miles from New Haven), the terminus of the branch, is a very pleasantly-located village, heavily engaged in the manufacture of cotton ducks, scythes, planes, rules, and other mechanics' tools, but chiefly noted as the birthplace of Clara Louise Kellogg, the prima donna.

Avon (37 miles) is a lovely country village, nestled among the hills, and is famed for its charming surroundings. Talcott Mountain, one of the highest peaks in the region, is especially noted, and a great resort in summer.

Granby (47 miles) was formerly the seat of the Connecticut State Prison, abandoned mines being used, instead of houses, for the confinement of prisoners. The horrors of these subterranean dungeons are beyond description. This is the last station in Connecticut.

Southwick (55 miles) is one of those old New England farming towns, situated among the hills, so famous in all New England history, with much of local interest, but little to recommend it to the stranger, save its lovely surroundings.

Westfield, Mass. (61 miles), pleasantly situated on the banks of Westfield River, surrounded by hills, is a most delightful spot. In the centre of the village is a neat public square, surrounded by churches and schools. Here is located one and the best of the State Normal Schools, and the public schools are noted far and wide. The town is celebrated for its manufacture of whips.

Easthampton (72 miles) is a large manufacturing town, cottons, buttons, suspenders, and rubber goods, being the specialties. It owes its growth and wealth largely to the energy and perseverance of Hon. Samuel Williston, who commenced the manufacture of buttons, and is now one of the most wealthy citizens of Massachusetts, and devotes his wealth freely to charitable and educational purposes, having founded here the Williston Seminary, and endowed it with several hundred thousand dollars. A fine hotel here is largely patronized by New-Yorkers.

Northampton (76 miles), the junction of Connecticut River Railroad with this road, is described on page 186.

Florence (79 miles) is a manufacturing village of note, being the birthplace of the Florence sewing-machine, which is manufactured here on a very large scale—from 1,500 to 2,000 being made each month. The sewing-silk manufacture is carried on extensively here, and at Leeds, two miles beyond.

Haydenville (83 miles), a manufacturing village, founded and named from ex-Lieutenant Governor Joel Hayden, is noted for its extensive manufactures of brass, etc.

Williamsburg (85 miles), the present terminus of the road, is delightfully located among the hills, has about 4,000 inhabitants, largely devoted to agriculture and manufactures, has stage-lines running to Cummington (the birthplace of Bryant), 8 miles, also to Goshen, Chesterfield, and Ashfield.

ROUTE IV.

FROM NEW LONDON TO STAFFORD SPRINGS, AND TO BRATTLEBORO, VERMONT, WHITE MOUNTAINS, LITTLETON, QUEBEC, MONTREAL, AND ALL PARTS OF VERMONT, WESTERN NEW HAMPSHIRE, NORTHERN NEW YORK, AND PROVINCE OF QUEBEC.

Via New London Northern Railway.

STATIONS.—New London, 126 miles from New York; Montville, 6 miles from New London; Norwich, 13 (connects with Norwich and Worcester division of Boston, Hartford, and Erie Railway); Yantic, 17; South Windham, 26; Willimantic, 30 (connects with Hartford, Providence, and Fishkill Railway); South Coventry, 35; Mansfield, 38; Tolland and Wellington, 44; Stafford, 50.

New London. (See page 148.)

Norwich, 13 miles (pronounced Nor-rij), one of the two shire-towns of New London County, had, in 1860, 14,000 inhabitants—now many more. It is an incorporated city, surrounded by many manufacturing villages, which lie along the banks of the *Yantic* and the *Shetucket*—two small rivers which unite to form the *Thames*—at a point commonly called "The Landing." Among the distinct neighborhoods which make up the town, are East Chelsea, West Chelsea (west side), Laurel Hill, the Falls, the Plain, Up-town, Bean Hill, Yantic, and Greeneville. The view of the Landing, as one comes up by rail or boat from the south, is interesting—street rising above street, upon the side of a steep hill, on which are placed three churches, a school-house, county jail, etc. Washington Street, Broadway, and the Plain, are lined with attractive dwelling-houses—some of them quite handsome—and all surrounded by shade-trees and gardens. The antiquarian tourist may visit with interest the Indian burying-ground in Sachem Street, where the *grave of Uncas* is marked by a granite obelisk; and the battle-field near Greeneville, where a plain granite block marks the site of Miantonomoh's capture. A drive of five miles toward New London leads to Mohegan, where a remnant of the aborigines still live. The *Falls in the Yantic*, three-quarters of a mile above the Landing, were once famous for their natural beauty, but are so much hidden by factories and the railroad bridge, that their attractions are much diminished. The manufactories are of cotton fabrics, worsted braid, blankets, carpets, envelopes, paper, hardware, etc.

The *Free Academy* is an admirable school for the older boys and girls of Norwich and vicinity. It was established and is maintained by private liberality, and ranks among the best institutions of its sort in the country. The building is situated near the parade-ground, on the Plain; is spacious, convenient, and well supplied with class-rooms, apparatus, library, etc. The public schools of a lower grade are also good.

HOTELS: The *Wauregan House* and the *American House*, and several small taverns.

CHURCHES.—The Second and Broadway Congregational Churches, and Christ Church (Episcopal), are substantial modern buildings; and two or three other new churches are projected.

The *Yantic Cemetery* and the old burying-ground up-town contain some interesting graves and monuments.

Willimantic (30 miles) is a large manufacturing town upon the *Willimantic River*, which is here a large stream having a fall of 100 feet in a mile, and thus affording a great water-power. There is an abundance of building-stone in the vicinity. The *Hartford, Providence and Fishkill Railway* connects here, and the *New York and Boston Air Line*, when completed, will pass through this place, making its distance from New York 120 miles, and from Boston 80 miles.

Mansfield (38 miles) is on the *Natchang River*, and is noted for its manufactures of sewing-silk, the business having been commenced as early as 1793. It also contains manufactories of other kinds.

Tolland and Willington (44 miles) are two adjacent manufacturing villages. The former is the county seat of Tolland County, and contains the public buildings, several churches, etc.

Stafford (50 miles). This is the last station in Connecticut; it is situated upon the Willimantic River, and is celebrated for the medical properties of its mineral springs. One of these, as analyzed by Prof. Silliman, contains a large proportion of hydrogen gas and sulphur, and a small portion of iron. The other, which is considered one of the best chalybeate springs in the United States, contains a solution of iron, sustained by carbonic-acid gas, some earthy substances, and an element called natron.

The springs and a large hotel (the *Stafford Springs House*) are close by the depot, on the west side of the track.

Stafford village is two miles distant.

(For continuation of this route, see Route VI. of MASSACHUSETTS.)

ROUTE V.

FROM NEW YORK TO WHITE MOUNTAINS, VIA NEW LONDON.

Via Norwich and Worcester and connecting Railways.

(Branch of Route I.)

STATIONS.—New London, 126 miles from New York; Norwich, 139 (connects with New London Northern Railway); Jewett City, 149; Plainfield Junction, 155 (connects with Hartford, Providence, and Fishkill Railway); Central Village, 159; Wauregan, 160; Danielsonville, 165; Daysville, 168; Putnam, 172; Thompson, 175; Grosvenor Dale, 177.

Jewett City (149 miles) is a flourishing place on the *Quinebaug River*, having a fine water-power and numerous manufactories.

Plainfield Junction (155 miles) is the intersection of the *Hartford, Providence and Fishkill Railway*.

Danielsonville (165 miles) is a village of *Killingly* township, which is the greatest cotton-manufacturing town in the State. It contains quarries of different kinds of stone, and beds of porcelain clay. Within the limits of the town is *Alexander's Lake*, the Indian name of which was *Mashapang*. The tradition of the Indians was, that when a tribe were indulging in a debauch, the Great Spirit became enraged, and caused the ground under their feet to sink, and water to take its place. Without comment on this tradition, we will state that the origin of the lake was the sinking of the ground, and that, when the water is smooth, the pine-forest can still be seen, some of the trees reaching almost to the surface.

Daysville (168 miles) is in Killingly township.

Thompson (174 miles) is a large and pleasant agricultural and manufacturing town. The *Chargoggagoggmanchigaggogg Pond*, which lies partly in this town, and partly in Massachusetts, has about 60 miles of coast, is studded with beautiful islands, and was considered the paradise of the *Nipmuck Indians*.

Grosvenor Dale (177 miles) is the last station in Connecticut.

(For continuation, see Route VII. of MASSACHUSETTS.)

ROUTE VI.

WATERBURY TO PROVIDENCE, R. I.

Via *Hartford, Providence & Fishkill Railway*.

THIS railway, connecting at Providence, R. I., with the *Boston and Providence Railway*, is intended to extend to Fishkill on the Hudson River, over which it is proposed to throw a bridge, thus making unbroken communication with the Erie Railway, and greatly shortening the route to the West. At present it is completed as far west as Waterbury. Work is in progress on the division between *Brewster's* on the Harlem Road and *Fishkill*. It was recently known as the "*Boston, Hartford and Erie Railway*."

In the following list of stations we will commence at the western terminus, so that, on leaving Connecticut, this and its connecting routes may be resumed in Rhode Island and Massachusetts:

STATIONS.—Waterbury (connects with Naugatuck Railway); Waterville, 3 miles; Hancock, 7; Ferryville, 11; Bristol, 15; Plainville, 19 (connects with New Haven and Northampton Railway); New Britain, 24; Newington, 28; Hartford, 33 (connects with New Haven, Hartford, and Springfield Railway, and with steamers for New York); East Hartford, 35; Manchester, 42 (connects with South Manchester Branch); Vernon, 45 (connects with Rockville Branch); Bolton, 49; Andover, 55; Willimantic, 64 (connects with New London Northern Railway); South Wyndham, 68; Waldos, 72; Baltic, 75; Lovett's, 79; Jewett City, 82; Canterbury, 85; Plainfield, 89 (connects with Norwich and Worcester Railway); Moosup, 92; Sterling, 96; Providence, 123 (connects with diverging railways).

Waterbury. (*See* page 150.)

Waterville (3 miles) is noted for its manufacture of pocket cutlery.

Terryville (11 miles) is a manufacturing village. The first manufactory of wooden clocks in the United States was started here by Mr. Terry.

Bristol (15 miles) is in the vicinity of a valuable copper-mine. It is noted for its manufactures, especially clocks.

Plainville (19 miles). (*See* page 156.)

New Britain (24 miles) is an important place, having a population, in 1860, of about 4,000. It is beautifully laid out and built, and is supplied with gas and water, the latter from a reservoir of 175 acres, at an elevation of 200 feet, which gives sufficient pressure to supersede the necessity of fire-engines. It is celebrated for its manufactures, and is the seat of the State Normal School.

Hartford (33 miles). (*See* page 154.)

East Hartford (35 miles) is on the opposite side of the river from Hartford, with which it is connected by a long bridge.

Manchester (42 miles) is noted for its varied and extensive manufactures.

South Manchester is at the terminus of a branch 2½ miles from Manchester. The principal silk-manufactory of the Cheney Brothers is located here, which produces some of the finest silk goods in the United States.

Vernon (45 miles) is where a road branches off to *Rockville*, a distance of 5 miles.

Rockville, on the *Hockannon River*, possesses a fine water-power, and is one of the most enterprising and flourishing of Northern Connecticut villages.

Willimantic (64 miles). (*See* page 158.)

Baltic (75 miles). This village is owned principally by the A. & W. Sprague Manufacturing Company, who have located here a cotton-mill 1,000 feet long, and running 60,000 spindles. This company has several other manufactories on the line of this road—at Quidwick, River Point, Cranslow, etc., with a capacity for producing 27,000 yards of printed goods daily.

Plainfield (89 miles). (*See* page 159.)

Sterling (96 miles), the last station in Connecticut, has manufactories of printed goods.

(For continuation of this route, *see* RHODE ISLAND, Route II.)

RHODE ISLAND.

Rhode Island adjoins Connecticut on the east and Massachusetts on the south. It is entitled to distinction as the smallest State in the Union, its entire area not exceeding 1,159 square miles, with an extreme length and breadth respectively of 47 and 37 miles. It is divided into five counties, and contained, in 1870, 217,393 inhabitants. Next to Providence, the largest towns are Smithfield, Newport, Warwick, Bristol, and Kingston.

The country is most pleasantly varied with hill and dale, though there are no mountains of any great pretensions. Ample compensation for this lack in the natural scenery is made by the numerous small lakes which abound everywhere, and especially by the beautiful waters and islands and shores of the Narragansett Bay, which occupy a great portion of the area of the State. The Pawtucket, Pawtuxet, and Pawcatuck, are the most considerable streams. Its capitals, Providence and Newport, are among the most ancient and most interesting places in the United States, and the latter has long been one of the most fashionable American watering-places.

The State of Rhode Island was first settled at Providence, in 1636, by Roger Williams. To the enlightened and liberal mind of Williams in Rhode Island, and to the like true wisdom of Penn in Pennsylvania, and of Lord Baltimore in Maryland, America owes its present happy condition of entire freedom of conscience, perfect religious toleration having been made a cardinal point in the policy of those colonies. Rhode Island proper was settled (1638) by Governor Coddington and others, at Pocasset (now Portsmouth). It was purchased of the Indians, by whom it was called *Aquid-neck*, "Isle of Peace." Subsequently it was called "Isle of Rhodes" (whence Rhode Island), from the beautiful island of that name in the Mediterranean. The people of Rhode Island were early and active participants in the War of the Revolution, and many spots within her borders tell thrilling tales of the stirring incidents of those memorable days.

Rhode Island is emphatically *the* manufacturing State of the Union; the amount and variety of manufactures within her borders by far exceeding those of any other State in proportion to the number of inhabitants, and the area of territory. From careful returns obtained through the instrumentality of the "National Association of Cotton Manufacturers and Planters," and recently communicated to the "Rhode Island Society for the Protection of Industry" by Mr. Henry Lippitt, we derive the following statistics: There are in Rhode Island 130 cotton-mills, containing about 1,200,000 spindles; and this number is exceeded only by the State of Massachusetts, where 2,500,000 spindles are running. In the United States there are about 7,000,000 spindles in operation, and more than half of these are found in Massachusetts and Rhode Island. The largest special item of the cotton manufacture is printing cloths; more than 2,000,000 spindles were producing this description of goods in New England and New York during the year 1849. More than one-half the product of these spindles found a market in the city of Providence, the sales of that class of goods for the year 1849, in Providence, being 4,200,000 pieces, of the value of about $14,000,000. In Rhode Island, there are also 70 woollen-mills, containing about 500 sets of woollen machinery, and consuming not less than 20,000,000 pounds of raw wool per annum. The total value of the manufactures of the State is estimated as follows, in 1869:

Manufactures of cotton $40,000,000
" wool 25,000,000
" metal 35,000,000

Total..................$100,000,000

We have been unable to obtain the statistics for 1870.

ROUTE I.

STONINGTON, CT., TO PROVIDENCE.
Via Stonington and Providence Railway.

THIS is a portion of one of the principal routes from New York to Boston, and is a continuation of Route I. of Connecticut.

STATIONS.—Stonington, 138 miles from New York; Westerly, 6 miles from Stonington; Charlestown, 10; Richmond Switch, 14; Carolina, 17; Kingston, 23; Wickford, 30; Greenwich, 36; Hill's Grove, 41; Elmville, 44; Providence, 50 (188 from New York).

Stonington. (*See* page 149.)

Westerly (6 miles) has now become an important centre of manufactures, upon the Pawtucket River, navigable to this point for vessels of from 40 to 50 tons' burden. Has an excellent hotel.

Kingston (23 miles). Visitors to *Narragansett Pier* leave the cars at this point. (*See* page 163).

Wickford (30 miles), on an arm of Narraganset Bay, has a good harbor. Is noted for its cotton and woollen manufactures.

PROVIDENCE.

HOTELS: The *Aldrich House*, near the railroad depot, and the *City Hotel*, near Broad Street, are the principal houses. The latter has been recently refitted and refurnished throughout.

Providence, one of the most beautiful cities in New England, and surpassed only by Boston in wealth and population, is the chief city of Rhode Island. It is pleasantly situated on the northern arm of the Narraganset Bay, called Providence River. It is an ancient town, dating as far back as 1636, when its founder, Roger Williams, driven from the domain of Massachusetts, sought here that religious liberty which was denied to him elsewhere.

This city makes a charming picture seen from the approach by the beautiful waters of the *Narraganset*, which it encircles on the north by its business quarter, rising beyond and rather abruptly to a lofty terrace, where the quiet and gratefully-shaded streets are filled with dainty cottages and handsome mansions. Providence was once a very important commercial depot, its rich ships crossing all seas, and at the present day the city is mainly distinguished for its manufacturing enterprise. In this department it early took the lead, which it still keeps, the first cotton-mill which was built in America being still in use, in the adjacent town of *Pawtucket*, and some of the heaviest mills and print-works of the Union being now in operation within its limits. It has also extensive manufactories of machinery and jewelry. The workshops of the American Screw Company are the best appointed of their kind in the country.

Providence is the seat of *Brown University*, one of the best educational establishments in America. It was founded in Warren, Rhode Island, in 1764, and removed to Providence in 1770. Its library is very large and valuable, and is remarkably rich in rare and costly works.

The *public schools* have been brought to a high degree of perfection. Not only are the ordinary branches taught, but instruction is also given in music and sewing. There are, in all, about 230 teachers, and 10,000 pupils.

On the east side of the Seekonk River is the yearly meeting boarding-school belonging to the Society of Friends.

The *Athenæum* has a fine reading-room, and a collection of over 31,000 books.

The *Providence Historical Society*, incorporated 1822, has a library of 8,000 volumes.

Rhode Island Hospital, in the southwestern suburb, is one of the finest structures in the State.

The *Butler Hospital for the Insane*, upon the banks of Seekonk River, is an admirable institution, occupying large and imposing buildings.

The *Dexter Asylum for the Poor* stands

upon an elevated range of land east of the river.

The *Home for Aged Women*, and the *Children's Friend Society*, possess great interest.

The *Reform School* occupies the large mansion, in the southeast part of the city, formerly known as the Tockwotton House.

The *Custom-House* (Post-Office, and United States Courts) is a handsome granite structure, and one of the principal architectural ornaments of the city. The railroad depot, some of the banks, and many of the churches of Providence, are imposing structures.

Swan Point Cemetery, a spot of great rural beauty, is near the Butler Hospital for the Insane, upon the banks of the Seekonk River.

RAILWAYS.—The railways diverging from Providence, besides the one just described, are the *Providence and Worcester*, 43 miles, to Worcester, Mass.; *Hartford, Providence, and Fishkill*, 123 miles, to Waterbury, Conn.; *Boston and Providence*, and the *Providence, Warren, and Bristol*.

ROUTES.—There are six distinct routes from Providence to New York: two by rail, via Hartford and New London; and four by steamboats, via the *Stonington, Norwich*, or *Fall River*, and the direct through-line from Providence.

VICINITY.

What Cheer Rock. Upon the immediate edge of the city, on the shore of a charming bay in the Seekonk River, stands the famous What Cheer Rock, where the founder of the city, Roger Williams, landed from the Massachusetts side, to make the first settlement here.

At *Hunt's Mill*, three or four miles distant, is a beautiful brook with a picturesque little cascade, a drive to which is among the morning or evening pleasures of the Providence people and their guests. *Vue de l'Eau* is the name of a picturesque and spacious summer hotel, perched upon a high terrace four miles below the city, overlooking the bay and its beauties, for many miles around.

Gaspee Point, below, upon the opposite shore of the Narraganset, was the scene of an exploit during the Revolution.

Some citizens of Providence, after adroitly beguiling an obnoxious British revenue craft upon the treacherous-bar, stole down by boats in the night and settled her business by burning her to the water's edge.

Rocky Point, equidistant between *Providence* and *Newport*, is an attractive summer retreat, among shady groves and rocky glens, upon the west shore of the bay. In summer-time boats ply five times a day on excursion-trips from Providence to various rural points down the bay, charging 50 cents only for the round trip. Rocky Point is the most favored of all these rural recesses. Thousands visit it in the course of the season, and feast upon delicious clams, just dug from the sand, and roasted on the shore in heated seaweed, upon true and orthodox "clambake" principles. Let no visitor to Providence fail to eat clams and chowder at Rocky Point, even if he should never eat again. Here is a good hotel with celebrated bathing-houses attached, and a tower 170 feet high, from which is a charming view of the bay and land.

Marked Rock is another famous excursion-place, a few miles higher up the bay. It is reached in forty minutes from Providence by boat. The towns of *Warren and Bristol* are across the bay. (*See* page 164.)

Narraganset Pier, in the town of Kingston, on the west side of the bay, within a few years has become a place of great resort, during the summer months, and a large number of hotels and boarding-houses have been erected there. The wonderful salubrity of the air, the facilities for ocean bathing and fishing, and the beauty of the rocky shore, combine to make this one of the most attractive spots on the shore of the Atlantic. It is reached from *Providence* by steamer, or by rail to *Kingston* station on the *Stonington and Providence* Railroad. From New York by railway to Kingston (*see* Route I.).

Down the Bay. In a trip down the bay, besides the points above mentioned, we pass *Mount Hope* (*see* page 164), and *Fall River*. (*See* Route VIII. of MASSACHUSETTS.)

Off on our right, as we still descend toward the sea, is *Greenwich*, and near

by it the birthplace and home of General Nathaniel Greene, the Revolutionary hero; and just below is the township and (lying inland) the village of *Kingston*. In this neighborhood once stood the old snuff-mill in which Gilbert Stuart, the famous American painter, was born.
Prescott's Headquarters is a spot of Revolutionary interest on the western shore of the large island, filling the lower part of the bay, after which the State is named.

ROUTE II.

WATERBURY AND HARTFORD, CONNECTICUT, TO PROVIDENCE.

Via Hartford, Providence & Fishkill Railway.

THE portion of this route in Connecticut has been described as Route VI. of CONNECTICUT.

STATIONS.—Waterbury; Hartford, 33 miles; Summit, 101; Nipmac, 106; Anthony, 109; River Point, 112; Natick, 114; Cranston, 119; Providence, 123 (connects with all diverging routes).

Natic (114 miles), 9 miles from Providence, upon the Pawtuxet River, is celebrated for its prints.

Cranston (119 miles) is noted for its manufactures.

Providence (123 miles). (*See* page 162.)

ROUTE III.

PROVIDENCE TO BRISTOL.

Via Providence, Warren, and Bristol Railway.

THIS is a road of only 14 miles in length, forming a connection with the Bristol line of steamers to New York.

Warren (10 miles), on the east side of *Narraganset Bay*, has a good harbor and a number of manufactories.

Bristol (14 miles) is on a peninsula extending into Narraganset Bay. It is situated on an elevated plain extending gently to the shore, and having a fine harbor, easy of access, and of sufficient depth for large-sized vessels. During the Revolutionary War, Bristol was bombarded by the British, and a large portion of it destroyed. It is now much resorted to in summer, on account of its fine sea air. It is connected with New York by the Fall River line of steamers.

Mount Hope, the famous home of the renowned King Philip, the last of the Wampanoags, is just below Bristol, upon Mount Hope Bay, an arm of the Narraganset on the east. From the crown of this picturesque height is beheld a fine panorama of the beautiful Rhode Island waters. Upon the shore of Mount Hope Bay, opposite, is the busy manufacturing town of Fall River, Massachusetts.

ROUTE IV.

PROVIDENCE TO NEWPORT.

NEWPORT is reached from Providence by steamers; from New York by steamer of the Fall River line, from pier 30, North River, at 5 P. M. daily, and from Boston by the *Old Colony and Newport Railway, via* Taunton (67 miles); or by rail to Providence, and thence by boat down Narraganset Bay. A new Route to New York is to be opened by ferry to Wickford, connecting with the Stonington and Providence Railway.

If Newport were not, as it is, the most elegant and fashionable of all American watering-places, its topographical beauties, its ancient commercial importance, and its many interesting historical associations, would yet claim for it distinguished mention in these pages. The approach seaward is charming. Coming in from the sea round Point Judith, a few miles bring the traveller into the waters of the Narraganset Bay, where he passes between *Fort Wolcott*, on Goat Island, and the stronghold of *Fort Adams*, upon Brenton Point on the right, and enters the harbor of the ancient town, once among the commercial capitals of the Union. As late as 1769 Newport exceeded New York in the extent of her foreign and domestic commerce. In the Revolution, the British held possession of the place, during which time, and at their departure (1779), it became almost desolate. Before leaving, they destroyed 480 buildings, burned the light-house, cut down all the ornamental and fruit trees, broke up the wharves, used the churches for riding-schools and the State House for a hospital, and carried off the church bells and the town records to New York; disasters which reduced the population from 12,000 to 4,000. But the incidents of this period have left some pleasant memories for the present day, and remembrances of the fame of Commodore Perry, the gallant commander on Lake Erie, who was born in Narragansett, across the bay, and whose remains lie now in Newport; of the residence of Rochambeau, and other brave officers of the French fleet, and of the visits of General Washington, and the *fêtes* given in his honor—the venerable buildings associated with all these incidents being still to be seen. Newport was settled in 1637, and incorporated in 1700. *Pocasset*, or *Portsmouth*, at the northern extremity of the island, had been settled the year previous. The old town lies near the water; but, of late years, since the place has become popular as a summer residence, a new city of charming villas and sumptuous mansions has sprung up, extending far along upon the terraces which overlook the sea. Of the old buildings, and of those which belong to Newport *per se*, instead of in its character of a watering-place, are the ancient *State House* (for Newport is a semi-capital of Rhode Island), the *Redwood Library* and *Athenæum*, the *Old Stone Mill*, said to have been erected by Icelanders before the days of Columbus; *Tammany Hall Institute*, *Trinity Church*, the *Vernon family mansion*, the *Perry monument*, Commodore *Perry's house*, built in 1763, and long known as the "Granary;" the fortifications in the harbor, *Fort Adams*, *Fort Wolcott*, *Fort Brown*, and the *Dumplings*. Fort Adams, on Brenton's Point, is one of the largest works in the United States. It mounts four hundred and sixty guns. The chief picturesque attractions of the town and its immediate vicinity are the fine ocean-shores, known as the First, the Second, and the Third Beach. It is the First which is chiefly used as a bathing-ground by the Newport guests. It is half a mile from the Ocean House. Stages run during bathing hours. At the Second Beach are the famous rocks called *Purgatory*, and the *Hanging Rocks*, within whose shadow it is said that Bishop Berkeley wrote his "Minute Philosopher." The *Glen* and the *Spouting Cave* are charming places to ride to, when the weather invites. *Lily Pond*, the largest sheet of spring-water on the island, is easily reached from Spouting Cave.

Newport was the birthplace of the gifted miniature painter Malbone; and Gilbert Stuart's place of nativity may be seen in Narraganset, across the bay. Stuart made two copies of his great Washington picture for Rhode Island, one of which may be seen in the State House at Newport, and the other in that at Providence. Among the interesting relics to be found in the town are: Franklin's printing-press, imported by James Franklin in 1720. It is in the office of the Newport *Mercury*, established in 1758. Upon this press the first newspaper issued (1732) was printed. The *Chair of State*, in which Benedict Arnold sat at the reception of the charter in 1663, is in possession of the Gould family. The *First Baptist Church*, founded in 1638, and claimed as the oldest church in Rhode Island, is worthy a visit. The bell in the tower weighs half a ton. One daily newspaper (*News*), and the *Mercury*, the oldest weekly newspaper but one in the United States, are published in Newport.

The leading hotels are the *Ocean House*, *Atlantic*, *Perry*, *Aquidneck*, and *United States*.

The American Steamboat Company's steamers, "Bay Queen," Captain Allen, and "City of Newport," Captain Kelley, make excursions daily (Sundays excepted) between Providence, Rocky Point, and Newport.

DISTANCES.—To Providence, 30 miles; Fall River, 18; Point Judith, 15; Block Island, 30.

ROUTE V.

PROVIDENCE TO WORCESTER, MASS.
Via Providence and Worcester Railway.

STATIONS.—Pawtucket, 4 miles; Valley Falls, 6; Lonsdale, 7; Ashton, 9; Albion, 11; Manville, 12; Woonsocket, 16; Blackstone, 18 (crossing of Boston, Hartford and Erie Railway); Millville, 20; Uxbridge, 25; Whitins, 26; Northbridge, 35; Farnum's, 33; Grafton, 34; Sutton, 36; Millbury, 37; Worcester, 43 (connects with Boston and Albany; Norwich and Worcester; Fitchburg and Worcester; and Worcester and Nashua Railways).

Pawtucket (4 miles) is a flourishing manufacturing town on the *Pawtucket River*, which furnishes a fine water-power. The first cloth manufactory operated by water, in this country, was established here in 1790. The place has numerous important manufactures, and is especially noted for its steam fire-engines and the prints of the Dunnel Manufacturing Company. It has an important commerce. Among the public buildings the *Masonic Temple* and *Manchester Hall* are fine architectural specimens.

Woonsocket (16 miles) is a flourishing manufacturing town, famous for its cotton manufactories, of which there are over twenty. Woonsocket comprises, under one general name, the villages of Hamlet, Jencksville, Globe, and Union, and lies on both sides of the *Blackstone River*. In the rear of Berou is an eminence commanding a beautiful view of the village. Many of the most beautiful residences are grouped upon the swells of high land, which rise in various directions. It lies on the line of the Airline Railway, to be built between Boston and New York. This is the last station in Rhode Island.

MASSACHUSETTS.

MASSACHUSETTS, one of the original thirteen States, and the most populous and wealthy of the New England or Eastern States, is bounded on the north by New Hampshire and Vermont; east by the Atlantic Ocean; south by Connecticut and Rhode Island, and west by New York. Its greatest length, from east to west, is 145 miles, and its mean breadth 70 miles. It embraces 4,992,000 acres, and is divided into 14 counties.

The landscape is of varied character, often strikingly beautiful, embracing not a few of the most famous scenes in the Union. In the southeastern part of the State the surface is flat and sandy, though the sea-coast is, in many places, very bold, and charmingly varied with fine pictures of rocky bluff and cliff. It abounds in admirable summer resorts, where the lovers of sea-breezes and bathing may find every means and appliance for comfort and pleasure. In the eastern and central portions, the physical aspect of the country, though agreeably diversified, is excelled in attraction by the taste and architectural beauty of its numerous cities, villages, and smiling homesteads, nowhere so abundant and so interesting as here. The Green Mountains traverse the western portions of Massachusetts in two ridges, lying some 25 miles apart, with picturesque valley-lands between. Here are the favorite summer resorts of Berkshire, and other parts of the Housatonic region. Saddle Mountain, 3,505 feet high, is a spur of the most western of the two ridges we have mentioned, known as the Taconic or the Taughkannic Hills. Mount Washington, another fine peak of this line, has an altitude of 2,624 feet. It rises in the extreme southern corner of the State, while Saddle Mountain stands as an outpost in the northwest angle. The more eastern of the two hill-ranges here is called the Hoosic Ridge. Noble isolated mountain-peaks overlook the winding waters and valleys of the Connecticut—some of them, though not of remarkable altitude, commanding scenes of wondrous interest, as Mount Holyoke and Mount Tom, near Northampton. North of the middle of the State is the Wachusett Mountain, with an elevation of 2,018 feet. On Hudson's Brook, in Adams township, Berkshire County, there is found a remarkable natural bridge, 50 feet high, spanning a limestone ravine 500 feet in length. In New Marlborough, the tourist will see a singular rock poised with such marvellous art that a finger can move it; and on Farmington River, in Sandisfield, he will delight himself with the precipices, 300 feet high, known as the Hanging Mountain. Massachusetts has some valuable mineral springs, though none of them are places of general resort. In Hopkinton are mineral waters impregnated with carbonic acid, and carbonates of iron and lime; in Winchendon, a chalybeate spring, and one in Shutesbury, containing muriate of lime. But we need not make further mention of those points of interest here, as we shall have occasion to visit them all, under the head of one or other of the group of New England States, as we follow the net-work of routes by which they may be reached.

The history of the State began with the landing of the Pilgrim Fathers from the May Flower at Plymouth, on the memorable 22d of December, 1620.

The most memorable events of the

Revolutionary struggle within the State were the battles of Lexington and Bunker Hill, and the siege of Boston.

BOSTON.

THIS is one of the most interesting of the great American cities, not only on account of its thrilling traditionary and historical associations, dating from early days in the discovery and colonization of the Western Continent, through all the trials and triumphs of the childhood, youth, and manhood of the republic—but for its dauntless public enterprise, and its high social culture; for its great educational and literary facilities; for its numerous and admirable benevolent establishments; for its elegant public and private architecture, and for the surpassing natural beauty of its suburban landscape. Boston is divided into five sections—Boston proper, East and South Boston, the Highlands (formerly Roxbury), and Dorchester. The old city is built upon a peninsula of some 700 acres, very uneven in surface, and rising at three different points into an eminence, one of which is 138 feet above the sea. The Indian name of this peninsula was Shawmut, meaning "Living Fountain." It was called by the earlier inhabitants Trimount or Tremont, which latter name it still retains in one of its principal streets. The name of Boston was bestowed on it in honor of the Rev. John Cotton, who came hither from Boston in England. The first white inhabitant of this peninsula, now covered by Boston proper, was the Rev. John Blackstone. Here he lived alone until John Winthrop—afterward the first Governor of Massachusetts—came across the river from Charlestown, where he had dwelt with some fellow-emigrants for a short time. About 1635, Mr. Blackstone sold his claim to the now populous peninsula for £30, and removed to Rhode Island. The first church was built in 1632; the first wharf in 1673. Four years later a postmaster was appointed, and in 1704 (April 24th) the first newspaper, called the *Boston News-Letter*, was published. The city was incorporated February 23, 1822, with a population of 45,000. It is divided into 16 wards, and contains a population of 253,924.

168

Boston Harbor is large, and contains numerous islands, and in depth of water and availability is surpassed by none on the coast. A narrow isthmus, which is now called the "Neck," joins the peninsula of Old Boston to the main-land on the south, where are now the Highlands, formerly the suburb of Roxbury. The name "Neck" has lost its former appropriateness by reason of the great additions of "made land" upon either side. It is now both thickly and widely built upon.

South Boston extends some two miles along the south side of the harbor, from Old Boston to *Fort Independence*. Near the centre, and two miles from the State House, are *Dorchester Heights*, memorable as having been occupied and fortified by Washington in anticipation of an attack by the British, March 4, 1776. A fine view of the city, of the vicinity and the sea, may be obtained from these Heights. Here, too, on Telegraph Hill, is a large reservoir of the Boston waterworks. The *Perkins Institute* (Blind Asylum) should be visited. Admission on Saturday mornings. Permits granted at No. 20 Bromfield Street. *Independence Square* contains 6¼ acres.

East Boston (the "Island Ward") is in the western part of Noddle's Island. It was the homestead of Samuel Maverick, while John Blackstone was sole monarch of the peninsula, 1630. Here is the deepest water of the harbor, and here the ocean-steamers chiefly lie. The wharf formerly used by the Cunard steamers is 1,000 feet long. East Boston is connected by two ferries with the city proper. It is the terminus of the *Grand Junction Railroad*, by which several lines of inland railroad are brought to deep water. *Chelsea* is near by.

The principal sights in and around Boston are Bunker Hill Monument, Faneuil Hall, the Common, the Public Garden, the State-House, the Public Library, Old South Church, famous for its historical associations, Athenæum, on Beacon Street, Natural History Buildings, Institute of Technology, Mount Auburn, and Harvard University Buildings, the Great Organ, the City Hospital, the City Hall, and one or two other public buildings. The granite warehouses on the prin-

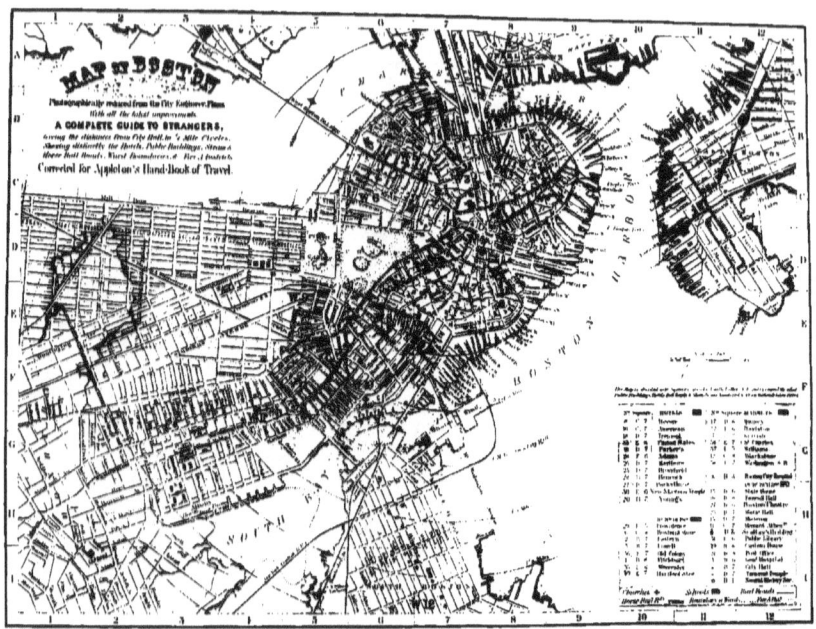

cipal streets, such as Commercial, State, Franklin, Pearl, Summer, etc., are worth visiting, as are also the streets on the "Back Bay" occupied by dwelling-houses. The streets in the older portions of the city are irregular and generally narrow. Washington and Tremont Streets are the principal thoroughfares. In 1867 Roxbury was annexed to this city, and in 1868 Dorchester was also absorbed. The suburban town and villages of Cambridge, Charlestown, Chelsea, and Brookline, are chiefly occupied as the residences of Boston merchants. Boston is well supplied with water from Cochituate Lake, 3½ miles long, situate in Framingham and Natick townships, 21 miles from the city. To Chestnut Hill reservoir, now in process of construction in Brookline, is a favorite drive.

HOTELS, RESTAURANTS, AND CLUBS.

HOTELS : The most fashionable and best-kept houses are the *Revere*, on Bowdoin Square, the *Tremont*, on Tremont Street, the *St. James*, on Newton Street, and the *Commonwealth*, on Washington Street.

Parker's, in School Street, is conducted on the European plan. The restaurant attached to this house is one of the best in the country.

The *American House*, in Hanover Street, is centrally located, and well conducted, and has upward of 300 rooms.

The *United States Hotel*, immediately opposite the New York and Albany Depot, is a convenient and well-appointed house.

Among the other hotels in the city are the following :
Adams House, 371 Washington Street.
Albemarle, Camden Street.
Boston, Harrison Avenue, corner Beach.
Central, 9 Brattle Square.
City, 55 Brattle Street.
Continental, Washington Street.
Coolidge House, Bowdoin Square.
Everett House, corner Washington and Camden.
Sherman House, Court Square.
Hotel Pelham, Boylston Street, corner Tremont.
Marlboro' Hotel, 227 Washington.
Norfolk House, Eliot Square, Boston Highlands

Parks House, 187 Washington Street.
Quincy House, 1 Brattle Square.
Sturtevant House, East Boston.
St. James Hotel, Newton Street, facing Franklin Square.
Waverley House, Charlestown.
Wilde's Hotel, 46 Elm Street.
Winthrop House, 34 Bowdoin Street.
Young's Hotel, Cornhill Court, Washington Street.

RESTAURANTS.—Among the best restaurants are : *Charles Copeland's*, in Tremont Row ; the restaurants of *Parker's*, the *Tremont*, and the *Revere*. The *Cornhill Coffee-House* (Young's) in Cornhill Road, leading from Washington Street, is a well-appointed and much-frequented establishment. Good restaurants are connected with all the railway stations.

CLUBS.—There are several clubs, admission to which is obtained by members' introduction. The *Union* and *Somerset* are among the largest and best.

CONVEYANCES.

RAILWAYS.—The means of "getting about" in Boston are quite as plentiful, and generally better, as well as cheaper, than in most American cities. *Scollay's Building*, corner Tremont and Court Streets, Bowdoin Square, and near *Horticultural Hall*, and the Tremont House, on Tremont Street, and No. 12 Broad Street, are the principal starting-points for the city railway cars. We append a list of the main car-lines and of the hack-fares.

Tremont Street and Depots.—From Scollay's Building, through Court to Green, Leverett, and Causeway Streets, by the Lowell, Eastern, and Fitchburg Railroad Stations, and return by a different route.

East Boston and Camden Street.—From Scollay's Building to Hanover, Fleet, and Commercial Streets, across East Boston Ferry, through Meridian Street to Chelsea ; return by a different route.

Providence Depot and Chelsea Ferry.—From Providence Depot, Pleasant Street, through Boylston, Tremont, Court, Hanover, Richmond, North, and Commercial Streets, to Chelsea Ferry ; return by a different route.

Boston and Roxbury.—The Norfolk House, Warren and Tremont Streets line of cars leave station at Scollay's Building, and reach Roxbury through Harrison Avenue and Washington Street, or Tremont Street.

The Mount Pleasant, Dorchester (via Grove Hall), Brookline, Jamaica Plain, Forest Hills, and Eggleston Square cars, leave from corner of Tremont and Montgomery Place, and reach Roxbury through the same routes as above.

The "Meeting-house Hill and Mount Bowdoin Branch" cars leave corner of Federal and Summer Streets.

The Dorchester and Milton and Quincy cars run from the corner of Broad and State Streets.

South Boston and City Point.—From Scollay's Building, passing the Albany and Old Colony Railway Depots.

Charlestown, Somerville, and Medford cars run from Scollay's Building, across Charlestown Bridge, and return *via* Warren Bridge. (Route to Bunker Hill.)

Lynn and Chelsea (*via* Charlestown) cars leave Scollay's Building and 71 Cornhill, running across Charlestown Bridge, and returning *via* Warren Bridge.

Cambridge and Boston.—Harvard Square, Prospect Street, Broadway, and North Avenue cars leave Bowdoin Square, opposite Revere House, running across Cambridge Bridge; return the same way.

Mount Auburn, Brighton, Newton Corner, West Cambridge, and Watertown, same as above. Stages from Watertown for Waltham every alternate hour.

East Cambridge and Boston.—Cambridge Street and East Cambridge cars leave Bowdoin Square, opposite Revere House, and pass over Craigie's Bridge to East Cambridge, and return.

The railway stations in Boston are eight in number, and are generally accessible by one or other of the lines of street cars.

Old Colony and Newport, on Kneeland Street, South End.

Boston, Hartford, and Erie, foot of Summer Street.

Providence, Pleasant Street, foot of the Common.

Boston and Maine, Haymarket Square, end of Union Street.

Eastern, Causeway Street, near Andover Street.

Fitchburg, Causeway Street (near Warren Bridge).

Lowell, Causeway Street (near Lowell Street).

Boston and Albany, Albany and Beach Streets.

FARES.—Every licensed hack is compelled to keep a copy of the law regulating the rates of fare, posted in a conspicuous place for the information of passengers.

Complaints of overcharges should be made to the Superintendent of Hacks, City Hall.

The *Soldiers' Messenger Corps*, established in 1865, deliver small packages, letters, etc., promptly. The messengers wear scarlet caps. They will generally be found round the principal hotels. Tariff of charges, 15 to 20 cents in the city, 25 cents outside.

BRIDGES AND WHARVES.

BRIDGES. — Seven free bridges link Cambridge, Charlestown, Chelsea, and South Boston, with the Peninsula. These structures are among the peculiarities of the place, in their fashion, their number, and their length. The first one which was built was that over Charles River to Charlestown, 1,503 feet long. It was opened for travel, June 17, 1786. The *Old Cambridge Bridge, or West Boston*, across the Charles River to Cambridge, 2,758 feet in length, with a causeway of 3,432 feet, was completed 1793. The *Federal Street Bridge*, which leads from the Neck to South Boston, is 1,550 feet long; *Mount Washington Avenue Bridge*, leading to South Boston. The *Canal Bridge*, between Boston and East Cambridge, is 2,796 feet, and from East Cambridge another bridge extends 1,820 feet, to Prison Point, Charlestown. *Dover Street*, to South Boston, is 500 feet; and *Warren Bridge* to Charlestown is 1,390 feet. Besides these bridges, a causeway of a mile and a half extends from the foot of Beacon Street to Sewell's Point, in Brookline. This causeway is built across the bay upon a substantial dam. Other roads lead into Boston over special bridges, connecting the city with the main as closely as if it were a part thereof. Thus the topography of Boston is quite anomalous as a "mountain city in the sea."

WHARVES.—The wharves of Boston are among the finest in the United States, and are attractive to the commercial and shipping man. The principal are, *Long*, *Central*, *India*, and *Commercial Wharves*.

Steamers for the several eastern ports leave these wharves daily.

PLACES OF AMUSEMENT.

The theatres and other places of popular amusement in Boston are more numerous in proportion to the population than in most cities, and are well conducted and much frequented.

Boston Theatre, on Washington Street, is one of the best conducted and deservedly popular temples of the drama in the country. The audiences at this theatre are generally large and select.

Boston Museum, on Tremont, between Court and School Streets, is a spacious edifice. (Curiosities and dramatic entertainments.)

Howard Athenæum, 34 Howard Street, near Tremont Row, with sittings for 1,200 persons, occupies the site of the Millerite Tabernacle, destroyed by fire.

Theatre Comique (Old "Aquarial Garden"), 240 Washington Street.

The *Globe Theatre*, 364 Washington Street.

Olympic, 572 Washington Street.

Lyceum, 165 Washington, near Milk Street, on what was once the Province-House estate.

Boston Music Hall, erected 1852, main entrance on Winter Street (organ, etc.). This organ, built by G. F. Walcker, of Ludwigsburg, Germany, is believed to be the second largest instrument in the world. The elaborate cabinet-work is by the Brothers Herter, of New York. The entire cost was $80,000.

Boston Athenæum, Beacon Street (statuary and paintings).

Horticultural Hall, 100 Tremont Street, is a beautiful edifice of dressed granite, much admired for its classic style and elegant proportions. The annual exhibitions of the "Massachusetts Horticultural Society" are held here.

The rooms of the *Boston Society of Natural History*, and the *Institute of Technology*, on Boylston Street, are places of interest, as also the libraries and Museums connected with Harvard University.

CHURCHES.

The churches of the city are 130 in number. The following list embraces those most conspicuous for their age, historical associations, or architecture:

Christ Church, in Salem Street, is an ancient structure, having been erected in 1722.

Trinity Church (Episcopal), erected in 1734, is at the corner of Summer and Hawley Streets.

King's Chapel (Unitarian), at the corner of Tremont and School Streets, is generally visited by strangers. It was founded in 1686. The present building is a plain granite structure, erected 1750–'54. The stained-glass windows over the altar, added in 1862, are much admired. The cemetery attached to the church is the resting-place of Johnson, "the Father of Boston," and of Governor John Winthrop.

Old South Church, at the corner of Washington and Milk Streets, is an object of much interest. It is of brick, was erected (1730) on the site of the original church (1670), which was of wood, and has one of the loftiest spires in the city. This church was used as a place of meeting by the heroes of '76, and was subsequently converted into a riding-school for Burgoyne's troops. The *Prince Library*, formerly kept in this church, is now deposited in the Public Library, subject to the control of the Old South Corporation. The building in Milk Street, opposite the church, is said to mark the site of Franklin's birthplace.

Brattle Street Church (Unitarian) is an ancient-looking Revolutionary structure, frequently visited by strangers. It was consecrated July 25, 1773, and occupies the site of the old wooden structure, founded 1699. The "round shot" fired from the American guns at Cambridge, during the evacuation of Boston by the British, can be seen in the church walls. The late Edward Everett once presided over this church.

St. Paul's Church (Episcopal), facing the Common, between Winter and West

Streets, built in 1820, is of gray granite, 112 by 72 feet, in the Græco-Ionic style. The pillars supporting the portico are of Potomac sandstone.

Tremont Temple, used for devotional purposes, is on Tremont Street. The large hall has sittings for 3,000 people.

Park Street Church (Congregational), facing Tremont Street, near the Common, founded in 1809, occupies a fine position, and has a beautiful spire.

The *Arlington Street Church* (Unitarian) is a fine edifice. It fronts the "Public Garden."

The *Central Church* (Congregational-Trinitarian), corner of Berkeley and Newbury Streets, is probably the most elegant church edifice in New England.

The *Church of the Immaculate Conception* (Roman Catholic), in Harrison Avenue, is an imposing structure, and an immense cathedral is in process of erection in Washington Street.

SQUARES, MONUMENTS, ETC.

Boston Common is a large and charming public ground in a central portion of the city proper. The fence enclosing it is 1½ miles in length. It contains nearly 50 acres, of every variety of surface, with inviting walks, grassy lawns, and grand old trees. It is the pride of the city, and is much admired by strangers.

A pond and fountain, the site of the ancient "Frog-Pond," sometimes called Cochituate Lake, occupy a central point in the grounds, overlooked by Beacon, Tremont, Boylston, and Park Streets, on which stand many of the old mansions of the place. On the upper corner, the massive, dome-surmounted walls of the State Capitol are seen to great advantage. The *Old Elm*, near the pond, is an object of much interest, as one of the oldest and largest trees in the country. It is believed to have existed before the settlement of the city, having attained its full growth in 1722. It was nearly destroyed by a storm in 1832. Since 1854 it has been protected by an iron fence.

The Common drops from Beacon Street, the southeastern declivity of Beacon Hill, by a gentle descent to Charles and Boylston Streets. Adjoining the Common, fronting on Charles Street, is the Public Garden. This embraces 24 acres, and is ornamented with walks, ponds, and parterres of flowers, Powers's statue of *Edward Everett*, the admirable equestrian statue of *Washington*, by Thomas Ball, the beautiful monument in honor of the discovery of ether as an anæsthetic agent, and other pieces of statuary, and a conservatory. While in this vicinity, the pedestrian tourist will be repaid by a visit to the new streets and buildings on what is called the "Back Bay." Arlington Street and Commonwealth Avenue are handsome promenades. A statue to Hamilton, of granite, stands on the latter. The new buildings of the Societies of Natural History and Technology are located here.

Blackstone Square and *Franklin Square* are small but ornamental grounds on Washington Street, passed on the way to the Highlands and the Cemetery of Forest Hills.

Concord, Chester, and *Fort Hill Squares* are smaller public grounds.

The *Riverside Trotting Park*, 3 miles from the city, is reached by the Western Avenue.

A bronze statue of *Benjamin Franklin* stands in the yard of the City Hall, on School Street.

Bunker Hill Monument, commemorative of the eventful battle fought on the spot, is in Charlestown, occupying the site of the old redoubt on Breed's Hill. The observatory at the top of this structure commands a magnificent view, embracing a wide extent of land and water scenery. The journey up is somewhat tedious, traversing nearly 300 steps. The dedication of this monument took place June 17, 1843, in the presence of President Tyler and Cabinet, on which occasion Daniel Webster delivered an oration, which is considered his finest oratorical effort. On the hill is a stone marking the spot where Warren fell. Horse-cars run from the head of Tremont Street to the monument.

PUBLIC AND PROMINENT BUILDINGS AND PLACES NOT OTHERWISE CLASSIFIED.

STATE AND MUNICIPAL.

Faneuil Hall.—This famous edifice, called the "Cradle of Liberty," is in "Faneuil Hall Square," its main entrance being upon Merchants' Row East. It is 125 years old, and is an object of deep interest to Americans. Here the fathers of the Revolution met to harangue the people on the events of that stirring period; and often since that time the great men of the State and Nation have made its walls resound with their eloquence. It was presented to the city by Peter Faneuil, a distinguished merchant, who, on the 4th of July, 1740, made an offer, in a town-meeting, to build a market-house. The building was begun the following year, and finished in 1742. The donor so far exceeded his promise, as to erect a spacious and beautiful Town Hall over it and several other convenient rooms. The dimensions of the original building were 100 by 40. Destroyed by fire in 1761, it was rebuilt in 1763, and enlarged to its present dimensions in 1805. A full-length portrait of the founder, together with the pictures of Washington, by Stuart, and of Webster, by Healey, occupy places upon the west wall. Portraits of President Lincoln, by Ames, and of Governor Andrew, by Hunt, and of many other distinguished men, are also to be seen. *Faneuil Hall Market*, to the east of the Hall, is a substantial and imposing granite edifice. It was commenced August 20, 1824, is 585 feet in length, and covers an area of 27,000 feet. *Quincy Hall*, over the market, is a handsome apartment, surmounted by a dome.

The *State-House* occupies a commanding site on the summit of Beacon Hill, overlooking the "Common." Access by Beacon and Park Streets. Its foundation is 110 feet above the level of the sea. Length, 173 feet; breadth, 61. The edifice was commenced July 4, 1795, and completed in 1798, at a cost of $133,330. It was enlarged in 1855 at a cost of $243,204. On the entrance floor (Doric Hall) is to be seen Chantry's *statue of Washington*. Near by is the staircase leading to the dome, where visitors are required to register their names, and from the top of which is obtained a fine view of the city, the bay, with its islands, and the suburban towns. Bronze statues of Daniel Webster and Horace Mann occupy places on the east front facing the Common. In the *rotunda* of the building is a collection of flags carried by the State troops in the rebellion of 1861–'65, and two brass cannon captured in the war of 1812. The *tablets* on the eastern wall of this apartment are interesting. The *library* contains 25,000 volumes.

The *Old State-House*, at the head of State Street, is an object of considerable interest. Here more than a century ago the "Great and General Court of Massachusetts" sat when the colonists confronted in council the officers of the British crown.

The *Court-House* is a fine building in Court Square, fronting on Court Street. It is built of Quincy granite, and is 185 feet long by 50 feet wide. The corner-stone was laid September, 1833. In this building are held the State, County, City, Probate, and Police Courts. In the basement is the City Lock-up or "Tombs." In the rear of the Court-House are two large brick buildings known as *Massachusetts Block* and *Barristers' Hall*. The U. S. Circuit and District Courts are held at 140 Tremont Street.

The *City Hall*, fronting on School Street, near the Court-House, is a stately edifice, though seen to poor advantage in that confined locality. It is of New Hampshire granite. The corner-stone was laid December 22, 1862, and the building dedicated September 17, 1865. Bryant & Gilman, architects. Cost, $505,-191. A colossal bronze statue of Benjamin Franklin, who was a native of Boston, erected September, 1856, stands in front of the building. This fine work was modelled by R. B. Greenough. The headquarters of the Chief of Police and Chief Engineer of the Fire Department are in the City Hall.

The *State-Prison* is in Charlestown. In the old grave-yard adjoining it is the monument to John Harvard. It is of granite, 15 feet high, and was erected September 26, 1828, by the graduates of Harvard University.

The *City Jail*, on Charles Street, near the Medical College, is an octagonal-shaped granite structure, with four wings, conducted on the "Auburn plan."

The *Beacon Hill Reservoir*, City Water Works, completed in 1849, is a massive granite structure, 200 feet long and 66 feet high, fronting on Derne Street.

MASSACHUSETTS.

NATIONAL.

The *Custom-House* is well located at the foot of State Street, between the head of Long and Central Wharves. The foundation rests on 3,000 piles. It was commenced in 1837 and finished in 1849, at a cost of $1,000,000. It is cruciform, constructed of granite, and has an extreme length of 140 feet, and breadth 95 feet. The longest arms of the cross are 75 feet wide, and the shortest 67 feet, the opposite fronts and ends being all alike. The portico on either front is supported by six fluted Doric columns, 32 feet high, and weighing each 42 tons. The entire height to the top of the dome is 90 feet. A fine view of the harbor and bay is had from the roof.

The *United States Navy-Yard*, extending between the mouths of the Charles and Mystic Rivers, and embracing about 100 acres in extent, is near the Bunker Hill Monument. It contains among other things a rope-walk, the longest in the country. The *Dry Dock*, opened June 24, 1833, is 341 feet long, and cost $675,000.

(For *Post-Office* and *Sub-Treasury*, see *Merchants' Exchange*.)

EDUCATIONAL AND CHARITABLE.

Harvard University.—This venerable seat of learning is at Cambridge, three miles from the city of Boston. It was founded in 1638, by the Rev. John Harvard. The University embraces, besides its collegiate department, law, medical, and theological schools. The buildings are 15 in number, all located in Cambridge, except that of the Medical School in North Grove Street, in Boston. *Gore Hall*, and *University Hall*, are handsome edifices. The former containing the library and the latter the chapel, lecture-rooms, etc. *Holden Chapel* contains the Anatomical Musuem. The Observatory and telescope are of very great interest.

At the foot of Bridge Street is the *Massachusetts Medical College*, attached to Harvard College. The *Warren Anatomical Cabinet* and *Medical Library* are worth visiting. In the laboratory of this building, the fatal altercation between Prof. Webster and Dr. Parkman occurred. The *Zoological Museum*, under the care of Prof. Agassiz, is connected with the university, and its extensive collections very attractive to the naturalist.

Public Schools.—Many of the public schools of Boston are attractive to those interested in the cause of education. The Latin and English High Schools are among the most prominent, while many of the school-houses are models of their class. The former was established in 1635, and the latter in 1821. There are 25 grammar and 49 primary schools in Boston, occupying 638,540 feet of ground, and costing in the aggregate $2,988,260. The office of the Superintendent of Public Schools is in the City Hall.

The *Massachusetts General Hospital*, incorporated 1811, covers an area of four acres on Charles River, between Allen and Bridge Streets. It is constructed of Chelmsford granite.

The *City Hospital* is a conspicuous granite edifice, surmounted by a lofty dome. It stands on Harrison Avenue, opposite Worcester Square, and cost $408,844, exclusive of the grounds.

Marine Hospital.—Located on an elevated site in Chelsea, overlooking the harbor and surrounding country, is the United States Marine Hospital, devoted to invalid seamen.

Asylum for the Blind.—The Perkins Institution and Massachusetts Asylum for the Blind occupies the summit of Mount Washington, in South Boston.

The *Carney Hospital*, with Eye and Ear Infirmary, are excellent institutions.

Mechanic Building is a fine structure at the corner of Bedford and Chauncey Streets, belonging to the Massachusetts Charitable Mechanics' Association.

LITERARY, SCIENTIFIC, AND EDUCATIONAL INSTITUTIONS.

Boston, so long and highly distinguished for its literary character, as to have won the name of the "Athens of America," has, besides its innumerable libraries and institutions of learning, more than 100 periodical publications and newspapers, dealing with all themes of study, and all shades of opinion and inquiry.

The *Boston Public Library*, instituted in 1852, is on Boylston Street, facing the Common, near Tremont Street. The pres ent building was erected in 1856, from designs by Charles Kirby, at a cost of $250,000. It possesses, at this time, about 130,000 volumes.

The *Boston Athenæum* occupies an imposing edifice of Paterson freestone, in the Palladian style, on Beacon, near Tremont Street. It was incorporated in 1807, and is one of the best endowed literary establishments in the world. There are in the library 90,000 volumes, and an extensive collection of tracts. The Athenæum possesses a fine *gallery of paintings* (third story), in connection with which the annual displays of art are made. The *sculpture gallery*, 80 feet long, in the first story, contains several fine specimens of art. Tickets to picture and sculpture galleries, 25 cents.

The *Mercantile Library*, founded 1820, is at 16 Summer Street, corner of Hawley. It has 19,000 volumes and a lecture-hall.

The *Congregational Library*, 40 Winter Street, is rich in historical and ecclesiastical literature, and has a good reading-room.

Spacious *reading-rooms* are attached to the *Public, Mercantile,* and *Athenæum Libraries,* which are free to strangers.

Among the other reading-rooms of the city are the *Merchants' Exchange,* 55 State, *Young Men's Christian Association*, 5 Tremont Temple; the *Church*, 10 Studio Building, and the *New Church*, 21 Bromfield Street.

The *Massachusetts Historical Society*, 30 Tremont Street, organized in 1791, possesses 12,000 volumes, and many valuable manuscripts, coins, charts, maps, etc.

The *New England Historical and Genealogical Society*, 17 Bromfield Street, has a valuable library.

The *American Academy of Arts and Sciences*, one of the oldest societies of the kind in the country (1780), has 20,000 volumes. It occupies an apartment in the Athenæum.

Besides these libraries, Boston has many others; as, the *State Library*, the *Social Law Library, General Theological Library*, 41 Tremont Street, organized April 20, 1860, etc.

The *Lowell Institute*, founded by John Lowell, Jr., Washington Street, provides for regular courses of free lectures upon natural and revealed religion, and many scientific and art topics. We may mention among the foremost literary, scientific, and art societies of the city, the *Institute of Technology*, and the *Natural History Society*, on Berkeley and Boylston Streets (admission Wednesday and Saturday afternoons, free).

The *La Fresnaye Collection* of Birds in the Museum of Natural History numbers 8,989 specimens. The School of Technology is not yet complete. It is modelled on the plan of the *Conservatoire des Arts et Métiers*, and the *École Centrale*, of Paris, and, when finished, will embrace three departments, to be respectively known as the "Society of Arts," "Museum of Industrial Art and Science," and "School of Science and Art."

The *American Statistical* and the *Handel and Haydn Societies* are flourishing institutions.

ART GALLERIES.

The *Studio Building*, where many artists have rooms, is at the corner of Tremont and Bromfield Streets. No stranger should leave Boston without visiting the picture-galleries of Williams & Everett, No. 234 Washington Street; Child & Co., Tremont Street, and Doll & Hendrickson, Summer Street.

OTHER BUILDINGS AND PLACES OF INTEREST.

The Exchange, or *Merchants' Exchange*, 55 State Street, was completed in the fall of 1842, at a cost of $175,000. It is 70 feet high and 250 feet deep, covering about 13,000 feet of ground. The front is built of Quincy granite, with four pilasters, each 45 feet high, and weighing 55 tons each. The roof is of wrought-iron, and covered with galvanized sheet-iron; and all the principal staircases are fire-proof, being constructed of stone and iron. The centre of the basement story is occupied by the *Post-Office*. The great central hall, a magnificent room, is 58 by 80 feet, having 18 beautiful columns in imitation of Sienna marble, with Corinthian capitals, and a skylight of colored glass, finshed in the most ornamental manner. This room is now occupied by the *United States Sub-Treasury*.

The *Masonic Temple*, completed 1866,

175

is a handsome granite structure of six stories. It occupies a prominent position at the corner of Tremont and Boylston Streets, and is generally admired. The old Masonic Temple, dedicated May 30, 1832, stands farther up Tremont Street, on the site of the old Washington Garden. It is now used for the purposes of the United States courts.

Ordway Hall, in Province-House Court, in provincial times, was the residence of the colonial governors.

Horticultural Hall, in Tremont Street, between Bromfield Street and Montgomery Place, is an ornamental granite Gothic building lately erected, much admired for its chaste architectural design and finish.

CEMETERIES.

Mount Auburn Cemetery, about a mile from Harvard University, and about four miles from Boston, by the road from Old Cambridge to Watertown, constitutes one of the sights of Boston, and should be seen by every visitor. It is the property of the Massachusetts Horticultural Society, was consecrated September 24, 1831, and contains 140 acres. It is the oldest and by many considered the most beautiful of American rural burying-places, embellished by landscape and horticultural art and taste, and many elegant and costly monuments. Cars run from the station in Bowdoin Square, via Cambridge (Harvard College), every 15 minutes, during the day, and until half-past eleven o'clock at night. The gateway is of Quincy granite, and cost $10,000. *Central, Maple, Chapel, Spruce,* and other leading avenues, afford a circuit of the entire grounds, with a view of the principal monuments. The *Chapel*, an ornamented Gothic edifice of granite, with stained-glass windows, contains statues of Winthrop, Otis, John Adams, and Judge Story. *The Tower*, 60 feet high, in the rear of the grounds, is 187 feet above Charles River, and commands a wide and charming view for many miles. It is reached by Central, Walnut, and Mountain Avenues. *Forest Pond* and *Dell Pond,* and the numerous fountains, lakes, and ponds in different parts of the cemetery, form a novel and not altogether appropriate feature of Mount Auburn. The *Spurzheim Monument* and the *Bowditch Statue* are in Central and Chapel Avenues.

Forest Hill, in West Roxbury, next to Mount Auburn, is most visited of the Boston cemeteries. It has an imposing entrance of 160 feet front on Scarborough Street. It was consecrated June 28, 1848. A fine view is had from *Snow-Flake Cliff*. *Mount Hope Cemetery*, in West Roxbury, was purchased by the city (1857), for $35,000.

Woodlawn, four miles north of Boston, and two miles from Chelsea, incorporated 1850, has many attractive features as a rural burying-ground. The gate-house is a Gothic structure, 56 feet high. *Rock Tower* commands a fine view of the Bay, islands, and sea. *Granary Burying-Ground*, adjoining Park Street Church, between Tremont and Beacon Streets, contains a monument to the parents of Franklin. It is of Quincy granite, 25 feet in height. The *Cemetery* attached to King's Chapel, at the corner of Tremont and School Streets, contains the remains of Johnson, the "Father of Boston," as he has been termed; and of Governor John Winthrop.

Mount Hope Cemetery, in West Roxbury, is in care of the city.

SHORT PLEASURE EXCURSIONS.

Boston Harbor.—The harbor of Boston, as elsewhere remarked, is among the best and most spacious on the coast, and to the summer visitor affords one of the most striking features of the city. The most important and noteworthy fortified works in and around Boston are to be seen in a sail up or down the beautiful harbor. They are, *Fort Independence,* on Castle Island ; *Fort Winthrop,* on Governor's Island, and *Fort Warren,* on George's Island. Deer (*House of Industry, etc.*), Long, Rainsford, Spectacle, Gallop, and Thompson's Islands, are also passed. A visit to these islands and defensive works constitutes one of the pleasantest features of the summer tourist's experience in Boston. Frequent excursions take place in the summer season. Steamers make several trips daily between Boston and Hingham, and other places of interest along the coast. As these boats vary their routes and times of departure, tourists should consult the daily papers of Boston for particulars.

Beyond Hingham is the rocky coast of Cohasset, opposite which is the famous Minot's Rock Light-house. The present stone light-house takes the place of one constructed on iron piles, which was swept away in a severe gale on the night of the 16th of April, 1851, when two of the keeper's assistants were lost.

Nahant.—This once fashionable and still pleasant watering-place is situated about 12 miles from Boston, by water, and 14 by land. (*See* page 196.) During the summer season, a steamboat plies daily. (Fare 25 cents.) This is a most agreeable excursion, affording an opportunity, in passing through the harbor, for seeing some of the many beautiful islands with which it is studded. The peninsula is divided into Great and Little Nahant, and Bass Neck. On the south side of Great Nahant is the dark cave or grotto, called the *Swallow's Cave*, 10 feet wide, 5 high, and 70 long, increasing, in a short distance, to 14 feet in breadth, and 18 or 20 in height. On the north shore of the peninsula is a chasm 20 or 30 feet in depth, called *Spouting Horn*, into which, at about half tide, the water rushes with great violence and noise, forcing a jet of water through an aperture in the rock to a considerable height in the air. *Castle* and *Pulpit Rocks* and *Irene's Grotto* are visited by tourists.

Copp's Hill, near the Fitchburg Depot, is frequently visited. In the burying-ground is the vault of the Mather family. Roxbury, 2 miles, and Jamaica Plain, 3¼ miles, are pleasant places on the Providence Railway. *Longwood* and *Brookline* are pleasant residence spots, between 3 and 4 miles on the road to Worcester. *Sharon*, 17¼ miles, occupies the highest land between Boston and Providence. *Mr. Cushing's Garden*, a place of great beauty, is a short distance beyond Mount Auburn, in Watertown. Tickets may be obtained, gratis, on application at the Horticultural Hall, on Tremont Street. *Fresh Pond*, another charming place of resort, is about four miles from Boston, and about half a mile from Mount Auburn. The other sheets of water in the vicinity of Boston, frequented by visitors, are *Horn*, *Spot*, *Spy*, and *Mystic Ponds*.

Phillips's Beach, a short distance northeast of Nahant, is another beautiful beach, and a noted resort for persons in search of pleasure or health.

Point Shirley, five miles from Boston, affords a pleasant drive. The most direct route is *via* the East Boston Ferry. Excellent fish and game dinners and suppers are obtained here. (*Tuft's* Hotel.)

Brighton, a station on the Albany Railway, 5 miles west of the city, is famous for its cattle-market.

Nantasket Beach, 12 miles from Boston, is situated on the east side of the peninsula of Nantasket, which forms the southeast side of Boston Harbor. The beach, which is remarkable for its great beauty, is four miles in length, and celebrated for its fine shell-fish, sea-fowl, and good bathing.

Chelsea Beach, about three miles in length, is situated in the town of Chelsea, and is another fine place of resort, with good accommodation for visitors. A ride along this beach on a warm day is delightful. It is about five miles from Boston, and may be reached through Charlestown over Chelsea Bridge. *Swampscott* and *Phillips's Beach* may be reached on the same road.

Boston Water-Works.—These works draw their supplies from Lake Cochituate, situated in the towns of Framingham, Natick, and Wayland, about twenty miles distant from Boston.

The Brookline Reservoir is a beautiful structure of 38 acres, the water surface being about 22½ acres. Its capacity is about 100,000,000 gallons.

The Chestnut Hill Reservoir, on the boundaries of Brookline, Brighton, and Newton, is of recent construction, and a place of much resort.

The South Boston Reservoir, on Mount Washington, is an interesting locality. This spot was formerly known as Dorchester Heights, from which Washington compelled the evacuation of Boston by the British troops.

In arranging the routes for this State, the different routes from New York to Boston will first be given, then those connecting with the Connecticut routes, lastly the roads diverging from Boston in all directions.

ROUTE I.

NEW YORK TO BOSTON.
Via New York and Boston Express Line.

FROM New York to New Haven, see Route I. of CONNECTICUT. From New Haven to Springfield, see Route IV. of CONNECTICUT.

STATIONS.—Springfield, 136 miles from New York (connects with Connecticut River Railway and with Boston and Albany Railway); Indian Orchard, 142; Wilbraham, 145; Palmer, 151 (connects with New London Northern Railway); Warren, 161; West Brookfield, 165; Brookfield, 167; Spencer, 172; Charlton, 177; Rochdale, 181; Worcester, 190 (connects with Providence and Worcester, Worcester and Nashua, and Norwich and Worcester Railways); Grafton, 196; Westboro', 202; Southville, 206; Cordaville, 207; Ashland, 210; Framingham, 213 (connects with branches to Millbury and Milford); Natick, 217 (connects with branch to Saxonville); Wellesley, 219; Grantville, 221; Auburndale, 224; West Newton, 225; Newton Corner, 227; Brighton, 229; Boston, 234.

Springfield (136 miles) is upon the Connecticut River, 26 miles north of Hartford, 98 miles from Boston, and 138 from New York. The approach by this route up the bank of the Connecticut affords a fine view of the city. It was settled 1635, under its Indian name of Agawam, which was changed in 1640 to its present name. The *United States Arsenal*, located here, is the largest in the Union. It is charmingly perched upon Arsenal Hill, looking down upon the beautiful town, the river, and the fruitful valley. This noble panorama is seen with still better effect from the tower which rises from one of the arsenal buildings. This establishment employs nearly 800 hands, and 175,000 stand of arms are kept constantly on hand. Upward of $12,000,000 were paid out for the construction of arms here during the rebellion.

This is a famous gathering-point of railroads. The Connecticut River route starts hence, and furnishes one of the pleasantest lines of travel from New York to the White Mountains, through Northampton, Brattleboro, Bellows Falls, to Wells River and Littleton, N. H. (*See* Route No. V.) The Boston and Albany Railway passes through Springfield also, and continues our present route to Worcester. Below the city is the Agawam Ferry, leading over to the present town of Agawam, the birthplace of Senator Ben Wade. Springfield was incorporated as a town in 1646, and as a city in 1852. The manufactures of the place are peculiar, consisting not only of cotton or woollen factories, but of large workshops devoted to paper collars, jewelry, book-making, fire-arms, railway-cars, and similar unique industries. The city ranks third in the State in the value of its churches, which are of unusual architectural splendor and correctness. The *Cemetery*, on Maple Street, *Hampden Park*, and *Long Hill*, afford pleasant rides or walks. *Brightwood*, the residence of Dr. Holland, the author, is in the neighborhood of the city. The leading hotels are the *Massasoit House*, *Hayne's Hotel*, and *Cooley's Hotel*.

Indian Orchard (142 miles) is a manufacturing village on the Chicopee River, within the city limits of Springfield. It is noted for the success with which the experiment of half-time schools has been introduced among the operatives.

Wilbraham (145 miles) is the seat of the Wesleyan Academy, a well-known educational institution.

Palmer (151 miles) is the junction of the Boston and Albany with the New London Northern Railway, which has recently been extended north to South Vernon, Vt., thus becoming a through-line. Within sight of the station is the State almshouse in Monson, an imposing collection of buildings.

In this township are three streams, the Chicopee, Swift, and Ware Rivers, which furnish power for numerous manufactories.

Warren (161 miles) is a very pretty manufacturing village on the Chicopee River.

West Brookfield (165 miles) is noted for its boot and shoe factories. In 1675 it was the scene of a desperate fight between the whites and the Indians, when the town was destroyed. What is now called West Brookfield is the oldest portion of the town, where the primitive village existed.

Brookfield (167 miles) is especially noted for the large number of boots and shoes made in the factories located there. In the neighborhood are several ponds.

Worcester (190 miles) is a flourishing city, 45 miles from Boston, in the centre of one of the most productive agricultural regions of Massachusetts. It was settled in 1713, and incorporated as a city in 1848. It is noted for its schools and manufactures, and for its public institutions. The *American Antiquarian Society*, founded (1812) by Isaiah Thomas, has a fine building in the Italian style. The library, of 50,000 volumes, contains some rare works. The Public Library, established in 1859, has a library of about 23,000 volumes. *Mechanics' Hall* has a fine organ, and seats for 2,500. The *State Lunatic Asylum*, established in 1832, and the *Oread Institute*, are prominent edifices. The Jesuit *College of the Holy Cross* is about two miles south of the city. *Quinsigamond Lake*, a beautiful sheet of water, usually the scene of the annual races between the Yale and Harvard crews, is two miles east of Worcester.

In a southeasterly direction from the city is a conspicuous building, with turrets, which was erected for a medical college, but is now the *Worcester Academy*, so called, a Baptist institution. On the north side of the city are the new and elegant buildings of the *Worcester County Free Institute of Industrial Science*, recently endowed by private liberality. It has about 80 pupils, learning to become master-workmen in the various mechanic arts. A little farther north, and not in sight, is the well-known *Highland Military School*. The spacious rooms of the Natural History Society are filled with a choice collection of specimens. The city has commenced the erection of a new high-school building, to be one of the finest in the State. There are two large and handsome cemeteries containing many expensive monuments. The habits of the people are strongly marked with enterprise and public spirit. The *Bay-State House* is a first-class hotel.

The population is a little over 41,000.

Quite a net-work of railways connects the city with all parts of the country—the *Boston and Albany* Railroad; the *Worcester and Nashua*, communicating through other routes with the St. Lawrence River; the *Worcester and Providence*; the *Norwich and Worcester*; and the *Boston and Worcester*, which we now follow to the end of our present journey.

Westborough (202 miles) is a prosperous farming town, with some mechanical and manufacturing business. About three miles southeast of the station are the *Hopkinton Mineral Springs*. There is a large water-cure establishment not far from the station. The State Reform School, for boys, is established here.

Framingham (213 miles) is a thrifty town, having various mechanical and manufacturing establishments. In the vicinity are the State Normal School, and the Middlesex County Fair Grounds. It is also near the head of Cochituate Lake, the source of the water-supply of Boston. Two branch roads diverge here.

Natick (217 miles) is a large manufacturing village near the foot of Cochituate Lake, along the bank of which the railroad runs for about a mile. The Saxonville branch diverges here.

Wellesley (219 miles) is composed principally of residences of persons doing business in Boston. Not far from the station is Wauban Lake, around which are a number of elegant residences. From this point to *Boston* the villages through which the road passes may be considered suburbs of the city, and the general remark, that they are filled with handsome suburban residences, will suit them all. In coming into Boston, the railroad passes along the south bank of the Charles River, affording splendid views of the city and vicinity.

ROUTE II.

NEW YORK TO BOSTON.

Via Shore Line, Stonington, & Providence, and Boston & Providence Railways.

FROM New York to Stonington, see Route I. of Connecticut. From Stonington to Providence, see Route I. of RHODE ISLAND.

STATIONS.—Providence, 188 miles from New York; Pawtucket, 192; Attleborough, 200; West Mansfield, 205; Mansfield, 207 (junction of Taunton Branch); Foxborough, 210; Sharon, 214; Canton, 217; Readville, 223; Boston, 231.

Providence (188 miles). (*See* page 162.)

Pawtucket (192 miles). (*See* page 166.)

Attleborough (200 miles) is noted for its manufacture of jewelry, in addition to which there are numerous other branches of manufacturing carried on.

Mansfield (207 miles) possesses a fine water-power, derived from the Cocasset, Rumford, and Canoe Rivers. It is noted for the number and variety of its manufactures, and is the junction of the branch road to Taunton on the *New Bedford & Taunton Railway.*

Foxborough (210 miles) is a large manufacturing village, the principal establishment being the Union Straw Works, which give employment to an army of employés.

Canton (217 miles) is in the great manufacturing township of the same name. The granite viaduct of the railway at this point is noticeable, being 600 feet long and 63 feet high. To the east of the railway, between *Canton* and *Readville,* is *Blue Hill,* a commanding eminence.

Readville (223 miles), is in the town of Dedham, about two miles from the village of the same name, which is reached by a branch road, and is the county seat of Norfolk County. It has a number of manufactories, some fine public buildings, and a number of elegant residences.

ROUTE III.

NEW YORK TO BOSTON.

Via various Steamboat Lines.

Stonington Line.— This route is by steamer daily from pier 18, North River, round the Battery to the East River, and thence through Long Island Sound to Stonington, Connecticut, whence it is by rail as in Route II. (For places of interest seen from the steamboat, consult "Trip Down the Bay," and "Trip up the East River," pages 29 and 30 of NEW YORK.)

Norwich Line.— Steamer daily from pier 39, North River, *via* East River and Long Island Sound to New London, Connecticut; thence by Route V. of Connecticut to Worcester, and by Route I. of Massachusetts to Boston.

Fall River Line.—Steamer daily from pier No. 3 North River, through East River and Long Island Sound to Newport; thence by *Old Colony and Newport Railway.* (*See* Route VIII. of MASSACHUSETTS.)

Providence & New York Steamship Company.—Steamer daily, at 5 P. M., from pier 27, North River, to Providence, R. I., connecting there with all morning trains for the North and East.

The most expeditious routes are those marked I. and II.; though in pleasant summer weather the steamboat lines are much pleasanter, as they afford the traveller a most favorable opportunity of seeing Jersey City, Brooklyn, New York, and the various objects of interest described in a "Trip up the East River," page 30. The boats run on these lines are large, fast, splendidly furnished, and usually provided with a fine band of music. The Fall River Line has the best boats.

ROUTE IV.

NEW YORK TO THE HOUSATONIC REGION, TO PITTSFIELD, HOOSIC TUNNEL, ETC.

Via Housatonic, and Pittsfield and North Adams Railways.

(*Continuation of Route II. of Connecticut.*)

THE route traversed by this railway is very circuitous, and the traveller is for the greater part of the trip hemmed in by the steep sides of the mountains. At Sheffield the valley is quite broad, becomes narrower at Great Barrington, and then the train winds very slowly around the base of Monument Mountain to Stockbridge, where the valley is broader. The rest of the route is through a narrow valley, only occasionally widening into limited meadows.

In fact, "from *Salisbury* to *Great Barrington*," says Mr. Beecher, "the road lies along the base of the mountains, and, indeed, is called the under-mountain road." This route, as far as Bennington, in Vermont, runs through what the same writer calls "a country of valleys, lakes, and mountains, that is yet to be as celebrated as the lake district of England and the hill country of Palestine."

STATIONS.—Bridgeport, 59 miles from New York; Ashley Falls, 134; Sheffield, 138; Great Barrington, 144; Van Deusenville, 146 (branch to West Stockbridge and State line); Housatonic, 148; Glendale, 151; Stockbridge, 152; South Lee, 154; Lee, 158; Lenox, 161; Deweys, 165; Pittsfield, 169 (connects with Boston and Albany, and Pittsfield and North Adams Railways); Coltsville, 172; Berkshire, 175; Cheshire, 178; Cheshire Harbor, 181; South Adams, 183; North Adams, 189 (stages leave North Adams for Williamstown, etc., on arrival of trains).

Bridgeport (59 miles). (*See* page 146.)

Ashley Falls (134 miles) is the first station in Massachusetts. (For all stations between *Bridgeport* and *Ashley Falls*, *see* Route II. of CONNECTICUT.)

Sheffield (138 miles), upon the Housatonic River, is a quiet town at the base of the mountains. It was the first town settled in the county. Its main street is broad and well shaded. The dwellings convey the idea of quiet ease. The town is large, containing numerous valuable farms, but otherwise there is little business, except in quarrying marble. Orville Dewey, D. D., formerly of New York city, a distinguished author and Unitarian preacher, resides here. There are Congregational and Methodist Churches of good size, and a small Episcopal Chapel. In matters of education the place is backward.

Great Barrington (144 miles) is noted for its educational advantages, and for the quarries of variegated marble in the vicinity. It was first settled by the Dutch, from Kinderhook, N. Y., and their names are still prominent among the esteemed citizens. It was the county seat for a number of years, until it was succeeded by Lenox, and in 1869 by Pittsfield. Rev. Samuel Hopkins, from whom the adjective Hopkinsinian is derived, was once pastor of the Congregational Church. The poet Bryant formerly resided here. The president of the Housatonic Railway, David Leavitt, formerly a noted financier in New York city, has an elegant mansion here, and his great barn has long been a local curiosity. John Milton Mackie, the author, has a charming residence overlooking the valley. The town is not remarkable for its public buildings, but the *Congregational* and *Episcopal Churches*, and the new High School, are ornaments to the place. The Berkshire Woollen Company has large and well-built stone structures for its works. The *Berkshire House* is a good hotel.

Mr. Beecher, in his "Star Papers" (which we will quote more than once in the description of this route), says: "Great Barrington is one of those places which one never enters without wishing never to leave. It rests beneath the branches of great numbers of the stateliest elms. It is a place to be desired as a summer residence."

Van Deusenville (146 miles) is the junction of the branch to *West Stockbridge* and the *State Line*. There are extensive iron-works here, and a large Episcopal Church. It is a part of Great Barrington.

West Stockbridge, through which the State Line Branch passes, is a township in which is located a village of the same name; it is noted for its beds of iron-ore, and for its inexhaustible quarries of marble. It contains iron-works and flouring-mills, which create much business. There are several churches of different denominations. The somewhat famous C. Edwards Lester was once pastor of a church here. It was originally a part of Stockbridge.

Housatonic (148 miles) is a man-

181

ufacturing village of Great Barrington, and is rapidly increasing in importance and wealth. It is the seat of the mills of the Owen Paper Company, and of other thriving manufacturing establishments.

South Egremont, in Berkshire County, 4 miles to the west of Great Barrington, is reached by stage from Great Barrington, and also by 6 miles' staging from Hillsdale, on the Harlem Railway. It is a quiet village, in the midst of mountain scenery and well-stocked trout-streams. There are fine drives in the vicinity. The *Mount Everett House* is a very good summer hotel.

Stockbridge (152 miles) is "famed for its meadow-elms, for the picturesque beauty adjacent, for the quiet beauty of a village which sleeps along a level plain just under the river of the hills." It contains many elegant country-seats, among which are those of David Dudley Field, and the Rev. Henry Martin Field, of New York, and of Mrs. Henry D. Cone. The house in which Jonathan Edwards wrote his celebrated metaphysical works is occupied by the *Edwards Place School*, for boys. There is a neat cemetery, a fine soldiers' monument, and an elegant Italian fountain. The principal public buildings are the Public Library (with a good collection of books), the Congregational and Episcopal Churches. The pastor of the latter is a son-in-law of Mrs. Harriet Beecher Stowe, and that lady is one of the summer visitors here. The early mission to the Indians here was aided by the English *Society for the Promotion of the Gospel in Foreign Parts*, to the funds of which the celebrated Dr. Watts, hymn-writer, contributed. Stockbridge has an early history of great interest, having had many patriotic and learned sons and daughters. There is a good high-school. The *Laurel Hill Association*, founded in 1853, has had a great influence in beautifying the town. Southwest of the town is *Monument Mountain*, celebrated in Bryant's verse, and northward is *Rattlesnake Mountain*. "*Stockbridge Bowl* is a sweet lakelet, on the borders of which are several summer residences. If you wish to be filled and satisfied with the serenest delight, ride to the summit of this encircling hill-ridge, in a summer's afternoon, while the sun is but

an hour high. The Housatonic winds, in great circuits, all through the valley, carrying willows and alders with it wherever it goes. The horizon on every side is piled and terraced with mountains. Abrupt and isolated mountains bolt up here and there over the whole stretch of plain, covered with evergreens."
In the vicinity of Stockbridge are many delightful spots where picnic and other excursions are of frequent occurrence—among them the *Ice Glen*, where in the warmest weather may always be found a store of ice. The *Stockbridge House* is an excellent hotel, only open in summer.

Glendale (151 miles) is a manufacturing village, containing a woollen-factory and paper-mills, which are not very active.

Lee (158 miles) is a flourishing town on the *Housatonic River*, owing its prosperity to extensive paper-mills and woollen-factories. The *Morgan House* is a small but neat and well-kept hotel.

Lee is celebrated for its marble—among the best in the world. Large quantities of it were used in constructing the new portions of the United States Capitol at Washington. Its roads are not excelled. Its High School, in charge of Abner Rice, A. M., is widely celebrated for its high grade of scholarship, and in its other schools and churches the town compares favorably with any other. There are many drives about the town that are very attractive to the lover of Nature. That down the valley of the Hopbrook and up the mountain to Monterey is said not to be excelled in beauty in any part of Europe. The Congregational Church is one of the most elegant wooden structures in the State. The *Episcopal Church* is a small Gothic structure of white marble. There are also *Baptist*, *Methodist*, *Catholic*, and two *African Churches*, besides two Union chapels. The *High School* is the most prominent building, standing on elevated ground, near the Methodist Church. Among the residences are those of Alexander Hyde, a prominent writer and lecturer on agriculture, William Taylor, and Elizur Smith. The latter is chief owner of the paper-mills in the village. The *Lee Bank* is a well-managed institution, with a good building. Thomas A. Durant, the builder of the Pacific Railway, is a native of this town.

South Lee contains the mills of the South Lee Paper Company, which are well managed and thriving.

Lenox (161 miles) is a favorite resort of Bostonians and New-Yorkers, and is provided with good hotels, the chief of which is *Curtis's*. It is a place of little business, except in that part called the Furnace, which lies on the railway. There are extensive manufactories of window-glass, rough and polished plate-glass, and iron. This is the only place in the country at which polished plate-glass is made. It is in no respect inferior to the French article, as the passenger on the Housatonic Railway may see in the latest-made through-car, the windows of which are glazed with it. There are numerous pleasant excursions from Lenox, as that, for example, to Bald Mountain (carriages all the way), which gives a very fine view of the village and valley to the south, including Monument Mountain. Among the summer residences here are those of F. F. Dorr, Messrs. Woolsey and Aspinwall, Colonel Auchminty, Richard Goodman, J. D. F. Lanier, Dr. Dunning, Mrs. Schermerhorn, and General John F. Rathbone, of Albany. The last is on the site occupied by Henry Ward Beecher, is very expensively adorned, and unexcelled for its view in Berkshire. Mr. Beecher's "Star-Papers" were written in the house on the lower side of the highway, opposite General Rathbone's. At that time the road ran directly over the hill, and Mr. Beecher's house stood near where the general's now is. The stone wall on which *Dog Noble* barked has been removed also. To quote the "Star-Papers" again, it is "known for the singular purity and exhilarating effects of its air, and for the beauty of its mountain scenery." Mrs. Fanny Kemble Butler, who long resided here, said of the grave-yard at Lenox: "I will not rise to trouble any one if they will let me sleep there. I will only ask to be permitted, once in a while, to raise my head and look out upon this glorious scene."

Pittsfield (169 miles) is a large manufacturing and agricultural town, elevated 1,100 feet above the level of the sea. It is 151 miles west from Boston, and 49 east from Albany. The village is beautifully situated, and contains many elegant public edifices and private dwellings. In this village there was standing, until July 24, 1864, in the park opposite the Congregational Church, one of the original forest-trees—a large elm, 120 feet high, and 90 feet to the lowest limb—an interesting relic of the primitive woods, and the pride of the village. The necessity of cutting it down was esteemed a public calamity. The concentric rings in the trunk showed it to be 340 years old. The town received its present name in 1761, in honor of William Pitt (Earl of Chatham). The *Young Ladies' Institute* occupies several admirable buildings, surrounded by well-embellished grounds. The *New Roman Catholic Cathedral* is the finest in Western Massachusetts. Pittsfield is a large depot of manufactures, being extensively engaged in the production of cotton and woollen goods, machinery, fire-arms, and railroad-cars. The railway station here is one of the most elegant in the country, and has a really good restaurant attached. The chief hotels are *Burbank's* (well kept) and the *United States*, near together. On the principal square are the First Congregational Church, a Gothic structure of stone, erected in 1853, of which Dr. John Todd, the author, is pastor; and one of the finest business blocks to be found out of our great cities. The Berkshire Medical School, which formerly flourished here, is discontinued. Pittsfield is the new county seat of Berkshire, and very elegant and costly public buildings are in process of erection on the square. Some of the private residences are very large and in fine taste. Representative Dawes lives in a pleasant house half a mile east of the square. The drives in the vicinity are very fine, especially those to Williamstown (20 miles) (*see* page 184); to *Lebanon Springs* (15 miles) (*see* page 47). On the road to *Lebanon Springs* is *Lanesboro Pond*, near the head-waters of the Housatonic, surrounded by beautiful scenery.

At Pittsfield, the *Housatonic Railway* connects with the *Boston and Albany* and *Pittsfield and North Adams Railways*, the latter of which we follow to its terminus.

Lanesboro, distant 5 miles from Pittsfield, is noted for the beauty of its mountain scenery, and the healthfulness of its climate. It was the residence of the late Governor George N. Briggs.

Cheshire (178 miles) is one of the important towns on this road. It is famous for butter, cheese, lumber, and glass. The inhabitants for 50 years were almost unanimous in their Democratic politics. To show their appreciation of President Jefferson, they made him a present, on January 1, 1802, of a famous cheese, weighing 1,450 pounds. It was presented by Rev. John Leland, an eccentric Baptist preacher of the place. The south line of the town has a great many angles, the boundaries having been established to suit the religious views of the people, leaving the Presbyterian families in Lanesboro, and taking the Baptist families into Cheshire.

North Adams (189 miles), the terminus of the road, which, from Pittsfield, passes through a primitive but beautiful region, is one of the largest and most prosperous manufacturing villages in Berkshire County. It was originally called *East Hoosac*, and was owned by a company of Bostonians, of whom Hon. James Otis was one. This company used to meet at the *Bunch of Grapes* tavern in Boston, and Otis presided, as the lots were divided, and arrangements made for settling. The name was changed to Adams, in honor of the Governor of Massachusetts of that name. South Adams is a village of considerable importance in the southern part of the town. Rev. Washington Gladden, of North Adams, has published a little guide, entitled "From the Hub to the Hudson," which contains full accounts of the northern part of Berkshire, the Hoosac Tunnel, and other matters. He is quite enthusiastic in speaking of the natural beauties of the region, rather neglecting southern Berkshire, with which he is less acquainted. It is near *Grey Lock Mountain*, a noble peak having an elevation of 3,500 feet, the highest point in Massachusetts. There is a notable natural bridge upon Hudson's Brook, near the village. The *Wilson House* is a very large and well-furnished hotel, the property of Allen B. Wilson, the inventor of the Wheeler and Wilson sewing-machine. About a mile from the hotel is the *Natural Bridge*, a curiosity of considerable interest. The *Cascade* is 1¼ miles from the hotel. Liberal provision is made for education, and the High-School building is the most costly in the county. The Congregational Church here is flourishing, and the other denominations are also. This is the point of connection with the *Troy and Boston Railway*, for the stations on which line see "Route IX. of New York."

Williamstown (5 miles from North Adams, and 43 from Troy), upon the *Troy and Boston Railway*, is the seat of *Williams College*. It is a beautiful village in the midst of the Berkshire Mountains.

Mills's Park is an enclosure of 10 acres, in which a marble shaft, surmounted by a globe, marks the spot where Samuel J. Mills and his associate students met by a hay-stack in 1807, to consecrate themselves to the work of foreign missions. This was the beginning of this work in America.

The residence of President Hopkins (the oldest college-president in America, and a native of Stockbridge) is directly opposite *West College.*

Among the many attractive spots in the vicinity are *Flora's Glen*, where Bryant wrote "Thanatopsis," *Sand Spring*, the *Cascades*, a beautiful fall, and *Snow Hole*, a gorge in the mountains where the snow never entirely melts. The Hoosac Tunnel is within 7 miles. *Greylock*, the central eminence of *Saddle Mountain*, is frequently ascended by parties of gentlemen, but is considered impracticable for ladies. The *Mansion House* is the best hotel, but not very well kept. *Greylock Hall* was opened June 1, 1870, at the celebrated Sand Springs, and is capable of accommodating 100 guests. It has an observatory overlooking the valley. The waters are efficacious in curing cutaneous diseases.

The college buildings are worthy of notice, among which the Gymnasium, the gift of J. Z. Goodrich, of Stockbridge, is the most costly. There is a bronze soldiers' monument on a granite pedestal, in the main street.

The Hoosac Tunnel is two

miles from North Adams, and is well worth a visit. When completed it will be the longest in the world, with the exception of the one under the Alps, at Mont Cenis, which is 7½ miles in length. The cost will be over $9,000,000. The railway between Boston and Albany does not take the shortest route between those cities. The Hoosac Mountain, with its eastern and western peaks, stands directly across the straight path, and ever since 1825 the ingenuity of man has been working in vain to devise a way to get through the mountain. The present tunnel was begun in 1855, and has been in charge of different contractors, who have had varying success.

F. Shanly & Brother, of Canada, the present contractors, are confident they will have completed their great undertaking before the expiration of the contract time, January 1, 1874.

The tunnel may be approached either from Adams, or from Greenfield on the Connecticut River. The town of Florida occupies the mountain-top. The views on the stage-trip over the mountains are extremely picturesque and sublime. The tunnel may be examined by ladies without danger.

ROUTE V.

NEW YORK TO THE CONNECTICUT RIVER VALLEY, WHITE MOUNTAINS, FRANCONIA MOUNTAINS, etc.

Via Connecticut River Railway.

(*A continuation of Route III. of Connecticut.*)

STATIONS.—Springfield, 136 miles from New York (connects with Boston and Albany Railway); Chicopee Junction, 140; Willimansett, 143; Holyoke, 144; Smith's Ferry, 149; Mount Tom, 151; Northampton, 153 (connects with New Haven and Northampton Railway); Hatfield, 157; North Hatfield, 160; Whately, 162; South Deerfield, 164; Deerfield, 169; Greenfield, 172 (connects with Vermont and Massachusetts Railway); Bernardston, 179; South Vernon, 186 (connects with Ashuelot and Vermont and Massachusetts Railways, and with the New London Northern); Vernon, 191; Brattleboro, 196 (connects with Rutland and Burlington Railway).

Springfield (136 miles). (*See* page 178.)

Chicopee (140 miles) is a township on the Connecticut and Chicopee Rivers, noted for its manufactories, the principal of which are those of the *Dwight Manufacturing Company*, devoted to the production of prints, sheetings, etc., and the *Ames Manufacturing Company*, which makes machinery, fire-arms, bronze cannon and ornaments, swords, silver and plated ware. Here were cast the bronze doors of the Senate wing of the Capitol at Washington, after designs by Crawford, and Ball's equestrian statue of Washington, in the Public Garden at Boston.

Holyoke (144 miles) possesses the greatest water-power in Massachusetts, being the site of the large dam of the Holyoke Water-Power Company, formerly the Hadley Falls Company. The Connecticut River, which here has a fall of 60 feet in three-quarters of a mile, is dammed by an immense structure over 1,000 feet in length and 30 feet in height. This dam is built of wood, spiked to the rock of the river-bed, and covered with plates of boiler-iron. The constant pouring of the water wore away the rock to such an extent as in 1869 as to imperil the existence of the dam, and it was found necessary to construct an apron or inclined plane, which, while it has robbed the fall of much of its beauty, has answered the preservative purpose for which it was designed. The canal (3 miles in length) around the falls was made in 1792, being the first ever constructed in this country for purposes of navigation.

The village of Holyoke is comparatively new, is very pretty, regularly laid out, and noted for its numerous paper-mills and other manufactories, as are the villages on the opposite bank of the river.

Smith's Ferry (149 miles) is where visitors to *South Hadley* cross the river.

South Hadley is where the celebrated *Mount Holyoke Female Seminary* is located. This seminary, founded by Miss Mary Lyon, in 1837, furnishes at a moderate cost a practical education, the duties of housekeeping being an especial feature in the system of instruction. The pupils of this institution are fitted for teachers. South Hadley has many spots which afford most agreeable prospects. Standing on the elevated bank of the river and facing the northwest, you look directly up the Connecticut, where it passes between Holyoke and Tom—those mountains rising with precipitous boldness, on either side of the valley; through the opening, the river is seen for two or three miles, enlivened by one or two lovely islands, while over the rich meadows, that adorn the banks, are scattered trees, through which, half hidden, appears in the distance the village of Northampton, only its more conspicuous edifices being visible.

Northampton (153 miles) was settled in 1654, by planters from Hartford and Windsor. The Indian name is *Nonotuck*. It is in every way one of the most charming villages in New England, and none other is more sought for summer residences. It lies about a mile west of the Connecticut, surrounded by rich alluvial meadows, sweeping out in broad expanse from the base of the grand mountain-ridges. The village is not too large for country pleasures, the population of the township falling within 6,000; yet its natural advantages are so great, and so many pleasant people have established themselves here in such attractive places, and the hotels are so admirable, that the tourist will not miss either the social or the physical enjoyments of his city home. Even the little business part of Northampton has a cosy, rural air, and all around are charming villas, nestled on green lawns, and among fragrant flowers. Among the specialties of Northampton are several water-cure establishments, the chief of which is that known as *Round Hill*, a large and beautiful place, upon the fine eminence after which it is named, just west of the village. The schools here have always been in very high repute. The *State Lunatic Asylum* is a large and elegant structure, built in 1858. This is also the seat of the *Clarke Institution for Mutes*, endowed by the late John Clarke with $300,000. This school was the first in this country to teach articulation to mutes, instead of signs, thus abandoning the old or Hartford system of instruction.

The vicinage of Northampton is, perhaps, the most beautiful portion of the Connecticut valley, the most fertile in its intervale land, and the most striking in its mountain scenes; for it looks out directly upon the crags and crests of those famous hills, Mount Holyoke and Mount Tom. *Florence*, a thriving manufacturing point two miles west of the centre of the town, is where the celebrated Florence sewing-machines are made.

The hotels are the *Mansion House*, the *Warner House*, and *Round Hill Institute*. This is the junction with the *New Haven and Northampton Railway*.

Mount Holyoke is directly across the river from Northampton; a carriage-road three miles long winds to the summit, 1,120 feet above the sea, where there is a little inn and an observatory. There are not of its kind many scenes in the world more beautiful than that which the visitor to Mount Holyoke looks down upon: the varied features of the picture —fruitful valleys, smiling villages and farms, winding waters, and, far off, on every side, blue mountain-peaks innumerable—will hold him long in happy contemplation. Mount Holyoke is a part of a ridge of greenstone, commencing with West Rock near New Haven, and proceeding northerly across the whole of Connecticut; but its elevation is small until it reaches Easthampton, when it suddenly mounts up to the height of nearly 1,000 feet, and forms Mount Tom. The ridge crosses the Connecticut, in a northeast direction, and, curving still more to the east, terminates 10 miles from the river, in the northwest part of Belchertown. All that part of the ridge east of the river is called Holyoke, though the *Prospect House*, built in 1821, stands near its southwestern extremity, opposite Northampton, and near the Connecticut. This is by far the most commanding spot on the mountain, although several distinct summits, that have as yet received no uniform name, afford delightful prospects. An inclined railway, 600 feet long, down the mountain-side, connects with horse-cars to the Connecticut River, where passengers take boat.

Mount Tom, upon the opposite side of the river, is not yet so much visited as are its neighboring cliffs of

Holyoke, though it is considerably higher, and the panorama from its crest is no less broad and beautiful. It is more frequently called by its Indian name *Nonotuck* by the people of the valley. Its height is 1,200 feet.

Easthampton, on the Granby Railway (five miles from Northampton), is situated on the west side of Mount Tom. It contains a very extensive button-manufactory, well deserving of a visit from those who can appreciate mechanical ingenuity. The principal feature of the place, however, is its noble seminary for the youth of both sexes, which was founded and liberally endowed by the Hon. Samuel Williston, at an expense of $55,000, and has been in successful operation upward of 20 years.

Hadley, the birthplace of General Joe Hooker, is famous for its manufacture of brooms, first introduced in 1790. It is connected with Northampton by a bridge over the Connecticut. The river immediately above the town, leaving its general course, turns northwest; then, after winding to the south again, turns directly east; and, thus having wandered five miles, encloses, except on the east, a beautiful intervale containing between two and three thousand acres. On the isthmus of this peninsula lies the principal street (West Street), the handsomest, by nature, in New England. It is a mile in length, running directly north and south; is sixteen rods in breadth; is nearly a perfect level; is covered during the fine season with a rich verdure; abuts at both ends on the river, and yields everywhere a delightful prospect. Hadley was settled in 1650, by a colony from Hartford, Windsor, and Wethersfield, Connecticut. In this town resided for fifteen or sixteen years Whalley and Goffe, two of those who composed the court for the trial of King Charles I., and who signed the warrant for his execution. They came to Hadley in 1664. When the house which they occupied was pulled down, the bones of Whalley were found buried just without the cellar wall, in a kind of tomb formed of mason-work, and covered with flags of hewn stone. After Whalley's death, Goffe left Hadley, and went, it was thought, to New York, and finally to Rhode Island, where he spent the rest of his life with a son of his deceased *confrère*. Four miles east of Hadley is *Amherst College* (see page 189).

The *Great Bend* of the *Connecticut* is reached a mile north of Northampton, and here we take our last view of the river until we reach South Vernon.

Whately (162 miles) is a small village, just beyond which the

Sugar-Loaf Mountain comes into view, as we journey on up the valley. This conical peak of red sandstone rises almost perpendicularly five hundred feet above the plain, on the bank of the Connecticut, in the south part of Deerfield township. As the traveller approaches this hill from the south, it seems as if its summit were inaccessible. But it can be attained without difficulty on foot, and affords a delightful view on almost every side. The Connecticut and the peaceful village of *Sunderland* on its bank appear so near, that one imagines he might almost reach them by a single leap. This mountain overlooks a spot which was the scene of the most sanguinary conflict that occurred during the early settlement of this region. A little south of the mountain the Indians were defeated in 1675 by Captains Lathrop and Beers; and one mile northwest, where the village of Bloody Brook (*South Deerfield*) now stands (which derived its name from the circumstance), in the same year, Captain Lathrop was drawn into an ambuscade, with a company of "eighty young men, the very flower of Essex County," who were nearly all destroyed. A stone slab marks the spot where Captain Lathrop and about thirty of his men were interred; and a *marble monument*, about 20 feet high and 6 feet square, is erected in front of the *North Church.* Among other relics of the pioneer warfare, there is preserved at Deerfield an old door—all that remains of the block-house to which the early settlers were wont to flee for protection. It is of massive wood-work and bears numerous tomahawk-scars and bullet-pits. *Table Rock* and *King Philip's Chair* are on the eastern side of the mountain.

South Deerfield (164 miles) is a little village principally noted as the site of the battle-field of *Bloody Brook* described in the preceding paragraph.

Deerfield (164 miles) is noted for

the beauty of its principal street, which is shaded by numbers of large and handsome trees.

Deerfield Mountain, rising some 700 feet above the plain on which the village stands, commands a wide view. The alluvial plain on which Deerfield stands is sunk nearly 100 feet below the general level of the Connecticut valley; and at the southwest part of this basin Deerfield River is seen emerging from the mountains, and winding in the most graceful curves along its whole western border. Still farther down is the village, remarkable for its regularity, and for the number and size of the trees along the principal street. Upon the whole, this view forms one of the most perfect rural pictures that can be imagined. *Pocumtuck Rock* commands a fine view of the valley. The *bridge* over the Deerfield River, just beyond the station, is 750 feet long and 90 feet above the water. Three miles north of Deerfield, and in the same valley, but on higher ground, can be seen the lovely village of Greenfield.

Mount Toby lies in the north part of Sunderland and the west part of Leverett townships, and is separated from Sugar-Loaf and Deerfield Mountains by the Connecticut River. On various parts of the mountain interesting views may be obtained, but at the southern extremity of the highest ridge there is a finer view of the valley of the Connecticut than from any other eminence. Elevated above the river nearly 1,200 feet, and but a little distance from it, its windings lie directly before you; and the villages that line its banks, Sunderland, Hadley, Hatfield, Northampton, and Amherst, appear like so many sparkling gems in its crown.

Mount Warner is a hill of less altitude than any before named, being only 200 or 300 feet in height, but a rich view can be had from its top of that portion of the valley of the Connecticut just described. It lies in the north part of the town of Hadley, not more than half a mile from the river, and can be easily reached by carriage.

Greenfield (172 miles) is a pleasant and thriving place. The wonted New England quiet, however, is all around it, in elm-shaded streets and garden-surrounded villas. The hill-ranges in the neighborhood open fine pictures of the valleys and windings of the great river. Being connected with the railway systems of the West and of the Northwest, it is a desirable place for tourists to rest a while ere starting upon fresh fields of adventure and exploration. Green River, which flows near the village, is a pretty stream, and hard by are the Deerfield and Greenfield Rivers. Cutlery is extensively manufactured here. The neighborhood abounds in pretty drives. Hotel—the *Mansion House*. The *Vermont and Massachusetts Railway* comes in here from the east, and the *Troy and Greenfield* from the west. The latter is the route to the Hoosac Tunnel, which is much visited by tourists. Directly east on the Connecticut is Turner's Falls, the site of an immense water-power, second only to that of Holyoke. It was purchased early in 1870, by General B. F. Butler and others, and a new Lowell has already been laid out and begun.

Bernardston (179 miles) is the last station in the State, and the seat of *Power's Institute*. Soon after leaving the station we come in sight of the Connecticut River again.

Brattleboro (196 miles). (*See* the continuation of this route under the title of Route I of VERMONT.)

ROUTE VI.

FROM NEW LONDON TO BRATTLEBORO, WHITE MOUNTAINS, LITTLETON, LAKE MEMPHREMAGOG, QUEBEC, MONTREAL, AND ALL PARTS OF VERMONT, WESTERN NEW HAMPSHIRE, NORTHERN NEW YORK, AND PROVINCE OF QUEBEC.

Via New London Northern and Vermont and Massachusetts Railways.

(*Continuation of Route IV. of Connecticut.*)

STATIONS.—New London, 126 miles from New York (*see* page 148); Monson, 61 miles from New London; Palmer, 65 (connects with Boston and Albany Railway, and Ware River Railway); Belchertown, 76; Amherst, 85; North Amherst, 88; Leverett, 90; South Montague, 95; Grout's, 100; Northfield Farms, 103; Northfield, 109; South Vernon, 111 (connects with Ashuelot and Connecticut

River Railways); Vernon, 116; Brattleboro, 121 (connects with Vermont Central, Vermont and Canada Railway).

New London. (*See* page 148.)

Monson (61 miles) is 5 miles beyond the boundary-line between Connecticut and Massachusetts. It is situated in a valley, and is a prosperous place. The stone bridges in this vicinity are built without cement or mortar, the stones being kept in position by the peculiar manner in which they are laid.

Monson Academy is a flourishing institution.

Flynt's *Granite Quarry* is seen a short distance north of the station. Many of the finest buildings at Amherst and Springfield are constructed of this stone, and large quantities are now being transported to Albany for the new State-House.

Palmer (65 miles). (*See* page 178.)

The Ware River Railway, from Palmer to Ware and Gilbertville (important manufacturing villages), was completed in June, 1870, and was at once leased to the New London Northern.

This road will be rapidly extended to Barre, Winchendon, Peterboro', N. H., etc.

Belchertown (76 miles). Just after leaving this station, a fine view of the Connecticut Valley and Mount Holyoke (*see* page 186) appears on the west of the road.

Amherst (85 miles) is charmingly situated, and is noted for its colleges, its beautiful surroundings, and its refined and cultivated society. It is irregularly built upon a hill, commanding extensive views of the Connecticut Valley and adjacent mountain-ranges. The town contains five Congregational churches, as also one Baptist, and one Episcopal. There are two hotels, the *Amherst House*, near the centre of the village, and the *Orient House*, about two miles east of the railroad depot.

Amherst College, one of the chief seats of learning in New England, is located here. It was founded in 1821, and numbers (1869–'70) 19 instructors and 255 students. The buildings occupy an eminence in an amphitheatre of 100 miles in extent, and command a prospect of exceeding beauty. The college cabinets, with their rich and varied collections in zoology, botany, geology, mineralogy, etc., are open daily, and well repay a visitor's attention. The college recitation-rooms are said to be the finest in the country, some of them being embellished with numerous and costly works of art.

The *Massachusetts Agricultural College*, with its extensive dormitories and greenhouses, is located about a mile north of Amherst College, and possesses, with other objects of interest, the *Durfee Plant-House*, which is well stocked with rare and beautiful plants. Since its opening, in 1866, this institution has become the largest and most successful agricultural school in the country.

Leverett (90 miles) is in the midst of some delightful scenery. Tourists to enjoy it should take the left side of the cars going north, and the right side going south.

Grout's (100 miles) is the terminus of the *New London Northern Railway*, the cars running the rest of the way to Brattleboro on the track of the *Vermont and Massachusetts Railway*, which extends east to Fitchburg, and west to Greenfield and the Hoosac Tunnel.

Northfield (109 miles) is an attractive village, and the last station in Massachusetts. After leaving the station the road crosses the Connecticut River, fine views of which are had from the bridge.

Brattleboro (121 miles). (*See* page 223.)

This is continued as Route I of VERMONT.

ROUTE VII.

NEW LONDON TO WORCESTER AND FITCHBURG.

Via Norwich and Worcester Railway.

(*Continuation of Route V. of Connecticut.*)

STATIONS.—New London, 126 miles from New York; Webster, 57 miles from New London; North Webster, 58; Oxford, 62; North Oxford, 64; Auburn, 68; Worcester, 73 (junction of the Western Railway); Sterling Junction, 85 (junction of the Worcester and Nashua Railway); Fitchburg, 99.

New London. (*See* page 148.)

Webster (57 miles) and **North**

Webster (58 miles) almost form one continuous village. They are both supported by their extensive manufactures, deriving their power from several millstreams, the water-supply of which is rendered constant by a large storage reservoir about a mile east of North Webster, called *Chabanakongkomun Pond.* This is destined to be a large and populous manufacturing town.

Oxford (62 miles) and **North Oxford** (64 miles) are two villages of Oxford township. The first of these is a quiet and pleasing village. The principal street is broad, and is fronted by many attractive residences. In the township are several woollen and cotton mills, and many boot and shoe factories. Two miles southeast of the station is *Fort Hill,* upon which are the remains of an old fort, built by the Huguenots, who were the first settlers in the township.

Worcester (73 miles). (*See* page 179.)

Sterling Junction (85 miles) is the intersection of the Worcester and Nashua Railway, forming the connecting link with the net-work of railways in Northeastern Massachusetts.

Fitchburg (99 miles) is a very enterprising manufacturing place, and the semi-capital of Worcester County. It contains a town-house, with a capacious public hall, several churches, a number of very good schools and many manufactories of various kinds, the *Nashua River* furnishing a fine water-power. A handsome court-house was erected in 1870. The *Fitchburg* and *American* are good hotels. At this point the road connects with the *Fitchburg and Boston* and the *Vermont and Massachusetts Railways.*

ROUTE VIII.
BOSTON TO PLYMOUTH, NEW BEDFORD, NEWPORT, CAPE COD, AND VICINITY.

Via Old Colony and Newport, and connecting Railways.

[THIS route will not be a continuous one, as the system of short roads and branches will involve numerous digressions. The stations will be given at the head of each branch, and not as usual at the head of the route.]

STATIONS.—Boston; Neponset, 5 miles; Quincy, 8; Braintree, 10 (connects with South Shore Railway); South Braintree, 12; Randolph, 15; Stoughton, 19; North Easton, 22; Easton, 24; Raynham, 30; Taunton, 33; Weir, 34; North Dighton, 38; Dighton, 41; Somerset, 44; Fall River, 49; Tiverton, 53; Bristol Ferry, 55; Newport, 67.

Neponset (5 miles) is a flourishing village on Dorchester Bay. It has a fine harbor, and is an important suburb of Boston.

Quincy (8 miles) is upon an elevated plain, and is remarkable for its neatness and beauty. The buildings of note are a church known as "Adams Temple," containing a monument to John Adams, a noble town-hall of granite, and the ancestral home of the Quincy family. A short distance from the village are the celebrated quarries of the Quincy granite. John Adams and John Quincy Adams, both Presidents of the United States, and John Hancock, a signer of the Declaration of Independence, were born here.

Braintree (10 miles) is a manufacturing place, though in the vicinity the land is highly cultivated. The *South Shore Railway,* 22 miles in length, connects here.

Weymouth is a fine town, having three stations on the *South Shore Railway,* named respectively *Weymouth, East* and *North Weymouth.* There is a good harbor in the town, and the last two stations named are manufacturing and business places. The former is a favorite residence for Bostonians, and contains many handsome dwellings.

Hingham, on the South Shore road, is a town noted for its beautiful scenery. It is a popular summer resort, possesses a good hotel, and in summer a steamer makes regular trips to Boston, affording fine views of the bay.

Nantasket, on the South Shore road, is in the town of *Hull,* 7 miles from the principal village. The town is a favorite watering-place, having a beautiful beach 4 miles long. (*See* page 177.) There are several good hotels, and there is also steamboat communication with Boston several times a day.

Cohasset, the terminus of the road, is a pleasant village, romantically situ ated on a rocky coast. The celebrated Minot's Ledge Light-house is located here. *Marshfield*, the home of Daniel Webster, is 8 miles distant, and can only be reached by private conveyance. Having completed this digression, we will return to the main line.

South Braintree (12 miles) is a charming village, in the midst of beautiful scenery. The *Plymouth Branch* diverges here.

South Abington (21 miles), on the Plymouth Branch, is noted for its shoe-manufactories. A short branch connects it with Bridgewater.

Plymouth (37¼ miles), the terminus of the branch, is noted as the landing-place of the Pilgrim Fathers, December 22, 1620, and as being the site of the first house ever built in New England. *Plymouth Rock*, the great attraction, is now reduced to a small area, with the surface just visible above the ground. The most noticeable buildings are, Pilgrims' Hall, the Court-House, and one of the churches. The former building contains many relics, among them a chair belonging to Governor Carver, the sword-blade of Miles Standish, and the cap of King Philip. It also contains Colonel Henry Sargent's valuable painting of the May Flower. The harbor is large but shallow. The environs and views are delightful, and in the township are about 200 ponds, one of the largest, *Billington Sea*, being well stocked with fish. The *Samoset* is a good hotel. The stations of *Randolph*, *Stoughton*, *North Easton*, and *Easton*, are merely manufacturing towns.

Raynham (30 miles) is noted as the place where two brothers, named Leonard, started the first establishment on this continent for forging iron. The original Leonard mansion, built in 1670, is still occupied by a member of the family.

Taunton (33 miles) is on Taunton River, at the junction of Mill River, and at the head of navigation. It is one of the most beautiful towns in the State, and is noted for its manufacture of "Britannia" ware. This is the junction with the *Cape Cod*, *Middleboro'*, *and Taunton Railway*. Taunton Green and Mount Pleasant Cemetery are attractive spots. The *State Lunatic Asylum* is located here. The *New Bedford and Taunton Railway*, from Mansfield, on the *Boston and Providence Railway*, connects here.

Dighton (41 miles) is on the Taunton River. Near here is the celebrated *Dighton Rock*, an insulated mass of granite, covered with inscriptions, which are so worn that they cannot be deciphered. They are supposed to have been cut by Norwegian adventurers, who are thought to have visited this coast about the year 1000.

Fall River (49 miles) is one of the leading towns of the State, and is especially noted for its manufactures, having the largest number of spindles of any town in the State. All the mills, formerly run by water-power from Fall River, are now run by steam. The view from the hill is very beautiful. Fall River, upon which the city is situated, descends 130 feet in less than half a mile, over a granite bed and between granite banks. The harbor, which strictly is a part of Narragansett Bay, is a fine one, with sufficient depth of water to float the largest vessels. The quarries of granite in the vicinity are very valuable, and most of the stone used in the construction of the forts at Newport came from them. Fall River is noted for the number of its churches. It has also several good hotels. *Mount Hope*, the home of King Philip, is seen across the bay. This is the terminus of the Fall River line of Sound steamers to New York.

Newport, R. I. (*See* page 164.)

We will now return to South Braintree and follow the other branch.

STATIONS.—East Randolph, 15 miles from Boston; East Stoughton, 17; North Bridgewater, 20; Campello, 22; Keith's, 24; East and West Bridgewater, 25; Bridgewater, 27 (connects with Abingdon and Bridgewater Branch); Titicut, 31; Middleboro', 35 (connects with Cape Cod and Middleboro, and Taunton Railways); Lakeville, 37; Myricks, 42 (connects with New Bedford and Taunton Railway); Assonet, 45.

Bridgewater (27 miles) is the connection with the *Abingdon and Bridgewater Branch* to South Abingdon, 7 miles. It is an ancient town. The site was granted as a plantation to the town of Duxbury in 1642. It was then called

"Saughtuchquett" (Sawtucket), and was sold (1645) to Captain Miles Standish by "Onsamegum," chief of the Wampanoag Indians. The *Bridgewater Iron-Works* are among the largest on the continent. They consume 10,000 tons of iron annually, and employ about 600 men. The manufacture of small-arms in New England was commenced here.

Middleboro' (35 miles) is a prosperous town, pleasantly situated upon the Taunton River. It is the seat of a very popular scholastic institution. Here the *Cape Cod* and *Taunton Branches* leave the main line. The *Fairhaven Branch* also diverges for Mattapoisett and New Bedford, 61 miles.

Myricks (42 miles) is where the *New Bedford and Taunton Railway* diverges.

New Bedford (61 miles) stands on the west side of the Accushnet River, which empties into Buzzard's Bay. The situation, upon ground rising rapidly from the water's edge, is very advantageous, and affords fine views of the harbor and *Fair Haven*, opposite. While the town, as a rule, is neatly built, *County Street* is noted for its unrivalled combination of natural and artificial beauties. The Town Hall and Custom-House are both imposing buildings, as are some of the churches. The educational advantages are good, and there is a fine public library. There is also a large theatre. The fisheries have always been a source of prosperity, and now to them is added a large and important manufacturing interest. This city has recently constructed water-works, at an expense of about $700,000, although the supply of well-water has always been plentiful and pure. The drive around Clark's Point is a very attractive one for the visitor. It is about 5 miles long, its whole distance on the margin of the bay and river, 80 feet wide, and kept perfectly smooth. New Bedford, although its fleet is less than half its former tonnage, is still deserving of the title of the Whaling City. Various manufactories are taking the places of the whaling fleet in the business operations of the city, and the Wamsutta Mills, whose product of cotton cloth is not excelled in the country, is one of the largest of the manufactories of New England. There are charming drives, and rare facilities for sea-bathing and all aquatic sports. It is connected by lines of steamers with *Boston*, *Providence*, and *Fall River*. There is also a regular steamer to *Nantucket*, touching at *Wood's Hole*, in *Falmouth*, and *Holmes's Hole*, on *Martha's Vineyard*.

HOTELS: *Parker House*, *Mansion House*, and others. About 10 miles from New Bedford, on *Great Hill*, near the shore of Buzzard's Bay, is an excellent hotel.

Martha's Vineyard is an island in the Atlantic Ocean, about 30 miles from New Bedford, and is a delightful resort, the trip by steamer being very charming, affording passengers a view of the islands in the bay, among them *Naushon*, the summer headquarters of the New York Club. This is a regularly-organized camp-meeting ground, a grove being especially laid out for the purpose, cottages having been erected in large numbers. These meetings are held every August, and there are often from 15,000 to 20,000 people upon the island at one time.

Gay-Head, the westerly end of Martha's Vineyard, is a spot well worth the attention of the visitor to this island. It is of volcanic origin, and has been pronounced by Prof. Hitchcock one of the most remarkable geological formations in America. "Never," said General Twiggs, as he looked from the top of this bold promontory, "since I stood on Table Rock, have I seen a sight so grand and beautiful as this!"

Nantucket is an island still farther out in the ocean, and can be reached by steamer either from *New Bedford* or *Hyannis*. There are good hotels, the *Ocean House* and *Adams House*, and numerous boarding-houses. The inhabitants are hospitable, and the evenings are spent in social visiting and pleasant dancing-parties. Here is to be had every pleasure that can be derived from the ocean, and as for fishing, every taste can be gratified, from catching the smallest of the finny tribe to the largest shark. The scenery is charming, and the air pure and bracing. The grand whaling fleet, once the pride of this island, and the wonder of the world, has departed, but *Siasconsett*, with its many and unique attractions, remains, and will never disappoint the seeker after health and pleasure.

We will now return to *Middleboro'*, and travel over the

CAPE COD RAILWAY.

STATIONS.—Middleboro', 35 miles from Boston; South Middleboro', 42; West Wareham, 45; South Wareham, 47; Wareham, 49; Agawam, 51; Cohasset Narrows, 54; Monument, 55; North Sandwich, 59; West Sandwich, 60; Sandwich, 62; West Barnstable, 70; Barnstable, 73; Yarmouth, 76 (connects with Cape Cod Central Railway); Hyannis, 79 (connects with steamer for Nantucket daily).

CAPE COD CENTRAL RAILWAY.

STATIONS. — South Yarmouth, South Dennis, North Harwich, Harwich, Brewster, East Brewster, and Orleans.

Without going into a detailed description of the roads, we will say, in general terms, that if one would like to visit that secluded portion of Massachusetts—Cape Cod—let him journey from "Plymouth Rock," the inner point, to Provincetown, the outer verge, and he will find novelties in both physical Nature and social life, which will more than compensate for the labor of reaching them.

BOSTON AND PROVIDENCE RAILWAY.

NEW YORK TO BOSTON.

This railway forms the connecting link between New York and Boston, by the route designated as I. of Connecticut, and continued from Stonington as I. of Rhode Island. It is also the last link in the routes by "Sound Steamers," via *Stonington Line* or *Bristol Line*.

STATIONS.—New York: Stonington, 138 miles; Providence, 188; Pawtucket, 192; Attleboro', 200; West Mansfield, 205; Mansfield, 207; Foxboro', 210; Sharon, 214; Canton, 217; Readville, 223; Boston, 231.

Providence, R. I. (188 miles). (*See* page 162.)

Pawtucket, R. I. (192 miles). (*See* page 166.)

Attleboro', Mass. (200 miles), one of the oldest settlements in the colony, and noted for its manufactures.

Sharon (214 miles) is the highest point between Boston and Providence. The natural scenery is beautiful and picturesque. One of its principal attractions is

Massapoag Lake, a beautiful sheet of water, and a popular summer resort.

Canton (217 miles) is in the midst of diversified and picturesque scenery, and is interesting on many accounts. The town contains *Punkapog Pond*, a pretty little lake, well stocked with fish, and *Blue Hill*, an eminence 630 feet high, from the summit of which superb views can be enjoyed of Boston and environs. The railroad viaduct, over one of the ponds and river at Canton, is one of the most elegant specimens of masonry in the United States.

Boston (231 miles). (*See* page 168.)

ROUTE IX.

BOSTON TO BELLOWS FALLS AND LAKE CHAMPLAIN.

Via Fitchburg, Cheshire, and connecting Railways.

STATIONS. — Boston: Charlestown, 1 mile; Cambridge, 3; Belmont, 6; Waltham, 10; Lincoln, 17; Concord, 20; South Acton, 25; Littleton, 31; Groton Junction, 35 (connects with Peterboro and Shirley, Worcester and Nashua, and Stony Brook Railways); Shirley, 40; Leominster, 46; Fitchburg, 50 (connects with Fitchburg and Worcester and Cheshire Railways); South Ashburnham, 60 (connects with Vermont and Massachusetts Railway); North Ashburnham, 64; Winchendon, 68; State Line, 71; Keene, N. H., 92 (connects with Ashuelot Railway); Bellows Falls, Vt., 114 (connects with Rutland and Burlington and Vermont Central Railways).

Boston, Charlestown, and **Cambridge.** (*See* description of Boston and vicinity, page 168.)

Watertown (8 miles by branch road) is the site of a United States Arsenal and Mr. Cushing's beautiful garden. The Charles River is navigable to this point for vessels of 6 feet draft.

Waltham (10 miles) is a flourishing manufacturing village on the Charles River. The first cotton-mill in Massachusetts was built here, and this is the site of the Waltham Watch-Works, the largest in the United States. A short distance from the village is Prospect Hill, which rises to a height of 500 feet, affording splendid views.

Concord (20 miles) is a manufacturing village, on both sides of the Concord River. April 19, 1775, the same day as the *battle of Lexington* (the first in the Revolutionary War), blood was shed at Concord. A granite obelisk, 25 feet in height, marks the spot.

Lexington (11 miles, by a branch road) is where the first blood was shed in the Revolutionary War. Eight Americans were killed, in memory of whom a monument has been erected by the State upon the village green.

Groton Junction (35 miles) is the point of intersection with the *Peterboro' and Shirley, Worcester and Nashua,* and *Stony Brook Railways.* In the village of *Groton* is the Lawrence Academy, a richly-endowed institution.

Leominster (46 miles), on the Nashua River, is the principal seat of the comb-manufactories of the State.

Fitchburg (50 miles), junction with *Fitchburg and Worcester,* and *Cheshire Railways.* We follow the latter road. (For Fitchburg, see page 190.)

South Ashburnham (60 miles) connects with *Vermont and Massachusetts Railway* for the *Hoosac Tunnel.*

Winchendon (68 miles), on Miller's River, is the last station in the State. It is a manufacturing town.

(For the continuation of this route, see Route IV of NEW HAMPSHIRE.)

ROUTE X.

BOSTON TO THE WHITE MOUNTAINS, MONTPELIER, VT., GREEN MOUNTAINS, LAKE CHAMPLAIN, THE ADIRONDACKS, LAKE MEMPHREMAGOG, AND CANADA.

Via Boston and Lowell, and connecting Railways.

STATIONS.—Boston : Medford, 5 miles ; Winchester, 8 (Woburn Branch Railway diverges) ; East Woburn, 9 (connects with Stoneham Branch Railway); Woburn W. S., 10 ; Wilmington, 15 ; Billerica, 19 ; North Billerica, 22 ; Lowell, 26 (connects with Lowell and Lawrence, and Salem and Lowell Railways); North Chelmsford, 29 (junction of Stony Brook Railway); Tyngsboro' and Dunstable, 33 ; Concord Depot, 39 ; Nashua, 40 (connects with Concord Railway of New Hampshire, and Worcester and Nashua Railways).

Medford (5 miles) is a suburb of Boston and the seat of Tufts College, a Universalist institution, which is located on an eminence known as Walnut Hill. This is the head of navigation on the Mystic River and is noted for its shipbuilding. It is also reached by branch of *Boston and Maine Railway.*

Winchester (8 miles) is where the Woburn branch diverges to *Woburn,* a pleasant manufacturing village 2 miles distant.

East Woburn (9 miles) is where the Stoneham Branch Railway diverges to *Stoneham* (2 miles), a place noted for its large boot and shoe manufactories. From this point to Lowell the scenery is uninteresting.

Billerica (19 miles) is a station midway between the villages of *Billerica* and *Tewksbury.* At the former of these is located the *Howe School,* and at the latter the *State Pauper Institution,* where such paupers as do not properly belong to any particular town are cared for.

Lowell (26 miles) is one of the largest and most noted manufacturing cities in the Union, and is a place of the greatest attraction to any one interested in the subject of the production of prints, cottons, and carpets. The Pawtucket falls, the source of the city's prosperity, have a descent of 33 feet, and around them runs a canal, which, originally intended for purposes of navigation, was purchased in 1821, and devoted to the use of a mill-race. In 1846 the present grand canal from the outlet of Lake Winnipisseogee was commenced. The mills of the *Merrimac Manufacturing Company* are of great extent, and their process of printing calicoes very interesting. The *Lowell Manufacturing Company* manufacture carpets on a large scale, and a visit to their works is highly entertaining. Another place of interest is the *Lowell Bleachery.*

There are over 50 mills in operation at

Lowell, employing many thousand operatives, and representing a capital of many millions of dollars. The *Mechanics' Association* has a library of 10,000 volumes. A monument to Ladd and Whitney, of the Sixth Massachusetts regiment, killed in Baltimore, April 19, 1861, stands in the public square.

The principal hotels are the *Washington*, *Merrimack*, and *American*.

The Boston and Lowell Railway here connects with the *Lowell and Lawrence* and *Salem and Lowell Railways*.

North Chelmsford (29 miles) is the junction with the Stony Brook Railway to Groton Junction.

Tyngsboro' and **Dunstable** (33 miles) are the last villages, upon this route, in Massachusetts, and agricultural in their character.

This trip will be resumed as Routes I. and III. of NEW HAMPSHIRE.

ROUTE XI.

BOSTON TO PORTSMOUTH, N. H.; PORTLAND, ME.; THE ROADS CENTRING AT THOSE CITIES; AND THE PRINCIPAL PLACES IN NORTH-EASTERN MASSACHUSETTS.

Via Eastern Railway, Branches and Connections.

THE Shore line to Portland, running parallel with the coast, communicates with several popular and attractive watering-places, among which Nahant, Swampscott, Marblehead, Beverly, Rockport, and Rye Beach, may be specified.

The cool sea-breezes, the freedom from dust, the varied scenery and picturesque views, afford great attractions to the summer tourist in search of health and recreation.

STATIONS.—Boston: Somerville, 2 miles; Everett, 3 (Saugus Branch Railway diverges); Chelsea, 4; North Chelsea, 6; West Lynn, 10; Lynn, 11; Swampscott, 12; Salem, 16 (Marblehead Branch diverges, Junction of Lawrence and South Reading Branches, and Salem and Lowell Railway); Beverly, 18 (Gloucester Branch diverges); North Beverly, 20; Wenham, 22; Ipswich, 27; Rowley, 31; Newburyport, 36 (Junction of Newburyport Railway); East Salisbury, 38 (Amesbury Branch diverges); Seabrook, 42; Hampton Falls, 43; Hampton, 46; North Hampton, 49; Greenland, 51; Portsmouth, 56 (Junction of Concord and Portsmouth, and Portland, Saco and Portsmouth Railways); Portland, 108.

Everett (3 miles), on the Malden River, was formerly called *South Malden*. The Saugus Branch diverges here.

Chelsea (4 miles) is one of the pleasantest of the Boston suburban cities. The *Naval Hospital*, *Marine Hospital*, and *Town Hall*, are prominent buildings. *Powder-Horn Hill* and *Mount Bellingham* command fine views. Population, 18,547. *Woodland Cemetery* is two miles beyond.

Lynn (11 miles) is a well-built city of 28,231 inhabitants, according to the United States census of 1870, on the northeastern shore of Massachusetts Bay, surrounded by a beautiful variety of scenery. This is a very ancient settlement, having been first made in 1629, one year before that at Boston. In this place was begun the prosecution of the now vast iron interests of the country; the earliest forge and smelting works having been erected here in 1643, upon the banks of Saugus River. In this place also is a picturesque locality, known as *Dungeon Rock*, a spot of many legendary associations, much frequented in later years by those holding the spiritualistic faith, where a large cave has been artificially excavated in search of supposed treasure. *High Rock*, in the centre of the city, is a fine eminence, affording a very beautiful panoramic view of the surrounding country, and remarkable as being the residence, though not the original home, of the celebrated Hutchinson family of vocalists. In this city are numerous churches, including a large and flourishing branch of the Society of Friends.

The City Hall, containing also the Free Public Library, is a building of great elegance and much admired.

The school system is of a high rank, giving the most valuable opportunities for education. In this city, the great feature, however, is the manufacture of ladies' shoes, in which it takes the lead of the whole country. This business was begun here about 1750, under the instruction of John Adam Dagyr, a native of Wales. The immense manufactories now in operation are at once its pride and strength.

Nahant (4 miles from Lynn) is a charming peninsula, or a pair of rocky islands connected with each other and the main-land by a series of unsurpassed beaches. A large and splendid hotel there, in 1819, and numerous summer residents, filled the place with their cottages, and made it the most fashionable watering-place in New England. This hotel was, however, burned in 1861, and since then the tide of pleasure-seekers has gone in other directions, especially toward Swampscott. The chief business now prosecuted is fishing; and this, at present, is largely, if not wholly, in the taking of lobsters, which abound here, and enable the fishermen of Nahant to supply the Boston market to a very great extent. The attractions of Nahant to the geologist, and to the marine botanist and zoologist, are very great. Prof. Agassiz has here his summer residence. Population in 1865, 313. Omnibuses run to and from the central station in Lynn, in connection with many of the trains of the Eastern Railroad.

Swampscott (12 miles) is to Boston what Long Branch is to New York, that is to say, the favorite resort of its wealthiest citizens. The beach is neither large nor attractive, and the walks and drives are not particularly beautiful, yet *fashion* has set its stamp upon it, and its fortune is made. The coast here is particularly dangerous to the mariner, the beaches being very short and the bluffs high and long. The bathing here is excellent, with no undertow. The permanent residents are principally engaged in the cod and haddock fishing, which is principally done in dories or smacks, and supply the market with fresh fish. Population in 1865, 1,619.

The leading hotels are the *Great Anawam*, the *Little Anawam*, the *Lincoln House*, and the *Ocean House*.

Salem (16 miles) is the principal shire town in Essex county, and the first permanent settlement in the old Massachusetts Colony. Roger Conant and others, on breaking up the "fishing plantation" at Cape Ann, in the autumn of 1626, removed to Naumkeag, now Salem. John Endicott arrived in 1628, Rev. Francis Higginson in 1629, and John Winthrop in 1630, who soon after removed to Charlestown and Boston. The year 1692 is remarkable for the prevalence of the *witchcraft delusion*, at Salem village, now Danvers, for which several persons were tried and executed. In the court-house are deposited the papers and other documents that relate to the trials. The house is standing, in which some of the preliminary examinations were made, and, having been the home of Roger Williams, adds an additional interest. The place of execution is in the western part of the city, an eminence overlooking the city, the harbor, and the surrounding shores, and is known as "*Gallows Hill.*" A pleasant drive of some five or six miles will enable the visitor to examine the several places of interest mentioned in Mr. Upham's work on the subject. Salem has a convenient and well-protected harbor, with good anchorage. Previous to the Revolution the people were largely engaged in the fisheries, and during that period in privateering. After the restoration of peace, this spirit of enterprise was directed to voyages of exploration and trade with distant ports in the East, and was conducted with so much success that an extensive commerce sprung up. This business has of late considerably declined, many of the cargoes formerly received here being discharged at the ports of Boston and New York. Manufacturing industries have, for some years past, been successfully introduced, that of the leather very extensively; also, though not to the same extent, cotton, jute, white lead, chemicals, etc., etc. Many interesting historical associations cluster around Salem, and every period in her annals, from the landing of Conant, Endicott, and Higginson, has recorded some important event, and enrolled illustrious names.

Plummer Hall was erected in 1856, from funds bequeathed to the proprietors of the *Salem Athenæum*, by the late Miss Caroline Plummer, of Salem, a lady of great literary accomplishments. In this elegant building are deposited the library of the *Athenæum*, which contains 14,000 volumes; and the library of the *Essex Institute*, containing some 25,000 volumes and a large collection of newspapers, pamphlets, manuscripts, and various historical relics. The Institute has an extensive scientific collection, which is deposited with the Trustees of the *Peabody Academy of Science*, in the *East India Marine Hall;* and has published ten volumes of Historical Collections, six volumes of Proceedings, and one volume of the Bulletin.

East India Marine Hall was erected in 1825, for the accommodation of the museum of the East India Marine Society. This society was organized in 1799, and possesses a very valuable museum. In 1867, George Peabody placed in the hands of nine trustees the sum of $140,000, for the promotion of science and useful knowledge in the county of Essex. In 1868, an act of incorporation was obtained, under the name of "The Trustees of the Peabody Academy of Science." They have purchased the East India Marine Hall, and have received on permanent deposit the museum of the East India Marine Society, and the scientific collections of the Essex Institute; they have been rearranged under their direction, thus forming a very extensive museum, open to the public, free, on Wednesday, Thursday, Friday, and Saturday of each week, from 10 A. M. to 5 P. M. One of the State Normal Schools is located in this city, and was opened for the admission of pupils in September, 1854. The other educational facilities are of a high character.

The rides in the vicinity are pleasant, and its proximity to Marblehead, Swampscott, and Nahant on the one side, and to the Beverly and Manchester shores, with the charming lands adjacent, render it a pleasant summer residence. The harbor affords good opportunities for boating and sailing.

The tourist should not fail to take the horse-cars to *Peabody* (distance 2 miles), to visit the *Peabody Institute*, in which are deposited many interesting works of art, and the various memorials of the founder, George Peabody, of which may be mentioned the portrait of Queen Victoria, Congress medal, etc., etc. A short distance in one direction from the Institute Building is the house in which Mr. Peabody was born, and about the same distance in an opposite direction, within the limits of *Harmony Grove Cemetery* (Salem), are deposited his mortal remains.

The *Marblehead Branch* diverges at Salem, and it is also the junction of the *Lawrence* and *South Reading Branches* and of the *Salem and Lowell Railway*.

Marblehead, 4 miles from Salem, population in 1865 (State census) 7,330; the terminus of the Marblehead Branch, is situated on a rocky promontory, and has an excellent harbor. At the commencement of the Revolution it had a large foreign trade, and was the second town in the colony.

There are several old mansions worthy of note, especially that of Dr. Daniel Gill, the birthplace of Vice-President E. Gerry; and the old Bank Building: this last exhibits the peculiar architecture and decorations of an aristocratic residence of a century since; even the paper was imported from England, and is supposed to have been built in 1768 for Colonel Jeremiah Lee; like the Sparhawk and Pepperell houses at Kittery, Me., it is a fine specimen of the palatial mansions of the nabobs of the last century. The fishing business has not, of late, been vigorously prosecuted. Other branches of industry have been introduced, particularly that of the manufacture of boots and shoes. The schools are in excellent condition. The academy, founded in 1788, where Judge Joseph Story was prepared for college, is yet vigorous. The churches, benevolent, literary, and other institutions, indicate the advancement of the people in culture and refinement. *Marblehead Neck*, easily reached by boats across the harbor, or a circuitous ride of a much greater distance, is a favorite resort; hither hundreds from Nashua, Lowell, Worcester, and other places, come and pitch their canvas tents and spend a few weeks of the heated term—recently a few temporary wooden structures have been erected.

Beverly (18 miles), population in 1865 (State census) 5,944, is on the opposite side of Ann Harbors from Salem, with which it is connected by a bridge, built in 1788. While the manufacture of shoes has increased rapidly during the past ten years, some attention is yet given to commerce and the fisheries. The strip of territory adjoining the coast from the village to Manchester has, within the past twenty-five years, attracted the notice of the wealthy denizens of our cities, who have selected the most eligible sites, erected beautiful residences, and otherwise improved the grounds in the highest style of landscape gardening. The *Gloucester Branch* diverges here.

Gloucester (28 miles), population in 1865, 11,938, has a capital harbor, which is one of the best on the coast. The town is pleasantly situated and compactly built. Its interests are commercial, and it has a greater amount of tonnage in the fisheries than any other place in the United States. It was the first place settled on the north shore of Massachusetts Bay. Robert Conant established a fishing colony in 1624, which in 1626 he abandoned.

Rockport is the terminus of the Branch Railroad, and has lately increased in population and importance. The extensive granite quarries are a great source of wealth, and furnish employment for a large number of men. The picturesque scenery, fine sea-views, and facilities for out-door sports and recreation, have rendered it a very attractive and favorite place of resort for summer tourists. Additional accommodations are made every year to meet the increasing demands of the travelling public.

Wenham (22 miles), as in days of yore, is a pleasant town; it was called by John Dunton, in 1686, "a delicious paradise." *Wenham Pond*, so famous for its ice, large quantities of which are exported, and probably the only one of our charming little lakes that has a European reputation, is a beautiful sheet of water, having a surface of about three hundred and twenty acres, and is the source from which the city of Salem derives the water for the use of her citizens. Wenham was formerly a part of Salem, and the early settlers called the village *Enon;* when incorporated in 1643 its name was changed to the present name. The old burial-ground, about half a mile from the Town-Hall, contains many interesting inscriptions.

Ipswich (27 miles), the birthplace of Nathan Dane and Rufus Choate. Its Indian name was *Agawam*, or *Fishing Station*. It is situated on both sides of Ipswich River, which is crossed by two stone bridges, one built in 1764, the other in 1861. It contains, in addition to a number of fine churches and stores, a county *Asylum for the Insane* and a *County House of Correction*, a *Female Seminary* organized by Miss S. P. Grant and Miss Mary Lyon in 1828, now in successful operation; and a *Grammar School* for classical instruction, established in 1650. There are several factories and mills, but the town is principally noted for its hay crop. A few years since the late Augustine Heard, Esq., erected at his own expense a beautiful brick structure, deposited therein some six thousand volumes of choice works, and left a fund for its support as a free public library.

Newburyport (36 miles) is a city located upon the Merrimac River, and is considered one of the most beautiful in New England, standing upon a gentle declivity, and having a wide avenue running along the summit, with fine large mansions on each side. Previous to 1764 it constituted a part of Newbury. During the close of the last and the beginning of the present centuries few places were more flourishing—the embargo and afterward the great fire of 1811 had a very depressing influence. The city contains a custom-house, a court-house, a very handsome City-Hall, and a number of churches of the different persuasions. School privileges are good. The harbor is large and deep, but the entrance is obstructed by a sand-bar.

Among the objects of interest may be specified the *Old Presbyterian Church*, the scene of Whitefield's labors, a monument to his memory, and other sacred relics; the elegant and costly *Memorial Chapel*, built by the late Rev. Dr. Horton, as a monument to his only daughter, in connection with *St. Paul's Church*, one of the oldest of the Episcopal churches; the house where Jacob Perkins lived, and the building where he prepared the first steel bank-note plates now generally used; the old *Garrison House*, a great curiosity, built of brick and stone, and having loop-holes for musketry, near the green in *Oldtown*, and built by an ancestor of the late President Pierce; the *Tracy House*, once honored by the presence of Washington, Lafayette, and others, recently purchased and fitted up for the use of the *Free Public Library*, which was founded by Josiah Little in 1854, and contains some 13,000 volumes; the *Oak-Hill Cemetery*, with its imposing gateway, the gift of Mr. Tappan, of New York, a son of this place—from the elevated portions are beautiful and extensive views of the surrounding country. The old burial-places contain many quaint inscriptions, and are always interesting to the antiquarian.

The chief natural curiosity is a series of limestone-pits, about two miles south of the city, known by the name of *Devil's Den*. They were formerly wrought to advantage, but have long since been abandoned, and are still regarded with interest on account of a number of minerals to be found there, some of which are of rare occurrence. *Plum Island*, connected by a causeway and bridge, distance some three miles, is a place of interest, especially to the lovers of wild-game. It is a narrow island, about eight miles long, and consists of yellow sand thrown up by the wind into fantastic hillocks, and bearing scarcely any vegetation except thickets of juniper and the plum from which it derives its name. Two light-houses on the northerly end.

The principal hotel is the *Merrimac House*. The Newburyport Railway for Georgetown, etc., connects at this point.

East Salisbury (38 miles) is where the *Amesbury Branch* diverges. It is near *Salisbury Beach*, a well-known resort. The Essex County towns are rich in beautiful scenery, and in historical associations of the most interesting character, and there are none more so than the closely-connected communities of Amesbury and Salisbury. Poet and painter have celebrated the picturesque views of the Merrimac. In Amesbury the poet Whittier has resided for thirty years, and it is the birthplace of Josiah Bartlett, one of the signers of the Declaration of Independence. In Salisbury is pointed out the site of the birthplace of Abigail Eastman, the mother of Ezekiel and Daniel Webster; the ancient house where Caleb Cushing was born; the site of the ancient court-house of old Norfolk County; and the plain little room in a country tavern (preserved in its primitive condition) where the king's commissioners met in 1699, and where the members of the General Court assembled in 1737 to adjust the boundary-line between Massachusetts and New Hampshire. The ancient graveyards, where lie the mouldering remains of eminent divines, and men of note in their day, should not be neglected. This is the last station on this line in Massachusetts.

(For continuation, *see* Route V. of NEW HAMPSHIRE.)

ROUTE XII.

BOSTON TO LAWRENCE, TO THE WHITE MOUNTAINS, TO PORTLAND, MAINE, AND TO THE NORTH.

Via Boston and Maine Railway, and Connections.

STATIONS.—Boston: Somerville, 2 miles; Medford Junction, 4; Malden, 5; Melrose, 7; Wakefield Junction, 9 (connects with South Reading Branch, and with Danvers Branch Railway to Newburyport); Wakefield, 10; Reading, 12; Wilmington Junction, 18 (connects with Salem and Lowell Railway); Ballardvale, 21; Andover, 23; South Lawrence, 26 (connects with Lowell and Lawrence, Concord, Manchester and Lawrence, and Lawrence Branch of Eastern Railways); North Lawrence, 27; North Andover, 28; Bradford, 32 (connects with Newburyport Railway); Haverhill, 34.

Malden (5 miles) is on the Malden River, which is navigable for vessels of 300 tons to within half a mile of the village. It is quite a manufacturing place, and is connected with Charlestown by a bridge 2,420 feet long.

Wakefield Junction (9 miles) is the connecting point of the junction of the *South Reading Branch* and the *Danvers Branch Railway* to Newburyport, described on page 198.

Reading (12 miles) is noted for its manufactories of boots and shoes.

Wilmington Junction (18 miles) is the point of intersection of the *Salem and Lowell Railway*. This is a famous hop-producing region.

Andover (23 miles) is pleasantly situated; has a population of not far from 5,000. Besides a large area devoted to agriculture, there are three manufacturing villages along the Shawsheen, which passes through the town. In 1844 a large tract, lying on its northerly border, by the Merrimac, was set off to form the new city of Lawrence, in connection with a similar section taken from Methuen, on the opposite side of the river. Within the bounds of Andover are several beautiful ponds, with much besides to make its scenery attractive.

In 1778, while the Revolutionary War was at its height, *Phillips Academy* was incorporated, and located on its beautiful site here, where for nearly a century it has been widely known as one of the largest and best classical schools of New England.

Thirty years later, in 1808, a *Theological Seminary* was endowed, and opened under the same board of trustees with the academy, located on the same hill, and helping largely to carry out the design with which the academy was organized.

There is also in the immediate vicinity a large *Seminary for Young Ladies*, well patronized, and effectively administered. Usually, in the three institutions, there are from 400 to 500 members.

Within the limits of the town there are 8 churches—5 Congregational, 1 Baptist, 1 Methodist, 1 Episcopal.

Trains connect Andover with Boston seven to ten times daily; with Lawrence, the same; with Lowell, three or four times; and with Salem and Newburyport as often.

During the summer months, many find it a pleasant retreat from city life; while for its permanent inhabitants, its general healthfulness, its excellent society, its rare educational advantages, and its high moral and religious atmosphere, make it a choice home.

Lawrence (26 miles) one of the leading manufacturing cities of the United States, dates the commencement of its prosperity from 1845, when a dam was thrown across the Merrimac River (on both sides of which the city is built), giving a fall of water of 28 feet, and furnishing the power for the numerous mills and factories located here. A canal, over a mile long, 14 feet deep, and gradually diminishing in width from 100 feet at the head to 60 feet at the foot, distributes the water to the various factories, etc.

A second canal, of about the same length, is partially completed upon the opposite side of the river. Among the leading manufacturing companies are the Pacific, Washington (formerly Bay State), Atlantic, Everett, Pemberton, Lawrence Woollen, and Arlington. There are also numerous paper, flour, and other mills.

The Common is a handsome public park of 17¼ acres. The City Hall, High-School House, Court-House, *Lawrence American*, and Post-Office Block, churches, and mills, are the most noteworthy buildings.

Among the literary and educational institutions are the Franklin Library, the "White" Lecture and Library Fund, Pacific and Atlantic Mills Libraries, the High, Oliver Grammar, and other public schools. The city is lighted with gas, and the mills, their boarding-houses, and the city fire-hydrants, are supplied with water from a reservoir on Prospect Hill. Population in 1845, 100; in 1870, 30,000. Valuation in 1870, $17,500,000.

The railroad connects at this point with the *Lowell and Lawrence*, *Concord*, *Manchester*, and *Lawrence*, and the *Lawrence Branch of the Eastern Railway*.

North Andover (27 miles), a flourishing manufacturing village, incorporated (formerly part of Andover) in 1854. A small stream, the outlet of Great Pond, furnishes water-power. Population, 3,500.

Railroad connects with Lawrence Branch of Eastern.

Bradford (32 miles) is the junction of the *Newburyport Railway*. It contains the famous Female Academy, founded 75 years ago, and noted as the *Alma Mater* of Mrs. Judson and Harriet Newell, of missionary memory. The institution is flourishing, a new academy and dormitory having been recently erected at a cost of $150,000, and capable of accommodating 150 pupils. The town is connected with Haverhill by a bridge across the Merrimac, 680 feet long.

Haverhill (33 miles) is the last station, on this route, in Massachusetts. It is a manufacturing city, upon the *Merrimac River*, with a population of 13,000, and contains, among other noteworthy buildings, fifteen churches, two of which are remarkably handsome; one of them modelled after an Italian temple; the other built in the Gothic-Arabic style. The schools are high in their standard.

It contains a fine Soldiers' Monument, erected in 1869.

The city is built on a gentle slope, and the surrounding scenery is picturesque and beautiful. It is noted in Indian history as being the home of Hannah Dustin, who, being carried into captivity by the Indians, killed nine of them while they were asleep in camp, near Concord, N. H., scalped them, and returned home, down the Merrimac, in a bark canoe, bringing her trophies with her. It is also the birthplace of John G. Whittier, the American Quaker poet. Just back of the city, within a circuit of six miles, are three beautiful lakes, nestling among the hills, one of which was named by Mr. Whittier, *Kenoza*, which is the Indian name for pickerel. It is this beautiful sheet of water, and the surrounding scenery, which are referred to by him in the poem of "The Barefoot Boy," as "the sand-rimmed pickerel-pond," and "the walnut slopes beyond." On the shore of this lake is located *Kenoza Hall*, a stone building, built for social and picnic purposes by an incorporated association of gentlemen, and is a popular summer resort for an hour of recreation.

The *Newburyport Railway* to Newburyport (*see* page 199), and to Georgetown, diverges here.

Georgetown is a manufacturing town. Its principal attraction is the *Memorial Church*, built by George Peabody, and presented by him to the town.

(For remainder of this route, *see* Route II. of NEW HAMPSHIRE.)

ROUTE XIII.

BOSTON TO ALBANY.

Via Boston and Albany (Western) Railway.

STATIONS.—Boston: South Framingham, 21 miles; Worcester, 44; Worcester Junction, 45 (connects with Providence and Worcester, Worcester and Nashua, and Norwich and Worcester Railways); Rochdale, 53; Charlton, 57; Spencer, 62; East Brookfield, 64; Brookfield, 67; West Brookfield, 69; Warren, 73; Brimfield, 79; Palmer, 83 (connects with New London Northern Railway); Willbraham, 89; Indian Orchard, 92; Springfield, 98 (connects with New Haven, Hartford and Springfield, and Connecticut River Railways); West Springfield, 100; Westfield, 108 (connects with New Haven and Northampton Railway); Russell, 116; Huntington, 119; Chester, 126; Middlefield, 131; Becket, 135; Washington, 138; Hinsdale, 143; Dalton, 146; Pittsfield, 151 (connects with Pittsfield and North Adams and West Stockbridge and Pittsfield Railways); Shaker Village, 154; Richmond, 159; State Line, 162 (connects with Housatonic Railway); Canaan, 167; East Chatham, 172; Chatham, 177 (connects with Harlem and Hudson, and Boston Railways); Chatham Centre, 181; Kinderhook, 184; Schodack, 192; Greenbush, 199 (connects with Troy and Greenbush Railway); Albany, 200 (connects with divergent routes).

(This route, from *Springfield* to *Boston*, has been described as Route I.)

Westfield (108 miles). (*See* page 157.)

Chester (126 miles) is a manufacturing town.

Middlefield (131 miles) has several mills for the manufacture of satinets and broadcloths.

Dalton (146 miles) has manufactories of cutlery, machinery, paper, and woollen goods.

Pittsfield (151 miles), connection with *Pittsfield and North Adams*, and *West Stockbridge and Pittsfield Railways*. (*See* page 183.)

State Line (162 miles) is the connection with the *Housatonic Railway*.

(For a description of this section of the country, *see* Route II. of CONNECTICUT, and Route IV. of MASSACHUSETTS.)

From Chatham to Albany, this road follows the same general line as the *Harlem Railway* (Route II. of NEW YORK).

ROUTE XIV.

BOSTON TO THE HOOSAC TUNNEL.

Via Fitchburg and Vermont and Massachusetts Railways.

THE Fitchburg Railway has already been fully described in Route IX.

VERMONT AND MASSACHUSETTS RAILWAY.

STATIONS.—Boston: Fitchburg, 50 miles (connects with Fitchburg Railway, Boston, Clinton and Fitchburg, and Fitchburg and Worcester Railways); Wachusett, 53; Westminster, 55; Ashburnham, 61 (connects with Cheshire Railway); Gardner, 65; Templeton, 69; Baldwinville, 71; Royalston, 77; Athol, 83; Orange, 87; Wendell, 90; Erving, 92; Grout's Corner, 98 (connects with New London Northern Railway); Montague, 102; Greenfield, 106 (connects with Connecticut River Railway); Shelburne Falls, 119; Charlemont, 128; Zoar, 132; Hoosac Tunnel, 136.

Fitchburg (50 miles). (*See* page 190.)

Ashburnham (61 miles), connects with the *Cheshire Railway* for *Bellows Falls*, etc.

Gardner (65 miles) is noted for its chair-manufactories.

Athol (83 miles) is on Miller's River, which furnishes a fine water-power for a number of manufactories.

Erving (92 miles) is on the east side of the Connecticut River. (The scenery of this section of the State is described in Route V.)

Grout's Corner (98 miles), connects with *New London Northern Railway*. (*See* page 189.)

Montague (102 miles), on the east side of the Connecticut, is where the railway crosses the river by a bridge. In the north part of the township are *Turner's Falls*, where there is a dam, furnishing an immense water-power. There is a canal, with 75 feet of lockage, around the falls, which is used for purposes of navigation.

Greenfield (106 miles). Connects with the *Connecticut River Railway*. (*See* page 188.)

Shelburne Falls (119 miles) is a flourishing manufacturing village upon the north side of *Deerfield River*.

Charlemont (128 miles) is on the Deerfield River, in the midst of charming scenery, the Hoosac Mountains being in full view.

Hoosac Tunnel (136 miles) has already been described. (*See* page 184.)

NEW HAMPSHIRE.

NEW HAMPSHIRE, one of the original thirteen States, is bounded north by Canada, east by Maine and the Atlantic, south by Massachusetts, and west by Vermont. The first settlements were made at Dover, in 1623. It contains some of the grandest hill and valley and lake scenery in America, and is yearly visited by a larger number of tourists than perhaps any State in the Union. The White Mountains here are popularly supposed to be the highest land east of the Mississippi River, as indeed they are, with the single exception of Black Mountain, in North Carolina. These noble hills occupy, with their many outposts, a very considerable portion of the State, and form the specialty in its physical character. The reader will find a detailed mention of all these features, and of the beautiful intermediate lake-region, in subsequent pages.

On his route from Boston to the mountain-regions, the tourist will find much to interest him, if his interest lies that way, in the enterprising manufacturing towns of the lower part of the State. In its historical records, New Hampshire has no very striking passages—no important reminiscences, either of the Revolutionary War, or of the later conflict with Great Britain in 1812.

The principal rivers of New Hampshire are the Connecticut, which forms the whole western boundary of the State, dividing it from Vermont, the Pemigewasset, the Merrimac, Contoocook, Upper and Lower Ammonoosuc, and the Saco. Lake Winnipiseogee, near the centre of the State, is its principal inland water. The railway lines of New Hampshire are numerous enough to give ready access to all sections of her territory, and to the neighboring States. Occasions will occur for ample mention of the facilities which they afford for travel, as we follow them, severally, hither and thither.

ROUTE I.

BOSTON TO THE WHITE MOUNTAINS, LAKE MEMPHREMAGOG, AND CANADA.

Via Boston and Lowell and connecting Railways.

(*Continuation of Route X. of Massachusetts.*)

THE stations on the *Boston and Lowell Railway*, as far as Nashua, N. H., were described in Route X. of MASSACHUSETTS, and we now resume the trip at Nashua, taking the *Concord Railway of N. H.*

STATIONS.—Boston : Nashua, 40 miles (connects with Worcester and Nashua Railway, also with Boston and Lowell and Nashua and Lowell Railways); Thornton's Ferry, 46 ; Reed's Ferry, 49 ; Goff's Falls, 53 ; Manchester, 57 (connects with Manchester and North Weare Railway, and Manchester and Lawrence Railway); Martin's Ferry, 62 ; Hooksett, 66 ; Suncook, 67 ; Concord, 75 (connects with Boston, Concord, and Montreal Railway, for the White Mountains, also with Concord and Portsmouth, Concord and Claremont, and Northern N. H. Railways); East Concord, 77 ; North Concord, 80 ; Canterbury, 85 ; Northfield, 88 ; Tilton, 93 ; Union Bridge, 97 ; Laconia, 102 ; Lake Village, 104 ; Weir's, 108 (steamer Lady of the Lake, during the season of navigation, leaves for Centre Harbor, Wolfboro', etc., on arrival of each train); Meredith Village, 112 ; Fogg's Road, 116 ; Ashland, 120 ; Bridgewater, 123 ; Plymouth, 126 (stages leave Plymouth

203

and Littleton for White Mountains and Franconia Notch, Sanbornton for New Hampton and Gilmanton, Meredith Village for Conway, and Littleton for Lancaster and other places); Quincy, 132; Rumney, 134; West Rumney, 137; Wentworth, 142; Warren, 146; East Haverhill, 154; Haverhill and Newbury, 159; North Haverhill, 164; Woodsville, 168; Wells River, 168 (connects with Connecticut and Passumpsic Rivers Railway); Bath, 173; Lisbon, 178; North Lisbon, 183; Littleton, 188.

Nashua (40 miles) is an important manufacturing city, situated on both sides of the Nashua River. It contains numerous first-class residences, is supplied with water and gas, and its streets are plentifully ornamented with shade-trees. For railways connecting at this point, consult the list of stations at the head of this route. The leading hotels are the *Indian Head*, *Tremont*, and *Central*.

Amherst (8 miles from Nashua), near the Wilton Branch, is situated upon the *Souhegan River*, and was the birth-place of Horace Greeley. There are numbers of mineral springs in the vicinity, one of which, *Amherst Spring*, is becoming popular. A hotel stands at the spring, which is three miles from the station. There is a line of stages from the station to the spring and to the principal village. Amherst was formerly the Hillsborough county seat; but the courts have been taken from it in part and carried to Manchester and Nashua. A new hotel has been built at the main village.

Wilton (16 miles from Nashua), the terminus of the branch, is situated in the Souhegan valley, in the midst of a fine dairy region. There are numerous factories here, and in the neighborhood are granite quarries. This is a favorite summer residence for Bostonians, there being pleasant walks, drives, etc., in the vicinity. *Barnes Falls* are 2 miles distant. The *Whiting House* is a good hotel.

Manchester (57 miles) is one of the principal manufacturing cities of the New England States, including within its limits the villages of *Piscataquay* and *Amoskeag*. The Merrimac River furnishes a good water-power for numerous factories, among which are the "Amoskeag," "Manchester Print Works," "Langdon Mills," and "Stark Mills," the "Locomotive," and "Fire Engine Manufactories," and others. The population of the city, by the census of 1870, is 23,509. The *Manchester House* is a good hotel.

(For railroad connections, see list of stations.)

Hookset (66 miles) is upon the Merrimac River, and the site of the "Hookset Manufacturing Company" for cotton goods and other manufactories. The railroad-bridge across the river at this point is 550 feet long. To the west of the railroad is *Pinnacle Mountain*.

Suncook (67 miles), at the falls of the Suncook River, where it empties into the Merrimac, is principally noted as containing the mills of the "Pembroke," "Webster," and "China" companies. The "China" mill is new, and is one of the largest in New England.

Concord (75 miles) is the capital of the State, and contains among other buildings of interest the following: The *State Capitol*, occupying the entire square bounded by Main, State, Park, and Capitol Streets. It is built of the celebrated Concord granite. The *City Hall* and *Court-House* on Main Street is about a quarter of a mile from the Capitol. The *State Prison*, a granite structure, is upon State Street. The *Asylum for the Insane* is upon the westerly side of the city in the midst of attractive grounds, and is a large and flourishing institution.

One of the principal beauties of Concord, which is located on the level but gradually-rising land on the west bank of the Merrimac River, is the abundance of trees shading its regularly-laid-out streets. The city is a place of extensive trade, and is celebrated for its carriage-manufactories and the superior quality of the granite quarried in the vicinity, some of the finest structures in the Eastern cities being built of it. The railroads connecting at this point are enumerated in the list of stations at the head of this route.

The *Concord and Claremont* and *Contoocook River Railways*, diverging here, lead to *Contoocook* (11 miles), *Bradford* (26 miles), and *Hillsborough Bridge* (30 miles from Concord); they pass through fine farming towns particularly attractive to the tourist. Hillsborough and Bradford both possess good hotels and are both connected with *Bradford Springs* by lines of stages.

We here take the *Boston, Concord and Montreal Railway*.

From Concord to Wells River the route passes through some of the most romantic portions of the State, now skirting the shores of Lake Winnipiseogee and now running at the base of lofty mountains, crossing and recrossing the dancing mountain-streams until it reaches the White Mountains themselves.

Tilton (93 miles) is upon Winnipiseogee River, the outlet of the lake of the same name, and was called *Sanbornton Bridge* until 1869. It is a pretty place, is delightfully located, and contains the *New Hampshire Conference Seminary and Female College*, which is located upon the rising ground west of the railway, the buildings being surrounded by attractive grounds. *Barnes's Hotel* is half a mile from the depot.

Laconia (102 miles) is a flourishing manufacturing village in a picturesque region upon *Great Bay*. The hotel is *Willard's*. Before reaching this station the views commence to be charming, the contrast between the clear waters of the lake and the frowning mountains in the distance being of rare beauty.

Lake Village (104 miles) upon a small arm of the lake, is a thriving manufacturing village from which a steamer runs daily to *Alton Bay*, connecting with the Dover and Winnipiseogee Railway to Dover and Portsmouth. The hotel is the *Lake House.*

Weir's (110 miles) is upon Lake Winnipiseogee, is the point of departure of the steamer "Lady of the Lake" for Centre Harbor, *Wolfborough, Diamond Island*, and other points, giving the tourist an opportunity to view the beauties of this charming sheet of water. Near *Wier's* is the *Endicott Rock*, supposed to have been set up as a monument, or boundary, by the surveyors sent out by Governor Endicott, of Massachusetts.

Lake Winnipiseogee, the largest and most beautiful sheet of water in the State, is about 25 miles in length, and varies in breadth from 1 to 10 miles. Its waters are very pure and translucent. It is studded with islands and surrounded by mountains. Edward Everett, in writing of this lake, says: "I have been something of a traveller in our own country—though far less than I could wish—and in Europe have seen all that is most attractive, from the Highlands of Scotland to the Golden Horn of Constantinople, from the summit of the Hartz Mountains to the Fountain of Vaucluse, but my eye has yet to rest on a lovelier scene than that which smiles around you as you sail from Wier's Landing to Centre Harbor." In the lake trip, *Belknap Mountain*, with its two peaks 2,500 feet high, is upon the right, and opposite upon the north rises *Ossipee*, while farther on is *Red Hill*. In the distance, on the right as the steamer approaches Centre Harbor, is seen *Mount Chicorua*, 3,600 feet in height, and in a clear day even Mount Washington.

Centre Harbor (10 miles from Wier's) is a very small village, but, being a very popular summer resort, has a commodious hotel so located as to command the most charming views of the lake and vicinity. This is the *Senter House;* another but smaller hotel, the *Moulton House*, is well kept. The chief objects of interest in the vicinity are *Red Hill* and *Squam Lake*. Red Hill, a remarkably beautiful eminence, about 2,500 feet high, is situated northwest of the lake. The ascent to the summit, although steep and arduous, can be effected for a portion of the distance in carriages, and all the way on horseback. From the southeast there is a fine panoramic view of the lake and the adjacent country. In order to obtain the finest views of the lake and adjacent landscape, the ascent should be made in the forenoon, or in the evening from 3 to 5 o'clock. At the latter hour, on a fine September day, the view of the lake and its islands is charming. Beyond the lake extends "a slumbrous stretch of mountain-land far seen."

On the south ascends *Mount Major*, a ridge of a bolder aspect and loftier height. On the northeast the great *Ossipee* raises its chain of elevations, with a bold sublimity, and looking down in conscious pride upon the regions below;

while *Kearsarge* and *Monadnock* are plainly seen to the southwest.

Squam Lake, lying west from Red Mountain, and two miles northwest from Winnipiseogee Lake, is another splendid sheet of water. It is about six miles in length, and in its widest part not less than three miles in breadth, and, like its neighbor, is studded with a succession of romantic islands. This lake abounds in trout of the finest kind.

From *Centre Harbor* a line of stages runs to *Conway* and the *White Mountains*, that trip being described as Route II.

We will now return to *Weir's* and resume our trip by rail.

Meredith Village (114 miles) is a manufacturing village upon Lake Winnipiseogee. After passing this station, we leave the lake and pass along the borders of *Winnebago*, or *Measly Pond* and *Long Pond*.

Ashland (120 miles) formerly called *Holderness*, is a manufacturing village upon Squam River, near the *Pemigewasset River*, and has a good hotel, the *Squam Lake House*.

Squam Lake, 3 miles distant, has been described under the head of *Centre Harbor*.

Plymouth (126 miles) is on the Pemigewasset River, surrounded by noble mountain scenery, being on the southern verge of the Franconia range. The finest hotel and station-house on the road has been built here by the company, and, through the season, music is furnished by a good band, during the stoppage of the through-trains.

Mount Prospect affords more extended views, commanding from its summit, which is reached by a carriage-road, a view of 30 miles, within which distance are many beautiful lakes and hills.

Livermore Falls, two miles from the village, are remarkable in their character, and should not be passed without a visit.

The village is something of a manufacturing place. The *Pemigewasset House* is a good hotel.

From this point diverges the stage-route to the White Mountains.

Rumney (134 miles), in the valley of the Baker River near *Bald* and *Rattlesnake Mountains*, is noted for its saw-mills and for the manufacture of charcoal.

Warren (146 miles), though a small manufacturing town, is a place of great interest from its proximity to *Moosilauke*, or *Mooschillock* Mountain, an isolated peak, 4,600 feet in height, and commanding from its summit (a ride of nine miles from the station) the most extensive views in all directions. This is the highest mountain in the State, outside of the Franconia and White Mountain groups. From the *Prospect House* may be seen the Valley of the Connecticut, the White and Franconia Mountains, and the whole of Vermont and New Hampshire. There is a good hotel, which is a popular resort.

East Haverhill (154 miles) is where the road passes *Owl's Head*, a rocky cliff several hundred feet high, and said to resemble the object for which it is named.

Haverhill and Newbury (159 miles). Haverhill is one of the county seats of Grafton County, and has extensive marble quarries and works. It is at the point where the road enters the Connecticut Valley. *Newbury* and *Bradford* on the opposite bank of the river will be described in Route I. of VERMONT. The mountain seen in the rear of *Newbury* is Mount Pulaski.

North Haverhill (164 miles) is situated east of what is known as the *Great Ox-bow* of the Connecticut River, from the peculiar course of the channel. The railroad runs at a considerable elevation at this point, affording the traveller fine views of the valley.

Woodsville (168 miles) is where the trains of this road and of the *White Mountain Branch* cross the Connecticut to *Wells River*, Vermont. The views from the bridge are fine.

Wells River, Vt. (168 miles), connects with *Connecticut and Passumpsic River Railway* and with *White Mountain Branch*. (For Wells River, see Route I. of VERMONT.)

Bath (173 miles) is upon the *Connecticut* and *Ammonoosuc Rivers*, the latter of which has the reputation of being "the wildest and most impetuous river in New Hampshire." It is a wonderfully beautiful stream, and is crossed by the railroad several times between Wells River and Littleton.

vi

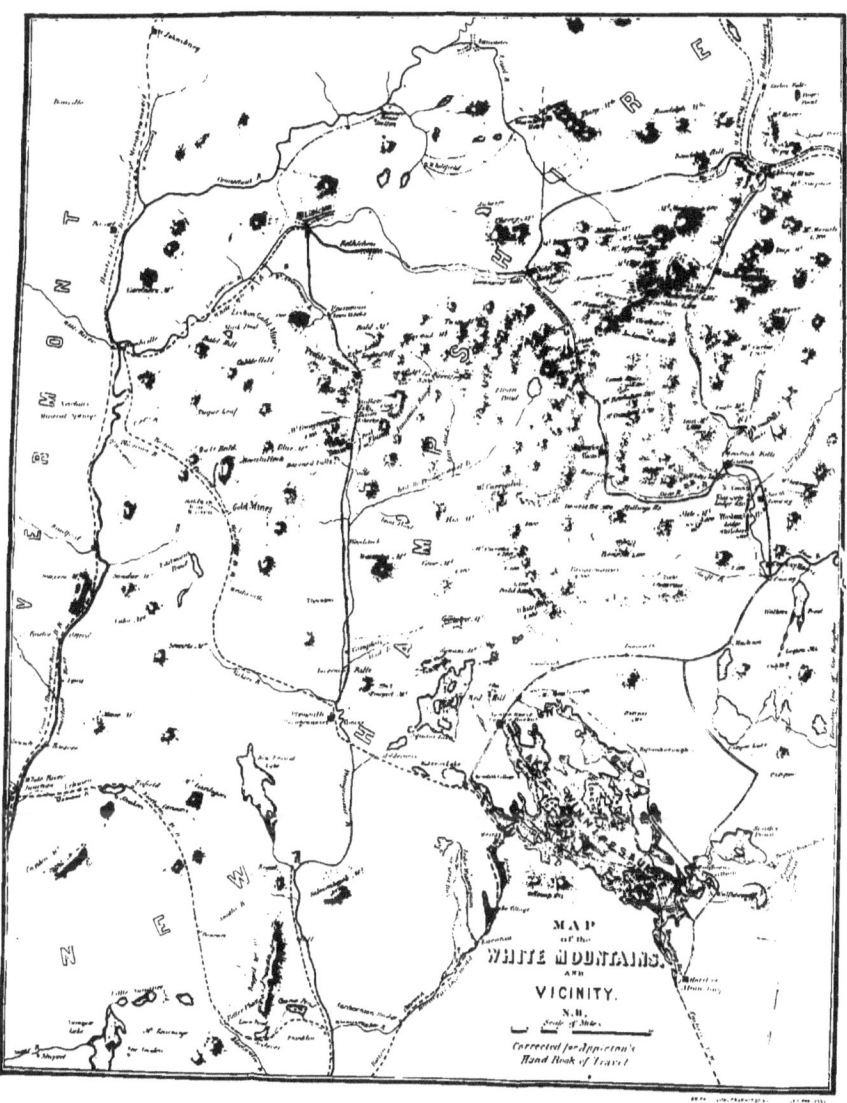

Littleton (188 miles) is a village on the *Ammonoosuc*, and is a pleasant place. We here reach the end of our journey by rail, and are fairly in the mountains. *Thayer's Hotel* is a well-managed house, where carriages with good teams and competent drivers can always be obtained. The stage-route from here to the *Profile House* is 11 miles, and to the *Crawford House* 22 miles. This is the best point from which to reach the *Mount Washington Railway*. Near *Lisbon Village*, a few miles below Littleton, are *gold-mines* in full and successful operation.

THE WHITE MOUNTAINS.

THESE mountains cover an area of about 40 square miles, in Grafton and Coos Counties, Northern New Hampshire; though the name of White Mountains is, in the neighborhood, given to the central group only—the half-dozen lofty peaks, of which Mount Washington is the royal head and front. These noble hill-ranges have earned for this region the title of the "Switzerland of America." Their precise latitude is 40° 16' 34½" north, and longitude 71° 20' west. The western cluster is contradistinguished as the Franconia range. The White Mountains (specifically so called) extend from the Notch in a northeasterly direction, some 14 miles, increasing from each end of the line gradually in height toward Mount Washington, in the centre. These respective elevations are, in the order in which they stand, beginning at the Notch: Mount Webster, 4,000 feet above the level of the sea; Jackson, 4,100; Clinton, 4,200; Pleasant, 4,800; Franklin, 4,900; Monroe, 5,300; Washington, 6,285; Clay, 5,400; Adams, 5,800; Jefferson, 5,710; and Madison, 5,361. They were first visited by whites, according to Belknap, the State historian, by Walter Neal, in 1632. Their aboriginal name was *Agiochook* or *Agiocochook*, signifying "Mountain of the Snowy Forehead and Home of the Great Spirit."

Although the route by which we have come is not so popular as the one via *Conway*, next to be described, the entry into the mountains may as well be made *via Littleton*, as anywhere else, if one wishes to see them all. We are now in

The Franconia Hills, which, though in popular estimation inferior in interest to the eastern cluster, are really not so, except it be in the wonders of the mountain ascents; and, even in this, the panorama, from the summit of *Lafayette*, is scarcely less extensive or less imposing than the scene from the crown of Mount Washington, while the exquisite little lakes, and the singular natural eccentricities in the Franconia group, have no counterpart in the other. In this, as in other ranges of the White Hills, the mountains are densely wooded at their base, while their rock-ribbed summits are barren, and scarred by time and tempest. The hills approach, at one point, to within half a mile of each other, and form the wild Procrustean portal, called the Notch

Profile House.—Taking a stage at Littleton, a ride of 11 miles over the hills brings us to the Profile House, a large and well-kept hotel in the immediate vicinity of the most striking and attractive portions of the *Franconia* group. It is upon a small, level plain in the bosom of the hills. Immediately behind the hotel is a *cascade*, which, when the brook is swollen by a recent rain, is very charming.

Echo Lake, one of the greatest charms of this part of the mountain-region, is a diminutive, but very deep and beautiful pond, north of the hotel, entirely enclosed by high mountains. From the centre of this fairy water, a voice, in ordinary tone, will be echoed distinctly several times, and the report of a gun breaks upon the rocks like the roar of artillery. The Indian superstition was, that these echoes were the voice of the Great Spirit, speaking in gentleness or in anger.

Eagle Cliff is a magnificently bold and rocky promontory, almost overhanging the hotel. It casts its dark shadows down many hundred feet into the glen, traversed by the road beneath.

Profile, or Cannon Mountain, 2,000 feet above the road and 4,000 above the sea, is directly opposite Eagle Cliff, and forms the western side of the Notch. Away up upon its crown is a group of mighty rocks, which, as seen from the Profile House below, bear an exact resemblance to a mounted cannon.

It is upon this mountain, also, that we find that marvellous freak of Nature— **The Profile Rock; or, the Old Man of the Mountain.**— This wonderful eccentricity, so admirably counterfeiting a human face, is 80 feet long from the chin to the top of the forehead, and is 1,200 feet above the level of the road, being yet far below the summit of the mountain. This strange apparition is formed of three distinct masses of rock, one making the forehead, another the nose and upper lip, and a third the chin. The rocks are brought into the proper relation to form the profile at one point only, namely, upon the road through the Notch, a quarter of a mile south of the Profile House. The face is boldly and clearly relieved against the sky, and, except in a little sentiment of weakness about the mouth, has the air of a stern, strong character, well able to bear, as he has done unflinchingly for centuries, the scorching suns of summer and the tempest-blasts of winter. Passing down the road a little way, the "Old Man" is transformed into a "toothless old woman in a mob cap;" and, soon after, melts into thin air, and is seen no more. Hawthorne has found in this scene the theme of one of the pleasantest of his "Twice-told Tales," that called "The Great Stone Face."

Bald Mountain.—There is a carriage-road from the hotel to the summit of Bald Mountain, 2½ miles distant, whence a noble view is obtained without undergoing the fatigue consequent upon the ascent of the more lofty peaks.

Profile Lake is a beautiful little pond, lying at the base of the mountain, and immediately under the ever-watchful eye of the stern "Old Man." This lakelet is sometimes called the "Old Man's Washbowl." It is full of the finest trout.

Mount Lafayette, or the Great Haystack, is the monarch of the Franconia kingdom, towering skyward to the height of 5,280 feet. Its lofty pyramidal peaks are the chief objects, in all views, for many miles around. The summit is reached by a long but not wearisome road, commencing at a point on the road about 2¼ miles below the *Profile House.* Horses are kept at the foot of the mountain. On the summit stands a comfortable house, erected as a shelter for visitors. From here is obtained "a view more beautiful, in some respects, though it may be less grand and majestic, than that from Mount Washington."

Walker's Falls.—This fall, which is reached by following, for half a mile, a rivulet which crosses the road 2½ miles below the hotel, is one of the most picturesque of the mountain cascades, though the volume of water is not very great, nor the height of the fall at all remarkable. Half a mile farther up there is a longer and more picturesque fall.

The Basin, another remarkable scene of this neighborhood, is five miles south of the Notch. It lies near the roadside, where the Pemigewasset has worn deep and curious cavities in the solid rocks. The basin is 45 feet in diameter, and 18 feet from the edge to the bottom of the water. It is nearly circular, and has been gradually made by the whirling of rocks round and round in the strong current. The water, as it comes from the basin, falls into most charming cascades. At the outlet, the lower edge of the rocks has been worn into a very remarkable likeness of the human leg and foot, called the "Old Man's Leg." Across the brook, at the outlet of the basin, is thrown a bridge of logs, which enables the visitor to reach a path leading, in the course of some 200 rods, to a succession of the most exquisitely lovely cascades in this whole region. These cascades should be followed to the point where they end in a waterfall between 20 and 30 feet in height.

The Flume is one of the most famous of all the Franconia wonders. Leaving the road, just below the Basin, we turn to the left among the hills, and, after a tramp of a mile, reach a bare granite ledge 100 feet high, and about 30 feet wide, over which a small stream makes its varied way. Near the top of this ledge we approach the ravine known as the Flume. The rocky walls here are 50 feet in height, and not more than 20 feet apart. Through this grand fissure comes the little brook which we have just seen. Except in seasons of freshets, the bed of the stream is narrow enough to give the visitor dry passage up the curious glen, which extends several hundred feet, the walls approaching, near the upper extremity, to within 10 or 11 feet of each other. About midway, a tremendous bowlder, several tons in weight, hangs suspended between the cliffs, where it has been caught in its descent from the mountain above. A bridge, dangerous for a timid step, has been sprung across the ravine, near the top, by the falling of a forest-tree. The *Cascade*, below the Flume, is a continuous fall of more than 600 feet, the descent being very gradual. The *Flume House*, near the Flume, occupies a most charming site opposite Mount Liberty.

The Pool is a wonderful excavation in the granite rock, as though hewn by human beings. It is about 150 feet wide and 40 feet deep, the water entering by a cascade, and escaping through the rocks at its lower extremity; from the top of the rocks above to the surface of the pool, the distance is nearly 150 feet. This spot is reached by a walk of three-quarters of a mile from the hotel.

Georgiana Falls, or **Harvard Falls,** as they are sometimes called, are of greater magnitude than any others yet discovered in these mountains. They make a sheer leap of 150 feet, and are reached by a path from a small farm-house about 2 miles below the Flume House, on the Plymouth road. This completes the visit to the *Franconia Hills*, and, on our return to the Profile House, we can choose between a visit to the *Mount Washington Railway via Littleton*, or, by taking the road *via Bethlehem* to the Crawford House, the headquarters of the *White Mountain region proper*. We will take this latter road, and, descending from the hotel only to cross another high and weary hill, will take our last, lingering look at the Franconia Notch, in all its beauty, and then descend to

Bethlehem, a beautiful village, famed for its views of the whole White Mountain range. It is a flourishing place, only 5 miles from Littleton, and has a good hotel, the *Sinclair House*.

Two or three miles beyond Bethlehem the road crosses the *Ammonoosuc* on a strong wooden bridge, and then follows the course of the stream several miles to *Lower Ammonoosuc Falls*, one of the most attractive cascades in this river. It is near enough the road to be seen from the coach.

The **White Mountain House** is a pleasantly-situated hotel, having fine views of the White and Franconia Mountains. The *White Mountain Railway* runs from this point to the summit of Mount Washington, to be described hereafter. A carriage-road extends from the hotel to within about two miles of the summit, and another to the summit of *Mount Prospect*, or, as it is now designated, MOUNT PEABODY, the name having been changed in August, 1869, in honor of the great philanthropist. This is the only point on the west slope of the mountains whence comprehensive views may be obtained from hills of moderate elevation. **The Giant's Grave** is a mound rising some 60 feet from the plain, and from its summit is obtained a magnificent view of the surrounding mountains. It is about half a mile from the *White Mountain House*.

We now cross the Ammonoosuc, and ascend some four miles to the

Crawford House, the headquarters of the White Mountains proper. — It is a most excellent establishment, and bears the name of the earliest hosts of these mountain-gorges. The story of the adventures and endurance of the early settlers here is extremely interesting—how Captain Eleazer Rosebrook, of Massachusetts, built a house on the site of the Giant's Grave, four miles from the Notch, afterward occupied by Fabyan's Mount Washington Hotel — how his nearest neighbors were 20 miles away, excepting the Crawford family, 12 miles down in the Notch valley, the site of the present old Crawford House, at the base of the mountains coming from Conway, on the southeast—how the Rosebrook children were often sent, for family supplies, over the long and dangerous path to Crawford's, returning, not unfrequently, late at night—how Ethan Allen Crawford was heir to the Rosebrook estate, and how he became known as the "Giant of the Hills"—how he and his family made the first mountain-paths,[*] and were for long years the only guides over them of the rare visitors which the brief summers

---

[*] The first bridle-path was cut by Ethan Allen Crawford, in 1821.

209

brought—and how they have since seen their home thronged, for weeks together, like a city saloon, with beauty and fashion. The Crawfords are a large, athletic race. Abel, the father, called the "Patriarch of the Mountains," would walk five mountain miles to his son's before breakfast, at the age of 80. At 70, he made the first ascent ever made on horseback to the top of Mount Washington. His sons were all over six feet tall; one of them was six and a half feet, and another, Ethan Allen, was seven feet in height.

Before making the ascent of Mount Washington, the tourist will do well to visit the less prominent places in the vicinity, among which are the following:

Mount Willard.—This mountain is easy of ascent, either in carriages or on foot, to a height of 2,000 feet above the *Crawford House*. Speaking of the view of the *Notch* from this mountain, Bayard Taylor says: "As a simple picture of a mountain-pass, seen from above, it cannot be surpassed in Switzerland." Near the summit of the mountain is the "*Devil's Den*," a dark, cold cave, about 15 feet high, 20 wide, and 20 deep, only accessible by means of ropes.

Gibbs Falls.—This name has been given to the most striking of a series of romantic cascades reached by a walk of half an hour from the hotel along the aqueduct by which it is supplied with water, the falls being about a quarter of a mile from where the aqueduct issues from the brook.

Ascent of Mount Washington.—There are three modes of ascending Mount Washington from the *Crawford House*: 1. By bridle-path. 2. By carriage-road via *White Mountain House*. 3. By the railway from the *White Mountain House*; and still another, to the sturdy pedestrian, on foot. We shall in this instance take the first, which carries us over several intermediate mountains, and secures us many magnificent views which we would otherwise lose.

Mount Clinton, the first mountain over which we pass, is so near the hotel that we traverse but a few rods of ground before we commence the ascent, which is steep and at times over corduroy-roads (round logs laid close to each other, across the road), dangerous in wet weather. We pass through a dead forest, and then emerge at the summit, 4,000 feet elevation. Here the first noble mountain-view bursts upon us, and we descend the narrow ridge which connects this mountain with the next. On the right, 2,000 feet below us, is *Mount Washington River*, and at the left at the same distance, the *Ammonoosuc*. *Mount Pleasant*, the next of the chain, is traversed by two roads, one directly over the summit, and the other (the one usually taken) round the southern side. Height of summit, 4,800 feet.

Mount Franklin, the third in the series, 4,900 feet in height, is an irregular flattened peak, the ascent of which is extremely difficult, but which when accomplished amply repays the adventurer by the sublimity of the view, especially toward the southeast.

Mount Monroe, the next mountain to be traversed, is only the inferior of *Mount Washington* in height, not in beauty. The passage is made round, not over, the summit, and by a comparatively easy road. *Oakes Gulf* is on the right. Winding round Monroe we come in view of *Mount Washington*, its summit nearly 1,500 feet above us.

The *ascent of the last peak* on this road is made from the southwestern side, and it is not necessary to walk until near the summit. In fact the horses are only abandoned for the convenience of the guides. The summit is an acre of comparatively level ground, upon which is the *Tip-Top House*, and a little below it the *Summit House*, the former used as a dining-room, the latter as a hotel.

The view from this point has been thus described: In the west, through the blue haze, are seen, in the distance, the ranges of the Green Mountains; the remarkable outlines of the summits of *Camel's Hump* and *Mansfield Mountains* being easily distinguished when the atmosphere is clear. To the northwest, under your feet, are the clearings and settlement of *Jefferson*, and the waters of *Cherry Pond;* and, farther distant, the village of *Lancaster*, with the waters of *Israel's River*. The Connecticut is barely visible; and often its appearance for miles is counterfeited by the fog arising from its surface. To the north and northeast, only a few miles distant, rise boldly the great northeastern peaks of the White Mountain range—*Jefferson*, *Adams*, and *Madison*—with their ragged tops of loose, dark rocks. A little farther to the east are seen the numerous and distant summits of the mountains of Maine. On the southeast, close at hand, are the dark and crowded ridges of the mountains of *Jackson ;* and beyond, the conical summit of *Pequaket*,[*] standing by itself, on the outskirts of the mountains; and, farther over, the low country of Maine and *Sebago Pond*, near Portland. Still farther, it is said, the ocean itself has sometimes been distinctly visible. The White Mountains are often seen from the sea, even at 30 miles' distance from the shore; and nothing can prevent the sea from being seen from the mountains, but the difficulty of distinguishing its appearance from that of the sky near the horizon. Farther to the south are the intervals of the Saco, and the settlements of *Bartlett* and *Conway*, the sister ponds of *Lovell*, in Fryeburg; and, still farther, the remarkable four-toothed summit of the *Chocorua*, the peak to the right being much the largest, and sharply pyramidal. Almost exactly south are the shining waters of the beautiful *Winnipiscogee*, seen with the greatest distinctness on a favorable day. To the southwest, near at hand, are the peaks of the southwestern range of the White Mountains; *Monroe*, with its two little alpine ponds sleeping under its rocky and pointed summits; the flat surface of *Franklin*, and the rounded top of *Pleasant*, with their ridges and spurs. Beyond these, the *Willey Mountain*, with its high, ridged summit; and, beyond that, several parallel ranges of high, wooded mountains. Farther west, and over all, is seen the high, bare summit of *Mount Lafayette*, in Franconia. Visitors to Mount Washington should always go well clad. The range of the thermometer even in midsummer is from 30° to 45°. It frequently falls as low as 25°, and sometimes to 20°, or 12° below freezing.

The *carriage-road* takes the tourist directly to the base of the mountain, leaving only three miles of horseback-riding, a saving of six miles of distance, but at the expense of much splendid scenery.

The Mount Washington Railway, the easiest mode of ascent, was commenced in 1866. The grade is enormous, being 3,596 feet in 3 miles, and in places 1 foot in 3. The track is of three rails bolted to a trestlework of heavy timber. The third or centre rail is like a wrought-iron ladder with rounds 4 inches apart. Into this fits a cog-wheel which fairly pulls the train up the mountain. The seats for the passengers are so swung as to be horizontal, whatever may be the inclination of the track. The safety of the train is secured by independent, self-acting breaks.

Having finished our visit to the Crawford House and vicinity, we will make a trip through the *Notch* to the *Glen House*, another celebrated resort.

The Great Notch is seen to the best advantage as approached from this direction. It is a gorge or rift in the mountains which rise on either side to the height of 2,000 feet, and which in one spot, called the "Gateway," are only 22 feet apart. The Saco River runs through the Notch.

The Flume is a portion of a little mountain-stream crossed by a bridge not far from the hotel. It rushes rapidly through a deep and narrow gorge. Next we come to

The Silver Cascade, sometimes called the "Second Flume;" it is a favorite scene, about half a mile south of the entrance to the Notch. It is one of the most charming waterfalls imaginable, seen from the piazza of the hotel, at a distance of two miles, bubbling down the mountain-side, 800 feet above the neighboring valley. The best view is from the bridge. Passing down the Notch between the *Willey Mountain* and Mount Webster, and oppressed by the grandeur of the scene, we come to the *Willey House*, where the whole Willey family, nine in number, were crushed by an avalanche from which they were trying to escape, August 28, 1826. A rock thirty feet high split the avalanche and saved the house from which they fled to their death.

---

[*] *Pequaket* is often confounded with *Kearsarge*, which is in Merrimac County, and after which was named the vessel that sunk the Alabama.

Sparkling Cascade and **Sylvan Glade Cataract** are two wild and beautiful waterfalls on a brook emptying into the *Saco*, below the Willey House. This brook is sometimes called "*Ripley*," and sometimes "*Avalanche Brook*."

As we proceed down the Saco we come in succession to the *Giant Stairs*, 3,500 feet high; *Mount Resolution*, 3,400 feet; and *Mount Crawford*, 3,200 feet. We next come to the *Mount Crawford House*, half a mile beyond which we cross "*Nancy's Brook and Bridge*," so named after a young woman who perished here from exposure when in pursuit of a faithless lover. The ravine over which this bridge is thrown is a beautiful specimen of a trap-dike.

At **Sawyer's Rock** the road turns to the east, and we see on our right the three peaks of *Tremont Mountain*, and behind them, in the distance, *Pequaket Mountain*.

Goodrich Falls.—After leaving the Saco valley, and crossing the trestle-bridge over the *Ellis River*, a good view of the Goodrich falls may be obtained. This is the largest vertical fall in the mountains, and at times of high water very imposing.

Jackson, one mile beyond these falls, is at the foot of *Essex Mountain*. The *Jackson Falls Hotel* is a quiet house within three minutes' walk of the falls, a romantic cascade on the *Wild Cat Brook*. From the hotel looking south, *Iron Mountain* (2,900 feet) is seen upon the right, and *Tin Mountain* on the left. From a point south of the hotel, the two peaks of *Doublehead* come into view. Among the mineral resources of Jackson are mines of iron, copper, and tin. In the vicinity is excellent trout-fishing, and between here and *Goodrich Falls* the views of the *Washington* range are grander than from any other point.

The route is now up the *Ellis River*, through the *Pinkham Notch*, and down the *Peabody River*, to our destination, the two rivers running respectively south and north from the summit of the Notch.

The Glen House is one of the largest and best of the mountain houses. It fronts the Peabody River and Washington range, and, with the aid of the glass, parties ascending and descending Mount Washington can be watched. This place is nearer the Mount Washington range than any other hotel in the mountains, four of the highest peaks being in full view from the portico. They are *Washington*, *Clay*, *Adams*, *Madison*, and *Jefferson*. In the vicinity of the hotel are many points of great interest, the principal of which will be mentioned, without any detailed description.

Garnet Pools, in the Peabody River, about half a mile from the hotel, are a series of basins, some of them 15 or 20 feet deep, worn in the granite rock by the action of the water.

Thompson's Falls are a series of cascades in an affluent of the Peabody River, 2 miles from the hotel on the road to Conway. The view of Mount Washington and Tuckerman's Ravine, from the upper fall, is the finest that is obtained from any point.

Emerald Pool, noted for its quiet beauty, is a short distance from the road, just before reaching Thompson's Falls.

Glen Ellis Fall is four miles from the hotel, near the road to North Conway and the Notch. In this fall the Ellis River slides at a very sharp angle, of 20 feet, and then leaps 60 feet more.

Crystal Cascade is about a mile from *Glenn Ellis* fall, on the way back to the hotel. Its source is from the heights opposite to those which feed the Ellis River, part of its water coming through Tuckerman's Ravine from the dome of Mount Washington. The height of this fall is 80 feet, and it has been tersely described as "an inverted liquid plume."

Tuckerman's Ravine is a marvellous place, seen in the ascent of the mountains, by the *Davis Road*, leading from the Crawford House. It lies upon the right in passing over the high spur directly southeast of Mount Washington. Turning aside, the edge of the precipice is reached, and may be descended by a rugged pathway. It is a long, deep glen, with frowning walls, often quite inaccessible. It is filled, hundreds of feet deep, by the winter snows, through which a brook steals, as summer suns draw near, gradually widening its channel, until it flows through a grand snow cave, which was found, one season, by measurement, to be 84 feet wide on the *inside*, 40 feet high, and 180 feet long. The snow forming the arch was 20 feet thick. The engineers of the carriage-road dined in that snow-arch July 16, 1854. The ravine may be reached by climbing directly up the stream of the *Crystal Cascade* by *Thompson's Path*, diverging from the carriage-road about two miles up Mount Washington, or to descend into it from or near the summit, the latter being the more usual method.

The Ascent of Mount Washington by the road from the Glen, until the completion of the steam railway, was the easiest and most popular of all the different routes, as, since 1861, a smooth carriage-road from the Glen to the Summit has enabled any one to visit the Tip-top House without the fatigue of walking or riding on horseback. The average grade is 12 feet in 100, and the steepest, which is 2¼ miles from the base, is 16 in 100 for a short distance only. For 4 miles the road winds through the woods, until it emerges at the ledge, and thence runs upon the verge of the ravine between Washington, Clay, and Jefferson, the upper end of which is known as "*Great Gulf*." Leaving this, it passes to the easterly side of the mountain, overlooking the valley of the Peabody and Ellis Rivers. The views from the *Summit* have been mentioned in the description of the *Ascent from the Crawford House* (page 210). Tourists frequently make the ascent from one of these hotels and the descent to the other, without making the trip through the *Notch*.

We will now leave the *Glen House*, and take a pleasant ride of 8 miles to *Gorham*, on the Grand Trunk Railway, 91 miles from Portland, and finish our account of the *White Mountains* by describing the places of interest in the vicinity.

Gorham is the northeastern gateway to the White Mountains, and is a thriving village.

The *Alpine House*, located here, is one of the largest hotels in the mountain region, and is admirably kept, having accommodations for from 200 to 300 guests. It is situated in a valley at the junction of the *Androscoggin* and Peabody Rivers,

800 feet above the sea. The ascent of Mount Washington from the Alpine House is by the same road, and at the same expense as from the *Glen House*.

The scenery in the vicinity of the hotel is remarkably striking both in the views of the mountain-ranges, of isolated mountains, and of rivers and waterfalls. From *Lead Mine Bridge*, 4 miles from the Alpine House, a striking view is obtained of the *Androscoggin*, dotted with islands in the foreground, with the mountains in the distance.

Randolph Hill is about 600 feet higher than the hotel, is reached by a pleasant carriage-ride of five miles, and when the summit is gained a superb view is obtained of the whole northerly wall of the Mount Washington range.

Berlin Falls, where the whole volume of the Androscoggin descends nearly 200 feet in the course of a mile, is one of the most striking rapids in the country. It is reached by a drive of six miles along the west bank of the river.

Mount Moriah is 4,700 feet in height, but now can only be ascended by a foot-path, though there was once a good bridle-path. From the summit, "the eye must travel far to the southwest to rest upon any level extent of land. Northern New Hampshire, Vermont, and Maine, are a vast panorama of solid surges. On the west the distant view is barred by the heavy forms of the great White Mountain range proper."

Mount Surprise, directly in front of the *Alpine House*, is 1,200 feet in height, and is a spur of Mount Moriah. Its ascent is easy, and there is no other point so near the highest mountains where such an impression of their sublimity can be obtained as from here.

Mount Hays is in the rear of the Alpine House. It can only be ascended by pedestrians. "If there were a bridle-path to the top of this eminence it would soon be celebrated as affording the grandest landscape view of Madison, Adams, and Washington, to be obtained in New Hampshire."

Mount Madison.—There is only a *blazed* path up this mountain, but the tourist, who is willing, in charge of a competent guide, to attempt the ascent, will be more than repaid for the expense and fatigue he will have to submit to, when he once reaches the summit.

We have now completed the circuit of the Franconia and White Mountains, and have mentioned all the most noteworthy objects, but we have omitted much that would doubtless be of great interest. We have drawn largely for facts, and occasionally for description, from "*The White Mountain Guide Book*," published by E. C. Eastman, of Concord, N. H. Having described the White Mountain region, we now propose to give in detail all the routes by which it may be reached, including the one we have just traversed.

I. BOSTON to LITTLETON *via Boston and Lowell, Concord Railway of N. H., Concord and Montreal Railways.* (Route X. of Massachusetts and I. of New Hampshire.)

II. BOSTON to DOVER, N. H., Alton, N. H., Centre Harbor, North Conway, etc., *via Boston and Maine,* and *Dover and Winnipiscogee Railways,* steamer on *Lake Winnipiscogee,* and stage *via North Conway.* (Routes XII. of Massachusetts and II. of New Hampshire.)

III. BOSTON to FLUME HOUSE. Same as Route I. to Plymouth: thence by stage to *Flume* and Crawford Houses.

IV. BOSTON to PORTLAND, Maine, and GORHAM, N. H., *via Boston and Maine* and *Grand Trunk Railways.* (Routes XII. of Massachusetts, II. of New Hampshire, and II. of Maine.)

V. BOSTON to LITTLETON *via Boston and Lowell, Concord, Northern, Central, and Connecticut and Passumpsic Valley Railroads.*

VI. NEW YORK to WHITE MOUNTAINS, *via* any route from *New York to Boston,* thence by any of the foregoing routes from Boston to the White Mountains.

VII. NEW YORK to WHITE MOUNTAINS *via New Haven, Hartford, Springfield, etc.* (Routes I., III. of Connecticut, V. of Massachusetts, and I. of Vermont.)

VIII. NEW YORK *via New London.* Steamer from New York to New London, or railway (Route I. of Connecticut), thence *via* Route IV. of Connecticut, Route IV. of Massachusetts, and I. of Vermont.

IX. NEW YORK *via New London.* Steamer or cars to New London, thence *via* Route V. of Connecticut, VII. of Massachusetts, IX. of Massachusetts, IV. of New Hampshire, and I. of Vermont.

X. NEW YORK *via* Albany, steamer, Hudson River Railway or Harlem Railway to Albany (Routes I. and II. of New York), thence *via* Rutland and Washington (Route IX. of New York), or Bennington and Rutland (Route V of Vermont), to Rutland, and Rutland and Burlington, and Vermont Valley, to Bellows Falls, thence by Route I. of Vermont.

ROUTE II.

BOSTON TO THE WHITE MOUNTAINS.

Via Boston and Maine and Dover and Winnipiscogee Railways, steamer on Lake Winnipiscogee and stages to Conway.

(*Continuation of Route XII. of Massachusetts.*)

STATIONS *on Boston and Maine Railway.* —Boston: Haverhill, 33 miles; Atkinson, 37; Plaistow, 38; Newton, 41; East Kingston Depot, 45; Exeter, 50; South Newmarket, 54; Newmarket 57 (connects with Concord and Portsmouth Railway); Durham, 62; Madbury, 65; Dover, 68 (connects with Dover and Winnipiscogee Railway).

STATIONS *on Dover and Winnipiscogee Railway.*—Gonic, 76 miles; Rochester, 78 (connects with Great Falls and Conway Railway); Farmington, 86; New Durham, 92; Alton, 95; Alton Bay, 96.

Haverhill (33 miles). (*See* page 200.)

Exeter (50 miles) is delightfully situated on the Exeter River, at the head of navigation. At this point there are falls which afford a great water-power for a number of mills and factories. The Phillips Academy, founded in 1781, is a richly-endowed institution. The "Robinson Female Seminary," with an endowment of $250,000, is a new institution.

New Market (57 miles) is a manufacturing town at the junction with the *Concord and Portsmouth Railway.* It is located upon the Piscassick River.

Durham (62 miles), on the Piscataqua River, is a manufacturing village at the head of tide-water. The falls at this point furnish a good water-power. In the vicinity are fine granite quarries.

Dover (68 miles) is a beautiful and flourishing city, situated on both sides of the Cocheco River, at the lower falls, the head of sloop navigation. The river having a fall of 32 feet, furnishes a fine water-power for the numerous mills and manufactories located here, the principal of which are the cotton-mills of the well-known *Cocheco Manufacturing Company.* Dover is the oldest town in the State, having been settled in 1623. It contains a handsome city hall, a number of churches, and several hotels, the principal of which are the *American House* and the *New Hampshire Hotel.*

Rochester (78 miles) is an important manufacturing town.

Farmington (86 miles) is upon the Cocheco River. Not far from the village was a rock of from 60 to 80 tons weight, so nicely balanced upon two other rocks as to be easily made to vibrate by the pressure of one's hand. It has within a few years been overthrown by some Vandal.

New Durham (92 miles) is a township containing within its limits five small lakes or ponds. The largest of these, *Merrymeeting Pond,* is ten miles in circumference. The Cocheco and Ela's Rivers both have their sources here. *Mount Betty, Cropple Crown,* and *Straws Mountain,* are all in this township. On the northeast side of Straws Mountain is a remarkable cave in the solid granite. A part of the Ela's River runs over a fountain which is regarded as a great curiosity. By sinking a small-mouthed vessel in this fountain, water may be procured, exceedingly cold and pure.

Alton Bay (96 miles), upon *Winnipiseogee Lake,* is the terminus of the railway. The town consists of scarcely any thing but the hotel, the railway buildings, and the steamboat wharf. In the vicinity are a number of pleasant and interesting places to visit, the roads being good, and conveyances to be obtained at the hotel.

Sharp's Hill is one of the attractive places in the vicinity. From the top a fine view is had of the lake.

Longee Pond, about 6 miles from Alton Bay, is noted for its tame fish.

Mount Belknap is in the neighborhood, and an excursion to its summit is very pleasant. This will occupy one entire day.

We here take a steamer for *Centre Harbor* at the other end of the lake, and thus have an opportunity of seeing the whole of this beautiful island-dotted, hill-surrounded lake, which has been partially described on page 205.

Wolfborough, 10 miles by steamer from *Alton Bay* and 106 from Boston, is delightfully situated upon two slopes of land rising from a bay. It is a favorite summer resort, being noted for its boating, fishing, and charming surroundings. The *Pavilion* is a large and comfortable hotel.

Cropple Crown Mountain, 5 miles from Wolfborough, is ascended by carriage-road to within a mile of the summit, the balance of the way being traversed on horseback. The view from the summit is delightful. Adjoining this mountain on the northeast is a smaller one called " *Tumble-down Dick*," from which the views are very fine.

Stages leave Wolfborough for Conway, etc.

Diamond Island is a pleasant resort, about equidistant from Alton Bay, Wolfborough, and the Weirs. The *Island House* is a good hotel. The steamer always stops here.

Centre Harbor. (*See* page 205.)

The steamer is left at Centre Harbor by those wishing to visit the White Mountains *via* Conway, and the rest of the trip is made in stages, the road running through the towns of *Moultonborough, Sandwich, Tamworth, Madison,* and *Conway.*

Sandwich is a noted farming town, and has also numerous boot and shoe manufactories. The *Sandwich* and *Squam Mountains* are in this township.

Tamworth (16 miles from Centre Harbor) ranks as one of the best grazing-towns in the State, the surface being uneven but not mountainous.

From this point the road runs along the shore of " *Six-mile Pond* " for quite a distance.

Conway is reached after a ride of 14 miles from Tamworth, during the latter part of which a fine view is obtained of *Chocorua* ("the Old Bear") *Mountain,* 3,358 feet high, and destitute of vegetation. Conway possesses but few objects of interest, except the trout-brooks in the vicinity, though most of the objects of interest in North Conway can be reached from here.

North Conway (5 miles from Conway), in the valley of the Saco, is the favorite resort of New England artists, and is also much frequented by families. On the east is *Middle Mountain*, on the north *Pequaket*, and on the west can be seen *Moat Mountain*, and in the distance *Chocorua*. Looking up the valley of the *Saco*, with *Mount Washington* in the distance, the view is exceptionally beautiful.

There are many pleasant walks and drives in the vicinity, among which those to the following places:

Artist's Falls is reached by taking the road to Conway for a short distance to a bridge, at the foot of the hill. After crossing the bridge, turn to the left, and a walk of half a mile will enable one to reach these charming falls. *Echo Lake, Cathedral,* and *the Ledges,* are all to be seen in one excursion. They are about 3 miles distant, on the opposite side of the river. *Echo Lake* is very beautiful, and is at the foot of *Moat Mountain.* Its name suggests its greatest attraction. The *Cathedral* is a cavity in the rock, which forms one side and an arched roof, 80 feet high, forest-trees forming the other side. The *White Horse,* visible from the village, is the picture of a horse upon the side of the cliffs. *Diana's Bath* is a little to the north of the Cathedral. It is a charming place. *Mount Pequaket,* 3,367 feet high, is about 3 miles from the village. The ascent is by no means difficult, and the view is remarkably fine. The hotels at North Conway are, the *Washington House, Kearsarge House, North Conway House, McMillan House,* and *Cliff House.*

Just after leaving North Conway, the road reaches *Bartlett,* which, together with the whole White Mountain region, has been described in Route I.

ROUTE III.

BOSTON TO MONTPELIER, VT., THE GREEN MOUNTAINS, LAKE CHAMPLAIN, THE ADIRONDACKS, AND MONTREAL.

Via Route X. of Massachusetts to Nashua, Route I. of New Hampshire to Concord; thence by Northern New Hampshire and connecting railways.

This road (the Northern New Hampshire) passes through the New Hampshire mountains, and presents very varied scenery, the first 20 miles being among the meadows of the Merrimac Valley, after which the mountains, with their rugged defiles and rushing torrents, are passed, and then the eastern slope of the Connecticut Valley is reached.

STATIONS.—Boston: Concord, 75 miles (connects with the numerous railways diverging from Concord); Fisherville, 82; Boscawen, 85; North Boscawen, 89; Franklin, 94 (branch for Bristol, 15 miles, connects); East Andover, 100; Potter Place, 106; West Andover, 107; Danbury, 113; Grafton, 118; Canaan, 126; Enfield, 133; East Lebanon, 138; Lebanon, 142; White River Junction, 144 (connects with Vermont Central, and the Connecticut and Passumpsic River Railways).

Concord (77 miles). (*See* page 204.)

Fisherville (84 miles) is a small village at the junction of the Merrimac and Contoocook Rivers. After leaving the station, the road crosses the river by two bridges, an island interposing. This (Dustin's Island) is noted as the place where Mrs. Dustin, of Haverhill, Mass., and a nurse, killed nine Indians who had taken them prisoners, and escaped in a canoe.

Boscawen (87 miles) is a town settled in 1734. It contains two villages, two ponds of some note, and is watered by the Merrimac and Blackwater Rivers, the latter of which furnishes a fine water-power for numerous mills and factories. The meadows along the Merrimac are noted for fine groups of elms.

Franklin (96 miles) is situated at the point where the *Pemigewasset* and *Winnipiseogee* unite to form the *Merrimac*. It is quite a manufacturing place, and is very picturesque in its appearance. There is a famous peat-bog in the town. The branch to *Bristol* (15 miles) diverges here.

At **Lower Franklin** (formerly a part of Salisbury) Daniel Webster was born. Here he had a residence and one of the finest farms in the Merrimac Valley. The house stands within eight rods of the railway.

Bristol (121 miles), a town at the terminus of the Bristol branch, is watered by three rivers, the *Pemigewasset*, *Smith's*, and the *Newfound* Rivers. The latter is the outlet of *Newfound Lake*, a sheet of water 7 miles long, and 3 broad. Graphite (plumbago) has been discovered in large quantities and of superior quality.

East Andover (102 miles) is a farming town. For nearly two miles before reaching this point, the road runs along the bank of *Chance* or *Webster's Pond*, a beautiful sheet of water.

Andover (106 miles) is on the banks of *Eagle Pond*, a charming little lake, about 4 miles long, on the opposite side of which is *Ragged Mountain*. There are other ponds in the township, which is also watered by the *Blackwater River*.

Potter Place (108 miles). From this point the scenery is quite wild. This is the point of departure for Mount Kearsarge.

Kearsarge Mountain received its name from the earliest explorers of the State, and was so designated on the maps made by them. It is about 4 miles from *Potter Place Station*, and lies in the towns of Warner, Sutton, Wilmot, and Salisbury—all cornering near its summit. It stands alone—no other considerable height in its vicinity—and is over 8,000 feet high. About halfway from its base to its summit is situated the *Winslow House*, a commodious summer hotel, which from its unusual elevation commands a splendid view of the west, and from its verandas a grand panorama of mountain and water scenery is presented to the eye, rarely seen from a summer-house. Among the points in sight are *Sunapee Lake*, *Lovells* and *Sunapee Mountains*, and *Ascutney* and *Mansfield Mountains* in Vermont. The view from the summit is not excelled, for variety, by any point in the State. Lakes *Winnipiscogee* and *Sunapee*, besides some 30 ponds, may be seen—Merrimac River, a host of villages, and a great portion of the mountain scenery in the State, from *Monadnock* on the south, to *Mount Washington* in the north, and, in the west, the *Green Mountains* of Vermont. The hotel, situated half-way up its side, is reached by a good carriage-road, and the remaining distance—about a mile—can be made on horseback or on foot, over a good road. The war-vessel that sunk the Alabama was built at Portsmouth, N. H., and received its name from the mountain at the suggestion of Major Henry McFarland, a paymaster in the U. S. A., and one of the proprietors of the *New Hampshire Statesman*. The hotel received its name from the commander of the Kearsarge, *Captain Winslow*.

A mountain near North Conway, properly called *Pequaket*, from the name given to a range to which it belongs, and receiving its name from a tribe of Indians inhabiting the vicinity in the valley of the Saco, has sometimes been called Kearsarge; and the attempt has been made to wrest from and get for it the reputation and *name* made famous by the great national victory of our war-ship Kearsarge over the Alabama. The glory of that victory largely belongs to New Hampshire. The ship was built from her yard, named by a New Hampshire man, from the name of a favorite mountain in his own country; and the chief executive officer, Lieutenant Thornton, a grandson of one of the New Hampshire signers of the Declaration of Independence, planned the attack, and fought his ship to a glorious victory.

Within ten miles square lying to the southeast, and at the foot of this mountain, were reared Ezekiel and Daniel Webster, General Dix, William Pitt Fessenden, Farmer, the electrician, the Bartlett family, one of the most distinguished in New Hampshire, besides many others of note.

Grafton (120 miles) is a township containing 5 ponds, and a remarkable ledge called the *Pinnacle*, on the south side of which the ground rises gradually, while on the north there is an almost vertical descent of 150 feet. At *Glass Hill* are the most famous mica-mines in the country, from which large quantities of mica are mined annually.

Canaan (128 miles) contains a very curious sheet of water, called *Heart Pond*, which is surrounded by a natural embankment, which gives it the appearance of being set on a hill. After leaving the station, the *Mascomy River* is frequently crossed, and much beautiful mountain scenery is visible from the car-windows.

Enfield (135 miles) is watered by a number of ponds and streams, which lend great beauty to the landscape. There are three families of Shakers in the township, who carry on extensive manufactures, having 10 mills. They also are noted for their attention to agriculture and stock-raising. After passing the station, the road passes along the shore of *Enfield*, or, as it is sometimes called, *Pleasant Pond*.

Lebanon (142 miles) is a township having for its western boundary the Connecticut River, and also being watered by the *Mascomy River*. A medicinal spring, a lead-mine, and a vein of iron-ore, have been found. The principal village is at the head of the falls of the Mascomy River. The village of *West Lebanon* is on the Connecticut River, and contains some handsome buildings as well as the *Tilden Seminary for Young Ladies*. The railway here crosses the Connecticut by a bridge, from which fine views from the river are had.

White River Junction, N. H. (146 miles), is the junction with the Vermont Central and the Connecticut and Passumpsic River Railways.

Hanover is four miles north of White River Junction. It occupies a broad terrace, 180 feet above the water. Here is the venerable *Dartmouth College*, founded in 1769, and named in honor of William, earl of Dartmouth. Webster, Choate, Woodbury, and Chase, present Chief Justice, were of the alumni of this institution.

The college buildings are grouped around a square of 12 acres, in the centre of the plain upon which the village stands. A new hall and gymnasium have just been erected. The *Observatory* should be visited.

(For continuation, see Route II of VERMONT.)

ROUTE IV.

BOSTON TO BELLOWS FALLS AND LAKE CHAMPLAIN.

Via Route IX. of Massachusetts, and the Cheshire Railway and Connections.

STATIONS.—Boston: Fitchburg, 50 miles; Fitzwilliam, 77; Troy, 82; Marlborough, 86; South Keene; Keene, 92 (connects with Ashuelot Railway); East Westmoreland, 100; Westmoreland, 104; Walpole, 110; Cold River; Bellows Falls, 114 (connects with Vermont Central, Vermont and Canada Railway).

Fitchburg, Mass. (50 miles). (*See* page 190.)

Fitzwilliam (77 miles) is the first town, on this line, in New Hampshire. It is hilly, is watered by several streams and ponds well stocked with fish. Near the centre of the town is a hill from which a romantic prospect is obtained. *Gap Mountain* is partly in this and partly in Troy township. There are granite quarries here.

Marlborough (86 miles) is a manufacturing town in which are several ponds. It has a hotel.

Keene (92 miles) is called one of the handsomest villages in New England. It is situated on a flat, east of the Ashuelot River, and is noticeable for the extent, width, and uniform level of its streets. In early times the inhabitants had considerable trouble with the Indians. It has always been a place of inland trade, but since the completion of the railroads has greatly increased, the manufacturing interests being flourishing. The Ashuelot Railway runs from here to South Vernon, at the junction of the Connecticut River and Vermont and Massachusetts Railways.

Walpole (110 miles) is a beautiful town having a great variety of landscape. It contains, among other objects of interest, a hill about 750 feet in height, a part of Mount Toby. It is called *Fall Mountain*. The villages are *Walpole* and *Drewsville*.

Bellows Falls (114 miles) is a famous railway junction. Railways come in from Boston on the east, from the valley of the Connecticut on the south, from

Vermont and Canada on the north, and from Albany and Troy, via Rutland, on the west.

The Falls are a series of rapids in the Connecticut, extending about a mile along the base of a high and precipitous hill, known as *Mount Kilburn*, which skirts the river on the New Hampshire side. At the bridge which crosses the river at this place, the visitor can stand directly over the boiling flood; viewed from whence, the whole scene is very effective. The Connecticut is here compressed into so narrow a compass that it seems as if one could almost leap across it. The water, which is one dense mass of foam, rushes through the chasm with such velocity, that, in striking on the rocks below, it is forced back upon itself for a considerable distance. In no place is the fall perpendicular to any considerable extent, but in the distance of half a mile the waters descend about 50 feet. A canal half a mile long, with locks, was constructed round the falls, many years since, at an expense of $50,000. The first bridge across the Connecticut was built here in 1785. In the immediate neighborhood are the *Abenâquis Springs*, highly tonic and possessing medicinal properties. *Fall Mountain Hotel* is located near the springs at the base of Fall Mountain, and is a pleasant resort for invalids. There is a good path from the hotel to *Table Rock* on the top of the mountain, from which an extended view of the valley of the Connecticut is had.

The *Island House* at Bellows Falls is an excellent hotel.

SULLIVAN RAILWAY.

The Sullivan Railroad extends from Bellows Falls through Charlestown, Claremont, and Cornish, and crosses the Connecticut at Windsor, Vt., to White River Junction and the White Mountains via Littleton. The towns are not mentioned.

Claremont is a manufacturing place, and is the largest town, except *Keene*, in the valley of the Connecticut, north of Springfield, Mass. It develops one of the finest and most picturesque water-powers, and is one of the most beautiful villages in the State.

Cornish, opposite Windsor, Vt., is the birthplace of Salmon P. Chase.

(For continuation, *see* Route III of VERMONT.)

ROUTE V.

BOSTON TO PORTSMOUTH, NEW HAMPSHIRE, PORTLAND, MAINE, TO THE WHITE MOUNTAINS, VIA PORTSMOUTH, OR VIA GRAND TRUNK RAILWAY, TO QUEBEC AND TO ALL PARTS OF MAINE.

Via Eastern Railway and connections.

(*Continuation of Route XI. of Massachusetts.*)

STATIONS.—Boston; Seabrook, 42 miles; Hampton Falls, 43; Hampton, 46; North Hampton, 49; Greenland, 51; Portsmouth, 56 (connects with Portland, Saco, and Portsmouth, and Concord and Portsmouth Railroads).

Seabrook (42 miles) is so named from the number of brooks and rivers by which the township is traversed. Whale-boat building is the most important manufacture.

Hampton Falls (43 miles), **Hampton** (46 miles), and **North Hampton** (49 miles), are in the rear of the celebrated bathing resort known as *Hampton Beach*, which will be described under the head of *Portsmouth*. A stage runs from *Hampton* to the beach and to *Rye Beach* on the arrival of the trains. Many eminences in the vicinity afford fine views of the ocean, the *Isles of Shoals*, and the coast.

Greenland (50 miles) is noted as a fruit-growing town. A stage runs from the station to *Rye Beach* on the arrival of trains.

Portsmouth (56 miles) stands upon a peninsula on the south side of *Piscataqua River*, and, excepting the narrow strip connecting it with the mainland, is surrounded by water; the ocean, an inlet, and the Piscataqua, touching it on three sides. The harbor is deep, safe, and never frozen, and ships of any size may enter with safety. The main entrance is on the northeast, and is well protected by forts. The other entrance is on the south of New Castle on Grand Island and is called *Little Harbor*. There are many islands in the harbor, some accessible by bridges.

The city is an interesting place for the tourist to visit, and one cannot fail to be

charmed with the shaded streets, ancient buildings, large gardens, and home-like residences. Among the objects of peculiar interest are the *Church of St. John*, the *Athenæum*, the *residence* of *Governor Langdon*, and the *tomb* of *Sir William Pepperell*, which is near the Navy-Yard.

The *United States Navy-Yard* is admirably located upon *Continental Island*, and contains, besides theusual ship-houses and other buildings required in such a place, a very fine balance dry-dock, which is an ingenious affair and with its appendages cost about $800,000. *Seavys Island* has been added to the Navy-Yard as a site for officers' quarters. A steamer runs hourly between the yard and the foot of *Daniel Street*. The *Portsmouth Steam Factory* and the *Sagamore Mills* are large and of great interest to visitors. *Auburn Cemetery* and *Harmony Grove Cemetery* are tastefully laid out and ornamented, and are usually visited.

The HOTELS are the *Rockingham House*, the *Philbrick House*, the *City Hotel*, and the *Franklin*.

THE RAILROAD CONNECTIONS at this point are with the *Portland, Saco*, and *Portsmouth Railway* (for all parts of Maine, and for the *White Mountains* via Gorham on the *Grand Trunk Railway*), and with the *Concord and Portsmouth Railway*. Passengers for the *White Mountains* via Lake *Winnipiscogee* take this latter road to New Market, where they connect with Route 11. (*See* page 214.)

VICINITY.

In the vicinity are many charming resorts, speedily and easily reached. Among them the following are the principal:

Rye Beach is seven miles by an excellent road, but it may also be reached from the stations previously mentioned. The bathing is good, and the beaches are growing in popularity. The hotels are the *Ocean House, Washington* and *Surf Houses* at one end of the beach, and the *Atlantic* and *Farragut* at the other. At the southern end of Rye Beach is *Boar's Head*, an abrupt eminence extending into the sea and dividing it from Hampton Beach.

Hampton Beach is not as fashionable as Rye, but was very celebrated many years ago. The hotels are good, the bathing and fishing are capital, the scenery charming, and the rides in the vicinity pleasant. This beach can be reached from the stations on the railway already mentioned, and by the carriage-road from Portsmouth.

The Isles of Shoals are reached by steamer from Portsmouth, from which they are distant 10 miles. They are a group of rocks, or rather mere ledges, seven in number, and named as follows: *Duck, Star, Smutty Nose, White, Hog, Malagar,* and *Londoner* Islands. They are organized as a town under the name of Gosport.

To make the trip to these islands enjoyable, choose a pleasant summer day; then with the waves dancing in the bright sunshine, and your heart palpitating with pleasurable expectation, you start from Portsmouth Harbor on your journey. As you near the Isles of Shoals, you discern that the white, thready line that separated their surfaces from the sea is a lashing, roaring surf, which, in fair weather and foul, seems to pelt and fight these everlasting rocks, as if they were intruders in the pathway of the great deep. With some difficulty, and amid the screams and taunts of the crazy sea-birds, you make the desired landing, and find yourselves on *terra firma*. The clear, bracing atmosphere has made your blood dance with invigoration, your appetite becomes sharp-set, your spirits are exhilarated, and every thing is joyous. The edible treasures of the sea, with the additions of choice luxuries of the land, are at your service, in the order of an extemporized picnic, and you eat and are merry as you never were before: and the Isles of Shoals, with their quaint people, their lone position, their queer old houses, their numerous craft, are impressed upon your mind so indelibly that, in all future time, you contrast each similar recreation but to more pleasantly recall the happy hours spent upon these resting-places of the deep sea.

The hotel is the *Appledors*, is well conducted, and is a pleasant place to spend a few days, or weeks, and indulge in fishing, hunting, bathing, and boating, to one's heart's content.

(For continuation of this route, *see* Route I. of MAINE.)

ROUTE VI.

PORTSMOUTH TO MANCHESTER, TO THE WHITE MOUNTAINS, VIA LAKE WINNIPISEOGEE, OR VIA LITTLETON, TO THE CONNECTICUT VALLEY, THE GREEN MOUNTAINS AND LAKE CHAMPLAIN.

Via Concord and Dover, and connecting railways.

STATIONS.—Portsmouth: Greenland, 4 miles; New Market Junction, 10 (crossing of Boston and Maine railway); Epping, 17; Raymond, 23; Candia, 29; Manchester, 40 (connects with roads centring here); Suncook, 52; Concord, 59 (connects with Boston, Concord, and Montreal, and other railways diverging from Concord).

Greenland (4 miles). (*See* page 219.)

New Market Junction (10 miles). Point of departure for *Lake Winnipiscogee*, and the *White Mountains*. (*See Route* II., page 214.)

Raymond (23 miles) contains a natural curiosity called the *Oven*. It is a natural excavation in a ledge, is about 5 feet high, 5 wide, and 15 deep, and closely resembles the object for which it is named.

Candia (29 miles) is on the ridge between the Merrimac River and the ocean, and commands a view of the White Hills, the Wachusett, and several other mountains, the light-house on Plum Island, and the ocean.

Manchester (40 miles). (*See* page 204.)

Suncook (52 miles). (*See* page 204.)

Concord (59 miles). Point of departure for White Mountains, via *Route I.*, or for Connecticut Valley, Green Mountains, and Lake Champlain, via Route III. (*See* pages 204 and 216.)

ROUTE VII.

BOSTON TO THE WHITE MOUNTAINS AT GORHAM, AND TO THE ST. LAWRENCE RIVER.

Via Grand Trunk Railway.

(*Continuation of Route II. of Maine.*)

STATIONS.—Portland, 108 miles from Boston; Shelburne, 86 miles from Portland; Gorham, 91; Berlin Falls, 98; Milan, 103; West Milan, 109; Northumberland, 122; North Stratford, 134; Island Pond, 149; Norton Mills, 166.

Shelburne (86 miles) is one of those picturesque towns on the flanks of the White Mountains, abounding in rugged scenery. Within the limits of the town are *Mount Moriah* and *Moses's Rock*, an extensive mine of lead, and rich deposits of zinc-ore. The *Androscoggin*, and some smaller streams pass through the town.

Gorham (91 miles). (*See* page 213.)

Berlin Falls (98 miles). (*See* page 213.)

Milan (103 miles) is upon the *Androscoggin River*, and is noted for its saw-mills. The surface is uneven, but not mountainous.

Northumberland (122 miles) is watered by the Connecticut and Upper Ammonoosuc, and contains *Cape Horn*, a mountain about 1,000 feet in height. At the falls in the Connecticut a dam has been erected, at each end of which is a village, that in Vermont being Guildhall. A handsome bridge connects the two.

North Stratford (134 miles) is the last station in New Hampshire, the road here crossing the northeast corner of Vermont into Canada.

The Dixville Hills are in the extreme northern portion of the State, and are as yet but little known. The readiest access is to leave the railway at North Stratford, and thence up the Connecticut River, via Colebrook, to the *Monadnock House*. *Dixville Notch* is ten miles from Colebrook.

The only two stations in Vermont are the following:

Island Pond, Vt. (149 miles). Though chartered in 1781, it owes its growth entirely to the railway, which was first opened to this point in 1852. A village at once sprang up, which contains two hotels, stores, saw-mills, passenger depot, a custom-house, etc, etc. On both sides of this station the road runs through dense woods.

Norton Mills is the last station in the United States at the eastern end of the railway.

VERMONT.

VERMONT, named from the French *Vert Mont*, i. e., "Green Mountains," is the most northwestern of the New-England States. It lies between 42° 44' and 45° north latitude, and between 71° 25' and 73° 26' west longitude; and is bounded north by Canada; east by New Hampshire, from which it is separated by the Connecticut River; south by Massachusetts; and west by Lake Champlain and New York. It is 157¼ miles in length, and 90 in its greatest breadth, its south line being 41 miles, embracing an area of 10,000 square miles. Vermont was first settled by Massachusetts emigrants at Fort Dummer (Brattleboro) in 1724, Brattleboro being chartered in 1753, and was the first member of the Confederacy added to the original thirteen States, March 4, 1791. In this State occurred the battle of Bennington (August 16, 1777), in which the British were defeated. The State is divided into 14 counties. Montpelier is the capital, and Burlington, Rutland, Brattleboro, St. Albans, Middlebury, and Woodstock, are the chief towns. Population in 1870, 330,235.

The thousand points of interest among the Green Mountains of Vermont have not yet received their due meed of favor from tourists, but their claims to attention are now generally admitted. The mountain-chain extends from near New Haven, in Connecticut, northward through Massachusetts and Vermont, into Canada; though, properly speaking, it lies in Vermont alone, where are the chief summits of Mansfield, Camel's Hump, Jay Peak, Shrewsbury Mountain, South Peak, Killington Peak, Ascutney Mountain (on the Connecticut), and others. After the White Mountains of New Hampshire, the Green Mountains rank with the noblest mountain-groups east of the Rocky Mountains —with the Blue Ridge in North Carolina, Georgia, and Virginia, the Alleghanies in Pennsylvania, and the Kaatskills and the Adirondacks in New York.

ROUTE I.

NEW YORK TO THE CONNECTICUT RIVER VALLEY, WHITE MOUNTAINS, FRANCONIA MOUNTAINS, GREEN MOUNTAINS, LAKE MEMPHREMAGOG, ETC.

Via Vermont Central, Vermont & Canada, and connecting railways.
(*Continuation of Route V. of Massachusetts.*)

THE Vermont Central, Vermont and Canada Railway, consists of nine separate railways, which were consolidated in 1870, the termini being Grout's Corners, Mass., Montreal, Canada, and Ogdensburg, N. Y.

STATIONS.—New York: Brattleboro, 196 miles; Dummerston, 201; Putney, 205; East Putney, 208; Westminster, 216; Bellows Falls, 220 (connects with Cheshire Railway, and all railways diverging from this point); South Charlestown, 224; Charlestown, 228 (stage connections); North Charlestown, 234; Claremont, 238 (stage connections); Windsor, 246; Hartland, 250; North Hartland, 254; White River Junction, 260 (connects with Northern New Hampshire, and Connecticut and Passumpsic Rivers Railway). The Vermont Central Railroad extends from Windsor to Lake Champlain. Norwich, 264; Pompanoosuc, 270; Thetford, 275; North Thetford, 277; Fairlee, 282; Bradford, 289 (stage connections); South Newbury, 293; Newbury, 296; Wells River, 300 (connects with White Mountains and Boston, Concord and Montreal Railways); Ryegate, 304; McIndoes, 308; Barnet, 311; McLeran's, 314; Passumpsic, 318; St. Johnsbury, 321; St. Johnsbury Centre, 323; Lyndonville, 328; West Burke, 337; South Barton, 345; Barton, 350; Barton Landing, 355; Coventry, 360; Newport, 365 (steamer leaves Newport daily, during the pleasure-travel season, for Magog, connecting with coaches for Grand Trunk Railway [*Sherbrooke Station*], arriving at Montreal or Quebec same evening); North Derby, 370.

Although this route passes over so many different lines of railway, the only change of cars between New York and Lake Memphremagog is at Springfield, and none between Boston and Lake Memphremagog.

The section we are about to traverse, running as it does along the boundary of Vermont and New Hampshire, is sometimes in one State and sometimes in the other, but chiefly in Vermont.

Brattleboro (196 miles) is on the west side of the *Connecticut*, at the mouth of *Whetstone Creek*. It is a favorite summer resort, the scenery and drives in the vicinity being romantic and pleasing. The *Asylum for the Insane* is located here. From Cemetery Hill a fine view is had of the Connecticut Valley, and of *Wantasticut Mountain*, on its eastern bank, rising 1,100 feet. The hotels are the *American*, the *Revere*, and the *Wesselhœft House*.

The *Glenwood Ladies' Seminary* is at *West Brattleboro*, 2 miles distant.

Hinsdale, N. H., on the opposite bank of the river, is connected with Brattleboro by a bridge. It is on the *Ashuelot Railway*, which connects Keene, N. H., and Vernon, Vt., and is watered by the Connecticut and Ashuelot Rivers, and by numerous brooks and springs. *Mine Mountain* extends the whole width of the town. In it are found iron-ore, minerals, and fossils. Its highest point is 900 feet above low-water mark. The remains of an old Indian fortification still exist on a hill not far from the Connecticut.

Dummerston (201 miles) is a small village. *Black Mountain* is in the centre of this township.

Putney (205 miles) is a village a short distance from the station. The township is interesting on account of its geological character. It contains *Sacket's Brook*, a mill-stream which falls 150 feet in 100 rods.

East Putney (208 miles) is opposite *Westmoreland*, New Hampshire, on the *Cheshire Railway*, which is in sight from the station.

Westminster (216 miles) is the scene of what is known as the massacre of March 13, 1775, when the citizens resisted the authority of New York, and were fired upon by the military, under order of the sheriff. This was one of the acts which greatly aggravated the feeling that led to the Revolutionary War.

Bellows Falls (220 miles) has been described on page 218. Passengers for the *Green Mountains* and *Lake Champlain*, via Rutland, take the Rutland and Burlington Railway here. From this point the Sullivan Railway, in New Hampshire, proceeds to connect with the Vermont Central, at Windsor, Vt.

South Charlestown, N. H. (224 miles), **Charlestown** (228 miles), and **North Charlestown** (234 miles), are all stations in Charlestown township, which is somewhat celebrated in the annals of the French and Indian wars. The *south village* is delightfully situated about half a mile from the river. The *centre village* has a bank and some manufactories. From the *north village* a fine view is had of *Ascutney Mountain*, Vt.

Claremont Station (238 miles) is 2 miles from the village, which is a prominent manufacturing place, containing, among others, the following manufactories: *Monadnock Mills* (cotton), *Claremont Manufacturing Company* (paper and books), *Machine Works*, *Cutlery Company*, and others. *Sugar River* passes through the village, and falls 150 feet in three-quarters of a mile, furnishing an immense water-power. The township contains fine beds of iron-ore and limestone. After leaving the station the road crosses Sugar River by a bridge 600 feet long, and 105 above the water.

Windsor (246 miles) is on the west bank of the river, which is crossed by the railway at this point. The village stands on elevated ground, is compactly

223

and elegantly built, and will compare favorably with the most attractive villages in the country. The scenery is picturesque, and the town is the centre of a fine agricultural and wool-growing region. A gun-factory is established here. The *State Prison* is located at this point. There is a good hotel. Opposite the town are the Cornish Hills, in New Hampshire.

Hartland (250 miles) is a rich farming town, watered by the *Connecticut* and *Queechee Rivers* and *Sull's Brook*.

North Hartland (254 miles) is a small station near the falls of the *Otta Queechee River*, which is here crossed by a bridge 650 feet in length and 80 in height. The falls can be seen to the west of the road.

White River Junction, in the township of Hartford (260 miles), is just south of the junction of *White River* with the *Connecticut*. This place is the connecting point for several railways, and has a good hotel, the *Junction House*. There is a restaurant in the depot. Passengers for the Green Mountains and Lake Champlain leave Connecticut River here.

Norwich (264 miles). After leaving White River Junction, the Connecticut and Passumpsic Railway crosses White River, and follows the valley of the Connecticut to *Norwich and Hanover Station*, which is about three-quarters of a mile from Norwich village, and the same from Hanover. The village was formerly the seat of Norwich University, since removed to Northfield. The only free bridge across the Connecticut leads to *Hanover*, the seat of *Dartmouth College*. (See page 218.)

Pompanoosuc Station (270 miles), in the town of Norwich, is reached after crossing the *Ompompanoosuc River*. Near this point is an old Indian burying-ground.

Thetford (275 miles) possesses an excellent water-power. There is a curious pond here upon an elevation 100 feet high, the base of which is only 4 rods from the Connecticut River. The pond is 9 acres in extent, has neither outlet nor inlet, and is well stocked with fish. *Thetford Academy* ranks high.

North Thetford (277 miles) is the point from which the copper-ore mined by the *Corinth Copper Company* is shipped.

Fairlee (282 miles) contains a pond of the same name, which is famous for its pickerel-fishing. On the left of the road, beyond the station, is a ledge of rocks several hundred feet high. *Orford*, N. H., is connected with Fairlee by a bridge across the *Connecticut*.

Bradford (289 miles) is an important manufacturing town, possessing a good water-power. The Bradford Academy, founded in 1820, has a high reputation. Soon after leaving the station, the village of Haverhill, N. H., and Moose Hillock, Sugar Loaf, and Black Mountains, are seen. Passengers for *Topsham, Corinth, Orange, Washington,* and *Piermont*, take stages here.

South Newbury (293 miles). The scenery in this vicinity is very interesting.

Newbury (296 miles) is one of the most attractive towns in the Upper Connecticut Valley. The village, which is upon a terrace about 100 feet above the flats which skirt the river, contains the churches, and the inevitable academy, which are to be found in almost every New-England town of considerable size. This place is greatly frequented on account of its celebrated *Sulphur Springs*, and its beautiful scenery. The great *Ox-bow* of the Connecticut, and *Mount Pulaski*, are both in this township. There are two good hotels here.

Wells's River, in the town of Newbury (300 miles), is noted for its magnificent views. It is here that the visitor to the White Mountains takes the cars for Littleton, the present terminus of the White Mountain Railway. (See page 207.) It is something of a railway centre. HOTELS: *Wells's River House* and *Union House*.

Ryegate (304 miles) is where, by a natural dam, the waters of the river are set back so as almost to form a lake, at the foot of which are *Dodge's Falls*. The views in this vicinity are charming.

McIndoe's (308 miles) is near McIndoe's Falls, on the Connecticut, which afford a good water-power. Just beyond the station is a boom in which generally large quantities of logs may be seen. Above this boom are *Beard's*

Falls, above which are a number of islands. Still above these islands are the well-known *Fifteen-Mile Falls*, which, however, are not visible from the cars.

Barnet (311 miles) is a village at the mouth of *Stevens River*, which is crossed just before reaching the station. The township is a romantic place, and contains three ponds, the largest of which is 300 acres in extent.

McLeran's (34 miles) is where the Passumpsic breaks through a narrow gorge of black, slaty rocks. In Barnet the railway leaves the Connecticut and proceeds up the valley of the Passumpsic.

Passumpsic (318 miles) is in the neighborhood of some beautiful falls.

St. Johnsbury (321 miles) is the most important and attractive place in this portion of the State. Many of the dwellings in the village are elegant, and surrounded by spacious grounds. The most prominent of these are the residences of the Messrs. Fairbanks, whose celebrated scale manufactories are located here. The *Court-House* is a handsome building. In front of the Court House stands the *Soldiers' Monument*, a statue of America by Larkin G. Meade, upon a pedestal of Vermont marble, bearing the names of 81 soldiers who lost their lives during the war of the rebellion. The new *Library Building* is near the Court-House. *Reservoir Hill*, near the village, is a point from which a charming but not very extensive view can be obtained.

St. Johnsbury Centre (323 miles) is a village in the town of St. Johnsbury.

Lyndonville (328 miles) is one of the three villages in the town of Lyndon. The scenery is picturesque and interesting, and within the limits of the town are two falls of the Passumpsic River, one of 65 and the other of 18 feet, called respectively *Great* and *Little Falls*. The general offices and repair-shops of the Connecticut and Passumpsic River Railways are here. From a hill near the station there is a fine view of *Burke Mountain*, 3,500 feet high.

West Burke (337 miles) is in Burke township and is the point of departure for *Willoughby Lake*.

Willoughby Lake, in the town of Westmore, reached by stages from *West Burke*, is a remarkably attractive summer resort. It is crescent-shape, 6 or 7 miles long, and from one quarter to two miles in width. Its depth is unknown, a sounding-line of 700 feet having failed to reach bottom. The lake lies between two mountain-peaks with nearly perpendicular faces, from the summit of the highest of which a magnificent view is obtained. This mountain is a fine field for the botanist, rare varieties of plants and flowers growing here.

The hotel is the *Willoughby Lake House*.

South Barton (345 miles), **Barton** (350 miles), and **Barton Landing** (355 miles), are all villages in the same township. The first is called the summit, as it is on the dividing ridge between the St. Lawrence and the Connecticut. The view from here embraces *Jay Peak*, 4,000 feet high, and other mountains in the vicinity. The second village (Barton) is at the foot of *Crystal Lake*, which furnishes a good water-power. There are people still living in this place who remember the attempt, June 6, 1810, to lead the waters of Long Pond, situated partly in Glover, and partly in Greensborough, through Mud Pond into the Barton River. The attempt was so successful that the entire volume of the water in the pond rushed out at once, forever draining it and causing a very disastrous freshet. The stage road to Montpelier passes through the bed of the pond. There is a daily line of stages from this place to Montpelier, *Hardwick*, *Glover*, and *Craftsbury*. The last of the three villages was, during the War of 1812–'15, a great resort for smugglers from Canada.

Coventry (360 miles) contains several manufactories.

Newport (365 miles) is upon a hill-side near the south end of Memphremagog. This is the best place for visitors to the lake to stop, the *Memphremagog House* being a good hotel, and all points of interest being easily accessible. From *Prospect Hill*, near the hotel, a fine view of the lake is obtained. There is a steamer upon the lake which makes daily trips to *Magog* in Canada, whence passengers for Montreal or Quebec take stages for *Sherbrooke Station* on the Grand Trunk Railway.

North Derby (370 miles) is the present terminus of the road, and is on the *Canada* line. The *Massiwippi Railway* is now building from this point to Lennoxville, on the Grand Trunk Railway.

Lake Memphremagog is a beautiful sheet of water, situated partly in Vermont and partly in Canada. It is 35 miles long, and varies from 2 to 5 miles in width. Its shores are rockbound, and indented with beautiful bays, between which jut out bold, wooded headlands, backed by mountain-ranges. Numerous picturesque islands dot its surface. *Muscalonge trout* are taken here in great perfection.

Newport, at the head of the lake, has two hotels and several churches, and a population of about 1,000. The *Memphremagog House* is a well-kept hotel; Bush & Pender, proprietors. *Prospect Hill*, south of the village, commands a fine view of the lake and surrounding elevations, prominent among which are *Owl's Head*, *Mount Elephantis*, *Mount Orford*, *Jay Peak*, and *Willoughby Mountain*. The steamer "Mountain Maid," Captain Fogg, leaves the hotel pier, Newport, every morning, and plies the entire length of the lake, touching at the *Mountain House* for the convenience of travellers wishing to ascend *Owl's Head* or *Bear Mountain*.

Jay Peak, 13 miles west of Newport, should be visited, if time permits. It is 4,018 feet high, and commands a fine view of the entire range of the Green Mountains, including Mount Mansfield, Camel's Hump, and Killington Peak, Ascutney Mountain, near Windsor, White and Franconia Mountains, Kearsarge, Lake Champlain, and the Adirondacks.

Owl's Head rises 3,000 feet above the lake, and commands, in clear weather, an extensive view. Tourists can either proceed to Montreal or Quebec from the foot of the lake, or return to Newport on the boat the same day at 6 P.M. At and near the Mountain House are the best fishing-grounds on the lake. Boats supplied on application at the hotel.

In ascending the lake, *Indian Point*, the *Twin Sisters*, and *Province Island*, are passed within a few miles of Newport. East of *Province Island* and near the shore is *Tea-Table Island*, a charming rural picnic spot, and on the western shore the boundary-line between Vermont and Canada strikes the lake. *Fitch's Bay* and *Whetstone Island*, *Magoon Point*, *Round* and *Minnow Islands*, are in the vicinity of the Mountain-House, and afford pleasant picnic and excursion points for visitors sojourning there. *Skinner's Island* and *Cave*, said to have been the haunt of Uriah Skinner, "the bold smuggler of Magog," during the War of 1812, are also near by. *Balance Rock*, on the southern shore of Long Island, is frequently visited. The eastern shore of the lake, in this vicinity, is much improved and adorned with some handsome summer residences, among which are those belonging to Judge Day, William Molson, and Hugh Allen, of Montreal. *Mount Elephantis* (Sugar Loaf) is seen to advantage from Allen's Landing.

Concert Pond, west of Mount Elephantis, abounds in brook-trout, and attracts numerous visitors.

Georgeville, 20 miles from Newport and 12 from Magog, has a hotel and several stores. *Knowlton's*, on the opposite (west) side of the lake, is the landing for passengers to Stanstead and Montreal. The route thither is by stage to Waterloo, 20 miles, and thence by rail 42 miles to St. John's, and 63 to Montreal. A better route, though a longer stage-ride, for those who do not care to follow the beaten track of travel and visit Montreal first, is to proceed by the steamer on to Magog (Outlet Village), and thence by stage to Sherbrooke, *en route* to Richmond and Quebec.

(For continuation, see Route I of CANADA.)

ROUTE II.

BOSTON TO MONTPELIER, VERMONT, THE GREEN MOUNTAINS, LAKE CHAMPLAIN, THE ADIRONDACKS, ROUSE'S POINT, OGDENSBURG, AND MONTREAL.

Via Route X. of *Massachusetts*, *I. of New Hampshire* to Concord, *III. of New Hampshire* to White River Junction, thence via Vermont Central and Vermont and Canada Railroads.

STATIONS.—White River Junction, 143 miles from Boston; White River Village, 146; Woodstock, 147; West Hartford, 152; Sharon, 157; South Royalton, 162;

Royalton, 164; Bethel, 169; Randolph, 176; Braintree, 182; Roxbury, 191; Northfield, 198; Montpelier Junction, 208; Montpelier, 209½; Middlesex, 212; Waterbury, 217; Ridley's Station, 222; Bolton, 225; Jonesville, 228; Richmond, 231; Williston, 236; Essex Junction, 239; Winooski, 245; Burlington, 247 (connects with trains on Rutland Division for Middlebury, Rutland, Troy, Albany, etc.; and with steamers on Lake Champlain for Ticonderoga, Lake George, Saratoga Springs, etc.); Colchester, 244; Milton, 251; Georgia, 255; St. Albans, 265 (connects with trains over Ogdensburg and Lake Champlain Division for Potsdam, Ogdensburg, and the West); Swanton, 275; Alburg Springs, 282; Alburg, 285; West Alburg, 287; Rouse's Point, 289; East Swanton, 274; Highgate Springs, 278; St. Armand, 282; Moore's, 284; Stanbridge, 289; Des Rivières', 292; St. Alexandre, 299; Stanstead, Shefford, and Chambly Junction, 305; St. John's, 308 (connects with Montreal and Champlain Division of Grand Trunk Railway, and with Stanstead, Shefford and Chambly Division); Montreal, 320.

This is an attractive route, and forms one of the leading thoroughfares between the New-England States and Canada. The Vermont Central Railroad follows that lovely stream, White River, and one of its branches, until it reaches Roxbury Summit, then descends Dog River to the Winooski River near Montpelier, and thence down the Winooski, to Burlington. It leaves the river about a mile and a half from Lake Champlain, and passes through a tunnel to the lake-shore.

White River Junction (143 miles). (*See* page 218.)

White River Village (146 miles) is a pretty place in a fine farming region. Before reaching this station the road follows the right or south bank for a few miles, but crosses White River, or its branch from Bethel, several times before reaching Roxbury.

Woodstock Station (147 miles), just beyond the bridge, is 10 miles from *Woodstock Village*, which is reached by stages, and is to be connected with the main line by a branch road to White River Junction. The town itself is the shire-town of Windsor County, and is located in the valley of the Otta Quechee. It is the birthplace of several distinguished men, among them Hiram Powers, the sculptor.

West Hartford (152 miles) is a small village. As the passenger is riding to the next station, he cannot fail to be delighted with the scenery, or to notice the transparent purity of the river where it is crossed by the road.

Sharon (155 miles) is the town in which Joseph Smith, the founder of the Mormons, was born. The village stands on the opposite side of the river. Without specifying the details of the scenery at the different stations, or the particular points at which there are bridges, we may state that, for the first 50 miles, the road crosses and recrosses the river, passing through a succession of hills and valleys, the scenery becoming more and more bold and rugged as the mountains are approached.

South Royalton (162 miles), and **Royalton** (164 miles), are two villages of Royalton township, the former on the right and the latter on the left bank of the river. The south village contains a public square, on which fronts the hotel, the *South Royalton House.* There is a daily line of stages from *Royalton* to *East Bethel, East Randolph,* and *East Brookfield,* also to *Chelsea,* the shire-town of Orange County.

Bethel (169 miles) is an active business village in a narrow valley, surrounded by steep hills. The branches of White River, up one of which the railroad proceeds, meet at this place. Two or three miles after leaving the station a curious hill rises abruptly from a level plain. There are daily stages from *Bethel* to *Barnard, Woodstock, Stockbridge,* and *Rochester.*

West Randolph (176 miles) is an exceedingly active and prosperous village, and is connected by a daily line of stages with *Randolph Centre,* where the *Orange County Grammar School* is located, *Brookfield* and *Chelsea Cottage Hotel.* After passing the station we first come in sight of the highest peaks of the *Green Mountains.*

Braintree (182 miles). This comparatively insignificant village is surrounded by wild and rugged mountain-scenery.

GREEN MOUNTAINS.

We are now fairly in the mountains, which, though neither so attractive nor so well known as the White Mountains, possess numerous lofty peaks and points of interest, which will be taken up in detail as we approach them, but will not be grouped together as was done in the case of the *White Mountains*.

Roxbury (191 miles) contains the quarries of the famous *Verde Antique Marble*, said to equal any thing in the world, but there is not much done there at present. The road here leaves the branch of *White River*, and, crossing the summit of the pass through which it runs, reaches the source of *Dog River*, a tributary of the *Winooski River*. Before it reaches Northfield there is a long bridge 70 feet high.

Northfield (198 miles) formerly contained the railway repair-shops now located at St. Albans. The *Vermont Military Institute*, formerly the Norwich University, at Norwich, is located here. There are also quarries of valuable dark-colored slate. The hotel is the *Northfield House*.

Montpelier Junction (208 miles) is where the branch to Montpelier village (1¼ miles) diverges.

Montpelier (209¼ miles), the capital of the State, is upon the *Winooski River*, which furnishes a fine water-power. The village stands upon what evidently was the bed of a lake. The *State Capitol* is of granite, is 176 feet long, and has a dome 124 feet high. In the portico stands a marble statue of *Ethan Allen*, made by the Vermont sculptor, Larkin G. Mead, and in the building are historical and geological collections, a State Library, and the flags carried by the Vermont volunteers during the rebellion. The river is here spanned by a good bridge. The drives and views among the hills in the vicinity are attractive. The hotels are the *Pavilion* and *Bishop's Hotel*. Stages run from here to *Calais, Hardwick, Greensboro', Glover, Barton, Plainfield, Marshfield, Cabot, Danville, Barre, Orange*, and *Chelsea*.

Middlesex (212 miles) is a small station on the *Winooski River*. Stages from the village to *Moretown, Waitsfield*, and *Warren*.

The Winooski River traverses more than two-thirds the entire breadth of Northern Vermont. Rising in the south part of Caledonia County, its course is generally westward to Lake Champlain, 40 miles from which it passes through Montpelier. Some of its valley passages are scenes of great pastoral beauty, strongly contrasted with high mountain surroundings, the singularly-formed peak of Camel's Hump continually showing itself, sometimes barely peeping over intervening ranges, and again—as near the middle of the valley stretch—coming into full display. In places, the Winooski is a wild, turbulent water, dashing over stern precipices and through rugged defiles. It is found in this rough mood just above the village of Winooski, a few miles from Burlington, where the waters rush in rapid and cascade through a ravine 100 feet. This picture is favorably seen from the railway. Passing on into the open valley-lands, which succeed, Mount Camel's Hump comes finely into view, as the central and crowning point of one of the sweetest pictures of all this region.

Before reaching Middlesex, the river, on the left of the railway, passes over a series of ledges, and then leaps into the *Middlesex Narrows*, a channel 30 feet deep and one-fourth of a mile long, which it has cut for itself through the slate-rock.

Waterbury (217 miles) is an attractive resort for summer tourists, being in the immediate vicinity of *Mount Mansfield* and *Camel's-Hump Mountain*, and other places of interest to the tourist. The hotel is the *Waterbury House*. Stages run from here to *Stowe, Mount Mansfield, Hyde Park*, and *Craftsbury*.

Stowe is a very pleasant place for a summer residence. It is situated on a plain, surrounded by splendid mountain-scenery, and is eight miles from the summit of Mount Mansfield, which is in full view from the hotel, and is reached by stages. HOTEL: *Mansfield House*. Among the favorite excursions from the village are those to *Bolton Falls, Smuggler's Notch, Bingham's Falls, Moss Glen Falls*, and others.

Mount Mansfield, the loftiest (4,348 feet) of the Green Mountains, is 15 miles from Waterbury Station. It is easily reached from the village of Underhill Centre on the north, or yet more easily from the pleasant village of Stowe on the south, both of which points may be reached from the Vermont Central road—Underhill from Jonesville Station or Essex Junction, and Stowe from Waterbury. Stages leave Waterbury for Stowe (10 miles) on arrival of trains. Mansfield is 20 miles from Burlington. The views of the mountain itself, its cliffs and peaks, are very grand for many points in the path upward, and the panorama unfolded upon the summit is, if possible, finer than that from the Camel's Hump. Lake Champlain and the Adirondack peaks lie to the westward, while the White Mountains of New Hampshire are seen on the east; and again, the many crests of the Green Hills, with their intervening vales and lakes and villages, stretch out toward the south. In favorable conditions of the weather and atmosphere, the mountains near Montreal, 70 miles distant, can be seen with the naked eye. The *Mansfield House* and the *Summit House*, both owned by the Mansfield Hotel Company, are well-kept houses. The latter, which is 9 miles (three hours) from the Mansfield House, commands a most lovely view. The drive from the Mansfield House to Bolton Falls and the *Natural Bridge* (3 miles) is delightful.

Ridley's Station (222 miles) is the most convenient point of departure for *Camel's-Hump Mountain*, conveyances from here taking the visitor nearly to the summit, a drive of three miles. After reaching the station, the road passes *Bolton Falls*. Soon after leaving the station, the river is crossed and is seen on the south, while on the north all is rugged and rocky.

Camel's-Hump Mountain, the most salient feature in the Winooski landscape, is, next to Mansfield, the highest of all the Green Mountain peaks, having an elevation of 4,083 feet. It may be ascended, without much difficulty, from any side. The mountain is crowned by jagged, barren rocks, and the imposing scene which the lofty heights overlook is in no way obstructed by the forest veil, which often disappoints the hopeful climber of forbidding mountain-tops. *Bolton Falls* afford a pleasant excursion from the Hump.

Bolton (225 miles) is in a valley surrounded by rugged and precipitous mountains. The hotel is the *Bolton House*. Bolton Falls are a little below Ridley's Station.

Jonesville (228 miles) possesses the same general characteristics as the other mountain villages, being in the midst of picturesque scenery. Stages daily to *Huntington*, *Hinesburg*, and *Underhill Centre*.

Richmond (231 miles) is a thriving place in a more open section of country, and is the centre of a large butter and cheese trade for several towns. The bridge over the Winooski, just beyond the station, is 600 feet long.

Williston (236 miles). Coming now into a more open country, on the right are visible the summits of the Green Mountains; on the left, beyond Lake Champlain, those of the Adirondacks. From the bridge across the *Winooski*, beyond the station, a superb view is had of *Mounts Mansfield* and *Camel's Hump*. A yet finer one is had from Essex Junction.

Essex Junction (239 miles) is where the branch to *Burlington* diverges. Stages go from Essex Junction to *Jericho*, *Underhill*, *Mount Mansfield*, *Cambridge*, *Johnson*, *Irasburg*, and *Newport*.

Winooski village (in the town of Colchester, 245 miles) may be considered a suburb of Burlington. The *Winooski Falls*, at this point, are considered worthy of the tourist's attention. There are extensive factories and mills there. The lofty granite monument over the grave of *Ethan Allen* is to be seen on the high ground in Burlington, south of *Winooski* village.

Burlington (247 miles). (See page 57.)

Lake Champlain. (See p. 56.)
The Adirondacks. (See p. 58.)
Colchester (244 miles) is an active manufacturing town. From this

point the road continues to the north, with the Green Mountains constantly in view on the east, and Lake Champlain frequently in sight on the west.

Milton (251 miles) is a prosperous village near the falls of the *Lamoille River*, which furnish power for saw-mills, etc.

Georgia (255 miles) is connected by stages with *Fairfax* (the site of the *New Hampton Baptist Institution*) and *Fletcher*. Before reaching the station, the road crosses the *Lamoille* by a very high bridge.

St. Albans (265 miles) is built upon high ground, rising from the shore of Lake Champlain, and is noted as the market-place of the great butter and cheese business of Franklin County. The public square of four acres is an ornamental ground, surrounded by the principal buildings. The extensive shops of the Vermont Central and Vermont and Canada Railroads are at St. Albans. On the 19th of October, 1864, a band of robbers, in the interest of the Confederates, made a raid on St. Albans from Canada, and captured about $200,000 from the banks, besides a number of horses. $90,000 of the money was recovered. From its position, St. Albans was selected by the Fenians for one of their raids upon Canada. The view from *Aldis Hill*, in the rear of the town, is magnificent. The railway depot is large and admirably managed. Stages run from St. Albans to *Missisquoi Springs*, *Sheldon*, *Fairfield*, *Bakersfield*, *Enosburg*, *Berkshire*, *Richford*, and *Troy*. HOTEL: the *Weldon House* is a large, first-class hotel. The railway divides here, one branch running to *Ogdensburg*, and the other to St. John's, thence to Montreal. We will first visit the springs, and then, after a trip to *Rouse's Point*, resume our journey to Montreal.

Missisquoi Springs, in the town of Sheldon, 13 in number, are 10 miles from *St. Albans*, with which they are connected by stage. There are no two of them possessed of the same characteristics, all producing different effects. The waters of the Missisquoi Spring proper have accomplished many wonderful cures. It is a popular resort for invalids. A large first-class hotel, the *Missisquoi House*, and several smaller ones, have been erected. The views of the surrounding mountains are very fine.

Sheldon is a small village, 3 miles from the Missisquoi Springs. There are one or two mineral springs near the village. HOTEL: *Central House*. Swanton (275 miles) is the first station on the *Ogdensburg Division*. Just beyond, the road crosses *Missisquoi Bay*.

Alburg Springs (282 miles) are on a peninsula. There is a large hotel here; and, besides the springs, all the attractions of Lake Champlain are within the visitor's reach.

Alburg (285 miles). Here the road runs on the shore of the lake.

West Alburg (287 miles) is where the road crosses the lake on a bridge one mile in length, from which fine views are secured. *Fort Montgomery* is in the State of New York, and a little above the bridge across the lake.

Rouse's Point (288 miles) is in New York, and is the junction of the *Montreal and Lake Champlain* with the railway for Ogdensburg. (*See* page 85.) Returning to *St. Albans*, we will resume the route to *Montreal*.

East Swanton (274 miles) is reached just after crossing the *Missisquoi River*.

Highgate Springs (278 miles) are quite near the railroad. The *Franklin House* is a well-kept hotel, and a pleasant place to stay at in summer. This is the last station in the United States. The Canadian stations, St. John's excepted, are small, unimportant places.

Montreal (320 miles) and the *great Tubular Bridge* will be described in the chapter on CANADA.

ROUTE III.

BOSTON TO BELLOWS FALLS, RUTLAND, THE GREEN MOUNTAINS, SARATOGA SPRINGS, LAKE GEORGE, LAKE CHAMPLAIN, AND CANADA.

Via Route IX. of Massachusetts ; IV. of New Hampshire, and Vermont Central, Vermont and Canada Railways.

STATIONS.—Boston: Bellows Falls, 114 miles (connects with railways diverging from Bellows Falls); Bartonsville, 142; Chester, 128; Gassett's, 132; Cavendish,

136; Proctorsville, 138; Ludlow, 141; Healdville, 147; Summit, 148; Mount Holly, 151; East Wallingford, 154; Cuttingsville, 157; Clarendon, 160; Rutland, 167 (connects with Rensselaer and Saratoga, and Harlem Extension Railways, for Saratoga Springs, and all points along the Hudson River); Sutherland Falls, 173; Pittsford, 176; Brandon, 183; Whiting, 188; Salisbury, 193; Middlebury, 199; New Haven, 207; Vergennes, 213; North Ferrisburg, 218; Charlotte, 222; Shelburne, 227; Burlington, 234 (connects with steamers to Plattsburg, on Lake Champlain, connecting there with Montreal and Plattsburg Railway. There is a *Day and Night Express*).

This road passes through the marble district, through the Green Mountains, and along the shore of Lake Champlain, and is noted for the fine views along the whole line.

Bellows Falls (114 miles.) (*See* page 218.)

Bartonsville (124 miles) is where the ascent to the mountains commences. Between this and *Chester* is a deep ravine spanned by a bridge.

Chester (128 miles) is built upon the crest of the hills, along the base of which runs the *William's River*. HOTEL: *Chester House*.

Gassett's (132 miles) is merely the station for *Springfield*. The village (7 miles distant) is at that great natural curiosity, the *Black River Falls*, which, if possible, should not be passed without a visit, to observe the peculiar action of the water upon the rocks. Springfield is an active manufacturing village.

Proctorsville (138 miles) is a manufacturing village, after leaving which the Green Mountains come into view on the right.

Ludlow (141 miles) is a large manufacturing village, containing several churches and schools. The railway passes over what is called the "*Hog-Back*," the peculiar formation of which is a subject of much speculation.

Healdville (147 miles) is a small village. On the right of the railway there are a ravine and several cascades.

Summit (148 miles) is the highest point on the line, which descends 1,000 feet in the 18 miles between here and *Rutland*.

Mount Holly (151 miles) is where the road reaches Mill River, the course of which it follows to Rutland.

Clarendon (160 miles) is well known for its mineral springs, and for *Clarendon Cave* in its southwestern portion. Stages run to the springs from *West Rutland Station*, 4 miles south of Rutland. The medicinal virtues of these waters, the varied and beautiful scenery, the pleasant drives around, and the excellent hotel accommodations, make this watering-place a very desirable summer halt.

Rutland (167 miles) is a pleasant town, especially noted for its marble-quarries and works. It is a place of over 10,000 inhabitants, does a large business, and contains handsome dwellings and stores. *Shrewsbury*, *Killington*, and *Pico Peaks* of the Green Mountains, *Clarendon Springs*, and other places in the vicinity, contribute to the attractions of Rutland. The hotels are: the *Bardwell House*, *Bates House*, *Stevens House*, and the *Central House*. The road here connects with the *Rensselaer and Saratoga*, and *Harlem Extension Railways*, all three using the same depot.

Killington Peak, rising grandly on the east of Rutland, is the third in rank of the mountains of Vermont. A visit to this peak makes a pleasant excursion from the neighborhood. To the foot of the mountain the distance is 7 miles, and 2 miles more to the summit. On the north side is a perpendicular ledge of 200 feet, called *Capital Rock*. *Mount Ida*, too, is hereabouts, and beyond Killington Peak, as seen from Rutland, and northward, are *Mount Pico* and *Castleton Ridge*, shutting out the view of Lake Champlain.

Sutherland Falls (173 miles) of Otter Creek are on the right of the track, but no idea of their beauty can be had from the glimpse obtained from the cars. The marble-works here are extensive. The railway at this point runs for a distance upon a hill-side, gradually descending to the meadows at the base.

Pittsford (176 miles) is on the north of a beautiful valley, and is noted for its beds of iron-ore and its marble-quarries.

231

Brandon (183 miles) contains a scale factory, a marble-quarry, and manufactories of mineral paints. Minerals of fine quality are found in this town. There are here two curious caverns formed of limestone, the larger containing two apartments, each from 16 to 20 feet square. It is entered by descending from the surface about 20 feet. Stages for *Lake Dunmore*, 9 miles distant, leave here on the arrival of the trains.

Lake Dunmore is a beautiful sheet of water, 30 miles above Rutland. It is 8 miles (by stage) from Middlebury, and 9 from Brandon. Dunmore is a wonderfully picturesque lake, surrounded at most points by bold hills, seen here in verdant slopes, and there in rocky bluff and cliff. The lake is about 5 miles in length and 3 in breadth, and affords capital fishing. A good summer hotel and several cottages are on the west bank.

Whiting (188 miles). A fine view of the *Green Mountains* is had from this station, and a short distance beyond the Adirondacks come in sight. Stages run to *Orwell*.

Middlebury (199 miles) is upon the Otter Creek, near some fine falls on that stream, and a few miles only from Lake Dunmore. It has a population (the township) of some 4,000, and, like nearly all the villages in Vermont, is a very beautiful place, surrounded at all points by most attractive mountain-scenery. It is distinguished as one of the first manufacturing towns in the State, and also as the seat of *Middlebury College*, founded in 1800. Its chief edifice is 100 feet long and four stories high, built of stone. Extensive marble-quarries are in the neighborhood. *Camel's Hump* and *Mount Mansfield*, described on page 229, are in sight, to the right. After leaving the station, *New Haven River* is crossed in sight of some rapids. At *Belden's Falls* there is a great marble-mill.

Vergennes (213 miles), the oldest city in Vermont (there are only two), was incorporated in 1783, and is at the head of navigation on Otter Creek. There is a United States Arsenal here, and here Commodore McDonough's fleet was fitted out in 1812. The *Addison House* is the hotel. The *Fort Cassan House*, a few miles distant, is a summer resort.

The Otter Creek Falls, at Vergennes, are upon the Otter Creek, about seven miles from Lake Champlain. The brook is 500 feet in width, divided by a fine island, on either side of which the fall leaps some 30 or 40 feet. There are many other beautiful cascades in the Otter Creek; some at Middlebury, above Rutland; and, a few miles below Middlebury, still others of yet greater interest. The *Elgin Spring* is in the neighborhood of the Otter Creek cascades.

Charlotte (222 miles) is a village some little distance from the station. The fossil remains of a whale were found here in 1849. The skeleton is in the State Geological Collection at Montpelier.

Shelburne (227 miles) is a small village overlooking the lake.

Burlington (234 miles). (For description, *see* page 57. This route here connects with Route II.)

ROUTE IV.

NEW YORK TO RUTLAND. THE GREEN MOUNTAINS, LAKE CHAMPLAIN, AND CANADA.

Via Route VIII. of *New York, and Harlem Extension Railway.*

STATIONS. — New York: Petersburg Junction, 178 miles (connects with Troy and Boston Railway); Bennington, 190; North Bennington, 194; Arlington, 206; Manchester, 215; East Dorset, 220; Mount Tabor and Danby, 227; Wallingford, 236; Rutland, 245 (connects with Vermont Central, Vermont and Canada, and Rensselaer and Saratoga Railways).

The above distances are *via Harlem Railway* to *Chatham Four Corners*.

Petersburg Junction (178 miles). (*See* page 85.)

Bennington (190 miles), and **North Bennington** (194 miles), are both in *Bennington Township;* it also contains *Bennington Centre*, which is the Revolutionary village. This township, being situated several hundred feet above the sea and surrounded by mountains, is delightfully cool in summer and possesses other attractions. In the old village stands the "Catamount Tavern," containing intact the room in which the "Council of Safety," then the only government in the State, held its sessions in the times of the Revolution. Ethan Allen's house still stands next door. *Hoosac*, New York, the adjoining township, was the scene of the battle of Bennington (August 16, 1777), in which a detachment of the British forces, under Colonel Baum, was terribly beaten by the Green Mountain Boys, led by the intrepid General Stark. It was upon the occasion of this memorable engagement that Stark is reported to have made the famous address to his troops: "See there, men! there are the red-coats! Before to-night they are ours, or Molly Stark will be a widow!" The manufactories of the United States Pottery Company at Bennington are well deserving of a visit. Fine porcelain and Parian ware are made here, the vicinage yielding the necessary materials in abundant and excellent supply.

About two miles from the hotel in *Bennington* is *Mount Anthony*, which can be reached by a foot-path, or by a carriage-road, which more than doubles the distance. Upon the summit is a tower 100 feet in height, from which a splendid view is obtained. There are numerous pleasant drives in the vicinity, among them those to *Petersburg* and *Prospect Mountains* and to *Big Pond*. There is good trout-fishing in the neighborhood.

HOTEL: *Mount Anthony House*.

Arlington (206 miles) is a rich agricultural town, well watered by Green River and several small brooks, which furnish a good water-power. It contains *West* and *Red Mountains*, extensive quarries of marble, a medicinal spring, and a cave which is about 13 rods long, with an average width and height of 8 feet. It is in some places very narrow, but in others expands into large rooms. Near the extremity is a room more than 50 feet high, incrusted with stalactites. This cave is entered by a narrow passage in a hill-side, descending 20 feet. A stream of water runs through the cavern.

Manchester (215 miles) is a beautiful village, in a valley between the *Green* and *Equinox Ranges*, and is noticeable for its white-marble pavements, there being many quarries in the vicinity. It is a pleasant resort, from the many attractions in the vicinity, among which may be mentioned fine scenery, trout-fishing, and driving.

Mount Dorset, in which is the cave mentioned under the head of *Arlington*, is 5 miles from the village.

Stratton Gap, a beautiful glen, and the subject of one of A. B. Durand's best paintings, is near by. *Mount Equinox*, 3,813 feet above tide-water, and 2,917 above the village, is noted for its glorious views, the following points being visible from its summit when the weather is clear: Lakes George and Champlain, Kearsarge and the Franconia Mountains in New Hampshire, Graylock Mountain in Massachusetts, Killington Mountain in Vermont, and the Catskill Mountains and Saratoga village in New York. *Skinner Hollow* is a deep indentation on the south side of the mountain, containing a cave in which the snow never entirely melts, a stream which finds an outlet through a cavern, and a marble-quarry.

East Dorset (220 miles) is in *Dorset Township*, which contains *Dorset Mountain*, and a part of *Equinox Mountain*. There are several very remarkable caverns in this town, as well as a number of marble-quarries.

Wallingford (236 miles) is a town containing three handsome mountain-ponds, the largest of which, *Hiram's*, has an area of 350 acres, and is on very elevated ground. There are marble-quarries in the town. *Green Hill* is composed of quartz, and is near the centre of the town. *White Rocks*, part granite and part quartz, belong to the Green Mountain range. At the foot of them are cavities called the *ice-beds*, in which the ice never melts. The village on the banks of Otter Creek presents some picturesque scenery.

Rutland (245 miles). Connects with Route III. (For description, *see* page 231.)

The branch of the *Rensselaer and Saratoga Railway*, which connects at this point, has been described as Route IX. of NEW YORK, as far as the State line, but there are two stations in Vermont which should be mentioned here.

Castleton (11 miles from Rutland) is neatly built, and rich and beautiful in scenery. The township in which it is located is noted for its slate-stone, from which is made an imitation marble, "so perfect that it challenges the closest scrutiny." "It has six times the strength of marble, and its appearance is much superior."

Poultney, 28 miles from Rutland, on the Rutland and Washington Railway, is an attractive summer residence. The scenery is varied and picturesque, the roads are capital, and the air is dry and pure. Board can be had at *Ripley College* during the months of July and August. Among the many pleasant places in the vicinity are Lake Bombazine and Lake Austin.

Lake Bombazine is a beautiful sheet of water, 9 miles in length, famed for its boating and fishing. There are two hotels at *Heath's Ferry*.

Lake Austin is another attractive spot. The hotel is the *Saint Catharine House*.

In Castleton and Poultney are many slate-quarries, where slate of a variety of colors and great excellence is extensively quarried.

MAINE.

Maine, the largest of the New-England States, and the most easterly in the Union, is bounded on the north by the Dominion of Canada, on the east by New Brunswick and the Atlantic Ocean, on the south by the Atlantic Ocean, and on the west by the Dominion of Canada and New Hampshire. It is 250 miles long, and 190 broad in its greatest dimensions, and includes an area of 31,766 square miles, of which only about 4,300 are improved.

The coast-line of Maine is bold and picturesque, but inland for some ten or twenty miles the surface of the country is flat and marshy.

The general character of the surface of the State is hilly and diversified. It is heavily timbered with pine, hemlock, spruce, maple, birch, and ash, and this staple forms its chief industry. In the winter great numbers of lumbermen are employed in felling the trees and dragging them over the snow to the rivers, where they lie until the breaking up of the ice in the spring, when they are floated down to the mills and places of export.

The rivers of Maine are thus highly important, as forming the means of inexpensive transportation for its lumber, and, fortunately, they are numerous and extensive.

The Penobscot and Kennebec, flowing into the Atlantic, are the most important of these water-courses, their length being from 200 to 300 miles each.

The Androscoggin, the Saco, the St. John, and the St. Croix, are also valuable water-powers.

The coast of Maine is indented by many inlets, and possesses the largest number of fine harbors of any State in the Union, while these are guarded by numerous islands, large and small, forming a complete breakwater against the vast Atlantic.

Among the principal lakes of Maine may be mentioned *Moosehead*, *Cheuncook*, *Umbagog*, and *Sebago*. It is estimated that one-tenth of the surface of the State is covered with water.

The climate of Maine is very severe in winter, and the northeast winds from the Atlantic, in the spring and early summer, are extremely injurious to health. The summers, however, never reach the extremity of heat, but are mild and genial. The agricultural products of the State comprise wheat, rye, Indian corn, oats, barley, and potatoes; but there is little rich land, and the chief products of the State are live-stock, butter, and wool.

The mineral resources of the State are not specially noticeable, nor do her manufactures compare with the other New-England States. Indeed, at present, Maine is chiefly important for her vast quantities of lumber, and such will doubtless be the case for many years to come.

MOUNTAINS AND LAKES.

The most interesting route for the tourist in Maine to take is perhaps that which leads through the hills, lakes, and forests of the north; but we warn him beforehand that it will not be one of ease. Rugged roads and scant physical comforts will not be his most severe trial; for, in many places, he will not find road or inn at all, but must trudge along painfully on foot, or by rude skiff over the lakes, and trust to his rifle and his rod to supply his larder. In these wildest regions the exploration may be made with great satisfaction by a party well provided with all needed tent-equipage, and with all the paraphernalia of the chase; for deer, and the moose, and the wild-fowl, are abundant in the woods, and the finest fish may be freely taken in the waters. Still he may traverse most of the mountain-lands and lakes by the roads and paths of the lumbermen, who have invaded all the region; and he may bivouac, as comfortably as should content an orthodox forester, in the humble shanties erected by the hardy backwoodsman. The mountains of Maine are broken and distinct peaks. Along the western side of the State extends an irregular continuation of the White Mountains, diverging finally to the northeast, and including some lofty peaks, of which Mount Katahdin, 5,385 feet above the level of the sea, is the highest. The scenery among these mountains is highly beautiful, diversified by charming lakes and spreading forests. This chain divides the waters which flow north into St. John's River from those which pass southward to the Atlantic. Many beautiful lakes lie within this territory. The wilderness of Northern New York (see ADIRONDACKS) has many features in common with the northern mountain and lake region of Maine. The internal improvements of the State are few, but important. Portland is the chief commercial city and railway centre of the State, and thence diverge the leading routes to every section within its limits, and in the neighboring provinces of Canada.

ROUTE I.

BOSTON TO PORTLAND, AND ALL PARTS OF MAINE, AND TO THE WHITE MOUNTAINS AND CANADA, VIA GORHAM, N. H.

Via Routes XI. and XII. of Massachusetts, II. and V. of New Hampshire, and the Portland, Saco, and Portsmouth Railway.

STATIONS. — Boston: Portsmouth, 56 miles; Kittery, 58; Elliott, 63; Junction Great Falls Branch, 67 (Portsmouth, Great Falls and Conway Railway); South Berwick Junction, 70 (junction of Boston and Maine Railway); North Berwick, 74; Wells, 80; Kennebunk, 85; Biddeford, 93; Saco, 95; West Scarborough, 99;

Scarborough, 102; Cape Elizabeth, 106; Portland, 108 (connects with Portland and Kennebec, Maine Central, Grand Trunk, and Portland and Rochester Railways).

Portsmouth (56 miles). (See page 219.)

Kittery (58 miles) is on the Piscataqua River, opposite Portsmouth, with which it is connected by a bridge. It is also connected by bridge with the United States Navy-Yard.

South Berwick Junction (70 miles) is the point of union of the two lines from Boston to Portland. There is a prosperous village at this point, and the manufactures are increasing rapidly.

Wells (80 miles) is noted for its fine beach, 6 miles in length, and covered with snipe and curlew. In the woods are partridges and woodcock. A large trout-stream crosses the beach. This is not a fashionable place, but is a great rendezvous for sportsmen. *York Beach* and *Bold Head Cliff* are next to the south, and not far from Wells Beach, and can be reached from Portsmouth or Wells Beach by private conveyance. They are favorite points for excursion-parties.

Agamenticus Mountain is a mile from *Cape Neddick*, from the summit of which can be seen the White Mountains, and the harbors of Boston, Portsmouth, and Portland.

Kennebunk (85 miles) is noted for its ship-building, carried on mainly at the "Port," at the mouth of the Kennebunk River.

Biddeford (93 miles) is opposite Saco, near the mouth of *Saco River*, which at this place has three falls of 16 feet each, and one of 7 feet, thus furnishing a fine water-power to both places. On the Biddeford side there are, among others, the mills of the following well-known companies: *Laconia, Pepperell,* and *Saco.*

The Pool, which is in Biddeford, though generally spoken of in connection with Saco, is a deep basin scooped out in the solid rock, about a quarter of a mile from the sea, with which it is connected by a narrow passage. It is emptied and filled with each changing tide.

Saco (95 miles) is a noted manufacturing place, and the celebrated York

Mills are located here. It is also a place of resort on account of its fine beach a few miles east. Fine bathing and fishing make this a favorite place for excursions, picnics, etc., while sufficient game is always to be found to tempt the sportsman.

On *Foxwell's Brook*, in Saco township, there is a waterfall 60 feet in height, surrounded by wild and striking scenery.

Laurel Hill Cemetery is a place generally visited. The lumber interest, both at Biddeford and Saco, is important.

Cape Elizabeth (106 miles) may be considered a part of Portland. It is a delightful summer resort, with excellent bathing and fishing.

HOTELS: *Cape Cottage* and *Atlantic House*.

Portland (108 miles), the commercial metropolis of Maine, is handsomely situated on a peninsula, occupying the ridge and side of a high point of land, in the southwest extremity of Casco Bay, and, on approaching it from the ocean, is seen to great advantage. The harbor is one of the best on the Atlantic coast, the anchorage being protected on every side by land, while the water is deep, and communication with the ocean direct and convenient. It is defended by *Forts Preble, Scammell*, and *Gorges*, and dotted over with lovely islands. These islands afford most delightful excursions, and are among the greatest attractions of the vicinity. On the most elevated point of the peninsula is an observatory, 70 feet in height, commanding a fine view of the city, harbor, and islands in the bay. The misty forms of the White Mountains, 60 miles distant, are discernible in clear weather. The original name of Portland was *Machigonee*. It was first settled by the whites as an English colony in 1632, just two centuries before the charter of the present city was granted. On the night of the 4th of July, 1866, a fire occurred which swept away nearly one-half of the whole business portion of the city. The entire district destroyed by the fire has been since rebuilt, most of the stores and dwelling-houses having Mansard roofs, which give a most picturesque and charming appearance to the city.

Portland is elegantly built, and the streets beautifully shaded and embellished with trees, and so profusely, that before the fire they were said to number no less than 3,000. *Congress Street*, previous to the fire the main highway, follows the ridge of the peninsula through its entire extent. Among the public buildings of Portland, the *City Hall*, the *Court-House*, and some of the churches, are worthy of particular attention. The collection of the *Society of Natural History*, organized 1843, was totally destroyed by the fire; but is rapidly building up again, and now comprises a fine cabinet, containing specimens of the ornithology of the State, more than 4,000 species of shells, and a rich collection of mineralogical and geological specimens, and of fishes and reptiles. The *Athenæum*, incorporated in 1826, has a library of 12,000 volumes; and the *Mercantile Library* possesses also many valuable books. The *Marine Hospital*, erected in 1855, at a cost of $80,000, is an imposing edifice. Brown & Co.'s extensive sugar-refinery, wholly destroyed by the fire, was rebuilt and in full operation in 60 days. Within the past year water has been introduced into the city from *Sebago Lake*.

HOTELS: The *Falmouth, Preble House, United States, American*, and *St. Julian*.

In the vicinity are pleasant drives, (notably the one to *Cape Elizabeth*), and the islands in the harbor furnish material for delightful water picnics and excursions. The principal of these is *Cushing's Island*, noticed hereafter.

The leading routes of travel from Portland are the *Grand Trunk* (Canada), *Portland, Saco, and Portsmouth; Portland and Kennebec, Portland and Bangor* (Maine Central), and the *York and Cumberland*. The last-named is a short line, extending from Portland south, *via* Morrill's, Saccarappa, Buxton Centre, to Saco River, a distance of 18 miles.

Besides these lines, there is the International Line of steam, making three trips per week, Monday, Wednesday, and Friday—leaving Portland at 5 P. M., connecting at St. John with steamer for Kinno, Digby, and Annapolis, to Halifax. There is also the connection with the New Brunswick Western Extension Railway, which extends from Fairville, on the left bank of the St. John River, westward,

237

88 miles, to the Maine boundary on the St. Croix River. This connection has been pushed forward by the Maine companies, from Bangor to Mattawamkeag Point, on the Penobscot; and a farther distance of 21 miles from the St. Croix River is under contract by them. There remain only 35 miles of railway to be built to make a continuous line from Bangor to Shediac, on the Gulf of St. Lawrence. And, in 1871, this whole line, including the Nova Scotia branch, will be completed, thus closely uniting New York with Halifax, and shortening the distance between New York and Liverpool. A new line of railroad, called the Portland and Ogdensburg Railroad, has been contracted for and a portion of it built. This road will run directly through the "Notch" in the White Mountains, and thence west to Ogdensburg, and is designed to facilitate the transportation of grain from the West, without breaking bulk, and its exportation abroad.

Cushing's Island is three miles from the city, and contains about 250 acres. It commands magnificent ocean-views. On both sides of the island are fine beaches for bathing; and as for fishing, there is every variety, from that at the shore to the deep-sea fishing 10 miles out. The *Ottawa House* is a first-class hotel, and is principally frequented by a class of people who think more of comfort and real pleasure than of the dissipations of fashion.

Casco Bay is one of the finest on the American coast. It lies between Cape Elizabeth and Cape Small Point, a distance of 20 miles, while its indentation is about 15 miles. Within it are some fine harbors. It contains numerous islands, some of them large and well cultivated, and it is seen to advantage from the high grounds in Portland, Falmouth, Cumberland, or Yarmouth.

ROUTE II.

BOSTON TO THE WHITE MOUNTAINS, CANADA, AND THE WEST.

Via Grand Trunk Railway.

(Continuation of Route I.)

STATIONS.—Boston; Portland, 108 miles; Falmouth, 5; Yarmouth, 11;

Yarmouth Junction, 12 (connects with Portland and Kennebec Railway); New Gloucester, 22; Danville Junction, 27 (connects with Maine Central Railway); Mechanic Falls, 36 (connects with Portland and Oxford Central Railway); Oxford, 41; South Paris, 47; Bryant's Pond, 62; Bethel, 70; Gilead, 80; Shelburne, 86; Gorham, 91.

This important thoroughfare connects the navigable waters of Portland Harbor with the St. Lawrence and the Great Lakes. Its route passes through a fertile and productive country, generally under fine cultivation, the streams in its vicinity abounding in water privileges of the first importance. From Portland, passing onward, five miles, through Falmouth, on the Presumpscott River, to Danville Junction, the valley of Royal's River and the valley of the Little Androscoggin. It strikes and crosses the latter river at Mechanic Falls. Pursuing its course upward, it passes in the vicinity of the "Mills" on its way to Paris Cape, in the neighborhood of South Paris, drawing in upon it the travel and business of that rich and populous region. Still following up the valley of the Little Androscoggin, passing on the way two important falls, and reaches Bryant's Pond, the source of that river. This point is 15 miles from Rumford Falls, on the Great Androscoggin, one of the most valuable and available water-powers in the State. Passing hence into the valley of Alder stream, the route strikes the Great Androscoggin, near Bethel. Crossing that stream, it follows up its picturesque and romantic valley, bordered by the highest mountains in New England, till, in its course of about 20 miles from Bethel, it reaches Gorham, New Hampshire, the point of departure for Mount Washington, eight miles distant.

From the valley of the Androscoggin the road passes into the valley of the Connecticut, reaching the banks of that river at North Stratford, New Hampshire. Following up this rich and highly-productive valley 32 miles, the road reaches the parallel of 45° north latitude, the boundary-line between the United States and Canada. The route thence lies through what are known as the Eastern Townships of Canada, *via* Richmond to Quebec, and up the St. Lawrence, via Montreal, to Toronto on Lake Ontario, and thence to Detroit, Michigan, via Port Sarnia, at the foot of Lake Huron.

Yarmouth Junction (12 miles) is the crossing of the Portland and Kennebec Railway.

New Gloucester (22 miles), upon *Royal's River*, has a fine water-power and a number of mills. It is a flourishing farming town, and contains a Shaker settlement.

Danville Junction (27 miles) is the Junction with the Maine Central Railway for Bangor and the valley of the Penobscot.

Mechanic Falls (36 miles), junction of *Portland and Oxford Central Railway* for *West Minot, Bearce Road, East Hebron, Buckfield*, and *Hebron*. The road here crosses the *Little Androscoggin River*.

Oxford (41 miles), upon the *Upper Androscoggin*, is a flourishing village in the township of the same name.

South Paris (47 miles), on Little Androscoggin River, is one of the principal points on the line; a great amount of business is done here, and several lines of stages are run to neighboring villages and towns. It is in Paris township, which also contains another village, *Paris Hill*, and the following hills, *Singepole, Mount Mica*, and *Streaked Mountain*, the latter being much resorted to by local pleasure-parties.

Bryant's Pond (62 miles) is the source of the *Little Androscoggin*.

Bethel (70 miles) is one of the pleasantest villages in the State, and is rapidly growing. It has a seminary, with an annual attendance of from 200 to 300 scholars. Tourists are beginning to treat this as a place worthy of attention on account of the romantic, Swiss-like character of the scenery, the fine fishing in the neighboring ponds and streams, and its central position in regard to several attractive places; among them the following: *Screw-Auger Falls* (14 miles), *Rumford Falls* (20 miles), Partridge Falls (4 miles), and White Mountains (25 miles). Near Rumford are *White Cap Mountain*, 500, and *Glass Face Mountain*, 400 feet above the surrounding country.

Gilead (80 miles) is the last station in Maine.

Shelburne (86 miles). (*See* page 221.)

Gorham (91 miles) is one of the principal entrances to the White Mountain region. (*See* page 213.)

(For continuation of this route, *see* Route VII. of NEW HAMPSHIRE.)

ROUTE III.

PORTLAND TO AUGUSTA AND THE VALLEY OF THE KENNEBEC.

Via Portland and Kennebec Railway.

STATIONS. — Portland: Woodford's, 3 miles; Westbrook, 5; Cumberland, 12; Yarmouth, 16 (crossing of Grand Trunk Railway); Freeport, 22; Brunswick, 30 (junction of Bath Branch and of Androscoggin Railway); Bath, 40; Bowdoinham, 38; Richmond, 46; South Gardiner, 51; Gardiner, 56; Hallowell, 61; Augusta, 63; Vassalborough, 75; Winslow, 80; Waterville, 81; Kendall's Mills, 83 (junction with the Maine Central Railway); Somerset Mills, 87; Pishon's Ferry, 92; Skowhegan, 100.

Westbrook (5 miles) is in the flourishing town of the same name, which is noted for the superior quality of its working-cattle. It contains two villages, lumber, cotton, and other mills and manufactories. The scenery about the falls on the Presumpscott is very pleasing.

Yarmouth (16 miles) is the intersection of the Grand Trunk Railway.

Brunswick (30 miles) is an important town on the Androscoggin River, at the head of tide-water. It is very largely interested in the lumber-trade, and has numerous saw-mills, and several factories, a fall of 50 feet in the river furnishing an inexhaustible water-power. It is connected by bridge with Topsham, on the opposite side of the river. The *Bath Branch* and *Androscoggin Railway* connect at this point.

Bowdoin College, in the township of Brunswick, founded in 1794, is situated upon a plain with a grove of pines in the rear. Two of the buildings are occupied as dormitories, the others as chapel, lecture-rooms, library, museum, the Bowdoin Gallery of Paintings, etc., etc.

The *Medical Department* has a fine library, anatomical cabinet, etc.

Bath (40 miles), the terminus of the Bath Branch, is a flourishing city, 14 miles from the mouth of the Kennebec River, on its west bank. The city extends for about 5 miles along the river, which at this point is 900 yards wide, with an average depth of 8 fathoms of water. It is a beautiful place, and was noted for the extent of its ship-building interest, which at present shares the general depression in that branch of industry. The leading hotel is the *Sagadhock House*.

Richmond (46 miles) is noted for the extent of its ship-building in proportion to its size. It is upon the Kennebec River.

Gardiner (56 miles), at the junction of the *Cobbesseeontee* with the *Kennebec*. It is noted for its extensive manufactures, and the fine water-power furnished by the *Cobbesseeontee*, across which are 8 stone dams in the space of a mile. The business part of the city is upon a flat along the river, but the residences are upon a gentle rise, beautifully located and commanding a fine prospect; some of them are of superior architecture.

Hallowell (61 miles) resembles *Gardiner* in the manner in which it is built, and in general characteristics. The views from the higher portions are uncommonly good. Steamboats run between here and Boston. In the neighborhood are quarries of light-colored granite. There are several factories at this place, which are run by steam.

Augusta (63 miles), the capital of the State, is at the head of sloop navigation, though steamboats run to *Waterville*, 18 miles above. The city lies on both sides of the river, the two portions being connected by a bridge 520 feet long. It is well laid out, is handsomely built, and owes much of its loveliness to a great abundance of shade-trees and shrubbery. Among the prominent buildings in the city are the *State-House*, built of white granite, and considered as next to that in *Montpelier, Vermont*, the handsomest in New England; the *Court-House*, which is the best and most convenient in the State; and the *Maine Insane Asylum*, a splendid granite structure. The *United States Arsenal*, with its well-arranged grounds and buildings, is always an object of interest.

The great dam of the Kennebec at this point is 1,000 feet long, has canals at each end, and furnishes an immense water-power.

Vassalborough (75 miles) is a large and flourishing town, the station being only one of several villages within its limits. It contains several large and attractive ponds, which, with the streams, supply power to numerous manufactories. On a beautiful elevation near the centre of the town, and shaded by a grove, is *Oak Grove Seminary*, under the charge of the Friends. Vessels of considerable size can pass from here to the ocean by means of the canals round the *Kennebec Dam*.

Waterville (81 miles) is on the Kennebec, at *Ticonic Falls*, which are 18 feet in height and the whole width of the river, which is spanned by a bridge 550 feet long. The educational institutions are *Waterville College*, a Baptist, and *Liberal Institute*, a Universalist institution. The water-power in the vicinity is immense. Taking the Ticonic Falls as a centre, there are, within a radius of 5 miles, the two falls across the *Kennebec* at Kendall's Mills, two falls 5 miles distant on the *Sebasticook*, and an indefinite series of falls upon the *Emerson Stream*, besides numerous rapids on all these streams, which could easily be dammed. The *Maine Central Railway* connects at this point.

Emerson Falls are at West Waterville, on *Emerson Stream*, a tributary of the Kennebec. They are the highest in the State; and, being in the midst of picturesque scenery, are much resorted to.

Skowhegan (100 miles), having a fine water-power, is the centre of an extensive trade, and is the site of a great number of mills. There is much delightful scenery about the village, which is neatly built. It is connected with *Bloomfield*, on the opposite bank of the Kennebec, by bridges; between the two villages is a small island.

ROUTE IV.

PORTLAND TO BANGOR AND THE VALLEY OF THE PENOBSCOT.

Via Maine Central Railway..

STATIONS.—Portland: Danville Junction, 28 miles (junction with Grand Trunk Railway); Auburn, 34; Lewiston, 35; Greene, 42; Leeds, 45 (junction of Androscoggin Railway); Monmouth, 48; Winthrop, 54; Readfield, 60; Belgrade, 68; West Waterville, 77; Waterville, 83 (crossing of Portland and Kennebec Railway); Kendall's Mills, 86; Clinton, 92; Burnham, 97; Pittsfield, 104; Detroit, 107; Newport, 111 (connects with Dexter and Newport Branch); East Newport, 114; Etna, 119; Carmel, 123; Hermon Pond, 128; Bangor, 138 (connects with European and North American Railway, late Bangor, Old Town, and Milford Railway).

Danville Junction (28 miles) connects with Grand Trunk Railway.

Lewiston (35 miles) is an important manufacturing village, situated upon the left bank of the Androscoggin River, which is crossed by a bridge 1,700 feet long. The waterfall here is one of exceeding beauty. The entire volume of the Androscoggin is precipitated 50 feet over a broken ledge, forming in its fall a splendid specimen of natural scenery. The river immediately below the fall subsides into almost a uniform tranquillity, and moves slowly and gracefully along its course, in strange though pleasing contrast with its wild and turbid appearance at and above the cataract. The peculiar formation of the ledge over which the river falls enables this immense water-power to be utilized by means of two dams, and a system of canals, locks, etc. The manufactures are large, and growing in number and importance, the cotton interest being the most important. Educational interests are closely watched and fostered; there are ample school accommodations, and the *Maine State Seminary* is intended to afford instruction of the highest grade. The leading hotel is the *De Witt House.*

Leeds (45 miles) is the junction of the *Androscoggin Railway.* It is a neat and pleasant village, and is near a large pond, which furnishes a good water-power.

Monmouth (48 miles) is a pleasant village, near the sources of the Cobbesseecontee. It contains a flourishing academy.

Winthrop (54 miles) is a desirable summer retreat. It is in the form of a crescent, at the union of the *North* with the *South Lake.* There is a water-cure here, which is much frequented. The township contains another (*East*) village and six beautiful ponds, the largest being 10 miles long, and from 1 to 3 miles wide. It is also traversed by the Cobbesseecontee and some of its tributaries. The environs of the ponds are generally beautiful; the waters deep, clear, and well stocked with a variety of fish.

Belgrade (68 miles)' is a prosperous village. In the town are three large and beautiful ponds or lakes. They are connected, and find an outlet at *Waterville.*

Waterville (83 miles) connects with *Portland and Kennebec Railway.* (*See* page 240.)

Clinton (92 miles) is a village at the falls of the *Sebasticook.*

Pittsfield (104 miles) is on the *Sebasticook River.* Stages daily to *St. Albans, Harmony,* and *Cambridge.*

Newport (114 miles) is the point of departure for *Moosehead Lake.* (*See* page 245.) Connects with *Dexter and Newport Railway.*

Dexter (128 miles), the terminus of the *Dexter and Newport Branch,* is at the outlet of a pond of 1,000 acres, from which issues a small stream, clear as crystal, never failing, never freezing, and never exposed to freshets. The fall is 150 feet in three-quarters of a mile.

Carmel (123 miles) is an active place of business. In this town are found fine specimens of petrified shells, showing that it once was the bed of an ocean, though now 150 feet above the Penobscot.

Bangor (138 miles), one of the largest cities in Maine, is at the head of navigation, on the west side of the *Penobscot River,* at the mouth of the *Kenduskeag.* It lies on both sides of the latter river, which is crossed by several bridges, and affords a good water-power. The tide in the basin where the ships lie, at the mouth of the *Kenduskeag*, usually rises and falls 17 feet. The buildings in the city are constructed with neatness and taste, many even with elegance. The granite *Custom-House* is a striking building. The *Bangor Theological Seminary*, situated in the higher part of the city, and several of the churches, are noticeable edifices. The "specialty" of Bangor is lumber, of which it is, next to Chicago, the greatest depot on the continent. All the vast country above, drained by the Penobscot and its affluents, is covered with dense forests of pine, and hemlock, and spruce, and cedar, from which immense quantities of lumber are continually cut and sent from the numerous saw-mills, down the river to market at Bangor. During the eight or nine months of the year through which the navigation of the river is open, some 2,000 vessels are employed in the transportation of this freight. Not unfrequently 200,000,000 feet are received in a single year. The whole industry of Bangor is not, however, in the lumber-line, as she is also engaged in ship-building, has a large coasting trade, and a considerable foreign commerce.

There are two lines of steamers between *Bangor, Portland, and Boston*, leaving on Monday, Wednesday, and Friday. At this point connection is made with the EUROPEAN AND NORTH AMERICAN RAILWAY. This railway is to form the only all-rail route between the cities of Bangor, Maine (where it connects with the Maine Central Railroad), and the city of St. John, New Brunswick, distance 200 miles. Sixty miles from Bangor to Mattawamkeag is finished, and trains running; 88 miles is also finished and trains running between St. John and the St. Croix River, thus leaving a gap of 52 miles (now in course of construction) to finish the line.

This gap is now filled by two first-class stage-lines, one *via* Houlton, the other *via* Calais.

STATIONS.—Veazie, 5 miles from Bangor; Orono, 8; Webster, 9; Oldtown, 12; Milford, 13; Costigan, 18; Olamon, 27; Passadumkeag, 31; Enfield, 35; Lincoln, 45; Winn, 56; Mattawamkeag, 58.

Orono (8 miles), and **Oldtown** (12 miles), are in the valley of the *Penobscot*, which here furnishes an unrivalled water-power, by means of which the mills at these points are enabled to manufacture the great bulk of the lumber which finds a market at *Bangor*. The Bangor and Piscataquis Railway diverges at Oldtown.

Milford (13 miles) is to be the point where the branch of this road to *Calais*, as yet unfinished, is to connect.

Passadumkeag (31 miles) lies at the junction of the *Passadumkeag River* with the Penobscot. The river, after which the town is named, is a charming stream, about 40 miles long. At present little is generally known of this section of country, but, as facilities for travel and hotel accommodations increase, it is destined to become popular with tourists.

Winn (56 miles) is a beautiful village, and abounds in ponds and streams which are well stocked with fish. Game is found in the surrounding woods in great variety. It is also the location of the largest tannery in New England. It has an excellent hotel.

Mattawamkeag (58 miles) is the present terminus of the road.

BANGOR AND PISCATAQUIS RAILROAD.

This road branches from the European and North American Railway at Oldtown, and runs through the towns of Oldtown, Alton, La Grange, Orneville, Milo, and Sebec, to Dover and Foxcroft. It is 40 miles long, traverses a farming and lumbering region, and, after crossing the Piscataquis River at Milo, runs near to the vast slate-deposits of Piscataquis County, the products of which are transported over this line and the European road to a market.

This road furnishes the easiest route by far to *Moosehead Lake*, and to those vast forests lying above and beyond it, sought by tourists and sportsmen in the season of summer travel, the ride from the Dover and Foxcroft station being up the beautiful valley of the Piscataquis, and some four miles less staging than by any other route.

The distances given are from Bangor, which is 138 miles from Portland.

Pea Cove is in the town of Oldtown, and is the site of the main boom for logs on the Penobscot River. Here all the logs that have been cut on the river above are collected, assorted into the different ownerships, and run down to the mills in the towns below.

Alton (20 miles) is a farming town, the only village in which is 3½ miles from the railroad station.

La Grange (32 miles) is a very prosperous farming town, having also good water-privileges on two considerable streams running through it from the north to the south, separated by a remarkable moraine, or horse-back, which has excited the curiosity of the most eminent scientific men and naturalists.

Orneville (35 miles) is principally devoted to farming and lumbering.

Milo (39 miles), where the road crosses the Piscataquis River, is a flourishing farming town. Here the principal slate-quarries make their depot. The slate produced ranks in quality above that from any other localities, and the deposit occupies a territory of some 40 or 50 miles east and west, by about 15 north and south. The iron from the Katahdin Iron-Works, situated eighteen miles north of this point, also strikes the road here. This mine is in one of the beautiful ranges of the *Ebeeme Mountains*.

Sebec (45 miles) contains two thriving villages, the principal one of which is situated at the foot of *Sebec Lake*, a beautiful sheet of water of some 15 miles in length, by about 3 miles in its widest part. This lake is much sought by tourists in the summer season for its beautiful scenery, its excellent fish, and abundant game and berries. There is upon it a small steamboat for the use of pleasure-parties, and a number of sail-boats.

Dover and Foxcroft (52 miles), the present terminus of the road, are beautiful and thriving villages situated on either side of the Piscataquis River. *Dover* is the shire town of Piscataquis County, and has one of the best hotels in the region. *Foxcroft* has also a very excellent hotel, well arranged for families, and admirably kept. From this point it is but 4 miles to Sebec Lake, and 32 to Moosehead Lake.

The route to Moosehead Lake is through the flourishing villages of Guilford and Abbott, on the Piscataquis River, Monson on an affluent to the latter stream, and Shirley to Greenville, at the foot of the lake. At *Greenville* are excellent houses, well kept, furnishing to the traveller and tourist a home for the season.

Moosehead Lake. (*See* page 245.)

Bar Harbor and Southwest Harbor.—The distance from Bangor to either Bar or Southwest Harbor per stage route is 48 miles (26 from Bangor to Ellsworth, and 22 miles from there to either of the above-mentioned harbors). The route is a pleasant one, over a good road, and past fine scenery. *Bar Harbor* is on the east, and Southwest Harbor on the southerly side of Mount Desert Island.

Southwest Harbor is one of the finest in the United States, and presents from different points a combination of scenery to be found at no other place in this country, and unsurpassed for beauty and grandeur. Good mail facilities either east or west. Telegraph-office at one of the public-houses. Steamboats twice a week, Wednesdays and Saturdays, from Boston and Portland. There are three well-kept public-houses.

ROUTE V.

FROM BRUNSWICK TO FARMINGTON.

Via Androscoggin Railway.

STATIONS.—Brunswick, 30 miles from Portland; Little River, 8 miles from Brunswick; Lisbon, 12; Crowley's, 14; Lewiston (Branch Road), 19; Sabattisville, 19; Leeds Crossing, 26; Leeds Centre, 34; North Leeds, 36; Strickland's Ferry, 39; East Livermore, 41; Livermore Falls, 46; Jay Bridge, 48; North Jay, 52; Wilton, 56; East Wilton, 58; Farmington, 63.

Brunswick. (*See* page 239.)

Lisbon (12 miles) lies at what are called the "*Ten-Mile Falls*" of the Androscoggin River. The township is important in an agricultural point of view.

Croley's (14 miles) is where the branch to *Lewiston* diverges.

Lewiston (19 miles). (*See* p. 241.)

Leeds Crossing (26 miles, junction with *Maine Central Railway*), **Leeds Centre** (34 miles), and **North Leeds** (36 miles), are all pleasant villages. (*See* page 241.)

Livermore Falls (46 miles) is a pleasant manufacturing village at the falls of the *Androscoggin*, after which it is named.

Wilton (56 miles), and **East Wilton** (58 miles), are villages in one of the finest agricultural towns in the State.

Farmington (63 miles), at the junction of the *Sandy* and *Little Norridgewock Rivers*, is the terminus of the railway. It is one of two villages in the rich agricultural township of the same name.

PLACES OF INTEREST, LAKES AND MOUNTAINS, NOT ON ANY RAILWAY ROUTE.

Belfast, on Penobscot Bay, 30 miles below *Bangor*, has a capacious harbor, easy of access, and well protected by islands. The city is somewhat irregularly built, but many of the streets are shaded with trees, and the private residences indicate taste and wealth. During the season of navigation, steamers connect Belfast with Portland, Boston, and Bangor, and at all times there is stage communication. Like most other seaport towns, it enjoys the advantages of bathing, fishing, and boating; besides which, the islands in the bay form the destination of many pleasant picnics and excursions.

Castine, 12 miles from *Belfast*, on the opposite side of the bay, is a village in the township of the same name, formed by a peninsula that jets out into Belfast bay. It occupies a fine maritime position. It was named after Baron *Castine*, whose house, still standing, is regarded as one of the curiosities of the place.

Belfast Bay, which lies between these two places, is dotted with islands easily reached from either of them, and which afford pleasures without number; one can sail, row, swim, fish, or hunt, to his heart's content.

Eastport, upon the waters of Passamaquoddy Bay, at the extreme eastern point of the territory of the United States, is well deserving of a visit from the tourist in quest of the beautiful in nature; for more charming scenes on land and on sea than are here can rarely be found. From the hills in the rear of the village a view is obtained which has few superiors, for from this position the eye commands the blue waters of *Passamaquoddy*, with its countless island-gems.

Eastport is 234 miles northeast of Portland, and is reached thence and from Boston by regular steamboat communication to and from St. John, N. B. A steamer also leaves Portland twice every week, for Halifax, Nova Scotia, making the trip in about 36 hours. Steamboats run to Calais and places *en route*, 30 miles above, at the head of navigation on the St. Croix River. The town is charmingly built on Moose Island, which embraces 2,000 acres, and is connected with the main-land of Perry by a bridge; and by ferries with Pembroke, Lubec, and the adjoining British islands. It is protected by *Fort Sullivan*.

It was expected that, at the time of the first Fenian invasion of Canada, one column would start from here, but these anticipations were not realized.

Campo Bello Island, opposite the city and between it and the ocean, should geographically belong to the United States, but is really a part of New Brunswick. A person who does not care for the comforts of a popular resort, can enjoy himself for a short time on this island. The water is too cold for bathing, and fogs are frequent, but in their absence the air is delightful. The scenery is beautiful, the boating excellent, and out-of-door attractions numerous. The residents, too, are extremely hospitable. A curious collection of rocks, called the "*Friar's Face*," are still attractive, though their effect has been sadly injured by being used for a target for the guns of an English man-of-war. There are many other romantic spots upon the island to which the residents can direct the visitor.

The traveller may see Eastport and its vicinage, and then go home, if he pleases, for it is the place beyond which the stars and stripes give place to the red cross of England.

Calais is at the head of tide-water on the *St. Croix River*, which is the boundary between the United States and New Brunswick. The tide here rises 20 feet. There are a number of handsome buildings in the city, which is connected with the other side of the St. Croix River by numerous bridges. The lumbering interests are the great business of the place.

Mount Desert Island is situated in *Frenchman's Bay*, about 40 miles southeast from Bangor. It is 15 miles long, 12 broad, and contains an area of about 100 square miles. It contains six small villages and several good harbors. The scenery of the island is very grand and beautiful. The greater part of its surface is covered with nearly twenty granite mountains, whose highest peak, *Mount Adam*, attains an altitude of about 2,200 feet. High up among the mountains are many beautiful lakes, the largest of which is several miles in length. These lakes, and the streams that flow into them, abound in trout. The southeast coast of the island is lined with stupendous cliffs, several hundred feet in height, the most remarkable of which are *Great Head* and *Schooner Head*. The *Porcupines* are five rocky islands in Frenchman's Bay, on the east side of Mount Desert.

Mount Desert Rock, the site of a noted light-house, is about 20 miles to the south, in the open ocean.

Mount Desert is connected by steamer with Rockland, Bangor, Portland, and Boston.

There are a number of good hotels at *Bar Harbor* and other places upon the island.

Moosehead Lake, the largest in Maine, is among the northern hills. It is 35 miles long, and, at one point, is 10 miles in breadth, though near the centre there is a pass not over a mile across. Its waters are deep, and furnish ample occupation to the angler, in their stores of trout and other fish. This lake may be traversed in the steamboats employed in towing lumber to the Kennebec. A summer hotel occupies a very picturesque site upon the shore at the foot of the lake. The Kineo House, midway, is the usual stopping-place. There are numerous islands on the Moosehead Lake, some of which are of great interest. On the west side, Mount Kineo overhangs the water,

at an elevation of 600 feet. Its summit reveals a picture of forest beauty well worthy the climbing to see. The roads thither, lying through forest-land, are necessarily somewhat rough and lonely. This lake is the source of the great Kennebec River, by whose channels its waters reach the sea. The readiest approach from Boston or Portland is via *Bangor and Piscataquis Railroad* (see page 242), or *via Newport*, on the *Maine Central Railway* (see page 241).

Lake Umbagog is about 15 miles long, and in parts 10 miles wide, being but little inferior in beauty to Lake Winnipiseogee. The trout-fishing here is unrivalled. Its outlet passes into the *Androscoggin* by the *Morgalloway River*. There are no hotels, but board can be had at the farm-houses. It is best reached from *Gorham, New Hampshire*, on the Grand Trunk Railway. Androscoggin and Moosetocnoguntic Lakes are near Umbagog, and are noted for their fishing. They are reached by stage from *Bethel*, on the Grand Trunk Railway. There is a hotel at *Upton*, in which place lives a famous guide and trapper.

Sebago Pond is a charming lake, 12 miles long, and from 7 to 8 in width. It is connected with *Portland* by the *Cumberland and Oxford Canal*, and is on the stage-route to *Conway* and the *White Mountains*.

The Grand Lakes are in Washington County, and are celebrated for their salmon-trout. Reached by steamer to *Calais*, thence by rail to *Princeton*, where guides and information are obtained.

Mount Katahdin, with its peaks 5,385 feet above the sea, is the loftiest summit in the State. It is reached by *Bangor and Piscataquis*, and *European and North American Railways* (see page 242), or by stages from *Bangor* over the *Aroostook* road, starting in tolerable coaches on a tolerable road, and changing always in both from bad to worse. A pleasant route *for the adventurer* is down the West Branch of the Penobscot, in a canoe, from Moosehead Lake. "Birches," as the boats are called, and guides may be procured at the foot of Moosehead, or at the Kineo House, near the centre of the lake. By this approach, Katahdin is seen in much finer outlines than from the eastward.

Sugar-Loaf Mountain, upon the Seboois River, northeast of Mount Katahdin, is nearly 2,000 feet high, and from its summit a magnificent view is commanded, which embraces some fifty mountain-peaks and nearly a score of picturesque lakes. Bigelow, Saddleback, Squaw, Bald, Gilead, the Speckled Mountain, the Blue Mountain, and other heights, with intervening waterfalls and brooks, are in the neighborhood.

There are other lakes, rivers, mountains, islands, cascades, and springs in Maine, at present practically inaccessible, which will doubtless become popular resorts in course of time.

THE BRITISH PROVINCES.

The possessions of the British Crown in North America occupy nearly all the upper half of the continent; a vast territory, reaching from the Arctic seas to the domains of the United States, and from the Atlantic to the Pacific Oceans. Of this great region, our present explorations will refer only to the lower and settled portions, embracing the Canadas, New Brunswick, and Nova Scotia. The rest is, for the most part, yet a wilderness.

THE DOMINION OF CANADA.

On the first of July, 1867, by authority of the queen and the British Parliament, and with the consent of their respective legislative bodies, the four British Provinces, hitherto known as Upper and Lower Canada, New Brunswick, and Nova Scotia, were united under one government, and entitled the Dominion of Canada. The two provinces first mentioned assumed the names of ONTARIO and QUEBEC, the others retaining their former designations.

The Dominion, with Prince Edward Island, Newfoundland, the Northwest, and Hudson's Bay Territories, comprise the British possessions in America, and include an area of 3,369,345 square miles, being 30,000 square miles less than the United States, including Alaska.

The provinces of Ontario and Quebec, to which we will first direct the tourist's attention, occupy an area of 331,280 square miles, and extend along the northern border of the United States, from the Atlantic Ocean to the Mississippi and Lake Superior.

The entire frontier line of this tract of country extends about 1,300 miles, with a breadth varying between 200 and 300 miles.

The population of Ontario is, according to the latest estimate, in 1869, 2,047,334; of Quebec, 1,387,884.

DISCOVERY, SETTLEMENT, AND RULERS.—The earliest discovery of Canada (1497) is ascribed to Sebastian Cabot. Jacques Cartier, a French adventurer, spent the winter of 1535 at St. Croix, now the River St. Charles, upon which Quebec is partly built. The first permanent settlement, however, was at Tadousac, at the confluence of the Saguenay and the St. Lawrence. From that time (about 1608) until 1759, the country continued under the rule of France; and then came the capture of Quebec by the English, under General Wolfe, and the transfer, within a year thereafter, of all the territory of New France, as the country was at that time called, to the British power, under which it has ever since remained. The mutual disagreement which naturally arose from the conflicting interests and prejudices of the two opposing nationalities, threatened internal trouble from time to time, and finally displayed itself in the overt acts recorded in history as the rebellion of 1837. It was after these incidents, and as a consequence thereof, that the two sections of the territory were formed into one. This happened in 1840.

GOVERNMENT.—The Government of the dominion consists of the queen, governor-general, Senate, and House of Commons. Each province, however, retains its own lieutenant-governor and Legislature, as was formerly the case.

RELIGION.—The dominant religious faith in Lower Canada, or Quebec, is that of the Roman Catholic Church;

while in Ontario the creed of the English Established Church prevails.

LANDSCAPE.—The general topography of Upper Canada (Ontario) is that of a level country, with but few variations excepting the passage of some table-heights, extending southwesterly. It is the most fertile division of the territory, and thus, to the tourist in search of the picturesque, the least attractive. The Lower Province (Quebec) is extremely varied and beautiful in its physical aspect; presenting to the delighted eye a magnificent gallery of charming pictures of forest wilds, vast prairies, hill, and rock-bound rivers, rushing waters, and bold mountain-heights, everywhere intermingled, and their attractions embellished by intervening stretches of cultivated fields, rural villages, and villa homes.

MOUNTAINS.—The hill-ranges of Canada are confined entirely to Quebec. The chief lines, called the *Green Mountains*, follow a parallel course southwesterly. They lie along the St. Lawrence River, on its southern side, extending from the latitude of the city of Quebec to the Gulf of St. Lawrence. There is another and corresponding range on the north side of the river, with a varying elevation of about 1,000 feet. The *Mealy Mountains*, which extend to Sandwich Bay, rise in snow-capped peaks to the height of 1,500 feet. The *Wotchish Mountains*, a short, crescent-shaped group, lie between the Gulf of St. Lawrence and Hudson's Bay.

RIVERS.—Canada has many noble and beautiful rivers, as the *St. Lawrence*, one of the great waters of the world; the wild, mountain-shored floods of the *Ottawa*, the *Gatineau*, and the *Saguenay*; and the lesser waters of the *Sorel* or *Richelieu*, the *St. Francis*, the *Chaudière*, and other streams.

SPRINGS.

The Caledonia Springs. (*See* page 263.)
The St. Leon Springs. (*See* page 260.)
Massena Springs. (*See* page 259.)
St. Catharine's. St. Catharine's, Canada West, on the *Great Western Railway*, 11 miles from Niagara Falls, and 32 miles from Hamilton. (*See* page 257.)

WATERFALLS IN CANADA.
Niagara. (*See* page 70, STATE OF NEW YORK.)
Falls of Montmorenci. (*See* page 251.).
The Chaudiere Falls, on the Ottawa. (*See* page 264.)
The Chaudiere Falls, Quebec. (*See* page 252.)
The Rideau Falls. (*See* page 264.)
The Falls of Shawenegan. (*See* page 260.)
St. Anne's Falls are 24 miles below Quebec. (*See* page 251.)

ROUTES.

IN arranging the routes through Canada it will be impracticable to adopt the course pursued in the United States, where railroad communication is had with most points of interest, and where almost every town along the routes of a railway has something that will interest the traveller. We will, therefore, begin by assuming as our point of departure the city of *Quebec*, and follow the *Grand Trunk Railway* to the city of Detroit, Michigan. We will then take *Niagara Falls* as a base, and follow the *Great Western Railway* to Detroit.

These are the only two railroad routes that will be considered, and in them reference will only be made to the principal places, though the names of all stations will be given at the head of the route.

The Canadian stations passed on the various routes from the United States to *Quebec* and *Montreal* will not be described, not being of any note. (For means of access to Montreal and Quebec, *see* Routes from New York, Boston, and Portland.)

Having considered these routes, the rivers and isolated points will be taken up, the tour of the *Great Lakes* concluding the chapter.

From the immense extent of unexplored country in the British possessions, this account will necessarily be incomplete, still, it will open to the tourist—familiar with the beaten track—a novel and attractive field. Until recently the Upper St. Lawrence and the immediate vicinity of Montreal and Quebec have been the only portions of Canada visited by travellers.

ROUTE I.

QUEBEC TO MONTREAL, TORONTO, DETROIT, MICHIGAN, AND THE GREAT LAKES.

Via Grand Trunk Railway.

(THE distances given are from Portland, Maine, except the section from Quebec to Richmond, where they are from Quebec.)

All passenger trains, East and West, run to and from the city terminus, Bonaventure Street, Montreal. Trains are run between Portland and Island Pond by *Portland time;* between Montreal and Quebec, by *Montreal time;* between Montreal and Toronto, by *Montreal time;* between Toronto, London, and Sarnia, by *Toronto time;* and between Sarnia and Detroit, by *Chicago time.*)

STATIONS.—Quebec: Point Levi; Chaudière Junction, 7 miles; Craig's Road, 15; Black River, 20; Methot's Mills, 28; Lyster, 37; Beçancour, 41; Somerset, 49; Stanfold, 55; Arthabaska, 64 (connects with Arthabaska and Three Rivers Railway); Warwick, 71; Danville, 84; Richmond, 95 (connects with line from Portland).

(For stations on the line from Portland to Compton, the first station in Canada, see Routes II. of MAINE and VII. of NEW HAMPSHIRE. The following stations complete the line, the distances given being as previously mentioned from Portland. To obtain the distance of any station from Quebec, subtract 126 from the number given, that being the difference of distance from *Richmond* of Portland and Quebec.)

STATIONS. — Portland: Compton, 183 miles; Waterville, 186; Lennoxville, 193; Sherbrooke, 196; Brompton Falls, 203; Windsor, 211; Richmond, 221 (junction of Quebec division); New Durham, 231; Acton, 243; Upton, 249; Britannia Mills, 255; St. Hyacinthe, 262; St. Hilaire, 275; Belœil, 276; St. Lambert, 290; Montreal, 297 (connects with Montreal and Champlain division); Pointe Claire, 311; St. Anne's, 318; Vaudreuil, 321; Coteau Landing, 334; Lancaster, 351; Cornwall, 364; Dickinson's Landing, 374; Williamsburg, 389; Matilda, 396; Edwardsburg, 401; Prescott Junction, 410 (connects with St. Lawrence and Ottawa Railway); Brockville, 422 (connects with Brockville and Ottawa Railway); Lyn, 426; Mallorytown, 435; Landsdowne, 444; Gananoque, 452; Kingston, 469 (connects with mail line of steamers); Napanee, 495; Shannonville, 510; Belleville, 517; Trenton, 529; Brighton, 538; Colborne, 546; Grafton, 553; Cobourg, 561 (connects with Cobourg and Peterborough Railway); Port Hope, 567 (connects with the Midland Railway of Canada); Newtonville, 577; Newcastle, 583; Bowmanville, 587; Oshawa, 596; Whitby, 600; Duffin's Creek, 607; Frenchman's Bay, 609; Port Union, 613; Scarborough, 619; Don, 628; Toronto, 630 (connects with Northern Railway, Hamilton and Toronto Branch of Great Western Railway, also with steamers sailing from Toronto); Weston, 638, Georgetown, 659; Acton West, 665; Guelph, 678 (junction of Guelph Branch of Great Western Railway); Berlin, 693; Petersburg, 699; Hamburg, 705; Shakspeare, 712; Stratford, 718 (junction of Buffalo and Lake Huron division); St. Marys, 729 (branch to London); Loudon, 751 (connects with Great Western Railway, and London and Port Stanley Railway); Lucan, 744; Ailsa Craig, 751; Forrest, 776; Sarnia, 798; Detroit, 861 (connects with Michigan Central, Detroit and Milwaukee, and the Michigan Southern Railways, and with lake steamers).

QUEBEC.

QUEBEC may be pleasantly reached from New York, *via* Boston to Portland, Maine, and thence 317 miles by the *Grand Trunk Railway*—total distance, by this route, from New York to Quebec, 650 miles; or from New York by the *Hudson River Railway* or steamboats, or by the *Harlem Railway* to Albany; thence to Whitehall, thence on Lake Champlain to Plattsburg, thence by the *Montreal and New York Railway* to Montreal, and from Montreal by steamer down the St. Lawrence, or by the *Grand Trunk Railway*. Distance by railway, from Montreal to Quebec, 168 miles. There are other railway routes from Boston to Quebec, *via* Albany, or by the *Vermont Central* and Vermont and Canada lines through St.

Albans to Montreal. Another route is to go by way of Halifax and Picton to Nova Scotia, and thence by steamer direct to Quebec. (*See* NOVA SCOTIA.)

Quebec is the oldest, and, after Montreal, the most populous city in British North America. It is upon the left bank of the St. Lawrence river, and some 340 miles from the ocean.

The city was founded in 1608, by the geographer Champlain. It fell into the possession of the British in 1629, but was restored three years later. The English made an unsuccessful attempt to regain possession of it in 1690. It was finally captured by Wolfe, in 1759, after a heroic defence by Montcalm.

The city is divided into the Upper and Lower Town; the ascent from the latter being by a very steep and winding street, through Prescott Gate. The Upper Town occupies the highest part of the promontory, which is surrounded by strong walls and other fortifications; while the Lower Town is built around the base of Cape Diamond. The latter is the business quarter.

The *Citadel*, a massive defence crowning the summit of Cape Diamond (thus named from the circumstance of quartz crystals, sparkling like diamonds, being found in the dark-colored slate of which the cape is composed), covers about 40 acres with its numerous buildings. Its impregnable position makes it perhaps the strongest fortress on this continent; and the name of the "Gibraltar of America" has been often given to it, not inaptly. The access to the Citadel is from the Upper Town, the walls of which are entered by five gates. Near the Palace Gate is the Hospital and a large Guard-House. By St. Louis gate, on the southwest, the tourist will reach the memorable Plains of Abraham, the scene of Wolfe's victory and death, in the year 1759. The Prescott Gate is the only entrance on the St. Lawrence side of the fortress.

The view from the Citadel is remarkably fine, taking in, as it does, the opposite banks of the great river through many picturesque miles up and down. The promenade here, on the ramparts above the esplanade, is charming. In the public garden, on Des Carrières Street, there is an obelisk to the memory of Wolfe and Montcalm. At the foot of the Citadel stands a tower, over which now floats the British flag, on the spot where Montgomery and his soldiers all fell, swept by the grape-shot of a single gun manned by a Canadian artillerist.

The *Parliament House.*—Among the chief public edifices of Quebec is the New Parliament House, which supplies the place of the building destroyed by fire in 1854.

Durham Terrace is the site of the old castle of St. Louis, which was entirely consumed by fire in 1834.

The *Artillery Barracks* form a range of stone buildings 5,000 feet in length.

The *Roman Catholic Cathedral* was erected under the auspices of the first Bishop of Quebec, and was consecrated in 1666. It is 216 feet long, and 180 feet in breadth. There is in the Lower Town a chapel noticeable for its antiquity; it was built and used as a church before 1690. It is called *Notre-Dame des Victoires*.

The *Ursuline Convent* and the *Church of St. Ursula* are striking buildings, encompassed by pleasant gardens. This establishment was founded in 1639, and holds a high position in the public esteem. It accommodates a superior, 50 nuns, and 6 novices, who give instruction in reading, writing, and needlework. The building was destroyed by fire in 1650, and again in 1686. The remains of the Marquis de Montcalm are buried here in an excavation made by the bursting of a shell within the precincts of the convent.

The *English Episcopal Cathedral*, consecrated in 1804, is one of the finest modern edifices of the city. Tradition points to its site as the spot upon which Champlain erected his first tent.

St. Andrew's Church, in St. Anne Street, is in connection with the Scotch Establishment. The Methodists have a chapel in St. Stanislaus Street, and another in St. Louis suburb, called the Centenary Chapel.

The Lower Town.—It is in this portion of the city that the traveller will find the Exchange, the Post-Office, the banks, and other commercial establishments.

There are pleasant drives to *Spencer Wood*, the Governor-General's residence, and to *Château-Bigot,* an antique and massive ruin, standing in solitary loneliness, at the foot of the Charlesbourg Mountain.

When in Quebec the tourist should by all means take a run down to the Saguenay River, which magnificent trip can be performed by taking the railway at Point Levi for Rivière du Loup, and there crossing by steamer; or, during the summer months, he can take the steamer from Quebec direct to the Saguenay.

HOTELS: The leading hotels are the *St. Louis* and *Russell's;* they are the largest and most central, and are moderate in their terms.

VICINITY.

The *Plains of Abraham* may be reached *via* the St. Louis Gate, and the counterscarp on the left, leading to the glacis of the citadel hence toward the right; approaching one of the Martello Towers, where a fine view of the St. Lawrence opens. A little beyond, up the right bank, is the spot where General Wolfe fell on the famous historic ground of the Plains of Abraham. It is the highest ground, and is surrounded by wooden fences. Here stands the St. Foye monument, erected to the memory of Wolfe and Montcalm. It is of bronzed metal, standing on a stone base, and surmounted by a bronze statue of Bellona. On the pedestal are simple and appropriate inscriptions. Within an enclosure lower down is a stone well, from which water was brought to the dying hero.

Wolfe's Cove, the spot where Montgomery was killed, and other scenes, telling tales of the memorable past, will be pointed out to the traveller in this neighborhood.

The *Mount Hermon Cemetery* is about 3 miles from the city, on the south side of the *St. Louis* road. The grounds are 32 acres in extent, sloping irregularly but beautifully down the precipices which overhang the St. Lawrence. They were laid out by the late Major Douglas, of the United States Engineers, who had previously displayed his skill and taste in the arrangements of the Greenwood Cemetery, near New York.

Lorette.—To see Lorette may be made the object of an agreeable excursion from Quebec, following the banks of the St. Charles River.

Lake St. Charles is 4 miles long and one broad. It is divided by projecting ledges into two parts. It is a delightful spot in its natural attractions, and in the fine sport it affords to the angler.

The Falls of Montmorenci.—Nine miles below Quebec, the impetuous Montmorenci (so called after a French admiral of that name), after fretting itself a whirlpool route, and leaping for miles down the steps of a rocky bed, rushes with velocity toward the ledge, over which it falls, pouring its fleecy cataract 250 feet into the chasm below. The foam rising from the foot of the falls becomes frozen in winter, and the ice, accumulating layer upon layer, forms two cones, one of which not unfrequently attains the height of 100 feet, offering, to those who are courageous enough to ascend to its apex, a full front view of the edge of the precipice, and the still surface of the Montmorenci River sleeping in its icy bed. The second cone is much used for "tobogginning." Experts in this exclusively Canadian amusement climb to the top of the cone; and then, perching themselves on their "toboggins" (a sort of light Indian sleigh), dash down the glassy slope with a velocity which, increasing every instant, occasionally carries the hardy tobogginers a full half mile from the pinnacle whence they started. Before quitting the picturesque banks of the Montmorenci, the tourist should by all means visit the *Natural Steps,* 2 miles above the cataract. The limestone rock bordering the river is there formed, for half a mile, into a succession of steps, each about a foot in depth, as regularly arranged as if they had been hewn out by human hands. The "Mansion House," in which the Duke of Kent passed the summer of 1791, stands at a short distance from the falls.

The Falls of St. Anne, in the river St. Anne, 24 miles below Quebec, are in the neighborhood of great picturesque beauty. Starting from the city in the morning betimes, one may visit Montmorenci, and proceed thence with ease the same evening to St. Anne. Next morning, after a leisurely survey of these cascades, there will be most of the day left to get back, with any *détours* that may seem desirable, to Quebec.

The *Falls of the Chaudière* are reached *via* Point Levi. The rapid river plunges over a precipice of 130 feet, presenting very much the look of boiling water, whence its name of *chaudière*, or caldron. The cataract is broken into three separate parts by the intervention of huge projecting rocks, but it is reunited before it reaches the basin beneath. We now take our leave of Quebec, with its unique natural beauties and its winning stories, with the remembrance of some of the impressions it made upon Professor Silliman, when he visited it years ago : " Quebec," he writes, " at least for an American city, is certainly a very peculiar place. A military town, containing about 20,000 inhabitants—most compactly and permanently built—environed, as to its most important parts, by walls and gates, and defended by numerous heavy cannon—garrisoned by troops having the arms, the costume, the music, the discipline of Europe—foreign in language, features, and origin, from most of those whom they are sent to defend—founded upon a rock, and in its highest parts overlooking a great extent of country—between 300 and 400 miles from the ocean, in the midst of a great continent, and yet displaying fleets of foreign merchantmen in its fine capacious bay, and showing all the bustle of a crowded seaport—its streets narrow, populous, and winding up and down almost mountainous declivities —situated in the latitude of the finest parts of Europe, exhibiting in its environs the beauty of a European capital, and yet in winter smarting with the cold of Siberia—governed by a people of different language and habits from the mass of the population, opposed in religion, and yet leaving that population without taxes, and in the full enjoyment of every privilege, civil and religious."

Point Levi, opposite Quebec, is where passengers take the cars.

Arthabaska (64 miles) is the junction of a short road to *Three Rivers*, on the St. Lawrence.

Richmond (95 miles from Quebec and 221 miles from Portland) is a thriving village, on a branch of the *St. Francis River*. A bridge connects it with *Mel-* *bourne*. The Quebec division unites with the main line at this point.

MONTREAL.

Montreal (297 miles) may be reached daily from New York in from 15 to 18 hours, by the *Hudson River* or *Harlem Railway* to Troy ; rail to Whitehall, and steamer on Lake Champlain ; or by rail through Vermont, *via* Rutland, Burlington, and St. Albans to Rouse's Point, or *via* Plattsburg on Lake Champlain. From Boston, *via* Albany, or other routes to Lake Champlain, etc. ; or, *via Portland and the Grand Trunk Railway ;* time 30 hours.

Montreal, the metropolis of British North America, is situated on an island of the same name, about 30 miles long and 10 wide, which is formed by a branch of the Ottawa on the north and the St. Lawrence on the south, and lies at the foot of a mountain, to which Jacques Cartier, in 1535, surveying with delight the magnificent prospect, gave the name of " Mont Royal." The present site of Montreal was occupied, at the time of Cartier's first visit, by an Indian village called Hochelaga. In 1542 the first European settlers arrived, and just one century later the original Indian name, consequent on the consecration of the spot on which the future city was to stand, and its commendation to *La Reine des Anges*, gave place to the French one of " Ville Marie." This new name, in its turn, was replaced by the present one, in 1760, the date of British possession ; at which period Montreal had become a well-peopled and well-fortified town. Its population is now estimated at 125,000, and is rapidly on the increase. The main branch of the Ottawa, which is the timber highway to Quebec, passes north of Montreal Island, and enters the St. Lawrence about 18 miles below the city ; about one-third of its waters is, however, discharged into Lake St. Louis, and joining, but not mingling, at Caughnawaga, the two distinct bodies pass over the Sault St. Louis and Lachine Rapids—the dark waters of the Ottawa washing the quays of Montreal, while the blue St. Lawrence occupies the other shore. Nor do they merge their distinctive character until they are several miles below Montreal. The quays of Montreal are unsurpassed by those of any city in America; built of solid limestone, and uniting with the locks and cut-stone wharves of the Lachine Canal, they present for several miles a display of continuous masonry which has few parallels. Unlike the levees of the Ohio and the Mississippi, no unsightly warehouses disfigure the riverside. A broad esplanade or terrace, built of limestone, the parapets of which are surmounted with a substantial iron railing, forms the river front.

The houses in the suburbs are handsomely built in the modern style, and mostly inhabited by the wealthy merchants. Including its suburbs, of which it has several, the city stretches along the river for two miles, from southwest to northeast, and, for some distance, extends between one and two miles inland. St. Paul Street, the chief commercial thoroughfare, extends along the river the whole length of the city. Great St. James and Notre-Dame Streets are the fashionable promenades. Montreal, with its beautiful villas, its glittering roofs and domes (all the latter being covered with tin), its tall spires and lofty towers, and its majestic mountain in the background, bursting on the eye of the tourist, approach it from what direction he may, forms, together with the noble river, a vast and picturesque panorama that is, perhaps, unequalled in the whole of the American Continent.

The "ice-shove," a most imposing spectacle, may be witnessed by those travellers who arrive at Montreal toward the beginning of April. This strange phenomenon results from the crowding of the ice about a mile below the city, where the channel of the river is comparatively narrow; there it is *packed*, *piled*, and *frozen* into a solid mass of twenty to thirty feet in thickness, which, when lifted by the rising waters above, and set in motion again by the whole hydraulic power of the gigantic stream, rushes onward until again impeded by the banks of the narrowing river. The lateral pressure 't there exerts forces the *bordage* up on .he land, where it not unfrequently accumulates to the height of 50 feet.

HOTELS: The *St. Lawrence Hall*, Great St. James Street, a fine house, centrally located, and well kept; the *Donegana*, Notre-Dame Street; the *Ottawa*, Great St. James Street; and the *Montreal House*, Custom-house Square, and opposite the Custom-house. Besides these leading establishments, there are many other comfortable houses and *cafés*, where travellers of all ranks and classes may be lodged and regaled according to the varied humors of their palates and their purses.

PUBLIC BUILDINGS.

Montreal is conspicuous among the cities of the New World for the number and magnificence of her public buildings and churches.

The *Bonsecours Market* is an imposing Doric edifice, erected at a cost of $300,000, and, as regards the convenience of its arrangements and the spaciousness of its construction, it throws into the shade all similar structures on this continent. In one of the upper stories are the offices of the Corporation and Council Chamber, and a concert or ball room capable of accommodating 4,000 people. The view from the dome, overlooking the river and St. Helen's Isle, is truly grand.

The *Bank of Montreal* and the *City Bank*, the first a fine example of Corinthian architecture, stand side by side on the Place d'Armes.

The *Custom-House* is a neat building on the site of an old market-place, between St. Paul Street and the river.

The *Court-House* is one of the most striking of the architectural specialties of the city.

The *Post-Office* is in Great James Street.

The *Merchants' Exchange and Reading-Room* are in St. Sacrament Street. The latter is a large and comfortable room, well supplied with newspapers and periodicals, English and American, all at the service of the stranger when properly introduced.

The *Museum of the Natural History Society* is near the Crystal Palace. Admission 25 cents.

The *General Hospital* and *St. Patrick's Hospital* are in Dorchester Street, the latter, however, at the west end of the town.

The *Seminary of St. Sulpice*, adjoining the Cathedral of Notre-Dame, is 132 feet long, and 29 deep, and is surrounded by spacious gardens and court-yards.

CHURCHES.

The principal of these is the cathedral of *Notre-Dame*, said to be the largest church on the continent. The cost of the cathedral was $400,000, and it is capable of seating 10,000 persons. It is surmounted by two stately towers, each 220 feet high, from the top of which is a complete view of the city, the river St. Lawrence, the colossal tubular bridge, and the blue hills of Vermont in the distance. At certain hours of the day a chime of bells peal forth their merry notes from the northeast tower, and from the northwest is sometimes heard the hoarse, hollow tone of the "Gros Bourdon," which weighs 29,400 pounds. This noble edifice is 255 feet long and 135 broad.

The Jesuit church, in Bleury Street, has the most highly-ornamented interior to be found in the city.

St. Patrick's Church (Roman Catholic) occupies a commanding position at the west end of Lagauchetière Street.

The *Bishop's Church* (Roman Catholic), in St. Denis Street, is a very elegant structure.

The remaining Roman Catholic churches are the *Recollect* in Notre-Dame Street, the *Bonsecours*, near the large market, and *St. Mary's*, in Griffintown. There are also chapels attached to all the nunneries, in some of which excellent pictures may be seen.

The Episcopal churches are: *Christ Church Cathedral*, a beautiful edifice; *St. George's Church*, in St. Joseph Street; *St. Stephen's*, in Griffintown; *Trinity*, in St. Paul Street; and *St. Thomas's*, in St. Mary Street.

The Protestant churches worthy of notice are *St. Andrew's Church*, a beautiful specimen of Gothic architecture, being a close imitation of Salisbury Cathedral, in England, though of course on a greatly-reduced scale. This, with *St. Paul's Church*, in St. Helen Street, is in connection with the Established Church of Scotland.

The *Wesleyans* have a large and very handsome building in St. James Street, and also others in Griffintown and Mont-calm Street; the Independents formerly had two houses, but now only the one in Radegonde Street. This last was the scene of the sad riot and loss of life on the occasion of Gavazzi's lecture in 1852. The *Free Church* has two places of worship, one in Coté Street, and one in St. Gabriel Street; besides these, there are the *American* and the *United Presbyterian*, the *Baptist*, and the *Unitarian* churches; and a small *Jewish* synagogue, the last-named being classical in design.

NUNNERIES.

The *Gray Nuns*, in Foundling Street, was founded in 1692, for the care of lunatics and children. The *Hôtel Dieu* was established in 1644, for the sick generally. The *Black*, or *Congregational Nunnery*, in Notre-Dame Street, dates from 1659. The sisterhood, at this third and last of the conventual establishments of Montreal, devote themselves to the education of young persons of their own sex. The stranger desirous of visiting either of the nunneries should apply to the Lady Superior for admission, which is seldom refused.

MISCELLANEOUS.

The *Victoria Bridge*, which spans the great St. Lawrence at the city, is "the lion *par excellence* of Montreal, the eighth wonder of the world, the link of the *Grand Trunk Railway*, connecting (for railway purposes only) the city of Montreal, on the island, with the main-land to the south, giving to the ancient Hochelaga an unbroken railway communication of 1,100 miles in length, besides connections." It is one of the noblest structures on the continent. Its length is 9,194 feet, or nearly 2 miles. It rests, in this splendid transit, upon 24 piers and 2 abutments of solid masonry, the central span being 330 feet in length. The heavy iron tube through which the railway track is laid is, in its largest dimensions, 22 feet high and 16 feet wide. The total cost of this bridge was $6,300,000. It was formally opened, with high pomp and ceremony, amid great popular rejoicings, by the Prince of Wales, during his visit to America in the summer of 1860.

McGill's College is beautifully situated at the base of the mountain. The highschool department of the college is in Belmont Street. The city also possesses, besides the university of McGill's College, many excellent institutions for the promotion of learning—French and English seminaries, a royal grammar-school, with parochial, union, national, Sunday, and other public schools. It has numerous societies for the advancement of religion, science, and industry; and several public libraries.

The *Mount Royal Cemetery* is 2 miles from the city, on the northern slope of the mountain. From the high-road round its base, a broad avenue through the shaded hill-side gradually ascends to this pleasant spot. There are other romantic burying-grounds, both of the Catholic and the Protestant population, in the vicinity of Montreal, and other scenes which the visitor should enjoy—pleasant rides all about, around the mountain and by the river.

The *Nelson Monument*, an elegant column erected to the memory of that renowned naval hero, stands at the head of the Place Jacques Cartier.

The Water-Works, a mile or so from the city, are extremely interesting for their own sake, and for the delightful scenery in the vicinity.

St. Anne's (318 miles) is a village at the upper point of Montreal Island, where the railway crosses the river to the north bank.

Cornwall (364 miles) is the upper entrance to the Cornwall Canal.

Prescott Junction (410 miles) connects with *St. Lawrence and Ottawa Railway* for Ottawa, the capital of the Dominion of Canada, described on page 263. Passengers for *Ogdensburg* cross the St. Lawrence here.

Brockville (422 miles) is a town of some importance, and is one of the termini of the *Brockville and Ottawa Railway*.

Kingston (649 miles) the original capital of Canada, modern as it appears, looks far back for its history, as its advantageous situation attracted the notice of the early French discoverers. It was once occupied as a small fort called *Ca-taraqui*, otherwise known as *Frontenac*, in honor of the French count of that name, and was the scene of various sieges and exploits before it passed, with all the territory of the Canadas, from French to British rule. It was from this point that murderous expeditions were made by the Indians in the olden times against Albany and other English settlements of New York; which in turn sent back here its retributive blows. The present city was founded in 1783. It has now a population of about 16,000.

As a military station, it is only second to Quebec. Among its objects of interest are the fortifications of *Fort Henry*, on a hill upon the eastern side of the harbor; four fine Martello Towers off the town, and other defensive works; the *University of Queen's College;* the *Roman Catholic College of Regiopolis*, and the *Provincial Penitentiary*, a mile to the west of the city.

Royal Mail Line of steamers on *Lake Ontario* connects here.

Belleville (517 miles) is at the head of *Moira River* on rising ground, and in the distance looks remarkably well. From the surrounding country the view of the lake is very fine.

Cobourg (561 miles) is a place of about 5,000 population, and is one of the regular refreshment-stations of the road. *Victoria College*, a Wesleyan institution, located at this point, is a handsome building. There is also a fine town hall, and that necessary adjunct of civilization, a jail. The *Cobourg and Peterborough Railway*, running back into the woods, diverges here.

Port Hope (567 miles) is a very pretty town in a valley, the hills gradually rising one above the other on the western side of the town. The *Midland Railway of Canada* for *Beaverton*, on *Lake Simcoe*, diverges here.

Lake Simcoe is 30 miles long by 18 miles wide, and contains numerous islands, only one of which is inhabited, and that by Indians. The lake finds an outlet in the *Georgian Bay*, on *Lake Huron*. There is a steamboat upon this lake, and any tourist desirous of seeing Nature unimproved by civilization is advised to pay it a visit.

Toronto (630 miles) is the largest

and most populous city in Ontario. Some eighty years ago the site of the present busy mart was occupied by two Indian families only. In 1793, Governor Simcoe began the settlement under the name of York, changed, when it was incorporated, in 1834, to Toronto—meaning, in the Indian tongue, "The place of meeting." One of the principal thoroughfares, Yonge Street, extends, through a flourishing agricultural district, to Lake Simcoe, a distance of 36 miles. The population, in 1817, numbered only 1,200; in 1850, it had reached 25,000; and now it is upward of 75,000.

The *University of Toronto* stands in a large park with avenues of noble trees leading into two of the principal streets of the city. The style of the buildings, except in some minor details, is pure Norman. The massive tower in the centre of the south façade is 120 feet high.

The *Normal School*, on Church Street, and *Trinity College*, on Queen Street west, are both handsome buildings.

Osgoode Hall, in which the courts of law are held, combines with a pleasing exterior the most admirable interior arrangements.

The *Provincial Lunatic Asylum*, and the *Merchants' Exchange*, are places to be visited.

Among the notable churches are the English *Cathedral of Saint James*, and the Roman Catholic *Cathedral of St. Michael*. The new *Wesleyan Methodist Church*, on McGill Square, will be a splendid edifice, the finest in the Dominion.

The drives in the vicinity are not especially attractive, though one or two of them are quite pretty, especially the one along the lake, on a pleasant day, when the water is covered with steam and sail vessels of all kinds and sizes, from the royal mail-steamer to the "shell" of the oarsman.

The leading hotels are the *Rossin House* and *Queen's*.

The road here connects with the *Hamilton and Toronto Branch of the Great Western Railway;* with *steamers* sailing on *Lake Ontario*, and with the *Northern Railway* to *Lake Simcoe* and *Collingwood*. This latter road is a very desirable one for tourists having but little time, and desiring to visit *Mackinaw* and *Lake Superior*, as there is a line of steamers from *Collingwood* to *Chicago*, touching at Mackinaw.

Collingwood is on *Georgian Bay*, an immense arm of *Lake Huron*. It is a place of great importance as the *English Naval Depot* for the Northern lakes, and is connected with Detroit, Michigan, and Chicago, Illinois, by regular lines of steamers.

Guelph (678 miles) is a large and important town on *Speed River*, which here has a fall of 33 feet, furnishing power for a number of mills, factories, etc. It is built on hilly ground, and has a picturesque appearance. The limestone-quarries in the vicinity furnish the material out of which the court-house and many other buildings are constructed.

The *Guelph Branch of the Great Western Railway* connects here.

Stratford (718 miles) is pleasantly situated on the *Avon River*. It is the junction of the *Buffalo and Lake Huron Division of the Grand Trunk Railway*, from Buffalo to Goderich, on Lake Huron, intersecting the Great Western Railway at *Paris*.

St. Mary's (729 miles) is a thriving village. A branch diverges to *London* (22 miles), where it connects with the *Great Western* and *London and Port Stanley Railways*.

London (754 miles). (See page 258.)

Sarnia (798 miles) is the last station in Canada, and is some little distance from *Point Edward*, the actual terminus of the division, whence it is reached by stages. It is a busy, pleasant place, on the St. Clair River, opposite the city of *Port Huron*, Michigan. The Grand Trunk line of steamers leave here tri-weekly for Chicago and intermediate ports. At *Point Edward*, which is the point marking the spot where *Lake Huron* finds an outlet through the *St. Clair River*, passengers cross by ferry to *Fort Gratiot*, in Michigan. The current is remarkably swift, so much so that one can see the descent, though the water is very deep.

Occasionally passengers for the Upper Lakes can connect with a steamer at this point, but as a rule it is better to continue on to *Detroit*.

Detroit, Michigan (861 miles). Omitting all mention of the places in

Michigan (not one of which is visible from the cars), we will submit to a ride of 68 miles, through a densely-wooded country, until we come to the beautiful "City of the Straits." As this city is described in the WESTERN TOUR, we will omit all description here, merely saying: Go either to the *Russel House*, *Biddle House*, or *Michigan Exchange*, and you will find first-class hotels, with clerks glad to tell you what there is to see, and how to do it. If you have a day or two to spare before you start for the Upper Lakes, be sure and visit the *Put-in-Bay Islands*, in Lake Erie, one of the most charming summer resorts in the country. All particulars about them can be obtained at the hotels. The road connects here with the *Detroit and Milwaukee*, *Michigan Central*, and *Michigan Southern Railways*.

BUFFALO AND LAKE HURON BRANCH.

Distance from Buffalo to Detroit, 258 miles.

This branch runs from Buffalo, where it connects with all routes centring there, to Goderich, on Lake Huron, the cars being ferried across the Niagara River on a steamboat constructed especially for the purpose. The three principal stations are *Port Colburn*, *Paris*, and *Stratford*.

Port Colburn (19 miles from Buffalo) is the *Lake Erie* inlet of the celebrated *Welland Canal* around *Niagara Falls*. The road crosses the canal, and from the car-windows numbers of large vessels and steamers can be seen on both sides of the track.

Paris (83 miles) is where the road intersects the *Great Western Railway*. (*See* page 258.)

Stratford (115 miles) has been described on page 256. This is the junction with the main line, and here trains are divided, those cars with passengers for Detroit and intermediate points taking the main line; the others continuing on the branch.

ROUTE II.

NEW YORK TO DETROIT, MICHIGAN, CHICAGO, ILLINOIS, THE WEST, AND THE GREAT LAKES.

Via Route V. and the Buffalo Branches of Route VII. of New York, and Great Western Railway.

THE routes through Canada, from Buffalo to Detroit, are most uninteresting, with the exception of the country in the vicinity of Hamilton, on the Great Western Railway; but the cars are luxurious, and the roads in splendid order. If a tourist wishes to enjoy this trip thoroughly, we would advise him to take a sleeping-car, on a night-train, and indulge in a comfortable nap.

The distances given are from New York.

STATIONS.—Suspension Bridge, 448 miles; Thorold, 457; St. Catharines, 459; Jordan, 465; Beamsville, 470; Grimsby, 474; Winona, 479; Hamilton, 480 (connects with branch to Toronto); Dundas, 487; Copetown, 503; Lynden, 507; Harrisburg, 510 (connects with branch to Guelph); Paris, 520 (connects with Buffalo and Lake Huron Division of Grand Trunk Railway); Princeton, 527; Arnolds, 529; Eastwood, 534; Woodstock, 539; Beachville, 544; Ingersoll, 548; Dorchester, 558; London, 567 (connects with London and Port Stanley Railway, and with branch of Grand Trunk Railway to St. Mary's); Komoka, 577; Mt. Brydges, 583; Longwood, 589; Glencoe, 599; Newbury, 605; Bothwell (oil wells), 610; Thamesville, 618; Chatham, 633; Baptiste Creek, 647; Stoney Point, 652; Belle River, 661; Windsor, 678; Detroit, 679 (connects with Michigan Central, Michigan Southern, and Detroit and Milwaukee Railways).

Suspension Bridge (448 miles) is the station in Canada at the western end of the bridge. (For description of Niagara Falls, *see* page 70.)

Thorold (457 miles) is a milling and manufacturing town at the point where the railway crosses the *Welland Canal*, by means of which the largest vessels pass round the *Falls of Niagara*.

St. Catharines (459 miles) is famous for its mineral springs, which are

257

said to be a sovereign cure for many diseases, and to possess strong tonic qualities. The hotel accommodations and medical attendance are all that can be desired.

Hamilton (480 miles) is the only point on the road, with the exception of *Dundas*, where the scenery is sufficiently attractive to be called to the tourist's particular attention. It is situated upon *Burlington Bay*, at the western end of *Lake Ontario*. The streets are wide and well laid out, and the buildings are elegant, being constructed principally of white stone, there being large quarries near the city. The bay, which is one of the safest and most commodious harbors on Lake Ontario, is five miles long, two broad, and everywhere navigable to within a few yards of the shore. It abounds in pike, bass, perch, and eels. In the vicinity are several pretty drives, and from the "mountain" beautiful views are to be had. Among the pleasant resorts in the neighborhood are "*Ocklands*" and "*the Beach*," reached by ferry-boats. *Watertown, Flamborough Heights, Wellington Square*, "*Burning Springs*," *Ancaster*, etc., are all just far enough to be reached by pleasant drives over fine roads. Looking back from the cars as the train goes west, or forward as it approaches from the west, *Dundurn*, the castle of the late Sir Allan McNab, is to be seen high up on the mountain overhanging the bay.

The principal hotels are the *Anglo-American* and the *City Hotel*.

Hamilton is connected with Toronto by a line of steamers and by a branch railway.

Dundas (487 miles) is at the head of the *Desjardins Canal*, and is celebrated for its manufactories and its rural scenery. It is the residence of many Hamilton merchants.

Paris (520 miles) is situated at the junction of the *Nith* and *Grand Rivers*, is an important place, and possesses an excellent water-power. There are several petrifying springs and a mineral spring in the vicinity. Duck-hunters can find rare sport, in the season, by taking a team to *Long Point*, on Lake Erie (49 miles), *via Simcoe*. The *Buffalo and Lake Huron Division* of the *Grand Trunk Railway* intersects at this point.

London (567 miles) is a city of fine appearance, with streets running at right angles to each other and lined with excellent buildings. It is the northern terminus of the railway to *Port Stanley*, on Lake Erie, and is also the junction of a branch road connecting with the *Grand Trunk Railway* at *St. Mary's*.

Bothwell (610 miles) is the principal town of the oil-regions. The country here is flat and uninteresting, the air redolent with the scent of petroleum, and the landscape ornamented with the huge derricks which are to be found wherever oil-wells exist.

Chatham (633 miles) is a place of considerable business, and, besides the railway, is connected with Detroit by a regular line of steamers. It is principally noted for the large African element in its population.

Windsor (678 miles), opposite Detroit, is the western terminus of the road, and, though only divided by the river from the United States, is to all intents and purposes as thoroughly a "last century village," although really an incorporated city, as though it was located on an inaccessible island. It has, to be sure, a few modern stores, and the railway buildings give their immediate neighborhood an air of life, but outside of this the peculiar inertia of the colonists shows itself everywhere, and the French pony drawing an awkward old cart is met exactly as it might have been seen one hundred years ago. There is one beautiful drive along the river-bank, but let no traveller stop in Windsor to enjoy it; let him cross the river to Detroit, stop at one of the fine hotels with which the city is provided, and then, if he wishes to enjoy the drive, let him hire his carriage at the hotel where he stops.

Through-passengers cross the river, without change of cars, on a steam ferryboat, which transports a whole train at one load.

Detroit (679 miles). (*See* page 256.)

ROUTE III.

TRIP DOWN THE ST. LAWRENCE.

WE will consider, for the purposes of this trip, that we are at Kingston (see page 255), whither we have come either by rail or steamer, and are about to make the descent of the St. Lawrence in one of those stanch steamers which, under the care of bold and skilful pilots, brave all the dangers of the roaring rapids.

The Thousand Islands.—The first 40 miles of the St. Lawrence, after leaving Lake Ontario, are known as "The Lake of the Thousand Isles," from the continuous groups of islands and islets through which the steamboat threads its tortuous way toward Ogdensburg. There are said to be as many as 1,800 of these islands, of every imaginable shape, size, and appearance, some being mere dots of rock a few yards in extent, others covering acres, thickly wooded, and in summer and early autumn presenting the most charming appearance of rich foliage conceivable.

The passage through the thousand islands is generally made in the early morning, and nothing is more delightful than to watch them as they appear and disappear, and wonder at the accuracy with which the boat makes the abrupt turnings and twistings necessary to elude them.

The Rapids.—Passing Ogdensburg (see page 85) and Prescott (see page 255), you are soon made aware of the increasing swiftness of the current, and discover that you are about to experience that celebrated sensation of the tourist, known as "shooting the Rapids."

Until 1840 this passage was considered impossible; but, by watching the course of rafts down the river, a channel was discovered, and steamboats then attempted it, for the first time, under the guidance of the Indian pilot, *Teronhiahéré*. The pilots are still Indians, and their accuracy in the performance of their dangerous duties is really marvellous. Yet no one need fear the undertaking, for there has never yet occurred a fatal accident in making this course.

These Rapids are known by the following names: "The Gallopes" (four in number), the "Plate," "Depleau," "Long Sault," "Coteau," "Cedars," "Cascades," and "La Chine"—the shortest, but the most alarming in its appearance, of all. Passing that, we behold the towers of Notre-Dame and the Victoria Bridge at Montreal.

Having now taken a comprehensive view of the Rapids as a whole, we will treat of the places along the river-bank. The first point of interest below Prescott and Ogdensburg is *Louisville*, whence stages run to *Massena Springs*, 7 miles distant.

Massena Springs, on the banks of the river Racket, are five in number, the largest being named *St. Regis*, in honor of the tribe of Indians who discovered its virtues. These springs are a place of popular resort, their attractions being greatly enhanced by the beautiful surroundings and their proximity to the *Long Sault Rapids*, some 4 or 5 miles distant. The *United States Hotel* is a large house.

Dickinson's Landing is at the head of the Long Sault Rapids, which are 9 miles in length, and through which a raft will drift in forty minutes. The *Cornwall Canal*, 11¼ miles in length, has its inlet at this point. It is used by vessels bound up the river, to enable them to go round the Rapids. There is no difficulty in descending these rapids. The scenery here is very beautiful.

Cornwall is at the foot of the *Long Sault Rapids*, and is the lower terminus of the *Cornwall Canal*. There is excellent duck-shooting in the autumn. Just below this place the St. Lawrence, now entirely in Canada, expands into a lake, called *St. Francis*. It is about 25 miles long and 5 wide, and is dotted with islands, especially at the lower end.

Coteau du Lac is 30 miles below Cornwall, and is at the head of the *Coteau Rapids*, which, 9 miles below, take the name of the *Cedars*, and, still farther on, the *Cascades*. At the foot of the *Cascades* is *Beauharnois*, at the lower end of a canal, 11¼ miles long, around the Rapids. The village is prettily situated on a bay, and is a favorite resort for picnics from Montreal. The expanse of the river from this point to the head of the *Lachine Rapids* is called *Lake St. Louis*. One of the most noticeable places in this lake is *Nun's Island*, 5 miles below Beauharnois. It is of a peculiar shape, and was formerly an Indian burying-ground, though now in a high state of cultivation. Its name is derived from the fact that it is the property of the Grey Nunnery of Montreal.

Lachine is at the head of the Lachine Rapids, which, though the shortest, are the most turbulent and dangerous on the river. It is connected with Montreal by railway.

Caughnawaga, at the foot of the Lachine Rapids, is a small station on the south bank, where passengers from Plattsburg to Montreal cross the St. Lawrence.

Montreal. (*See* page 252.)

Varennes (15 miles below Montreal) lies between the St. Lawrence and Richelieu Rivers. It is connected with Montreal by a steamboat line, and is coming into notice on account of its mineral springs.

Sorel (45 miles from Montreal) is the first point at which the through-steamers for Quebec make a landing. This is a small place, but there is good fishing in the vicinity, and in the autumn excellent snipe-shooting. Five miles below the river expands into *Lake St. Peter*, which is 25 miles long, 9 wide, and is very shallow, except in the main channel, which is crooked and narrow, but which will permit the passage of the largest ships.

Three Rivers is about half-way between Montreal and Quebec, and is the third city in the eastern section of the province. It is at the mouth of the *St. Maurice River*, which runs through a rich lumber-district, and brings to *Three Rivers* every year large quantities of logs and manufactured lumber, which here find a market. There are founderies as well as saw-mills here.

St. Leon Springs, on the *Rivière du Loup (en haut)*, are reached by a stage-ride of 26 miles from *Three Rivers*.

Falls of the Shawenegan. —Very little is known of the country through which the St. Maurice runs, except that it is a perfect net-work of lakes abounding in fish and game, and that the scenery is charming. By taking a conveyance from Three Rivers to the *Portage des Grais*, where a canoe, *which must be previously engaged*, awaits the tourist, the trip to the Falls of the Shawenegan can be made in a primitive but satisfactory manner. About 30 miles from *Three Rivers* is the confluence of the *Shawenegan River*, and a little above, though on the *St. Maurice*, are the falls of which we speak. They have a sheer descent of 150 feet, and in magnitude are second only to Niagara. Of these falls the *Canadian Hand-book and Tourists' Guide* * says: "Notwithstanding the numerous rapids below the falls, there is much less difficulty in ascending than might be expected; for, while a current runs down the mid-channel, at the rate of five or six miles an hour, there are opportunities of taking advantage of an eddy on either side running up, by shooting rapidly across the main stream. When the water is high, in April and May, there are three distinct falls, unconnected with each other, and meeting in a large basin. The rocks that separate the fall are respectively called '*La Grand-Mère*' and '*Le Bonhomme.*' In the chasm below, where the waters of the different falls meet, the scene is sublime and terrific, giving the appearance of an enormous mass of snow, violently agitated. There are large fissures in the precipitous rock, into which the waters are driven with great force, and which rebound again in sheets of spray, with deafening sound. Immediately above the falls the current is unbroken and quiet, though very rapid."

A few miles above are "the *Falls of the Grand-Mère*, which, though not equal to those below them, are well worthy of a visit. The length of the St. Maurice is estimated at about 400 miles, though nothing definite is known about its headwaters."

Doucet's Landing, opposite Three Rivers, is the terminus of the *Arthabaska* branch of the Grand Trunk Railway.

Quebec. (*See* page 249.)

A description of the points of interest to the tourist on the Lower St. Lawrence would consume too much space, and we will merely enumerate them, with a word or two of comment.

Ste. Anne River.—This river enters the St. Lawrence from the north, through a ravine, of which one writer says a bolder or finer is scarcely to be found in the world. In the village is the church of *St. Anne,* where miraculous cures are said to be effected by the saint. The

* M. Longmore & Co., Montreal.

neighborhood is replete with places of interest.

Crane Island, Goose Island, and four others, form a group in the river 36 miles below Quebec. They are the resort and breeding-place of myriads of duck, geese, and teal, to say nothing of smaller game.

From *Goose Island* to the *Saguenay River* the St. Lawrence is about 20 miles wide. The water is salt, but clear and deep, and the spring-tides rise and fall 18 feet. The black seal, the white porpoise, and the black whale, are abundant.

Murray Bay, just below these islands, is a quiet watering-place, surrounded by wild scenery, and noted for the fine fishing in *Murray River.* A daily steamer from Quebec makes it easy of access.

La Baie des Rochers is 24 miles below *Murray Bay.* There is a lofty cape here, which has never been scaled by man, and upon the summit of which is a raven's nest, which is said to have been observed by the first missionaries that ever came to Canada.

Of the north bank of the river we may say that it is lined with game of all kinds, both winged and four-footed, and that the list of fish to be caught in the river and its affluents is almost unlimited. For detailed information, we refer the sportsman to local guides. For the purpose of seeing the *Lower St. Lawrence*, the tourist had better take a coasting steamer from Quebec for the Gulf, descending the north and ascending the south side of the river. In this trip he will be enabled to visit

Gaspe, the most easterly extremity of the province, jutting out into the Atlantic, a peninsula of frowning cliffs, at whose base is no accessible beach except at intervals, where streams have cut a passage for themselves to the ocean. This whole coast is a great fishing-station.

Cap Desespoir, one of the extremities of *Gaspe,* is the most dangerous spot on the coast. In 1811, 8 transports and 884 officers, soldiers, and seamen, were lost in one storm.

Perce Rock, near *Cap Desespoir,* is a natural arch, under which a fishing-smack may pass at full sail.

We will now cross the Gulf and return to Quebec by the south shore.

Metis, 200 miles from Quebec, is the site of the largest and longest government wharf. It is also a whale-fishing station.

Rimouski, 20 miles above *Metis,* has an extensive government wharf, and contains a number of elegant houses and a good hotel. This is a place at which the tourist should stop, for the scenery in the valley of the Rimouski is beautiful and the trout-fishing unrivalled.

Trois Pistoles (140 miles above Quebec) is at the mouth of the river of the same name, famed for its fish.

Rivière du Loup (*en bas*) is 114 miles below Quebec, and the terminus of one of the branches of the Grand Trunk Railway, and is a popular summer resort. It is at the mouth of the river after which it is named, and commands a fine prospect of the St. Lawrence, which at this point is 20 miles wide. About a mile from the village is a waterfall where the Du Loup, after rushing for a while over a rocky bed, dashes in a sheet of foam over a precipice of from 80 to 100 feet in height.

Lake Temiscouata is to be reached from *Rivière du Loup* by the Grand Portage Road, a distance of 36 miles. Only two or three cabins dot the shores of this lovely lake, and it is just the place for the seeker after solitude and trout. On the road is a curious collection of granite bowlders extending for about 2 miles, and probably deposited by a glacier.

Kakouna or **Cacouna** (it is spelled both ways) is the favorite watering-place of the Canadians, and is a very fine village, combining picturesque scenery, good hotels, fine hunting and fishing, and admirable sea-bathing, for at this point the water of the St. Lawrence is very salt. *St. Lawrence Hall* is a large, first-class hotel, overlooking the river.

Grand Falls of the River St. John.—" At these falls the river * makes a sudden turn, and, becoming contracted to the width of about 50 yards, makes a plunge of perhaps 40 feet, mostly in a solid mass. Below this, and extending for perhaps a mile, is a succession of falls, which make the entire descent some 80 feet. The water rushes

---

* The Canadian Hand-book and Tourists' Guide.

through what might be termed a winding chasm, whose sides are perhaps 150 or 200 feet high, perpendicular, and composed of a bluish slate. Generally speaking, the entire distance, from the first fall to the last, presents a sheet of foam, though around every jutting point is a black and apparently bottomless pool, teeming with fish. There is a comfortable stopping-place here kept by a *Mrs. Russell.*"

Reached from *Rivière du Loup* or *Kakouna* by stage. A trip to these falls and return will occupy three days.

Kamouraska is on the St. Lawrence, 90 miles from Quebec. It was formerly a popular resort, but has been supplanted by other places.

Grosse Isle (29 miles from Quebec) is the quarantine station. It is in daily communication with the city by means of a small steamer. Passes may be obtained from the superintendent or head emigration agent.

After passing the *Isle au Coudres* and the Island of Orleans, we find ourselves once more at Quebec.

LIST OF SALMON AND TROUT RIVERS BELOW QUEBEC.
(Fom the *Canadian Hand-book and Tourists' Guide.*)

	MILES
From QUEBEC to MURRAY BAY	78

The Saint Lawrence here furnishes a few salmon and many fine trout.

From MURRAY BAY to the SAGUENAY. 44
The fishing here is for the white porpoise, and has been mentioned in the article on the St. Lawrence.

River ESCOUMAIN............... 23
Between this and the Saguenay are two branches of the Bergeronne, both furnishing a few salmon and many trout.

River PORTNEUF................ 26
Plenty of trout and salmon.

SAULT AU COCHON.............. 9
Impassable for salmon, but full of trout.

LA VAL......................... 2
Superior salmon and trout.

BERSEMIS....................... 24
In all its tributaries are many fine salmon; between it and La Val are the Columbia, Plover, and Blanche, all poor salmon streams.

	MILES
River OUTARDES	11
MANICOUAGAN	16
MISTASSIMI	12
BETSCIE	3
GODBOU	15

A celebrated salmon river, one of the best in Quebec Province.

| TRINITY | 15 |

Good salmon and trout.

LITTLE TRINITY	10
CALUMET	3
PENTECOST	14

Not a salmon river.

| SAINTE MARGUERITE | 36 |

One of the best for both salmon and trout.

| MOISIE | 23 |

Celebrated for fine, large salmon.

| TROUT | 7 |
| MANITOU | 35 |

Good trout-fishing; salmon obstructed by falls.

| SHELDRAKE | 16 |
| MAGPIE | 22 |

Only a few salmon.

| SAINT JOHN | 5 |

An admirable salmon stream.

| MINGAN | 16 |

Probably the best salmon river in Quebec Province, and excellent for trout.

TRIP UP THE OTTAWA.

To describe the beauties of this trip would require a volume in itself; and we will be compelled, after giving a sketch of the river as a whole, to make a mere skeleton trip, describing a few of the most prominent points, and leaving the tourist to gain a knowledge of the details from personal experience or local guide-books.

The Ottawa River flows 800 miles, and enters the St. Lawrence on both sides of the Island of Montreal, traversing in its way *Lake Temiscaming, Grand Lake,* and others. Rapids and falls greatly impede the navigation of its waters, but lend to them wonderful beauty. It is a wild forest-region, but little occupied heretofore by others than the rude lumbermen, though numerous settlements are now springing up, and its agricultural capacities are being developed. Near the city of Ottawa the *Rideau* empties into the *Ottawa*. A mile lower it receives, from the north, its greatest tributary, the *Gatineau*, which, with a course probably of 420 miles, drains an area of 12,000 square miles. For about 200 miles the upper course of this river is in the unknown northern country. At the farthest point surveyed, 217 miles from its mouth, the Gatineau is still a noble stream, a thousand feet wide, diminished in depth but not in width. Eighteen miles lower down, the *Rivière au Lièvre* enters from the north, after running a course of 260 miles in length, and draining an area of 4,100 miles. Fifteen miles below it, the Ottawa receives the *North* and *South Nation Rivers* on either side, the former 95 and the latter 100 miles in length. Twenty-two miles farther, the *River Rouge*, 90 miles long, enters from the north. Twenty-one miles lower, the *Rivière du Nord*, 160 miles in length, comes in on the same side; and, lastly, just above its mouth, it receives the *River Assumption*, which has a course of 130 miles. From Ottawa the river is navigable to *Grenville*, a distance of 53 miles, where the rapids that occur for 12 miles are avoided by a succession of canals. Twenty-three miles lower, at one of the mouths of the Ottawa, a single lock, to avoid a slight rapid, gives a passage into Lake St. Louis, an expansion of the St. Lawrence above Montreal. The remaining half of the Ottawa's waters find their way to the St. Lawrence by passing in two channels, behind the Island of Montreal and the Isle of Jesus, in a course of 31 miles. They are interrupted with rapids; still it is by one of them that all the Ottawa lumber passes to market. At *Bout de l'Isle*, therefore, the Ottawa is finally merged in the St. Lawrence, 130 miles below the city of Ottawa.

The route up the Ottawa from Montreal is as follows: Take the cars from Montreal to Lachine, and then change to a steamboat running through *Lake St. Louis* (an expansion of the St. Lawrence), and then up the river. We first pass the village of *Sainte Anne*, where the Grand Trunk Railway crosses the river on a bridge supported by 16 stone piers. Two miles beyond is an expansion in the river called the *Lake of the Two Mountains*.

Carillon is the outlet of the canal from *Grenville*, built to avoid the rapids called the *Carillon*, *Chute à Blondeau*, and *Long Sault*. From this point the river forms the boundary-line between Quebec and Ontario. The tourist does not usually pass through the canal, but takes the cars for *Grenville*, 12 miles.

Grenville.—Here another change is made, and a steamboat is ready to convey him up the river, through the densely-wooded country, much of which is still in its primitive state.

L'Original (6 miles from Grenville) is where visitors to *Caledonia Springs* leave the steamer.

Caledonia Springs (9 miles from L'Original) possess valuable curative properties, especially in cases of rheumatic or cutaneous diseases; and the water is largely exported, under the name of "Plantagenet Water." These springs are in a quiet locality, and are sufficiently frequented to have pleasant society in the season (August).

Buckingham (20 miles below Ottawa), at the mouth of the *Rivière du Lièvre*, is a lumbering-town. Here is the place to stop to see the beauties of the

Rivière du Lièvre.—This river is destined to become a very popular resort, and a few words of description will not be out of place. Procuring guides at the hotel (a good one) in Buckingham, first visit the two waterfalls known as the *Upper* and *Lower Falls*—the first being 40, and the second 70 feet high—then take a carriage, or—what is far better—a canoe, and proceed up the river 25 miles, to the *High Falls*, which have a clear leap of 150 feet. They greatly resemble *Montmorenci*. Above these falls is *White Fish Lake*, on the shore of which is a remarkable cave, called "the Church." In the lake is an island very rich in metallic ore. Blacklead and antimony have been discovered in the neighborhood.

Ottawa, the capital of Canada, stands on the river of the same name, 54 miles distant from Prescott, and 126 from Montreal. It was originally called Bytown, in honor of Colonel By, of the Royal Engineers, under whose command it was laid out in 1823, and is divided into *Lower Town*, *Central Town*, and

263

Upper Town. On *Barrack Hill*, which rises almost vertically from the river to a height of 350 feet, and is in many respects a counterpart of the citadel of Quebec, are situated the *Parliament and departmental buildings.* These are all in the Italian-Gothic style, and are built of a kind of stone found in the vicinity. There is connected with the legislative halls a library capable of containing 300,000 volumes. When these buildings are completed, and the surrounding grounds are improved and decorated, as now contemplated, they will compare favorably with any in the world. Among the other principal public edifices may be mentioned the *Roman Catholic Church*, one of the handsomest in Canada; the *Queen's Printing-House*, and numerous other buildings, contributing to the stable appearance of the city. Ottawa is connected with Lake Ontario by the Rideau Canal, the entrance being at Kingston, 95 miles distant. It is the emporium of the Canadian staple, lumber. The scenery in the vicinity is of unsurpassed beauty.

The Chaudière Falls are situated in the western portion of the city, and are named after those near Quebec. "They are 40 feet in height, and over 200 in width; they are situated near the centre of the river; and the waters that flow over them are strongly compressed by rocks, that stretch out and impede them. In the great *Chaudière* (or Caldron) the sounding-line has not found bottom at 300 feet." Immediately below the falls is a suspension-bridge, from which a superb view is obtained.

Rideau Falls. — These falls, on the *Rideau River*, are in the northeast portion of the city, are two in number, and are very attractive, though eclipsed by the grandeur of the Chaudière.

"*Lumber-Shoots.*"—It being impossible safely to run lumber over the falls, *shoots*, or inclined planes, are constructed, down which the rafts rush with amazing velocity. It is exciting to witness the passage of a raft down these "shoots," but to ride on one of them is said to combine in one the experiences of balloon, diving-bell, and the Rapids of the St. Lawrence.

One mile above the city are the *Little Chaudière Falls*, a pretty fall of 13 feet, and two miles above the rapids known as

The Remoux. The *De Cheine Rapids*, 8 miles above Ottawa, have a fall of 9 feet.

Aylmer (9 miles) is at the foot of an expansion of the river 26 miles long, called *Lac de Cheine*, and navigable for the largest vessels.

Chats Portage, or **Chats Falls** (35 miles), are a series of cascades descending 50 feet in 3 miles. At one point thirteen falls are visible at once. A canal around these falls was commenced, but has never been finished.

Lac des Chats.—This portion of the river is 20 miles long, and 1 mile broad, and commences immediately above the falls. In places its bays increase the width to 3 miles.

Arnprior (40 miles), at the mouth of the *Madewasea River*, is a station on the *Brockville and Ottawa Railway.* Regular trains run between here and Brockville. (*See* page 255.)

Portage du Fort is where the river is divided into several channels by a group of islands, and is also crossed by a reef of crystallized limestone, forming the falls.

Calumet Falls is where the next reach of navigable water is reached. Navigation is again interrupted at *Chapeau Rapids*, on the north side of *Alumette Island*, and at *Hawley's Island*, in the south channel, 2¼ miles below Westmeath.

Pembroke (70 miles) is where the last navigable section of the river commences, extending to *Des Joachim*, 40 miles above, passing through *Upper* and *Lower Alumette Lakes* and *Deep River*, where mountains rise 600 feet from the edge of the water, the depth of which nearly equals their height.

At a distance of 100 miles above Ottawa, the last house is reached, above which is unbroken wilderness.

TRIP UP THE SAGUENAY.

The Saguenay is the largest tributary of the St. Lawrence, and unquestionably one of the most remarkable rivers on the continent. Its head-water is Lake St. John, 40 miles long, which, although eleven large rivers fall into it, has no other outlet than the Saguenay. The original name of this river was *Chicoutimi*, an Indian word signifying deep water;

and its present one is said to be a corruption of *Saint-Jean Nez*. The first place of interest to point out to the traveller is

Tadoussac, lying a short distance above *Pointe aux Vaches*, 140 miles from Quebec. Apart from its pleasant situation as a watering-place, it is interesting from the circumstance of having been the spot on which stood the first stone-and-mortar building ever erected on the Continent of America. The scenery here is wild and romantic in the extreme; and the waters all round abound in excellent salmon and trout. Just in the rear of Tadoussac, and at the *Bergeronnes*, and on the opposite side of the Saguenay, among the *Canard Lakes*, and at the *Little Saguenay, St. John, Grand Bay,* and *Chicoutimi, Kenogami*, and other lakes, the trout are only too plenty, very large, and glad to be caught. Seal-hunting is also a favorite sport for those who resort to these shores; several varieties of the animal are here met with in abundance.

The journey up the Saguenay may be made semi-weekly by steamer from Quebec, or by the *Grand Trunk Railway*, 101 miles to St. Paschal, Rivière du Loup, opposite the mouth of the Saguenay, and thence by steamer. The course of the Saguenay—between lofty and precipitous heights, and, in its upper part, amid rushing cataracts—is 126 miles from Lake St. John to the St. Lawrence, which it enters 140 miles below Quebec. Large ships ascend 60 miles. In the trip from Quebec to the Saguenay beauties, there are many interesting points to be noticed in the preceding journey of 120 miles down the St. Lawrence—the ancient-looking settlements on its banks, and the not less picturesque *habitans* of the country. A day's sail lands the voyager at *Rivière du Loup*, where he passes the night on board his steamer, waiting for the following morning to resume his journey. The Saguenay is a perfectly straight river, with grand precipices on either side. It has neither windings nor projecting bluffs, nor sloping banks, nor winding shores, like other rivers, nor is its stern, strange aspect varied by either village or villa. "It is," says a voyager thither, "as if the mountain-range had been cleft asunder, leaving a horrid gulf of 60 miles in length and 4,000 feet in depth, through the gray mica schist, and still looking fresh and new. One thousand five hundred feet of this is perpendicular cliff, often too steep and solid for the hemlock or dwarf-oak to find root; in which case, being covered with colored lichens and moss, their fresh-looking fractures often appear, in shape and color, like painted fans, and are called the pictured rocks. But those parts more slanting are thickly covered with stunted trees, spruce and maple and birch growing wherever they can find crevices to extract nourishment; and the bare roots of the oak, grasping the rock, have a resemblance to gigantic claws. The bases of these cliffs lie far under the water, to an unknown depth. For many miles from its mouth no soundings have been obtained with 2,000 feet of line; and for the entire distance of 60 miles, until you reach Ha-ha Bay, the largest ships can sail, without obstruction from banks or shoals, and, on reaching the extremity of the bay, can drop their anchors in 30 fathoms. The view up this river is singular in many respects; hour after hour, as you sail along, precipice after precipice unfolds itself to view, as a moving panorama; and you sometimes forget the size and height of the objects you are contemplating, until reminded by seeing a ship of 1,000 tons lying like a small pinnace under the towering cliff to which she is moored; for, even in these remote and desolate regions, industry is at work, and, although you cannot clearly discern them, saw-mills have been built on some of the tributary streams which fall into the Saguenay. But what strikes one most is the absence of beach or strand, except in a few places where mountain torrents, rushing through gloomy ravines, have washed down the *detritus* of the hills, and formed some alluvial land at the mouth; no coves, nor creeks, nor projecting rocks are seen in which a boat could find shelter, or any footing be obtained. The characteristic is a steep wall of rock rising abruptly from the water; a dark and desolate region, where all is cold and gloomy; the mountains hidden with driving mist, the water black as ink, and cold as ice. No ducks nor sea-gulls sitting on the water, or screaming for their prey. No hawks nor eagles soaring overhead, although there is an abundance of what might be called 'eagle cliffs.' No deer coming down to drink at the streams, no squirrels nor birds to be seen among the trees. No fly on the water, nor swallows skimming over the surface. Two living things you may see, but these are cold-blooded animals; you may see the cold seal, spreading himself upon his clammy rock, watching for his prey. You may see him make his sullen plunge into the water, like to the Styx for blackness. You may see him emerge again, shaking his smooth oily sides, and holding a huge living salmon writhing in his teeth; and you may envy the fellow faring so sumptuously, until you recollect that you have just had a hearty breakfast of fresh-grilled salmon yourself, and that you enjoyed it as much as the seal is now enjoying his raw morsel. And this is all you see for the first twenty miles, save the ancient settlement of *Tadoussac* at the entrance, and the pretty cove of *L'Ance à l'Eau*, which is a fishing-station. Now you reach *Cape Eternity, Cape Trinity*, and many other overhanging cliffs, remarkable for having such clean fractures, seldom equalled for boldness and effect, which create constant apprehensions of danger, even in a calm ; but if you happen to be caught in a thunder-storm, the roar, and darkness, and flashes of lightning, are perfectly frightful. At last you terminate your voyage at *Ha-ha Bay*—that is, *Smiling* or *Laughing Bay*, in the Indian tongue— for you are perfectly charmed and relieved to arrive at a beautiful spot, where you have sloping banks, a pebbly shore, boats and wherries, and vessels riding at anchor; birds and animals, a village, a church, French Canadians, and Scottish Highlanders." After duly enjoying the pleasant "let down" from the high tragic tone of the landscape you have been so long gazing upon and wondering at, formed in the comparatively pastoral character of this upper region of the Ottawa, you return to your steamer, and, descending the stern and solemn river, come again, at nightfall, to the Rivière du Loup, from whence you started in the morning. This is the second day of your journey, and on the third you are back once more in Quebec.

After leaving these delightful scenes, and returning to Quebec, those who choose so to do, can set out for home either by rail, *via* Richmond, Portland, Boston, and New York, or *via* Richmond by rail to Sherbroke, thence by coaches to Magog, connecting with steamer for New York (*see* LAKE MEMPHREMAGOG), thence by *Passumpsic Railway* to White and Franconia Mountains, Boston, or New York.

NEW BRUNSWICK.

NEW BRUNSWICK, the third Province of the Dominion, lies upon the eastern boundary of the State of Maine. The landscape is of great variety and of most picturesque beauty ; the whole Province (excepting the dozen miles lying directly on the sea) being broken into attractive valleys and hills, which northward assume a very marked and sometimes a very rugged aspect. Much of its area of 230 miles in length and 130 in breadth is covered with magnificent forests, which, as in the neighboring State of Maine, constitute its chief source of industry and wealth.

The hills are nowhere of a very wonderful height, but they often rise in precipitous and sharp acclivities, which give them an almost Alpine aspect; all the more striking in contrast with the peaceful plains and vales which they protect from the tempests of the sea.

Like the neighboring Province of Nova Scotia, New Brunswick so abounds in lakes and rivers, that ready water access may be had, with the help of a short portage now and then, over its entire area. Thus a canoe may easily be floated from the interior to the Bay de Chaleur, the Gulf of St. Lawrence, and the ocean on the north, or to the St. John River, and thence to the Bay of Fundy on the south.

The St. John River is the largest in New Brunswick, and one of the most remarkable and beautiful in America. It rises in the highlands which separate Maine from Canada, not very far from the sources of the Connecticut. For 150 miles it flows in a northeast direction, to the junction of the St. Francis. From the mouth of the St. Francis, the course of the St. John is irregularly east-southeast to the Grand Falls; at which point it makes a descent of from 70 to 80 feet, presenting a splendid picture for the gratification of the tourist. The leap of the Grand Falls passed, the river makes its way almost southward for some distance, after which it turns abruptly to the eastward, and so continues its way for 100 miles, passing Fredericton, to the outlet of the Grand Lake, in the southern central part of the Province. From Grand Lake its passage is in a wide channel, due south to Kingston, and thence southwest to St. John, at its mouth in St. John Harbor, on the Bay of Fundy.

The entire length of this beautiful river is about 600 miles, and from the Grand Falls to the sea, 225 miles, its course is within the British Territory. The river and its affluents are thought to afford 1,300 miles of navigable waters. Very much of the shores of the St. John is wild forest-land. In some parts, the banks rise in grand rocky hills, forming in their lines and interlacings pictures of wonderful delight.

The chief tributaries of the St. John, besides the St. Francis and other waters already mentioned, are the Aroostook, the Oromocto, the Eel, on the west; and the Salmon, the Nashwaak, the Tobique, the Kennebecasis, and the Washedemoak, on the east.

The coast, and bays, and lakes, and rivers of New Brunswick abound with fish of almost every variety and in immense supplies. The fisheries of the Bay of Fundy are of great value, and employ vast numbers of the population. In the harbor of St. John alone there have been, at one time, 200 boats with 500 men taking salmon, shad, and other fish. Nearly 600 fishermen have been seen at one period at the Island of Grand Manan; while at the West Isles, about 700 men have been thus employed at one moment; and so on at many of the other countless fishing grounds and stations of the New Brunswick and the Nova Scotia coasts.

The climate here is healthful, but subject to great extremes of heat and cold; the mercury rising sometimes to 100° in the daytime, and falling to 50° at night.

INTERNAL COMMUNICATION.—Besides the steamers and stages which connect the various towns and cities of New Brunswick and Nova Scotia, lines of railway are in active progress, which will unite the two Provinces, and both to the Canadas and the States. A portion of the *European and North American Railway* was opened (August 1, 1860) from St. John to Shediac, 106 miles, while the "Western Extension" is now completed from St. John to within 21 miles of Bangor. From Shediac steamers connect with Charlottetown, P. E. Island; Pictou, N. S.; the northern ports of New Brunswick, and Quebec. This line opens up new and pleasant ground to the tourist. Another road is to extend from St. Andrews to Woodstock, and thence to Quebec. The magnetic telegraph already connects New Brunswick, Nova Scotia, and Prince Edward's Island, with the States. The connection between Nova Scotia and Prince Edward's Island is by a submarine cable, nine miles from Cape Tormentine to Cape Traverse.

St. John.— HOTELS: *Waverley House* and *Stubbs's*.

ROUTES.—From Boston, Mass., every Monday and Thursday, at 9 A. M., by steamer. From Halifax, *via* Windsor, N. S., 45 miles by rail, and thence by steamer, 110 miles, to St. John, every Wednesday and Saturday, connecting with steamboats for Portland.

St. John, at the mouth of the St. John River, is the principal city of New Brunswick, with a population of over 30,000. It is superbly situated upon a bold, rocky peninsula, and is seen very imposingly from the sea. The scenery of the St. John River is very striking, in the passage immediately preceding its entrance into the harbor, and a mile and a half above the city. It makes its impetuous way here in a chain of grand rapids, through rugged gaps, 240 feet wide and 1,200 feet long. The passage is navigable only during the very brief time of high and equal tides in the harbor and the river; for at low water the river is about 12 feet higher than the harbor, while at high water the harbor is five feet above the river. It is thus only, when the waters of the harbor and of the river are on a level, that vessels can pass; and this occurs only during a space of from

broad, and for the most part macadamized. Viewed from the water, or from the opposite shore, the city is prepossessing and animated. In front, the town is lined with wharves, which, from the number of vessels constantly loading and discharging, always exhibit a spectacle of great commercial activity. Warehouses rise over the wharves, or tower aloft in different parts of the town, and dwelling-houses and public buildings rear their heads over each other, as they stretch along and up the sides of the hill. The spires of the different churches, the building above the town, in which the town-clock is fixed, a rotunda-built church, the signal-posts on *Citadel Hill*, the different batteries, the variety of style in which the houses are built (some of which are painted white, some blue, and some red); rows of trees showing themselves in different parts of the town; the ships moored opposite the dock-yard, with the establishments and tall shears of the latter; the merchant-vessels under sail, at anchor, or along the wharves; the wooded and rocky scenery of the background, with the islands and the small town of *Dartmouth* on the east shore—are all objects most agreeable to see.

Of the public buildings, the chief is a handsome edifice of stone, called the *Province Building*, 140 feet long by 70 broad, and ornamented with a colonnade of the Ionic order. It comprises suitable chambers for the accommodation of the Council and Legislative Assembly, and also for various Government offices. The *Government House*, in the southern part of the town, is a solid but gloomy-looking structure, near which is the residence of the military commandant. The admiral's residence, on the north side of the town, is a plain building of stone. The north and south barracks are capable of accommodating three regiments. The *Wellington Barracks* (in the northern part of the town), which comprises two long ranges of substantial stone and brick buildings, is the most extensive and costly establishment of the kind in North America. There is also a military hospital, erected by the late Duke of Kent. *Dalhousie College* is a handsome edifice of freestone. Among the churches of various denominations are several of the English establishment, and of the Presbyterian order, and two of the Roman Catholic faith. The *Court-house* is a spacious freestone structure, in the southern part of the town. In the suburbs is a new hospital. The banking establishments are four in number. The hotels and boarding-houses are not of the highest order. The inhabitants of Halifax are intelligent and social, and travellers will remark a tone of social society here more decidedly English than in most of the other colonial cities. Hollis and Sackville Streets are the principal business-thoroughfares, and these have of late years been greatly improved by the erection of fine structures, which will compete with those of our American cities.

The harbor opposite the town is more than a mile wide, and has, at medium tides, a depth of 12 fathoms. About a mile above the upper end of the town it narrows to one-fourth of a mile, and then expands into Bedford Basin, which has a surface of ten square miles, and is completely land-locked. On an island opposite the town are some strong-mounted batteries. The harbor is also defended by some other minor fortifications. The *Citadel* occupies the summit of the heights commanding the town, and is a mile in circumference. It is a costly work, and, after that of Quebec, is the strongest fortress in the British North American colonies.

Halifax, ever since its settlement in 1749, has been the seat of a profitable fishery. Its trade, which is in a very prosperous condition, is principally with the West Indies and other British colonies, with the United States, and the mother country. It is also the chief rendezvous and naval depot for the British navy on the North American station. The British Government having made Halifax one of the stopping-places of the Cunard line of steamers, in their trips either way across the Atlantic, has added greatly to its importance as a maritime city, as well as advanced its commercial prosperity.

The chief portion of the fishing interest is confined to the ports of Digby and Yarmouth, and the more southern shores of the province.

From Halifax the traveller can return

to New York by rail to Windsor, and thence by *International Steamship Line* to Portland or Boston, thence by rail or steamer to New York. From Pictou, steamers sail regularly for Charlottetown, Prince Edward Island; for Sydney, Cape Breton; and for Quebec. The "Inman" steamer for Liverpool calls at Halifax every fortnight.

CAPE BRETON.

The traveller in this direction should not return to his home without making a visit to the Island of Cape Breton, where is to be found some of the most magnificent scenery on this continent.

"Bras d'Or" lake, an inland sea of salt water, covering an area of 500 square miles, and surrounded by lofty and abrupt promontories and precipices, is alone well worthy a visit from the artist or tourist. At the Margaree River, on the southern shore of the island, is found the finest trout-fishing known, and in June this locality is much frequented by British officers from Quebec and Montreal, in pursuit of this exciting sport.

TRIP TO THE UPPER LAKES.

As this trip will be fully described in the Western Tour, where it properly belongs, we will merely allude to its most prominent features.

The best point of departure is *Detroit, Michigan*, reached by Grand Trunk or Great Western Railway. (*See* page 256.)

The steamers running to Lake Superior are, with but one or two exceptions, screw-steamers elegantly fitted up, and in most cases supplied with a good brass and string band, nothing being omitted which will conduce to the comfort of the passengers. The route is up the *Detroit River*, across *Lake St. Clair*, and thence up the St. Clair River to *Lake Huron*, which is traversed throughout its entire length.

Mackinaw, in the Straits of Mackinaw, is a charming island, rich in natural attractions. It is provided with very good hotels.

Sault Ste. Marie, a village at the Falls of the river Ste. Marie, is where steamers and vessels pass into Lake Superior through the great ship-canal, which is blasted from the solid rock.

The steamers in making the round trip stop long enough at all places of interest to allow passengers to visit the copper and iron mines and other desirable points. Passengers will find good hotels at all the principal places, with competent guides if they wish them.

SKELETON TOURS.

₊ THE following trips have been arranged with a view to informing the tourist how to see the most desirable places in the country, in the most economical and expeditious manner. For many of the tours given, those where prices are mentioned, excursion tickets for the round trip are issued by the railroad companies, which may be obtained at any of the general ticket-offices.

Grand Round Trips from New York.

I. *Via* Hudson River Railway, People's or Day Line of Steamers to Albany, and New York Central Railway to Niagara Falls; rail or steamer from Niagara Falls to Toronto; Grand Trunk Railway or Royal Mail Line of Steamers on Lake Ontario and River St. Lawrence, passing Thousand Islands and Rapids by daylight to Montreal; Grand Trunk Railway or Royal Mail Line of Steamers to Quebec; Grand Trunk Railway to Sherbrooke; stage to Lake Memphremagog; steamer on lake to Newport; rail to Wells River Junction and Littleton; stage to Profile House, Crawford House, and Littleton, including White Mountains and Franconia Hills; rail to Concord, Nashua, and Boston; Boston to New York, *via* rail and Sound steamers. Fare, $58.45.

II. Same as I. to Montreal, thence by rail to St. Johns and Burlington; Lake Champlain steamers to Ticonderoga and Lake George; rail to Saratoga and Albany; and Day Line of Steamers on Hudson River to New York. Fare, $37.85.

III. Same as I. to Montreal, thence Grand Trunk Railway to Gorham (White Mountains); stage to Glen House; stage to Crawford House; stage to Profile House; stage to Littleton; rail to White River Junction and Burlington; steamer on Lake Champlain to Ticonderoga; and steamer on Lake George to Caldwell; stage to Moreau; and rail to Saratoga Springs. Fare, $57.20.

IV. Same as I. to Montreal, thence Grand Trunk Railway to Portland; rail or steamer to Boston; and Boston to New York *via* rail, and any of the lines of Sound steamers. Fare, $37.45.

V. Same as I. to Montreal, thence by rail to Plattsburg; Lake Champlain steamers to Whitehall; rail to Saratoga Springs; rail to Rutland, Bellows Falls (passing through the Green Mountains), Fitchburg, and Boston. Fare, $36.45.

VI. Same as I. to Wells River Junction, thence down Connecticut valley to New Haven by rail; rail or Sound steamer to New York.

VII. Same as VI. to Brattleboro, Vt., thence rail to New London, and steamer or rail to New York.

VIII. New York to Niagara Falls *via* Erie Railway, thence as in II. to Saratoga and Albany, N. Y. Central Railway, and Grand Trunk or Great Western Railway to Detroit; steamer from Detroit to all points on Lake Superior; rail from Marquette to Escanawba on Green Bay, Wisconsin; steamer from Escanawba to Green Bay; rail from Green Bay to Chicago; rail to Pittsburg and through coal and iron regions of Pennsylvania and New Jersey to New York.

IX. Same as I. to Albany; Albany and Susquehanna Railway to Sharon Springs; thence *via* Binghamton and Buffalo to Niagara Falls, returning *via* Buffalo and Erie Railway. Fare, $18.85.

X. *Via* Erie Railway to Ithaca; steamers on Cayuga Lake to Cayuga; N. Y. Central Railway to Niagara Falls, and re-

SKELETON TOURS.

turn to New York *via* Buffalo and Erie Railway. Fare, $17.80.

XI. *Via* Erie Railway to Watkins; steamers on Seneca Lake to Geneva; N. Y. Central Railway to Niagara Falls, and return to New York *via* Buffalo and Erie Railway. Fare, $17.75.

XII. *Via* Erie Railway to Cleveland; Cleveland, Detroit and Lake Superior Line of steamers to Marquette, Portage Lake and Duluth, passing the famous Pictured Rocks, the Falls of Ste. Marie, and the celebrated Iron Mountains of that region; thence to New York *via* Green Bay, Fort Howard, Chicago, Detroit, Niagara Falls, and Buffalo. Fare, $68.60.

XIII. *Via* Erie Railway to Cleveland; Cleveland, Detroit, and Lake Superior Line of Steamers to Marquette and Portage Lake, and Duluth, and back to Sarnia, Canada; thence *via* Grand Trunk Railway and N. Y. Central Railways to Albany; and thence to New York *via* rail or Hudson River steamer.

XIV. *Via* Erie Railway to Cleveland, Ohio; steamers to Detroit, Mich.; rail *via* Chicago, Ill., to Green Bay; steamer to Escanawba; rail to Marquette, Lake Superior; steamer down Lakes Superior and Huron to Sarnia; thence return to New York as in XI. Fare, $65.40.

Short Round Trips from New York.

I. *Via* Hudson River steamers to Albany, Albany and Susquehanna Railway to Sharon Springs; returning to New York *via* Binghamton and Erie Railway. Fare, $10.50.

II. *Via* Hudson River steamers to Albany, Albany and Susquehanna Railway to Sharon Springs, and thence *via* Binghamton and Owego to Ithaca, returning to New York *via* Erie Railway. Fare, $13.40.

III. *Via* Erie Railway to Owego, and thence direct to Cayuga *via* Ithaca and steamers on Cayuga Lake; returning to New York by rail to Geneva; steamers on Seneca Lake to Watkins; rail to Elmira, and thence *via* Erie Railway. Fare, $14.30.

IV. *Via* Hudson River steamer to Catskill, thence by steamer to Hudson; rail to Hoosic Falls and Tunnel; thence by Troy and Boston, Housatonic, and New York and New Haven Railways, to New York.

V. *Via* Erie Railway to Binghamton, Delaware, Lackawanna, and Western Railway to Scranton, Delaware Water-Gap, and Manunka Chunk; thence by Morris and Essex Division of same road to New York. This trip includes some of the finest mountain and river scenery in the country.

VI. *Via* Central Railway of New Jersey to Easton, Pa.; Lehigh Valley Railway to Wilkesbarre, the Wyoming Valley, and Scranton; returning as in preceding trip *via* Delaware Water-Gap and Manunka Chunk.

VII. *Via* steamer or rail to Long Branch, rail to Philadelphia; thence to Williamsport, Pa., by the route described on page 125; thence by Northern Central Railway to Elmira, Erie Railway to Binghamton, returning to New York as in trip V.

VIII. *Via* Fall River steamer to Newport, rail to Boston, steamer to Portsmouth, N. H., and Isles of Shoals; steamer to Portland, Me.; steamer to Mount Desert Island; steamer to Bangor, Me.; rail and stage to Moosehead Lake. Return by rail, *via* Springfield.

IX. Steamer to Bridgeport, Conn.; Housatonic Railway to Pittsfield; rail to Boston and New Bedford; steamer to Martha's Vineyard and Nantucket; steamer to Newport and Providence, R. I. Return by Fall River Line of steamers.

X. Rail to White River Junction, Vt.; thence by rail to Burlington, Vt.; trip on Lake Champlain in steamer to Vergennes; rail to Bellows Falls and New London. Return by Sound steamers.

XI. Rail to Lake Memphremagog; stage to Sherbrooke; rail to Portland; steamer to Boston; rail to New York.

Trips to the White Mountains.

Trips through the White Mountains are given on page 214—the tourist having the choice of ten different routes, besides those already mentioned in the "Grand Round Trips."

SKELETON TOURS.

Trips from Boston.

As Boston is included in the trips numbered **I.**, **IV.**, and **V.** of New York, any of the three can be made from that city at the same price.

Any of the other New York trips can be made from Boston, the extra expense being the fare by steamer or rail from Boston to New York.

(For a pleasant short trip from Boston, see Route VIII. of MASSACHUSETTS, page 190.)

Trips from Philadelphia.

All the New York trips, at the additional expense of the fare between the two cities.

I. *Via* Belvidere Delaware Railway to Easton; thence, as in short trip No. VI. from New York, extending the return trip *via* New York to Long Branch, and thence by rail back to Philadelphia.

II. *Via* Pennsylvania Central Railway (Route I. of PENNSYLVANIA, p. 118) to Pittsburg; thence by Pittsburg and Erie Railway to Erie, returning *via* Philadelphia and Erie Railway. (*See* page 128.) This is a superb trip.

III. *Via* Pennsylvania Central Railway to Harrisburg, Northern Central and Branch to Gettysburg, back to Harrisburg by same road; thence to Williamsport by Northern Central to Wilkesbarre, the Wyoming Valley and Scranton, by Lackawanna and Bloomsburg Railway, and return to Philadelphia *via* Delaware, Lackawanna, and Western, and Belvidere Delaware Railways.

IV. *Via* Philadelphia & Reading Railway to Reading, Lebanon Valley Branch to Harrisburg, Northern Central to Northumberland, Lackawanna and Bloomsburg to Scranton, Lehigh Valley to Easton, and Belvidere Delaware to Philadelphia.

V. *Via* Philadelphia and Erie Railway to Lockhaven, Tyrone and Lockhaven Railway to Tyrone. Return by Pennsylvania Central.

VI. *Via* rail to Baltimore, Md., Northern Central and Gettysburg Railways to Gettysburg; Northern Central and Lebanon Valley to Reading. Return by Philadelphia and Reading Railway.

VII. *Via* Pennsylvania Central Railway to Huntingdon, Huntingdon and Broad Top Railway to Broad Top and Dallas Mountains and Bedford Springs, back to Huntingdon; Pennsylvania Central to Tyrone; Tyrone and Lockhaven to Lockhaven, and Philadelphia and Erie to Philadelphia.

By consulting the map and the chapter on Pennsylvania, many pleasant variations of these routes can be made.

In all the foregoing skeleton trips fares have been omitted except where the railway companies have advertised season excursion tickets, though it is very probable that such tickets will be issued for many of the other trips. Time-tables and rates, however, will always be found in APPLETONS' RAILWAY GUIDE, which is published semi-monthly, and which is an almost indispensable aid to the tourist.

Tickets can be procured at the principal ticket-offices of the roads interested in the excursion system.

INDEX.

NORTHERN AND EASTERN TOUR.

DAYS, FALLS, ISLANDS, LAKES, MOUNTAINS, RIVERS, AND VALLEYS, ARE INDEXED IN GROUPS.

Adirondack Region, Routes into, 61.
Afton, N. Y., 75.
Albany, N, Y., 48.
Albion, N. Y., 69.
Alburtis, Pa., 139.
Alleghany City, Pa., 125.
Allentown, Pa., 134, 139.
Alton, Me., 243.
Alton Bay, N. H., 215.
Altoona, Pa., 122.
Amenia, N. Y., 52.
Amherst, Mass., 189.
Amherst, N. H., 204.
Amherst College, 187, 189.
Andover, Mass., 199.
Andover, N. H., 217.
Ansonia, Conn., 150.
Arlington, Vt., 233.
Arnprior, Can., 264.
Arthabaska, Can., 252.
Ashbury, N. J., 95.
Ashburnham, Mass., 202.
Ashland, N. H., 206.
Ashley Falls, Mass., 181.
Atco, N. J., 93.
Athens, N. Y., 48.
Athol, Mass., 202.
Atlantic City, N. J., 93.
Attica, N. Y., 82.
Attleborough, Mass., 180, 193.
Auburn, N. Y., 68.
Augusta, Me., 240.
Auburn, Pa., 127.
Avon, N. Y., 82.
Avon, Conn., 157.
Aylmer, Can., 264.

Babylon, L. I., 87.
Bainbridge, N. Y., 75.
Baltic, Conn., 160.
Bangor, Me., 241.
Bar Harbor, Me., 243.
Barnet, Vt., 225.
Barton, Vt., 225.
Barton Landing, Vt., 225.
Bartonsville, Vt., 231.
Bath, N. Y., 82.
Bath, N. H., 206.

Bath, Me., 240.
Batavia, N. Y., 64.
BAY.
Baie des Rochers, Can., 261.
Belfast, Me., 244.
Burlington, Can., 253.
Casco, Me., 238.
Ha-ha, Can., 266.
Minas, N. S., 269.
Murray, Can., 261.
Narraganset, R. I., Trip down, 163.
New York, Trip down, 29.
Bay Side, L. I., 37.
Beacon Falls, Conn., 150.
Belchertown, Mass., 189.
Belfast, Me., 244.
Belgrade, Me., 241.
Belleville, Can., 255.
Bellows Falls, Vt., 218,223,231.
Belvidere, N. J., 99.
Bennington, Vt., 232.
Bergen Point, N. J., 94.
Berlin, Conn., 154.
Bethel, Me., 239.
Bethel, Vt., 227.
Bethlehem, Pa., 133, 134, 139.
Bethlehem, N. H., 209.
Beverly, Mass., 197.
Biddeford, Me., 236.
Billerica, Mass., 194.
Binghamton, N. Y., 80.
Birmingham, Pa., 125.
Black Rock, Conn., 145.
Blairsville Intersec., Pa., 122.
Bloomingdale, N. Y., 38.
Bloomsburg, N. J., 95.
Bold Head Cliff, Me., 236.
Bolton, Vt., 229.
Boonton, N. J., 96.
Bordentown, N. J., 91.
Boscawen, N. H., 216.
Boston, Mass., 168.
Bothwell, Can., 258.
Bound Brook, N. J., 94.
Bowdoin College, Me., 239.
Bradford, Mass., 200.
Bradford, Vt., 224.
Braintree, Mass., 190.

Braintree, Vt., 227.
Brandon, Vt., 232.
Branford, Conn., 147.
Brattleboro, Vt., 188, 189, 223.
Brewster's, N. Y., 52.
Bridgeport, Conn., 146, 150, 152, 181.
Bridgewater, Mass., 191.
Brighton, Mass., 177.
Brinton's, Pa., 123.
Bristol, Pa., 90.
Bristol, Conn., 159.
Bristol, R. I., 164.
Bristol, N. H., 217.
British Provinces, 249.
Broadway, N. J., 97.
Brockport, N. Y., 69.
Brockville, Can., 255.
Brookfield, Conn., 149, 152.
Brookfield, Mass., 179.
Brookline, Mass., 177.
Brooklyn, N. Y., 31.
Brown University, 162.
Brushville, L. I., 35.
Brunswick, Me., 239.
Buckingham, Can., 263.
Buffalo, N. Y., 65.
Bull's Ferry, N. Y., 38.
Burlington, N. J., 91.
Burlington, Vt., 57, 229, 232.

Caconha, Can., 261.
Calais, Me., 244.
Caldwell, N. Y., 54.
Caldwell's Landing, N. Y., 42.
Callicoon, N. Y., 79.
Camden, N. J., 91.
Cameron, Pa., 129.
Canaan, Conn., 152.
Canaan, N. H., 218.
Canandaigua, N. Y., 69.
Candia, N. H., 221.
Canton, Mass., 180, 193.
Cap Desespoir, Can., 261.
CAPE.
  Elizabeth, Me., 237.
  May, N. J., 98.
  Neddick, Me., 236.
  Vincent, N. Y., 85.

275

INDEX.

Carillon, Can., 263.
Carlisle, Pa., 140.
Carmel, Me., 241.
Cascade Bridge, N. Y., 79.
Castine, Me., 244.
Castleton, Vt., 85, 233.
Catasauqua. Pa., 135.
Catawissa, Pa., 127.
Catskill (see K).
Caughnawaga, Can., 260.
CAVE.
 Arlington, Vt., 233.
 Cathedral, N. H., 216.
 Clarendon, Vt., 231.
 Howes, N. Y., 75.
 Oven, N. H., 221.
Cayuga, N. Y., 68.
Cedarmere, L. I., 36.
Centre Harbor, N. H., 205, 215.
Chambersburg, Pa., 140.
Charlemont, Mass., 202.
Charlestown, N. H., 223.
Charlotte, Vt., 232.
Chateaugay Woods, N. Y. Routes into, 61.
Chatham, N. Y., 52.
Chatham, N. J., 96.
Chatham, Can., 258.
Chatham Four Corners, N. Y., 84.
Chat's Portage, Can., 264.
Chelsea, Mass., 195.
Chelsea Beach, Mass., 177.
Cherry Valley, N. Y., 66.
Cheshire, Mass., 184.
Cheshire, Conn., 156.
Chester, Mass., 201.
Chester, N. J., 96.
Chester, Vt., 231.
Chicopee, Mass., 185.
Chittenango, N. Y., 63.
Christiana, Pa., 119.
Claremont, N. H., 219.
Claremont, Vt., 223.
Clarendon, Vt., 231.
Clarksville, Pa., 131.
Clinton, N. J., 94.
Clinton, Me., 241.
Coatesville, Pa., 119.
Cobleskill, N. Y., 75.
Cobourg, Can., 255.
Cohasset, Mass., 190.
Cold Spring, N. Y., 44.
Colchester, Vt., 229.
Collins, N. Y., 75.
Collingwood, Can., 256.
Collinsville, Conn., 156.
Columbia, Pa., 119.
Columbia Cross Roads, Pa., 143.
Concord, Mass., 194.
Concord, N. H., 201, 216, 221.
Convent Station, N. J., 96.
Conway, N. H., 215.
Cooperstown. N. Y., 66.
Cornish, N. H., 219.
Corning, N. Y., 81.
Cornwall, Can., 255, 259.
Cornwall Bridge, Conn., 152.
Cornwall Landing, N. Y., 44.
Corry, Pa., 130.
Coteau du Lac, Can., 259.
Coventry, Vt., 225.

Coxsackie, N. Y., 48.
Crawford, N. J., 94.
Cranston, R. I., 164.
Crawford House, N. H., 209.
Croton, N. Y., 41.
Croton Falls, N. Y., 51.
Crown Point, N. Y., 57.

Dalton, Mass., 201.
Danbury, Conn., 149.
Danielsonville, Conn., 159.
Danville, Pa., 127, 139.
Danville Junc., Me., 239, 241.
Dartmouth College, N. H., 218.
Daysville, Conn., 159.
Deal, N. J., 93.
Deerfield, Mass, 187.
De Kalb Junction, N. Y., 85.
Delaware, N. J., 137.
Denville, N. J., 96.
Deposit, N. Y., 79.
Derby, Conn., 150.
Detroit, Mich, 256, 258.
Dexter, Me., 241.
Dickinson's Landing, Can., 259.
Dighton, Mass, 191.
Dillerville, Pa., 119.
Dobb's Ferry, N. Y., 40.
Dominion of Canada, 247.
Doucet's Landing, Can., 260.
Dover, N. J., 96.
Dover, N. H., 214.
Dover, Me., 243.
Dover Plains, N. Y., 52.
Downington, Pa., 119.
Drakesville, N. J., 96.
Dummerston, Vt., 223.
Duncannon, Pa., 121.
Dundas, Can., 258.
Dunkirk, N. Y., 81.
Dunnellen, N. J., 94.
Dunning, Pa., 137.
Dunstable, Mass., 195.
Durham, N. H., 214.

Eagle Bridge, N. Y., 85.
Eagle Cliff, N. H., 207.
East Andover, N. H., 217.
East Dorset, Vt., 233.
East Hampton, L. I., 36.
Easthampton, Mass., 157, 187.
East Hartford, Conn., 159.
East Haven, Conn., 147.
East Haverhill, N. H., 206.
East Liberty, Pa., 125.
East Mahanoy Junction, Pa., 127.
Easton, Pa., 134, 139.
Eastport, Me., 241.
East Putney, Vt., 223.
East Salisbury, Mass., 199.
East Swanton, Vt., 230.
East Wilton, Me., 244.
East Woburn, Mass., 194.
Elmira, N. Y., 81, 143.
Elizabeth, N. J., 88.
Elizabethport, N. J., 91.
Emporium, Pa., 129.
Enfield, N. H., 218.
Erie, Pa., 130.
Erving, Mass., 202.

Essex Junction, Vt., 229.
Exeter, N. H., 214.

Factoryville, Pa., 138.
Fairfield, Conn., 145.
Fair Haven, Conn., 147.
Fairlee, Vt., 224.
Fairview, Pa., 136.
FALLS.
 Artist's, N. H., 216.
 Barre's, N. H., 204.
 Bash-Bish, Conn., 153.
 Beard's, Vt., 224.
 Berlin, N. H., 213, 221.
 Black River, Vt., 231.
 Bolton, Vt., 229.
 Buttermilk, N. Y., 43.
 Calumet, Can., 264.
 Canaan, Conn., 153.
 Chats, Can., 264.
 Chaudière (Ottawa), Can., 248, 264.
 Chaudière (Quebec), Can., 248, 252.
 Cocheco, N. H., 215.
 Corinth, N. Y., 61.
 Crystal Cascade, N. H., 212.
 Dodge's, Vt., 224.
 Du Lièvre, Can., 263.
 Du Loup, Can., 261.
 Emerson, Me., 240.
 Fifteen miles of the Conn., Vt., 225.
 Flume, N. H., 208.
 Foxwell's, Me., 237.
 Genesee, N. Y., 64.
 Georgiana, N. H., 209.
 Gibbs, N. H., 210.
 Glen Ellis, N. H., 212.
 Glen's, N. Y., 54.
 Goodrich, N. H., 212.
 Grand-Mère, Can., 260.
 Hadley, Mass., 185.
 Harvard, N. H., 209.
 Jackson, N. H., 212.
 Kaaterskill, N. Y., 46.
 Lamoille, Vt., 230.
 Little Chaudière, Can., 264.
 Livermore, N. H., 206.
 Lower Ammonoosuc, N. H., 209.
 McIndoe's, Vt., 224.
 Mascomy, N. H., 218.
 Moer's, Pa., 135.
 Montmorenci, Can., 248, 251.
 Niagara, N. Y., 70, 248.
 Norton's, Conn., 153.
 Otta Queechee, Vt., 224.
 Otter Creek, Vt., 232.
 Passaic, N. J., 98.
 Passumpsic, Vt., 225.
 Portage, N. Y., 82.
 Rapids of the St. Lawrence, Can., 259.
 Rideau, Can., 248, 264.
 Rumford, Me., 239.
 Saco, Me., 236.
 Ste. Anne's, Can., 248, 251.
 Saint John, Can., 261.
 Sawkill, N. Y., 78.
 Screw-Auger, Me., 239.
 Sebasticook, Me., 241.
 Shawanegan, Can., 248, 264.

INDEX.

FALLS.
Silver Cascade, N. H., 211.
Sparkling Cascade, N. H., 212.
Sutherland, Vt., 231.
Sylvan Glade Cataract, 212.
Taghkanic, N. Y., 68, 83.
Thompson's, N. H., 212.
Ticonic, Me., 240.
Trenton, N. Y., 66.
Turner's, Mass., 188, 202.
Walker's, N. H., 208.
Winooski, Vt., 229.
Yantic, Conn., 158.
Fall River, Mass., 191.
Falls Village, Conn., 152.
Farmingdale, N. J., 93.
Farmington, Conn., 156.
Farmington, N. H., 215.
Farmington, Me., 244.
Far Rockaway, L. I., 37.
Fisherville, N. H., 216.
Fishkill Landing, N. Y., 44.
Fitchburg, Mass., 190, 194, 201, 218.
Fitzwilliam, N. H., 218.
Flatbush, L. I., 37.
Flushing, L. I., 37.
Fordham, N. Y., 51.
Fort Adams, R. I., 165.
Fort Lee, N. J., 38.
Fort Plains, N. Y., 63.
Fort Washington, N. Y., 39.
Foxborough, Mass., 180.
Foxcroft, Me., 243.
Framingham, Mass., 179.
Frankfort, N. Y., 63.
Franklin, N. H., 216.
Franklin, Pa., 132.
Freehold, Pa., 130.
Freeport, Pa., 123.
Frederickton, N. B., 268.

Gainesville, N. Y., 83.
Gallitzin, Pa., 122.
Gap, Pa., 119.
Gardiner, Me., 240.
Gardner, Mass., 202.
Garrison's, N. Y., 43.
Gaspé, Can., 261.
Gaspee Point, R. I., 162.
Gassett's, Vt., 231.
Geneva, N. Y., 69.
Georgia, Vt., 230.
Georgetown, Mass., 201.
Georgeville, Vt., 226.
Gettysburg, Pa., 141.
Giant's Grave, N. H., 200.
Gilead, Me., 239.
Glen Cove, L. I., 36.
Glendale, Mass., 182.
Glen House, N. Y., 84.
Gloucester, Mass., 198.
Gold Mines, N. H., 207.
Gorham, N. H., 213, 221, 239.
Grafton, N. H., 217.
Granby, Conn., 157.
Grassy Point, N. Y., 42.
Gravesend, L. I., 38.
Great Barrington, Mass., 181.
Great Bend, N. Y., 80, 138.
Great Neck, L. I., 37.
Greenbush, N. Y., 49.

Greenfield, Mass., 188.
Greenland, N. H., 219, 221.
Greenport, L. I., 36.
Greensburg, Pa., 123.
Greenwich, Conn., 145.
Greenwich, R. I., 163.
Greuville, Can., 263.
Greycourt, N. Y., 78.
Grosvenor Dale, Conn., 159.
Groton, Conn., 148.
Groton Junction, Mass., 194.
Grout's Corner, Mass., 189, 202.
Guelph, Can., 256.
Guilford, Conn., 148.
Gwynedd, Pa., 133.

Hackensack, N. J., 98.
Hackettstown, N. J., 97.
Hadley, Mass., 187.
Hagerstown, Md., 140.
Hallowell, Me., 240.
Halifax, N. S., 269.
Hamburg, Pa., 127.
Hamilton, Can., 258.
Hammondsport, N. Y., 84.
Hampton Beach, N. H., 219, 220.
Hampton Falls, N. H., 219.
Hancock, N. Y., 79.
Hanover, N. H., 218.
Hanover Junction, Pa., 141.
Healdville, Vt., 231.
Hellertown, Pa., 133.
Hell Gate, N. Y., 31.
Hempstead Village, L. I., 35.
Herkimer, N. Y., 63.
High Bridge, N. J., 95.
Highlands of Navesink, N. J., 92.
Hingham, Mass., 199.
Hinsdale, N. H., 223.
Holyoke, Mass., 185.
Hookset, N. H., 204.
Hoosac Tunnel, Mass., 184, 202.
Hornellsville, N. Y., 81.
Housatonic, Mass., 181.
Howell's, N. Y., 78.
Hudson, N. Y., 47.
Hummelstown, Pa., 140.
Huntingdon, Pa., 121.
Hunt's Mill, R. I., 163.
Hyde Park, L. I., 35.
Hyde Park, N. Y., 45.
Harrisburg, Pa., 120, 140, 142.
Hartford, Conn., 151, 159.
Hartland, Vt., 224.
Hastings, N. Y., 40.
Haverhill, Mass., 200, 214.
Haverhill, N. H., 206.
Havana, N. Y., 84.
Haverstraw, N. Y., 41.
Haydenville, Mass., 157.

Indian Harbor, Conn., 145.
Indian Orchard, Mass., 178.
Ipswich, Mass., 198.
Irvineton, Pa., 129.
Irvington, N. Y., 40.
ISLAND.
Bedloe's, N. Y., 30.
Blackwell's, N. Y., 31.

ISLAND.
Campo Bello, N. B., 244.
Cape Breton, N. S., 271.
Coney, N. Y., 30, 38.
Constitution, N. Y., 43.
Crane, Can., 261.
Cushing's, Me., 238.
Diamond, N. H., 215.
Ellis, N. Y., 30.
Fire, L. I., 37.
Goose, Can., 261.
Governor's, N. Y., 29.
Grosse Isle, Can., 262.
Long, N. Y. (*See* L.)
Mackinaw, Mich., 271.
Martha's Vineyard, Mass., 192.
Mount Desert, Me., 245.
Nantucket, Mass., 192.
Nun's, Can., 259.
Plum, Mass., 199.
Randall's, N. Y., 31.
Shoals, Isles of, N. H., 219, 220.
Staten, N. Y., 30.
The Thousand of the St. Lawrence, Can., 259.
Ward's, N. Y., 31.
Island Pond, Vt., 221.
Islip, L. I., 37.
Ithaca, N. Y., 69, 83.

Jackson, N. H., 212.
Jamaica, L. I., 35, 36.
Jamesburg, N. J., 91.
Jamestown, N. Y., 130.
Jersey City, N. J., 88.
Jewett City, Conn., 158.
John Brown Tract, Routes into, 62.
Johnstown, Pa., 122.
Jonesville, Vt., 229.
Junction, N. J., 95.

Kaatskill, N. Y., 46.
Kakouna, Can., 261.
Kamouraska, Can., 262.
Kane, Pa., 129.
Katonah, N. Y., 51.
Keene, N. H., 218.
Kennebunk, Me., 236.
Kent, Conn., 152.
Kinderhook Land'g, N. Y., 48.
Kingston, N. Y., 45.
Kingston, Pa., 138.
Kingston, R. I., 162, 164.
Kingston, Can., 255.
Kirkwood, N. Y., 80.
Kiskiminetas, Pa., 123.
Kittery, Me., 236.
Knowlton's, Vt., 226.

Lachine, Can., 260.
Lackawaxen, Pa., 79.
Laconia, N. H., 205.
La Grange, Me., 243.
LAKES, PONDS, AND POOLS.
Alexander's, Conn., 159.
Alumette, Can., 264.
Austin, Vt., 234.
Avalanche, N. Y., 60.
Basin, The, N. H., 208.

277

INDEX.

LAKES, PONDS, AND POOLS.
Billington Sea, Mass., 161.
Bombazine, Vt., 231.
Bras d'Or, N. S., 271.
Bryant's, Me., 239.
Budd's, N. J., 96.
Canandaigua, N. Y., 69.
Cayuga, N. Y., 68.
Chabanakongkomum, Mass., 190.
Champlain, N. Y., 56, 229.
Concert, Vt., 226.
Crooked, or Keuka, N. Y., 84.
Crystal, Vt., 225.
Dunmore, Vt., 232.
Eagle, N. H., 217.
Echo, N. H., 207, 216.
Emerald Pool, N. H., 212.
Enfield, N. H., 218.
Fresh, Mass., 177.
Garnet Pools, N. H., 212.
George, N. Y., 54.
Grand, Me., 245.
Greenwood, N. Y., and N. J., 77.
Heart, N. H., 218.
Henderson, N. Y., 60.
Hoptacong, N. J., 96.
Lac des Chats, Can., 264.
Long, N. Y., 60.
Long, Conn., 152.
Lough Neah, N. Y., 59.
Luzerne, N. Y., 60.
Macopin, N. Y., 77.
Mahopac, N. Y., 51.
Mashapang, Conn., 159.
Massapoag, Mass., 193.
Memphremagog, Vt., 226.
Merrymeeting, N. H., 215.
Moosehead, Me., 243, 245.
Newfound, N. H., 217.
Oneida, N. Y., 63.
Onondaga, N. Y., 64.
Otsego, N. Y., 66.
Owasco, N. Y., 68.
Pleasant, N. Y., 60.
Pool, The, N. H., 209.
Profile, N. H., 208.
Punkapog, Mass., 193.
Quinsigamond, Mass., 179.
Rockland, N. Y., 41.
Ronkonkoma, L. I., 36.
Rossignol, N. S., 269.
Saint Charles, Can., 251.
St. Francis, Can., 259.
Saint Louis, Can., 259.
Saint Peter, Can., 260.
Saint Regis, N. Y., 60.
Saltonstall, Conn., 146.
Sanford, N. Y., 60.
Saranac, The, N. Y., 59.
Sebago, Me., 245.
Seneca, N. Y., 69.
Simcoe, Can., 255.
Sinnipink, N. Y., 42.
Six-mile, N. H., 215.
Skeneateles, N. Y., 68.
Spectacle, Conn., 152.
Squam, N. H., 205, 206.
Stockbridge Bowl, Mass., 182
Temisconata, Can., 261.

LAKES, PONDS, AND POOLS.
Tupper's, N. Y., 59.
Twin, Conn., 153.
Umbagog, Me., 245.
Wawayandah, N. Y., 77.
Webster's Pond, N. H., 217.
Wenham, Mass., 198.
White Fish, Can., 263.
Winnebago, N. H., 206.
Winnipiscogee, N. H., 205, 215.
Willoughby, Vt., 225.
Lake Village, N. H., 205.
Lambertville, N. J., 99.
Lancaster, Pa., 119.
Landisville, Pa., 120.
Lanesborough, Mass., 184.
Landsdale, Pa., 133.
Lansingburg, N. Y., 85.
Lawrence, Mass., 200.
Leaman Place, Pa., 119.
Lebanon, Pa., 140.
Lebanon, N. J., 94.
Lebanon, N. H., 218.
Lee, Mass., 182.
Leechburg, Pa., 123.
Leeds, Me., 241, 244.
Lehighton, Pa., 135.
Lehigh University, Pa., 133.
Lehigh Water-Gap, Pa., 135.
Lenox, Mass., 183.
Leominster, Mass., 194.
Leonia, N. J., 97.
Leverett, Mass., 189.
Lewiston, Me., 241.
Lewistown, Pa., 121.
Lexington, Mass., 194.
Lime Ridge, Pa., 134, 139.
Linden, N. J., 89.
Lisbon, N. H., 207.
Litchfield, Conn., 151.
Little Falls, N. Y., 63.
Littleton, N. H., 207.
Livermore Falls, Me., 244.
Lockport, N. Y., 69.
Lockhaven, Pa., 128.
London, Can., 256, 258.
Long Branch, N. J., 92.
LONG ISLAND, N. Y.
 Brooklyn, 31.
 Description, 31.
 Trip No. 1, 35.
  "   " 2, 36.
  "   " 3, 37.
  "   " 4, 38.
Longwood, Mass., 177.
L'Original, Can., 263.
Lowell, Mass., 194.
Lower Franklin, N. H., 217.
Ludlow, Vt., 231.
Lyndonville, Vt., 225.
Lynn, Mass., 195.
Lyons, Pa., 139.

McIndoe's, Vt., 224.
McLeran's, Vt., 225.
Maine, 235.
Madison, N. J., 96.
Malden, Mass., 199.
Mamaroneck, N. Y., 145.
Manchester, Conn., 150.
Manchester, Vt., 233.
Manchester, N. H., 204, 221.

Mansfield, Conn., 158.
Manunka Chunk, N. J., 137.
Marblehead, Mass., 197.
Marblehead Neck, Mass., 197.
Marked Rock, R. I., 163.
Marshfield, Mass., 191.
Martha's Vineyard, Mass., 192.
Massachusetts, 167.
Mattawamkeag, Me., 242.
Mattituck, L. I., 36.
Mauch Chunk, Pa., 135.
Meadville, Pa., 130, 132.
Mechanic Falls, Me., 239.
Medford, Mass., 194.
Medina, N. Y., 69.
Meredith, N. H., 206.
Meriden, Conn., 153.
Metis, Can., 261.
Middleborough, Mass., 192.
Middlebury, Vt., 232.
Middlefield, Mass., 201.
Middlesex, Vt., 228.
Middletown, Conn., 154.
Middletown, N. Y., 78.
Middletown, Pa., 120.
Mifflin, Pa., 121.
Milan, N. H., 221.
Milburn, N. J., 95.
Milford, Conn., 146.
Milford, Me., 242.
Millerton, N. Y., 52.
Milo, Me., 243.
Milton, Pa., 127, 128.
Milton, Vt., 230.
Monmouth, Me., 241.
Monmouth Junc., N. J., 89.
Monroe, N. Y., 78.
Monson, Mass., 189.
Montpelier, Vt., 228.
Montpelier Junction, Vt., 228.
Montague, Mass., 202.
Montreal, Canada, 230, 252.
Morristown, N. J., 96.
Moscow, Pa., 137.
MOUNTAIN RANGES.
 Adirondack, 58, 60, 229.
 Alleghanies, Pa., 122.
 Blue, Pa., 137.
 Dixville Hills, N. H., 221.
 Franconia, N. H., 207.
 Green, Can., 248.
 Green, Vt., 228.
 Highlands, N. Y., 42.
 Kaatskill, N. Y., 46.
 Kittatinny, Pa., 137.
 Mealy, Can., 248.
 Taconic, Conn., 153.
 West, Vt., 233.
 White, N. H., 207.
 White, N. H. Ten Routes to the, 214.
MOUNTAIN.
 Adams, N. H., 211.
 Agamenticus, Me., 236.
 Anthony, Vt., 233.
 Anthony's Nose, N. Y., 42.
 Ascutney, Vt., 233.
 Bald, N. H., 206, 208.
 Belknap, N. H., 205, 215.
 Betty, N. H., 215.
 Black, Vt., 223.
 Blue Hill, Mass., 180.

INDEX.

Mountain.
Brace, Conn., 154.
Breakneck, N. Y., 43.
Burke, Vt., 223.
Butter Hill, or Storm King, N. Y., 44.
Camel's Hump, Vt., 229.
Cape Horn, N. H., 221.
Chicorua, N. H., 205.
Chocorua, N. H., 215.
Clay, N. H., 212.
Clinton, N. H., 210.
Crawford, N. H., 212.
Cro' Nest, N. Y., 44.
Cropple Crown, N. H., 215.
Deerfield, Mass., 188.
Dorset, Vt., 233.
Doublehead, N. H., 212.
Dunderberg, N. Y., 42.
Elephantis, Vt., 226.
Equinox, Vt., 233.
Fall, N. H., 218.
Franklin, N. H., 210.
Gap, N. H., 218.
Giant Stairs, N. H., 212.
Glass Face, Me., 239.
Glass Hill, N. H., 217.
Grey Lock, Mass., 184.
Hayes, N. H., 213.
Holyoke, Mass., 186.
Independence, Vt., 57.
Iron, N. Y., 212.
Jay Peak, Vt., 225, 226.
Jefferson, N. H., 211.
Katahdin, Me., 245.
Kearsarge, N. H., 217.
Killington Peak, Vt., 231.
Kimo, Me., 245.
Lafayette, N. H., 210.
Madison, N. H., 211-213, 213.
Major, N. H., 205.
Mansfield, Vt., 229.
Marcy, or "Tahawus," N. Y., 60.
Marlborough, N. H., 218.
Mine, N. H., 223.
Moat, N. H., 216.
Monroe, N. H., 210.
Monument, Mass., 182.
Mooschillock, N. H., 206.
Moriah, N. H., 213.
North, N. Y., 46.
Ossipee, N. H., 205.
Owl's Head, Vt., 226.
Pequaket, N. H., 216, 217.
Pinnacle, N. H., 204.
Pisgah, Pa., 135.
Pleasant, N. H., 210.
Profile, N. H., 207.
Prospect, N. H., 206.
Pulaski, Vt., 206, 224.
Ragged, N. H., 217.
Randolph Hill, N. H., 212.
Rattlesnake, Mass., 182.
Rattlesnake, N. H., 206.
Red, Vt., 233.
Red Hill, N. H., 205.
Resolution, N. H., 212.
Riga, Conn., 152.
Saddle, Mass., 184.
Sandwich, N. H., 215.
Schooley's, N. J., 97.
Shawangunk, N. Y., 78.

Mountain.
South, N. Y., 46.
Squam, N. H., 215.
Straw's, N. H., 215.
Sugar Loaf, Mass., 187.
Sugar Loaf, Me., 246.
Surprise, N. H., 213.
Tin, N. H., 212.
Toby, Mass., 188.
Tom, Mass., 186.
Torn, N. Y., 77.
Tumble-down Dick, N. H., 215.
Wantasticut, N. H., 223.
Warner, Mass., 188.
Washington, N. H., ascent from Crawford House, 210.
Washington, N. H., ascent from Glen House, 213.
White Cap, Me., 239.
Willard, N. H., 210.
Willey, N. H., 211.
Mount Hope, R. I., 164.
Mount Bethel, Pa., 137.
Mount Holly, Vt., 231.
Mount Joy, Pa., 120.
Mount St. Vincent, N. Y., 39.
Mount Union Station, N. Y., 121.
Mount Vernon, N. Y., 145.
Murray Bay, Can., 261.
Myrick's, Mass., 192.
Mystic, Conn., 149.

Nahant, Mass., 177, 196.
Nantasket, Mass., 190.
Nantasket Beach, Mass., 177.
Nantucket, Mass., 192.
Narragansett Pier, R. I., 163.
Narrowsburg, N. Y., 79.
Nashua, N. H., 204.
Natic, R. I., 164.
Natick, Mass, 179.
Natural Bridge, Mass., 184.
Naugatuck, Conn., 150.
Neponset, Mass., 190.
Newark, N. J., 95.
New Britain, Conn., 159.
New Brunswick, N. J., 89.
New Brunswick, Province of, 266.
Newburg, N. Y., 44.
Newburg Junction, N. Y., 77.
Newbury, Vt., 206, 224.
Newburyport, Mass., 198.
New Bedford, Mass., 192.
New Durham, N. H., 215.
New Jersey, 87.
New Gloucester, Me., 239.
New Hamburg, N. Y., 45.
New Hampshire, 203.
New Hartford, Conn., 156.
New Haven, Conn., 146, 153.
New London, Conn., 148, 157, 189.
New Market, N. H., 214.
New Market Junction, N. H., 204, 221.
New Milford, Conn., 149, 152.
Newport, Me., 241.
Newport, Pa., 121, 136.
Newport, R. I., 164.
Newport, Vt., 225, 226.

New Rochelle, N. Y., 145.
New Windsor, N. Y., 44.
New York, 5.
New York City, 6.
Norristown, Pa., 118, 126.
North Adams, Mass., 184.
Northampton, Mass., 157, 186.
North Andover, Mass., 200.
North Bennington, Vt., 232.
North Charlestown, N. H., 223.
North Chelmsford, Mass., 195.
North Conway, N. H., 216.
North Derby, Vt., 226.
Northfield, Mass., 189.
Northfield, Vt., 228.
North Hampton, N. H., 219.
North Hartland, Vt., 224.
North Haverhill, N. H., 206.
North Oxford, Mass., 190.
North Stratford, N. H., 221.
North Thetford, Vt., 224.
Northumberland, Pa., 128, 139.
Northumberland, N. H., 221.
North Webster, Mass., 190
Norton Mills, Vt., 221.
Norwalk, Conn., 145, 149.
Norwich, Conn., 157.
Norwich, Vt., 224.
Nova Scotia.
  Coast, 269.
  Description, 268.
  Game, 269.
  Rivers, Lakes, and Bays, 269.
Nunda, N. Y., 82.
Nyack, N. Y., 40.

Oakland, Pa., 137.
Oceanport, N. J., 92.
Ogdensburg, N. Y., 85.
Oil City, Pa., 132.
Oil Creek, Pa., 131.
Oil Regions, Pa., 131.
Oldtown, Me., 242.
Oneida, N. Y., 63.
Orange, N. J., 95.
Orford, Vt., 224.
Orneville, Me., 243.
Orono, Me., 242.
Oswego, N. Y., 86.
Otisville, N. Y., 78.
Ottawa, Can., 263.
Owego, N. Y., 80.
Oxford, Mass., 190.
Oxford, Me., 239.

Palatine Bridge, N. Y., 63.
Palenville, N. Y., 47.
Palmer, Mass., 178, 189.
Paoli, Pa., 118.
Paris, Can., 257, 258.
Parkesburg, Pa., 119.
Passadumkeag, Me., 242.
Passumpsic, Vt., 225.
Patchogue, L. I., 37.
Paterson, N. J., 98.
Pawtucket, R. I., 166, 180, 193.
Pea Cove, Me., 242.
Peekskill, N. Y., 42.
Pembroke, Can., 264.
Penn Haven Junction, Pa., 135.

279

INDEX.

Pennsylvania, 100.
Penn Yan, N. Y., 84.
Petersburg, Pa., 121.
Perth Amboy, N. J., 89.
Petersburg Junction, N. Y. 85, 232.
Philadelphia, Pa., 101.
Philips's Beach, Mass., 177.
Phillipsburg, N. J., 95.
Phœnixville, Pa., 126.
Piermont, N. Y., 40.
Pierrepont Manor, N. Y., 85.
Pittsburg, Pa., 123.
Pittsfield, Mass., 183, 201.
Pittsfield, Me., 241.
Pittsford, Vt., 231.
Pittston, Pa., 136, 138.
Plainfield, Conn., 159, 160.
Plainfield, N. J., 94.
Plainfield Junction, Conn., 159.
Plainville, Conn., 156, 159.
Plattsburg, N. Y., 57.
Pleasure Bay, N. J., 93.
Plymouth, Pa., 138.
Plymouth, Conn., 151.
Plymouth, Mass., 191.
Plymouth, N. H., 206.
Point Levi, Can., 252.
Point Shirley, Mass., 177.
Portage, N. Y., 82.
Portage du Fort, Can., 264.
Port Chester, N. Y., 145.
Port Clinton, Pa., 127.
Port Colburn, Can., 257.
Port Henry, N. Y., 57.
Port Hope, Can., 255.
Port Jervis, N. Y., 78.
Port Kent, N. Y., 57, 58.
Port Monmouth Pier, N. J., 92.
Portland, Me., 237.
Portsmouth, N. H., 219, 236.
Portsmouth, R. I., 165.
Pompanoosuc, Vt., 224.
Potter Place, N. H., 217.
Pottstown, Pa., 126.
Pottsville, Pa., 127.
Poughkeepsie, N. Y., 45.
Poultney, Vt., 234.
Prescott Junction, Can., 255.
Prescott's Headquarters, R. I., 164.
Princeton, N. J., 89.
Proctorsville, Vt., 231.
Profile House, N. H., 207.
Profile Rock, N. H., 208.
Providence, R. I., 162, 164, 160, 193.
Putney, Vt., 223.

Quakake, Pa., 127.
Quebec, Can., 249.
Queenstown, Can., 74.
Quincy, Mass., 190.
Quogue, L. I., 36.

Rahway, N. J., 89.
RAILWAYS.
Albany & Susquehanna, 75.
Allentown Line, 139.
Androscoggin, 243.

RAILWAYS.
Bangor and Piscataquis, 242.
Belvidere Delaware, 99.
Bennington & Rutland, 232.
Boston and Albany (Western), 201.
Boston and Lowell, 194, 203.
Boston and Maine, 199, 214.
Boston and Providence, 193.
Boston, Hartford, and Erie, 159, 164.
Camden and Amboy, 90.
Camden and Atlantic, 93.
Cape Cod, 193.
Cape Cod Central, 193.
Catawissa, 125.
Central of New Jersey, 93.
Cheshire, 193, 218.
Concord and Dover, 221.
Connecticut and Passumpsic Rivers, 222.
Connecticut River, 185.
Cumberland Valley, 140.
Danbury and Norwalk, 149.
Delaware, Lackawanna, and Western, 136.
Dover and Winnipiseogee, 214.
Eastern (Mass.), 195, 219.
Erie, 76, 97, 130, 132.
European and North American, 242.
Fitchburg, 193, 201.
Grand Trunk, 221, 238, 249.
Great Western, 257.
Housatonic, 152, 180.
Hudson and Boston, 84.
Hudson River, 50.
Lackawanna and Bloomsburg, 138.
Lake Shore, 130.
Lehigh & Susquehanna, 136.
Lehigh Valley, 134, 139.
Long Branch and Sea Shore, 91.
Maine Central, 241.
Morris and Essex, 95.
Mount Washington, 211.
Naugatuck, 150.
New Jersey, 87.
New Jersey Southern, 91.
New London Northern, 157, 188.
New Haven and Northampton, 156.
New Haven, Hartford, and Springfield, 153.
New York and Boston Express Line, 178.
New York and Harlem, 51.
New York and New Haven, 144.
New York and Oswego Midland, 86.
New York Central, 62.
Northern Central, 140.
Northern of New Jersey, 97.
Northern New Hampshire, 216.
North Pennsylvania, 133.
Norwich and Worcester, 158, 180.

RAILWAYS.
Ogdensburg and Lake Champlain, 85.
Oil Creek and Alleghany River, 132.
Old Colony and Newport, 190.
Oswego and Syracuse, 86.
Pennsylvania Central, 118.
Philadelphia and Erie, 128.
Philadelphia and Reading, 125.
Portland & Kennebec, 239.
Portland, Saco, and Portsmouth, 236.
Providence and Worcester, 165.
Providence, Warren, and Bristol, 164.
Rensselaer & Saratoga, 52.
Rome, Watertown, and Ogdensburg, 85.
Rutland & Burlington, 230.
Rutland & Washington, 85.
Shore Line, 144, 180.
Stonington and Providence, 162.
Sullivan, 219, 222.
Syracuse, Binghamton, and New York, 86.
Troy and Boston, 85.
Vermont and Canada, 226.
Vermont and Massachusetts, 188, 201.
Vermont Central, 222, 226.
Vermont Valley, 222, 230.
Warren and Franklin, 131.
West Jersey, 98.
Ramapo, N. Y., 77.
Raritan, N. J., 94.
Raymond, N. H., 221.
Raynham, Mass., 191.
Reading, Mass., 199.
Reading, Pa., 126, 140.
Readville, Mass., 180.
Red Bank, N. J., 92.
Reno, Pa., 133.
Renovo, Pa., 128.
Rhinebeck Landing, N. Y., 45.
Rhode Island, 161.
Richland, N. Y., 85.
Richmond, Can., 252.
Richmond, Me., 240.
Richmond, Vt., 229.
Ridgefield, Conn., 149.
Ridgeway, Pa., 129.
Ridley's Station, Vt., 229.
Rimouski, Can., 261.
RIVER.
Ammonoosuc, N. H., 206.
Androscoggin, N. H., 213.
Annapolis, N. S., 269.
Ausable, Walled Banks of the, N. Y., 58.
East, Trip up, 30.
Hudson, Source of the, 59.
Hudson, Trip up, 38.
Juniata, Pa., 121.
Ottawa, 262.
Ottawa, Trip up the, 262.
Rivière du Lièvre, Can., 263.
Rivière du Loup (en bas), Can., 261.

INDEX.

RIVER.
Saguenay, Can., 264.
Saguenay, Trip up the, 264.
Sainte Anne, Can., 260.
Saint John, N. B., 266.
Salmon and Trout Rivers of Canada, 262.
Susquehanna, Pa., 142.
Winooski, Vt., 228.
River Head. L. I., 36.
Rochester, N. H., 215.
Rochester, N. Y., 63.
Rockaway Beach, L. I., 37.
Rockaway, N. J., 96.
Rockport, Mass., 198.
Rockville, Conn., 160.
Rocky Point, R. I., 163.
Rome, N. Y., 63.
Rondout, N. Y., 45.
Roselle, N. J., 94.
Rouse's Point, N. Y., 85, 230.
Roxbury, Vt., 228.
Royalton, Vt., 227.
Rupert, Pa., 139.
Rumney, N. H., 206.
Rutland, Vt., 231, 233.
Rye, N. Y., 145.
Rye Beach, N. H., 219, 220.
Ryegate, Vt., 224.

Sackett's Harbor, N. Y., 85.
Saco, Me., 36.
Saint Andrew's, N. B., 268.
Sainte Anues, Can., 255.
Saint Catharines, Can., 257.
Saint John, N. B., 267.
Saint Johnsbury, Vt., 225.
Saint Johnsbury Centre, Vt., 225.
Saint Johnsville, N. Y., 63.
Saint Mary's, Pa., 129.
Saint Mary's, Can., 256.
Salamanca, N. Y., 81, 130.
Salem, Mass., 196.
Salisbury, Conn., 152.
Saltsburg, Pa., 123.
Sandwich, N. H., 215.
Sandy Hook Pier, N. J., 92.
Saranac Region, N. Y., Routes into the, 61.
Saugerties, N. Y., 45.
Sault Ste. Marie, Mich., 271.
Sawyer's Rock, N. H., 212.
Schaghticoke, N. Y., 85.
Salem, N. Y., 85.
Schenectady, N. Y., 62.
Schoharie, N. Y., 75.
Schuylkill Haven, Pa., 127.
Scotch Plains, Fanwood, N. J., 94.
Scranton, Pa., 136, 133.
Seabrook, N. H., 219.
Sellersville, Pa., 133.
Seneca Falls, N. Y., 69.
Seymour, Conn., 150.
Shark River, N. J., 93.
Sharon, Mass., 177, 193.
Sharon, Vt., 227.
Sheffield, Mass., 181.
Sheffield, Pa., 129.
Shelburne Falls, Mass., 202.
Shelburne, N. H., 221, 239.
Shelburne, Vt., 232.

Shickshinny, Pa., 139.
Schohola, Pa., 79.
Sing Sing, N. Y., 41.
Skeneateles, N. Y., 68.
Skeleton Tours, 272.
Skowhegan, Me., 210.
Slatington, Pa., 135.
Sleepy Hollow, N. Y., 46.
Sloatsburg, N. Y., 77.
Smith's Ferry, Mass., 185.
Somerville, N. J., 94.
Sorel, Can., 260.
South Abingdon, Mass., 191.
South Amboy, N. J., 91.
South Ashburnham, Mass., 194.
South Barton, Vt., 225.
South Berwick Junction, Me., 236.
South Braintree, Mass., 191.
South Charlestown, N. H., 223.
South Deerfield, Mass., 187.
South Egremont, Mass., 182.
South Hadley, Mass., 185.
Southington, Conn., 156.
South Lee, Mass., 183.
South Malden, Mass., 195.
South Manchester, Conn., 160.
South Newbury, Vt., 224.
South Norwalk, Conn., 149.
South Paris, Me., 239.
Southport, Conn., 145.
South Royalton, Vt., 227.
Southwest Harbor, Me., 243.
Southwick, Conn., 157.
Spragueville, Pa., 137.
SPRINGS.
Abenâquis, N. H., 219.
Alburg, Vt., 230.
Amherst, N. H., 204.
Arlington, Vt., 233.
Ballston, N. Y., 52.
Bedford, Pa., 121.
Bradford, N. H., 205.
Caledonia, Can., 248, 263.
Clarendon, Vt., 231.
Clifton, N. Y., 69.
Columbia, N. Y., 48.
Cressou, Pa., 122.
Elgin, Vt., 232.
Ephrata, Pa., 119, 140.
Highgate, Vt., 230.
Hopkinton, Mass., 179.
Massena, Can., 248, 259.
Newbury Sulphur, Vt., 224.
New Lebanon, N. Y., 47.
Oak Orchard Acid, N. Y., 64.
Richfield, N. Y., 66.
Saint Catharine's, Can., 248, 257.
Saint Leon, Can., 248, 260.
Sand, Mass., 184.
Saratoga, N. Y., 52.
Sharon, N. Y., 66.
Stafford, Conn., 158.
Vallonia, N. Y., 75.
Springfield, Mass., 178, 185.
Spruce Run, N. J., 95.
Stafford, Conn., 158.
Stamford, Conn., 145.
Stanhope, N. J., 96.

State Line, Mass., 201.
STEAMBOAT LINES.
Fall River, 180.
Norwich, 180.
Providence and New York, 180.
Stonington, 180.
Sterling, Conn., 160.
Sterling Junction, Mass., 190.
Stewartsville, N. J., 97.
Stockbridge, Mass., 182.
Stockport, N. Y., 48.
Stonington, Conn., 149, 162.
Stowe, Vt., 228.
Stratford, Conn., 146.
Stratford, Can., 256, 257.
Stroudsburg, Pa., 137.
Succasunna, N. J., 96.
Suffern's Station, N. Y., 77.
Summit, N. J., 95.
Summit, Vt., 231.
Sunbury, Pa., 128, 143.
Suncook, N. H., 204, 221.
Sunnyside, N. Y., 40.
Suspension Bridge, Can., 257.
Suspension Bridge, N. Y., 69.
Susquehanna, N. Y., 80.
Swampscott, Mass., 196.
Syracuse, N. Y., 63.

Tadoussac, Can., 265.
Tamaqua, Pa., 127.
Tamworth, N. H., 215.
Tarrytown, N. Y., 40.
Taunton, Mass., 191.
Terryville, Conn., 159.
Thetford, Vt., 224.
Thompson, Conn., 159.
Thorold, Can., 257.
Three Rivers, Can., 260.
Throgg's Point, L. I., 31.
Ticonderoga, N. Y., 56.
Tilton, N. H., 205.
Titusville, Pa., 133.
Tivoli, N. Y., 45.
Tobyhanna, Pa., 137.
Tolland, Conn., 158.
Tom's River, N. J., 93.
Toronto, Can., 255.
Towanda, Pa., 136.
Trenton, N. J., 90.
Trois Pistoles, Can., 261.
Troy, N. Y., 49.
Tunkhannock, Pa., 136.
Turner's, N. Y., 78.
Tyngsborough, Mass., 195.
Tyrone City, Pa., 121.

Undercliff, N. Y., 44.
Union City, Conn., 150.
Unionville, Conn., 156.
United States, 1.
Utica, N. Y., 63.

VALLEYS, GLENS, and MOUNTAIN-PASSES.
Dixville Notch, N. H., 221.
Great Gulf, N. H., 213.
Housatonic, Conn., 152.
Mountains, N. H., 212.
Notch of White Mountains, N. H., 211.

INDEX.

VALLEYS, GLENS, and MOUNTAIN-PASSES.
Pinkham Notch, White Stratton Gap, Vt., 233.
Tuckerman's Ravine, N. H., 212.
Watkins Glen, N. Y., 69, 76.
Wyoming, Pa., 138.
Valley Forge, Pa., 126.
Valley Station, N. J., 95.
Van Deusenville, Mass., 181.
Varennes, Can., 260.
Vassalborough, Me., 240.
Venango, Pa., 130.
Venango City, Pa., 133.
Vergennes, Vt., 232.
Vermont, 222.
Vernon, Conn., 160.
Verona, N. Y., 63.
Verplanck's Point, N. Y., 42.
Viaduct, the Starucca, N. Y., 80.
Wakefield Junction, Mass., 199.
Wallingford, Conn., 153.
Wallingford, Vt., 233.
Walpole, N. H., 218.
Waltham, Mass., 193.
Warehouse Point, Conn., 156.
Warren, Mass., 178.
Warren, N. H., 206.
Warren, Pa., 129.
Warren, R. I., 164.
Warsaw, N. Y., 83.
Washington, N. J., 97.
Washington's Crossing, N. J., 99.
Waterbury, Conn., 150, 159.
Waterbury, Vt., 228.
Waterloo, N. J., 97.
Watertown, Conn., 151.
Watertown, Mass., 193.
Watertown, N. Y., 85.

Waterville, Conn., 151, 159.
Waterville, Me., 240, 241.
Watkins, N. Y., 83.
Waverly, N. J., 88.
Waverly Junction, N. Y., 136.
Webster, Mass., 189.
Weir's, N. H., 205.
Wellesley, Mass., 179.
Wells, Me., 236.
Wells River, Vt., 206, 207, 224.
Wenham, Mass., 198.
Wernersville, Pa., 140.
West Alburg, Vt., 220.
Westborough, Mass., 179.
West Brook, Me., 239.
West Brookfield, Mass., 178.
West Burke, Vt., 225.
Westerly, R. I., 162.
Westfield, N. J., 94.
Westfield, Mass., 157, 201.
West Hartford, Vt., 227.
West Haven, Conn., 146.
West Lebanon, N. H., 218.
Westminster, Vt., 223.
West Point, N. Y., 43.
Westport, N. Y., 57.
West Randolph, Vt., 227.
West Rutland, Vt., 231.
West Stockbridge, Mass., 181.
West Troy, N. Y., 49.
Wethersfield, Conn., 155.
Weymouth, Mass., 190.
Whately, Mass., 187.
Whitehall, N. Y., 56.
Whitehaven, Pa., 136.
Whitehouse, N. J., 94.
White Mountain House, N. H., 209.
White Plains, N. Y., 51.
White River Junction, N. H., 218, 224, 227.
White River Village, Vt., 227.

Whiting, Vt., 232.
Whiting's, N. J., 93.
Wickford, R. I., 162.
Wilbraham, Mass., 178.
Wilcox, Pa., 129.
Wilkesbarre, Pa., 136, 138.
Wilkinsburg, Pa., 123.
Williamsburg, Mass., 157.
Williams Bridge, N. Y., 51.
Williams College, Mass., 184.
Williamsport, Pa., 127, 143.
Williamstown, Mass., 184.
Willimantic, Conn., 158, 160.
Willington, Conn., 158.
Williston, Vt., 229.
Wilmington Junction, Mass., 199.
Wilton, Me., 241.
Wilton, N. H., 204.
Winchendon, Mass., 194.
Winchester, N. H., 194.
Windsor, Can., 258.
Windsor, Conn., 156.
Windsor, Vt., 228.
Winn, Me., 242.
Winooski, Vt., 229.
Winsted, Conn., 152.
Wolcottville, Conn., 151.
Wolfborough, N. H., 215.
Womelsdorf, Pa., 140.
Woodstock, Vt., 227.
Woodsville, N. H., 206.
Woonsocket, R. I., 166.
Worcester, Mass., 179, 190

Yale College, Conn., 146.
Yarmouth, Me., 239.
Yarmouth Junction, Me, 239.
Yonkers, N. Y., 39.
York, Pa., 142.
York Beach, Me., 236.

ADDITIONAL.

Bedford, N. Y., 51.
Boston Corners, N. Y., 51.

Chappaqua, N. Y., 51.
Cohoes, N. Y., 50.
Copake, N. Y., 52.

Everett, Mass., 195.

Guymard, N. Y., 78.

Hillsdale, N. Y., 52.

Lausingburg, N. Y., 50.

Melrose, N. Y., 51.
Mount Kisco, N. Y., 51.

Pawlings, N. Y., 52.

RAILWAYS.
Harlem Extension, 232.
Hartford, Providence, and Fishkill, 159, 161
Vermont Central, Vermont and Canada, 222.

INDEX OF ROUTES.

ROUTES.

CANADA.
I.—Quebec to Montreal, Toronto, Detroit, Mich., and the Great Lakes, 249.
II.—New York to Detroit, Mich., Chicago, Ill., and the Great Lakes, 257.
III.—Trip down the St. Lawrence, 258.

CONNECTICUT.
I.—New York to New Haven, Stonington, Rhode Island and Massachusetts, 144.
II.—Bridgeport to Pittsfield, Mass., 152.
III.—Connecticut River Valley from New Haven to Lake Memphremagog and the White Mountains, 153.
IV.—New London to Stafford Springs and all parts of New Hampshire, Vermont, and Canada, 156.
V.—New York to White Mountains, *via* New London, 158.
VI.—Waterbury to Providence, R. I., 159.

MAINE.
I.—Boston to Portland, Me., White Mountains and Canada, *via* Gorham, N. H., 236.
II.—Boston to White Mountains and Canada, 238.
III.—Portland to Augusta and the Valley of the Kennebec, 239.
IV.—Portland to Bangor and the Valley of the Penobscot, 241.
V.—Brunswick to Farmington, 243.

MASSACHUSETTS.
I.—New York to Boston, 178.
II.—New York to Boston, 180.
III.—New York to Boston, 180.
IV.—New York to Housatonic Region, 180.
V.—New York to Connecticut River Valley and White Mountains, 185.
VI.—New London, Conn., to White Mountains, Lake Memphremagog and Canada, 188.
VII.—New London, Conn., to Worcester and Fitchburg, 189.
VIII.—Boston to Plymouth, Newport, Cape Cod, etc., 190.
IX.—Boston to Bellows Falls and Lake Champlain, 193.
X.—Boston to White Mountains, Green Mountains, etc., 194.
XI.—Boston to Portsmouth, N. H., and Portland, Me., 195.
XII.—Boston to White Mountains, *via* Portland, Me., 199.
XIII.—Boston to Albany, N. Y., 201.
XIV.—Boston to the Hoosac Tunnel, 201.

NEW HAMPSHIRE.
I.—Boston to White Mountains and Canada, 203.
II.—Boston to White Mountains, *via* Conway, 214.
III.—Boston to Green Mountains, Lake Champlain, Adirondacks, and Canada, 216.
IV.—Boston to Bellows Falls and Lake Champlain, 218.
V.—Boston to Portsmouth, N. H., Portland, Me., the White Mountains, and Canada, 219.
VI.—Portsmouth to the White Mountains, the Connecticut Valley, the Green Mountains, and Lake Champlain, 221.
VII.—Boston to White Mountains at Gorham, and to the St. Lawrence River, 221.

NEW JERSEY.
I.—New York to Philadelphia, 87.
II.—New York to Philadelphia, 90.
III.—New York to Long Branch, Atlantic City, and Philadelphia, 91.
IV.—Jersey City to Eastern Pennsylvania, Delaware Water-Gap, Wilkesbarre, etc., 93.
V.—Jersey City to Eastern Pennsylvania and Delaware Water-Gap, 95.
VI.—Jersey City to Piermont, 97.
VII.—Jersey City to Paterson, 97.
VIII.—Philadelphia to Cape May, 98.
IX.—Philadelphia to Manunka Chunk and Delaware Water-Gap, 99.

NEW YORK.
I.—Trip up the Hudson, 38.
II.—New York to Albany (Harlem Railway), 51.
III.—Albany to Saratoga, Lakes George and Champlain, 52.
IV.—Trips to the Adirondack Region, 58.
V.—Albany to Buffalo and Niagara Falls, 62.
VI.—Albany to Binghamton, 75.
VII.—New York to Buffalo and Dunkirk, 76.
VIII.—Hudson to Rutland, Vt., 84.
IX.—Troy to Castleton, Vt., 85.

PENNSYLVANIA.
I.—Philadelphia to Harrisburg and Pittsburg, 118.
II.—Philadelphia to Reading and Williamsport, 125.
III.—Philadelphia to Erie and the Oil Regions, 128.

283

INDEX OF ROUTES.

IV.—Philadelphia to Lehigh and Wyoming Valleys, Delaware Water-Gap, Coal and Iron Regions, and Erie Railway, 133.
V.—Philadelphia or New York to Delaware Water-Gap, Binghamton, and Sunbury, 136.
VI.—Easton to Harrisburg and the Cumberland Valley, 139.
VII.—Baltimore, Md., to Gettysburg, Pa., and Elmira, N. Y., 140.

RHODE ISLAND.

I.—Stonington, Conn., to Providence, 162.
II.—Waterbury, Conn., to Providence, 164.
III.—Providence to Bristol, 164.
IV.—Providence to Newport, 164.
V.—Providence to Worcester, Mass., 165.

VERMONT.

I.—New York to Valley of the Connecticut, the White Mountains, Lake Memphremagog, etc., 222.
II.—Boston to Montpelier, Vt., Green Mountains, Lake Champlain, and Canada, 226.
III.—Boston to Bellows Falls, Green Mountains, Saratoga, Lake Champlain, Canada, etc., 230.
IV.—N. York, Rutland, Green Mountains to Lake Champlain, and Canada, 232.

THE END

To Tourists and Pleasure Travellers!
ALLUREMENTS UNAPPROACHED!!

With the annual recurrence of the pleasure season, the question naturally resolves itself in the minds of many, "Where shall we spend a few days of recreation this summer?" We answer: If you prefer the enjoyment of rural scenery, the solitude of some inland resort, to the glitter and confusion at our fashionable watering-places, where health succumbs to their attendant allurements to dissipation,

THE ERIE RAILWAY

offers some of the most attractive interior excursions this season ever presented those in the pursuit of pleasure, or a season of retirement from active duties. And these excursions are to places of unusual interest, some of which are to thousands as yet comparatively unknown (see page 272 of this Guide.) The trip to Watkins Glen —which is located within half a mile of the village of Watkins, at the head of Seneca Lake, 22 miles north of Elmira, and 296 miles from New York—

AFFORDS

an opportunity of witnessing some of the most sublime and magnificent of American scenery. This glen, no less renowned for its salubrious and invigorating atmosphere than for its utterly unapproachable allurements to travellers for pleasure, is annually attracting the attention and visits of thousands of admirers of Nature's beauties, who see in it

ALL THE

notable features of resorts of greater distinction—more to admire, more to amuse, and more to instruct, and which must inevitably, ere long, command for it great prominence in the public esteem. But, not here does the Erie Railway Company stop in its preparation of short, cheap, and interesting excursions; nor is there here concentrated all the rare loveliness, all the majestic grandeur of scenery for which the Empire State is so justly celebrated. Ithaca, Sharon Springs, Niagara Falls, and Saratoga, each possesses in itself

LUXURIES

peculiarly its own. Saratoga has its magnificent hotels, health-giving mineral springs, and delightful drives; and so, too, has Sharon Springs. Ithaca prides itself upon the beauty of its surroundings, the numerous cascades, waterfalls, etc., all within a short distance and of easy access; while the claims of Niagara upon the American and European traveller are too long and favorably known to require but a passing notice. In point

OF

interest the scenery on the line of the Erie Railway, extending almost its entire length, is unrivalled. So rapidly is it presented on either hand as you follow the tortuous windings of the Delaware, and the beautiful Susquehanna, while snugly ensconced in one of the

MODERN

drawing-room coaches built expressly for this line, that you are spell-bound in viewing its wondrous beauty, so diverse in character, so infinitely transcending any thing to be found on the line of any other railway. The scenery of the Erie Railway has done much to make it popular with the public as the great highway of

TRAVEL,

but its equipment, facilities, and accommodations, have done more. In no respect is it behind its rivals, while in many it takes precedence. As a route for *pleasure excursion parties* it must ever be popular, for the reason that it traverses some of the most beautiful passages in American scenery; and, as a route for *comfort*, it must ever be acknowledged, because it "affords all the luxuries of modern travel."

People's Line for Albany.

The largest and most magnificent River Steamers in the world,

THE ST. JOHN,
DREW, and
DEAN RICHMOND.

One of the above Steamers will leave *Pier 41*, North River, every afternoon (Sundays excepted) at *6 o'clock*, arriving at ALBANY in time to connect with Railroad Trains West and North. Returning, leave the Steamboat Landing at Albany on the arrival of connecting trains from the West and North. Through Tickets can be obtained at the OFFICE ON THE WHARF, and Baggage checked to its destination; also, at

DODD'S EXPRESS OFFICES,

944 Broadway, and No. 1 Court St., Brooklyn.

1870.

HUDSON RIVER BY DAYLIGHT!

Albany & New York Day Line of Steamboats.

C. VIBBARD and DANIEL DREW

Will leave New York from Vestry Street Pier at **8.45**, and Thirty-fourth Street at **9** A. M., daily. Returning, leave Albany at **9** A. M.

Landing at YONKERS, WEST POINT, CORNWALL, NEWBURG, POUGHKEEPSIE, RHINEBECK, CATSKILL, and HUDSON.

Connecting with the New York Central and Saratoga Roads for the North and West.

On and after June 15th a Special Train will leave, on arrival at Albany, of Broad-Gauge Cars to SHARON SPRINGS, affording the most pleasant, cheap, and expeditious route, avoiding stages.

The favorite Steamboat **MARY POWELL** leaves Vestry Street Pier daily at **3.30** P. M. for RONDOUT. Landing at COZZENS, WEST POINT, CORNWALL, NEWBURG, NEW HAMBURG, MILTON, and POUGHKEEPSIE.

Returning each morning, making the same Landings.

CROUCH & FITZGERALD,
Trunk Manufacturers,
(ESTABLISHED OVER THIRTY YEARS.)

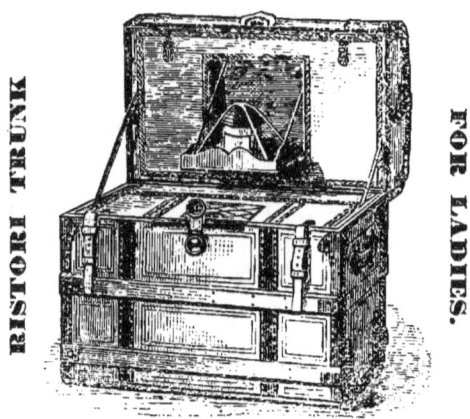

Patented September 29, 1868.

Keep constantly on hand the largest stock and best assortment of first-class goods, and made expressly for retail trade; comprising real SOLE LEATHER TRUNKS FOR GENTS' AND LADIES' USE, SOLE LEATHER VALISES, RAILROAD AND FANCY BAGS, LADIES' AND GENTS' TRUNKS of every description, suitable for either American or European travel.

Sole manufacturers of the RISTORI TRUNK, being the most complete and best arranged for ladies' use; also CROUCH'S PATENT CROSS-BAR SHAWL STRAPS for Ladies or Gents, superior to all others.

Illustrated Catalogues can be had on application.

Stores No. 1 MAIDEN LANE and 556 BROADWAY.
Factory, Nos. 352 & 354 West 41st St., New York.

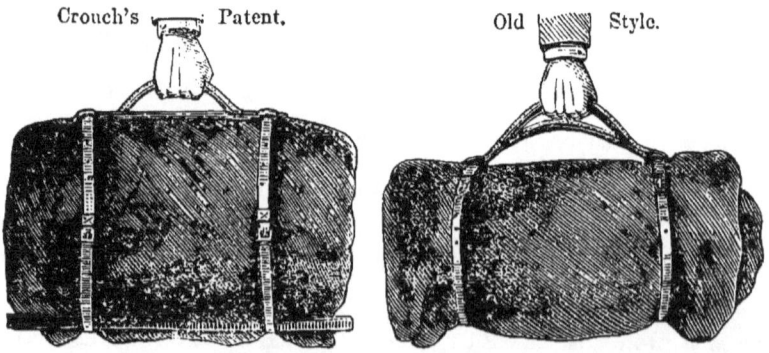

The Patent Cross-bar is warranted to carry 50 lbs. weight and retain its shape.

Central Railroad of New Jersey.

ALLENTOWN LINE TO THE WEST.

This Road offers superior facilities for persons seeking pleasant Suburban Residences within easy distance of New York.

20 Trains Daily to	....	GREENVILLE.
24 " "	....	BERGEN POINT.
30 " "	....	ELIZABETH.
13 " "	....	ROSELLE.
11 " "	....	CRAWFORD.
11 " "	....	WESTFIELD and FAIRWOOD.
13 " "	....	PLAINFIELD.
9 " "	....	DUNELLEN and BROAD BROOK.
12 " "	....	SOMERVILLE.

Connects at SOMERVILLE, for FLEMINGTON JUNCTION, with the DELAWARE, LACKAWANNA, and WESTERN ROAD.

" PHILLIPSBURG with LEHIGH and SUSQUEHANNA and BELVIDERE DELAWARE ROADS.

" EASTON with LEHIGH VALLEY ROAD and CONNECTIONS TO ALL PARTS OF PENNSYLVANIA and THE WEST.

Passenger and Freight Depot in New York,
At Foot of Liberty St., North River.

H. P. BALDWIN,
General Passenger Agent.

R. E. RICKER, Superintendent.

NEWARK AND NEW YORK RAILROAD,

Depot in New York, **Foot of Liberty St., N. R.**

26 Trains each way Daily between Newark and New York.

Narragansett Steamship Co.

FOR BOSTON,
VIA NEWPORT AND FALL RIVER.

1870.   **1870.**

SUMMER ARRANGEMENT.

The World-renowned Steamers

BRISTOL,
Commander A. G. SIMMONS,

PROVIDENCE,
Commander B. M. SIMMONS,

Having been thoroughly overhauled and refitted, will leave ALTERNATE DAYS, Sundays included,

At 5 P. M., from Pier 30, North River,
FOOT OF CHAMBERS STREET.

GRAND PROMENADE CONCERT

On each Steamer every evening, by

Hall's Celebrated Boston Brass, String, and Reed Bands.

The management being determined that nothing in the mode of transit of first class passengers shall surpass this line on a scale of grandeur and magnificence, adds this most expensive attraction and novelty, the engagement of the first orchestra of the country, which will be attached to each steamer on its passage.

Freight received up to 5 o'clock, P. M.

JAMES FISK, Jr., President.
M. R. SIMONS, Managing Director.
CHAS. B. KIMBALL, Gen'l Pass. Agent.
H. H. MANGAM, Freight Agent.

ST. CLOUD HOTEL,

On European Plan,

BROADWAY AND 42d STREET,

NEW YORK.

THE ONLY FIRST-CLASS HOTEL UP TOWN,

AND

Near Hudson River, Harlem, and Boston Railroads,

Being only four blocks distant from 42d St. Depots.

SEVERAL LINES OF HORSE-CARS RUNNING BY THE HOTEL,

DAY AND NIGHT,

BETWEEN CITY HALL AND CENTRAL PARK.

House new—Rooms large, elegantly furnished, and perfectly ventilated, and every Room supplied with Hot and Cold Water, Steam, and Gas.

For the convenience of guests, a patent "ATWOOD ELEVATOR" is at their service at all hours.

SUPERIOR ACCOMMODATIONS

For families or single persons, apartments being *en suite* or single.

T. B. RAND,
J. H. RAND,
G. W. RAND.

RAND BROTHERS,
PROPRIETORS.

www.ingramcontent.com/pod-product-compliance
Lightning Source LLC
Chambersburg PA
CBHW021205230426
43667CB00006B/563